Sensing and Perceiving

Sensing and Perceiving offers a comprehensive and highly accessible overview addressing two centuries-old questions: how are animals aware of the surrounding world, and how does this awareness enable everyday behaviors? Authors Julia J. C. Blau and Jeffrey B. Wagman provide a thorough description of the biological systems involved in these processes and examine both traditional and ecological approaches to understanding how these processes occur.

The book features a conversational and humorous writing style with everyday examples that introduce novice readers to sensing and perceiving processes. Key benefits include clear explanations of different theoretical assumptions, research questions asked, and conclusions drawn by the various approaches. The authors demonstrate how sensing and perceiving are actions we perform rather than passive experiences that happen to us, reflected in the book's unique title.

Sensing and Perceiving serves as an essential guide for students and professionals in sensation and perception, cognition, and biological psychology. This comprehensive textbook provides crucial foundational knowledge for undergraduate and postgraduate students exploring perceptual sciences, while offering valuable insights for researchers and practitioners in psychology, neuroscience, and related fields seeking to understand the active nature of sensory and perceptual processes.

Julia J. C. Blau is Associate Professor in the Psychological Sciences at Central Connecticut State University, New Britain, CT, USA. She is a member of the board of directors of the *International Society for Ecological Psychology*, an associate editor of the journal of *Ecological Psychology*, and she co-edits the series *Resources for Ecological Psychology* at Routledge.

Jeffrey B. Wagman is Professor of Psychology at Illinois State University, Normal, IL, USA. He is a member of the board of directors of the *International Society for Ecological Psychology*, an associate editor of the journal of *Ecological Psychology*, and he co-edits the series *Resources for Ecological Psychology* at Routledge.

"I am excited to use this textbook in my Sensation and Perception class. Information is presented in an engaged, familiar manner, and the authors use consistent characters and examples across chapters, which makes the text very easy to read. This writing style will allow students to understand traditional approaches and ecological approaches to perception equally, something that no other text does. This is a top-notch presentation of modern approaches to understanding perception. Even more, Blau and Wagman argue that sensing and perceiving are things that we do and not just things that happen to us, which is both novel and sure to spark student interest. The combination of coverage, writing style, and high-level execution makes this a textbook that will deepen any reader's appreciation for perception."

Brian Day, *Associate Professor of Psychology, Butler University*

"This textbook is a breath of fresh air for sensation and perception courses that provides a rigorous exploration of the ways organisms get to know the environment through their senses. And, even better, this is combined with an account of an ecological alternative to the mainstream views in the field. It is the perfect source to gather fundamental knowledge of sensation and perception as well as to understand the main theoretical positions and experimental results in their study. This book is a gamechanger both for students and professors interested in how we see, hear, and touch the world."

Vicente Raja, *Ramón y Cajal Research Fellow, Department of Philosophy, Universidad de Murcia, Spain*

Sensing and Perceiving

Julia J. C. Blau and Jeffrey B. Wagman

Routledge
Taylor & Francis Group
NEW YORK AND LONDON

Designed cover image: Photograph by Lynda James Carroll

First published 2026
by Routledge
605 Third Avenue, New York, NY 10158

and by Routledge
4 Park Square, Milton Park, Abingdon, Oxon, OX14 4RN

Routledge is an imprint of the Taylor & Francis Group, an informa business

ISBN: 978-1-032-69094-0 (hbk)
ISBN: 978-1-032-69091-9 (pbk)
ISBN: 978-1-032-69096-4 (ebk)

DOI: 10.4324/9781032690964

Typeset in Galliard
by Apex CoVantage, LLC

Contents

About the Authors

Julia J. C. Blau is Associate Professor in the department of Psychological Sciences at Central Connecticut State University, New Britain, CT, USA. She earned her doctorate in ecological psychology from the University of Connecticut, which is where she first created Fred and his adventures. Her research focuses on the fractality of event perception, as well as the ecological approach to film theory and aesthetics. She is a member of the board of directors of the *International Society for Ecological Psychology*, an associate editor of the journal of *Ecological Psychology*, and she co-edits the *Resources for Ecological Psychology Series* at Routledge.

Jeffrey B. Wagman is Professor of Psychology at Illinois State University, Normal, IL, USA. His research focuses on perception of affordances and perception by touch. He is the recipient of the Illinois State University College of Arts and Sciences Distinguished Lecturer Award, the Illinois State University Outstanding University Researcher Award, and a Japan Society for the Promotion of Science Invitation Fellowship for Research in Japan. He is a member of the board of directors of the *International Society for Ecological Psychology*, an associate editor of the journal of *Ecological Psychology*, and he co-edits the *Resources for Ecological Psychology Series* at Routledge.

Preface

Resources for Ecological Psychology

This series of volumes is dedicated to furthering the development of psychology as a branch of ecological science. In its broadest sense, ecology is a multidisciplinary approach to the study of living systems, their environments, and the reciprocity that has evolved between the two. Traditionally, ecological science emphasizes the study of the biological bases of energy transactions between animals and their physical environments across cellular, organismic, and population scales. Ecological psychology complements this traditional focus by emphasizing the study of information transactions between living systems and their environments, especially as they pertain to perceiving situations of significance to planning and execution of purposes activated in an environment.

The late James J. Gibson used the term "ecological psychology" to emphasize this animal-environment mutuality for the study of problems of perception. He believed that analyzing the environment to be perceived was just as much a part of the psychologist's task as analyzing animals themselves, and hence that the "physical" concepts applied to the environment and the "biological" and "psychological" concepts applied to organisms would have to be tailored to one another in a larger system of mutual constraint. His early interest in the applied problems of landing airplanes and driving automobiles led him to pioneer the study of perceptual guidance of action.

The work of Nikolai Bernstein in biomechanics and physiology represents a complementary approach to problems of the coordination and control of movement. His work suggests that action, too, cannot be studied without reference to the environment, and that physical and biological concepts must be developed together. The coupling of Gibson's ideas with those of Bernstein forms a natural basis for looking at the traditional psychological topics of perceiving, acting, and knowing as activities of ecosystems rather than isolated animals.

The purpose of this series is to form a useful collection, a resource, for people who wish to learn about ecological psychology and for those who wish to contribute to its development. The series will include original research, collected papers, reports of conferences and symposia, theoretical monographs, technical handbooks, and works from the many disciplines relevant to ecological psychology.

Jeffrey B. Wagman and Julia J. C. Blau, Series Editors
[Robert Shaw, William M. Mace, and Michael Turvey, Series Editors Emeriti]

Acknowledgments

A few years ago, we wrote our first book—*Introduction to Ecological Psychology*. One of the most common things we heard from our colleagues and students was, "This is great! When are you going to write a Sensation and Perception textbook?" First, thanks for the positive feedback! We appreciate it. Second, to answer your question—we just did. You are reading it. Thanks for the suggestion.

We are grateful to Kerry Marsh, who was among the very first people to suggest that we write this book. We also thank Madison Battey, Olivia Cornejo, MacKenna Duncan, Alison Guthrie, Sanako Hishinuma, Jullian McAuliffe, and Brayden Young who provided student perspectives on several chapters. Thanks also to Chris Pagano, Vincente Raja, Brian Day, Matthieu de Wit, Louie Favela, Tom Stoffregen, and Paula Silva who provided comments on drafts of individual chapters. And thanks to everyone who promoted our books (including this one) on podcasts and other platforms.

A very special thanks to Lynda James Carroll, who drew all the biological line drawings and who took several photographs and helped to adjust several others to illustrate the various concepts. JJCB is profoundly grateful to have you as a mother, fellow scholar, and inspiring presence in her life. Thanks also to Jeff Carroll for gamely playing the guitar and singing whenever we asked; and to Jason Kalter (and most of our friends and family) for letting us photograph their tongues like it was a totally normal thing to ask.

JJCB thanks Eric for the many walks and help sorting out the thorny bits, as well as emotional support when a chapter simply wouldn't do what it was told. She also thanks Grayson for asking *so many questions* and always being willing to listen to the answers, and Gwendolyn for periodically insisting on rest and fun. She could not have done this without you all. JJCB also thanks the wonderful friends that have been with her through thick and thin, it means everything.

JBW thanks Dawn for her love and support; Connor for helpful discussions of fantasy football, geography, and chess; and the family, friends, and pets that have provided support—the logically major and minor, the obvious and the non-obvious, the prolonged and the instantaneous, the recurring and the once only—for as long as he can remember.

And finally, we thank the *many* ecological psychologists who have come before us and together with us. The careful reader will notice that most of Fred's friends and family are named after some of these scientists. The exclusion of anyone was not deliberate—there were so many more names we simply could not find room for. To Claudia Carello (both authors' PhD advisor): we hope you don't mind us borrowing your name (again) for such a purpose. We are tempted to thank you (again) here but, after all, this (second) book is our (additional) thanks to you.

We hope that readers enjoy reading this book as much as we enjoyed writing it.

Julia J. C. Blau and Jeffrey B. Wagman

Part One

Biological Systems

1 Philosophy, History, and Introduction to Biological View

This book is an exploration of how we know stuff and how we do stuff. In particular, it is an exploration how we know about the world around us and about how this enables us to perform everyday behaviors. Both processes are often taken for granted. Think back to the minute or so before you started reading this book. Maybe you walked into a dim or dark room, reached out and knew that you had found the light switch (because you felt it), and you flicked it on. Then you knew that the book was across the room (because you saw it) and you knew that you could walk to it from where you were. As you began to walk in the direction of the book, you knew that your roommate was in the kitchen (because you heard her), you knew that she was making as snack (because you smelled it—*mmmm*), and you turned your head toward her (and her food). Then as you turned back and continued walking toward the book, you knew that your pet cat was suddenly in your path (because—*thank goodness*—you saw him). You (quite deftly) stepped over him and then around the coffee table, sat down on the couch, and knew that the book was within reach. You picked it up and started reading. Whew!

It is entirely possible (even likely) that you have never stopped to wonder how you are able to know all of these (and many, many other) things and perform all of these (and many, many other) everyday behaviors so easily. And why would you? You have other more important things to worry about! And it might not ever occur to you that knowing about the world around you and performing these everyday behaviors requires successfully *perceiving* your surroundings. How we perceive our surroundings in way that supports these abilities is a topic that frequently goes unexplored precisely *because* it is so often successful (Blau & Wagman, 2022).

The vast majority of the time, we find the light switch, know where objects are relative to us, know where and how to get from where we are to where we want to go, successfully find the source of a sound or smell, and even step over suddenly-appearing pet cats without any trouble at all. We may only stop to consider how we perceive our surroundings when something seems to go awry. Like when we experience an amusing illusion online or when we are embarrassingly unsuccessful at a seemingly simple everyday behavior—where did that bottom step come from, anyway!? We might wonder why we get it wrong at least some of the time.

As perceptual scientists, we are far more interested in how we get it *right most of the time.* Once you start to seriously consider this question, it becomes clear that the answers are . . . *complicated.* How we perceive our surroundings in ways that allow us to perform the everyday behaviors that feel so simple, that are so easily accomplished, is actually quite difficult to explain. After all, there are *entire* books about this—including this one.

To understand what we mean by this, we'd like you to meet Fred (see Figure 1.1). Reader, meet Fred. Fred, meet Reader. Fred is hungry and would like to have a snack. He is in luck, because on the other side of the field he is standing in, there is an apple tree. To solve his hunger problem, he must first perceive that there is a tree on the far side of the field, recognize

DOI: 10.4324/9781032690964-2

Figure 1.1 Fred would like to eat an apple from the tree. How does he learn about his environment so that he can accomplish this task?

both that it has apples on it, and that he could (at some point in the near future) walk from where he is to where the apples are and then (at some point shortly after that) reach, grasp, pluck, and eat those apples. We encounter (and overcome) situations like every day! And not just every day. All day long.

The study of how we perceive is ultimately the study of how we *know things* about our surrounding environment. How does Fred know where the tree is, how to get to it, and that he can reach and eat the apples? How did you know where your book was, how to get to it, how to grasp it, and how to turn the pages? The study of how we know things is called **epistemology**.

Epistemology the study of knowledge, particularly how it is acquired.

Socratic Question: Why is it important to understand how it is that we know about our surrounding environment? Why is it that this topic frequently goes unexplored?

The Nature of Assumptions

People have been studying the process of knowing for a very long time—literally *thousands* of years—and while we've made considerable progress, scientists still disagree (sometimes vehemently) about how this process occurs. Part of the disagreement over how to approach studying problems like Fred's—and the process of knowing more generally—is rooted in the **assumptions** that scientists make before they begin their investigations. Often (too often) the assumptions are made even without realizing it!

Assumption something believed to be true without proof.

Whether we realize it or not, all scientific investigations start with assumptions. Yes, *all* scientific investigations—including sciences such as biology, psychology, and ecology, but also such as physics, chemistry, astronomy, and geology. It is simply not possible to get very far in science without making at least some assumptions. And whether it is scientific investigations or our everyday lives, it is very easy to forget or overlook the assumptions that we make because they often seem so obvious and natural that questioning them feels silly—or because we don't even realize we are making assumptions at all! For example, we assume that gravity will keep working all day; that the light will turn on when we flip the switch, and that we won't suddenly forget how to use a fork. It would be very silly to be skeptical about these things!

Having said that, our assumptions dictate what questions we ask and how we ask them, and this is particularly important when doing science. For example, if we assume the sky is blue, we are going to ask questions like "why is the sky blue?" rather than asking "what color is the sky?" What questions we ask also changes what kind of answers we get. For example, if Fred approaches his best friend, Claudia, who looks visibly upset, he will get a different answer if he asks the question "how are you?" than if he asks, "what's wrong?"

Three Different Sets of Assumptions

This book covers three main approaches to the study of sensing and perceiving (see Figure 1.2). The first section describes the **biological approach**. It covers the anatomy of the sensory systems and goes into some

Biological approach the assumption that the entirety of lived experience (including perception) can be understood by understanding our biological systems.

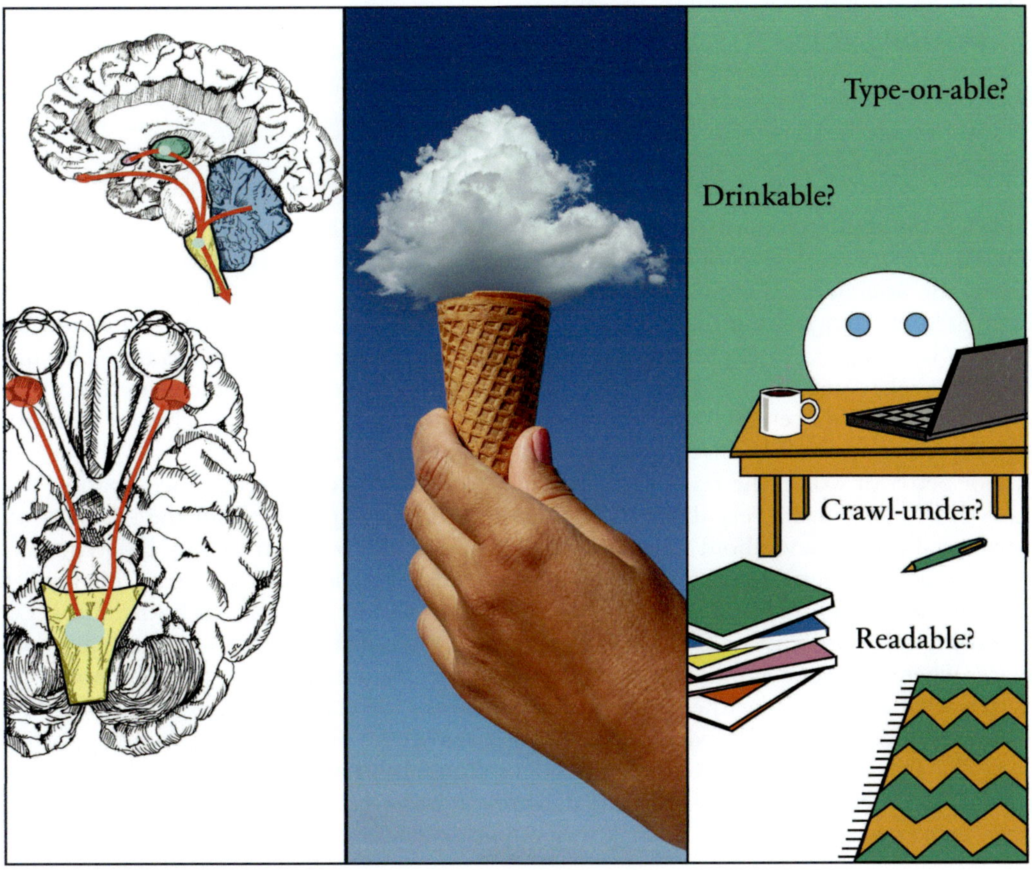

Figure 1.2 The understanding of perception can be approached many different ways. This book covers the biological approach (left), the traditional approach(es) (middle), and the ecological approach (right).

detail about what scientists understand about the neurological processing that occurs when those sensory systems are stimulated. Later in this chapter, we will cover the assumptions of the biological approach. In brief, this approach assumes that our entire lived experience (including how we know things) can be understood by understanding our biological systems.

The second section covers what we will call the **traditional approach**. We will cover the assumptions of this approach in Chapter 8. In brief, it starts from the assumption that the stimulation patterns available to the animal are not very informative about geometric and physical properties of nearby objects, and that these geometric and physical properties are the basis for how animals know things about the world. Since the stimulation itself is not very useful, most of the perceptual process is dedicated to interpreting the less-than-ideal stimulation so that animals can know about these properties of the world. Section Two covers the traditional approach to visual perception of properties such as size, distance, objects, and motion as well as the traditional approach to auditory perception of many of these properties.

Traditional approach(es) the study of perception as recovery-of-meaning from a meaningless impression on the senses. Largely (though not entirely) based on the work of Helmholtz.

The third (and final) section presents the **ecological approach**. Fair warning—the ecological approach is *a very different way* to think about the perceptual process. This is because it starts from *very different* assumptions. We'll cover the assumptions of the ecological approach in Chapter 13. In brief, the approach starts from the assumption that stimulation patterns available to the animal *are informative*—not about geometric and physical properties of the world, but about the *behaviors the organism can perform in the world*. And this is the basis for how animals know things about the world. Since the stimulation is already useful, the perceptual process is dedicated to exploring, detecting, and exploiting these patterns in performing everyday behaviors. Section Three covers the ecological approach to perceiving events and affordances; and perceiving by vision, hearing, and touch. It ends with a chapter dedicated to addressing commonly raised questions about the ecological approach.

Ecological approach the study of perceiving as an ongoing process continuous with action. Based on the work of Gibson.

For better or worse, the traditional and ecological views are inherently incompatible with each other. They make very different (often opposite) assumptions about the nature of the perceptual process and about science itself. Those assumptions lead to very different questions, which of course lead to very different answers. We will do our best in this book to present these views as clearly and correctly as possible (with the caveat that both authors take an ecological approach; see Blau & Wagman, 2022). We will also try to critically point out places where the views and the research do not fully explain a particular phenomenon.

For what it is worth, neither the traditional view nor the ecological view are incompatible with a biological approach, which is part of the reason we present the biological approach first. The two approaches make different assumptions about how to *understand* the biological data in the context of understanding perception; however, both "cognitive neuroscience" and "ecological neuroscience" exist as thriving fields of study.

Before we get to the various approaches, it will help to have a little bit of context for the psychological study of sensing and perceiving. The earliest work in this field wasn't in psychology—psychology didn't even exist as its own science until the late 1800s! But when psychology *did* emerge, the first questions that were asked were ones about how we perceive the world (see psychophysics section). Before that, people still studied the nature of knowing about stuff, they just didn't do it in a way that we would call science. We would more likely call their work *philosophy*, but what they did was the basis for all modern science—including psychology.

The Basics of Modern Science

One of the most fundamental shifts in scientific thinking started with the French philosopher Rene Descartes (pronounced ruh-NEH deh-KART, see Figure 1.3). In 1637, Descartes was getting frustrated with the unquestioned assumptions that scientists were making. He was aware that assumptions mattered a great deal, particularly if they blind you to questions you *should* be asking. He decided he was going to start over with *no assumptions at all* and figure out what—if anything—he was able to know without those assumptions. He recognized that eliminating all assumptions meant that he must doubt anything he knew by seeing, hearing, smelling, tasting, or touching because trusting this information would require him to make the assumption that his senses were reliable. Having done that, however, he realized that he had very little left that he could trust.

Descartes famously said, "Cogito, ergo sum", which translates as "I think, therefore I am". What he meant by this was that he was—at minimum—directly aware of his own thoughts (in this case, his doubts). This meant that there had to be something that was doing the doubting. That something was *him*! His *doubts* existed, therefore *he* must exist—what a relief! The problem was that he couldn't prove *anything else* existed! Not even his own body! Since he wasn't sure his senses could be trusted, it was possible the world around him was a figment of his imagination (or a trick being played on him by some supernatural entity), so the existence of his own mind was the only thing that was not in doubt.

Figure 1.3 Artist rendition of Rene Descartes, an influential 17th-century scholar.

The idea that the world is a figment of our imagination and nothing else exists except for our own minds is called **solipsism**. And honestly, it's not very helpful because if the world *is* a figment of our imagination, then we can't do science (because we can't ask questions about a world that doesn't actually exist). And we *like* doing science!

Instead, Descartes suggested (and all modern perceptual scientists agree with him) that the first assumption that we should make is that the world *does* exist. While we cannot necessarily *prove* that the world isn't a simulation, we need to start somewhere. So, scientists are all just going to have to agree (that is, we have to *assume*) that the world exists independently of our minds and is something we can investigate in a systematic way. This belief is called **realism.** Realism is great because it allows us to do science. Phew!

Solipsism the belief that the self is the only thing that exists.

Once we all agree that there is a world to know stuff *about*, we can start working on the question of *how* we know stuff. This is where the disagreements usually begin. One option is to assume that we are just born knowing everything we need to know—that is, that we have **innate knowledge** that helps us navigate our individual lives. And there are some philosophers and scientists who have argued for at least *some* innate knowledge—the notion of "instincts," for example, is the idea that there are some behaviors, drives, patterns of thought, and so on that are just part of what we know from the very beginning without having to learn them (see Box 1.1).

Realism the belief that the world exists independent of the self.

One the one hand, it might seem reasonable to assume that at least some of the knowledge that we have is innate. After all, newly born or hatched animals seem to know (how to do) lots of things almost immediately (Wundt, 1897). However, making this assumption is problematic on a couple of fronts. For one, it really just pushes the problem back a step. Think about it like this: our goal is to figure out how Fred knows about his environment, and how he knows what he can *do* in that environment. If we try to achieve that goal by saying "he just innately *knows stuff*", then we still have to answer the

Innate knowledge information that an organism has as part of their basic nature.

Box 1.1 Instincts and Constraints

It is important to distinguish inherited constraints from instincts. An "instinct" is a fully formed behavior that is assumed to be coded (somehow) into the DNA of the organism (see Box 1.2). It is like an unchanging computer program that is ready to run provided the prerequisites are met. This idea is unsupportable. For one, DNA does not contain instructions for behaviors (Carroll, 2005; Lewontin, 2001); also, if the environment of an organism changed even minimally from one generation to the next, the "instinctual" behavior might no longer work. For example, if an owl's instinctual hunting behavior relies on the zig-zag pattern that rodents make when they run away, then the owl would be unable to hunt it if a rodent suddenly starts running away in a straight line (see Figure 1.4). In other words, a small change in the environment could result in a species being unable to survive in the new environment. Evolutionarily speaking, that is extraordinarily disadvantageous in a world that is constantly in flux (VanValen, 1973).

Figure 1.4 An owl's hunting behavior has to be context dependent, or it would not survive.

It is the case that there are remarkable similarities in the way that organisms of a species behave across generations, but it does not follow that the behavior needs to be coded or programmed into their DNA. Instead, it could be that the shape, form, and capabilities of the body of the organism interact with shape, form, and possibilities of the environment to produce certain behaviors. A tall person will duck under a low barrier. That does not mean that "ducking" needs to be coded into the DNA, but rather that the constraints of the body coupled with the constraints of the environment will result in ducking behavior in order to avoid a headache.

question of where the innate knowledge *came from*. We haven't really solved the problem at all, just shifted the focus of the question!

Let's say, for the sake of argument, that we *were* willing to assume that Fred has at least some innate knowledge about the world. After all, he sure seems to know a bunch of stuff about the world, and he seemed to know some of it know right after he was born. Unless we want to assume that he got his knowledge from somewhere spooky (like God speaks to him, or he can read other people's minds), we have to assume that all of that knowledge was (somehow) inside of him in another way—maybe encoded into his genes through DNA. This is actually a pretty common assumption to make, even in 21st-century scientific investigations. People talk a lot about "nature" vs. "nurture", and when they do that what they are really saying is "DNA" vs. "experience". But the truth is that DNA just *doesn't work that way*; and even if DNA *could* encode full behaviors or outcomes, it wouldn't be particularly useful to us (see Box 1.2).

Box 1.2 DNA

The most well-known description of DNA is as a kind of "blueprint"—that is, the DNA contains a specific plan for every part of the body, and it feeds information to the body on how to form itself and how to function. Take Fred and his apple tree problem. This description of DNA suggests that some sequence of DNA markers tells his body what shape to be, another sequence tells him how to perceive a tree, and another sequence tells him how to move and grab an apple (see Figure 1.5, *top right*).

The problem is that this description of DNA is as an entirely feed-forward mechanism—meaning that is has an influence in only in one direction—DNA tells the body what to do, but the body can't give feedback to the DNA. For example, there might be a specific gene that tells the body how much to grow, another that tells the body how strong to make the muscles, and so on. *But it turns out that this is not really how any of this works.* How DNA influences any of these processes is actually complex and multi-directional rather than simple and linear (see Figure 1.5, *bottom*).

In fact, a person's height might be affected by environment, and that, in turn, might affect the DNA of the person in a way that might be inherited by their offspring. It is anything *but* straightforward and simple. There is an entire branch of science, called *epigenetics*, that studies the complex question of how genes express themselves in development (Gottlieb, 2000; Lewontin, 2001).

And that's just for an *outcome* like height—*behaviors* are another story. Even seemingly simple behaviors like withdrawing our hands from a hot stove (ouch!) require an understanding of the context for that behavior. For example, if the stove is *behind* us, we should move our hand *forward*, but if the stove is *in front* of us, we should move our hand *backwards*. A fully feed-forward system wouldn't be able to take those various contexts into account. None of this is intended to say that DNA doesn't have a role in our development, it's just unlikely that it is the source of our knowledge or our behaviors in any meaningful way.

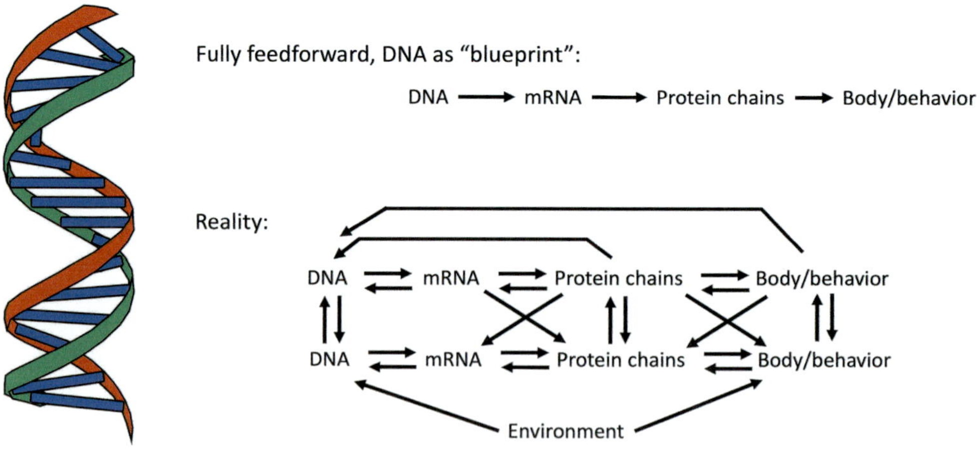

Figure 1.5 Left, a strand of DNA. Top right, in the DNA-as-blueprint model, DNA tells the body how to grow, how to perceive the environment, and how to move in that environment. Bottom right, the reality of the function of DNA is complex and multi-directional.

Figure 1.6 John Locke, empiricist philosopher who coined *tabula rasa* or "blank slate".

Instead of assuming knowledge is already there at birth (or even at conception), modern scientists commit to the notion that everything we know must be *learned*. That learning can (and probably does) start taking place sometime between conception and birth, but *all* learning comes from *experience*. That is, in addition to committing to realism, all the modern perceptual theories we present in this book strive to commit to the assumptions of the ***tabula rasa*** and **empiricism**.

The English philosopher John Locke (1690, see Figure 1.6) coined the phrase *tabula rasa* to capture the idea that organisms (and he particularly meant humans) start with no knowledge of the world around them and are instead a "blank slate" on which knowledge is written. That knowledge is (must be) written by *experience*. He also argued that all experience comes from the stimulation of our senses. Locke (and other empiricists like him) argued that our senses are a reasonably reliable way of knowing about the world. Besides, if we start with no knowledge—and if we are ruling out supernatural explanations—then the senses are the only game in town!

Tabula rasa literally "blank slate"; the idea that we start with no knowledge.

Empiricism the belief that all knowledge comes from experience

But, as we already mentioned, Descartes was not so sure. He was concerned about whether the senses provided reliable information about the world. And this concern is worth exploring! After all, we know that there are things in the world that our (human) senses just can't tell us about. Birds can use the magnetic fields of the earth to navigate, but we can't use them to do anything at all—unless we use a tool like a compass. Sharks can sense electrical fields; snakes can sense body heat; mosquitos can sense gradients of carbon dioxide (see Yong, 2022). The list goes on. Our senses just can't detect those kinds of energy, and so they can't provide us with reliable information about these aspects of the world. So, if our senses aren't telling us *everything* about the world, can we trust them to tell us *anything* about the world? And if we can't trust them to tell us anything about the world, are we back to the same place we were when we were deciding whether the world exists or not?

If we are going to assume that all knowledge comes in through our senses, the only way we can know about the world (the only way we can do science) is to assume that our senses are at least *reasonably* reliable about *at least some* aspects of the world. We have to assume that there is at least *some* correspondence between the patterns of energy that stimulate our sense organs and the world that we experience. If so, then we can use those senses to gather information about the world. We can use our senses to *know stuff*. Hooray! Where the perspectives in this book diverge is in how this process occurs, how reliable that process is, and what that process allows us to know about. As promised, we will start with the biological view and its assumptions. Well, really one main assumption that has many parts.

Socratic Question: What do the authors mean by the statement "Realism is great because it allows us to do science"? How do the competing assumptions of innate knowledge and empiricism affect how we might scientifically investigate the perceptual process?

The Fundamental Assumption of a Biological Approach: All Experiences Are Entirely Biological

The most fundamental assumption of the biological approach is that *all* experiences can be explained biologically. Our senses are the activities of organs; emotions are the movement of hormones; thoughts are the product of the brain. There's no room in a biological view for non-biological causes. This assumption runs counter to an idea that pervades a lot of modern science, so you'll have to forgive us here as we take a bit of an historical detour.

Dualism vs. Monism

Descartes (the same guy from before—he was quite prolific!) was interested in studying the human body. However, at the time, where it had power, the church was fully in control of what views and practices were acceptable. The church was of the firm belief that humans—being a creation of God—were not something that should be studied (at least, not in the same way that other soulless things like animals were studied).

To sidestep the issue, Descartes suggested an idea called **dualism**. That is, he suggested that humans were actually made of two parts: the body and the soul (see Figure 1.7, *left*). He convinced the church that while the soul could not be understood scientifically (because it was the purview of God), the body was of the earth and so it *could* be studied—sneaky! These days scientists don't tend to use the word "soul" (partially because of the religious connotations). Instead, the ones that believe in this dualism call the "not-body" part of us the "mind" or the "unconscious" or the "central executive".[1] Regardless of what you call it, the concept is the same: there are the passive, mechanical parts of the physical *body*, and there are the active, intelligent parts of the nonphysical *mind*. Further, the mind is the thing making decisions and controlling the body—like a captain might steer a ship or a puppeteer might control a puppet. And while it would be possible for us to poke you in the brain (because it is located in a particular place in your body), it would be impossible for us to poke you in the mind (because it is not).

Dualism the idea that something (here, the person) is divided up into two parts.

This assumption is *rampant* in modern science—especially psychology—and in society more generally. We talk about our bodies as if they are something we control or own (e.g., "my hand"). And movies in which two people's minds switch bodies imply that the body and the mind are separate and separable entities.

Many subfields of psychology rely on the central executive to explain stuff. The traditional approaches in the second part of this book certainly do! Biological (and ecological) psychology emphatically do *not*. They instead assume **monism**. That is, they assume that people are all one thing (see Figure 1.7, *right*). Specifically, they assume people are entirely physical, and

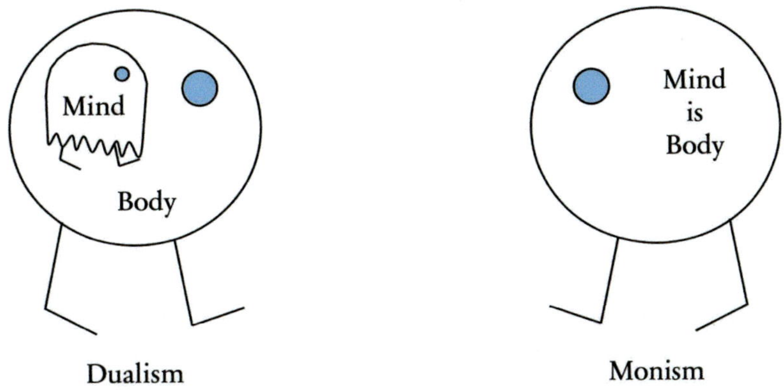

Figure 1.7 Left, dualism suggests that people are two different things, a physical body and a nonphysical mind (soul). Right, monism suggests that people are one thing, typically that they are all physical and that the "mind" is a property of the body.

any non-physical explanations of the body and how it works are impossible. The mind *is* the brain . . . we just might not understand *how* yet.

> **Monism** the idea that something (here, the person) is only made of one type of thing.

Body as Machine

When Descartes split the self in two (body and soul), he also asserted that the body was a **machine**. At the time (in the 17th century), there was a cultural obsession with making automata—mechanical devices that would perform complex behaviors. For example, there was an art installation of human-shaped automata in a park in the royal gardens at Saint-Germain-en-Laye. When viewers stepped on hidden pressure plates in the ground, it would open a series of valves, allowing water to flow through the automata in specific ways. The automata would then perform some action like tipping its hat or dancing. Amazing—especially for the 17th century!

> **Machine** a device that operates entirely based on immediate physical causes.

Descartes was inspired by these machines. He argued that we could consider the body in exactly the same way—a physical system that behaved entirely according to the laws of physics. Think of a series of dominoes placed in a line. Tipping over the first domino will cause the entire chain to fall over in sequence. To understand why any individual domino fell, you merely have to look to the one just before it. Descartes attempted to understand human behaviors as a sequence of dominos falling—each behavior caused by a mechanical precursor. For example, if a person removed their hand from a hot stove, that behavior could be understood like this: hand touches the hot stove -> sense organs register pain -> pain causes muscles to contract -> contracting muscles pull the hand away from the heat. In just this way, complex behaviors could be seen as a series of simple behaviors, each causing the next.

The "body-as-machine" metaphor is deeply influential in Western medical and scientific thought (Mattingly, 2011). If someone is sick, it is because part of their "machine" is broken.

The good news for people who apply this metaphor is that broken things can often be fixed! Medications and even organ transplants are a direct result of thinking of the body in the same way we think about cars—if a car is low on oil, we can add more; if a spark plug breaks, we can replace it with a new one.

Where Do These Assumptions Lead?

If *absolutely every* experience and behavior is biological, then it should be possible to identify the biological process behind *absolutely every experience that we have and behavior we perform.* This assumption means that if a psychological phenomenon hasn't been fully biologically explained, it's just because we haven't uncovered its biological root yet. It might mean we need to invent a new way of examining the body (hence all the tools explained in Box 1.3), or it might mean we have to better understand the findings we already have.

Assuming a fully biological cause for everything leads to questions like, "what part of the brain is responsible for the ability to plan complex tasks?", "what sequence of hormones is responsible for the feeling of love?", and "how does the processing of the brain change over the course of development?" All of these answers—and more!—are going to be found by looking at and measuring some part of the *body*.

Modern technology (see Box 1.3) has allowed an exploration of the body that early scientists could only *dream about*. These days we can understand the teeniest, tiniest parts of the body, we can watch as parts of the brain react *in real time*, we can edit DNA, alter the functioning of single cells, and change the distributions of hormones. What is important to remember as we marvel at the data gathered by these technological advancements, is that they were invented to answer very specific questions raised by the biological approach—and in this way, rest on the same assumptions made by a biological approach to understanding organisms.

Socratic Question: How do the assumptions of "monism" and "body as machine" lead to the fundamental assumption of the biological approach that *all* experiences can be explained biologically?

Box 1.3 How Do We Know That? Methodologies of Neurological Research

There are a lot of different methodologies for investigating the nervous system, including the brain and the sense organs. Each methodology reveals something different about how those systems work. What follows in an incomplete list to give you a sense of how we know what we know about such systems (see Figure 1.8):

*Lesions: whether by accident or on purpose, damage to one area of the brain can be informative about the function of that area of the brain. Damage to the hippocampus (as in the famous case of HM), for example, causes impairment in memory, which suggests that the hippocampus is involved in memory.

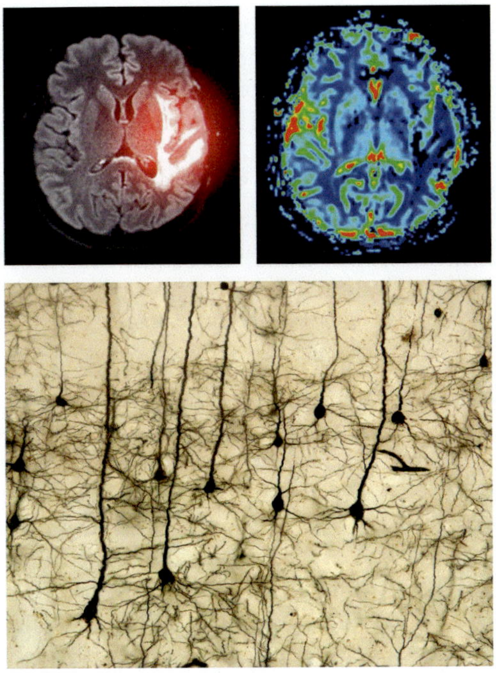

Figure 1.8 Modern technology allows insight into biological structure and function. Top left, a brain lesion; top right fMRI heat mapping; bottom, staining of neurons.

*Focal cooling: the electrical activity of the brain (see Chapter 3) cannot happen if the cells are too cold. Cooling one specific area of the brain essentially turns it off—temporarily anyway—and activity in "downstream" areas will be affected as well (sort of like turning off the water to Fred's house will stop his sink from working). This can be used to map the direction and location of processing.

*Functional magnetic resonance imaging (fMRI): measures the activity in the brain in (sort of) real time. Participants can be instructed to think of certain things, look at certain things, listen to certain things (etc.) and the activity of the brain in response can be measured and graphed as a "heat map" of activity.

*Transcranial magnetic stimulation (TMS): like focal cooling, TMS can "turn off" a specific area of the brain—again, temporarily—but instead of turning off a very small area (a few neurons, say) it turns off a larger area. It is essentially like a temporary lesion on the brain which allows for more systematic explorations of the effects of lesions.

*Microelectrodes: tiny (less than 1μm in diameter—the size of a single bacterium!) electrodes are inserted into a single or between two neurons to record the firing rate in real time. This is how Kuffler identified the receptive fields in the ganglia.

*Staining: after death, the brain is removed and sliced into thin slices. Different chemicals can be added to cause different things (e.g., cell walls, a particular chemical, a particular enzyme) to stand out. This is used to identify the microstructures of the brain.

Historically Popular Ideas

Once we get beyond the fundamental assumption of everything being biological (and its related assumptions), differences begin to emerge. Modern research has contradicted many of the other assumptions of the biological approach often enough that scientists have begun to doubt them (e.g. Strijkers, 2016; see Box 1.4 for more). Nevertheless, despite this doubt, these assumptions have been incredibly influential and are responsible for the vast majority of what we think we understand about the body. So, it's worth knowing what those assumptions were, even if they aren't really universally accepted anymore. To that end, what follows are described not as assumptions, but as 'historically popular ideas' instead.

Historically Popular Idea 1: Doctrine of Specific Nerve Energies

Let's return to Fred and his problem. He is standing in the field, admiring the apple tree. The sunlight is pouring down on him. He sees the light, but he can also *feel* the light (as warmth) on top of his head (he really should put on sunscreen—he's prone to sunburn). The qualitative experience he gets through his *eyes* is very different than the qualitative experience he gets through his *scalp*. In other words, the experience of *seeing* light is different than the experience of *feeling* light. For a while, this was a confusing problem. Why would the *same energy* (here, sunlight) cause a *completely different* experience? In other words, how could the same stimulus lead to a completely different sensation? Weird, right?

In the early 1800s, German physiologist Johannes Müller addressed this problem by suggesting that our awareness of the world wasn't *really* awareness of the world (Bridges, 1912). *Wait... what?* No really, bear with us (him) here; it kinda makes sense. Our sense organs (like our eyes and ears) react to stuff *out there* in the world, but they do so by activating nerves and brain areas *in here* in our bodies. And Fred's eyes and skin are attached to *different* nerves and *different* brain areas. Müller argued that Fred's awareness of the sunlight was really an awareness of the activations of his *nerves* rather than of the *world*. This is why the experience of seeing light and feeling light are different. In each case, different nerves and brain areas are being activated!

Part of the evidence for this is that stimulating the nerves attached to the different sense organs creates a very specific sensation associated with that sense organ. For example, if you stimulate the nerve attached to Fred's eye, he will "see light" even if there is no light there to be seen. You can try it right now! Close your eyes and (gently!) press on the side of your eye. You will see flashes of color with each press, or at least a change in the visual experience. In this case, the nerve isn't being stimulated by light; it's being stimulated by *pressure*, but you still "see light". Müller suggested that the reason we see with our eyes is because there's something about the character of the nerve *itself* that suggests "light" to the brain. The nerve is *specific* to that type of energy. He called this the **doctrine of specific nerve energies**.

> **Doctrine of specific nerve energies** The idea that all awareness of the world is actually awareness of the activity of nerves, and that nerves have their own specific "quality" that they convey (e.g., eye nerves convey light, tongue nerves convey taste).

Where Does This Popular Idea Lead?

If our awareness of the world is really awareness of the activations of nerves and brain areas, then the nerves and brain areas are the stars of the show. In other words, understanding our experiences requires examining the functioning of the nerves (and *not* by examining the world). This leads to questions like "what is the exact pathway of the nerves, from sense organ to brain area(s)?", "how are properties of the energy translated into patterns of nerve activation?", and "how can the brain figure out what out there in the world caused this particular pattern of nerve activation in the body?"

Historically Popular Idea 2: Hierarchical Processing

If we accept the assumption that we do not have direct access to the world and that our only awareness of the world is of the activation of nerves, it leads to a new problem. Specifically, all the information about the world (like the exact distance to Fred's tree, or the exact size of the apple) would need to be translated into a specific pattern of activation of the nerves and brain areas. Or in other words, how does the language of *light* become the language of the *brain*?

There are a lot of different ways we could imagine translating light information into the language of nerves, but the most popular has been **hierarchical processing**—the idea that all complex thoughts, perceptions, behaviors, and so on are built from simple to complex. Fred knows all about hierarchical processing because he is a fan of Lego building sets. He starts with a pile of blocks (each very simple), then builds them into an increasingly complex whole (see Figure 1.9).

> **Hierarchical processing** processing sensory input by starting with the simple elements and building to the more complex elements.

So how does his love for Legos help with understanding a biological approach to perception? Let's go back to Fred and his tree. In order for Fred to perform the action of grabbing an apple, he needs to see the tree. His brain needs to build a pattern of activation that means "apple tree". A hierarchical processing model would suggest that his sensory organs first identify simple elements—individual Lego pieces—and then build those simple elements into a complex experience of the whole—larger and larger groupings of connected Lego pieces. You could, for example, start by identifying the edges of the objects, then the orientation of those edges, then build those into shapes (see Figure 1.10).

The other implication of hierarchical processing is that it's, well, a *process* that produces *output*. Specifically, it's a *linear process* that leads to a *complex output*. What we mean by linear is that Input A leads to slightly more complex idea B, which leads to slightly more complex idea C, and so on in a line until you get the complex whole at the end. Just like how one Lego piece is connected with others until you have a more complex architectural masterpiece. In this perspective, perception is a process, and the **percept** is the output (see Figure 1.10).

> **Percept** The outcome of perception (when perception is considered as hierarchical processing).

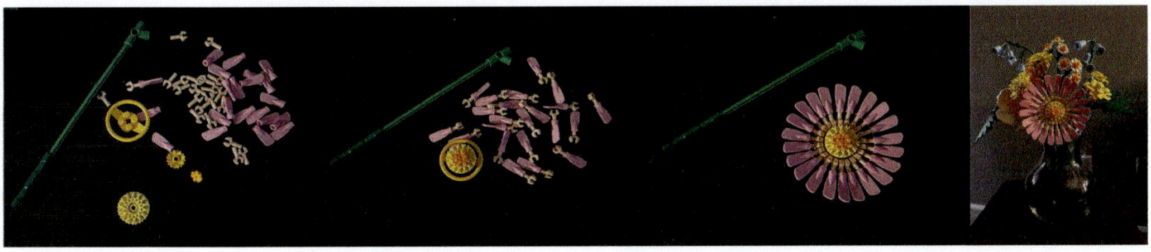

Figure 1.9 Simple building blocks, left, can create increasingly complex wholes, right.

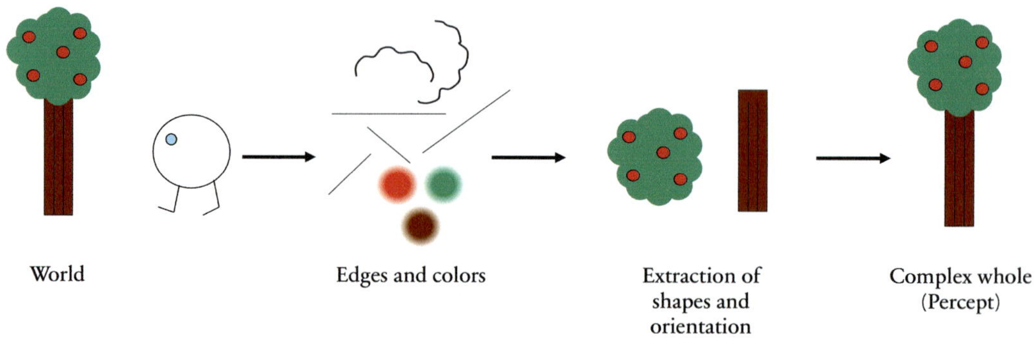

Figure 1.10 Hierarchical processing. In order to identify the tree, Fred's brain could first identify the edges, then figure out what orientation they are in, then piece together a larger whole.

Where Does This Popular Idea Lead?

If you start with the assumption that the system must first identify simple elements and then build them into increasingly complex ones, then it is going to change what you look for in the brain. You will expect that the "input" end—that is, the sensory organs—will be registering and transmitting simple elements; and you will expect that the "output" end—that is, the places farthest along in the processing chain will respond only to complex wholes. This popular idea leads to questions like "What are the simple elements that the sensory systems are identifying?", "What is the pathway of the processing of those elements?", and "Where is the 'output' of the processing, and what does it look like?"

Historically Popular Idea 3: Specificity of Neurological Areas

The first two popular ideas lead directly to the final popular idea: the specificity of brain areas. In this idea, every part of the brain has a single function, and every function of the brain takes place in a single area. Fred's brain will have an area for forming memories and a place for storing memories. In the area that stores memories, there will be an area that remembers what apple trees are and a part that remembers that he likes apples, and so on (see Figure 1.11).

Even when this was a *very* popular idea (it is far less so now), there was still considerable debate about it—but the debate was about *how* specific areas were. Does Fred need one part of the brain to remember skills like peeling an apple and a different part of the brain to remember events like being taught to peel an apple by his uncle Mike? Or can one part of the brain do both? Does he need one area to move his whole body, or do different parts of the brain move different parts of his body?

Where Does This Popular Idea Lead?

If you accept that each part of the brain has a specific function and each function is only in one part, then the job of a neuroscientist (someone who studies the brain) is to match every function to a part of the brain and/or to identify the function of every part of the brain. This leads to questions like "What does this part do?", "Where does this function happen?", and "And how about *this* part, what does *it* do?"

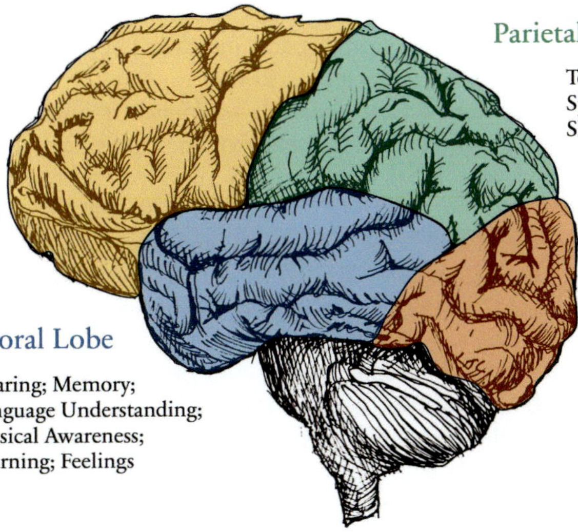

Figure 1.11 In the biological approach, the brain is often thought to have specific functions "housed" in specific parts of the brain.

Socratic Question: How do the historically popular ideas of doctrine of specific nerve energies, hierarchical processing, and specificity of neurological areas affect where and how scientists look for biological explanations for all experiences?

Box 1.4 What is Popular is Not Always Right, and What is Right is Not Always Popular

As we discussed at the beginning of the section on historically popular ideas, modern work in this field doesn't *fully* support those ideas anymore. Evidence against them has piled up to the point where it would be foolish to continue to believe them in their entirety. The following are (just some) of the findings that seem to contradict each of these popular ideas.

The processing of pain signals contradicts the doctrine of specific nerve energies. One time, Fred was teaching his pet baby elephant, Topsy, some tricks and he stumbled and fell, twisting his ankle. He tried to ignore the pain and kept walking around on it—Topsy *nearly* got the trick; he just wanted to keep working with her a little longer! Eventually, his ankle hurt so much that even touching his big toe on the ground caused pain to shoot up his leg (even though neither his toe nor the other parts of his leg were injured!). It turns out that if you ignore a pain signal and continue the behavior that is causing the injury, the pain signal will start recruiting *additional nerves* that don't usually carry pain signals. That's right: nerves that usually carry one type of signal (like touch) will carry a different type of signal (pain) instead. The nerve is *not* specific to the qualitative experience (e.g. Heinricher et al., 2009).

Hierarchical processing should be an entirely feedforward process and it's not. We're going to talk about this at some length in each of the biological chapters, but neurological pathways simply aren't linear like scientists initially expected. They loop back on themselves, split along different main pathways, and different pathways often communicate with each other both "up" and "down" the pathway. It's a complex process that is most certainly *not* linear (Strijkers, 2016). These days, the architecture of the brain is more often referred to as a "neural net" (short for network, but meant to make you think of the interconnecting strings of a fishing net).

Brain areas didn't turn out to be that specific, and functions are frequently distributed. Some functions proved impossible to pin to a specific area, and some areas proved to be involved in lots of different functions. Additionally, the brain (really, the whole nervous system) turned out to be much more *plastic* (that is, able to be changed) than previously thought. It is sometimes possible for someone to permanently injure the area involved in speech . . . and then, through practice, rewire their brain so language is processed in an entirely different area, allowing them to talk again. That plasticity means that there cannot be something special or unique about the area usually responsible for speech. Most modern biological behavioral scientists believe that function is *distributed* across many different areas in the brain, rather than entirely in one specific place (Parks et al., 1991).

Important Historical Distinctions

The study of sensation and perception (like most sciences) has a few core terms that come up with enough frequency that you have to know them in order to understand what people are talking about. That isn't to say that everyone agrees with them, or even that they end up being all that useful, but they're kinda everywhere and you'll feel lost if you don't know them. The following list is by no means a complete list of these core historical ideas, but these are terms and ideas we'll be using throughout the book, so it's enough to get started.

Distal vs. Proximal Stimulus

Let's return once more to Fred in the field (see Figure 1.12). The tree in the world is called the **distal stimulus**. It is the thing *out there* that is causing a pattern of activation on Fred's nerves. The pattern of activation on Fred's nerves is called the **proximal stimulus**. This distinction is going to be very important for the biological and traditional views (and not at all important for the ecological view). For the biological approach, the proximal stimulus is where most of the research is focused. The biological approach asks, "what is the pattern of stimulation (proximal stimulus) and how is that pattern related to the thing that caused it (the distal stimulus)?" As we'll talk about

Distal stimulus the object out in the world that is causing a reaction on the sense organs of the organism.

Proximal stimulus the pattern of reaction of the sense organs and nerves in response to some object in the world.

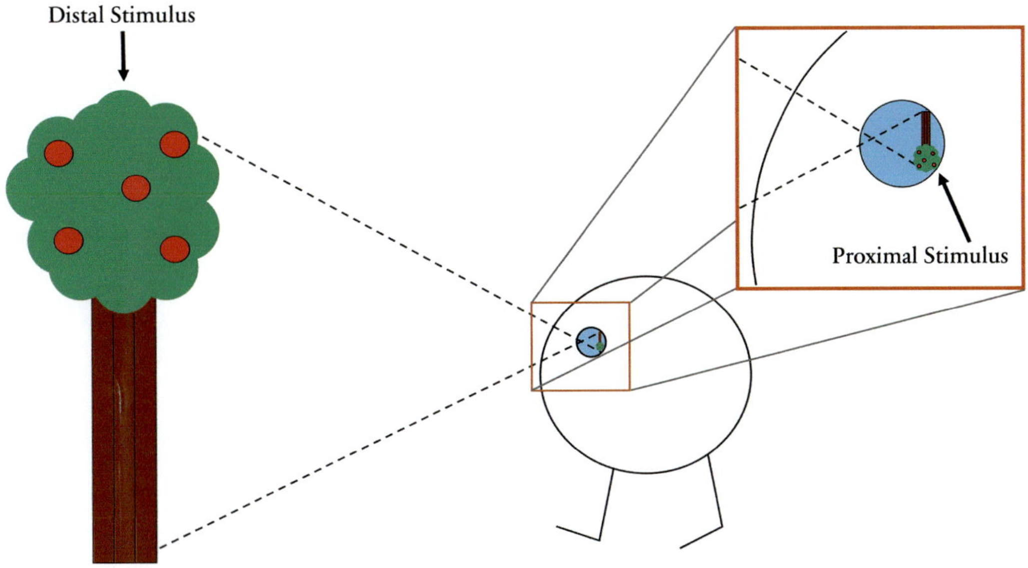

Figure 1.12 The distal stimulus is the object in the world; the proximal stimulus is the pattern of activation on the sense organs.

in Chapters 8 and 13, the other main approaches have different questions to ask about this distinction; for example, while this is an important distinction in the traditional approach, it is not in the ecological approach.

Near vs. Distance Senses

One of the distinctions often made in the literature is the difference between senses where the distal stimulus does not make physical contact with our sense organs and those where it does. Fred is not in contact with the tree, and yet he knows about the tree. He knows about something he *is not* in contact with (because he *sees* it). Fred also knows there is grass under his bare feet; he knows about something he *is* in contact with (because he can *feel* it). In this example, sight is a distance sense and touch is a near sense.

This is a distinction that, early in the study of sensing and perceiving, seemed like it was going to be useful. **Categorizing** in general seemed useful (check the next section for another example). Categorizing is the process of defining metaphorical "boxes" and sorting stuff into them. For example, I might sort my socks into two categories: "plain" and "have pictures of cats on them". That might help me understand my sock needs better (who doesn't need more cat socks?), but it isn't the *only* way I could sort them.

> **Categorizing** The process of inventing categories and sorting phenomena into them in order to better understand those phenomena.

Categorization felt like it was going to be useful in the early study of perception. This is particularly true for the early versions of the traditional views which saw near senses as easier to explain than distance senses. But as the science and our understanding has evolved, this

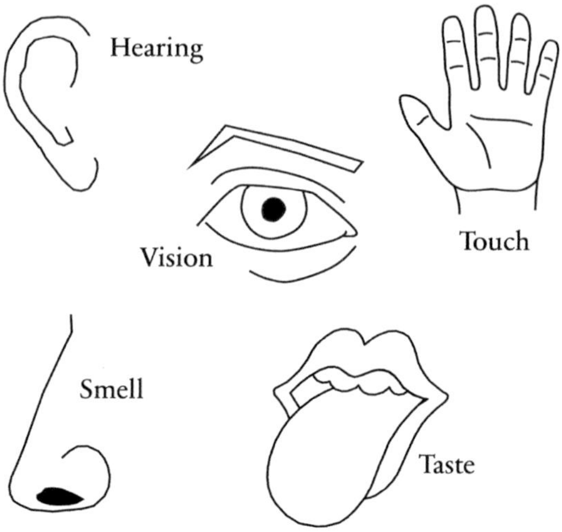

Figure 1.13 The classic idea of "five senses" is far too restrictive and may have hindered the study of perceptual processes.

distinction has meant less and less (and categorization more generally has seemed less and less useful). Neither the biological approach nor the ecological approach use this distinction at all. Nevertheless, it is still frequently discussed—especially in the traditional approach—and we didn't want you to be out of the loop.

Five Senses? Probably Not

When Fred was in kindergarten, he was taught about the five senses: touch, taste, smell, hearing, and sight (see Figure 1.13). You were probably taught these as well; your authors certainly were! What Little Fred did not know was that this list was first compiled by Aristotle in the 300s BCE. Aristotle was *very* into categorization. The problem, of course, is that it's all so much more complicated than that.[2] It depends on how you count, but some scientists claim that the senses are not separate *at all*, and others estimate that there are well over 30. *Wait . . . what?* Yup. You'll have to make your own mind up about what you think. The distinction among separate senses is much more important in the biological and traditional approaches and much less so in the ecological approach.

There are a number of senses that other organisms have that we do not—we already talked about the electric sense of sharks and the carbon dioxide sense of mosquitos, but there are a *lot* more examples. Even within humans, there is the problem that senses that *seem* distinct in theory—like taste and smell, for example—are actually very intertwined in practice (see Chapter 7). Trying to decide what the actual difference between those two is surprisingly complicated. For example, some animals taste with other parts of their bodies (like their feet), and some animals smell with their tongues. That means you can't just define taste as something that's done with the tongue and smell as something that's done with the nose. And in order to smell something, it has to dissolve into a liquid in your nose, just like in order to taste something, it has to dissolve in your saliva on your tongue. That means you can't say that smelling is in the air and taste is of a liquid. It's not such an easy problem! In fact, it's so thorny that one neuroscientist said, "I avoid thinking about it" (Yong, 2022, p. 47). While there may be some virtue in categorization, the myth of the five senses is one that might have held us back as a science. When you are sure (when you *assume*) that there are only five senses, you are only going to go looking for the machinery associated with those five, and nothing else.

> Socratic Question: Why might it be problematic to divide the senses into near senses and distance senses? Why might it be problematic to count exactly how many senses there are?

History

With all these assumptions, popular ideas and terminology in mind, let's talk about some of the historical work in this field. And here is where we get to tell you one of our favorite facts about the history of psychology—the first psychologists were studying sensation and perception. That's right! The first official psychology lab was started by a German scientist named Wilhelm Wundt. He was among the first to suggest that mental processes could be studied in the same scientific way as physics and chemistry. He applied the scientific method to the study of perceptual experience—specifically trying to understand the relationship between stimuli (distal stimuli, specifically) and the experience of the perceiver.

Psychophysics

Wundt's work is part of the field of **psychophysics**.[3] He wasn't the first psychophysicist, but he was the first to start a full lab based on it. Psychophysics is the scientific study of the relationship between a physical stimulus and the *experience* of that stimulus.

> **Psychophysics** the study of the relationship between physical stimuli and experience.

Of course, they did not have access to the same kind of modern technology that we do (see Box 1.3), so the inner workings of the human nervous system were basically unknowable. Well . . . kinda. Think about it like the top of Figure 1.14. Imagine Fred has a black box. He cannot see in it, and he doesn't know what it does. All he knows is that he can put in an input on one side and it will spit out an output on the other side. Hmmm . . . interesting! One way for him to guess what the black box does is to try a bunch of inputs one at a time and see what the box outputs each time. In the example shown in Figure 1.14, after trying a few inputs and seeing a few outputs, it looks like the pattern is that the black box multiplies the input by 2.

Psychophysics works on this black box principle. The sensory organs and neural pathways were not directly observable, so they were like the black box. To figure out what was going on inside people, the scientists varied the physical energy input (like dimmer and brighter lights, or quieter and louder noises) and measured the output (like the participant saying they could or could not see the light, or could or could not hear the noise). Note that this method requires the assumption that the black box does not change—it always performs the exact same function. It may seem rudimentary (particularly compared to our modern methods), but this technique revealed a lot of really interesting things about the way our sensory systems work.

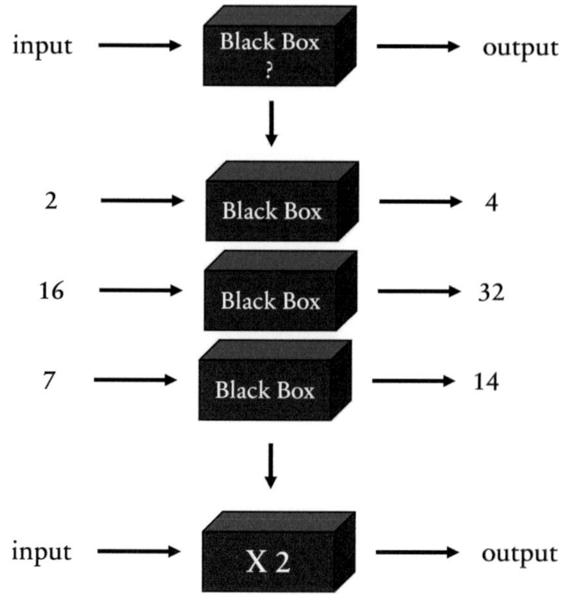

Figure 1.14 Black box logic. Although the workings of the black box cannot be directly observed, its function can be guessed at by varying the inputs, measuring the outputs, and looking for patterns.

Minimum threshold the smallest amount of energy that can be sensed.

Sensitivity the ability to respond to a stimulus.

Sensitivity vs. Acuity. The organs associated with each sense are detecting some kind of energy. Vision responds to light, hearing responds to sound, and so on. One of the first questions asked was "what is the smallest amount of energy that can be sensed?" What they are measuring is the **minimum threshold** of each sense, which is a measure of the **sensitivity** of the sense. They tested the sensitivity of all kinds of things. They tested how much salt had to be added to water before it could be detected, how bright a light had to be before it could be seen, and so on.

Difference threshold the smallest difference in a stimulus that can be noticed.

Acuity the ability to tell the difference between two stimuli.

In addition to the minimum threshold, psychophysicists also asked the question, "how different does the energy have to be before a change can be noticed?" That is, they were interested in **difference thresholds**, a test of the **acuity** of a sense. For example, they might gradually increase the brightness of a light and ask the participant to say when they notice a change, or they might increase the amount of salt in the water and ask if the participant could taste the difference. The results here were a lot less straightforward and (we think) a lot more interesting. It turned out that the difference threshold was not always the same; it wasn't always the same increase in brightness that could be seen, it

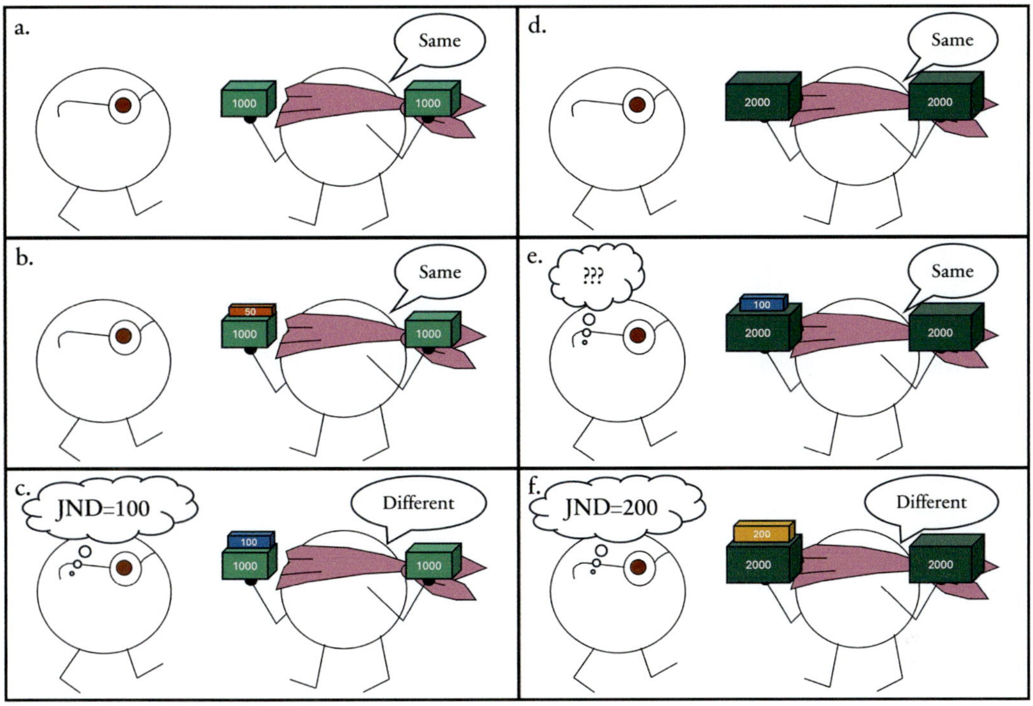

Figure 1.15 The just noticeable difference (JND) is dependent on the original stimulus. See text for details.

wasn't always the same amount of salt that had to be added before someone could tell the difference, and so on. The difference threshold entirely depended on the context.

Just Noticeable Differences (JNDs). Ernst Weber (a German physician) spent a lot of time investigating difference thresholds, which he named **just noticeable differences (JNDs)** and found a very interesting pattern of results. Let's talk about a specific example to understand the concept. In Figure 1.15a, Fred is holding two blocks weighing one kilogram (1000 grams or about the weight of a pineapple) each, one in each hand. They weigh the same amount; he says they feel the same to him. In Figure 1.15b, the experimenter has added 50 grams of weight (or half a slice of pineapple) to the block in his left hand, but Fred can't sense the difference between the two. They weigh different amounts, but Fred says they feel the same to him. In Figure 1.15c, the experimenter has added 100 grams (a whole slice of pineapple!) to the block in Fred's left hand, and he can now tell the difference. At this point, the experimenter says "100 grams is the just noticeable difference".

> **Just Noticeable Differences (JNDs)** the smallest difference between two stimuli that can be noticed.

But wait! In Figure 1.15d., Fred is holding two blocks weighing two kilograms (2000 grams, about the weight of a 2-liter bottle of water) each, in each hand. He once again says they feel the same to him. The experimenter adds 100 grams (a 100ml bottle of water; see Figure 1.15e) to the weight in his left hand—but this time, Fred can't sense that addition. The experimenter has to add *200* grams for Fred to notice (see Figure 1.15f)! The JND is 200 grams for this context.

So what's going on? Well, it turns out that the amount the weight has to change is dependent on the weight of the block to begin with. Specifically, the weight in the left hand has to be 10% heavier (or 10% lighter) before Fred will notice. The JND is a proportion of the original stimulus, not an absolute number. Weber formulated this equation:

$$\frac{\Delta I}{I_1} = k$$

In English, that formula says that the noticeable change in intensity (ΔI), divided by the original intensity (I_1), will always equal a constant (k). Weights have to be 10% heavier to notice a difference, so for weights, $k = 1/10$. The size of the Weber fraction, then, is a measure of the acuity of a sense. The following is a short list of some Weber fractions. Notice, for example, that our ability to sense changes in pitch is ***way better*** than our ability to sense the difference in light intensity.

Some Weber fractions:

Light intensity	1/10
Loudness of a sound	1/10
Taste of saltiness	1/20
Length of a line	1/100
Pitch of a sound	1/330

Socratic Question: Weber's law states that the just noticeable difference is a proportion of the original stimulus rather than the absolute stimulus. Why might it be helpful that the sense systems are sensitive to proportional change in a stimulus rather than absolute change in a stimulus?

Today, psychophysics is not its own field of study like it was in the 19th century, but you can think of it like the ancestor of the biological view of perception. It was the first rigorous attempt to understand our sensation and perception, and the field as a whole owes a lot to their work.

Explanation of the Features of This Book

Every chapter in this book (including this one!) will have a variety of features we hope will help the reader remember and understand the material better.

Socratic Questions

The Socratic method (named after the philosopher Socrates) teaches information by asking students to consider questions. Frequently, there are not "correct" answers to these questions. Instead, the act of considering the question helps the student draw parallels between different ideas, think more broadly (or more specifically!) about the topic, and/or consider another angle on the same ideas. In that spirit, throughout each chapter are questions that ask the reader to consider topics more deeply.

Terms

Each of the main terms is defined in a stand-out box. We don't recommend reading *only* the main terms, but collectively they should help anchor the ideas presented.

Summaries

At the end of each chapter is a summary of the points covered in the chapter. Obviously, by the nature of summaries, they will not contain enough detail to substitute for the chapter as a whole . . . but if you read them and they don't make any sense, it's a sign that you might want to revisit some sections of the chapter.

Science is not a straight line from ignorance to truth. In every scientific endeavor, there are pitfalls, dead ends, misinterpretations, reinterpretations, and contradicting views. The study of sensing and perceiving is no exception. Our goal with this text is to provide as comprehensive an overview as we can of the field. That means that sometimes we will present information that is contradictory with other parts of the text. That is just the nature of the beast. We hope you find this topic as interesting as we do!

Summary

The study of sensation and perception can be understood as the study of how we *know stuff* and how this allows us *to do* stuff. In the example of Fred trying to get a snack from an apple tree, perceptual scientists seek to understand how he knows where the tree is, what it means, and how he can use that information to get a snack. This book covers the three main approaches to this question: the biological approach, the traditional approach, and the ecological approach. To understand the differences between these approaches, you have to understand the assumptions of each approach. The first section of this book will cover the biological approach. The main assumption of the biological approach is that all experiences can be understood biologically.

Notes

1 This is mostly what we're going to call it for the remainder of the book.
2 "It's more complicated than that" is basically the main theme of this book.
3 Although Wundt wasn't the one to name it that; another German scientist named Gustav Fechner coined the term nearly 20 years before Wundt started his lab.

2 Light and the Eye

In Chapter 1, we introduced you to Fred's problem (see Figure 2.1). Fred knows stuff about the things that are in the field through all of his senses (however many there are). However, when it comes to knowing about things that are relatively far away (like the tree on the other side of the field), one of his best options is vision. While it may seem obvious to say, for Fred to see the tree there must be **light**. In Figure 2.1, we have traced the path of the light from the sun to the tree, and then from the tree to Fred's eye. In order to understand Fred's problem from a biological perspective, we need to start by understanding the *light itself*. Once we understand the light, we can start to understand what happens when that light makes contact with our eyes.

Light electromagnetic radiation structured in waves (and particles, and rays) over space.

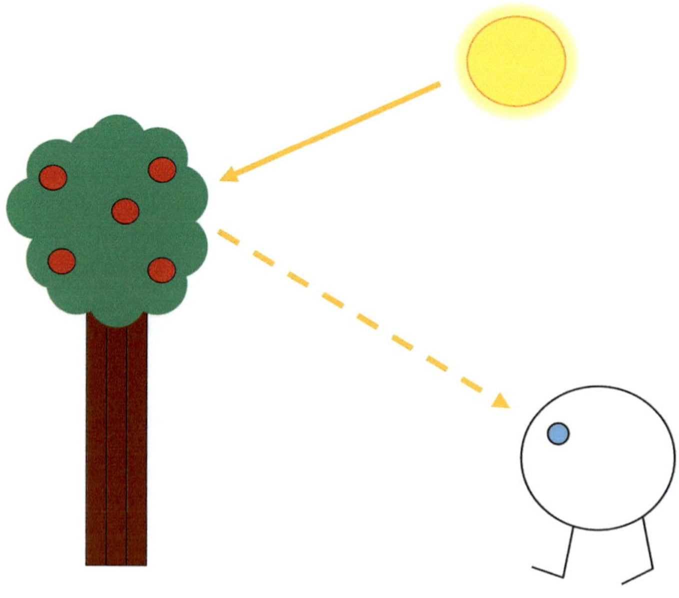

Figure 2.1 Fred's problem, with the pathway of the light depicted.

DOI: 10.4324/9781032690964-3

What is Light?

Light is most everywhere in some form or another. Go outside during the daytime and there it is. Flip on a light switch and there it is again. Glance at your cell phone and there it is yet again. You know this. And you know that you need light to see. Fred discovered this the hard way when he tried to walk across the room in a blackout and stubbed his toe on the coffee table—*ouch!* But what is light exactly? Technically speaking, light is electromagnetic radiation structured in waves (and particles, and rays) over space. Put that way, it sounds like it is the villain's weapon in a really bad science fiction movie or the technology behind a wacky product you might buy from an infomercial on late at night. It's neither, though, we promise—let's break the definition down piece by piece.

Part 1 of the Definition of Light—"Electromagnetic"

Energy comes in many different forms. There's thermal (heat) energy, kinetic (movement) energy, nuclear (from the nucleus of an atom) energy, and so on. Electromagnetism is just another form of energy. Specifically, it is the energy created by an electrically charged particle (like an electron). That energy is released and travels at tremendous speed (about 300,000,000 meters per second).[1] The sun produces vast amounts of electromagnetic energy of different kinds (collectively called the electromagnetic spectrum) which pours down on Earth. Visible light is only one part of this spectrum (other parts include radio waves and x-rays). We call the part of the electromagnetic spectrum that we can see "visible light" but truthfully, it's the light that's visible to *us*. Other organisms can see other parts of the electromagnetic spectrum that are invisible to us (more on this later in the chapter; see also Yong, 2022).

Part 2 of the Definition of Light—"Radiation"

In all likelihood, that word evokes images of accidents at Chernobyl or Fukushima or radiation warning symbols (see Figure 2.2); however, the word actually has a much more benign meaning. Radiation merely means energy of some kind coming from a source. Perhaps you have radiators in your house for heat. They are called that because heat *radiates* from them—it is an energy that comes from that source. Like heat, light radiates—it always comes from a source.

Figure 2.2 Radiation warning symbols make us think that "radiation" is a bad thing, but all it means is energy coming from a source. This symbol means *dangerous* radiation is nearby.

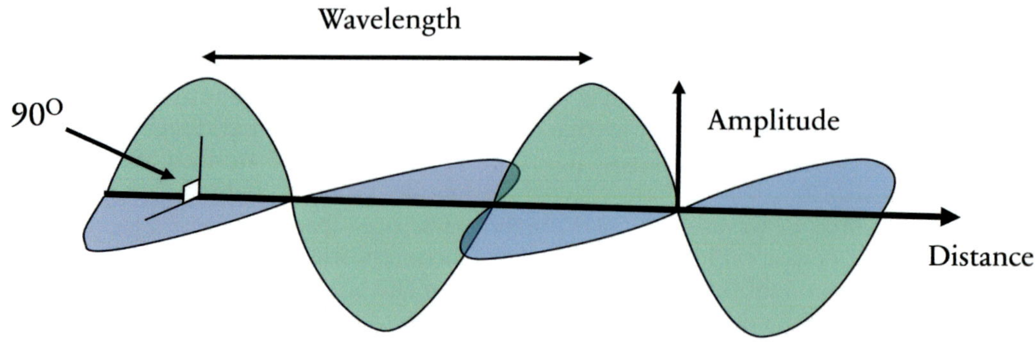

Figure 2.3 Light as a wave. The electric field oscillation (in green) is perpendicular to the magnetic field oscillation (in blue). Properties of the wave (wavelength, amplitude) have consequences for how they appear to us (color, brightness).

Part 3 of the Definition of Light—"Structured in Waves (and Particles, and Rays)"

Light is very, very fast. Faster than track star Sha'Carri Richardson. Faster than F1 driver Max Verstappen. Faster than time flies when you are having fun. In fact, it's the fastest thing we know.[2] Because it travels so fast, measuring its various properties is difficult. When scientists first started measuring it, they had to come up with a bunch of clever ways of doing so (see Box 2.1). But it turns out that it acts differently depending on how you measure it. When you measure light one way, it acts like a *wave* (that is, a regular repeating pattern). When you measure it a different way, it acts like a *particle* (that is, like a small portion of matter). Making things more complicated, when you are trying to understand how light bends and moves, it's best to describe it as a *ray* (like we did in Figure 2.1). For a full understanding of how the visual system is stimulated by light, you need to understand all three different ways of talking about it.

Light as a Wave

> **Wavelength** the distance from peak to peak in a repeating wave. Wavelength corresponds to experienced color of the light.
>
> **Amplitude** the height of repeating wave. The height corresponds to experienced brightness of the light.

Light travels through space in a wave pattern. When electrically charged particles travel through space, they produce waves of electric and magnetic energy. The two types of waves are perpendicular to each other, and equal in size (see Figure 2.3). Box 2.1 explains an experiment that shows how light acts like a wave.

Properties of the wave have consequences for how we perceive properties of the light. The distance from wave peak to wave peak is called **wavelength**. Differences in wavelength are perceived by humans as different colors. We know for sure that other animals (like dogs and cats and pet baby elephants) can see the differences in wavelengths, but it's hard to ask what their subjective experience of that is! The height of the wave is called the **amplitude**. Differences in amplitude are experienced (by humans anyway) as differences in the brightness of the light.

Light as a Particle

Light travels through space as a packet of energy called a **photon** and the amount of energy in that packet is measured in **quanta**. Einstein (1905) did a series of studies on light as a photon. He realized that each photon had different amounts of energy—that is, each photon had larger or smaller quanta. Furthermore, humans see larger or smaller quanta as different colors of light. Humans see photons with more energy (a larger quantum) as the violet end of the spectrum and less energy (a smaller quantum) as the red end of the spectrum. Ultraviolet light (which we cannot see, but many animals can) has *even more energy* still—which is why Fred gets a sunburn on his head when he spends too much time outside in the sun—*ouch*! Brighter sources (like the sun) emit more photons, dimmer sources (like a candle) emit fewer photons.

Photon (measured in quanta) photon is an elementary particle of light, the amount of energy in that particle is called a quantum (plural: quanta).

Box 3.1 Measuring Light

How Do We Know Light Is a Wave?

In 1801, Thomas Young demonstrated that light behaves as a wave in the famous double slit experiment. Well, famous to some people, anyway. You could actually set this up in your own house using a flashlight and a few notecards and prove it to yourself!

Light that comes from the sun is *incoherent*; that means that it is composed of all different frequences and intensities and is moving in all sorts of different directions. Imagine lots of different people talking to you all at once. Incoherent, right?

To perform the experiment, Young needed the light to be somewhat coherent (at roughly the same frequency and intensity moving in roughly the same direction). To get coherent light, he first passed sunlight through a single slit; this blocked the light traveling in directions other than pretty much straight ahead, and so the light that passed through was then (mostly) coherent. He then passed that coherent light through *two more* slits set up like in Figure 2.4 and then onto a surface. On that surface, he observed

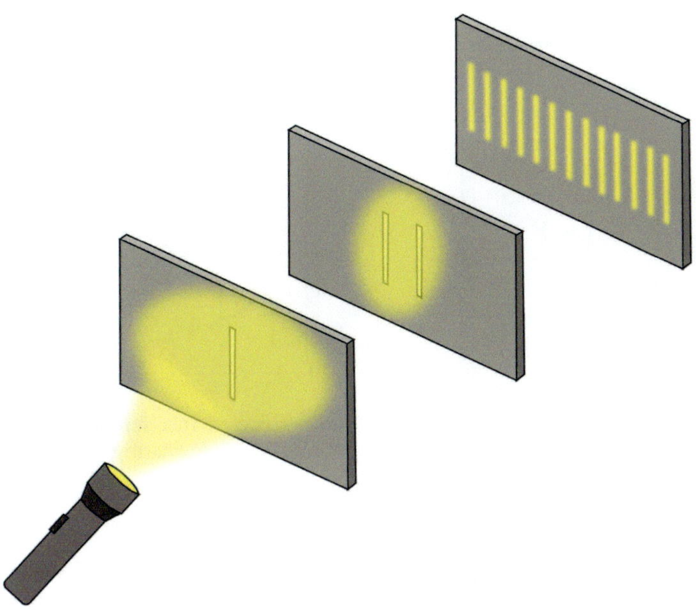

Figure 2.4 The double slit experiment. Incoherent light is passed through a slit so only coherent light falls on the double slit. The repeating pattern of light bars on the wall opposite the double slits is evidence that light travels like a wave.

several bars of light—like the beams of light passing through the slits somehow multiplied on their way to the surface (Young, 1832). Weird!

This can only happen if light is a wave—but why!? The beams of light didn't so much multiply as interact with each other. When two waves interact, they *interfere* with each other—if it helps, think about waves on the ocean. Waves that interact can show either constructive or destructive interference. In constructive interference, the waves are lined up peak to peak and trough to trough (see Figure 2.5, *top left*). When those waves interact, they *combine*. You end up with a higher amplitude way—one with an even *higher* peak and an even *lower* trough. In the case of light, that means a *brighter* light. In the case of an ocean wave, it means a bigger, stronger wave. In destructive interference, the waves are lined up peak to trough (see Figure 2.5, *top right*). That means that when those waves interact, they cancel each other out—in the case of light, that means darkness. In the case of an ocean wave, this means stillness.

So, what does this have to do with Thomas Young and his light experiment? Well, when the light passes through each of the two slits, it fans out in both directions. So, by the time the light strikes the surface, the light will have *repeating bands* of constructive and destructive interference. And this will produce repeating bands of brightness and darkness (see Figure 2.5, *bottom*). There is no explanation of this phenomenon if light is (only) a particle. Hence, light is (or can be considered) a wave.

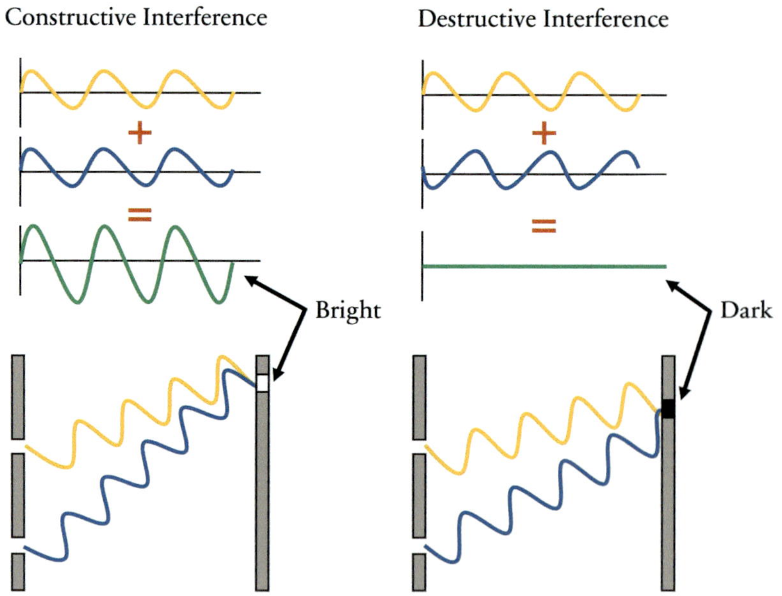

Figure 2.5 Top, constructive interference (left) and destructive interference (right). Bottom, how constructive and destructive interference result in alternating bands of dark and light.

How Do We Know Light Is (Also) a Particle?

It turns out understanding the light as a wave does not explain everything we know about light. Another way to understand light is as a particle. We know light can act as a particle due to something called the *photoelectric effect*. Maybe a *different* villain's weapon in a bad

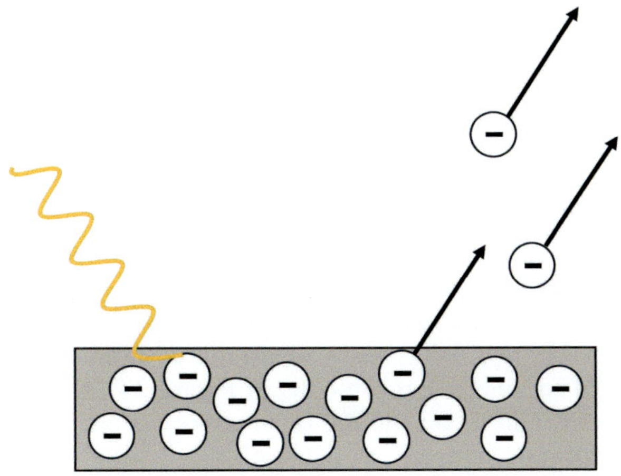

Figure 2.6 The photoelectric effect. Light striking a metal surface releases an electron.

science fiction movie? No, again. One of the properties of atoms that comprise metals is that they have lots of electrons. When light strikes a metal surface, the metal atoms release an electron.[3] If light were a wave, we would expect that certain changes in the light striking the surface would change the behavior of that escaping electron.

First, increasing the *amplitude* of the light (that is, making the light brighter) should increase the *energy* of the electrons released. Think about it like bouncing a ball off a wall—the harder you throw the ball at the wall, the harder it will bounce back at you. Look out!

Second, decreasing the *wavelength* of light (that is, changing the color of the light) which increases the *frequency* of peaks should increase the *number* of electrons released. In the ball analogy, the more balls you throw, the more balls will bounce back at you. Look out even more!

But when those predictions were tested, scientists found the *opposite* pattern of results: changing the brightness changed the *number* of electrons released and changing the color changed the *energy* of the electrons released (Hertz, 1887; Einstein, 1905). Weird! Again!

These results only make sense when you consider light as a particle—but why!? If light is a particle, then a brighter light means that *more packets of light* are hitting the surface.

In other words, a brighter light means that that packets of light are hitting the surface with greater frequency (more packets, more often). Just as in the previous analogy, throwing balls at the wall with greater frequency (more balls, more often) means that more balls will bounce back at you. Similarly, a higher frequency of packets of light means a higher frequency of electrons released.

And when light is considered as a particle, different colors of light have different *amounts of quanta*; that is, different colors have different amounts of energy. Just as in the previous analogy, throwing the ball with more energy at the wall means it will bounce back at you with more energy—that is, harder. A higher quantum releases electrons with more kinetic energy and vice versa.

These two (and other) experiments show that light acts as a particle *and* as a wave—even though our current understanding of those descriptions are mutually exclusive. It's one of those mysteries of the physical world that we just have to accept . . . for now.

For Our Purposes, Light Is (Best Described as) a Ray

Even though light can be understood as particle or as a wave, when trying to understand the way light interacts with the substances and surfaces of our environment, it is (most) helpful to think of it as a ray. This is because doing so means that we are able to draw the pathways of light as straight lines (or "rays"). Typically, we do this in summary form—one ray is drawn at each outer "edge" of an object. For example, in Figure 2.7, we have drawn one ray that radiates from the sun and reflects off the top of the tree and one that radiates from the sun and reflects off the bottom of the tree.

While light does travel in straight lines, these drawings are an oversimplification—and necessarily so. The light is radiating from the sun in *every* direction (remember incoherence?). Likewise, the light is bouncing off of the tree in *every* direction. That means that light fills all the spaces depicted in Figure 2.7; however, to understand how light behaves, it is helpful to just draw a very tiny portion of that light—the lines from the sun to the tree and from the tree to Fred's eye.

Socratic Question: What are the three ways in which light can be described? Which way is most helpful for understanding how light interacts with surrounding substances and surfaces? Why?

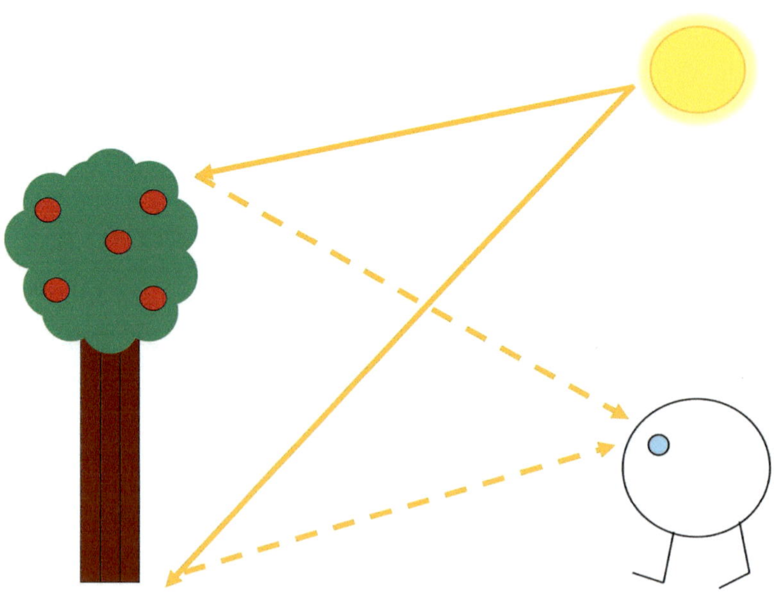

Figure 2.7 Fred's problem, with light rays depicted.

Part 4 of the Definition of Light—"Over Space"

Light travels. The way light travels makes it a particularly useful stimulation pattern for our visual system. In particular, it travels *far*. It travels *fast*. And it travels in *straight lines*.

Light Travels Far

Fred was hanging out with an astrophysicist friend of his, Dr. Smart, admiring the stars. (By the way, we hope that you have, at some point, done the same thing: stood outside on a clear night and looked at the stars—with or without an astrophysicist friend. If not, we are giving you that as homework. Go do that and come back.) Dr. Smart explained to Fred that each one of those stars is just like our own sun—massive balls of energy emitting (among other things) massive amounts of visible light. The light radiates from those stars in every direction, including the direction of Earth. That light travels for *billions of years* in some cases, just to be caught by Fred's eye.[4] If it hadn't hit his eye (or the Earth), it would have kept going. Light never runs of momentum; it just goes and goes and goes until it hits something.

For our purposes, that means we can use light to know about things that are far away.

Light Travels Fast

As we have already mentioned, light is the fastest thing we know. Over large distances—like from one end of the universe to the other—it might take billions of years for the light from a star to reach Fred's eye. However, on Earth (where Fred spends most of his time, and presumably you do, too!) the distances are much, *much* smaller. So much smaller that the light from the tree reaches Fred's eye imperceptibly fast.

For our purposes, that means we can see things (practically) instantaneously. Don't believe us? Go into a completely dark room and turn on the lights. Bam! (Virtually) instantaneous seeing!

Light Travels in Straight Lines

Light travels in straight lines whether it is traveling through a vacuum like outer space, or through a medium such as air or water. It can be bent by extreme gravity (called gravitational lensing), and it can be redirected by bouncing off of something or by passing through something (like water or a lens), but otherwise light will travel straight. Traveling in straight lines means that light rays that leave an object next to each other stay next to each other as they travel through the air. That is very important for making images (for reasons that will make sense later in the chapter).

For our purposes, that means that light can create clear images on surfaces.

The Light We Can See

The sun (our most abundant natural source of light) radiates energy with wavelengths that span the entirety of the electromagnetic spectrum. All of those different wavelengths of light hit our atmosphere. Not all of those wavelengths are able to make it *through* the atmosphere, however. In fact, the vast majority of the energy released by the sun is either scattered by or absorbed by the atmosphere. Human eyes (and those of other organisms) evolved sensitivity to those wavelengths of light that reliably make it through the atmosphere, strike the surfaces of the various surfaces on the planet *and* then bounce off of those surfaces.

The wavelengths of light that make up the so-called "visible light spectrum" are only a tiny portion of the full electromagnetic spectrum (see Figure 2.8). It is called "visible light" because it the light that humans can see (makes sense, right?). However—and this is a big however!—there are other organisms that can see ultraviolet (e.g., bees) and infrared light (e.g., snakes) in the same way we can see blue or green. And even those that see the same light we do (like Fred's pet baby elephant, Topsy) don't necessarily experience it the same way we do! You'll learn more about the different types of color vision in Chapter 4.

Another important thing to notice is that the visible light spectrum does not include white light. That is because there is no such thing as white light. *Wait . . . what?* Yep. When all the different wavelengths of light travel together, we perceive it as "white", but there is no singular wavelength that is white (Newton, 1730/1952). We only perceive it that way because of the way our eyes work (see Chapter 4 for why).

The different wavelengths of light don't really mix together; they just travel together in the same direction. So, the different wavelengths of light are less like cream in coffee and more like passengers on a bus. One way we know that this is true is that "white" light is easily broken into its **spectral components**—for example, by using a prism (see Figure 2.9). This is like opening the door on the bus to let all of the different passengers out!

Spectral components the different wavelengths that make up light.

Socratic Question: What is the difference between "light" and "visible light"? And why is there no such thing as "white light"?

How Is Light Structured?

Organisms live in cluttered environments. And we're not just talking about Fred's messy roommate, LeGrace—*all* organisms. What we mean is that just about all of the time, organisms are

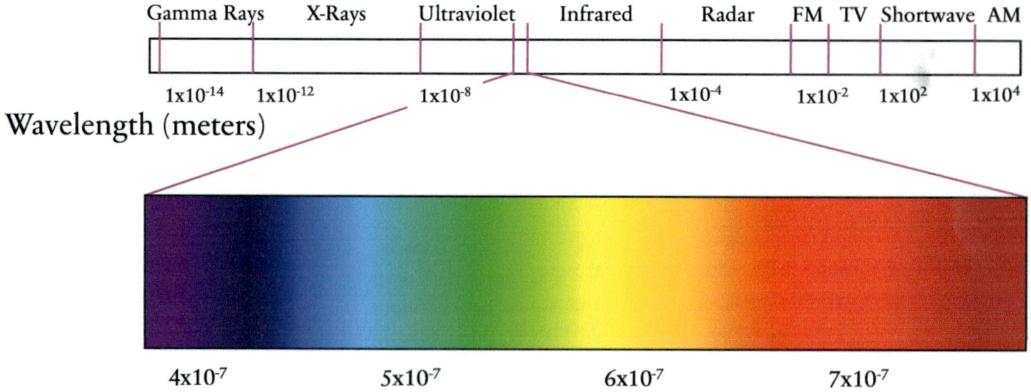

Figure 2.8 The electromagnetic spectrum. Only a tiny portion (called "visible light") can be seen by humans, but we are aware of (and use) other portions of the spectrum as well (e.g., X-rays, radiowaves).

Figure 2.9 White light is easily split into its spectral components by passing it through a prism. In addition to being pretty, this shows us that light does not mix, it only travels in the same direction for a while. When all of the colors of light travel together, we perceive it as "white".

surrounded by stuff—or more technically, by surfaces (it just might be *more* surfaces with a roommate like LeGrace!). When light strikes those surfaces, one of three things can happen: it can be absorbed, it can be reflected, or it can be transmitted. Which of the three happens depends on the properties of the surface. In this way, light is structured by its contact with the surfaces (see Box 2.2).

Absorption

One thing that can happen when light strikes a surface is that it can be absorbed by that surface. Light is energy, so when it is absorbed by the surface, it is absorbed as heat. If the surface absorbs more energy (like the black sock LeGrace left on the living room floor—*eww*!), less light will reflect and make its way to the eye; therefore, the surface will appear darker. If the surface absorbs less energy (like the white wrapper LeGrace left on the kitchen counter—also, *eww*!), more light will reflect and make its way to the eye; therefore, it will appear lighter (see Figure 2.10). This is why you are advised to wear light-colored clothing during hot weather. Lighter-colored surfaces reflect more light and therefore absorb less heat!

Surfaces also differ in *which light* energy they absorb (see Figure 2.11). As we have said, different wavelengths of light are perceived as different colors to us. When we say an object

Figure 2.10 These squares differ in how much light they absorb. The black square absorbs the most light, the white square the least.

Figure 2.11 These squares differ in which wavelengths of light energy they absorb.

"is yellow" (like the sneaker LeGrace left in the front hall. Again. *Ugh*!), what we mean is that it's surface is absorbing all of the light except a particular wavelength that we perceive as yellow. That particular wavelength bounces off the surface and to our eye, so the surface appears yellow. The red apples on Fred's tree appear red to him because there is a pigment in the apple's skin that absorbs all the light except red. So, red light is what bounces off the apple and to his eye. For more on color and color perception, see Chapter 4.

Mirror- and Scatter-Reflection

When light bounces off of an object, it can do so in one of two ways: mirror-reflection or scatter-reflection. Mirror-reflection means that the light bounces off the object at the exact same angle that it struck the object. This is the type of reflection that is happening when we look into a mirror. The light reflecting off of our face strikes the mirror at roughly a 90° angle to the surface. The light bounces directly back to our eye (at roughly a 90° angle to the surface) so we are able to see our face (roughly right in front of us). Good thing, too, or you'd never be able to see how those new glasses look on you (fantastic, by the way). Scatter-reflection means that the light bounces off the object at a different angle than it struck the object, like when light bounces off a rough surface like corduroy (see Figure 2.12, *top*). Objects that we see as "shiny" (like the gold earrings LeGrace left on the bathroom counter, *ugh* again) or glossy have more mirror-reflection and less

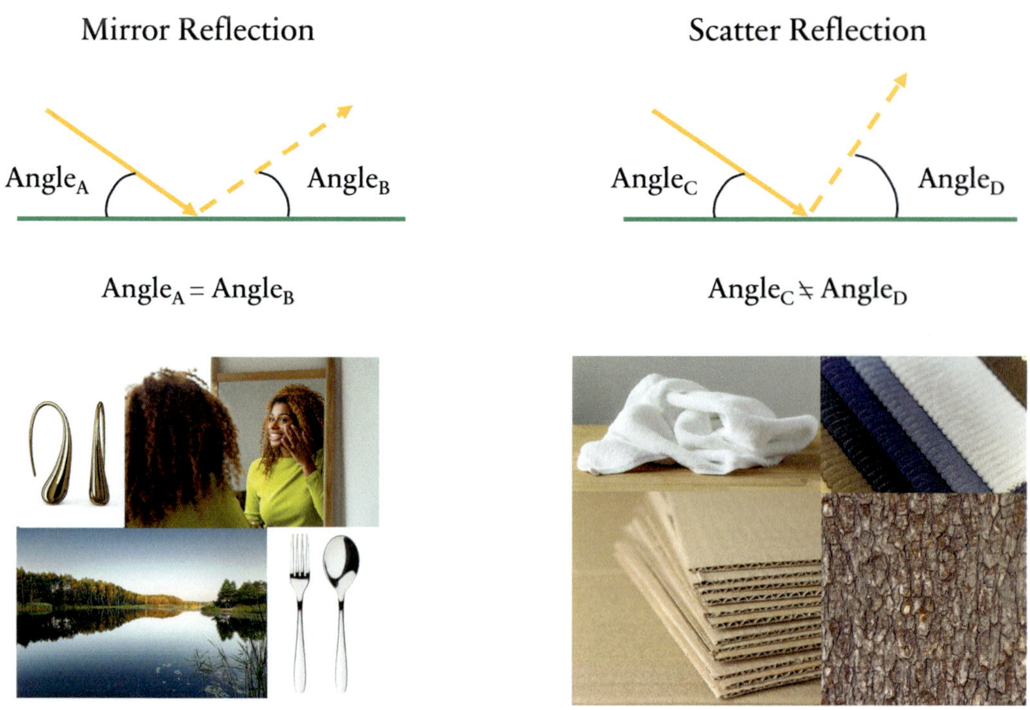

Figure 2.12 Top, mirror reflection vs. scatter reflection. Bottom, shiny surfaces have more mirror reflection, matte surfaces have more scatter-reflection.

scatter-reflection. Objects that we see as "matte" (like the towel LeGrace left on the floor, *eww* again) have less mirror-reflection and more scatter-reflection.

Transmission

The final thing that can happen when light strikes an object is that it can pass through that object—called **transmission**. This is why Fred can see out his window—all of the light transmits through the window. When light moves from a lower-density medium (like air) to a higher-density medium (like water) it slows down. The change in velocity causes the light to change direction. When light changes direction it is called **refraction** (see Figure 2.13).

> **Transmission** when light passes through an object. Objects that are either transparent or translucent have some amount of transmission.
>
> **Refraction** the change in direction of light when it passes from one medium to another. Caused by the change in velocity from moving from a lower-density medium to a higher-density medium.

In order for Fred to *use* any of the light that reflects off the various surfaces that surround him, he needs to be able to *detect* that structure. This is where having eyes comes in handy!

> Socratic Question: What are the three main things that can happen to light that strikes a surface? What makes a surface look shiny? What makes a surface look matte?

Figure 2.13 The pencil appears "broken" because the light leaving the water is refracted.

Box 2.2 The Optic Array

Optic array structured ambient light of different intensities in different directions.

From the ecological approach (and sometimes the biological and traditional approaches, depending on who you talk to), it is best to talk about light in terms of an **optic array**. After light leaves a source, but before it strikes an object, it is called radiant light. Radiant light is unstructured. Once the light strikes an object the properties of that object determine what happens to the light—what is absorbed, reflected, or transmitted. The light that leaves the substances and surfaces of the environment is *structured by* that environment. When an organism (in Figure 2.14, Fred) occupies a space in that environment, the light that surrounds him, called ambient light, has been uniquely structured by the environment around him. This is called the optic array (see Chapter 15).

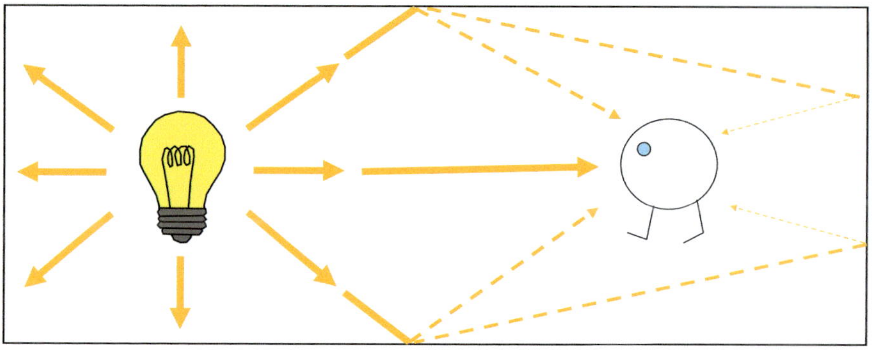

Figure 2.14 Radiant vs. ambient light.

Eyes

For light to be useful to the organism in terms of knowing anything about its cluttered environment, it has to have some way of detecting that light. Fortunately, there are a *lot* of ways of doing this. It's beyond the scope of this textbook to tell you about *all* of them, but to give you a sense of this diversity, we are going to talk about three of them: the eye cup, the compound eye, and the chambered eye. Regardless of the type of eye, light detection requires some type of **photopigment**. Photopigment is a substance that absorbs and reacts to light.

Photopigment a substance that absorbs and reacts to light. This reaction allows the visual system to respond to light.

Eye Cup

There are many organisms that have light sensitivity without having anything we would consider an "eye". Darwin was writing about the light-sensitive skin of earthworms way back

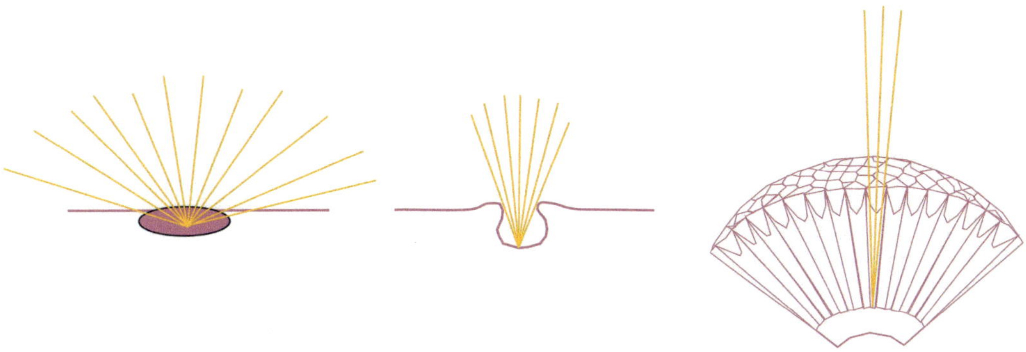

Figure 2.15 Left, light-sensitive patches do not allow for awareness of directionality. Middle, an eye cup allows some awareness of the directionality of the light. Right, a compound eye allows for even more directionality, although no image is formed.

in 1881. Their skin allows them to know when there are changes in light (which might indicate a predator, for example); however, this kind of light-sensitivity system cannot detect the *direction* of the light except in a very basic way. In Figure 2.15, *left*, the light-sensitive patch is not sensitive to the direction of light because it gathers light from all directions (except those blocked by the organism's own body). In order to have an awareness of *where things are*, an organism must be able to determine where the light is coming from. One way to do this is to have light-sensitive patches that collect light only from some directions but not others. In order to have some sensitivity to the *direction* of light, the light sensitive patch must *block* some of the light. In Figure 2.15, *middle*, the patch is deeper in the skin, creating an eye cup. This blocks light from some directions but not others and so provides some indication of direction. Nothing like an image is formed, but the organism could tell, for example, if there was a shadow *more to the right* of them rather than *more to the left* of them and act accordingly (hiding from a predator or approaching a food source, for example).

Compound Eye

Compound eyes are the most common type of eye among animals on Earth.[5] Just as having the light-sensitive part of the eye slightly deeper in the skin gives some directionality, putting the light-sensitive part at the bottom of a tube, called an **ommatidia**, gives *even more* directionality. A compound eye is a collection of these ommatidia, each has a crystalline cone at the top of the tube, and a photopigment at the bottom of the tube (see Figure 2.15, *right*). Importantly, while compound eyes convey *directionality* of light, they still do not produce an image.

> **Ommatidia** the tube-like structures that make up compound eyes.

> Socratic Question: What are the advantages of a compound eye over an eye cup? How might these advantages help animals with compound eyes? (Or put differently, why might it be so hard to swat a fly?)

Chambered Eye

Humans (and many, many other organisms)[6] have what are called chambered eyes. Unlike compound eyes which have individual tubes, each with its own photopigment, the chambered eye is like a sphere with an opening in the front and a light-sensitive surface on the back. This kind of eye collects the light that bounces off surfaces out in the world and focuses that light on the surface on the back of the eye in the form of an image. Given that light travels in straight lines, the spatial relationships in the world are preserved on this surface at least to some extent. That is, two points that are next to each other on the surface of the object will end up next to each other in the image that is formed in the eye. For the traditional approach (and many but not all biological approaches), this **retinal image** is the starting point for vision[7] (Kepler, 1604; see Chapters 9–11).

Retinal image (traditional) the image formed of the world by light on the back of the eye.

There are a lot of different kinds of chambered eyes, but all of them have *optical parts* and *translating parts*. The optical parts are responsible for capturing and focusing the light. The translating parts are responsible for receiving and reacting to the light and (in some cases) sending a signal to the brain. We are going to start by explaining the optical parts, and then we'll give an overview of the human eye anatomy. Finally, we'll give a brief overview of the translating parts with a fuller explanation in the next chapter (as you'll see, eyes are complicated things).

How the chambered eye creates an image on the retina is a little complex, so we are going to break it down into a series of questions. We'll start with:

How to Maintain Spatial Relationships When Light Diverges?

Let's revisit Fred and his tree. When light strikes the tree, that light reflects in every direction (which is why Fred can see the tree no matter where he stands relative to it—handy, right?). In other words, when the light reflects from the tree, it immediately **diverges**. If Fred held a sheet of paper up next to the tree, it would not form an image on the paper because of this divergence (see Figure 2.16, *left*).

Divergent light light rays moving away from each other over space.

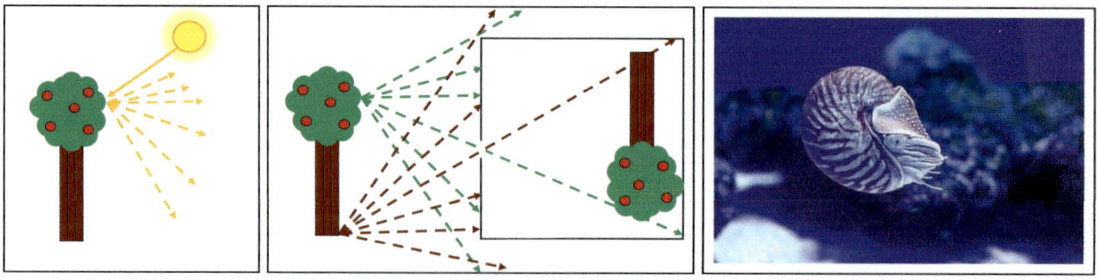

Figure 2.16 Left, after leaving a surface, reflected light diverges. Middle, a light-tight box with one small hole can collect light in such a way that an image is formed on the back wall. Right, the cephalopod nautilus has an eye that works like this.

> **Pupil** the opening in the front part of the eye. Light enters through this opening and projects on the back of the eye.

One way to deal with divergent light is to create a chamber where light can only get in through a very tiny hole (a **pupil**) in the front. This way, only light that was traveling at a very specific *angle* would pass through the hole and make it into the chamber. The rest of the light would bounce off the outside of the chamber (see Figure 2.16, *middle*). Remember that light travels in straight lines, so the light reflecting from the top of the tree will end up at the bottom of the eye and the light reflecting from the bottom of the tree will end up at the top of the eye. In other words, the image produced on the retina is upside down. By the same logic, the image is also left-right reversed—the light from the left side of the tree ends up on the right side of the image, the light from the right side of the tree ends up on the left side of the image. Weird, right?

A device (often an entire room) built with these features is called a *camera obscura*. A smaller version of this with film at the back is called a pinhole camera. A biological version with photopigments at the back is called a pinhole eye. The cephalopod nautilus has this type of eye (Colicchia, 2006; see Figure 2.16, *right*).

The retinal image produced by this type of eye is dim and blurry. That is because it does not let in much light. A few years ago, Fred had to make a pinhole camera as part of a project in art class for his teacher, Mr. Raoul. He learned pretty quickly that to make an image on the film, the shutter (the hole in the front) has to remain open for a *long time* in order to fully expose the film. But any movement *at all* during that time resulted in a blurry image. Rats! While that might work for the nautilus, other animals like humans are going to need more clarity and speed than that.

> Socratic Question: How is the retinal image formed? Why do you think that the retinal image is "the starting point" for at least some approaches to understanding vision?

How to Let in More Light and Still Preserve Spatial Relationships?

> **Convergent light** light rays moving toward each other over space.
>
> **Lens** a transparent substance with curved surfaces used for either diverging or converging light.

In order to increase the size of the opening at the front of the eye (and thus allow in more light), we need another way of handling the divergent light. Otherwise, we would never get a clear image to form; in other words, we need some way of getting the light to **converge**.

Earlier, we talked about refraction—how light changes direction when it travels from a less dense medium (say, air) to a more dense medium (say, water). A **lens** is a transparent substance that is denser than the surrounding material. When light passes through a lens, it changes direction in a specific way: if it is a *concave* lens, the light rays diverge. Concave lenses are used, for example, in flashlights to spread the light over a larger area. If it is a *convex* lens the light rays converge (see Figure 2.17, *top*). Convex lenses are used in magnifying classes and microscopes to make images appear larger.

If the light passes through a convex lens before or after entering the eye, it will refract in such a way that causes the divergent light to *converge*. In an eye that has a lens, the pupil can be larger and allow in more light. Score!

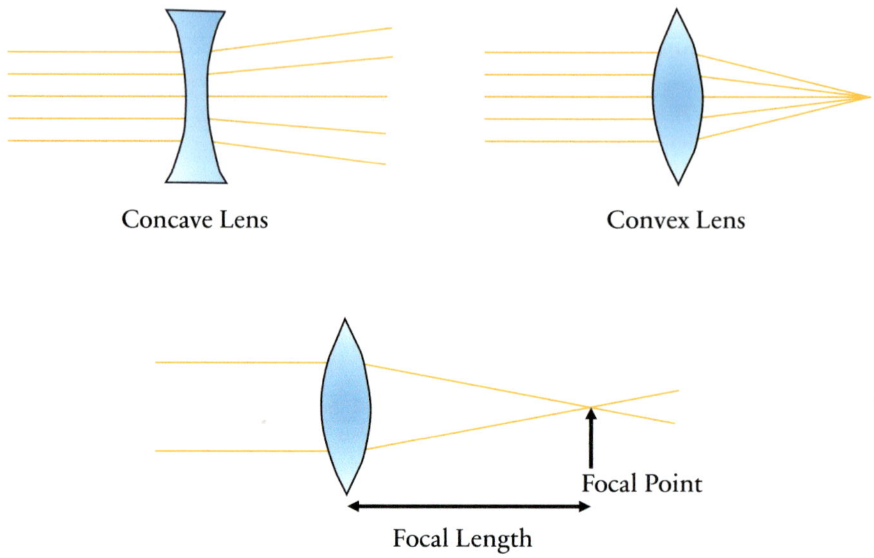

Figure 2.17 Top left, when light passes through a concave lens, it diverges. Top right, when light passes through a convex lens, it converges. Bottom, the focal length and focal point of a lens depend on its power.

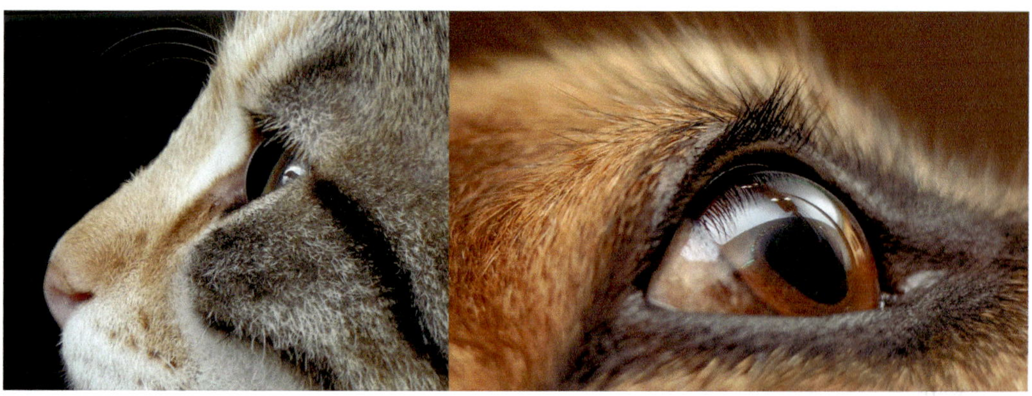

Figure 2.18 The cornea is fairly easy to see on cats and dogs.

The front part of the eye is called the cornea. If you have a pet dog or cat (or a willing friend), you can see the cornea fairly easily (see Figure 2.18) by looking sideways across the front of the eye. This curved surface acts as a lens to refract the light. The amount that a lens can change the direction of the light is called its **power**, and the power of a lens is measured in **diopters**.[8]

Power (of a lens) the amount that it refracts the light as it passes through.

Diopter a measure of the amount of refraction of light as it passes through a lens.

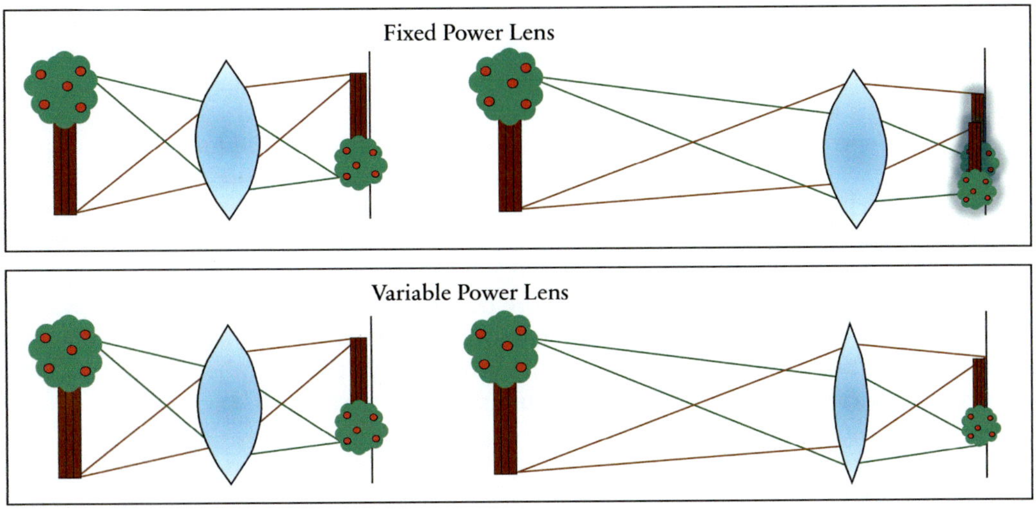

Figure 2.19 Top, with a fixed lens, only one distance will be in focus. Bottom, one solution is a variable lens, which accommodates for different distances by changing shape.

The place where the light converges past the lens is called the **focal point** and the distance from the lens to the focal point is called the **focal length** (see Figure 2.17, *bottom*). The focal point needs to land directly on the retina for the image to be in focus (i.e., not blurry).

Focal point the point where the light converges after passing through a lens.

Focal length the distance from the lens to the focal point.

How to Keep Objects in Focus Across Different Distances?

The farther away from an object you get, the more the light diverges (as you can see from the rays in Figure 2.16, *left*). As a consequence, the amount that the light needs to be bent in order to converge is a function of the distance of the object from the lens. If the power of the lens stays constant, only one distance will be in focus (see Figure 2.19, *top*). The eye must have some way to adjust for different distances. Otherwise, organisms would only be able to see things from a very specific distance. Inconvenient!

Different species have solved this problem in different ways. Some birds can change the shape of their cornea in order to change its power (Yong, 2022). This allows for changes in focus at far distances, but not for things up close (which is just fine for the bird).

Recall that a change in density of the medium causes the refraction of the light. For aquatic and amphibious animals, the light is passing from water through the cornea. The difference in density between the water and the cornea is not very large, so it does not refract the light very much. This is great, but what if you need more refraction than the cornea can provide? Well, another option is to have a secondary lens *inside* the eye that can change in some way (there are a couple of options) in order to alter how the light focuses on the back of the eye. For example, aquatic and amphibious animals compensate for their less-than-helpful cornea by having a very powerful (nearly spherical) lens inside the eye. To adjust for objects at a distance, it moves forwards and backwards (closer and farther away from the back of the eye) to move the focal point of the lens to land at the back of the eye. Amazing!

Humans (and reptiles, some birds, and mammals) also have a secondary lens inside the eye, but instead of changing *location*, the lens inside the eye changes *shape* to change its power (see Figure 2.19, *bottom*). The lens is surrounded by a circular muscle called the ciliary muscle. The lens is attached to the ciliary muscle by small fibers called zonular fibers. When the ciliary muscle contracts, it scrunches up closer to the lens, and reduces tension on the zonular fibers, which allows the lens to get fatter (and the surface more curved). When the ciliary muscle relaxes, it flattens out, which pulls on the zonular muscles and flattens out the lens (making the surface less curved). The more curved the surface, the more the lens refracts the light. Also amazing—but in a different way!

The light rays from farther objects are more or less parallel when they reach the eye, and so they require less refraction (a less curved surface). On the other hand, the light from closer objects is not parallel (the rays are at more of an angle to each other) when they strike the eye, and it requires more refraction (a more curved surface). The changes that occur in the lens to allow for focus of objects at different distances is called **accommodation**. Think about what this word means in a more everyday context. When you accommodate someone or something, you change what you are doing to help them out. That is exactly what the lens is doing by changing shape—changing what it is doing to help you see at different distances. In humans, at least, the accommodation is most useful for seeing things up close (see Chapter 9).[9] For objects more than about 6 meters away (about the length of full-sized car or a very large crocodile), the lens does not change shape (it stays at its flattest state).

Accommodation (in vision) adjusting the lens to allow for objects at varying distance to remain in focus.

There are a number of variations on this theme given the environmental requirements for vision for particular organisms. For example, diving ducks sometimes need to see in the air and sometimes need to see under water. In the air, their cornea can provide most of the refraction necessary to focus the light, but under water, the difference in density is minimal so the refraction by the cornea is minimal. To deal with this, these ducks can change the shape of their secondary lens so much that it bulges out past the pupil! Weird, right? The fish, *Anableps anableps* (colloquially known as the "four-eyed fish"; see Figure 2.20) has two eyes but *four* pupils. Two of the pupils work above the water, two work below. Accordingly, their lens is asymmetrical—flat above water, spherical below. Even weirder. But also amazing!

Why Would We Sometimes Want Less Light?

Go to a mirror in a room with a bright light (a bathroom usually works well for this). Look yourself directly in the eyes and examine the colored part of your eye (called the

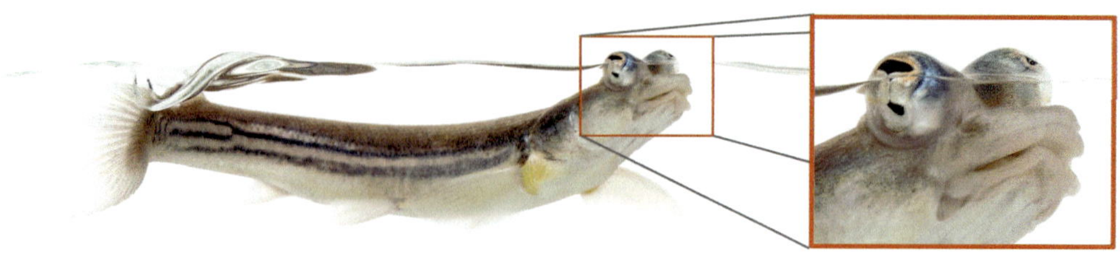

Figure 2.20 *Anableps anableps*, or the four-eyed fish, has two eyes, but four pupils.

Iris the colored part of the eye. It is a circular muscle with a hole in the center (the pupil); it can constrict to decrease the size of the pupil or relax to increase the size of the pupil.

iris). Cover your eyes with your hands (block out as much light as possible) and count to 10 (or 20 if you have nothing else to do). Uncover your eyes and quickly look in the mirror. If you did it right, the iris will change shape, changing the size of the pupil. When it is dark, the pupil gets much larger, collecting as much light as possible. When it is bright, the pupil gets much smaller, blocking some of the light. When you played peekaboo with the mirror, you were changing the amount of light reaching your eyes, and your irises acted accordingly.

But why would it do that? Why would the pupil change shape *at all*? Wouldn't we want as much light as possible to enter the eye all the time? Well no, not really, for a couple of reasons. Maybe you have been outside on a very bright day (say, a sunny day in a snowy landscape) and found yourself squinting in order to see clearly?

In very bright light conditions, having a wide-open pupil will actually *decrease* visibility. The reason why has to do with the way the lens refracts light. Because of its shape, different parts of the lens refract light to different degrees. The outer part of the lens refracts light much more than the center of the lens. In bright light, this creates blurriness around the edges of an image called **spherical aberration**.

Spherical aberration blurriness caused by the different parts of the lens refracting the light differently.

One possible solution would be to only allow light through the very center of the lens, which is exactly what the eye does in bright light conditions—by shrinking the size of the iris! Under *very* bright light conditions, however, the pupil can't get small enough to limit enough light, so we need to squint or wear ski goggles or sunglasses—and thereby decrease the light even further.

For some animals, a circular pupil does not restrict light enough in bright light conditions. A circular pupil can only get down to about 2mm in diameter (about the size of the point on a brand-new crayon). Animals who are more active at nighttime (and so have eyes geared to seeing in the dark) need even more dramatic light reduction in order for the light to focus properly during the day. This is why cats have vertical slit pupils; these pupils are able to close more tightly and so can block out more light (see Figure 2.21). And you thought it was just

Figure 2.21 Cat's pupils are vertical slits instead of circles (like ours). This is so they can get even smaller in bright light conditions.

to look cool! Under dimmer light conditions, they can also open far wider to allow more light in. And you thought that this was just to look cute!

Socratic Question: What is the main advantage of a chambered eye over other kinds of eyes? If the chambered eye is so great, why don't all animals have them?

How Do We Move Our Eyes?

Our eyes are in constant motion. As you read this book, your eyes move across the page rapidly. They are rotating in the **orbital cavity** (often called the eye socket), the cave-shaped bone that surrounds the eye and protects it. Three pairs of muscles (for a total of six) attach the eye to the socket. They maintain a ***dynamic*** balance meaning that small perturbations (like our constant body sway) will result in small counter-movements of the eye so that gaze remains steady. In other words, our eyes are never still (see Chapter 11). When moving our eye across a scene (like you are as you are reading this) our eyes do not turn smoothly. Instead, they fixate for a moment (stay still) then they jump quickly to the next fixation point. These jumps are called **saccades**. Our eyes *can* move smoothly—but only when they are tracking a smoothly moving object (like when Fred watched Topsy run across his yard).

Orbital cavity cave-shaped bone in the skull that surrounds and protects the eye, often called the eye socket.

Saccade quick movement of the eye in between fixations.

Anatomy of the Human Eye

Now that we have explained the function of many parts of eyes in general, we'll now discuss the anatomy of the human eye, in particular (see Figure 2.22). The human eye itself is roughly spherical and about the size of a ping pong ball. So far, we have discussed the iris, the pupil, the cornea, the lens, the ciliary muscle and zonule fibers, and the six muscles that move the eye (their names are the superior (top), inferior (bottom), medial (nasal), and lateral (outside) rectus; and the superior and inferior obliques). There is one more part of the eye that is visible from the outside (in addition to the iris and the pupil)—the so-called whites of the eyes. This part of the eye is a membrane, called the **sclera**, that surrounds most of the eye (including parts of the back portion of your eye that is fully inside your head). Part of the function of the sclera is to block out light except the light that enters through the pupil.

Sclera white fibrous tissue that covers and protects the eye.

At the front of the eye, between the iris and the cornea, is a small space called the anterior chamber (or "space in front"); the space around the lens (where the zonule fibers are) is called the posterior chamber (or "space in back"). Both chambers are filled with fluid (called aqueous humor).

Choroid middle layer of the wall of the eye. Filled with blood vessels and responsible for carrying nutrients to the eye.

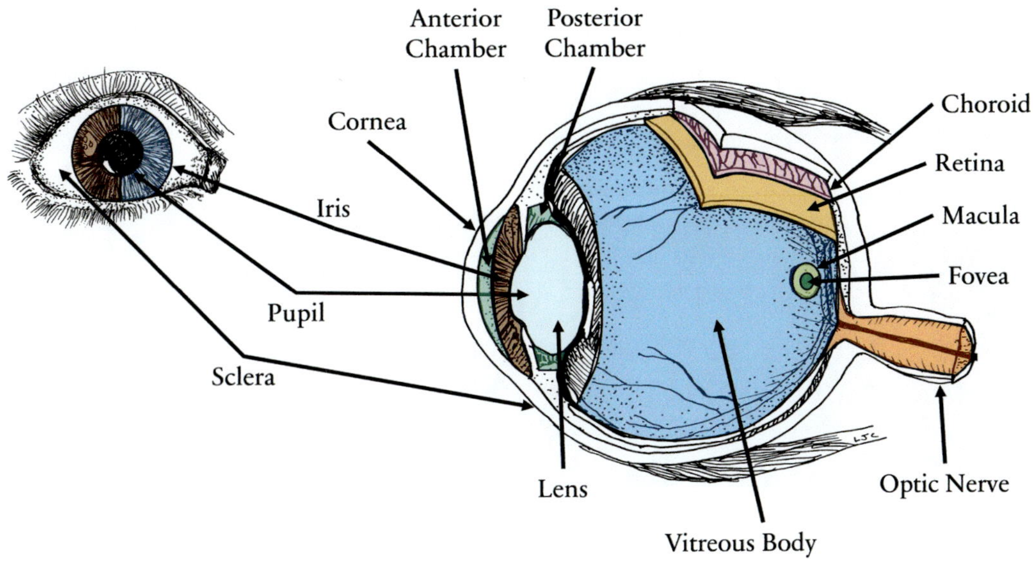

Figure 2.22 Anatomy of the human eye. See text for details.

The next layer in from the sclera is the **choroid**. This thin layer of tissue (0.2mm at its thickest, about the thickness of a thin sheet of paper) is filled with blood vessels that carry nutrients to the various parts of the eye (and carry waste away from the eye—you didn't know your eye produced waste, did you?). Inspecting these blood vessels is one reason why an optometrist or ophthalmologist looks into your eye through the pupil (see Figure 2.23 for a view of what an ophthalmologist might see). The choroid is dark red in color. When someone has "red eye" in a photo, it is because the light is reflecting off their choroid to the lens of the camera.

Retina innermost layer of the wall of the eye. Responds to light and translates it into the language of the brain.

The innermost layer of tissue is called the **retina**. The retina is a highly complex part of the eye, and we only understand some of its functions. It has (among other things) cells called **photoreceptors** that respond to light. That response is translated into the language of the brain (i.e., the language of **neurons**), and sent to the brain as a neural signal. Chapter 3 covers that process (and covers more of the retinal structures) in some detail.

Photoreceptors specialized cells that respond to light.

Neurons specialized cells that make up the nervous system, capable of sending and receiving neural signals.

The eye has a large chamber behind the lens (and before the retina) called the Vitreous (or "glass-like" or "clear") body. It is filled with fluid called vitreous humor (or "clear fluid"). Along with the aqueous humor (or "water-like fluid") in the anterior and posterior chambers, the vitreous humor maintains the spherical shape of the eye by having just the right amount of fluid to maintain the pressure—much like the air in a tire has just the right

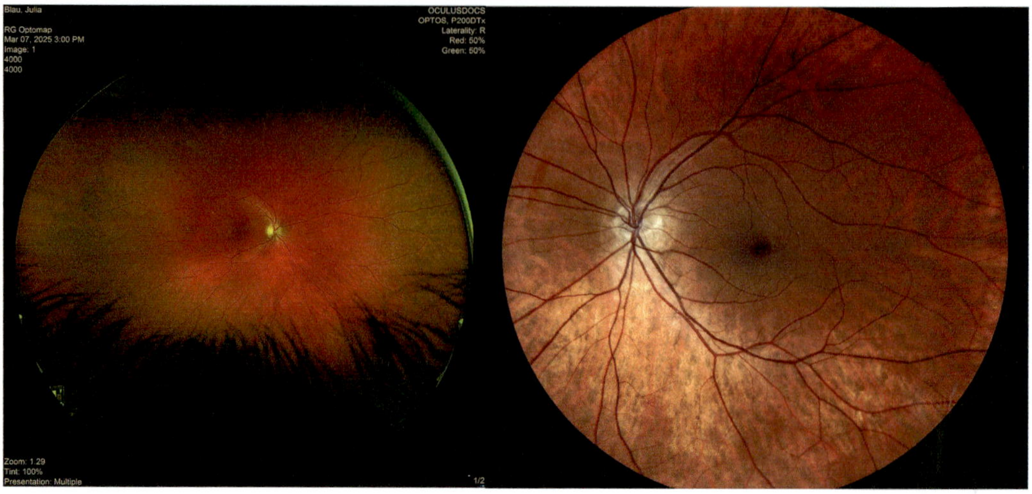

Figure 2.23 Left, Dr. Blau's retina. Right, Dr. Wagman's retina.

amount of air to maintain your tire pressure. Too much or too little can result in vision and other health problems (more on this at the end of the chapter). Sometimes bits of dead skin break off and float around in this space, causing shadows to fall on the retina. That is why you see "floaters" sometimes (see Figure 2.24). Don't worry—this is usually completely normal and harmless!

The size of the chamber allows the lens to have enough space to focus the light across all the distances we can see. Organisms with smaller chambers have a smaller range over which they can focus the light (called depth of field). This is one reason why very small animals—like insects—have compound eyes instead of chambered eyes. Insect-sized chambered eyes would be too small to see farther distances.

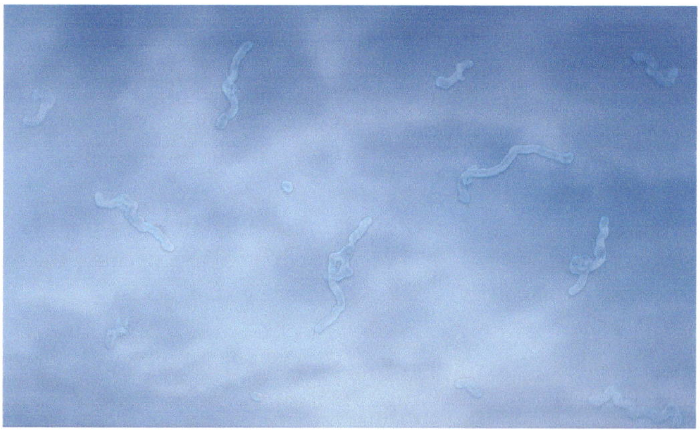

Figure 2.24 You may have seen "floaters" in your vision. Don't worry! They are just pieces of dead tissue floating in your eye, casting a shadow. They are normal and harmless.

The neurons in the retina send their signals to the brain. The pathway for that signal is called the **optic nerve**. The optic nerve leaves the eye through the same opening in which blood vessels enter the eye. There are no photoreceptors in this part of the eye, therefore any light that falls on this spot cannot be detected, and so this spot is often referred to as the "blind spot" (for more on this, see Chapter 3).

Optic nerve bundle of fibers that carries the visual signal from the eye to the brain.

Box 2.3 Non-Human Eyes

There is incredible diversity in the form and function of eyes. While this book focuses on the human eye (and human perception more generally), it's worth taking a moment to appreciate the different ways nature has addressed the ecological demands of different species (Land, 1999; Yong, 2022).

Tapetum lucidum reflective surface behind the retina of nocturnal animals that gives light a second chance to be absorbed by the photoreceptors.

Cats and other nocturnal animals have a reflective surface behind the retina called the **tapetum lucidum.** The light that does not get absorbed by the photoreceptors reflects off this surface and bounces back to those same photoreceptors—giving it a second chance to be absorbed. Even light deserves a second chance, right? This means that cats can see even in very dim light. This is also why their eyes appear to glow when the light hits them just right (see Figure 2.25)—the light is bouncing off the tapetum lucidum and out of the eye. And you thought this was just to look creepy!

Some animals with a chambered eye do not use a lens to focus the light. For example, in the scallop, the back of the eye serves as a concave mirror. The light bounces off this surface and the angle of the mirror means the light converges on the inside of the *front* of the eye (which is where the scallop has photoreceptors).

Snakes have a chambered eye that sees light, but they also have an eye cup (above their "normal" eye) that senses infrared light. It is essentially heat-vision. This allows them to track the path of their prey even after the prey is no longer present—the prey leaves a heat trail behind.

Figure 2.25 Cats' eyes appear to glow in the dark because they have a mirror-like membrane on the back of their eyes.

Socratic Question: Look at images of Dr. Blau's or Dr. Wagman's retinas in Figure 2.23. Identify the location of the fovea in each image. Identify the location of the "blind spot" in each image.

Disruptions in Eye Function

Why Do I Need Glasses?

Perhaps you wear glasses. Fred's friend Claudia wears glasses. Your authors wear glasses, too. Both Dr. Blau and Dr. Wagman need them both for seeing things that are far away *and* for seeing things that are up close. Glasses of all kinds are extremely common—one estimate is that 63.7% of adult Americans wear glasses.

In order for the light to focus properly on the back of the eye, the focal point must land precisely on the retina (see Figure 2.26). If the distance between the lens and the back of the eye is too short, the focal point will land *behind* the retina and make it difficult for the person to focus on objects up close. This is called **hyperopia** or, more colloquially, far-sightedness.

Hyperopia a condition where the eye is too small, so the focal point lands behind the retina, resulting in blurry vision of close-up objects.

If the distance between the lens and the back of the eye is too long, the focal point will land *in front* of the retina and make it difficult for the person to focus on objects that are far away. This is called **myopia** or, more colloquially, near-sightedness or short-sightedness. We sometimes call someone myopic if they are not thinking about things far enough in the future.

Myopia a condition where the eye is too large, so the focal point lands in front of the retina, resulting in blurry vision of far-away objects.

The lens in the eye continues to grow as we age (just like our nose and ears!), so people with myopia might find that their glasses don't need to be as strong as they age, as the larger lens can overcome the length of the eyeball and focus better. The lens also gets gradually less flexible with age. That loss of flexibility results in difficulty seeing things close up, called **presbyopia.** (Both

Presbyopia the gradual loss of up-close vision due to the stiffening of the lens with age.

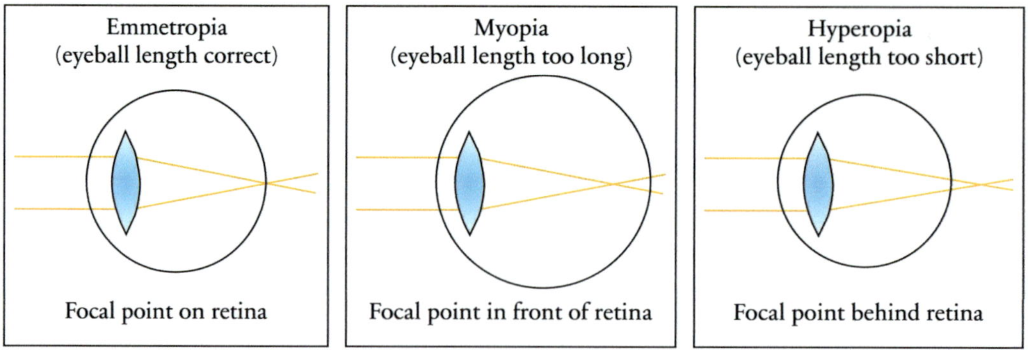

Figure 2.26 The focal point should land on the retina. In myopia, the eyeball is too big and the focal point is inside the eye. In hyperopia, the eyeball is too small and the focal point is behind the eye.

Dr. Blau and Dr. Wagman have myopia *and* presbyopia, which is why they have trouble seeing both far *and* near). The joys of middle age!

The cornea is supposed to be round—like the front part of a tiny basketball. If instead it becomes more like a tiny football in shape, the result is that different parts of the scene are refracted differently, resulting in a blurry image. It is particularly noticeable at night because of the directionality of the light. This is called **astigmatism.**

Astigmatism a condition where the cornea of the eye is slightly warped and so light doesn't focus as it should. Most noticeable at night when lights such as street lamps and car headlights cause "streaks of light".

Glasses can help with all of these conditions. In the case of presbyopia and hyperopia, the glasses are convex, which converges the light a little before it hits the eye. That way, the light doesn't have to converge as much once it's *in* the eye, which shifts the focal point forward so it lands on the retina. In the case of myopia, the glasses are concave, which diverges the light a little before it hits the eye. In that way, the amount of convergence needed is slightly *increased*, which means the distance needed for convergence gets a little longer—or in other words, it shifts the focal point backwards so it lands on the retina. For astigmatism, the shape of the lens is opposite to that of the cornea, evening out the image. Bifocals, worn by people who need help seeing both near and far (like Dr. Blau and Dr. Wagman), are concave on top and convex on the bottom.

Contacts do roughly the same thing as glasses, but they do so by changing the overall shape of the cornea. Laser surgery also changes the shape of the cornea, but permanently, by burning away parts of it.

Socratic Question: What kind of lenses would be necessary for someone who has myopia to see clearly? What kind of lenses would be necessary for someone with hyperopia or presbyopia to see clearly? How would these kind of lenses help in each case?

Diseases and Disorders

They eye is filled with *just enough* fluid to keep the parts in place. If too much fluid builds up in the eye, it can cause headaches, blurriness, and eventually blindness. This is called **glaucoma** and it requires treatment by a professional.

Glaucoma buildup of vitreous or aqueous humor in the eye, resulting in increased pressure and eventually damage to the eye.

The lens in the eye is normally clear—allowing light to pass through. Sometimes the proteins that make up the lens break down, making it cloudy. The cloudier it gets, the harder it is to see. These are called **cataracts** and are usually fixable through surgery.

Cataracts a breakdown in the protein of the lens resulting in cloudy lenses.

The six muscles in each eye (12 total) are linked together during childhood so that the two eyes are always focused on the same spot. Sometimes one of the eyes is much stronger than the other and dominates vision. This makes the weaker eye even weaker and so it stops coordinating with the strong eye. This condition is often referred to colloquially as a "lazy eye" but is properly called **amblyopia**. One way to treat this condition in childhood is to cover up the strong eye, forcing the weak eye to strengthen its muscles. Interestingly, this technique will not work in adulthood because the eyes have a critical period for learning to work together. In adulthood, doctors sometimes sever the muscles of the weak eye, which results in an aesthetic improvement, but does not help correct vision.

Amblyopia when the muscles of the two eyes are not coordinated, and they point in different directions.

The center of the retina has a small area called the **macula**. As people age, this area might break down, a process called **macular degeneration**. There are two forms of this, wet and dry. In wet macular degeneration, the retina starts to grow new blood vessels which block the light from being absorbed by the photoreceptors. In dry macular degeneration, fatty deposits grow under the retina, causing it to thin over time. In both cases, the vision loss is very gradual and usually painless. There are treatments, but only if it is caught early. Both also seem to have a genetic component.

Macula (eye) a small area in the center of the retina, responsible for the focus of vision.

Macular degeneration a condition where the macula breaks down, affecting focal vision.

For a bunch of reasons, the retina can become detached from the back of the eye (**detached retina**). These days doctors can reattach the retina by a variety of methods: by essentially squeezing the eye using a band so the internal pressure of the eye pushes the retina back into place, or by manually reattaching the retina using a laser, or even by injecting a bubble of air into the eye and then having the patient lie face down so the bubble pushes the retina back into place!

Detached retina when the light-sensitive layer of the eye separates from the back of the eye.

You might have noticed that we haven't talked about blindness—and that's because blindness is not all one thing! For example, it's possible to be legally blind—when your vision is so blurry that you cannot use it to safely navigate (Dr. Wagman is legally blind if he does not wear glasses or contacts). It's also possible to have eyes that didn't form correctly, or the nerve that connects the eyes to the brain does not carry the information the way that it should. It's even possible for the eyes and nerve to function properly, but to have something go awry with the brain's processing so you are unable to understand what you see. Any of these situations might be called "blindness", but they are not caused by similar issues or experienced in similar ways.

Summary

This chapter covered the physical properties of light and the biology of eyes. Light is electromagnetic radiation structured in waves (and particles and rays) over space. There are many different methods for detecting light. All have advantages and disadvantages. All have been shaped by millions of years of evolution. These means include covered eye cups, compound eyes, and chambered eyes. Humans have chambered eyes, which work well for preserving directionality and forming a clear image when looking at objects at different distances. The complexity of chambered eyes means that there are many ways in which vision can be impaired, but also many ways that it can be corrected.

Notes

1 This means that light could travel around the circumference of the earth about 7.5 times in a single second.
2 With the possible exception of quantum information, which might travel across vast distances instantaneously.
3 By the way, the photoelectric effect is how solar panels work. Light is turned into free electrons by having it bombard metal panels.
4 So, this means that looking at stars is one way to experience the distant past. Mind-blowing, right? This is one reason we gave you the homework assignment!
5 This is because all arthropods—like insects and crustaceans—have compound eyes, and there are more arthropods on Earth than any other kind of animal.
6 Including other primates, and all mammals, birds, fish, amphibians, and reptiles.
7 The ecological approach will reject the idea of the retinal image altogether, but we don't want to get ahead of ourselves here.
8 If you wear glasses or contact lens, your prescription is in diopters. This value will be negative if you are nearsighted and positive if you are farsighted. Dr. Wagman's prescription for contact lenses is *very* negative (–9.0).
9 You can feel the ciliary muscles work for yourself. Close your left eye and hold your right thumb at arm's length from your right eye. Now slowly bring your thumb toward your right eye and try to keep it in focus.

3 From the Retina to the Brain

In Chapter 2, we examined light and the organs that detect light. Humans have chambered eyes, specifically ones with a pupil in the front that lets in light that falls on the retina on the back. As we discussed in that chapter, the retina is a sheet of light-sensitive cells that translate light energy into the language of the brain (a process called **transduction**).

Transduction the process of changing some external stimulus (e.g., light, sound) into the language of the brain.

The full functioning of the retina is unbelievably complex and outside the scope of this book (curious readers are encouraged to read Rodieck (1998/2018), an *entire textbook* on the functioning of the retina!). We are going to cover the basics here, but you'll see that even the basics are pretty complicated! Given that the overall function of the retina is to translate the stimulation by the light into the language of the brain, we must first understand the language of the brain, at least a little. Let's start by covering the structures and functions of a neuron.

Neurons

Neurons are excitable cells specialized for sending information across the body (including to and from the brain). The adult human brain has between 86 and 100 billion neurons; in addition, there are about 20 billion neurons in the spine and another 15 billion neurons in the sensory, afferent, and motor neurons (Lent et al., 2012). Just for some context, there are about as many neurons in the entire body as there are stars in the Milky Way galaxy. Mind-blowing, right?

Neurons have branching fibers at each end, "receiving" and "sending" messages to thousands of other neurons. There are on the order of several *trillion* connections between the neurons in our brains, all of them relaying information continuously. Just for even more context, if you were to count all of these connections and counted one connection per second, you would not finish counting for over 30,000 years! *Even more* mind-blowing.

According to the biological perspective, every thought you have, every movement you make, every sensation you experience is a function of the communication between neurons. All of the various types of neurons (and there are a lot!) share the same basic physiology (see Figure 3.1). At one end of the neuron, the **dendrites** receive signals. The dendrites are attached to

Dendrites short branching fibers at the start of the neuron; responsible for receiving the electrochemical signal from the previous neuron.

DOI: 10.4324/9781032690964-4

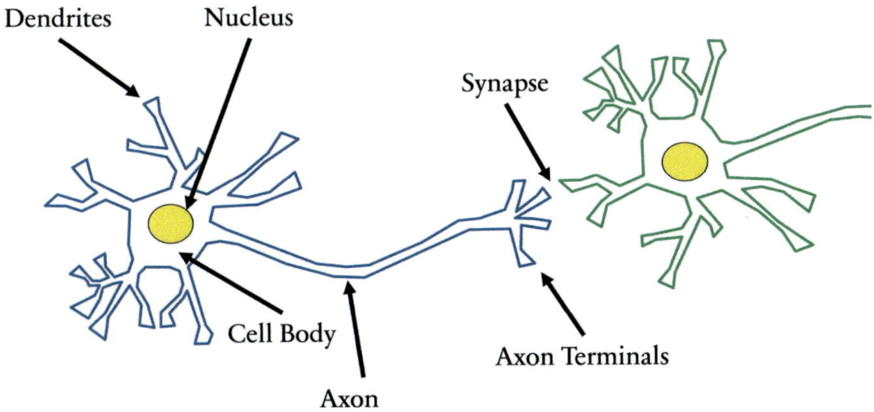

Figure 3.1 Parts of a neuron. This is a motor neuron (the kind that connects the brain and spinal cord to the muscles), but all neurons share the same parts, albeit in different arrangements.

the **cell body**; within the cell body is the **nucleus**; also attached to the cell body is the **axon**, which carries the signal to the **axon terminals.** The axon terminals send the signal across the **synapse** to the next neuron.

One thing to keep in mind as we go forward is that electricity is the movement of a magnetic charge. Neurons communicate by moving magnetically charged particles around, and so the "signal" they send can also be thought of (and measured) as an electrical signal. Electricity is magnets in motion! Communication between neurons occurs because the signal travels 'down' the axon and to the axon terminals of the "sending" (presynaptic) neuron. The signal travels along this path because of the magnetic charge of the fluids inside and outside of the neuron. Just like refrigerator magnets have a positive charge on one side and a negative charge on the other, the fluid inside and outside the cell have opposite magnetic charges. And you thought that your nervous system and refrigerator magnets had nothing in common!

Cell body main area of the neuron, contains the nucleus. The dendrites and axon are attached to it.

Nucleus a membrane-enclosed structure in the body of a neuron; contains the cell's genetic material

Axon tube-shaped structure that carries the signal from the start of the neuron to the end of the neuron; can be very short (a few micrometers) or very long (over a meter) depending on the needs of the cell.

Axon terminals branching fibers at the end of the axon; responsible for sending the electrochemical signal to other neurons.

Synapse small gap between the axon terminals of the "sending" neuron and the dendrites of the "receiving" neuron.

When the neuron sends its signal down the length of the axon (called the "action potential" or more colloquially, "firing"), there is specific movement of those charges. When the neuron is *not* firing, there is a net negative charge inside the neuron and a net positive charge outside the neuron.[1] When the neuron *is* firing, these relative charges trade places (through the movement of positively charged chemicals in and out of the cell) down the length of the neuron, all the way from dendrite to axon terminal. When the positive charge reaches the axon terminal, it releases **neurotransmitters**, which cross the synapse and may trigger the next neuron (the postsynaptic neuron) to fire (see Figure 3.2).

Neurotransmitters chemicals that cross the synapse and interact with neurons to either increase or decrease their rate of firing.

Measure the charge at any part of the axon while it fires and you will see that the neuron starts with a charge of -70mV (millivolts) and rises to +40mV and then goes back down to where it started—70mV, *every time it fires.* Not only that, it always takes the same amount of time to do this, *every time*. There is no way to make that process happen faster or slower or to make the charge inside the neuron higher or lower. This is why it's called an "all or nothing event" (Hodgkin & Huxley, 1939). Either it fires, and fires all the way, or it doesn't fire at all. Go big or go home, right?

While the strength and speed of the action potential can't change, the *rate* of firing can. Even when it's not receiving any outside stimulation, the neuron will fire at a particular rate, called its **baseline rate**. Incoming signals can either *increase* or *decrease* that rate to carry information.

Baseline rate (of neurons) the frequency of firing a neuron will exhibit when it is not receiving any stimulation. Information is conveyed by either increasing or decreasing frequency from this baseline.

It's not exactly the same, but you can think about it like electricity flowing down a wire to your lamp. If you changed the pattern of the flow, you could get the lightbulb to flicker on and off—maybe to signal using Morse code. In that case, the flickering—the changes in baseline rate—could carry information to whoever might be watching the flickering.

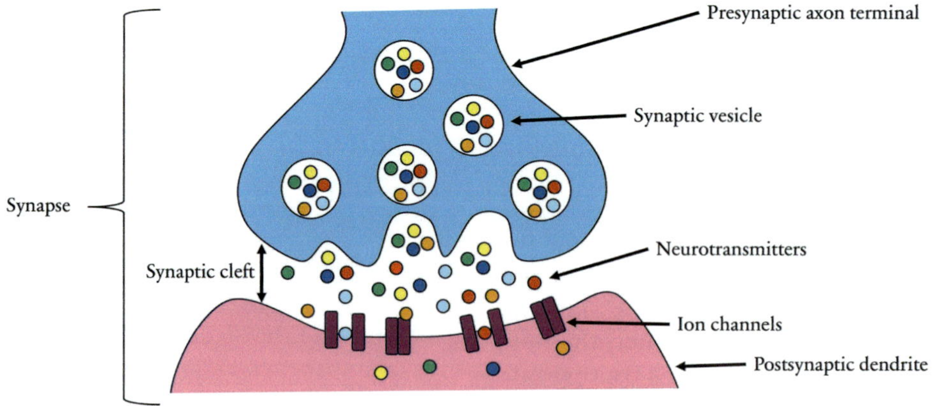

Figure 3.2 The synapse is how one neuron communicates with the next neuron. Synaptic vesicles carry neurotransmitters to the end of the axon terminal, where they are released. The neurotransmitters cross the synaptic cleft and enter the dendrite of the next neuron via the ion channels. If stimulated by enough neurotransmitters, the second neuron will change its firing rate.

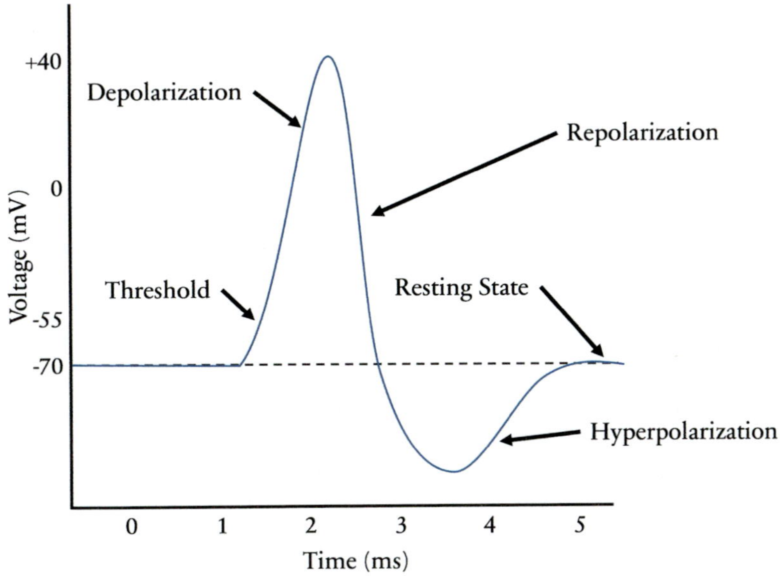

Figure 3.3 The measure of the magnetic charge inside a neuron during an action potential (while it is "firing"). See text for details.

Of course, neurons don't use Morse code. The language that neurons use to communicate is probably a lot more complex than our current understanding (and certainly a *lot* more complex than our discussion in this text). However, for our purposes, there are three elements that can change to convey information. They are (1) the rate of firing (increases *or* decreases), (2) the number of and type of neurons that are firing, and (3) which neurotransmitters are being released. You'll be surprised how much can be conveyed with just those three elements, all of which contribute to functioning of the retina.

One final note about neurons and other cells in the nervous system—and this has important consequences for perceptual experience—they all have a **refractory period**. That is, no matter how strongly they are stimulated, the neuron has to "reset" before it can fire again. This refractory period means there's an upper boundary on how frequently a neuron can fire. This limit will be very important going forward, so keep it in mind.

Refractory period (of neurons) the time during which, no matter the stimulation, a neuron cannot fire again. Sets the maximum frequency of firing for a single neuron.

Socratic Question: What is the "baseline rate" of a neuron? Why is it important to understand that neurons have a baseline rate when trying to understand the language of the brain?

Organization of the Retina

Armed with this information about how neurons work, let's (finally!) turn to the subject at hand: the retina. The retina is made up of several layers of different types of cells (see Figure 3.4). There are actually over 50 (!) different types of neurons in the retina, but we are going to focus our discussion on the six main types. Counterintuitively, the light passes *through* all of these types of cells before reaching the part of the photoreceptors that actually responds to light. That part of the photoreceptors is attached to the choroid (see Chapter 2). But all of these cells are very small and mostly clear, so the light is able to travel through them pretty easily. Once the light reaches the photoreceptors, the photoreceptors react and send a signal that travels back toward the direction of the light—back toward the front of the eye. Weird, right?

Once the photoreceptors are stimulated, they send the signal along a direct path to a type of neuron called **bipolar cells**, then to another type of neuron called **ganglia**, and then to the brain. You can think of this as the "vertical" path because it goes

Bipolar cells a type of neuron that responds to photoreceptors and horizontal cells and sends their signals vertically to ganglia and laterally to amacrine cells.

Ganglia a type of neuron that responds to amacrine cells and bipolar cells and sends their signals to the brain.

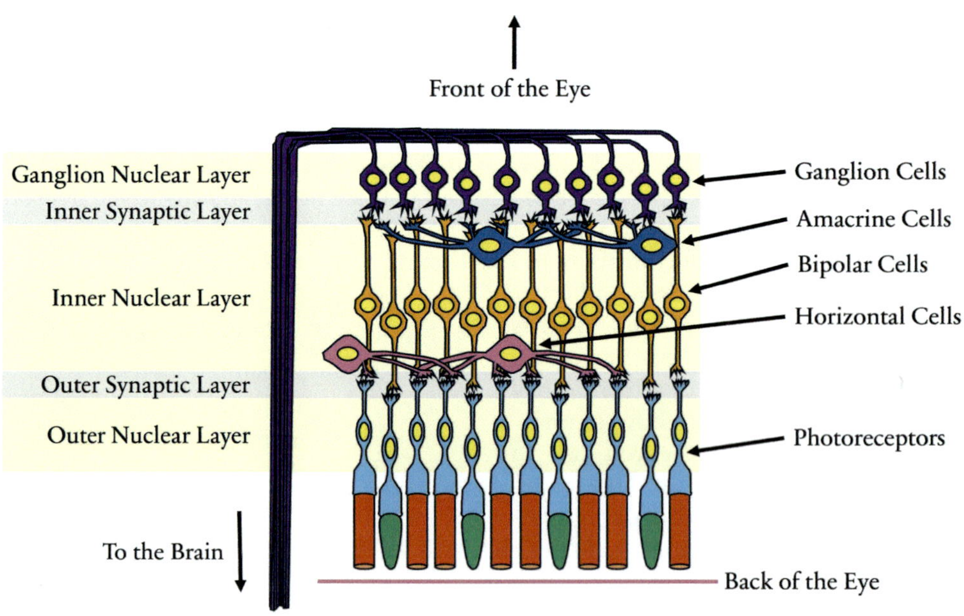

Figure 3.4 Layers of cells in the retina. Light passes through several layers of cells before reaching the photoreceptors attached to the back of the eye. From there, the signal travels both vertically and horizontally. Photoreceptors send signals to bipolar cells, which send their signal to ganglion cells (vertical signaling). Horizontal cells "listen" to photoreceptors and send signals to bipolar cells; Amacrine cells "listen" to bipolar cells and send signals to ganglion cells (horizontal signaling).

Figure 3.5 Close your left eye and look at the word "FRED". Move the book closer and farther away until the apple disappears. When that happens, the light from the apple is falling on your blind spot!

from the entry point (the photoreceptors) all the way "up" to the brain. **Horizontal** and **amacrine cells** are neurons that act sideways to this path. You can think of this as "horizontal", but more often people call this the "lateral" pathway.

Horizontal cells a type of neuron that responds to photoreceptors and sends their signals laterally to neighboring bipolar cells.

Amacrine cells a type of neuron that responds to bipolar cells and sends their signals laterally to neighboring ganglion cells.

The cells are organized in distinct layers, named for their location and what parts of each kind of cell are in that layer. There are three main nuclear layers that contain the nuclei of the cells in that layer. The outer nuclear layer contains the nuclei of the photoreceptors; the inner nuclear layer contains the nuclei of the bipolar, horizontal, and amacrine cells; the ganglion nuclear layer contains the nuclei of the ganglion cells. Between each layer are the two synaptic layers. The outer synaptic layer contains the synapses between the outer nuclear layer and the inner nuclear layer; the inner synaptic layer contains the synapses between the inner nuclear layer and the ganglion nuclear layer. So. Many. Layers.

The axons of all the ganglion cells group together to form the optic nerve (a bundle of axons is called a nerve) and leave the eye together (see Figure 2.22). Remember from Chapter 2 that there are no photoreceptors in this part of the eye so it cannot react to light, and so you are "blind" to light falling on that part of your retina. This is why it is called the "blind spot."

It might be hard to believe that you have a blind spot in your vision, but we can prove it to you! Close your left eye and look at the word "FRED" in Figure 3.5. Start with your face a couple of inches from the book and move the book slowly away from you. At a particular distance, the apple in the diagram will fall on your blind spot and disappear![2] If you keep moving back, it will fall off of your blind spot and reappear. Magic? No, something even better—science!

Now that we have a sense for the organization of the cells in the retina, let's work through how they convey information about light energy to the brain. We'll start with the cells directly responsible for responding to light: the photoreceptors.

Photoreceptors

Recently Fred and his best friend, Claudia, went to the movie theater. Fred lost the rock-paper-scissors match, so he was responsible for getting the popcorn while Claudia went and found seats. The line was long, so by the time he got into the theater, the lights were already off. It was so dark that he couldn't see a thing! After a minute of standing there looking for Claudia in the darkness, Fred finally saw her frantically waving at him and joined her at their seats—phew! Even though he could not see Claudia at all when he first stepped into the dark theater, by the end of the movie, Fred realized he could see Claudia just fine, almost as well as he could in full daylight.

Fred's situation illustrates a phenomenon known as **dark adaptation**, and studying it has been very informative about the cells in the retina. In a more controlled version of the movie theater scenario, scientists discovered that in the dark, the minimum amount of light needed to see (the ***minimum threshold***, see Chapter 1) decreases over time in a very particular way (Blanchard, 1918; see Figure 3.6, *left*). Specifically, it decreases quickly over the first few minutes (those first few moments before Fred could see Claudia waving) then levels off. Then it decreases slowly over the next 20–30 minutes until it takes very little light to see (which was why Fred could see Claudia so easily by the end of the film).

Dark adaptation the change in minimum threshold for light sensation over time spent in the dark.

Look at the changes in threshold over time in Figure 3.6 (*left*). Notice the kink in that function! That let researchers know that there wasn't just one type of cell on the retina—instead, there were *two*. One adapted quickly, but didn't adapt very much, and the other adapted slowly, but adapted *more* (see Figure 3.6, *right*). This second kind of cell could be used to see under very dim light conditions. We now know that these two types of cells—these two photoreceptors, called **rods** and **cones**—differ in a lot of ways.

Rods one of the two different types of photoreceptors present in most chambered eyes. Responsible for translating light into action potentials; more sensitive and less acute. Cannot sense differences in color; operates best in dim light.

Cones one of the two different types of photoreceptors present in most chambered eyes. Responsible for translating light into action potentials; less sensitive and more acute. Senses differences in color; cannot see in dim light.

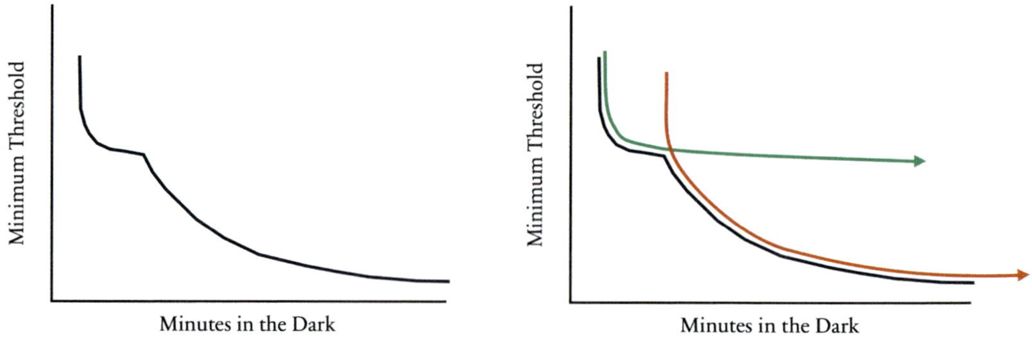

Figure 3.6 Left, the dark adaptation curve. Over time in a dark space, the minimum threshold decreases quickly at first, then levels out, then decreases again for about 30 minutes. Right, the kink in the curve suggests there are two different types of cells with two different adaptation curves.

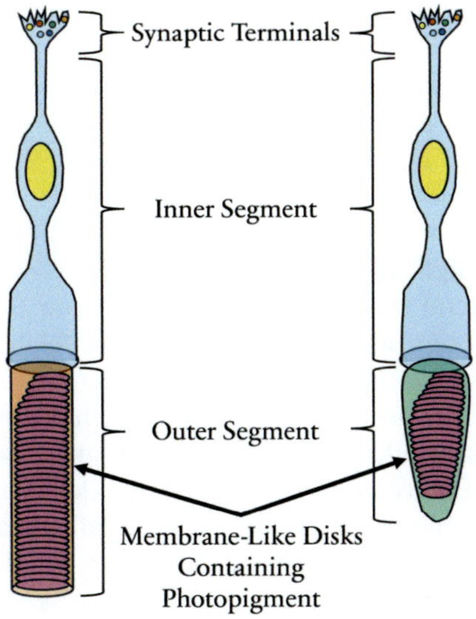

Figure 3.7 Rods (left) and cones (right) are named after the shape of the part of the cell that responds to light; the outer segment of rods is rod-shaped and the outer segment of cones is cone-shaped. Both types of cells respond to light by sending a neural signal to other cells.

Rods and Cones

Rods and cones are named after the shape of the part of the cell that responds to the light (see Figure 3.7), called the **outer segment**. The outer segment of the rods is long and roughly rod-shaped, whereas the outer segment of the cones is shorter and roughly cone-shaped (not surprising, right?). In the outer segment of both cells, there are membrane-like disks that contain photopigments (see Chapter 2). Each disk holds roughly 3 billion photopigment molecules.

> **Outer segment (of photoreceptor)** the part of the photoreceptor that responds to light, made out of a stack of disks filled with light-catching photopigments.

> Socratic Question: How did the kink in the dark adaptation curve depicted in Figure 3.6 suggest to researchers that there were two different types of cells with two different adaptation curves? What are those two different types of cells?

Photopigments

Photopigments are comprised of two parts—a large protein called an **opsin** and an organic molecule called a **retinal**. Think of the opsin as a lightning rod—catching the incoming energy and directing it at the retinal. The retinal uses that energy to change its shape—remember, light is energy! The energy in the light literally powers the transformation in the retinal. The change in shape is what is responsible for a biochemical cascade that, in turn, sends the neural signal (it's a fairly complicated process; we once again recommend the curious reader check out Rodieck, 1998/2018).

Opsin part of the photopigment, responsible for "catching" photons.

Retinal part of the photopigment, changes shape because of the energy caught by the opsin.

Different types of photoreceptors have different opsins. Each type of opsin is sensitive to a particular range of wavelengths. Humans have five different opsins in their photoreceptors—one in the ganglia, one in the rods, and three different kinds in the cones.

The opsin in the ganglia (melanopsin) is a broad-spectrum absorbing pigment. It is sensitive to a wide range of wavelengths of light just like broad spectrum sunblock protects Fred's head against a wide range of wavelengths of (ultraviolet) light. However, the signal from the photopigment in the ganglia isn't really used in seeing. Instead, it sends a signal to our pupil (to adjust for lighting conditions; see Chapter 2) and to the part of our brains that controls the sleep/wake cycle. Daylight tells our brains to wake up, and darkness tells our brains to go to sleep (this is how you eventually adjust when you change time zones).

Rods and cones have a different kind of opsin (rhodopsin) that has four different types. The rhodopsin in rods is most sensitive to (that is, it mainly absorbs) light that has a wavelength of 496 nm (what we see as greenish-aqua, see Figure 3.8).

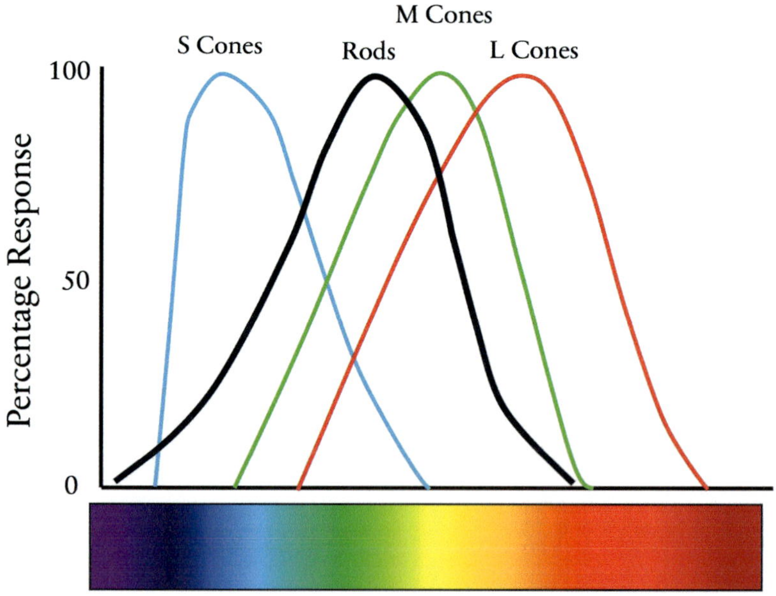

Figure 3.8 Response curves of the three different types of photoreceptors: three different types of cones, and one type of rods.

The rhodopsin in one of the three types of cones is most sensitive to 420nm, seen as blue. These are called S cones because they are sensitive to shorter wavelengths. The rhodopsin in a second kind of cone is most sensitive to 530nm, seen as green. These are called M cones because they are sensitive to **m**edium wavelengths. And the rhodopsin in the third type of cone is most sensitive to 560 nm, seen as red. These are called L cones because they are sensitive to **l**onger wavelengths (more on cone-specific functioning in Chapter 4).

The visual system has a difficult job to do under challenging working conditions. It has to work in very dim light, in very bright light, and even in rapidly changing light conditions (think about Fred stepping outside into the bright day after that movie with Claudia—**squint**). The visual system has to see small details, see quickly, and see different colors (sometimes under light that is changing color!). Thankfully, rather than relying on just one type of cell attempting to do all of that work under all of those conditions, the human visual system (and the sensory systems more generally) break the job up among different specialized cells.

Rods are longer and contain more disks, so they contain more photopigment. Consequently, they are able to absorb (and react to) as little as a single photon. This means they are very sensitive. That is, they have *a very low* minimum threshold (see Chapter 1). However, they cannot regenerate the opsins (that is, undo the change in shape) very quickly; their refractory period is 20–30 minutes. So, under bright light conditions, they quickly reach their response limit (they can only process about 100 photons per second). Consequently, they do not work very well in bright light.

Cones are shorter and contain less photopigment. As a consequence, they are less sensitive—their minimum threshold is about 30–100 photons. However, they are very quick to regenerate their opsins (only about 5 minutes), so they can continue to respond no matter how bright the light gets. In fact, studies show that cones will respond continuously right up until the point where the amount of light will physically burn the retina (like what would happen if you were to stare at the sun, which we strongly encourage you *not* to do)!

Human retinas have both rods and cones, which is known as a **duplex retina**. Most animals have duplex retinas, but there are some animals (lizards, snakes) that have retinas with only cones and other animals (deep sea fish, bats) that have retinas with only rods. It's a pretty safe bet that animals with only rods live in very dark places or are not active during the day—or both. For animals that have both types of cells, the proportion of rods and cones is related to the amount of time that particular species tends to spend in bright light—the more bright light they typically encounter, the larger the proportion of cones they have (Schultze, 1866). Importantly, this is not a *developmental* (i.e., change within a lifetime) difference; this is an *evolutionary* (i.e., changes over generations of an entire species) difference. You can't increase the proportion of rods in your eyes by spending more time in the dark!

> **Duplex retina** a retina that has both rods and cones.

Look again at the word "FRED" in Figure 3.5 (this time with both eyes open). When you do, light reflecting from the word "FRED" will fall on the center of each of your retinas, called the **fovea**. The rest of the retina is called the **periphery**. The fovea is mostly made up of cones, and the periphery is mostly made up of rods, though there is a gradual shift on your retina from one to

> **Fovea** center of retina, light from center of focus falls here.
>
> **Periphery (in eyes)** the part of the retina that is not the fovea or the blind spot.

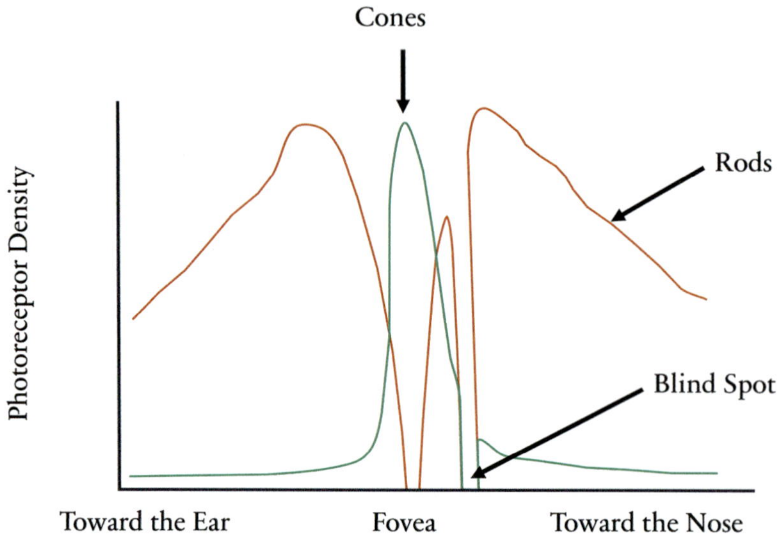

Figure 3.9 The distribution of rods and cones across the retina. Notice the high density of cones in the fovea, and how the density of the rods drops off the farther away from the fovea we look.

the other like how the suburbs sometimes create a gradual shift from the city to the country. If you go back to Figure 2.23, in each picture, you can see a darker smudge right next to the spot where the blood vessels come in. That's the fovea! It's very small—about the size of a flea. It's darker in the picture because the density of photoreceptors is highest in the fovea, so more light is being absorbed there. The density gradually drops off from there to the outer edges of the periphery (see Figure 3.9). In the center of the fovea, there are only cones and no rods (more on cone distribution in Chapter 4).

In the fovea, the vertical connections (the ones going to the brain) become less perpendicular to the back of the eye and more *diagonal* (see Figure 3.10), perhaps so that the cells can get out of the way of the light falling on the photoreceptors in the fovea. The organization is the same, just sort of shoved out of the way.

Just to be clear, not every kind of eye is organized this way! This is how the *human chambered eye* is organized, but as we've already pointed out, most animals don't have chambered

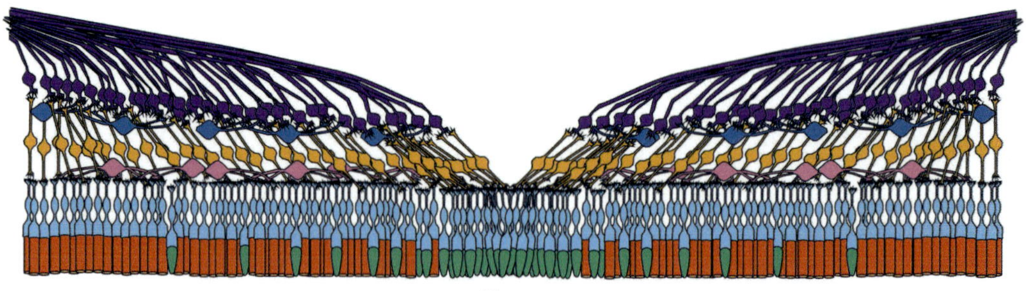

Figure 3.10 In the fovea, the vertically connected cells are shifted to the side (probably to allow more light to fall on the fovea).

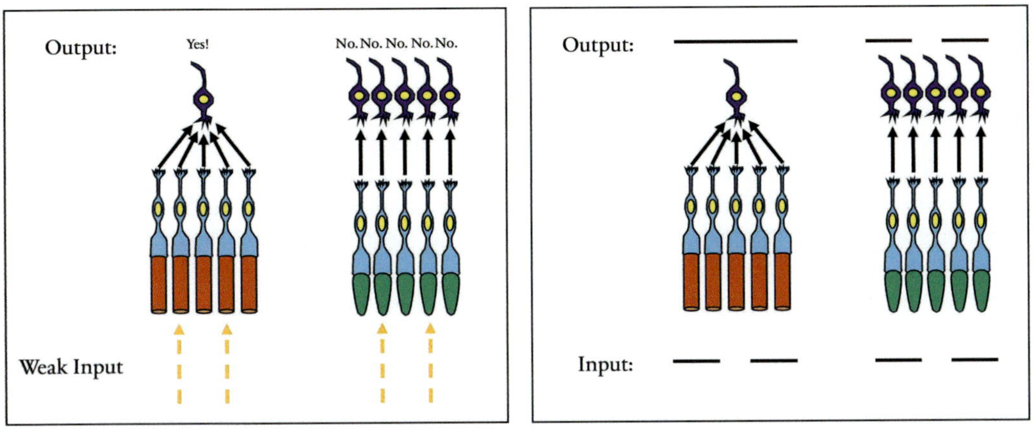

Figure 3.11 The way the rods and cones are connected to the next cells has consequences for sensitivity and acuity. Left: the rods pool their signals, and so they have better sensitivity (but less acuity). A dim light isn't enough for a single cone to get a single ganglion to fire (hence "no"); but when all those smaller signals are collected across the rods, it is enough (hence "yes"). Right: the cones keep their signals separate, so they have better acuity (but less sensitivity). A ganglion receiving signals from a group of rods can't tell the difference between a solid line and a line with a gap in it. But since individual cones send their signals to individual rods, that gap can be seen.

eyes. In addition, some animals with chambered eyes don't have a fovea, and some animals have two foveae in each eye! Animals that do not have a fovea usually live in very dark places, or at least spend most of their time in the dark, so they need eyes that are more sensitive to light (that is, eyes with more rods than cones). Animals with two foveae (like some fish; see Chapter 2) usually need to be able to focus in two directions at once—for example, below them looking for prey, above them looking for predators.

Sensitivity vs. Acuity

In the eye, there is a tradeoff between sensitivity and acuity (see Chapter 1). You can't have both in the same cells, but you can have both across *different* cells. And you need both for everyday life. The fovea and periphery differ in sensitivity and acuity. As we have already covered, the rods (mostly in the periphery) are more sensitive than the cones (mostly in the fovea). Conversely, the cones (mostly in the fovea) exhibit greater acuity than the rods (mostly in the periphery). In part, this is because of the shape, density, and functionality of the photoreceptors themselves, but it is also because of the way they are connected to the ganglia (see Figure 3.11).

A few years ago, Fred was spelunking,[3] and his flashlight ran out of batteries, leaving him in a pitch-black cave—eep! There was zero light, and he was starting to get worried—what would Topsy do if he never came home!? Would he ever get to see his girlfriend Carol again!? Then he saw a very dim light in his peripheral vision (what we sometimes call the "corner" of the eye). Although the light was so dim that the rods were barely responding, he was still able to see the light. Some 30–50 rods will combine their signals before sending them to the ganglia (by way of the bipolar cells; more on this later). How many rods pool their signals depends on the location—specifically, distance from the fovea—more rods are pooled together the farther from the fovea. In Fred's case, that pooling is why he was able to see the light—since a single ganglion was receiving the signal collected from 50 rod cells, the faint signal from each was pooled into a larger signal. That larger signal was enough to get the ganglion cell to fire, and for Fred to see the light in his periphery!

But then something weird happened: he tried to find the source of the light by looking directly at it . . . and it disappeared! *Poof!* He looked away again and it reappeared in the corner of his eye. What kind of sorcery is this? No kind, actually. Once again, it's something even better—science! When he looked directly at the light, the cone cells in his fovea were trying to do the work of detecting the faint signal. Just like with the rods, the light was so faint that the cones were barely responding to it. Unlike the rods, cones have a one-to-one (or very few-to-one) connection with ganglia (by way of the bipolar cells again). Since each ganglia cell is "listening" to a single (or very few) cones, that faintly responding cone was not sending a strong enough signal to get the ganglion cell to fire (see Figure 3.11, *left*). When Fred looked directly at the light, he could not see it.

The upshot is that the rods are more sensitive to light partly because of the way they are connected to the ganglia (Ramón y Cajal, 1894). So, if you're ever trapped in a very dark cave and need to see a very dim light in order to escape, look *just next to* it instead of right at it. The rod cells in the periphery of your retina will do a better job at allowing you to see whatever it is. Not that we're hoping or expecting that this will happen, but now you'll be prepared! This also works if you want to see a dim star in the night sky or a black cat in a dimly lit room.

At this point, you might be thinking that the rods have the best strategy for seeing. After all, they are the ones that are going to help you escape that very dark cave! Or find that pesky black cat. But there is a cost to pooling the signal. Put another way, there's a reason the cone cells *don't* pool their signals (at least, not as much). This is because the cone cells have a *different job*. Pooling information is great when you are trying to amplify a weak signal but not when you are trying to detect a *very precise* signal (i.e., acuity; see Figure 3.11, *right*).

Fred brought his best friend, Claudia, to get her vision checked (she has glasses already, but they need adjusting). The doctor asked her to read letters on a Snellen chart (see Figure 3.12). At the top of the chart, the letters start out quite large. Each successive row of letters gets smaller and smaller. Fred watches as Claudia starts to struggle with the smaller letters. Near the bottom of the chart, there is a letter "C" but Claudia reads it as an "O". Fred (who has perfect eyesight) is surprised, but the mistake is understandable. The difference between a "C" and an "O" is just a tiny gap, particularly when the letters themselves are so tiny! As we've already mentioned, the density of photoreceptors is highest in the fovea, and they are mostly cones (not rods), so the fovea has the best chance of detecting small gaps. This is why we look directly at things that we are trying to read (or see clearly, especially if it's tiny). In part, the reason the cones are better at detecting small gaps is because the signals from the cones are kept separated. They send individual signals to individual ganglia and to individual cells in the brain.

Fred focuses his eyes on the letter at the end of that same row (a "J") and realizes that, now that the C is in his periphery, he can't read it anymore! When he is focused on the "J" the light from the "C" is now falling on the periphery of his eye, where the rods are. And rods pool their signals. Got it? Maybe not? Maybe an analogy having to do with a choir will help.

In one of the scenes in his high school musical *From Cockney to Yankee*, Fred performed with a large choir. During one of the performances, Fred lost his place and stopped singing, but thankfully, the rest of the choir continued, and the audience did not notice any difference in the sound—whew! This is something like what happens when the ganglia are listening to

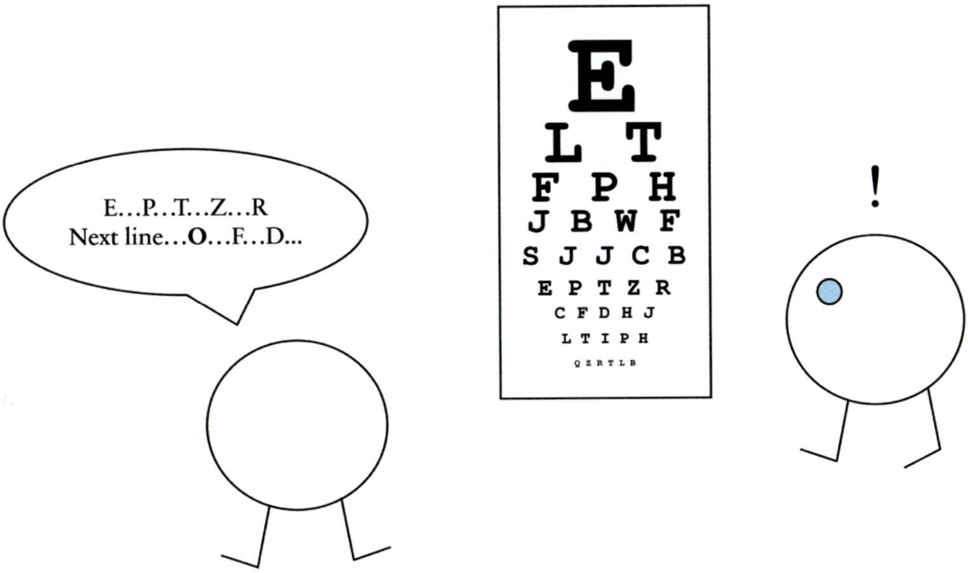

Figure 3.12 Claudia gets her eyes checked by reading a Snellen chart.

the rod cells "sing" about the details of the letter "C" in the periphery. Given that the signal is being pooled across so many rod cells, the ganglia responding to the rods can't tell the difference between a line with a gap in it and a line without a gap in it. They are listening to a choir when a few of the singers have stopped (or never started) singing. This is why if you go back to Figure 3.5, you won't be able to read the word "FRED" if you look at the apple (and why Fred couldn't read the C when he looked at the J). The pooling makes it harder to see detail. If instead you were listening to a solo singer, you would definitely notice if they stopped singing. This is why pooling the signal isn't always the best solution.

If you need to see detail in something (like reading, sewing, or inspecting a cool bug) you should look directly at it, so the light falls on your fovea and you are able to see the detail.

Socratic Question: What is the difference between sensitivity and acuity? How does the connection between the photoreceptors and the ganglia create a tradeoff between sensitivity and acuity?

Receptive Fields

The number of photoreceptors vastly outnumbers the number of bipolar cells, which in turn vastly outnumber the number of ganglion cells. There are roughly 120 million rods and 6 million cones in each human eye all feeding into about 1.5 million ganglion cells. This organization is called **neural convergence**. And neural convergence leads to *signal* convergence.

Neural convergence in the retina, neurons in each layer vastly outnumber the cells in the next layer of the signal chain. Some kind of editing or processing must be taking place.

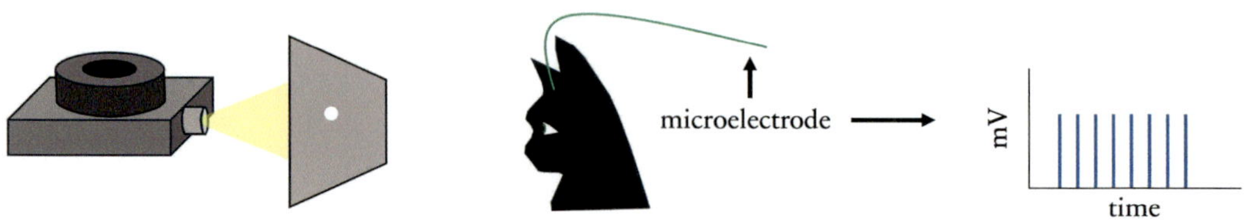

Figure 3.13 Schematic of Kuffler's setup. By inserting a microelectrode into a ganglion, he was able to observe its activity in real time.

Think about it like this: if we gave you a novel of over a thousand pages and then asked you to tell us what it was about, you could extract the important bits and give us a much shorter summary—say, five pages. The summary would contain a lot less information than the book, but it would be more concise and only the important bits would be in there. With so many more photoreceptors than ganglion cells, vision scientists from the biological approach assume some kind of summation—some kind of extracting of the important bits—must be taking place.

Importantly, the brain can't read the book in this metaphor (it doesn't receive signals directly from the photoreceptors). It can only listen to the summary (the important bits) it receives from the ganglia. The question then becomes: what does each layer of the visual system treat as the "important bits"?

In 1953, Stephen Kuffler discovered what the ganglia considered the important bits to include in the summary. He inserted a microelectrode (see Box 1.2) into a ganglion cell of a cat. He then placed the cat in front of a projector screen. Distressingly, the cat's eyes and body were paralyzed for this experiment, which meant they stayed focused where Kuffler wanted them. He then projected various stimuli onto the screen which would reflect light in specific patterns onto specific parts of the retina. He could then watch as the ganglia responded in real time (see Figure 3.13). This research (and more specifically, its methodology) was so influential that Kuffler became known as "the Father of Modern Neuroscience".

What he found was that without any stimulation, the ganglia would fire at a baseline rate (remember this from earlier?). When he projected particular patterns of light and dark that stimulated the retina in specific ways, the firing rate would *increase*. When he projected different patterns of light and dark that stimulated the retina in other ways, the firing rate would *decrease* (remember *this* from earlier?). In other words, *where* and *how* he stimulated it mattered.

A completely homogeneous screen—whether it was fully dark, fully light, or fully gray—resulted in a baseline firing rate. To the ganglion cell, overall luminance is *boring*. Spots of light that fell outside of a particular area of the retina *also* resulted in a baseline firing rate—*also* boring to the cell. However, when spots of light fell *within* that area of the retina, the ganglion cell responded in one of two different ways depending on its location. When the light was in the *center* of that area of the retina, the ganglion would fire *more* frequently than baseline—it was exciting to the cell! When the light was in the *outer part* of that area of the retina, it would fire *less* frequently than baseline—also exciting, but in a different way!

Ultimately, what he found is what we call "on-center, off-surround" organization (see Figure 3.14, *left*). In short, the ganglion cell fired more frequently when light fell on the center of the area (on-center) and less frequently when light fell on the outside part of the area (off-surround).

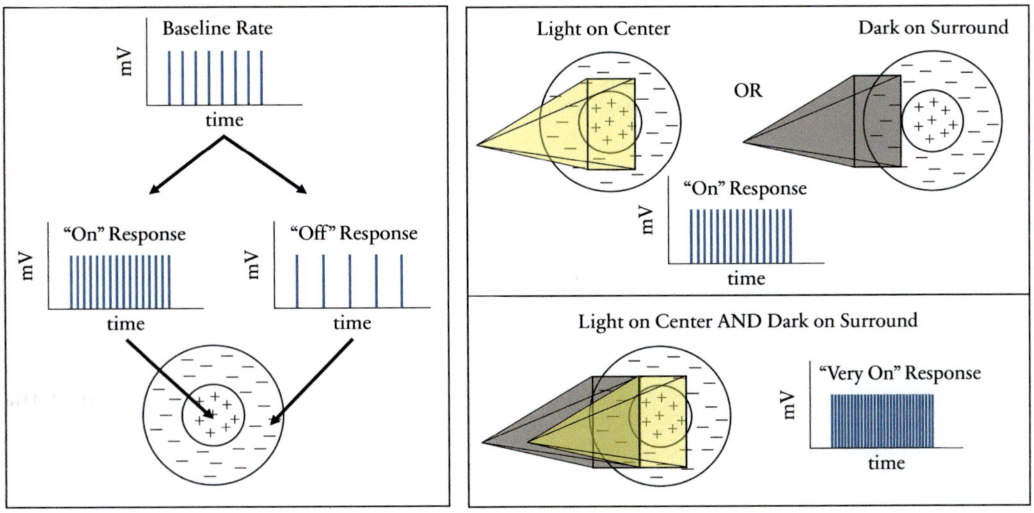

Figure 3.14 The "on-center, off-surround" organization of the ganglia cells. Left, a ganglion cell can increase its rate of firing (an "on" response) or decrease its rate of firing (an "off" response). Top right, light in the center provokes an "on" response, and light on the surround provokes an "off" response (the pattern is reversed for spots of dark). Bottom right, the on-center/off-surround organization is maximally stimulated by areas of contrast.

Let's take a step back and summarize what we've covered so far. One more time with feeling: the photoreceptors respond to light and send their signals to the bipolar cells and the horizontal cells. In turn, the bipolar cells send their signal to the ganglia and horizontal cells. The upshot of all that interconnected signaling is that a single ganglion is responding to the activity of a small group of photoreceptors distributed in a roughly circular pattern on the retina (that small group is called its **receptive field**). Specifically, when photoreceptors in the center of that circle respond to light, the ganglion cell increases its rate of firing, when the photoreceptors in the outer part of the circle (the surround) respond to light, the ganglion cell decreases its rate of firing. Additionally, when a spot of dark falls on the center of the receptive field, the ganglion cell decreases its rate of firing; when a spot of dark falls on the surround, the ganglion cell increases its rate of firing.

Receptive field the group of receptors or neurons that a neuron is responding to.

At this point, you might be asking yourself: why on *earth* would the ganglia have this organization?? It's not very straightforward, and it seems like simply registering the mere presence (or absence) of light would be easier! It might help to think about what kind of pattern on the photoreceptors would generate the largest response from a given ganglion cell. We know that light in the center of the receptive field would increase the rate of firing, and dark on the surround would also increase the rate of firing, so a pattern that has both would *doubly* increase the rate of firing (see Figure 3.14, *right*).

What kind of pattern has light in some areas and dark in other areas? One that has a lot of contrast. Or really, one that has a lot of *edges*. For the ganglion cell, edges are *not* boring! Edges are *very exciting*! Edges mark the border between things. They mark the border between one object and another or between an object and empty space. This is information your visual system needs. This is also a more general truth about all the sensory systems—they do not like sameness; sameness is *boring*. Our sensory systems like *change*; they like *differences*.

Kuffler's work also showed that the receptive fields are much, *much* smaller in the fovea than in the periphery (a finding that should make sense given our earlier discussions of sensitivity and acuity).

Socratic Question: How might the different size receptive fields in the fovea and the periphery contribute to differences in sensitivity and acuity of the photoreceptors located in each of these parts of the retina?

Lateral Inhibition

It turns out that the sideways connections provided by the horizontal and amacrine cells are responsible for the on-center, off-surround organization. How they do that is through a process called **lateral inhibition**. Stimulating one area of the retina with light will send an excitatory signal from those photoreceptors to their ganglion, but it will also send an *inhibitory* signal to all the ganglia surrounding that ganglion. The more stimulated the area, the more it inhibits the surrounding ganglia. That may seem absolutely *bizarre* at first, but let's work through a couple of examples of how it works, then it might make more sense as to why it works this way.

Figure 3.15 is a well-known illusion called the Mach band illusion. Each bar is a consistent shade of gray, meaning that the left side of each bar isn't any darker or lighter than the right side of each bar. However, it appears as though there is a gradient—that is, the left side of each bar looks slightly lighter than the right side of each bar.

Figure 3.16 shows what is happening at the level of the ganglia cells for the Mach band illusion. The lighter the color is, the more it stimulates the photoreceptors. The photoreceptors send their signal on the vertical path *and* the horizontal path. At the border between two grays, this means that the lighter gray inhibits the edge of the darker gray, making it look *even*

Figure 3.15 The Mach band illusion.

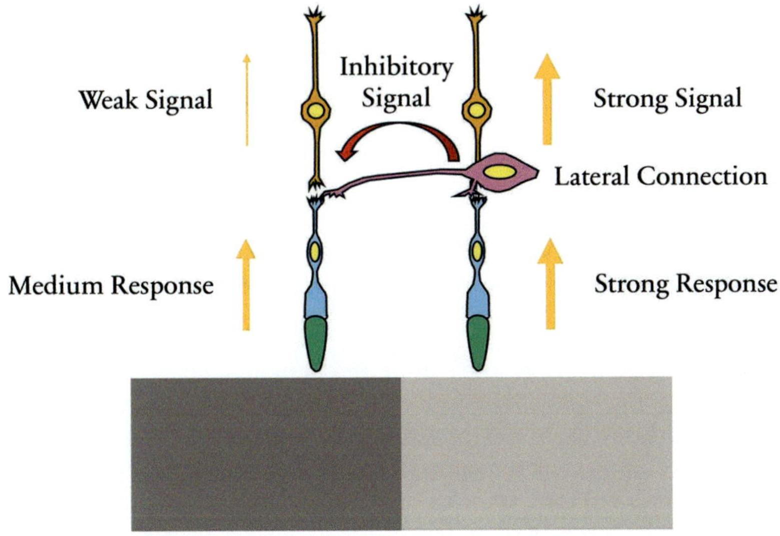

Figure 3.16 A schematic of the lateral inhibition happening in the Mach band illusion.

darker. The upshot of this system is that you can see the contrasts more easily. This system is built to highlight edges and enhance already existing boundaries.

This mechanism is particularly important in lower-light conditions when the differences between surfaces may be only minimal in terms of actual luminance. You still need to see edges (so you don't walk into the coffee table—ouch!), so your visual system makes the edges even easier to make out—and all before the signal even leaves the eye!

Neural Pathways

Retinotopic organization based on the spatial relationships of the retina.

As we discussed earlier, the axons of the ganglia bundle together and leave the eye as the optic nerve. At this point, the optic nerve is **retinotopic**. This means that the spatial arrangement of stimulation on the retina is preserved in the optic nerve. In other words, the optic nerve preserves a "map" of the retina. Stimulation patterns are next to each other on the retina are next to each other in the optic nerve. Handy, right?

Visual field (left or right) the total area visible to either the left or the right of a central fixation point. Visual information in the brain is sorted by visual field.

Very shortly after leaving the eye, there is a reshuffling of the nerve fibers to reorganize the signals by **visual field** rather than by eye. Look at the X in Figure 3.17. Everything to the left of that X is your Left Visual Field (LVF). Everything to the right of the X is your Right Visual Field (RVF). Both eyes see the LVF and the RVF. Confirm this for yourself by staring at the X then closing your eyes one at a time and notice that you can see both the red apple and Fred's pet baby elephant, Topsy, with either eye closed.

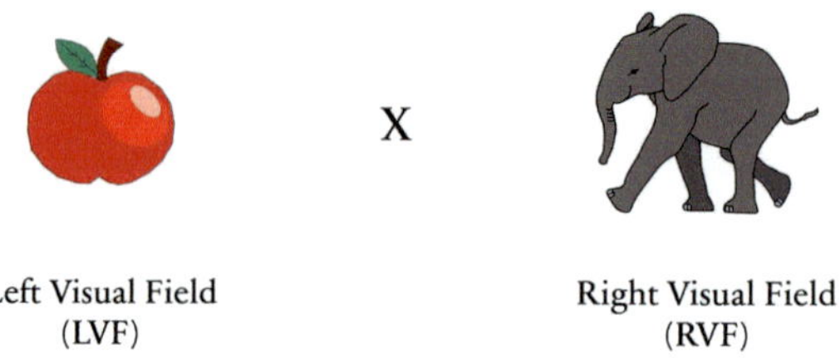

Figure 3.17 Demonstration of the visual fields. If you stare at the "X", the apple is in your left visual field and the baby elephant is in your right visual field.

In Figure 3.18, you'll see that (because light travels in straight lines) the light coming from the LVF actually ends up on the *right side* of both the retinas (as you look at this figure, keep in mind that the perspective of the image in the top left is from *underneath*, so the lefts and rights might get a bit confusing here). To get all the signals from the light in the LVF in the same place in the brain, some of the signals will have to cross over the midline. Since the image of the LVF is on the *right*, the signal from the right eye (the **ipsilateral** eye) stays on the right, but the signal from the left eye (the **contralateral** eye) will need to cross over to join it.

Ipsilateral on the same side.

Contralateral on the opposite side.

In the same way, the light coming from the RVF ends up on the left side of both the retinas. The signal coming from the left, ipsilateral, eye stays on the left, but the signal from

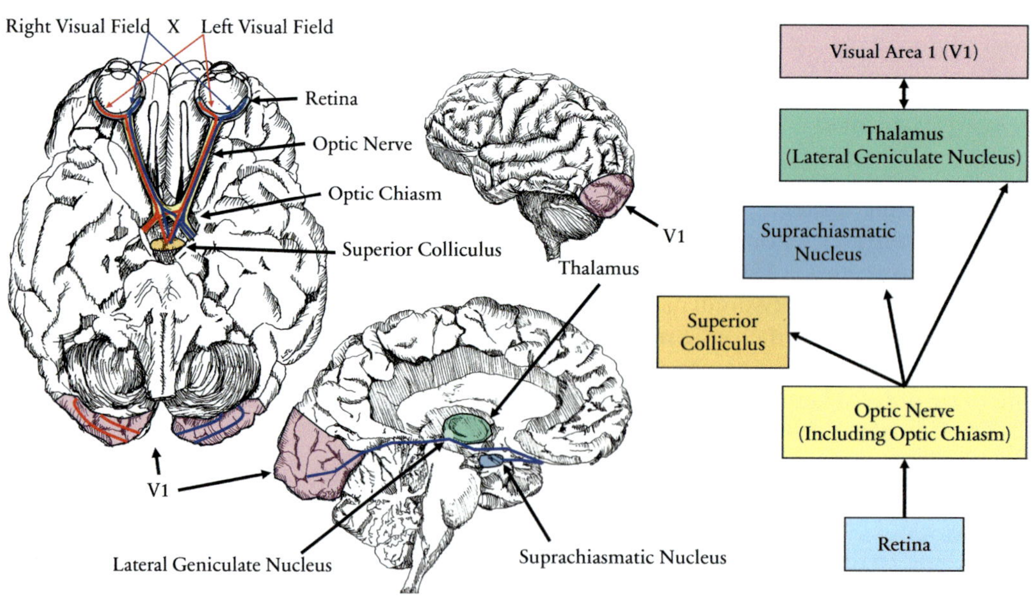

Figure 3.18 Pathways of the visual signal. Ventral view and side views of the brain showing the primary pathway (first sorting by visual field, through the lateral geniculate of the thalamus and to V1) and other areas that receive signals from the retina.

the right, contralateral, eye will need to cross over to join it. The place where the fibers cross the midline is called the **optic chiasm**.

Optic chiasm one of several bridges connecting the two hemispheres of the brain. Signals from the visual system cross the midline via this bridge to reorganize the signals by visual field rather than by eye.

The upshot of all this shuffling is that all the signals caused by light coming from LVF end up in the right hemisphere of the brain, and all the signals caused by light coming from the RVF end up on the left hemisphere of the brain. This probably sounds strange and a bit convoluted, but it's how most of our sensory systems work! The right hand is moved by the left motor cortex and a touch on the left knee is registered by the right somatosensory cortex. That's just how it is.

Primary Visual Pathway

After leaving the eye and reshuffling at the optic chiasm, the vast majority of the signal (90%) travels along the primary visual pathway (Ramón y Cajal, 1894), though not all (see Box 3.1). As you'll see is the case with most of our senses, the first stop is the thalamus.

Box 3.1 Pathways Other Than the Primary Visual Pathway

After the optic chiasm, the signal goes to several places in addition to the primary pathway (all these locations are marked in Figure 3.18). A little less than 10% of the signal travels to the *superior colliculus* or optic tectum (the former is what we call it in mammals, the latter in other warm-blooded vertebrates, but it does the same thing). This structure is in the midbrain and sends signals directly to the spine (bypassing the motor cortex of the brain). It is particularly responsive to movement and very quickly helps you orient your attention to anything moving (Gandhi & Katnani, 2011)—far quicker (around 40ms) than your conscious awareness of and ability to identify objects (around 200ms). Have you ever been in class and a person walked by the doorway to your room and before you could stop yourself, you looked over at the person walking by? This was likely aided by the action of your superior colliculus. It also receives information from your auditory and somatosensory systems and is fastest to respond to stimuli coming from all three.

Less than 1% of the signal goes to the *suprachiasmatic nucleus*, a tiny node right near the optic chiasm. This brain area is involved in our biological clock—a rhythmic cycle of hormones that regulates all kinds of things from sleep and hunger to cognitive clarity and insulin production.

A tiny fraction of the signal travels to the pretectum which is responsible for changing the size of the iris. And a tiny fraction travels to the *pregeniculate*, which is somewhat mysterious in its function. It might be involved in the biological clock, it might be an accessory to the optic system, and it might play a role in stabilizing the retinal image during head movements. Or maybe all three. No one is really sure!

Lateral Geniculate Nucleus of the Thalamus

The thalamus is one part of the limbic system (see Figure 3.18). There are two limbic systems: one in the left hemisphere of the brain, one in the right. The limbic system is on the inside of the hemisphere, the cortex (the wrinkly part) is wrapped around it. You can think of the thalamus like Grand Central Station[4] for the sensory systems. The signals come from all over the body from the various sensory systems to the thalamus and are then sent (usually we say "projected") to various areas of the cortex (depending on where those signals came from). This is a bit like how, every day, hundreds of thousands of people take commuter trains from the suburbs to Grand Central and then a subway to work somewhere in New York City.

Visual information travels to a specific part of the thalamus called the lateral geniculate nucleus (LGN). The retinotopic organization is maintained here just as it was in the optic nerve. So what does the LGN *do*? Well, it's not entirely clear. The cells of the LGN have the same on-center, off-surround receptive fields as the ganglia—they respond best to areas of contrast in a specific location on the retina. In this way, it might seem as though the LGN is just a conduit for the information about the location of edges. But there is more to it than that.

The LGN *also* gets input from other areas of the brain "further up" the processing pathway. In fact, it gets *three times* more input from the visual cortex (specifically V1) than from the retina.[5] Also, the strength of the signal that is sent from the LGN to the cortex is ***reduced*** from the signal that was sent from the eye to the LGN. There are several different interpretations of this reduction. The most common one is that the LGN's function is to weed out the signal from the noise (e.g., Mock et al., 2018). Remember that the eye is never still, and that ganglia sometimes fire without any stimulation of the retina. That means that there is a certain amount of "biological noise" that is masking the signal of "there's a tree across the field". It is possible that the LGN uses input from the visual cortex to see what signals persist over time and uses that to ignore the random fluctuations.

Visual Cortex—V1 and V2

After the signal leaves the LGN, it travels to the occipital lobe to an area called V1 (for **v**isual area **1**, also known as the primary visual cortex; see Figure 3.18). V1 is the outer layer of the occipital lobe and is only about 2mm thick.[6]

In 1981, David Hubel and Torsten Wiesel (who began their work as postdoctoral fellows in Kuffler's lab—small world, right?) won the Nobel Prize for their work discovering and describing the different kinds of cells in the visual cortex. Yay, science! Their work was performed on cats and macaque monkeys, but the work has since been replicated in human subjects using different techniques. They discovered (and named) three basic types of cells: simple, complex, and hypercomplex (which are now usually called end-stopped for reasons we'll explain later). They also discovered that those three kinds of cells are organized into groupings called columns and hypercolumns. Let's take those concepts one at a time.

SIMPLE CELLS

Hubel and Wiesel began with the hypothesis that the receptive fields of cortical cells would be circular (like those of the ganglia and LGN cells). They investigated the receptive fields of the cortical cells of a cat, using the same technique as Kuffler. In particular, they presented images of spots of light and dark on a screen using slides in a carousel slide projector,[7] testing the response of a specific cortical cell. However, regardless of where they put the spots, they were getting only mild responses from the cell—a kind of neural *meh*. They were starting to get frustrated

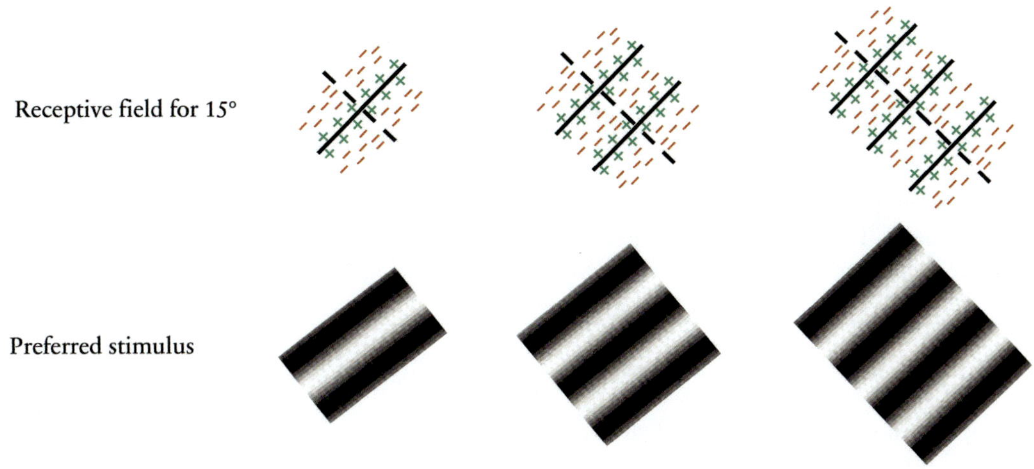

Figure 3.19 Top, the receptive fields (green plus signs and orange minus signs) of simple cells are maximally stimulated by sine wave gratings (repeating areas of black and white stripes, bottom).

when a slide got jammed in the projector. Instead of projecting a spot of light as they had intended, it projected *an edge at a slight angle*. This caused the cell to start firing "like a machine gun" (Hubel, 1982).

This accidental breakthrough led to the discovery of **simple cells**. The receptive fields of these cells look more like alternating bars, oriented in a particular way (see Figure 3.19). They seem to be most interested in what we call **sine wave gratings**—alternating bars of light and dark—at a particular angle and area of the retina.

Simple cells neurons in area V1 that respond to edges of a particular orientation in a particular area of the retina. They often prefer several edges in a row as in a sine wave grating.

Sine wave grating bars of alternating luminance.

COMPLEX CELLS

Complex cells are like simple cells in that they respond to repeating contrast areas of a particular orientation, but they are not picky about *where* that edge is on the retina. They are also not picky about whether the pattern is dark-light-dark or light-dark-light. They receive signals from both the LGN and the simple cells, so they are likely summing across both signals to look for global patterns.

Complex cells neurons in area V1 that respond to edges of a particular orientation but are not picky about the area of the retina or the exact pattern of contrast.

Both simple cells and complex cells actually prefer gratings that are *in motion* rather than ones that are static. Some cells care about the direction of movement, others do not. Some prefer a particular speed of movement, others do not. To each their own, right?

END-STOPPED (HYPERCOMPLEX) CELLS

Hubel and Wiesel called the final type of cell "hypercomplex" but, more recently, scientists have called them **end-stopped cells**. Hubel and Wiesel were working from one of those historically popular ideas we talked about in Chapter 1—specifically hierarchical processing (but see Box 3.2). They thought the cells worked in a step-by-step manner with signals moving from simple, to complex, to hypercomplex cells. However, scientists eventually discovered that hypercomplex cells are not really an entirely different kind of cell. Instead, they are just a simple or complex cell that has an additional component to their receptive field. These cells respond to stimulation that is both a particular orientation *and* a particular size, specifically one that fits inside the receptive field. Or in other words, they prefer the *end* or the *corner* of objects (Gilbert & Wiesel, 1990). That's why these cells are currently called "end-stopped". They tend to have the highest response when the *end* of the object *stops* in the receptive field.

Box 3.2 Cortical Cells as Fourier Transform Filter

Since most of the work in this field was based on the historically popular idea of hierarchical processing, the interpretations of Hubel and Wiesel's work tends to assume that these cells are first extracting simple forms and then building them into increasingly complex wholes (see Chapter 1). However, that is not the only option.

For example, the fact that areas of V1 increase their firing rate more to sine wave gratings than singular edges has led to a hypothesis that the function of the retina and V1 is as a kind of **Fourier transform** filter (Bruce et al., 2014). This might sound complicated, but we swear it's simpler than it sounds. A French mathematician named Joseph Fourier discovered that it is possible to break any pattern over space and/or time down into sine wave components. Those sine waves can then be added back together, and the original pattern recreated (see Figure 3.20).

Fourier transform the process of breaking a complex pattern over space or time into component sine waves. The original complex pattern can then be achieved by adding the sine waves together.

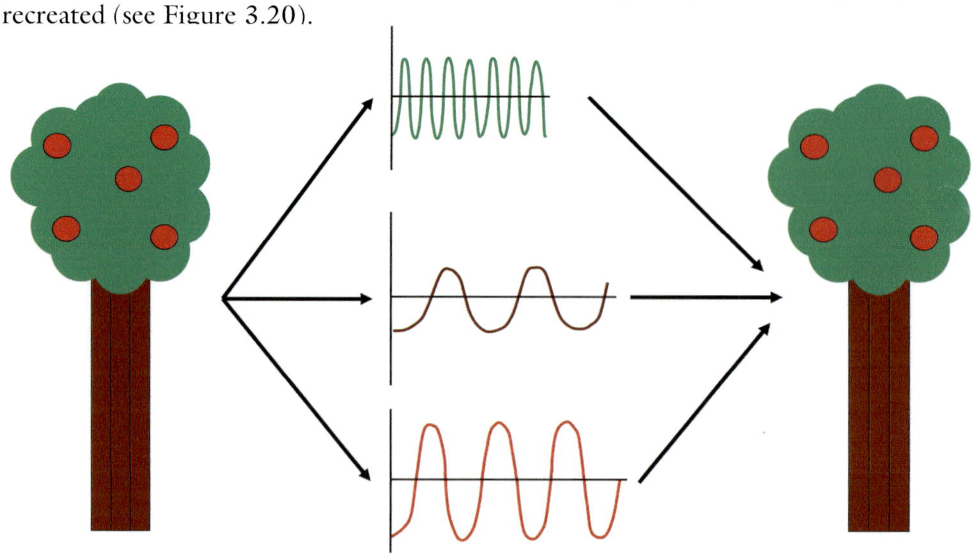

Figure 3.20 Spatial Frequency Analysis as a Fourier transform. Theoretically, any complex pattern can be broken down into simple sine waves and then recomposed by adding the sine waves together.

Theoretically, the sine-wave grating sensitivity of the simple, complex, and hypercomplex cells could act as a Fourier transform filter on the image and allow for recombination to a full image in the brain. Interestingly, this is almost certainly how sound is processed by the inner ear (see Chapter 5).

ORGANIZATION OF THE VISUAL CORTEX

Just like the optic nerve and the LGN, the visual cortex is retinotopic. However, one thing we have not mentioned just yet is that the scale of this map changes across the visual field. The fovea has far more area devoted to its processing than the periphery. To give you a sense of the disparity, the fovea makes up about 0.01% of the retina—the size of a flea compared to the size of a ping-pong ball. At the same time, 8–10% of V1 is dedicated to signals that originate in the fovea (Van Essen & Anderson, 1995). The brain is *way* more interested in stimulation that falls on your fovea that stimulation that is on the periphery. This phenomenon is called **cortical magnification**, and we will revisit this concept when we discuss the somatosensory system (see Chapter 6).

Cortical magnification when the relative area of the brain does not match the relative area of the sensory organ—usually an indication that that part of the sensory organ is being used to explore.

To understand the overall organization of V1, it might help to think of it like a flat surface that has been wrinkled up (like taking a piece of paper and crumpling it into a ball). If you flattened the cortex out on a table, the organization of the processing would be perpendicular to the table. That is, the cells are arranged in vertical columns.

Think again of Fred and his tree; let's assume that he's looking at one apple on the tree. One very tiny part of his retina is receiving light from one very specific part of the apple. All the signals that originate from that particular part of the retina go to the same part of V1, called a **hypercolumn**. The hypercolumn is made up of many **orientation columns** (see Figure 3.21).

Hypercolumn area of V1 that processes the light from a particular area on the retina. Made up of orientation columns.

Orientation column part of a hypercolumn, processes edges of a particular orientation of a particular location of the retina. Made up of two ocular dominance columns.

Each orientation column is made up of the simple, complex, and end-stopped cells we talked about. A particular orientation column cares about areas of contrast that are at a particular orientation. Say one orientation column cares about edges of 15°. It will respond maximally (but not exclusively) to an area of contrast at that particular orientation. So if along the edge of the apple there's one area that has a 15°, that column of cells will be firing in response.

Each orientation column is made up of two **ocular dominance columns** (we know, columns within columns within columns!). One of the pairs of ocular dominance columns

Ocular dominance columns part of an orientation column. Processes information of a particular orientation of a particular location of the retina of one of the two eyes.

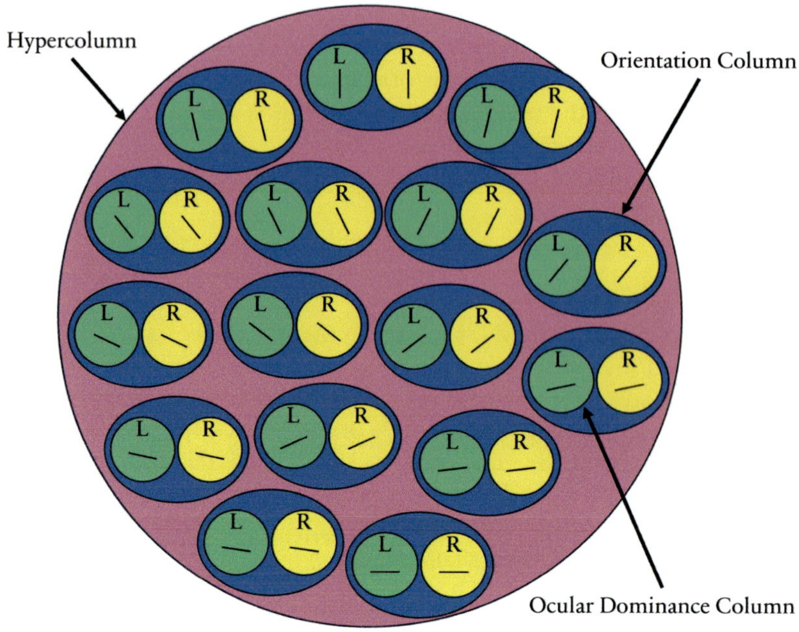

Figure 3.21 V1 is made up of hypercolumns, hypercolumns are made of orientation columns, orientation columns are made up of two ocular dominance columns (one for each eye). Nearby orientation columns have similar preferred orientations.

processes information (mostly) from the left eye, one processes information (mostly) from the right eye (from the same visual field). If Fred was looking at the 15° angle of the edge of that apple with both eyes, then both of these columns would be responding.

Orientation columns with similar sensitivities are located near each other within the hypercolumn. If one column is interested in edges of 15°, the next column over might be interested in edges of 20°, and so on. These columns are relatively small—a single column is roughly 0.5mm in diameter (about the thickness of a coat of paint).

Box 3.3 Vertically Reared Cats: Simple Cell Orientation Depends on Experience

You might be wondering how this complex organization of the cortex came to be. Is it merely encoded in our DNA as part of a genetic blueprint? It doesn't appear so. In 1970, Blakemore and Cooper took newborn kittens and put them in "vertical rooms" —rooms that only had vertical stripes on the wall. They placed Elizabethan collars (also known as cones of shame) on the kittens so that they could not see the floor of the room, which meant that they could only ever see vertical stripes.

Blakemore and Cooper used the same techniques developed by Hubel and Wiesel to map the visual cortex of these kittens after they had lived in the vertical rooms for

Figure 3.22 Left, a "vertical room" and a cat wearing an Elizabethan collar. Kittens raised in these conditions did not have the same cortical cells as kittens raised in a typical environment. Top right, the orientation of the receptive fields of cortical cells for a typically raised kitten. Bottom right, the orientation of the receptive fields of cortical cells for the kittens raised with vertical stripes.

a few months. They discovered that the receptive fields of the kitten's cortical columns did not have the same orientation variability as those of a typically reared cat. Instead of orientations ranging from horizontal to vertical, the orientations were clustered around the vertical lines with which they had been reared (see Figure 3.22). This suggests that the cortical organization is a result of experiences of the animal over the course of development, rather than the result of innate organization or genetic blueprint.

Socratic Question: Hubel and Wiesel won the Nobel Prize in 1981 for their work describing the receptive fields of cells in the visual cortex. What makes their work so valuable in understanding not just vision but the brain?

Streams of Processing

V1 sends information forward to V2. V2 sends information back to V1 and forward to many areas (more than 30!) in a complex and interconnected web (there are more than 300 known reciprocal connections between the various areas). We are not going to cover all of the complexities here, but instead we'll cover the two general pathways: the **dorsal pathway** and the **ventral pathway** (see Figure 3.23).

Dorsal pathway for most senses, after the primary processing area, the signal travels along the top of the brain towards the frontal lobe. Regardless of which sense, this pathway seems to be involved in perception for action (e.g., seeing so you can move).

> **Ventral pathway** for most senses, after the primary processing area, the signal travels along the bottom of the brain towards the temporal lobe. Regardless of which sense, this pathway seems to be involved in perception for scene synthesis (e.g., seeing so you can have a conscious awareness of the layout of surfaces).

Dorsal means "back" but in our case, it refers to the top of the head.[8] The dorsal pathway runs through V3 in the temporal lobe (with a large "backwards" projection to V4), then to the medial temporal (MT) and medial superior temporal (MST) areas, then up to the parietal lobe. Ventral means belly or abdomen, but in our case refers to the underside of the brain. The ventral pathway runs through V4 then to the inferotemporal (IT) areas in the temporal lobe (see Figure 3.23).

The first scientists to explore the functions of these two pathways, Mishkin et al. (1983), called the dorsal pathway the "where" pathway, and the ventral pathway the "what" pathway. That is, they suggested the dorsal pathway's function was to process spatial layout and motion (where things are and where they are going) and the ventral pathway's function was to process form, color, and identity of objects (what those things are).

The more modern interpretation of the two pathways was introduced by Goodale and Milner (1992; Milner & Goodale, 1995). They suggested that the ventral pathway was for building up a conscious representation of the visual scene (what things are and how they are oriented to each other and to you) and the dorsal pathway (which ends up directly next to the motor cortex) was responsible for controlling movement (how to interact with the things

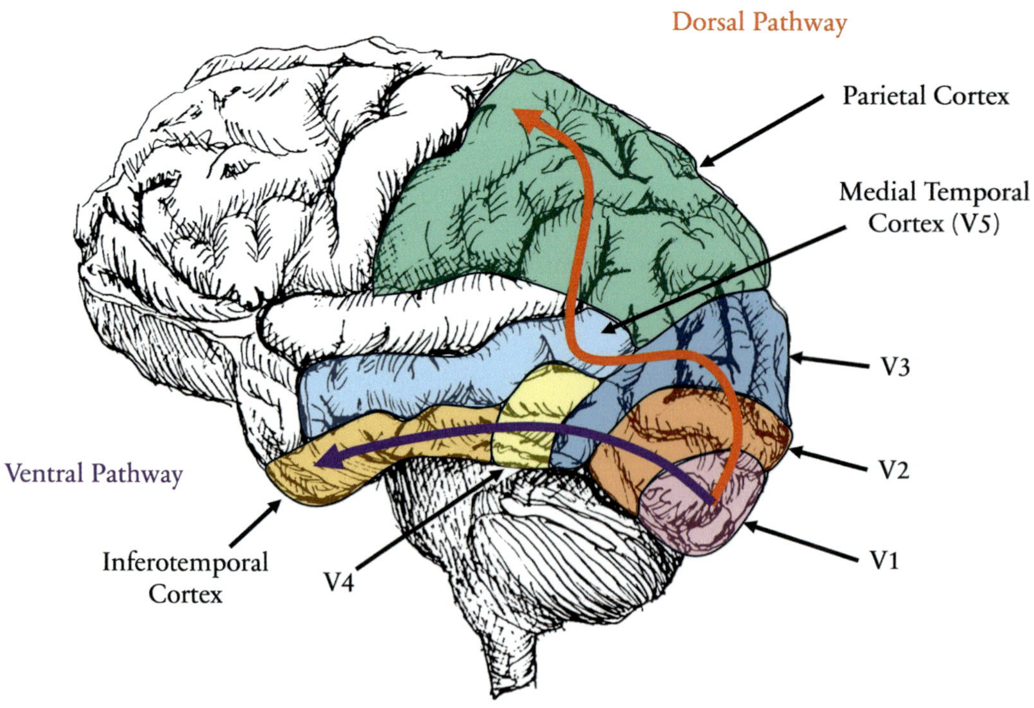

Figure 3.23 Dorsal and ventral streams of visual processing.

that you see). It is worth noting that whatever the two streams do, they do *not* process object properties in different ways—the two streams do not differ in their reactions to any object properties (shape, color, distance, etc.).

And—and this is important—there is a high degree of crosstalk between the two streams, so they really aren't as easily separated as this analysis would make it seem. Moreover, information flows *up* these pathways just as much as it flows *down*. It might be better to call them two interconnected *networks* rather than *streams*.

In addition to connections within brain hemispheres, there is a great deal of communication between brain hemispheres as well—mostly across a bridge of brain tissue called the corpus callosum. At every point along the visual processing pathways, the two hemispheres send signals across this bridge. The function of that communication is somewhat unclear, but it is hypothesized to be responsible for our unitary perception of the visual field as a *whole* rather than as *two halves*.

Socratic Question: What are the two visual streams of processing hypothesis? How has it evolved over time?

Summary

The brain is made up of excitable cells called neurons. These cells communicate with each other through electrochemical signals. In the eye, photoreceptors translate the language of light into the language of neural signals. Photoreceptors communicate with ganglia, and ganglia appear to extract edge information from that signal. The ganglia send their signals to the thalamus, and the thalamus sends the signal on to V1 in the cortex. The organization of V1 is a series of columns dedicated to particular areas of, and particular orientations within, the retina. V1 sends its signal to V2, and from there the signal splits in two: the dorsal pathway and the ventral pathway.

Notes

1 There are both positive and negatively charged ions inside and outside of the cell. Inside the cell, there are more negative than positive; outside the cell, there are more positive than negative.
2 You might wonder why you don't ever notice that you have a blind spot. There are a few different reasons for this, including that you have two eyes that are always moving . . . at least a little (see Chapter 11).
3 A delightful term that means exploring caves.
4 One of the largest and busiest train stations in New York City. Trains from the suburbs almost all go here, and many of the within-city lines intersect at this point.
5 Believe it or not, the lion's share (about 60%) of the incoming signal comes from other areas like the superior colliculus and reticular formation. This leads to another popular interpretation that this is a site of "top-down" processing (see Chapter 11).
6 About the thickness of a flea!
7 For our younger readers more used to a digital world—a carousel slide projector worked a lot like the projector your teachers use to project PowerPoint slides at a screen. However, instead of being hooked up to a computer, the light from the projector went through transparent slides so that the slides were visible on a screen. These usually had a cardboard border, which is what caused the shadow of an edge as it dropped into the machine.
8 Like the dorsal fin of a shark.

4 Color

The previous chapters focused on the ability of Fred's (and our) visual system to detect light and certain patterns in that light that might signify edges. But there's another ability that Fred's (and our) visual system has that is perhaps equally important: sensitivity to colors and differences in the color of the objects Fred (and we) are viewing. Differences in the *amplitude* of light (i.e., brightness contrast) help us to differentiate one surface from another, but differences in the *wavelength* of light (i.e., color contrast) help just as much—if not more so! To see what we mean, let's return to Fred and his apple tree.

If Fred is able to tell the difference between the colors of the different parts of the tree, he is going to have a lot easier time finding the apples on the tree. Look at Figure 4.1. Notice that in the picture that is in color (*left*), the apples are easy to see. In the black and white version (*right*), they are not! More than that, apples change color as they ripen so being able to see color allows Fred to know when a given apple is ready to eat. Yum!

Humans have the ability to distinguish about 10 million different colors (Morovic et al., 2012). No wonder Fred was overwhelmed by how many choices there were when he went to go paint his living room! Many animals can distinguish far fewer colors than these—which

Figure 4.1 The same picture in color (left) and black and white (right). The apples are easily visible when the picture is in color, and barely visible in the black and white photo.

DOI: 10.4324/9781032690964-5

is why Fred's pet baby elephant, Topsy, did not care nearly as much about what color paint Fred chose. But some animals can distinguish even *more* colors than we can, and some are even sensitive to wavelengths of light that we can't see at all. In fact, the *majority* of animals are able to see ultraviolet light (including insects and birds but also some mammals including dogs, cats, pigs, ferrets, and even reindeer); we are among the minority that can't! Flowers that are pollinated by bees usually have a "bullseye" pattern in the ultraviolet spectrum (see Figure 4.2—on the left is what we see; on the right are the same flowers photographed with a special camera that can register ultraviolet light in a color we can see).

Despite being sensitive to only a small portion of the electromagnetic spectrum, we can see a rather extraordinary number of different colors. But how? Well, it has a lot to do with the photoreceptors in the retina, specifically the cone cells. As we described in Chapter 3, cones are responsible for our ability to distinguish between different wavelengths of light.

Tri-Chromatic Color Theory

It would be inefficient (not to mention impossible) to have a different type of cone sensitive to each of the 10 million different colors we can see; we would need 10 million different cones at every point on the retina, and that simply isn't going to work! We need some way of getting all the very many colors out of far fewer receptors—kind of like how the hardware store can make all the colors of paint that they have to offer from just a few basic colors mixed

Figure 4.2 Many flowers have a "bullseye" pattern that reflects ultraviolet light. Left, what we see when we look at the flower; right, what a bee would see.

together a certain way (see the following). In Chapter 3, we mentioned that the three different cones were each sensitive to different parts of the electromagnetic spectrum (read: they are the most sensitive to specific colors of light; see Figure 3.8). To explain how we might get from just three sensitivities of particular wavelengths of light to all the millions of colors that we can see, we have to talk a little bit about color theory (see Box 4.1).

Box 4.1 Color Theory

One of Fred's favorite classes in elementary school was art class with his teacher, Mr. Raoul. In that class, Mr. Raoul had them experiment with mixing colors—swirling together finger paints, mashing pieces of Play-Doh into amazing technicolor mashups, the works! Fred eventually learned that there are just three *primary colors* (red, blue, and yellow). By mixing those colors in pairs, he could create the *secondary colors* (red and yellow make orange; yellow and blue make green; red and blue make purple). When he mixed all the colors together, he would get black (well, theoretically, anyway; Fred's mixtures usually came out more brown than black).

When Fred got a bit older, he took art classes in college. His teacher for Painting 101, Professor Riley, taught him that his understanding of primary and secondary colors was only *mostly* true. The *true* primary paint colors are not red, blue, and yellow, but *magenta*, *cyan*, and yellow (see Figure 4.3, *right*). Fred was really flummoxed by this! Yellow sounded about right, but *cyan*? *Magenta*? Yep.

Professor Riley encouraged Fred to go look at the colors of ink in his color printer. When he did, he found the three colors Mr. Riley said he would find! Amazing! Fred was even more surprised by the *secondary* colors. It turned out the secondary colors are not orange, green, and purple, but cobalt blue (a mix of cyan and magenta); lime green (a mix of cyan and yellow), and red (a mix of magenta and yellow). What in the name of Gustav Fechner is going on here!? Fred started to wonder if Mr. Raoul had lied to

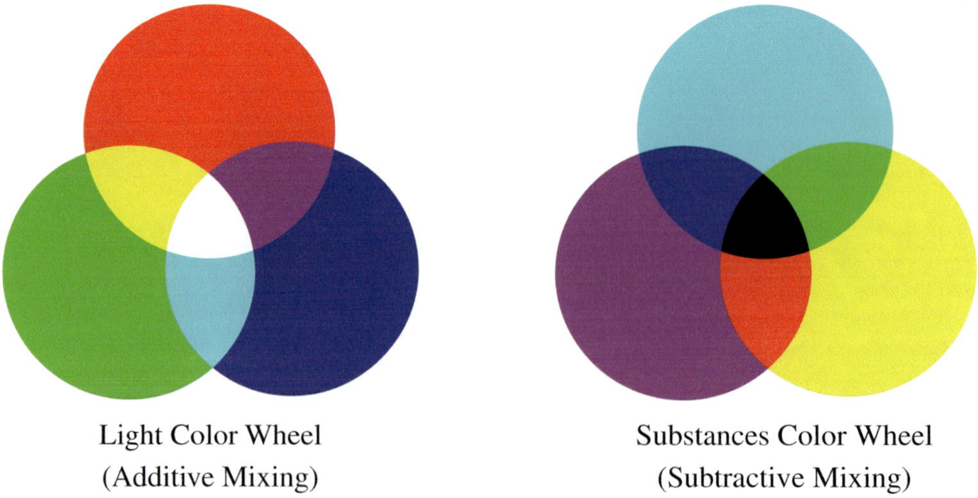

Figure 4.3 Left, light color wheel; right, paint color wheel.

him! Mr. Riley assured him that it wasn't a lie—rather, it's easier to teach a simplified version of color theory to children who are just learning what the different colors are. It also turns out that this is why his attempts to make black always ended up brown: the colors he was mixing with weren't *quite right*.

The following semester, Fred took a theater lighting class with Professor Profeta. And suddenly, he had to learn the primary and secondary colors *all over again*. It turns out that mixing *light* is very different than mixing *paint* (or any other colored substances, like Play-Doh).

Professor Profeta taught him that—just like in paint—he only needed three colors of light to create every conceivable color of light, but—unlike in paint—the three colors were red, lime green, and cobalt blue. From those, he could mix the secondary colors: red light and lime green light make yellow light; red light and cobalt blue light make magenta light; and lime green light and cobalt blue light make cyan light. Finally, when he mixed all of the colors of light together, he got *white* light.

Fred noticed that that the primary colors of light are the secondary colors of substances and vice versa. When he mentioned this to his teacher, Professor Profeta told him that *this is not a coincidence*! This is a consequence of the way our visual system works. If our eyes were different, the primary colors of substances and light would be different. If Fred's baby elephant were to take up painting or stage lighting, for example, he'd need a very different set of paints or colored lights to create his masterpieces.

Color Mixing

Subtractive color mixing the creation of different hues by combining different pigments that absorb different wavelengths (e.g., mixing paint).

Additive color mixing the creation of different hues by combining different wavelengths of light (i.e., mixing colors of light).

When mixing substances like paint or Play-Doh, you are doing something called **subtractive color mixing** which is . . . actually rather complicated. To explain it, it's easier to start with **additive color mixing**, which is what you are doing when you mix light. Late 18th- and early 19th-century British scientist Thomas Young suggested that to make any color we see, we only need to mix three colors of light: red, lime green, and cobalt blue. Mid-19th-century German scientist Hermann von Helmholtz later confirmed that with a series of experiments. He gave participants three different adjustable flashlights—one red, one lime green, and one cobalt blue— as well as a target color to match (see Figure 4.4 and Box 4.1). You can actually try this yourself—that is, if you happen to have adjustable red, lime green, and cobalt blue flashlights sitting around or if you have access to fancy stage lighting at your local theater.

In these experiments, the participants aimed their flashlights on a white surface (which reflects all visible light). If the participant shined a cobalt blue light on the surface, cobalt blue light would reflect back to the eye, and so the surface would appear cobalt blue. Makes sense, right? If the participant added a lime green light, the surface would reflect *both* cobalt blue *and* lime green light so it would appear as a combination of those two colors: cyan. And so on.

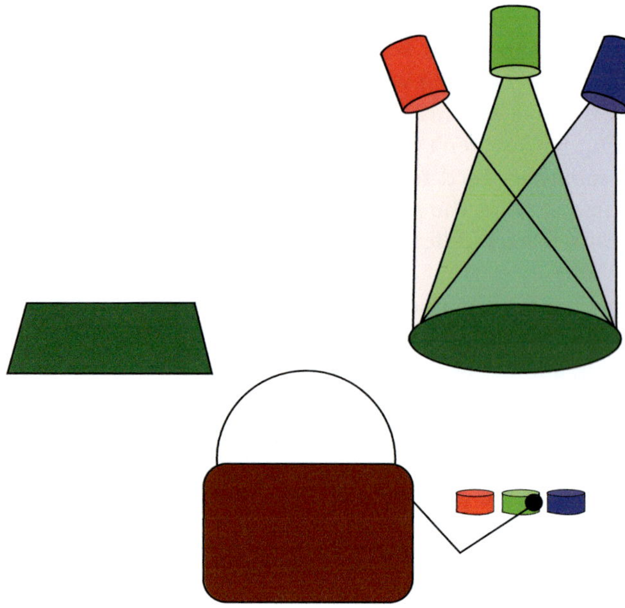

Figure 4.4 Young and Helmholtz suggested that we only needed three colors of light (red, cobalt blue, and lime green) to mix every possible color we can see. This was confirmed by giving participants three different lights to mix and having them match test patches.

Ultimately, Helmholtz found that pairings of the three primary colors of light (red, lime green, cobalt blue) would make the three secondary colors of light (yellow, magenta, and cyan). All three lights together would make white light (see Box 4.1). Moreover, the participants could use just those three primary color flashlights to match any color sample. They could, for example, match a greener cyan by adding more lime green, or a more orangey-red by adding more yellow, and so on.

This process is called **additive color mixing**—each time another color is added to the mix, it *adds* a new wavelength of light to be reflected back to the eye. Let's contrast this with what happens when mixing paint—**subtractive color mixing**. Before we can do that, we need to examine what makes yellow paint appear yellow. *Wait, what?* Yep. Trust us.

Yellow paint has a pigment in it that absorbs cobalt blue light (and reflects the rest of the colors). When white light, which has all of the colors in it (including the three primary colors: red, lime green, and cobalt blue; see Chapter 2) strikes the paint, the cobalt blue is absorbed. In other words, the cobalt blue is *subtracted* from the light that strikes the paint. Of the three primary colors, only lime green and red are left to reflect back to the eye. Remember that when mixing colors (look at the color wheel in Figure 4.3), lime green plus red equals yellow. So, if the paint absorbs cobalt blue, we see it as yellow. Easy peasy, right?

Now, let's look at a scenario where we combine yellow paint with cyan paint. Cyan paint appears cyan because it has a pigment in it that absorbs red light and so the paint reflects lime green and cobalt blue. The combination of those colors is cyan. In other words, if the paint absorbs red light, we see it as cyan. So, when we combine yellow paint and cyan paint, there are *two* pigments, one that absorbs red and one that absorbs cobalt blue. Mixing them together does not change what color each pigment absorbs, so the resulting mixture will absorb both red and cobalt blue. In that case, of the three primary colors of light, *only lime green* is not being absorbed. Therefore, lime green is the only color being reflected to the eye. In other words, mixing yellow and cyan paint will create lime green paint. Each time you add a color of paint, you are *subtracting* more wavelengths. That's why when you add all the colors together, you get black—in that case, *all* wavelengths of light are being absorbed. It's also why you can't make a color *brighter* by adding more paint. If you have made a color that is too dull, you have to start over. Pretty wild, right?

According to Young and Helmholtz's studies (among others), you only need three colors to generate all the many colors that we are capable of seeing. Rather than 10 million+ receptors, we would only need *three*: one sensitive to cobalt blue, one to lime green, and one to red. That's quite amazing, really. Just *three* components yield more than 10 million different outcomes. And looking back at Figure 3.8, it turns out three components is exactly what we have! This is known as the **Young-Helmholtz Trichromatic Color Theory**. "Tri" means three and "chromatic" means color. It's Three-Color Color Theory.[1]

Young-Helmholtz Trichromatic Color Theory in order to create all the colors we see, we can use a combination of just three colors (cobalt blue, lime green, and red) and so we have receptors (S, M, and L cones) wavelengths of light that correspond to each color.

Socratic Question: How is mixing Play-Doh (or paint) different than mixing colored lights? How did experiments on mixing colored lights lead to the development of Trichromatic theory?

As a reminder (see Chapter 3, in particular Figure 3.8), the cobalt blue sensitive cones are called S cones (because they are sensitive to short wavelengths); the lime green sensitive cones are called M cones (because they are sensitive to medium wavelengths); and the red

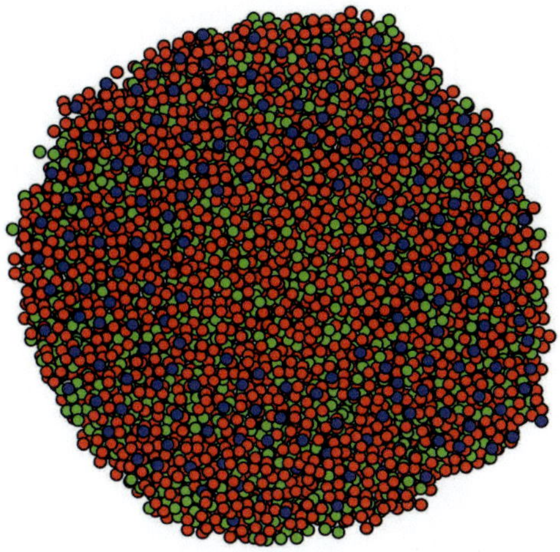

Figure 4.5 The distribution of different types of cones in the fovea. There are far more M and L cones than S cones. There are no S cones in the very center of the fovea, but unlike the M and L cones, they are in the periphery.

sensitive cones are called L cones (because they are sensitive to long wavelengths). There are far fewer S cones (accounting for only 5–10% of all cones). They are located across the entire retina except for the very center of the fovea (recall that the fovea is the center of the retina, see Figure 2.22 and 2.23). There are far more M and L cones, and they are located in the fovea, with a peak density right in the very center of the fovea (see Figure 4.5). Interestingly (to us, anyway), the distribution of M and L cones is not always the same across people. Most of the time, there are equal numbers of M and L cones, but sometimes people have far more L than M cones (Brainard et al., 2000). However, these differences don't usually result in differences in color *perception*.

How Trichromatic Theory Works

Trichromatic color theory is consistent what we know about cones and does a good job explaining how we are able to see most colors. In order to fully understand how this works, let's fully unpack a couple of examples. Let's say we see something yellow—maybe yellow paint, a lemon, or a patch of snow to be avoided! There are actually two different situations that could result in identical perceptions of that yellow something (see Figure 4.6, *left*). Thinking about Helmholtz's flashlight experiments again, you could shine a red flashlight and a lime green flashlight onto the same (white) surface *OR* you could just shine a yellow flashlight onto the same surface. In both cases, we would see it as yellow. Or in other words, the surface could appear yellow because it reflects only yellow light, or it could appear yellow because it reflects both red light and lime green light.

In Figure 4.6 (*right*), we've overlayed the two situations on the response curves from the cones. The yellow vertical line on the diagram indicates the situation where just yellow light is falling on the cones. Yellow light has with a wavelength of about 570nm which is very

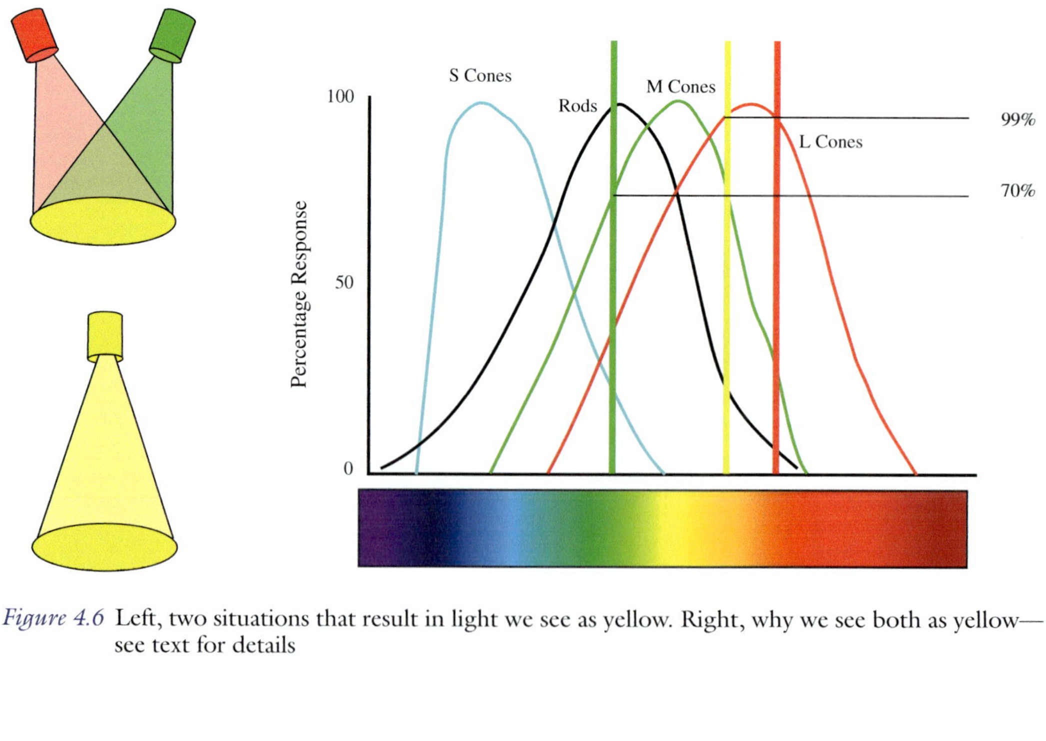

Figure 4.6 Left, two situations that result in light we see as yellow. Right, why we see both as yellow—see text for details

close to the most preferred wavelength of the L cones, so they respond at about 99% of their peak response. Meanwhile, this wavelength of light also stimulates the M cones, but since it's farther away from their most preferred wavelength (lime green), they respond at about 70% of their peak response.

Now consider the situation where both red and lime green light are being reflected to the eye. Red light has a wavelength of about 620nm (represented by the red vertical line in the diagram) so the L cones respond at about 99% (just like they did to yellow light). Green light has a wavelength of about 450nm (represented by the green vertical line in the diagram) and so the M cones respond at about 70% (just like they did to yellow light).

Imagine you are the brain—go you! You are getting a 99% response rate from the L cones and a 70% response from the M cones. You have no way of knowing what kind of light created this pattern. It could have been a yellow light on its own or a combination of a red light and a green light. In other words, two different physical stimuli could generate the same response from the cone cells. These are known as **metamers**—situations where different physical situations result in identical neural effects. In other words, metamers are situations when we end up with identical perceptions of different physical situations. In the Helmholtz study, the participants were *creating* metamers—finding combinations of the three primary colors that would match a single wavelength. The classical view of perception is very interested in this type of situation because it is an *ambiguity*—that is, a situation where different inputs result in identical outputs (see Chapter 8).

> **Metamers** different physical situations that result in identical neural effects.

One last point to make here is that there is no single wavelength that we see as magenta. It is what's called a **non-spectral color**. That is, it's a color that only exists in the combination of other colors. Weird, right? (Also in this category are brown and white, among others.)[2] There is no single wavelength that could stimulate both the L cones (red) at or near their peak, *and* the S cones (blue) at or near their peak. So, when this situation occurs, our visual system experiences magenta—a *reddish* blue or *bluish* red. Keep non-spectral colors in mind as you read the rest of the chapters in the biological view. It is an example of cross-fiber neural coding—a fancy term for how two colors blend into an *entirely different* color that does not look like the original colors (like how red and green make yellow). This concept will come up particularly in Chapter 7.

> **Non-spectral colors** colors that do not exist as specific wavelengths, we perceive them when two (or more) wavelengths travel together.

> Socratic Question: What are color metamers? How does Trichromatic theory explain the experience of color metamers?

Opponent-Process Theory

While the trichromatic color theory does an *okay* job explaining the basics of color perception, there are a few things it doesn't explain (which Helmholtz acknowledged when he wrote up the findings of his flashlight studies). First, perception of yellow is supposed to be a combination of the perception of lime green and red. Except that there are people who have difficulty distinguishing green and red (more on this later) and yet they have no trouble seeing the color yellow! If there are only three kinds of cones with sensitivities to (cobalt) blue, (lime) green, and red, then a person who cannot tell those two colors apart shouldn't be able to see a color that is created by mixing those two colors. Weird, right? It would be like giving someone just blue paint or just green paint and asking them to make yellow paint—good luck with that.

Afterimages and Hue Cancellation

Afterimage an image that appears to be on a white surface if you look at it after gazing at a colored image for a time. The image is an inverted color version of the original image.

And even for people with typical color vision, there is the issue of **afterimages**. To experience an afterimage, check out Figure 4.7. Stare at the center of the left photograph of weird bluish-aqua flowers for about 30 seconds. The more still you keep your eyes, the better this will work—so maybe stare at the very center of the image. After the 30 seconds, look at the center of the white box next to it. You should see an image that looks roughly like the photograph of reddish-orangish flowers on the right. What in the names of Young and Helmholtz is going on here?! So, by staring at an image that has certain colors in it for a little bit and then staring at a white space, you'll experience an image with different colors in it that isn't even actually there at all? Yup! This image is called an afterimage.

Trichromatic color theory can't explain why this happens (and, for what it's worth, Young and Helmholtz did mention these shortcomings in the original paper on the subject). Enter late 19th- to early 20th-century German physiologist Ewald Hering. He noticed that there were some combinations of colors that seemed impossible to see. You couldn't, for example, see a reddish green. You can't even imagine what it would look like. Not even Mr. Raoul or Mr. Riley could do so. You would think that with over 10 million colors, there would be a reddish green in there somewhere. But no. Reddish blue is possible, but not reddish green. Weird, right? Hering thought that it was weird, too. He suggested that rather than *three* primary colors, there were actually *four* primary colors that worked in pairs—red-green and blue-yellow. Keep in mind that Hering lacked the technology and knowledge about physiology that we have now—for example, he didn't know about cones and their spectral sensitivities. He (and many of the scientists who worked on investigating his theory) were basing

Figure 4.7 If you stare at the left photo for about 30 seconds, then stare at the white square (or any white surface), you will see a picture like the one on the right. This is an afterimage.

their ideas on careful observation and self-report. That's doing science the hard way, but it's how science was done!

In the 1950s, Dorothea Jameson and Leo Hurvich investigated Hering's theory of color vision as a possible explanation for afterimages. Specifically, they looked at something called **hue cancellation**. That is, if you shine a cobalt blue light on a white piece of paper and then add a yellow light, the two colors will "cancel" each other out and the surface will appear white. Moreover, if you shine a red light on a bluish green piece of paper (what we might call aqua), the surface will appear more bluish and less greenish. The red light "cancels" the green so only the blue is left.[3]

Hue cancellation the combination of two colors of light will cancel each other out (i.e., make them appear white)—suggesting they are connected in our physiology.

The implication here was that red and green on the one hand, and blue and yellow on the other were somehow connected in the physiology of our visual system. Red and green caused *opposing* reactions (or "processes"). Blue and yellow caused different *opposing* reactions (or "processes"). You cannot have a red response and a green response simultaneously, hence no reddish-green! This is called the **opponent process theory** of color perception (Hurvich & Jameson, 1957).

Opponent process theory there are three processes for color perception—one that detects red and green, one that detects blue and yellow, and one that detects the brightness of the light. The red/green and blue/yellow processes act in opposition to each other so cannot be activated simultaneously.

Socratic Question: How does the impossibility of certain colors (e.g., reddish-green) and the experience of afterimages provide evidence against trichromatic theory and in support of opponent-process theory?

Hering's observation was correct, but his description of the mechanism was not quite right. He assumed that one color (say green) would start a "building up" chemical reaction, and the opposing color (in this case, red) would start a "destructive" chemical reaction. Instead, as we now know, the opponent processes are increases and decreases in the rate of firing at the level of the ganglia (see Chapter 3).

Remember that the S, M, and L cones send their signals to the ganglia. In Chapter 3, we discussed how ganglia cells have a center-surround organization—the ganglia that receive the signals from the S, M, and L cones work the same way. A red center/green surround ganglia will have an "on" response to red in the center of its receptive field and an "off" response to green in the center of its receptive field. Conversely, it will have an "off" response to red in the surround and an "on" response to green in the surround. There are red center/green surround, green center/red surround, yellow center/blue surround, and blue center/yellow surround cells (see Figure 4.8).

There are a few differences between the color opponency ganglia and the bright/dark opponency type. First, the receptive fields of the color ganglia are much smaller than the

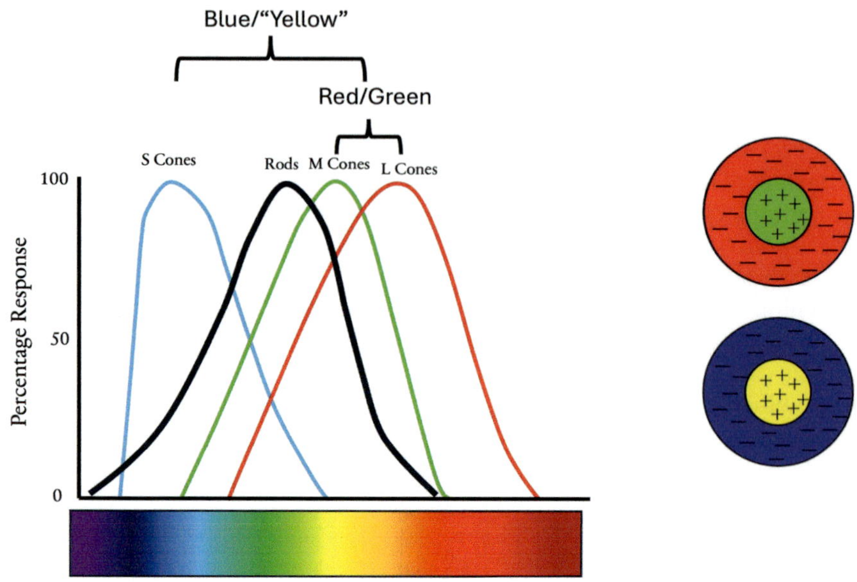

Figure 4.8 Center/surround organization of the ganglia. Red and green are paired and blue and yellow are paired.

receptive fields for the bright/dark ganglia—meaning that color discrimination acuity is much higher than simple bright-dark contrast acuity. *It better be, with over 10 million colors*! Second, there are a *lot more* color opponency ganglia than bright/dark ganglia, *eight times* as many in fact!

How Opponent-Process Theory Works

As we did with trichromatic theory, it's worth unpacking a bit more how opponent-process theory works. Let's say you are looking at a yellow flower with a green stem (see Figure 4.9). The light reflects from the yellow flower and onto a particular spot on your retina. Both M and L cones located at this spot are firing, the L cones are at 99% of their response rate, the M cones are at 70% of theirs (see Figure 4.9). These cells send their signals to the ganglia responsible for that area of the retina.

Since the M cones are only being mildly stimulated, they will send only mild signals to the ganglia, specifically a *mild inhibitory signal* to both the Blue/Yellow ganglia and the Red/Green ganglia and a *mild excitatory signal* to the bright/dark ganglia.[4] On the other hand, since the L cones are being strongly stimulated, they are going to send a strong signal to the ganglia, specifically a *strong inhibitory* signal to the Blue/Yellow ganglia, and a *strong excitatory signal* to both the Red/Green ganglia and the bright/dark ganglia. That means that the Blue/Yellow ganglia will receive *two* inhibitory signals, decreasing its firing rate well below baseline. This signals to the brain that there is yellow light.

Meanwhile, the light reflects from the green stem and onto a nearby spot on your retina. M cells are firing there as well. They are sending their signals to the ganglia responsible for this part of the retina (note that they are in a different location, these are different ganglia than the ones responsible for the "flower" part of the image). The M cones are sending a

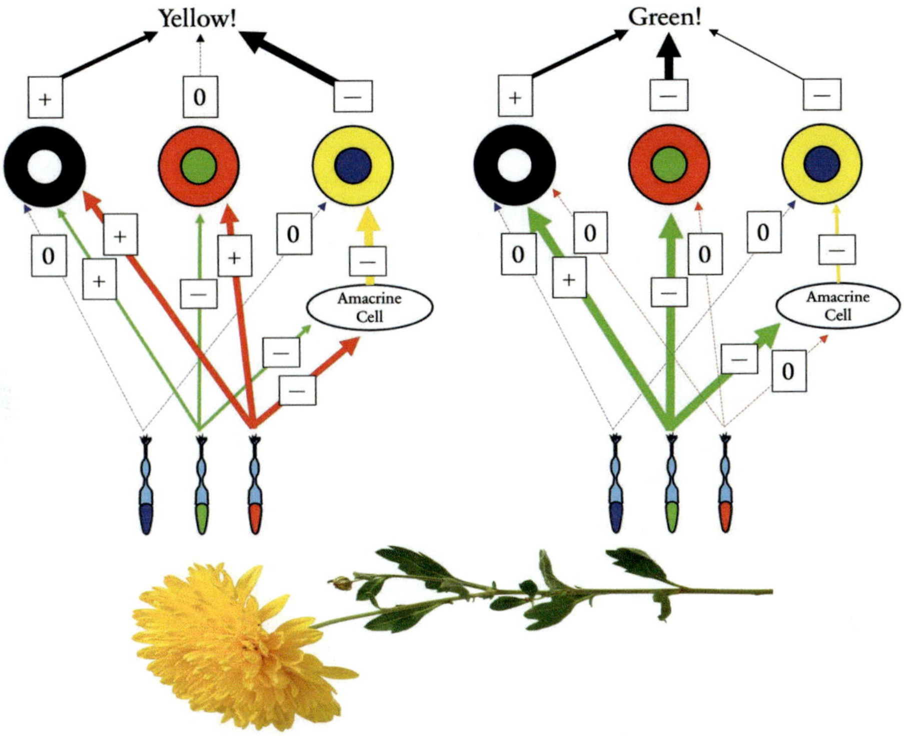

Figure 4.9 How the cones and ganglia react to a yellow flower with a green stem; see text for details.

strong inhibitory signal to both the Blue/Yellow ganglia and the Red/Green ganglia, and *a strong excitatory* signal to the bright/dark ganglia. That means that the Red/Green ganglia are receiving an inhibitory signal, which means that the signal that it is sending to the brain is about green (and not red).

Let's discuss one more situation—shining a blue flashlight and a yellow flashlight on the same patch of a white piece of paper. In this case, the S, M, and L cones would all be firing. The Blue/Yellow ganglia are getting an excitatory signal from the S cones, and an inhibitory signal from the M and L cones. Collectively, they cancel each other out. Consequently, the Blue/Yellow ganglia *does not respond*. Meanwhile, all those same cones are simultaneously sending an excitatory signal to the bright/dark ganglia. And so, the signal that it is sending to the brain will be about brightness (and not darkness), so the person would see white light.

Another way to think about what the ganglia are doing is that they are *comparing* different parts of the spectrum. The Blue/Yellow ganglia are comparing the blue portion of the spectrum to the rest of the spectrum (the red/green end). The Red/Green ganglia are comparing the green portion to the red portion. Having three cone types allows for exactly that many comparisons. If there were more cone types (or fewer cone types) there would be more (or fewer) comparisons to be made. Our color perception is thus *three-dimensional*. Just to be clear—we don't mean three-dimensional as in height, width, and depth. Instead, we mean that there are three spectrums (or dimensions) in which perceived color can vary. Any color we see can be recreated by mixing different amounts of the three main colors, red, green, blue (see Figure 4.10). If we had two cone types, our color perception would be

Figure 4.10 Left, three-dimensional color perception; right, two-dimensional color perception.

two-dimensional—any color could be matched by the specification along two dimensions of color. Four cone types would lead to four-dimensional color perception, and so on.

Why We Experience Afterimages

With all this information, we can now—finally!—understand why you saw red and yellow flowers after staring at green and blue ones for a while (that is, why we see afterimages). Recall that all cells that are part of the nervous system have refractory periods—after firing, they cannot fire again for a little while. Cones, of course, are cells that are part of the nervous system and so they have a refractory period, too. When staring at the blue flowers, your S cones were all firing, one after the other, until most (if not all) of them were in their refractory period. Meanwhile, they were sending signals to the Blue/Yellow ganglia, and you were seeing blue (see Figure 4.11, *left*). Go, you!

But now—after looking at those blue flowers for a while—you look at a white square. (Remember: white light has all the different wavelengths of light in it, including blue and yellow.) As we explained earlier—under typical circumstances—the S, M, and L cones would all respond to both blue and yellow light and send their signals to the Blue/Yellow ganglia. The opposing processes would cancel each other out and so the Blue/Yellow ganglia wouldn't respond at all. But since the bright/dark ganglia would be responding with an excitatory response, you would perceive the surface as white (see Figure 4.11, *middle*).

But since you just spent time staring at the blue flowers, the S cones are mostly in their refractory state! They got tired out by looking at all that blue. So. Much. Blue. They *don't* send a signal to the Blue/Yellow ganglia about the presence of blue. However, the M and L cones are still happily sending a signal to these ganglia about the presence of yellow. So the ganglia send a signal to the brain about yellow. Hence, you see the yellow afterimage (see Figure 4.11, *right*). Go, you?

We have a slightly better understanding of the spectral sensitivities of the different ganglia now than Hering did when he proposed them. The "Red/Green" ganglia are actually maximally sensitive to red and *bluish* green. The "Blue/Yellow" ganglia are actually maximally sensitive to *purplish* and a *yellowish* greenish (Ingling, 1977). Interestingly, even though the response at the level of the *cones* is maximized for these "ish" colors, the *perception* of these opponent colors is more "pure"—that is, the bluish green is seen as green, the purplish is seen as blue, and the yellowish greenish is seen as yellow. In other words, the colors that we actually see are closer to the colors Mr. Raoul taught Fred about in elementary school—maybe he knew what he was talking about after all!

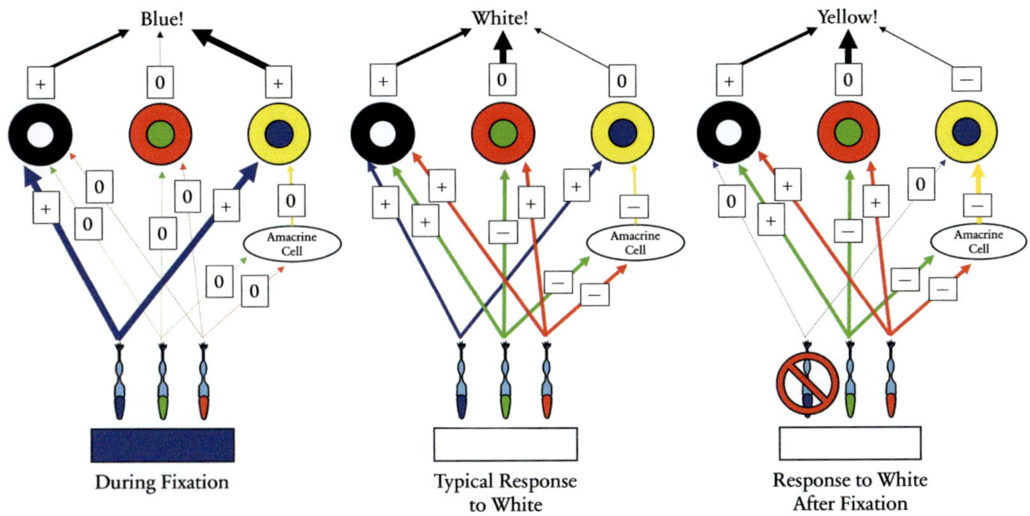

Figure 4.11 How color opponency ganglia account for afterimages. After lots of blue, the blue cones are all in their refractory state, and so the blue signal does not get sent to the ganglia even when it is present (as in white light). Since the red and green cones are still functioning, the ganglia exhibits the "yellow" response.

Color Constancy

The last time Fred picked an apple from his tree, he carried it around for a while before he ate it. He went for a hike in the bright sunlight, spent time inside a couple of different rooms in his house (some of which have new LED lights, and some of which still have the older incandescent light bulbs), and brought it to work (which has fluorescent lighting, ugh!). In every situation, he examined the apple trying to decide if he was hungry enough to eat it. In each of those situations, a very different set of wavelengths was reflecting off of the apple and into his eye. However, no matter where he brought the apple, it *appeared* as the same bright red color. This is known as **color constancy**.[5]

Color constancy the phenomenon where the perceived hue of surfaces remains the same regardless of sometimes dramatic shifts in the wavelengths reflected from the surface due to differences in lighting conditions.

Photometer device for measuring the amount and type of wavelengths being reflected by a surface. That is, it measures an object's spectral reflectance.

Spectral reflectance the amount of each wavelength that is reflected from a surface.

In Chapter 2, we discussed what happens when light strikes an object. Some of the light is absorbed, some is reflected, and—if it's a translucent object—some of the light passes through. We can measure what wavelengths of light are reflected off of any object using an instrument called a **photometer**. Every surface will have wavelengths it will absorb and wavelengths it will reflect and to what extent. Given that, we can graph the wavelengths of light reflected by a surface—its **spectral reflectance**. Note that spectral reflectance is independent of the available lighting and is *not* the same thing as how we

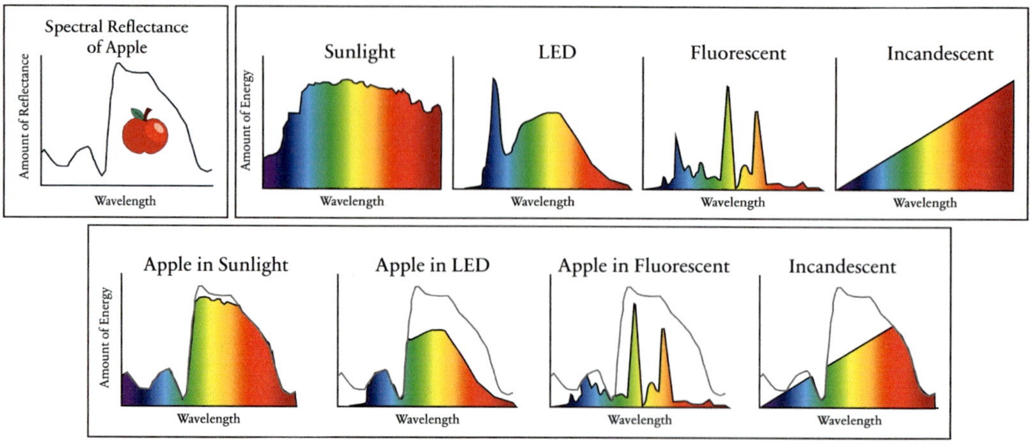

Figure 4.12 Top left, spectral reflectance of a red apple. Top right, spectral power of four different types of light—sunlight, LED, Fluorescent, and Incandescent. Bottom, what light would be reflected by the apple to the eye under the different lighting conditions (original spectral reflectance of the apple shown in gray).

perceive the object. Figure 4.12 (*top left*) is the spectral reflectance of a red apple.

Now look at Figure 4.12 (*top right*); this is the **spectral power** of the four different types of lighting that Fred encountered with his apple. Spectral power is the amount of each type of wavelength that is present in a given type of illumination (i.e., what colors of light are coming from a particular light source). Sunlight has all of the colors of visible light (a little less at the violet end, but still). That means there's plenty of red light there to bounce off the apple and to Fred's eye. So far so good. But now look specifically at the graph for the LED light. There's not a whole lot of red light there. While there is *some* red light there to bounce off the apple to Fred's eye, there isn't very much. And the fluorescent light has hardly any red at all! The incandescent light has lots of red light to reflect off of the apple, but not so much blue light to reflect off of his blue sweater. And yet, in all these situations, the (red) apple appears red to Fred, and his sweater appears blue to him. If all the eye is doing is relaying to the brain the exact wavelengths of light received, this is a bit puzzling.

Spectral power amount of each wavelength that is emitted by a light source.

The light reflecting from the apple to the eye is a consequence of both of the spectral power of the light illuminating the apple and the spectral reflectance of the apple (see Figure 4.12, *bottom*). Note that the light reflecting back to the eye is very, very different in the different lighting conditions. Yet, once again, the *perception* of the color of the apple is constant. The apple looks red in every context. Everything we've learned about color perception up to this point in the chapter has been geared toward the ways in which the cones might relay the *actual wavelengths* that are reaching the eye. But that falls apart when we start thinking about the everyday experience of color constancy—just like Fred's experience with the apple.

Socratic Question: What is color constancy? How is this phenomenon a challenge to theories of color perception that tightly link color perception to wavelengths of light reaching the eye?

Why Might Color Constancy Occur?

There are several possible explanations for why the apple appears the same color even though the actual wavelengths that reach the eye vary considerably. One is based on something we have already discussed—the refractory period of the cones. Let's imagine that Fred is looking at the apple under incandescent light—the kind coming from traditional pear-shaped light bulbs. This kind of lighting has a lot of light at the red end of the spectrum to reflect off of the apple, so Fred's red cones are working overtime. Eventually, many of the red cones end up in their refractory state, so they don't respond as frequently. So. Much. Red. Metaphorically speaking, the system has adapted to the constant presence of red by ignoring it. This process—called **chromatic adaptation**—was first suggested by Johannes von Kries (1853–1928). Except that . . . chromatic adaptation really only works as an explanation when everything in the *entire scene* is under a particular illumination (like an entire room lit by blue light). It doesn't really work when only *one part* of that scene is under that particular kind of illumination (like a room that is lit by sunlight, but has a blue light illuminating a single table). And color constancy still holds under those conditions (the apple on that table would still appear red). Drat.

> **Chromatic adaptation** an explanation of color constancy suggesting it is adaptation at the level of the retina that is responsible.

Another possible explanation relies on the fact that we rarely ever see just one surface at a time. Instead, we see many surfaces, each with their own spectral reflectance. If, under these circumstances, we compare the patterns of light reflecting from all the different surfaces, we can infer what kind of light is illuminating those surfaces. So, for example, if we see a lot more red light than we would expect reflecting from the surfaces, we can infer that this is fluorescent lighting (and not, say, LED lighting) and adjust our perception of the colors accordingly. Clever, huh? This is called **discounting the illuminant.**

> **Discounting the illuminant** an explanation of color constancy suggesting that it is inference based on an understanding of the spectral power of the illumination.

For this strategy to work, however, we have to know in advance what specific surfaces should look like under different kinds of lighting. Helmholtz suggested that we developed this knowledge from viewing the same surface under different lighting conditions (like Fred did when he carried the apple from place to place). Hering suggested it was because we have memory for various objects (like the exact color of stop signs or our favorite green shirt) and can use those objects as references.

Alternatively, we can assume that the brightest surface in any given room is white (Land, 1977). Seeing how the light reflects off *that* surface will tell us the spectral power of the light, which can then be used to adjust our perception of the rest of the surfaces. Modern cameras (like the one in your cell phone) work just this way. They assume the brightest part of the image is white and balance the rest of the photograph accordingly. Yay, technology!

Land (1977) suggested that this process is what is responsible for the color illusion in Figure 4.13. The paper second in from the left in both images is actually the exact same hue (the light pink of the box on the right), but it appears pinker in the top image and bluer in the bottom image. The wall behind the man is assumed to be white, so in the top image, the scene appears to be under a blue illumination and in the bottom image the scene appears to be under a pink illumination. The perceived color of the paper is shifted accordingly.

Even without a known reference color (white or otherwise), there is some physiological evidence for the proposal that we can use several surfaces in the room to infer the spectral

Figure 4.13 The second paper in from the left looks more pink in the top image (which has a blue illumination) than in the bottom image (which has pink illumination). However, both papers are the same shade of pink (matching the square on the right).

power of the light. Foster (2011) examined the responses of the cones to various surfaces under various types of illumination. He found that while a given type of cone might be more or less active under different lighting conditions, the *ratio* of activation remained the same under those conditions. That is, if the M cones responsible for responding to green grass were firing five times as often as the M cones responsible for responding to the yellow flower under sunlight, they would *also* do so under flourescent lighting. The *ratio* of response, therefore, could be used to keep color constant. Yay, ratios!

Of course, as Maloney and Wandell (1986) pointed out, this breaks down when there are too few surfaces (or no white surfaces), which is exactly what happened with the viral picture of The Dress (it went so viral, you can just search for "the dress" online and it will be the first hit; see Figure 4.14). If you (incorrectly) view the dress as being illuminated by just sunlight (visible in the back of the picture), then you will (incorrectly) see the dress as white and gold. If you (correctly) view the dress as being illuminated by both sunlight and the yellow light of the camera's flash, then you will (correctly) see the dress as black and blue. The luminant matters!

Unfortunately, color constancy doesn't get any easier to understand if we examine the responses in the different brain areas. Research shows that V1 cells respond proportionally to the signal sent by the eye. Or in other words, they respond to the *actual wavelengths* hitting the eye (meaning they would respond to the paper in Figure 4.13 as light pink in both images). In other words, V1 cells do *not* show color constancy. However, the V4 cells respond

Figure 4.14 The Dress (of internet fame) is an illusion created by confusions of the luminant.

proportionally to specific *perceived colors* regardless of illumination. Or in other words, they respond to the *perceived color* of the object, not the wavelength that reaches the eye (Zeki, 1980). That is, V4 cells demonstrate color constancy. If we assume the historically popular idea of hierarchical processing *and* if V1 doesn't have color constancy and V4 does, then we would have to assume that whatever processing allows for color constancy must happen somewhere between V1 and V4.

And yet! Newer research (Shapley & Hawken, 2011) makes it clear that color is not processed separately from any other property of the surface (e.g., form, distance). In that case, the V4 cells (which are also clearly involved in form perception) cannot be reacting to color independent of the surface, and in fact might be reacting to something far more complicated. In a general way, the neural construction hypothesis of vision (based on the historically popular idea of hierarchical processing) keeps hitting dead ends in just this way.

Socratic Question: Some theories of colors constancy rely on a phenomenon known as "discounting the illuminant". How does this phenomenon work and why might it not work under all conditions?

Box 4.2 Does Color Even Exist at All?

The existence of non-spectral hues, the phenomenon of color constancy, and the incredible variety of color systems all lead to a question: does color even exist at all? After all, if you could somehow look at a wavelength of light *outside* of a perceptual system, it would not have a color, per se. The difference between green and red at the level of the energy is just a difference in wavelength—longer or shorter, but not greener or redder. And these differences are ones that some animals cannot even detect! *And* magenta *only* exists in our experience—it is *not* a property of the wavelength itself.

As strange as it might be to consider, a lot of theorists conclude that color simply does not exist. Instead, it is a kind of shared hallucination that we have named and embraced. We don't even know if your hallucination is the same as mine. There's no way to tell if what I see as yellow is what you see as purple, but we've all agreed to call that color "yellow"!

We would like to suggest another possibility. Maybe there is such a thing a color, but it cannot exist independent of context. Think about it like friction—friction *absolutely exists*; it just can only happen as an interaction between surfaces. Perhaps color only exists as an interaction between an organism and an environment. Color could not exist independent of the organism viewing it. Color could not exist independent of the surface. That is, color (and our perception of it) cannot exist independent of a surface reflecting light, and it cannot exist independent of a viewer detecting that light. Color is a relational property (see Chapter 14 for other relational properties).

Socratic Question: Imagine there is a red balloon in front of you. We turn out all the lights so that it is now pitch-black (so you can't see the balloon at all). Is the balloon still red? What does it mean to say an object is red?

Purkinje Shift

Purkinje Shift: The change in brightness perception of different wavelengths as a result of the change in level of illumination.

Fred brought his red apple on a picnic date with his girlfriend, Carol. They ended up talking well past sunset and into the nighttime. Neither of them ended up eating the apple, so it was lying nearby during the whole date. When it was still fully bright daytime, the apple appeared much brighter than the surrounding grass. But an hour or so after sunset (when it was quite dark) the reverse was the case—the green grass appeared much brighter than the apple (see Figure 4.15). So much weirdness occurs with colors!

This shift from reds (and yellows) appearing the brightest in full illumination to greens (and blues) appearing the brightest in dim illumination is called the **Purkinje Shift**, named after Czech scientist Johannes Purkinje (1787–1869) who first wrote about it. This shift is a consequence of the types of cells that are responding under those different conditions: cones in bright light and rods in dim light.

Figure 4.15 The Purkinje Shift is a phenomenon where reds (and yellows) appear the brightest under full illumination (left), but greens (and blues) appear the brightest under low illumination (when we are essentially seeing in black and white as in the photo on the right).

Figure 4.16 Left, night scenes are tinted blue to mimic night vision. Right, red night lights are better than white night lights because they don't change the functioning of the rods and so preserve your night vision.

As we discussed in Chapter 3, the rods cease to function well once the light gets bright enough—essentially, in bright light, they are always in their refractory state. This means that cones are responsible for vision under bright-light conditions. Conversely, in dim light, there is not enough light to get a strong signal from the cones. This means that rods are responsible for vision under dim-light conditions. As we also discussed in Chapter 3 (we did a lot in Chapter 3!), rods are limited in the range of wavelengths to which they can respond. Specifically, they are most sensitive to the wavelengths that we see as blue/green and do not respond at all to the wavelengths that we see as red. Let's say that again for emphasis: *rods cannot respond to red light.*

Under dim light, the red-blind rods are functioning better than the cones. Because of this, vision is shifted to the blue/green end of the spectrum under dim light. Filmmakers take advantage of this and mimic it by color shifting night scenes to the blue end of the spectrum (see Figure 4.16, *left*). Next time you're watching a movie with a night scene, check it out! It will almost certainly have a blue tint.

In dim light, reds will appear black (just like the apple in Figure 4.15). Also, since the rod cells are not sensitive to red light, red light makes an excellent nightlight (see Figure 4.16, *right*). It will not interfere with any dark adaptation you have achieved and does not affect the circadian rhythms (or in other words, it won't wake you up as much). Preserving dark adaptation is one of the reasons that many military vehicles like submarines, helicopters, and ships use red lights for illumination at night.

Disruptions in Color Functioning

Earlier in this chapter, we mentioned a condition where a person has difficulty distinguishing the colors red and green, a condition often called *red-green colorblindness.* Colorblindness is a bit of a misnomer—it makes it sound as if people who are colorblind cannot see color at all, and that is not (usually) the case. A better term (the one we will be using here) is color deficiency. There are many different types of color vision, some that are atypical in humans but typical in other species (see Box 4.3).

Genetic Disruptions in Color Functioning

The genes responsible for the formation of cones are (mostly) on the X chromosome. The versions of the gene that result in color vision oddities are recessive, meaning that if you have at least one copy that is "typical", then your vision will be typical. All of your color vision chromosomes have to code for atypical vision in order for you to have atypical vision. Individuals with XY chromosomes (biologically male) have only one X; whereas individuals with XX chromosomes (biologically female) have two. Consequently, color vision oddities are *far* more common in people with XY chromosomes. Some kind of color deficiency occurs in about 8% of biologically male people but only 0.5% of biologically female people.

All variations in color deficiency have to do with the functioning of the cones. People who have three types of cones with typical spectral sensitivity are **trichromats**.

> **Trichromacy (trichromats)** color vision achieved by three cones with typical spectral sensitivities.

The vast majority of people who have color deficiency have what is called **anomalous trichromacy**. In this condition, one of the three types of cones is sensitive to the "wrong" part of the spectrum (or under-performs at the "correct" part). Remember that perceived color is achieved by contrasting one area of the spectrum with a different area of the spectrum. Having three cones that are sensitive to different parts of the spectrum allows us to contrast every color we can see. However, if one of those three is sensitive to a *different* part of the spectrum or has reduced sensitivity, there will be difficulty seeing color the same way as typical trichromats. If, for example, the M and L cones have their peaks too close together, they essentially act like one kind of cone instead of two. And so, color vision becomes *two-dimensional* instead of *three-dimensional.*

> **Anomalous trichromacy (Anomalous trichromats)** color vision achieved by three cones, but one of them has reduced or altered sensitivity resulting in color confusions.

Deuteranomaly is the most common form of anomalous trichromacy—a reduced sensitivity to green light (deficient M cones). **Protanomaly** is next most common, which is a reduced sensitivity to red light (deficient L cones). Finally, there is the extremely rare **tritanomaly**, which is a reduced sensitivity to blue light (deficient S cones). This is so rare because the genes that code for the S cones are on *both* the X and the Y chromosomes—regardless of biological sex, the person would have to inherit the atypical gene from *both* parents.

> **Deuteranomaly** reduced sensitivity to green light.
>
> **Protanomaly** reduced sensitivity to red light.
>
> **Tritanomaly** reduced sensitivity to blue light.

For people with anomalous trichromacy, the ability to see color distinctions might improve in brighter light and get worse under dimmer light. Also, those with deuteranomaly or protanomaly might be helped by special sunglasses that block out the part of the spectrum between the

> **Deuteranopes** missing green cones resulting in confusing mid-reds with mid-greens; blue-greens with grey and mid-pinks; bright greens with yellows; pale pinks with light grey/white; mid-reds with mid-browns; and light blues with lilac.

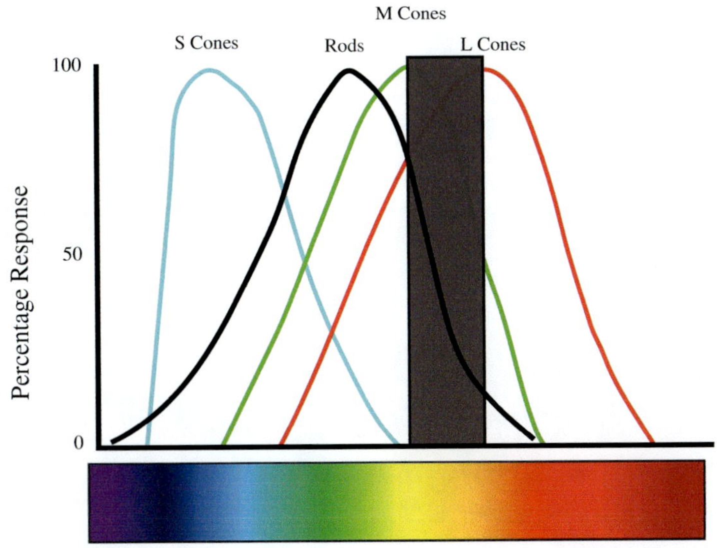

Figure 4.17 Deuteranomaly or protanomaly can be helped by glasses that block light from the part of the spectrum between the peaks of the response curves of the red and green cones. This enhances the separation between the two and allows for comparison at the level of the ganglia.

peak of the green receptor and the peak of the red receptor (see Figure 4.17). This increases the separation between the two, making comparisons easier for the ganglia to make.[6]

The same cannot be said for people with **dichromacy**. Rather than having an *underperforming* cone type, people with this condition are *missing* that cone type altogether. **Deuteranopes** are missing green cones, **protanopes** are missing red cones, and **tritanopes** are missing their blue cones (though again, this is extremely rare).

Protanopes missing red cones, resulting in confusing black with reds; dark brown with dark green/orange/red/blue/purple and black; blues with reds; purples with dark pinks, and mid-greens with some oranges.

Tritanopes missing blue cones resulting in confusing light blues with grays; dark purples with black, mid-greens with blues, and oranges with reds.

In Figure 4.18, you can see what the world looks like to people with the three different types of color deficiency. Notice that the pictures showing the experience of people with deuteranopia and protanopia are very similar—the ganglia only have one sample of that end of the spectrum and so are unable to make comparisons *within* that end of the spectrum. Reduced sensitivity to either red or green therefore results in what we tend to call "red-green color blindness". In the same way, reduced sensitivity to blue results in what we tend to call "blue-yellow color blindness". Without the blue signal, the ability to make comparisons to that end of the spectrum is affected (only the red/green comparison is possible).

It is also possible to be a **monochromat**—that is, having only one type of cone. However, it's the rarest of the color deficiencies; only about 1 person in 33,000 will be born with this (Pitt, 1944). Since color is about contrast, having only one type of cone means that

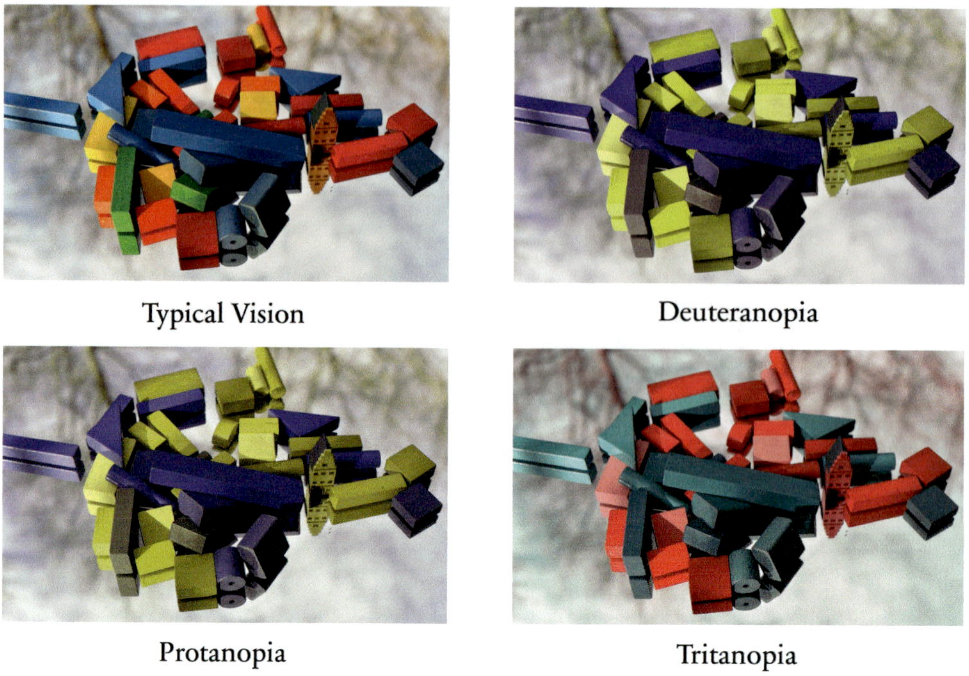

Figure 4.18 Colors appear differently to those with typical vision than to those with one of the typical color deficiencies.

monochromats really do see the world in black and white (regardless of which type of cone they have). More than that, however, their ability to see in bright light is severely hindered since most of their vision is achieved via the rods. They have to wear very dark sunglasses in order to keep the amount of light appropriate for the rod cells, and typically have very poor acuity.

Monochromacy vision is with only one type of cone, resulting in black and white vision.

Interestingly, both anomalous trichromats and dichromats have *better acuity* and *better contrast sensitivity* than those with typical vision. They are also far better at finding camouflaged figures even in black and white photographs or videos (Doron et al., 2019). They have vision superpowers!

Socratic Question: Why is "color-blindness" a misnomer? What is a better term? Why?

It's also possible to go in the other direction—to have *additional* color capabilities. **Tetrachromats** have an *additional* cone sensitive to the yellow-green part of the spectrum. True tetrachromats will also have opponent-process ganglia to compare the

Tetrachromacy (tetrachromat) color vision is achieved with four cones; this increases the ability to discriminate between different shades of color.

new part of the spectrum to the other parts, resulting in color vision that is *four-dimensional*. More vision superpowers!

In practice, that means that tetrachromats have better ability to discriminate between shades of color (some estimates say they can discriminate between 100 million different hues) in the visible light spectrum. It's a relatively rare phenomenon and almost all tetrachromats are biologically female. About 12% of biologically female people have the genes that would allow for the fourth cone, but not all are functioning tetrachromats (because they are missing the requisite opponent process ganglia). It's also worth noting that finding and diagnosing tetrachromacy is difficult because it requires testing colors the experimenter (probably) can't see!

Acquired Disruptions in Color Functioning

While all the conditions we have discussed so far are ones someone is *born with*, it is also possible to *acquire* color deficiency during one's life. Chronic illnesses (Alzheimer's, leukemia, sickle cell anemia, etc.), accidents/strokes (that damage the retina or the eye more generally), some medications (antibiotics, barbiturates, anti-tuberculosis drugs, etc.), exposure to certain chemicals (carbon disulphide, carbon monoxide, some lead-based chemicals, etc.), and most commonly aging (in addition to other aging effects, the lens yellows with age, changing the colors of light that reach the retina) can all affect color vision in a variety of ways. Typically, these mimic the conditions we've already covered.

Damage to the brain (via stroke, tumor, or some other injury) can cause several different color anomalies. Damage to the ventromedial occipital cortex can cause **cerebral achromatopsia**, in which people (like monochromats) see entirely in black and white. Unlike monochromats, however, their acuity and sensitivity to light is unaffected. Damage to other areas can cause color agnosia or anomia. People with color agnosia can see the color (which we know because they pass color discrimination tasks) but cannot understand what color *means*. People with color anomia could pick the correct color for an object (say, pick the yellow bananas when given an option of yellow, orange, or purple) but can't name the color (in this case, yellow).

> **Cerebral achromatopsia** complete loss of color vision due to damage to the ventromedial occipital cortex.

Our eyes (as they currently are) keep us from being able to see any colors outside of the visible light spectrum. The lens and the cornea both block shorter wavelengths of light, and longer wavelengths cannot be absorbed by the retina. This is not the case for some animals, however (see Box 4.3)!

Box 4.3 Color Perception in Non-Humans

There is a persistent myth that dogs are unable to see color. It is not true, however; they are *dichromats*. They have two cone types: one sensitive to blue and one to yellow. Their color vision is *two-dimensional*. They can see differences between those colors (similar to deuteranopic vision in humans) but cannot see reds or greens. Fred's pet baby elephant, Topsy (like all elephants), also has deuteranopic vision. However, while elephants have a "blue" cone like humans do, an elephant's blue cone has its peak response to a much shorter wavelength which allows them to see part of the UV spectrum (Yokoyama et al., 2005).

There's some evidence that the common ancestors of all vertebrates were tetrachromats, but then at some point, most vertebrate species became nocturnal. At some point after *that*, most of the now-nocturnal animals evolved into dichromats, likely because having only two cones increases the ability to see detail in the dark (Yong, 2022). Deer, for example, are dichromats. This is why deer hunters wear bright orange vests or orange camouflage patterns. The orange is visible to humans but not to the deer. Good for the hunters, bad for the deer. Some monkey and ape species then *re-evolved* trichromacy as they became more active during the daytime (including our ancestors). The exceptions to this are the so-called new world monkeys, in which males are dichromats and females are trichromats!

Tetrachromacy is also very prevalent in nature. Most fish and many species of birds (including chickens!) are tetrachromats. For some of those species, the additional dimension increases the ability to discriminate colors within the same spectrum as humans can see. For others, the additional cone extends color vision into the ultraviolet spectrum. For still others, it extends it into the infrared. In that case, the animals are additionally able to see combinations of the additional hues (so while we see magenta as a combination of cobalt blue and red, they might see a color as a combination of ultraviolet and blue, or of infrared and green).

And it doesn't stop there! Pigeons have pentachromacy (five cone types!) or higher in some cases. Bluebottle butterflies have 15, and the mantis shrimp famously have a whopping *16*. It's not clear that these species use their color capabilities in the same way as we do, however. Recall that human cones feed into an opponency system (red/green, blue/yellow) which is why we end up able to see over 10 million colors total. These animals may lack those opponency cells and so may not be seeing in 16 color *dimensions* but rather see only 16 colors *total*. Like an entire world colored in by just the small box of Crayola crayons.

And of course, there are the animals that can see other parts of the electromagnetic spectrum (remember "visible light" is what *humans* can see, but there's a lot more of the same type of energy) or other information in the same part of the spectrum. Snakes can see infrared, bees (and lots of other insects) can see ultraviolet. In both cases, that helps them find their food source (rodents and flowers respectively, see Figure 4.2). Many different animals (fish, birds, crustaceans, insects, etc.) can see the *polarization* of light. That is, they can tell the direction of the lateral displacement of the wave (see Chapter 2). This serves different functions for different animals, but our particular favorite is the (ever complicated) mantis shrimp; for them, the male's bodies polarize the light in a circular pattern, which acts as a mating display (Yong, 2022).

Socratic Question: What does the fact that many animals have very different color perception (from each other and from us) say about the "realness" of color (see Box 4.2)?

Summary

Humans have three different types of cones that are sensitive to three different parts of the electromagnetic spectrum. S-cones are sensitive to shorter wavelengths (which we see as cobalt blue); M-cones are sensitive to medium wavelengths (which we see as lime green);

L-cones are sensitive to longer wavelengths (which we see as red). Those three types of cones send their signals to three types of opponent-process ganglia—brightness contrast (black vs. white), blue vs. yellow, and red vs. green. While the pickup of wavelengths is relatively straightforward, it cannot explain color constancy—the fact that we see colored objects as being the same color, regardless of the lighting conditions. Color deficiency (typically called "color blindness") is a result of a missing or underactive type of cone; consequently, there are three different types.

Notes

1 Don't blame us for the repetition of "color" in the name. We are also not responsible for ATM machines or PIN numbers.
2 Think of a rainbow. Any color that is *not* in the rainbow is a non-spectral color.
3 There are makeup techniques based on this very idea—if a person's skin is too red, you can add green makeup and it will "cancel" the redness. Blue circles under the eyes can be "canceled" with yellow makeup. It sounds strange, but it works!
4 You might wonder why the bright/dark ganglia are involved at all—after all, we're talking about color here! Well, the bright/dark are how you are able to tell the difference between a bright yellow and a dark yellow, between a bright green and a dark green. They also help with edge detection, as talked about in Chapter 3.
5 Color constancy is an example of a many-to-one relationship. We will discuss these at length in Chapter 8 because the traditional theorists are very interested in them.
6 Absolutely worth looking up videos of people trying these glasses on for the first time. Trust us.

5 The Ear

Auditory and Vestibular Systems

After vision, probably the most studied sense is hearing. Unlike vision, we can never turn off our hearing. Even covering our ears only muffles sound rather than eliminating it altogether. In this chapter, we will follow a similar outline of topics as we did with our exploration of vision: we will start by examining the energy for hearing (sound), then move on to the machinery of the hearing system (preview: it's *way more* than just the odd-looking fleshy things on the sides of your head!). Finally, we will explore how the signals from the ear travel to the brain and then describe what the brain does with those signals. In the second section, we will give the same treatment to the vestibular system.

What is Sound?

Sound (or, more properly, **sound pressure**) is a mechanical disturbance in a **medium**. Just like the definition of light in Chapter 2, this definition sounds (pun absolutely intended) much scarier than it is, promise. Let's start with the idea of a medium. In order for sound to exist, there has to be something for it to exist *in*.[1] Most of the time when we are hearing things the medium is the air around us. Air may seem like it's a bunch of nothing, but actually it's a bunch of gas molecules swirling around. Sound can also travel through other media like solids and liquids, even through walls and floors (which is why Fred's upstairs neighbor, Miguel, is always complaining about Topsy's thumping feet and loud trumpeting!). The requirement of a medium is that it must be *elastic*. That is, the molecules have to be able to move closer together and farther apart. Air is easily able to do this, which makes it a great medium for sound.

> **Sound pressure** mechanical disturbance in an elastic medium resulting in patterns of denser and less dense molecules of that medium.
>
> **Medium (for sound)** the substance or material that carries sound. Air is the most common medium for sound.

One day, after asking Topsy to tiptoe and trumpet more softly at Miguel's request, Fred sat in his living room. It was quiet. Very, *very* quiet. So quiet it started to make Fred uncomfortable (see Figure 5.1, *top left*). At that moment, the air molecules around him were fairly evenly distributed. If he had been very high up (like on top of a mountain), the molecules would have been farther apart. If he had been very low down (like in a valley below sea level), the molecules would have been closer together. But his house is about at sea level, so the air molecules were an intermediate density.

DOI: 10.4324/9781032690964-6

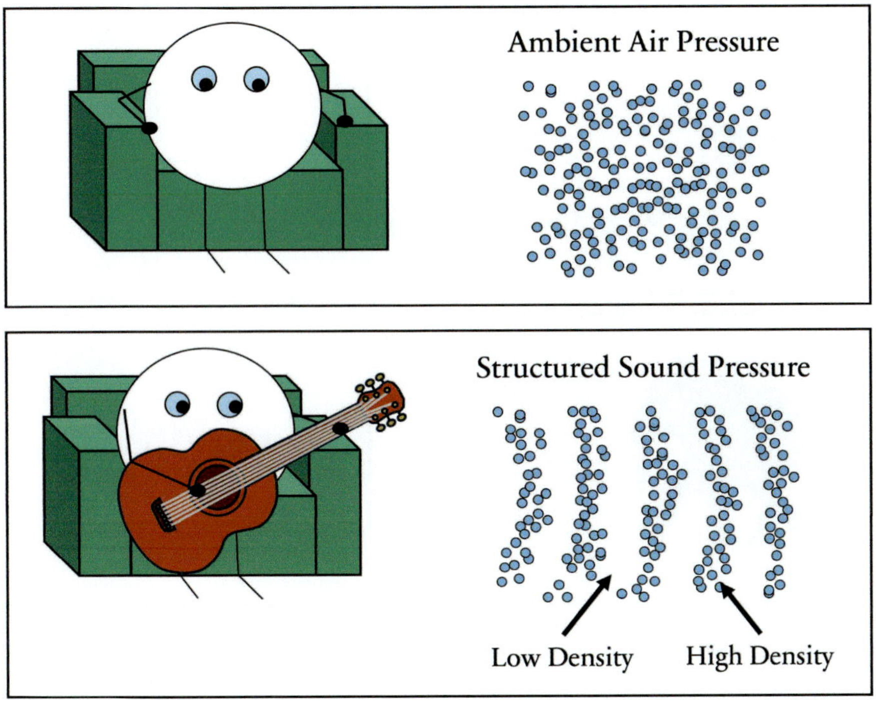

Figure 5.1 Top left, Fred sits in a quiet room. Top right, the air pressure in the quiet is roughly the same everywhere. That is called ambient air pressure. Bottom left, Fred plucks a string on his guitar. Bottom right, the vibrating string causes a pattern of high and low density in the air molecules.

Air molecules move around randomly (it's just what they do), and the speed of movement is related to the temperature.[2] If Fred had been in a hot place (like Arizona in the summer, phew!), the air molecules would have moved more quickly. If he had been in a cold place (like Vermont in the winter, brr!), the air molecules would have moved slower. But, fortunately, Fred's house is a nice comfortable temperature, so the air molecules were moving at an intermediate speed.

As he sat there in the quiet, the air molecules were evenly spread out in the room, and all were moving around randomly at roughly the same speed. This means that on average, there was the same *density*—that is, the same *air pressure* everywhere in the room. This is known as **ambient air pressure** (see Figure 5.1, *top right*).

> **Ambient air pressure** a measure of the density of undisturbed air at a given altitude and temperature.

Fred sat in the quiet as long as he could, but eventually he just couldn't stand it anymore. He got out his guitar (Miguel has indicated in the past that he doesn't find the guitar annoying) for some practice. He promised Carol he would learn her favorite song—*Enjoy Yourself (It's Later than You Think)*. First things first: he needs to tune it! He plucks one of the strings (see Figure 5.1, *bottom left*). When he does, the string vibrates back and forth. As it does, it disturbs the air. More specifically, when it moves in a direction, it pushes the air in that direction away from it with a great deal of force (for air molecules, anyway). Each time it moves in

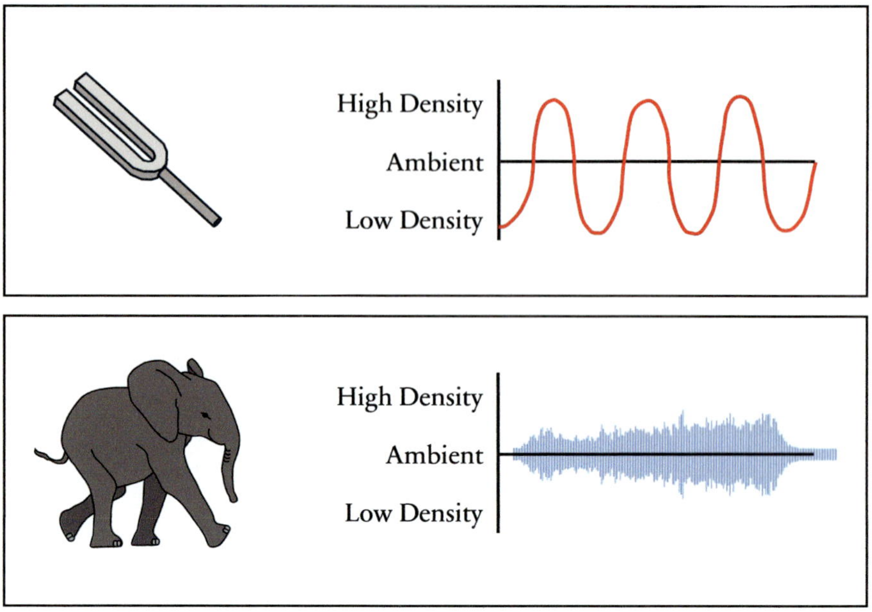

Figure 5.2 A tuning fork (top left) creates a pure tone (top right) when struck. A baby elephant, like Topsy (bottom left), on the other hand, will create a complex waveform (bottom right) when she trumpets.

a direction, it clusters the air molecules together and pushes them in that direction. That is, the kinetic (movement) energy created by releasing the string is transmitted from the string to this set of air molecules. This set of air molecules then bumps into the next set of molecules and transfer their energy to them and so on. The upshot is that Fred plucking a guitar string results in areas of tightly clustered air (high density of air molecules) and areas of less tightly clustered air (low density of air molecules). This pattern of low and high density air is *structured sound pressure* (see Figure 5.1, *bottom right*).

Just like with we did with light energy, we can depict sound energy in a graph. Specifically, we can graph the changing sound pressure relative to the ambient air pressure. This graph is called its **waveform**. In order to tune his guitar, Fred is going to use a tuning fork (see Figure 5.2, *top left*). A tuning fork is a fork-shaped metal object that, when struck on a surface, produces what we call a **pure tone**. That is, a waveform that is a perfect sine wave (see Figure 5.2, *top right*).

Waveform (sound) the curve that describes the sound pressure over time.

Pure tones sound that has a single frequency and a waveform that is a perfect sine wave.

Waveforms have three properties that we experience as properties of sound: frequency, amplitude, and complexity. Note on the waveform that there are peaks where the pressure is the highest. **Frequency** is the measure of how many peaks per second

Frequency (sound) number of peaks of high pressure per second, measured in Hertz (Hz).

there are, and we perceive differences in frequency as differences in *pitch*. The more peaks per second, the higher-pitched we perceive the sound to be (think the whine of a mosquito); the fewer peaks, the lower-pitched we perceive the sound to be (think of a foghorn). Frequency is measured in Hertz (Hz), named after Heinrich Hertz, a German physicist. To tune his guitar, Fred just needs to get the frequency (or pitch) of the string to match the frequency of his tuning fork: easy peasy!

The **amplitude** of the waveform is a measure of how tall the peaks are (measured from the ambient pressure up to the top of the tallest peak). We perceive differences in amplitude as differences in *loudness*. For the most part (more on this later), the higher the amplitude, the louder we perceive the sound to be (like that time Fred went to see Dio D. Vicen perform in concert with his rock band); the lower the amplitude, the quieter we perceive the sound to be (like that time Fred's friend Claudia whispered to him when they were studying in the library). Amplitude is measured in decibels (dB), named after Alexander Graham Bell, a Scottish-born, Canadian-American scientist (see Box 5.1).

Amplitude highest pressure of a sound wave, also called intensity, measured in decibels (dB).

Socratic Question: Sound and light are different kinds of energy patterns. Sound is mechanical energy and light is electromagnetic energy. But sound and light can both be treated as waveforms. How can sound be treated as a waveform? How do the properties of that waveform relate to properties of sound?

Box 5.1 The Decibel Scale

The vast differences between the pressure of a very quiet sound (like Claudia's whisper), and a very loud sound (like Dio D. Vicen's amplified wail) are hard to represent in a compact way. To give you a sense of the problem, imagine that the waveform for the quiet sound (*psst!*) is about ½ inch high; in that scale, the waveform for the loud sound (*Ohhhh yeeeeaaahh!*) would be *several miles high!* That would make the graphs awfully unwieldy.

To solve this problem, sound intensity is graphed on a *logarithmic* (log) scale. Without going into too much math detail, the decibel scale is a way of compressing the huge differences into much smaller differences. It makes representing the sounds on a graph much easier, but it does mean that reading those graphs isn't as straightforward. It might help to keep this in mind: for every 6 dB, sound pressure *doubles*. That is, a sound that is 6 dB louder than a quieter sound is roughly twice as loud as the quieter sound.

But where should the scale start? In other words, what should "0" be on a dB scale? Given our discussion about how "visible light" means "light that is visible to humans" it should come as no surprise that the scale starts at the quietest possible sound (the minimum threshold; see Chapter 1) humans can hear. That is, 0 dB is the minimum threshold for human hearing (Yost & Killion, 1997). But there are animals that can hear way quieter sounds than we can! So, when trying to understand the hearing abilities of those animals, the dB scale will include negative numbers. It doesn't mean negative sound, just quieter than humans can hear.

Very few things in real life produce a pure tone (aside from tuning forks, it's pretty much just computer-generated sounds that do this). Most sound-producing everyday objects create *complex* waveforms. For example, when Fred's pet elephant, Topsy (see Figure 5.2, *bottom left*) trumpets, the waveform would look more like the waveform in Figure 5.2 (*bottom right*).

In Chapter 3, we introduced the idea of a Fourier transform. As a reminder, it's a way of taking any complex pattern that changes over time and splitting it apart into several simpler sine waves. The sound of Topsy trumpeting can be put through that same Fourier transform. Any sound can. Each of the component sine waves has a particular frequency and amplitude. For a complex sound like an elephant trumpet, we can take each component frequency and measure its amplitude (often called its "intensity" or its "energy"). To get a sense of the overall sound, we can then graph the amplitude of each component frequency. This graph is a representation of the **complexity** of the sound.

Complexity (sound) the number and intensity of frequency components in a sound.

Satisfied with the tuning, Fred plucks the "A" string on his guitar. He sings the same note, trying to match the loudness as well. The two sounds—the guitar string and Fred's voice—theoretically have the same frequency and amplitude, but clearly sound different. If you were to perform a Fourier transform on the sound of the guitar, you might find something like Figure 5.3 (*left*). If you were to perform a Fourier transform on Fred's singing, you might find something like Figure 5.3 (*right*). The vertical lines in the figure indicate the particular set of frequencies that we call "A". The tallest peak (the one with the most energy) is the **fundamental frequency** of the sound. The fundamental frequency is the lowest (and usually dominant) frequency of a complex sound. Notice that both the guitar and the voice have peaks at almost every "A" frequency.

Fundamental frequency lowest frequency in a complex waveform.

Notice that both the guitar and the voice are making a lot more noises than just the "A" they thought they were making! All the other frequencies are **harmonics.** Harmonics are the result of the

Harmonics additional component frequencies that accompany the fundamental frequency.

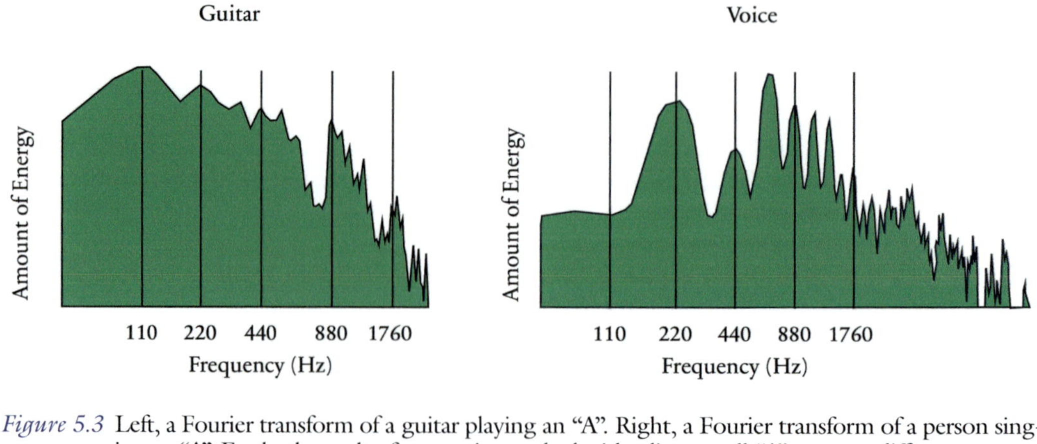

Figure 5.3 Left, a Fourier transform of a guitar playing an "A". Right, a Fourier transform of a person singing an "A". For both graphs, frequencies marked with a line are all "A" notes at different octaves.

properties of the object making the sound. When Fred plucks a guitar string, the string vibrates—but so does the body of the guitar, the neck, and even the tuning pegs! All of those vibrations produce frequencies that have a smaller amplitude than the sound of the string, but they still affect the overall sound that comes from the guitar. That's where the harmonics come from. When Fred sings a given note his vocal folds vibrate, but so do the other parts of his vocal tract. Obviously, Fred has different parts than his guitar, and so he produces a different set of harmonics. Even though they are both supposedly making the same note, the harmonics mean that the Fourier transforms of the guitar and Fred's voice have different shapes; they have different *complexity*. We perceive differences in complexity as differences in *object identity*; that is, that we perceive the sounds as having different **timber** (pronounced TAM-bur, or TIM-ber).

Timber also known as tone color or tone quality—the quality of a sound given to it by its harmonics that distinguishes the means of sound production (e.g., voice vs. guitar).

Socratic Question: What is a pure tone? How is a pure tone different from nearly all naturally occurring sounds?

Ears

Fred has been spending a lot of time with his niece, Eleanor. She's getting pretty good at naming body parts—he'll say, "where's your knee?" and she'll point right at her knee! "Where's your mouth?" She gets it right every time! When he asks, "where is your ear?", she points at the oddly shaped fleshy part on the outside of her head. Eleanor is not *wrong* exactly, but she's only pointing at one part of one section of her ear. The ear is actually quite a bit more extensive than just the parts you can see on the outside.

By convention, the ear can be divided into three sections (outer, middle, and inner), each with several parts (see Figure 5.4). Let's go through those sections one at a time.

Outer Ear

The part that Eleanor points to when Fred asks, "where's your ear?" is called the **pinna**. Its job is to collect the sound pressure and funnel it into the ear canal. The larger the pinna, the better it is at doing this—Topsy is *very* good at hearing! You can try this yourself: cup your hand behind your ear (making the pinna larger) and notice how sounds become louder. In fact, the first hearing aids were nothing more than extra-large funnels (see Figure 5.5)! Some animals can change the angle of their pinna to focus on a particular sound (think of your cat twisting their ears around searching for a sound). Mammals are the only animals that have pinnae—and not all mammals have them—but most animals hear just fine without them.

Pinna external part of the ear, responsible for collecting sound pressure and funneling it into the ear canal.

The pinna funnels the sound into the **ear canal**. The ear canal serves two

Ear canal the passage from the external ear to the tympanic membrane.

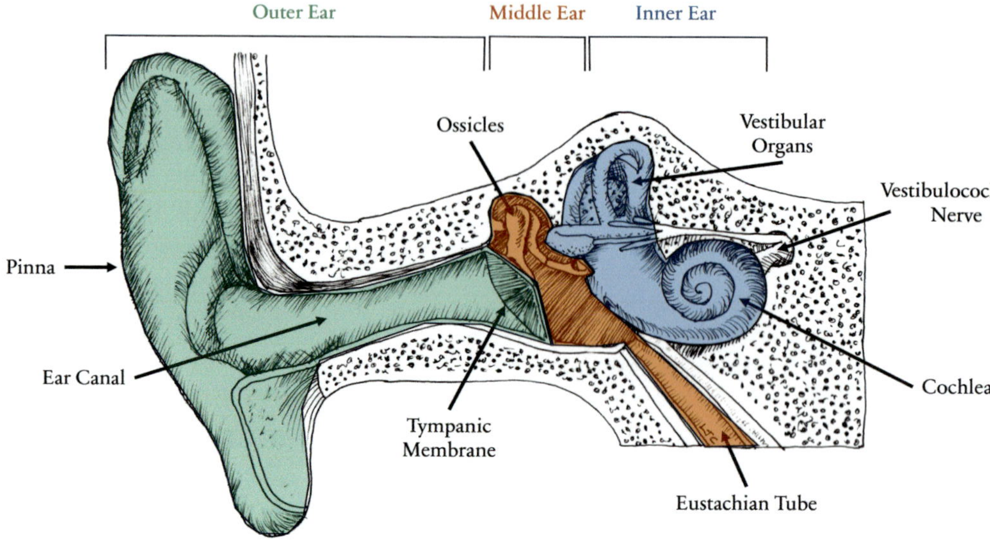

Figure 5.4 The outer ear consists of the pinna, the ear canal, and the tympanic membrane (the ear-drum). The middle ear contains the ossicles (the malleus, incus, and stapes). The inner ear contains the semicircular canals and the cochlea.

functions—first, it allows the next part of the ear (the tympanic membrane) to be further in the head, protecting it. The canal is also filled with hair and earwax, which stop debris and bacteria from making their way into the middle ear and giving you an infection (yup, earwax is actually a good thing!). Second, its shape and length amplify frequencies between (roughly) 2,000 Hz and 5,000 Hz by as much as 20 dB (making them a little over three times as loud; do Couto & Carvallo, 2009). As it so happens, this range of frequencies is also roughly the range of frequencies of human speech (see Chapter 12).[3]

The final part of the outer ear is the **tympanic membrane** (more colloquially known as the 'ear drum'). It is a relatively large membrane (in terms of the size of other things in the ear anyway; it's 10 mm across or about the size of a pea) at the end of the ear canal. When the sound pressure is funneled to it, it vibrates.

Tympanic membrane also known as the ear drum; thin membrane that vibrates in response to sound pressure.

Socratic Question: To some extent, the outer ear acts like a funnel for sound. But how is the outer ear more than just a funnel?

Middle Ear

The middle ear starts on the other side of the tympanic membrane. It is a small, enclosed space filled with moist air. Its job is to amplify the vibration of the tympanic membrane before

Figure 5.5 The first hearing aids amplified sound mechanically by increasing the size of the pinna with a trumpet bell.

passing it on to the inner ear. It needs to do this because the inner ear is filled with fluid (which is harder to move) rather than air (which is easier to move).

The three smallest bones in the human body, the **ossicles**, are part of the middle ear (and now you are prepared for that question on trivia night!). They are the **malleus** (Latin for "hammer"), the **incus** (Latin for "anvil"), and the **stapes** (Latin for "stirrup"). They are named for their shape (kinda), not for their function. The three bones are joined together in such a way that uses leverage (and their difference in size; see Figure 5.6) to amplify the vibration of the tympanic membrane before transmitting it to the inner ear. A small vibration of the malleus results in a large vibration of the stapes, and so a small vibration of the tympanic membrane results in a large vibration of the oval window.

Ossicles (Malleus, Incus, and Stapes) smallest bones in the human body, part of the middle ear. Responsible for amplifying and conducting the vibration of the tympanic membrane to the inner ear.

The two smallest *muscles* in the human body, the tensor tympani and the stapedius (connected to malleus and stapes, respectively) are also part of the middle ear (now you're *really* prepared for trivia night!). Their job is contract in response to loud sounds or in advance of sounds you make while eating or speaking (Edmonson et al., 2022). Keeping the bones from moving during loud sounds protects the more delicate parts of your middle and inner ears from harm. It takes about a half-second of a loud sound before the muscles can tense up, so they are of little protection for loud, abrupt sounds like a gunshot or a door slam but are very useful for attending loud concerts.

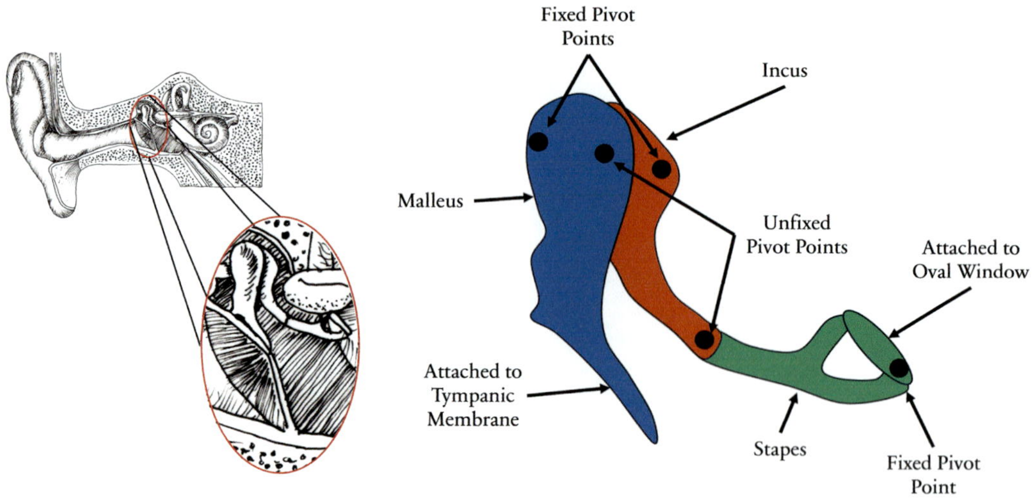

Figure 5.6 Left, an enlarged drawing of the ossicles. Right, a schematic showing how the smaller vibration of the malleus is converted into a larger vibration of the stapes via leverage.

Eustachian tubes passages leading from the middle ear to the throat, responsible for pressure equalization and drainage.

The final part of the middle ear is the **Eustachian tubes**. They are tubes that connect the middle ear to the throat. They serve two important functions. First, since the middle ear has to remain moist (so the bones do not dry out), it is prone to infections (bacteria love warm, damp places). The Eustachian tubes allow the middle ear to drain into your throat so it can continually refresh and keep itself clean.[4]

Second, they allow for pressure equalization. If you have ever gone up in an airplane or driven to the top of a large hill, you have probably experienced the sensation of your ears "popping". That was your Eustachian tubes allowing air in or out. Remember that altitude affects the spacing of air molecules. In particular, air molecules are more spread out at higher altitudes. So, when you go up to a higher altitude, the air molecules in your middle ear are going to try to spread out farther and will end up pressing on the walls of your middle ear (uncomfortable!). In response, your Eustachian tubes open and allow some of the air to escape, equalizing the pressure[5] (relief!). The reverse happens when decreasing altitude (or when scuba diving)—in that case, air needs to be let *in* in order to equalize pressure.

Inner Ear

Oval window membrane on the cochlea, vibrates in response to the movement of the stapes, pushes on the fluid in the cochlea.

Cochlea snail-shaped organ responsible for transducing sound.

The inner ear starts with the **oval window**, the membrane connected to the stapes. The organ of the inner ear has two main parts: the vestibular system (which we will talk about at length later in the chapter), and the **cochlea**. Look again at Figure 5.4; the cochlea is the part that is all curled up like a snail shell.[6] The oval window is in the side of the cochlea. It is responsible for the transduction (see Chapter 3) of the vibration of the oval window into the language of the brain.

Cochlea

The cochlea is a tiny organ, only about 4mm across in an adult human (about the size of a short grain of rice), but it is incredibly complex. To give you a sense of the structure of the organ, imagine a long flatish tube, wider and taller at one end (we'll call that the "head end") and thinner, shorter, and closed at the other end (we'll call that the "foot end"). If you rolled the tube up, starting with the foot end, that is the overall shape of the cochlea. It has a rigid exterior (like the snail's shell for which it is named) and cannot be uncoiled.[7]

The inside of the cochlea is separated into three spaces by two membranes that run along the length of the cochlea. In Figure 5.7, you can see a cross-section of the cochlea with the areas and membranes labeled. The top area, the **vestibular duct** (*scala vestibuli*), and the bottom area, the **tympanic duct** (*scala tympanic*) are joined at the "foot end" of the cochlea. They are filled with a fluid called perilymph, which has a chemical composition like cerebrospinal fluid. At the head end of the tympanic duct is the **round window** (another flexible membrane).

Vestibular duct perilymph-filled cavity in the cochlea, responsible for conducting vibration of oval window to Reissner's membrane.

Tympanic duct perilymph-filled cavity in the cochlea, responsible for releasing the pressure from inner-ear fluid vibrations.

Round window flexible membrane at the head-end of the tympanic duct, responsible for releasing pressure in the inner ear in response to fluid vibrations.

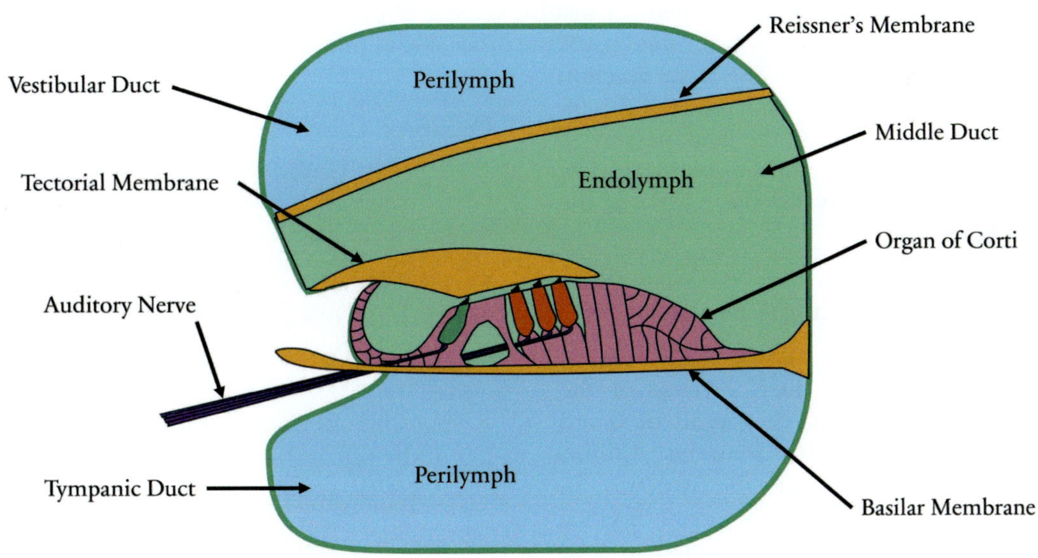

Figure 5.7 Cross-section of the cochlea. The fluid-filled cavity is separated into three areas (the vestibular duct, middle duct, and tympanic duct) by two membranes (Reissner's membrane and Basilar membrane).

The vestibular duct is separated from the **middle duct** (*scala media*, also sometimes called the cochlear duct) by **Reissner's membrane**. The middle duct is separated from the tympanic duct by the **Basilar membrane**. The middle duct is filled with a different type of fluid called endolymph, which has electrochemical properties that help aid in transduction.

There are other important structures here, but before we get into those, let's take a look at what happens when the oval window vibrates. The oval window is at the head end of the vestibular duct. When the oval window moves back and forth, it pushes the perilymph inside the vestibular duct back and forth. It's a bit like the time Fred gave Eleanor a bath when he was babysitting—she swished back and forth, back and forth, and eventually caused a huge wave in the tub. The oval window is like Eleanor sloshing back and forth, and the fluid in the vestibular duct is like the water in the tub that travels in waves in response to Eleanor's movements. Those waves push down on Reissner's membrane, which pushes on the endolymph, and that in turn pushes on the Basilar membrane. That's a lot of pushing!

Middle duct also known as the cochlear duct, an endolymph-filled cavity bounded above by Reissner's membrane and below by the Basilar membrane. Responsible for conveying the vibration of Ressiner's membrane to the Basilar membrane.

Reissner's membrane thin membrane separating the vestibular duct from the middle (or cochlear) duct. Responsible for transferring the vibration of the vestibular duct to the middle duct.

Basilar membrane stiff structural element of the inner ear, with a specific shape that allows for different resonant frequencies along its length. Responsible for mechanical Fourier transform of incoming sound vibration.

One thing to keep in mind is that, as a general rule, fluid is not compressible. That means it cannot be pressed into a smaller space than it currently occupies; push on one side, and it will *move* rather than *squish*. Also remember that the outside of the fluid-filled cochlea is rigid. That means that once the waves in the fluid reach the other side of this structure, those waves have to be able to *go somewhere*. This is the function of the tympanic duct and the round window. The duct conveys the fluid pressure to the round window, and the round window bulges out to allow for the release of the fluid pressure.

Organ of Corti and the Basilar Membrane

Inside the middle duct, on top of the Basilar membrane, is the **organ of Corti** (named after the Italian anatomist Alfonso Corti, who discovered the structure in 1851; see Figure 5.8). The organ of Corti is covered in hair cells arranged in four rows running down the length of the Basilar membrane. Three of the rows are made of **outer hair cells**, the remaining row is made of **inner hair cells**. On top of each

Organ of Corti structure on top of the Basilar membrane, contains rows of hair cells, responsible for transduction of sound vibration.

Outer hair cells receptor cells located in the organ of Corti. Arranged in three rows on the Basilar membrane, with their tops attached to the tectorial membrane. Responsible for amplification and cleaning of the signal from the inner hair cells.

Inner hair cells receptor cells located in the organ of Corti. Arranged in a single row on the Basilar membrane. Responsible for the mechanical transduction of sound vibration.

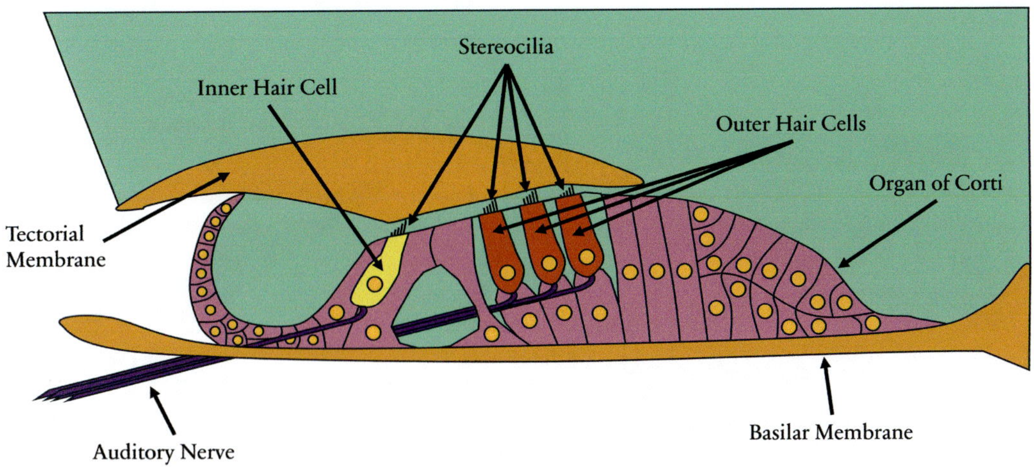

Figure 5.8 Cross-section of the Basilar membrane and the Organ of Corti. Movement of the Basilar membrane causes the hair cells in the Organ of Corti to bend over, which sends a neural signal to the brain.

hair cell are **stereocilia** (or, more colloquially, cilia which means hair) which look like little hairs (yes, these are hair cells with hairs on top).

The **tectorial membrane** is a stiff structure attached to the wall of the cochlea and resting on top of the hair cells. The cilia of the outer hair cells are attached to the tectorial membrane. The inner hair cells are not. As the movement of the fluid causes the basilar membrane to vibrate, this causes a pulling/sliding force (known as sheering) on the outer hair cells, forcing them to bend over. At the same time, the inner hair cells also move up and down in the fluid, which causes the cilia on top of those cells to bend over as they move up in the fluid (because of the friction between the hairs and the fluid).

The cilia are arranged by size (see Figure 5.9, *left*). Each cilium is connected to the one next to it by a very tiny filament called a **tip link**. The tip link is attached to an ion channel (remember these from Chapter 3?). When the sheering or friction forces cause the hair cells to bend over, it pulls on the tip link, opening the channel (see Figure 5.9, *right*), and allowing K+ ions to rush into the cell (Pickles, 1992). This depolarization releases neurotransmitters into the synapse with the auditory nerve fibers (which carry the signal to the brain).

Stereocilia often called cilia; hair-shaped projections on the top of the hair cells in the organ of Corti. When bent through mechanical disturbance, they release neurotransmitters to the auditory nerve.

Tectorial membrane stiff structure attached to the wall of the middle duct. The stereocilia of the outer hair cells are connected to this structure, so vibration of the Basilar membrane causes mechanical bending of the stereocilia.

Tip link tiny filaments connecting the tops of the stereocilia. When the group of cilia is bent, the tip links open ion channels, which starts the process of releasing neurotransmitters.

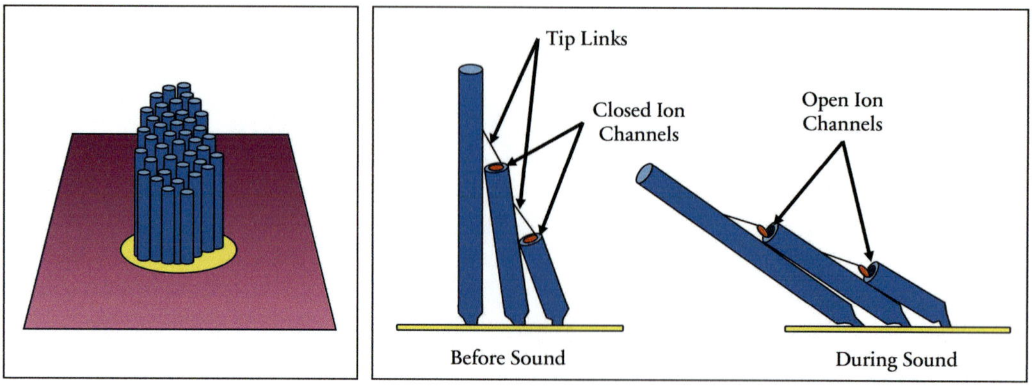

Figure 5.9 Left, a bundle of stereocilia. Right, when the Basilar membrane moves (due to sound vibration) the stereocilia bend over. This causes the tip links to open ion channels, allowing ions to rush into the cell (which starts an action potential).

It's important to recognize that all of this is happening with very tiny pieces moving very quickly. The cilia are only 0.05 mm wide, and the tip links are a tiny fraction of that. The quietest sounds that we can hear only cause the cilia to bend about 0.3nm (which is the diameter of *atoms*). It takes the hair cell about 10 microseconds (one microsecond is one *millionth* of a second) to respond to a sound. That reaction is much faster than the photoreceptors' response to light—probably because it relies on mechanical transduction rather than a chemical cascade. These hair cells are *tiny* and *quick*.

Conveying Frequency

Let's return to the movement of the Basilar membrane. First, the Basilar membrane is not terribly well-named. The word "membrane" brings to mind a sort of floppy barrier. The Basilar membrane, however, is relatively rigid. It also has a very particular shape that is responsible for the way it functions (more on this later). It is taller and thinner (about 0.1mm) at the "head end" and flatter and wider (0.5mm) at the "foot end", and it changes continuously along its length.[8] The upshot of having this particular shape is that every place along the Basilar membrane has a different **resonant frequency**.

> **Resonant frequency** the specific frequency at which an object vibrates when subjected to an outside force.

When Fred was cleaning up after Eleanor's bath one day, she found Fred's tuning fork and started playing with it. She eventually figured out it made a noise when she hit it on things—bong!— so she tried hitting it on a lot of stuff in a lot of ways. Bong! Bong! No matter what she hit it on, and no matter how hard or soft she hit it, as long as it was enough energy to get it to vibrate, the tuning fork always made the exact. Same. Tone. Bong! Specifically, it always vibrated at 110 Hz (the same "A" tone Fred and his guitar were making earlier). Fred told her to hold on the tuning fork so he could show her something cool. He got out his guitar and then asked Eleanor to bang the tuning fork again. Bong! But now, the A string on his guitar vibrated. Then he did it the other way around. He plucked the A string, and the tuning fork vibrated! 110 Hz is the *resonant frequency* of that tuning fork.

Everything has a resonant frequency—your cup of coffee, your book, the chair you're sitting in, everything! The reason your voice sounds like it does is because your vocal folds,

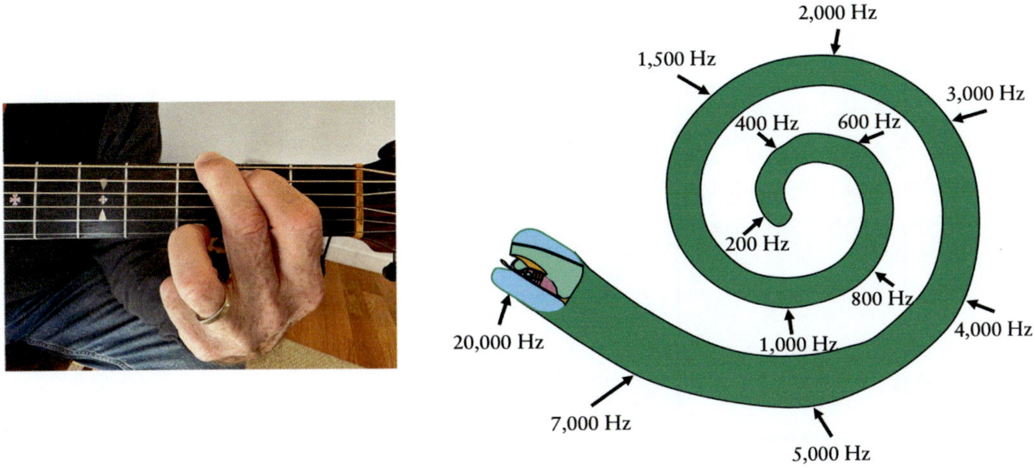

Figure 5.10 Left, a G chord on an acoustic guitar. Right, the locations of the resonant frequencies of the Basilar membrane.

skull, mouth, and face all have specific resonant frequencies. The combination of those frequencies is what makes your voice yours. This *also* explains why your voice might sound strange to you when hear it in on a recording. When you hear your voice as you are speaking, your auditory system is receiving the sound in two ways—through the air but also through your body. When you hear your voice on a recording (which is how other people hear your voice), your auditory system is only receiving the sound through the air.

Now look at Figure 5.10 (*left*), which is a photograph of one of your authors' dad playing a G major chord. That chord is the combination of several different notes:[9] three Gs, each an octave apart (97 Hz, 196 Hz, and 392 Hz); two Bs, each an octave apart (123 Hz and 247 Hz), and D (148 Hz). All of those frequencies combine in the air, and that complex sound makes its way to your ear where it is (eventually) translated into waves of the endolymph in the middle duct. The basilar membrane will vibrate in response, but in a *very specific way.* The part of the membrane that has a resonant frequency of 97 Hz will vibrate, the part of the membrane that has a resonant frequency of 196 will vibrate, the part of the membrane that has a resonant frequency of 392 will vibrate, and so on. Or in other words, the Basilar membrane will perform a kind of *biological Fourier transform* and separate the sound into its component frequencies (Von Békésy, 1960).

In Figure 5.10 (*right*), you can see the resonant frequencies of the Basilar membrane along the spiral. The *location* of the vibration causes the hair cells in that specific place to respond and send a signal to the brain. This is known as **Békésy place theory** after Hungarian scientist Georg von Békésy, who won the Nobel Prize in 1961 for this discovery. The G chord would make the marked *places* vibrate.

There is a lot of evidence at this point that Békésy was right—good thing that they gave him the Nobel Prize! This gets a bit complicated, but bear with us here. Much like the simple cells in the brain, researchers can

Békésy place theory description of how frequency of sound is conveyed by the inner ear. Since the different areas of the Basilar membrane have different resonant frequencies, the location of the stimulation is directly related to the frequency of the stimulus.

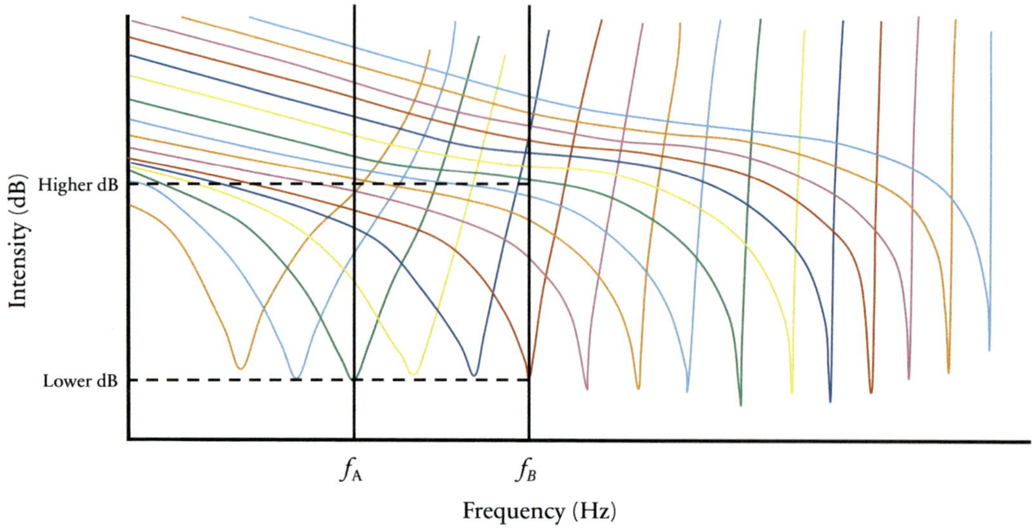

Figure 5.11 The colored lines are the characteristic curves for different hair cells. Each line represents the minimum threshold (of loudness) a particular frequency (pitch) must be in order for that cell to respond. Note that each line has one particular frequency where the threshold is very low. Also note that for a particular frequency (f_A or f_B), at a lower dB only one cell will respond. At a high dB, several cells will respond. In this way, the number of cells firing is directly related to the loudness of the sound.

insert microelectrodes into specific nerves along the Basilar membrane and measure their response to particular kinds of stimuli. Measuring the response at different places along the Basilar membrane reveals each inner hair cell's[10] **characteristic curve**. In Figure 5.11, each colored line represents the characteristic curve of a specific hair cell.

Characteristic curve threshold for response for a single hair cell to different frequencies. A given hair cell will be maximally (but not exclusively) responsive to a particular frequency.

The characteristic curve line represents the minimum threshold (see Chapter 1) for a cell to respond to a particular frequency. The lower the curve, the lower the threshold for responding to that frequency. In other words, the lower the curve, the smaller the amplitude (the quieter) a sound at that frequency can be and still elicit a response from the cell. Notice that the response curve gets narrower the higher the frequency. This means that the cells that respond to higher pitches are pickier about which sounds they respond to. Notice also that the shape of the curve for each cell indicates that a given cell does, in fact, respond to sounds at many different frequencies. However, for each cell, there is one particular frequency with the lowest threshold. Keep this in mind as we start looking at how the inner ear conveys amplitude information.

Socratic Question: How is the Basilar membrane organized? In other words, how does sensitivity to sound differ on different parts of the Basilar membrane? How is this different than how the retina is organized with respect to sensitivity to light?

Conveying Amplitude

On Figure 5.11, there is a vertical line marked "f_A". That is a lower-frequency sound (like a foghorn). If it is very quiet (say at the line marked "Lower dB"), only one cell will respond to that sound. If it is much louder (say at the line marked "Higher dB"), several different cells will respond to that sound. The same would be true for the higher frequency (marked f_B)—at lower dBs, only one cell will respond; at higher dBs, many will respond. Or in other words, these characteristic curves lead to a direct relationship between the number of cells responding and the loudness of the sound.

Note that these are responses of the *nerves*, not the responses of the *person*. As with vision, researchers can also manipulate the energy and ask participants what they perceive (see "Psychophysics" in Chapter 1). As the characteristic curves would predict, not all frequencies are perceived the same way. In addition, frequency (together with amplitude) affects perceived loudness. Look at Figure 5.12. The bottom-most curve is the **absolute threshold** for sound. It shows the smallest amplitude (the lowest dB) a given frequency (a given pitch) has to be in order for us to hear it. Notice that it's not a straight line! There are some frequencies that are easier for us to hear. For example, lower-pitched sounds have to be much louder in order for us to hear them.

> **Absolute threshold (hearing)** quietest sound that can still be heard. Varies by frequency.

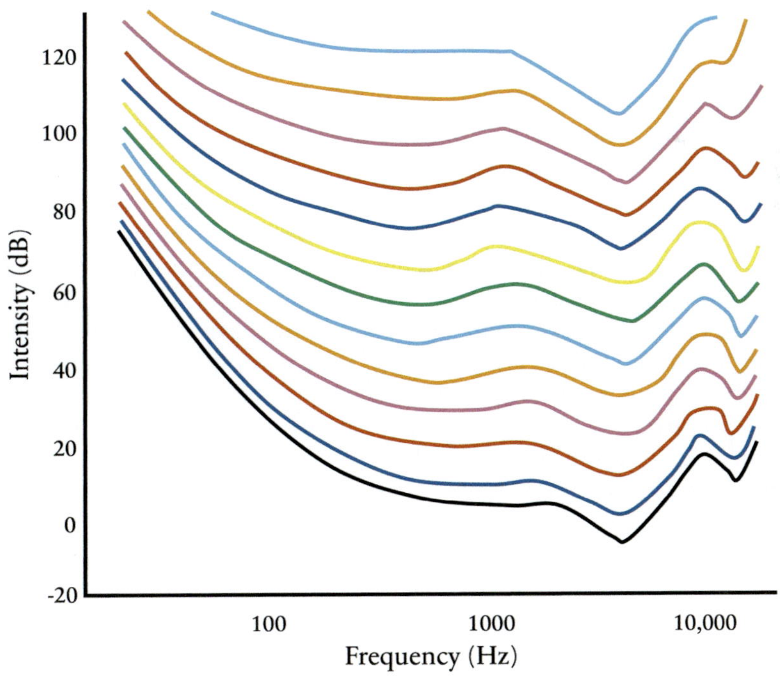

Figure 5.12 The bottom-most line is the minimum threshold for sound; note that it varies by frequency. Each of the lines represents sounds that are heard as equally loud.

Each additional line in Figure 5.12 indicates a line of equal **perceived loudness** (known as **equal loudness contours**). That is, if you were to play each sound along the green line, they would all sound the same amount of loud to a person. Notice that all of the curves have their lowest point around 2,000–5,000 Hz. This is likely related to our abilities to understand human speech sounds. The fundamental frequencies of speech tend to be lower-pitched than this, around 85 Hz–255 Hz. However, the sounds of speech that make a difference in what different words means (called "phonemes"; see Chapter 12) are in the range of highest sensitivity.

Perceived loudness how loud a sound seems to a listener. It is a function of both actual loudness and frequency.

Equal loudness contours a set of frequencies and amplitudes that are all perceived as the same loudness.

The shape of these contours is likely not due to the machinery of the inner ear, but rather the shape and length of the auditory canal. Remember from earlier—it amplifies sounds in the 2,000–7,000 Hz range.

Socratic Question: The same dB is perceived as different amounts of loudness (depending on the frequency). Different dBs are perceived as the same amount of loudness (depending on the frequency). Why might our bodies be wired this way? Is there an advantage to this?

Box 5.2 Non-Human Hearing

Hearing is not a universal experience. Many insects cannot hear at all, for example, and some mammals who live underground can only hear a little bit. Having said that, it does seem to be a relatively useful adaptation. Ears (or things like them) have evolved on at least 19 independent occasions on basically every body part you can imagine (Yong, 2022). Sound-sensing organs have been found on knees (crickets and katydids); abdomens (locusts, cicadas, and monarchs); mouths (hawkmoths); and smack in the middle of the chest (mantises).

One reason that so many different kinds of creatures have ears (or things like them) is that so many different kinds of creatures have another kind of organ—a stretch-sensing organ usually near joints. This type of organ has a thin membrane that stretches in response to movement and changes in location of the organism's limb. With only minor modifications (i.e., if it just becomes a *tiny bit thinner*) it will respond to vibrations in the air and voilà! That's an ear!

And the fact that ears (or things like them) are so common among different animal species comes in really handy for communication. It turns out the animal kingdom is a lot more chatty than we thought! Elephants communicate with each other over incredible distances by talking in very low-pitched rumbles (well below the threshold for human hearing). At the other end of the spectrum, mice sing to each other just as much as birds do—just at pitches too high for humans to hear. It's hard not to think of the generations of lab mice sharing their observations *about human behavior* with each other across cage walls.

Neural Pathways for Hearing

In this section, we are going to make a lot of references to the visual system in the brain (if you need a refresher, check out Chapter 3). There's a good reason for that, the two systems are very similar! In fact, with *all* the senses there are similar structures for similar processes. We started this book with a discussion of vision because scientists know the most about it, but also because it makes a good reference for understanding the biology of the other senses.

For example, one lesson learned by comparing multiple sense systems is that the neural organization (whether for vision, hearing, touch, etc.) depends on experience. In all cases, research has shown that the neural pathways develop in response to the stimulation patterns encountered in the environment and the behaviors that the organism performs in that environment (see Box 3.3 in Chapter 3) both in the short and long term. That's worth keeping in mind as we talk about the complex neural pathways for hearing.

After leaving the ear via the auditory nerve, the signal travels to both hemispheres of the brain. Unlike in the visual system, there is no separation by the location of the sound source in the world—the entirety of the signal from both ears travels to both hemispheres.

Take a look at Figure 5.13 and follow along as we trace the path of the signal and unpack what we know about the function of each step. Let's follow the signal coming in from the right ear (the left ear will do all the same things, just flipped right-to-left).

Brain Stem

The nerve fibers that are connected to the hair cells in the right ear bundle together with the nerves from the vestibular system (more on this later in the chapter) and project towards the brain stem. The signal enters the right half of the brain stem in an area called the **cochlear nucleus**. The cochlear nucleus is arranged much like the Basilar membrane—specific areas are interested in particular frequencies and cells that respond to similar frequencies are near each other. *And* similar frequencies exhibit lateral inhibition just like neighboring locations do in the eye (see Chapter 3). The function here is the same as it was there: to help sharpen contrasts between similar frequencies. The cochlear nucleus also seems to be more interested in the *starting* and *ending* of a given sound than in the rest of the sound. That is, the cells fire more frequently at the onset and offset of a sound.

> **Cochlear nucleus** part of the brainstem; entry point for signals from the cochlea.

The cochlear nucleus sends its signal to a few different areas within the brain stem. We'll talk more about sound localization in Chapter 12, but the brainstem areas are where localization of the sound in the horizontal direction starts. Think of this situation: Fred is standing and looking at his apple tree. Topsy (standing to his right) trumpets to get his attention. The sound hits Fred's right ear slightly *before* it hits his left ear. It's also slightly *louder* in his right ear than in his left (since his head is blocking some of the sound).

Since both ears are sending signals to the brain stem it is possible for the brain to have direct access to both the *timing* and differences in *loudness* of those signals. Both timing and loudness differences between the two ears help localize the sound (again, more about this in Chapter 12).

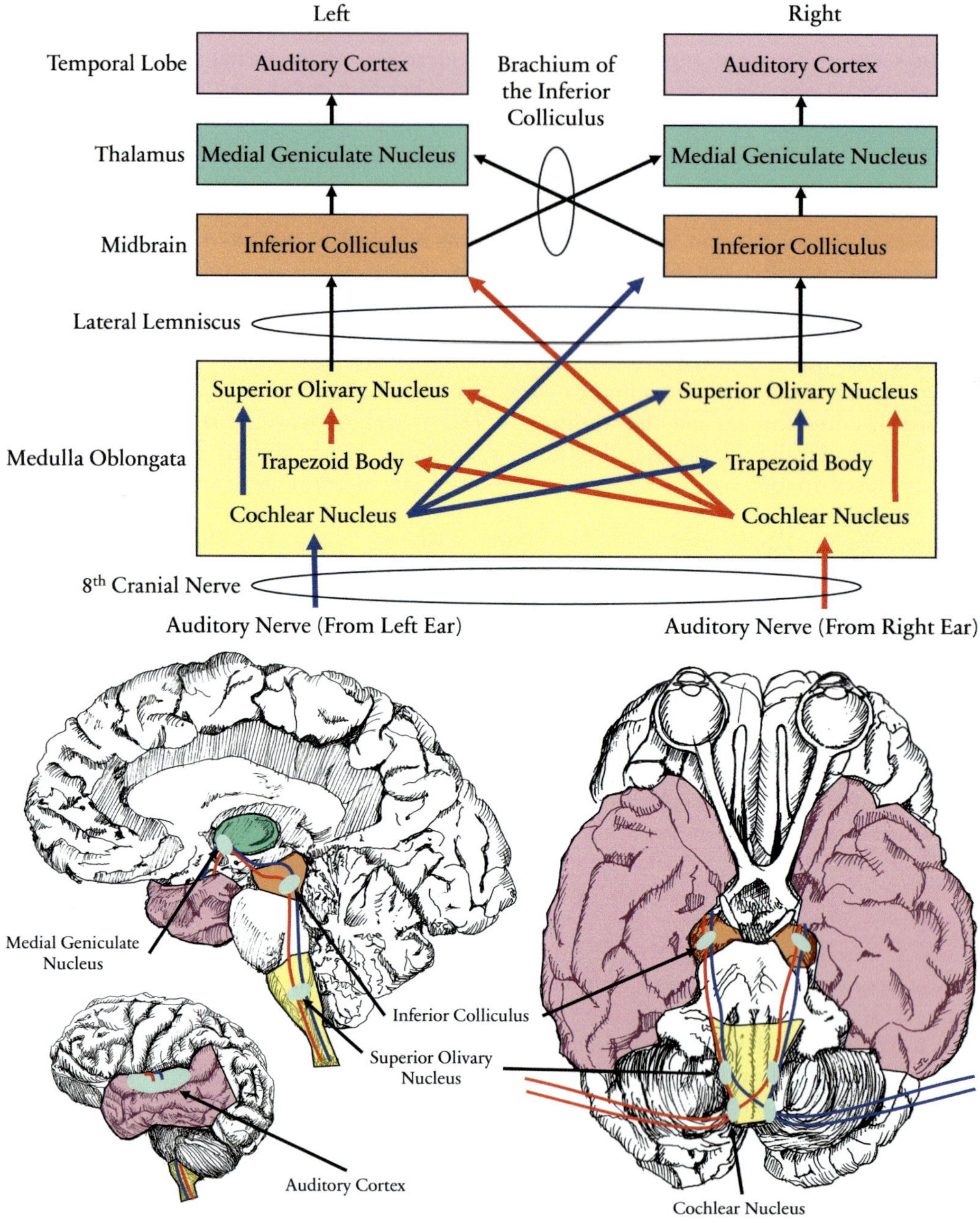

Figure 5.13 Neural pathways for hearing; see text for details.

Midbrain

The signal travels from the brainstem to the two midbrains, specifically the **inferior colliculi**. This structure is very like the superior colliculus we mentioned in

Inferior colliculus part of the midbrain. Responsible for unconscious orienting to sound.

Chapter 3—it is responsible for unconscious orienting to sound. If you hear a loud sound on your right and turn your head to look at it before you even realize it, you can thank your inferior colliculus.

Thalamus

Both inferior colliculi send their signal to their respective thalamus (remember the thalamus from Chapter 3?), specifically to a part called the **medial geniculate body**. The inferior colliculi *also* send their signals across a nerve bridge to the medial geniculate body on the contralateral side.

> **Medial Geniculate Body** part of the thalamus. Responsible for relaying sound information to the cortex.

The function of the medial geniculate body seems to be roughly the same as the LGN for the visual system: it's a conduit for the signals, possibly with some cleaning-of-the-signal function (Weyand, 2016). The LGN had retinotopic mapping, reflecting the spatial organization of the cells of the retina. Here, the medial geniculate body shows the same **tonotopic organization** as the nerve coming from the Basilar membrane. That is, it is sorted by the frequency of the tone, and specific areas respond best to pure tones rather than complex sounds.

> **Tonotopic organization** organization by frequency of sound.

> Socratic Question: Visual pathways in the brain show a retinotopic mapping. That is, spatial relations on the retina are preserved in the visual cortex. What kind of mapping does the auditory pathways in the brain show? What kind of relationships are preserved in the auditory pathways?

Temporal Lobe

The medial geniculate body in the thalamus sends the signal to the auditory cortex. Just like with vision, there is an area that receives the signal first called A1 (for **a**uditory cortex **1**). A1 is on the dorsal (top) side of the temporal lobe, tucked into the lateral sulcus (the big crevasse that separates the temporal lobe from the parietal and frontal lobes). The auditory cortex is organized like an avocado—a center area (like the pit of the avocado) surrounded by two layers (the edible part of the avocado and the skin; see Figure 5.14).

Core Areas

The center area has three tonotopically organized sections. Neighboring cells respond to similar frequencies, and each of the three areas shows an orderly progression from low to high. As with the medial geniculate body, the cells here respond best to pure tones.

Belt and Parabelt Regions

Together, the belt and parabelt regions form the auditory association cortex (that is, A2). These seem to perform roughly the same function as the extrastriate cortex for vision. That

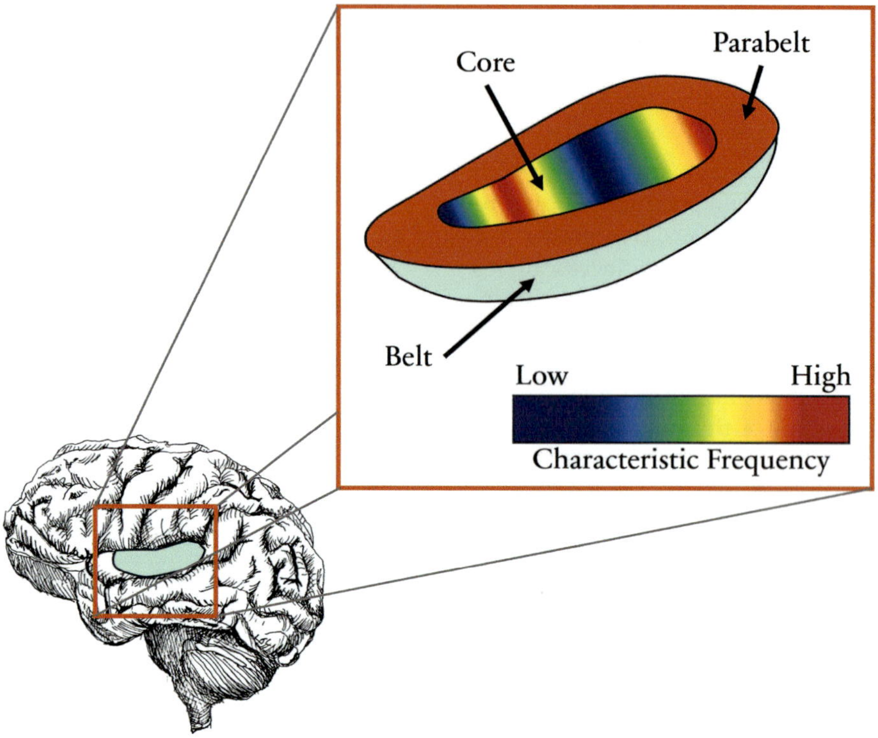

Figure 5.14 The auditory cortex is shaped like an avocado. The core area is surrounded by the belt and parabelt regions.

is, they perform more complex analyses of the auditory signal. The cells in these areas are less responsive to pure tones than to complex combinations of frequencies. The farther away from the core, the more complex the sound has to be to elicit a response.

Dorsal and Ventral Pathways

After leaving A2, the auditory pathway diverges into two directions (if this sounds familiar, that's because the visual pathways did the same thing; see Chapter 3) the *dorsal* (top) and *ventral* (bottom) streams. The dorsal pathway leaves the auditory cortex from the posterior (back) part of the belts; the ventral pathway leaves the auditory cortex from the anterior (front) part of the belts (see Figure 5.15).

After leaving the posterior of the belt regions, the dorsal pathway goes backward, then up, then forward. After leaving the anterior of the belt regions, the ventral pathway goes forward then up. Both end up in the frontal lobe, although in slightly different locations (the dorsal pathway ends up a bit higher and a bit farther back).

Just as with vision, it seems more likely that there is a *functional* difference between the pathways, rather than a *property-based* difference. Current research supports the idea that the dorsal pathway is involved in perception for the purpose of *action* (Rauschecker, 2018). That is, the dorsal pathway is how we synchronize our *behavior* with auditory events. In the same

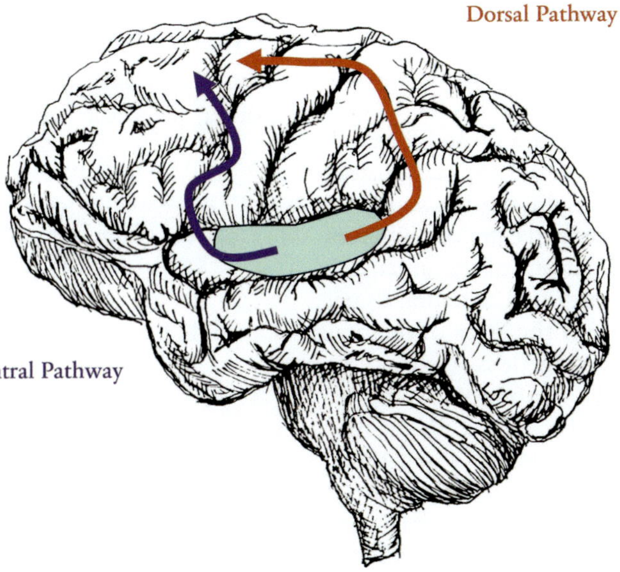

Figure 5.15 The dorsal and ventral streams of auditory processing.

way, it appears that the ventral pathway is involved in building up a conscious awareness of the auditory scene. It is worth mentioning that (just as with the two pathways for vision) there are numerous crossovers between the two pathways at all steps in the process, which means it's likely that even this functional distinction between the two pathways is too simplistic.

Descending Pathway

The preceding sections all describe the **ascending pathways**; that is, they describe the pathway from the ears to the various areas in the brain. Just like for vision (see Chapter 3), there is also a **descending pathway**; that is, the signal goes backwards from the brain back down to the ear. In some cases, the descending signal is *stronger* than the ascending signal! As we'll talk about in Chapter 8, these are thought to be involved in top-down processing, but they are also possibly involved in cleaning and amplifying the signal.

Ascending pathway pathway of the signal leaving the sense organ and moving to farther away (and theoretically more complex) processing areas.

Descending pathway pathway of the signal leaving the farther away (and theoretically more complex) processing areas, and moving back to the sense organ.

Disruptions in Hearing

In this section, we will only cover a couple of examples of hearing loss. Given all the very many structures involved in hearing, it's not surprising that there are very many ways to have hearing loss. For the most part, these are broken into two categories: **conductive hearing loss** and **sensorineural hearing loss**. The first category involves damage or malformations of the outer or middle ear—that is, those parts of the ear responsible for collecting and amplifying the sound to the inner ear. The second category involves damage or malformations of the inner ear, any of the nerves carrying the neural signal to the brain, or any of the areas of the brain responsible for processing the signal.

Conductive hearing loss hearing loss due to damage or malformations of the outer or middle ear.

Sensorineural hearing loss hearing loss due to damage or malformations of the inner ear or neural pathways.

Age-related hearing loss (known as **presbycusis**) results in the loss of higher frequencies first. The hair cells in the inner ear do not regenerate when damaged,[11] and they can be damaged by a variety of things (mostly exposure to very loud noises, but also certain recreational drugs, and some antibiotics). The part of the basilar membrane that resonates with the highest frequencies is right next to the oval window, which means it encounters more sound energy than any other part of the basilar membrane. All that energy causes wear and tear, resulting in loss of the highest frequencies first. Since high frequencies are what distinguish language sounds, this can be a very difficult and alienating condition. So what sounds are damaging? Anything above 85 dB. A general rule of thumb is that if you have to raise your voice to be heard over the sound, it's probably too loud. We strongly suggest turning down your music!

Presbycusis age-related hearing loss due to mechanical destruction of hair cells with use.

Fairly recently (in the early 2000s), a condition known as *hidden hearing loss* was identified (Kujawa & Liberman, 2009). In this case, the person will pass a hearing test but has great difficulty hearing in real life, particularly in loud places. The likely explanation is damage to the ascending/descending pathways that help clear and amplify the signal from the noise. Hearing aids designed to reduce background noise or ones with directional microphones can help.

Almost certainly you have experienced **tinnitus** at some point in your life. It's a high-pitched ringing in your ear that can last a few seconds to a few days. While annoying, it's mostly harmless and usually not indicative of anything serious. Scientists' best guess is that it is a misfiring of one of the auditory nerves. Very infrequently, it can last long enough and be loud enough to cause long-term issues in hearing. In those cases, audiologists can help with special hearing aids that block the sound using white noise.

Tinnitus high-pitched ringing in the ear, usually temporary and benign.

Some people are born deaf or hard of hearing. There are many possible causes for this, from genetics to maternal illness during pregnancy. Some forms of deafness can be treated with **cochlear implants** (a device that is surgically implanted and replaces the person's cochlea). It's worth mentioning that the use of cochlear implants is controversial in the Deaf community. Some in the community feel that the implication of the implants is that people who have this kind of hearing loss are *broken* and need to be *fixed*. Given the rich culture of the Deaf community, they do not see themselves that way. Regardless, early identification of hearing loss is vital to prevent language and other developmental delays. It is very common (and recommended!) for babies to have their hearing tested before they leave the hospital after birth.

> Socratic Question: Many people wear hearing aids for age-related hearing loss (presbycusis). These hearing aids need to do more than just amplify all sounds equally. Why?

Vestibular System

In Chapter 1, we introduced the idea that only having five senses was overly restrictive to our understanding of how we experience our worlds. This concern is particularly obvious when it comes to the vestibular senses. Even deciding which chapter to put them in was a struggle! We decided to put them here because of the location of the organ(s) and because the receptors involved are nearly identical to those in the hearing system. However, it would have also made sense to put them in with the touch senses (in Chapter 6); with the visual system (Chapters 2 or 3) for reasons that will become clear; as their *own* chapter; or several other options.

The vestibular system is sensitive to (minimally) three different movement-related properties: **angular motion**, **linear acceleration**, and **tilt** (also known as **graviception** or the perception of gravity). These three, in turn, contribute to (among other things) balance, stability of gaze, and even systems that regulate blood pressure. Take that, myth of the five senses!

The vestibular system is not just one organ but a collection of *five* organs. Together, these five organs are approximately the size of a large pea. The vestibular system is part of the inner ear along with the cochlea[12] and consists of three **semi-circular canals** and two **otolith organs** (see Figure 5.16, *left*).

> **Angular motion** perception of rotation about one of three axes.
>
> **Linear acceleration** perception of change in velocity.
>
> **Tilt (graviception)** perception of the self relative to gravity.

> **Semi-circular canals** three looped organs located in the inner ear. Responsible for perception of angular motion.
>
> **Otolith organs (utricle and saccule)** two sack-shaped organs located in the inner ear. Responsible for perception of linear acceleration and tilt (graviception).

> Socratic Question: How might the myth of the five senses have affected the scientific understanding of the vestibular system?

Semi-Circular Canals: Angular Motion

The name of these structures is based on their shape. Each is (more or less) a tube in the shape of a circle (like a doughnut; see Figure 5.16, right). Each tube is filled with endolymph, and at the base is a larger chamber called an **ampulla**. Inside, at the

> **Ampulla** larger chamber at the base of the semi-circular canal; houses the cupula.

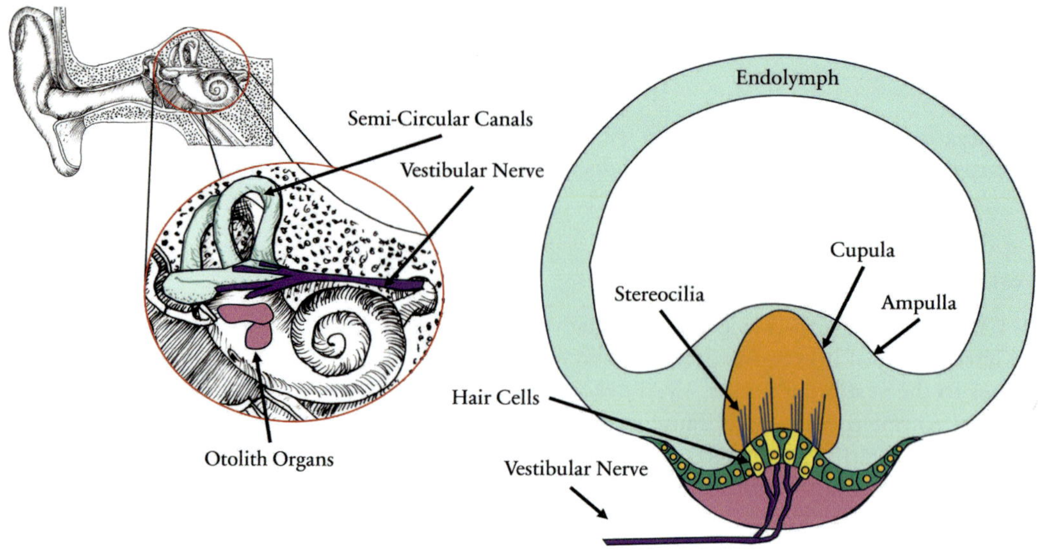

Figure 5.16 Left, the vestibular system is made of five total organs: three semicircular canals and two otolith organs. Right, the semi-circular canals are donut-shaped tubes filled with fluid. When the fluid moves, it stimulates the receptors in the lower part of the canal.

base of the ampulla, there are hair cells topped with stereocilia (like those in the cochlea). The largest cilia in each bundle is called the **kinocilium**, which has a more rigid structure than the rest of the cilia. Its function is not entirely clear as displacing it does not cause a change in the firing rate of the hair cell, but when it is removed or damaged the hair cell ceases to

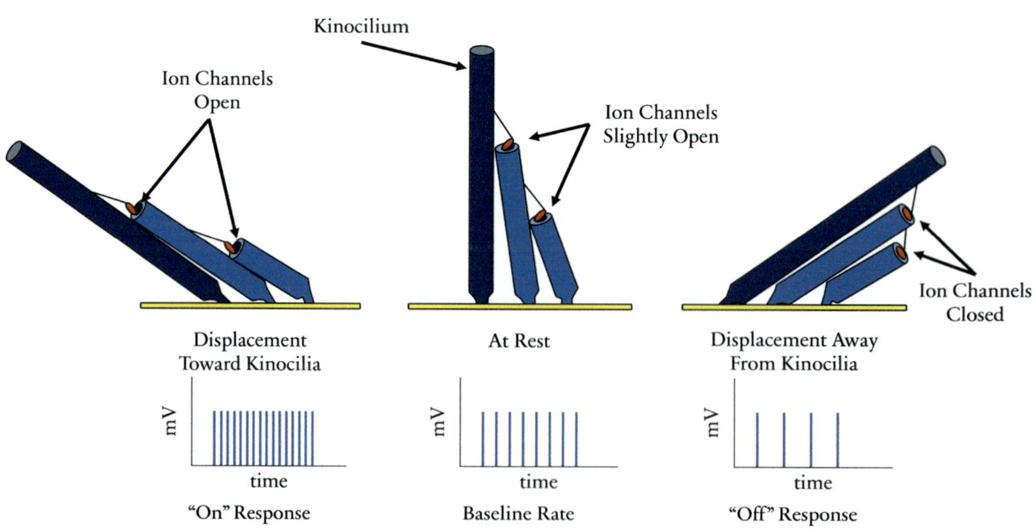

Figure 5.17 Displacing the stereocilia in the direction of the kinocilium (the tallest, stiffest stereocilium) increases the rate of firing of the hair cell. Displacement away from the kinocilium decreases the rate of firing.

function normally. The hair cells and cilia are enclosed in a gelatinous cone-shaped structure called the **cupula**.

Kinocilium largest stereocilia in the bundle on the top of the hair cell. Indicates the direction of response.

Cupula gelatinous cone-shaped structure housed in the ampulla. Contains the hair cell receptors.

When you move, the fluid sloshes around in these canals (remember Eleanor in the bath?). That sloshing pushes on the cupula and displaces the stereocilia. At rest, the hair cell has a base rate of firing. When displaced in the direction of the kinocilium, the tip links open the ion channels, depolarizing the cell and increasing the rate of firing. When displaced away from the kinocilium, the ion channels all close, hyperpolarizing the cell and decreasing the rate of firing. Or, in other words, movement in either direction results in a change in the rate of firing (see Figure 5.17).

There are three semi-circular canals, one for each axis of rotation (see Figure 5.18). To get a sense of the three axes, try three movements. First, tilt your head side to side as if trying to touch your ears to your shoulders. This is rotation about an axis that goes through your nose and out the back of your head (called the x-axis). Second, nod your head up and down as if saying "yes". When you do this, you are rotating your head about an axis that goes through one ear and out the other (called the y-axis). Third, shake your head back and forth as if saying "no"; this is rotation about an axis that goes through the top of your head down to your neck (the z-axis).

Any movement of the head can be understood as movement in one (or a combination of) these three axes. The three semi-circular canals are oriented in these planes and pick up on this exact kind of rotation.

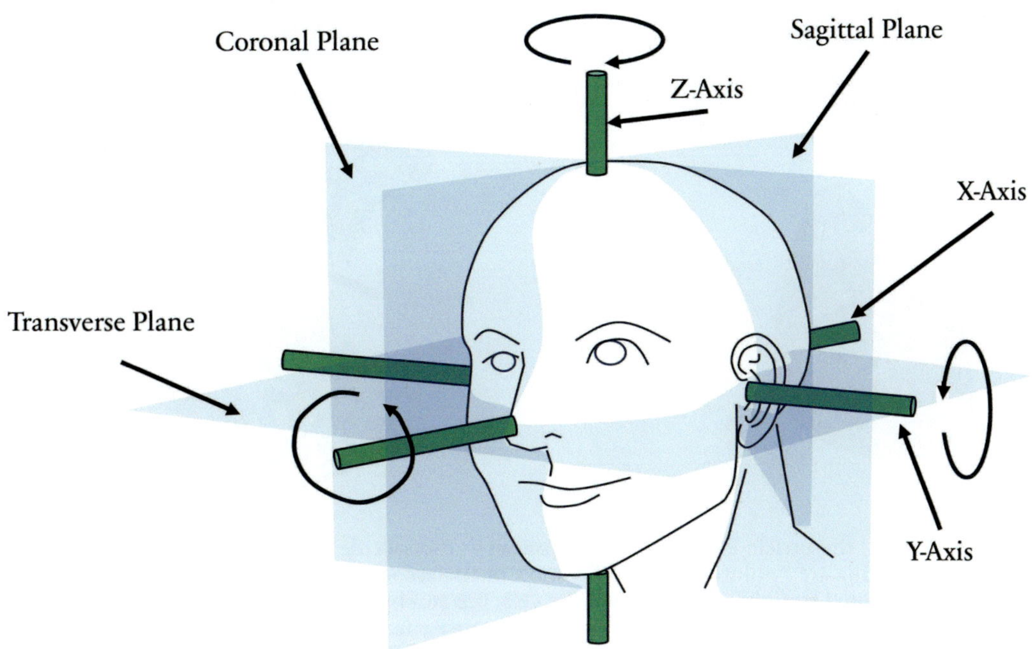

Figure 5.18 The head can rotate around three different axes. The semi-circular canals are oriented in these directions.

Otolith Organs

> **Macula (vestibular)** gelatinous structure embedded with hair cells and topped by otoconia.
>
> **Otoconia** small calcium crystals floating on top of the macula.

Each ear has two otolith organs: the **utricle** and the **saccule**. The utricle (Greek for "little pouch") is more or less horizontal; the saccule (Greek for "little sack") is more or less vertical. Both have an organ called the **macula**, which is a gelatinous structure with hair cells (with stereocilia on top) embedded in it. On the top of this are tiny crystals of calcium salts called **otoconia** (literally from the Greek for "ear stones"). Think of them like small chocolate chips floating on top of pudding.

Unlike the stereocilia in the semi-circular canals (which are all oriented in the same way), the stereocilia in the otolith organs are oriented in different directions. It helps to think of which side the kinocilia are on. Just as in the semi-circular canals, displacement of the cilia *towards* the kinocilia results in an *increase* in firing rate, and movement *away* from the kinocilia results in a *decrease* in firing rate. In Figure 5.19 (*left*), the direction of the arrow points towards the location of the kinocilia.

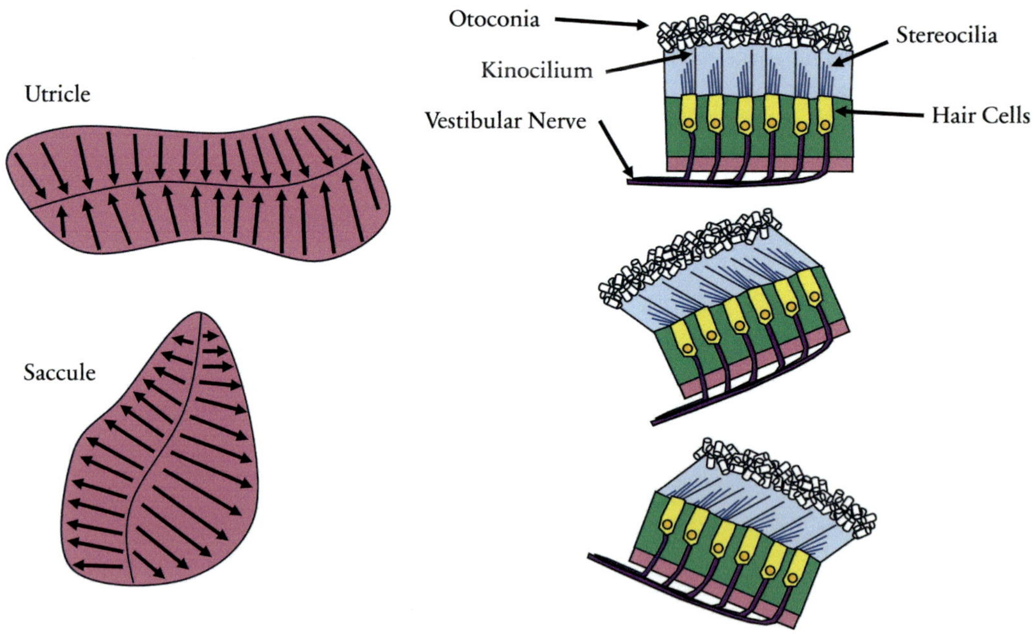

Figure 5.19 Left, the utricle is more or less horizontal; the saccule is more or less vertical. The stereocilia are "pointed" in the direction of the arrows. Top right, at rest the otoconia are oriented straight up and down; the cells fire at a baseline rate. Middle right, either looking up or increasing forward speed will cause the otoconia to slide backward, changing the rate of firing of some of the cells. Bottom right, either looking down or decreasing forward speed will cause the otoconia to slide forward, changing the rate of firing of some of the cells.

Tilt (Graviception)

Fred was hanging out one day when his upstairs neighbor, Miguel, started blaring his music. As any of us might do, Fred looked up at the ceiling in frustration, then sighed and looked down at the floor. Before the music started, when he was looking straight ahead, the macula in the utricles in his ears looked like Figure 5.18 (*top right*). The hair cells were "at rest" and were firing at a baseline rate. When he looked up at the ceiling, however, the heavier otoconia slid backwards, pulling on the gelatinous cap, displacing the hair cells (like in Figure 5.18, *middle right*). For some of the hair cells, the displacement was away from the kinocilia (decreasing the rate of firing); for some of them it was towards the kinocilia (increasing the rate of firing); for some of them it was sideways (no change in the rate of firing). Then, when he looked down at the floor, the heavier otoconia slid forwards, pulling on the gelatinous cap, displacing the hair cells in the opposite direction (like in Figure 5.18, *bottom right*). The response from the hair cells will be the opposite of what it was for looking up. Or in other words, tilting the head in either direction will change the rate of firing.

Linear Acceleration

Fred taught his neighbor's son, Ludovic, how to drive. It was an . . . interesting experience. Like many new drivers, Ludovic kept stomping on the gas and then slamming on the brakes. Whenever Ludovic would dramatically accelerate, both he and Fred would be slammed backward into their seats (technically what's happening there is that the car moves quicker than them and so they get pushed along by it until they can catch up). Whenever Ludovic would slam on the brakes, both he and Fred would both slide forward until their seatbelts caught them (again, what's really happening is that their bodies were still going forward, and they got held back by the seatbelts until their bodies slowed down). Eventually, Ludovic managed to get the car going at a constant speed (whew!). At that point, even though they (and the car) were moving along with the flow of traffic, both of them felt like they were just sitting in a chair (not moving at all). Speeding up and slowing down are both changes in velocity, also known as *linear acceleration*. Once the car is going at a constant speed, the linear acceleration is zero.

The otolith organs are like the people in the car (you are the car in this scenario). When you change your velocity, the otoconia slide around (like the people), pulling on the hair cells. Notice the ambiguity! The situation in Figure 5.18 (*top right*) can be caused by looking straight ahead *or* by moving at a constant velocity. The situation in Figure 5.18 (*middle right*) can be caused by looking up *or* by accelerating forwards. The situation in Figure 5.18 (*bottom right*) can be caused by looking down *or* by accelerating backwards. At the level of the individual organs, tilt and linear acceleration are ambiguous.

The horizontally oriented utricles respond to linear acceleration in the transverse plane (the plane defined by the X and Y axes). The vertically oriented saccules respond to linear acceleration in the sagittal plane (the plane defined by the X and Z axes; see Figure 5.18).

Neural Pathways for the Vestibular System

All the fibers from the vestibular system bundle together into the vestibular nerve. This nerve joins the auditory nerve (at which point it's called the vestibulocochlear nerve), and they project to the brainstem. The vestibular information projects to the vestibular complex, which is made up of several different nuclei. These nuclei also receive information from the visual system and from the muscles that control the eyes and neck. The vestibular complex projects to several areas: the oculomotor system, the thalamus, the medulla oblongata, the cerebellum (for the coordination of complex movements as well as motor learning), and the spine (to maintain an upright posture). As you read the next few sections, it might be helpful to reference Figure 5.19, which shows the neural pathways of the vestibular system.

Oculomotor System

Earlier, when Fred looked up at the ceiling in the direction of his noisy upstairs neighbor, his eyes and head coordinated in a very particular way. Try it yourself! Look up at the ceiling (or sky if you're outside). As you do, pay very close attention to the movements of your eyes and head. In all likelihood, you moved your eyes first, then followed with the head. At some point, your eyes fixated on a point, and the head continued to move to catch up. That last part—your eyes fixated on a point, head moving to catch up—requires deft control of your eye movements coordinated with your neck movements. And you did it without even thinking! This coordination is called the **vestibulo-ocular reflex** (**VOR**) and is one of the main purposes of the vestibular system (hence why we *could* have talked about this in one of the vision chapters).

Vestibulo-ocular Reflex (VOR) response of the eyes to vestibular information that keeps gaze steady during movements of the rest of the body.

The VOR is also responsible for your ability to have a stable gaze while running, shifting side to side in your seat while reading, or basically any motion that moves your head (and thus, your eyes). The VOR is controlled by the oculomotor system in the midbrain and is very fast—about 5ms to onset of movement.

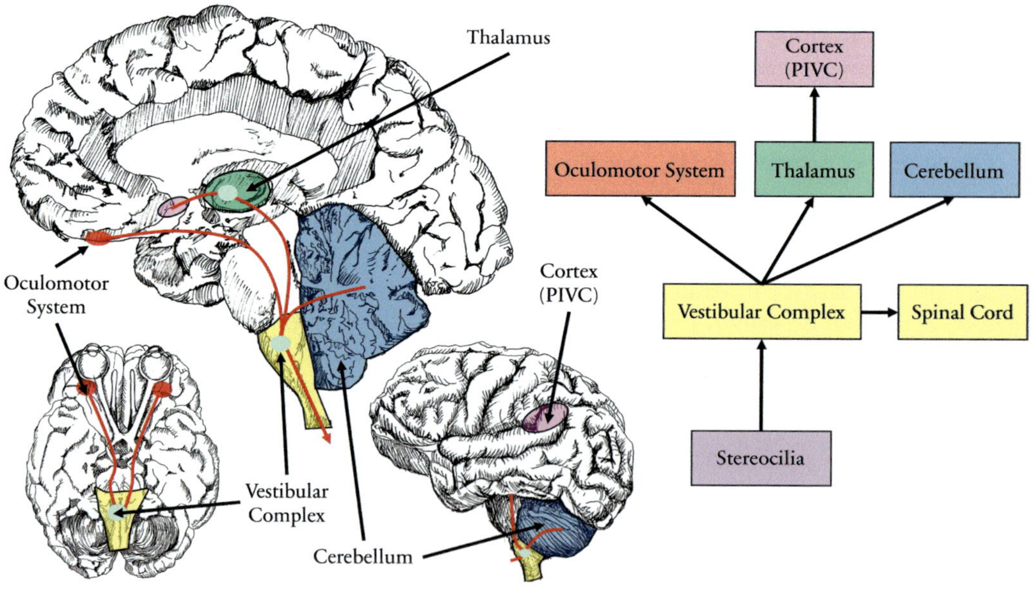

Figure 5.20 The neural pathways of the vestibular system; see text for details.

Thalamus and Cortex

Just like every other sensory system, the information from the vestibular system travels to the thalamus before heading to the cortex. Specifically, the vestibular system projects to the ventrobasal complex of the thalamus before traveling to several areas of the cortex, but most specifically to the **parietal insular vestibular cortex** (**PIVC**) deep in the lateral sulcus. The PIVC is thought to be responsible for the conscious feeling of equilibrium and the body's orientation in space.

Parietal insular vestibular cortex (PIVC) located in the lateral sulcus; responsible for the conscious feeling of equilibrium.

Medulla Oblongata

The signal also travels from the brain stem to the medulla oblongata, which regulates heartbeat and blood pressure. When you move (say, when you go from a seated position to standing), it is necessary for your circulatory system to change your blood pressure—otherwise, all the blood would rush away from your brain and you would faint. The medulla oblongata uses information from the vestibular system to know when and how to change your blood pressure in response to postural changes.

Disruptions of the Vestibular System

Just like most of our perceptual systems, we have a tendency to take the working of our vestibular system for granted. In fact, we pretty much don't notice it at all until it stops working properly. One of the most common instances of this is what is known as the **oculogyral illusion**, which is a very fancy way of saying dizziness caused by spinning around in circles—Topsy *loves* this feeling, but Fred does not. The illusion is that the world seems to move relative to the body even though it is not. It is caused by the suppression of the VOR, which happens when the body is moving faster than fixation can happen. Once you stop spinning, it takes a little while before the brain gets the message and starts the VOR up again.

Oculogyral illusion feeling of dizziness after spinning in a circle.

For people over the age of 65 (although it can happen at any age), another common cause of dizziness and loss of balance is **benign paroxysmal positional vertigo** (**BPPV**). BPPV is caused by one of the otoconia coming loose from the macula and finding its way into one of the semi-circular canals. There, it stimulates the hair cells, causing a feeling of rotation where there is none. It's not technically life-threatening (hence "benign"), but it is sometimes debilitating and very unpleasant! The most effective form of treatment is called the Epley maneuver—a series of positions that essentially guide the otoconia back where it belongs.

Benign paroxysmal positional vertigo (BPPV) feeling of imbalance caused by otoconia detaching from the macula and moving to the semi-circular canals.

Summary

Sound is the mechanical disruption of a medium (usually air) caused by the vibration of something. That pattern of disruption is captured by the outer ear, amplified by the middle ear, and changed into neural language by the inner ear. The part of the inner ear that translates sound into neural firings is called the cochlea—a spiral-shaped, fluid-filled organ. Inside the cochlea is the basilar membrane and the organ of Corti. These are responsible for conveying the pitch and loudness of the sounds to the brain. Also, part of the inner ear is the vestibular system. This system is made of five organs: three semi-circular canals that sense angular motion, and two otolith organs that sense tilt and linear acceleration.

Notes

1. Note that this means there is no sound in space—space is a vacuum, so there's no medium for the sound to travel through. All those science fiction movies that showed loud explosions happening in space were lying to you.
2. Technically, the movement of the molecules *is* the temperature.
3. It's not clear what came first evolutionarily—it's possible we developed ears that helped us hear each other, or it's possible we developed voices that took advantage of our particular ears.
4. This is why babies get so many ear infections—their Eustachian tubes are basically horizontal (they have no necks!) so the middle ear cannot drain properly.
5. This is why yawning or chewing gum helps—your jaw pushes against the tubes, encouraging them to open.
6. Fittingly, "cochlea" is Latin for snail shell.
7. If it *could*, it would be about 2mm in diameter on average and 35mm long.
8. Think of a tube of toothpaste.
9. These Hz are actual measurements from the actual guitar in the photo.
10. The inner hair cells are responsible for conveying the signal; the outer hair cells are responsible for cleaning that signal before transmission.
11. At least, not in humans. Fish, bird, and amphibian hair cells regenerate, no problem. They are much more suited to loud rock band concerts than we are.
12. In fact, before we knew what it actually did, scientists thought it was the *entrance* to the cochlea, hence the name "vestibular" from the Latin for "entrance".

6 Somatosensory Systems

Before we begin, we want you to get a feel for your surroundings. Like, literally *feel* your surroundings. Close your eyes and touch this book (or tablet, or whatever you are reading this on). Is it smooth or rough? What is its shape? Is it cool to the touch or warm? Relatively heavy or relatively light? Ok, now put the book aside and do some stretches (yes, with your eyes closed). Reach for your toes, lift your hands high into the air, cross your arms. How easy is for you to tell where your hands and arms are? Now pinch yourself. Maybe on the forearm or hand. Not too hard, mind you. But hard enough that you feel it, at least a little. What did the pinch feel like at first? Hurt a little, right? Maybe sharp? What does it feel like now? Hurts less, but also differently, right? Maybe throbby?

The myth of the five senses is particularly problematic when it comes to the sense of "touch", or what is formally called the **somatosensory system**. We lump a lot of very different experiences together under this one umbrella but a better way to think about it would be as several interconnected and overlapping senses responding to several interconnected and overlapping energy patterns. We feel the movements of our own bodies—the stretch of a muscle (ouch, but maybe the good kind), the bend of a joint (ouch, and maybe the bad kind), the pain of damage to the body (ouch, and *definitely* the bad kind), and so on. We also feel many different properties of the things we touch—texture, warmth, shape, and so on. And we can feel those properties by touching them with our hands, or by holding an object (say a pencil) and moving it across the same surface.

> **Somatosensory systems** commonly referred to as "touch". A collection of sensory systems that sense the body and nearby surfaces.

Because of the broad and overlapping nature of the somatosensory system, this chapter is going to be organized slightly differently than the previous ones. Rather than starting with what is *being felt*, we are going to start with *what is doing the feeling*. We will start with the sense organ with most of the somatosensory receptors—the skin. Then we will go through each of the different types of receptors in the somatosensory system, which *far* outnumber the types of receptors in the sense systems described in previous chapters. Combined. For each receptor, we will describe its physiology and what type of stimulation causes it to have the largest reaction. For some receptors, that will be a type of exploratory *movement* on a surface (see Box 6.1); for others it will be a type of energy or change in energy (like heat); and for still others it will be a type of movement of the body (like changing the position of the limbs) or damage to the body (like a cut).

DOI: 10.4324/9781032690964-7

Box 6.1 Types of Exploration by Touch

One night, during a storm, Fred's power went out. *Drat.* The first thing he did was try to find the flashlight he kept in his junk drawer (we all have one, right?). When he found the drawer and opened it, he started by pressing on each of the objects until he felt ones that were hard (he also keeps some of his stuffed animals in the same junk drawer, so he was ignoring all the squishy objects). Each time he felt a hard object, he would then run his fingers along the edges of the object to feel its contours and—hopefully—identify its shape. Eventually he found something that was both hard and roughly flashlight-shaped. Excellent! Of course, then he remembered that he actually has *two* flashlights. The one with the *smooth* handle was broken, and the one with the *rough* handle was working, but neither one of them had any batteries in them at the moment. *Drat (again).*

He ran his hand across the flashlight-shaped object that he found and realized that it was rough and not smooth. Good! Now he just needed to find the batteries. He knew that the flashlight takes AA batteries, but the drawer also has both AA and AAA batteries. When he found candidate batteries, he hefted each one in his hand. He figured that the slightly lighter batteries must be the AAAs and the slightly heavier ones must be the AAs. Almost there! Then he inserted the AA batteries (ensuring that they were oriented correctly), clicked the flashlight on, and . . . nothing. Too bad there is no way to tell whether or not batteries are dead just by feeling. Sigh. Again.

Before the power went out, Fred had been drinking tea in the living room. It was his third cup of the day, so he knew there were several cups on the table, only one of which had tea in it. He felt his way over to the table and then put the palm of his hand against each one to feel the temperature. Once he found the warm one, he decided to sit in the dark and drink his tea in peace.

Fred's experience illustrates what Lederman and Klatzky (1987) found: that people explore surfaces using different ways depending on the property of the object or surface they want to perceive. Try it yourself! To perceive hardness, people tend to poke or push on an object. To identify shape, people will run their fingers around the outside of the object (called contour following). To identify surface texture, people will run their hands over the object in a lateral (i.e., side-to-side) motion. To perceive weight, typically people will hold the object flat in their hand or hands and heft it (i.e., lift it up and down a bit). Finally, to determine temperature, people will typically hold their hands (or more likely their fingers) steady against the object.

All of these situations describe what Gibson (1962) called *active touch*—when a perceiver actively explores a surface or object by touching it. This is opposed to *passive touch*—when the perceiver is *being touched* by something. While some research (particularly early research) focused on passive touch, the vast majority has focused on active touch (see Chapter 18).

Socratic Question: How does Fred's experience during the power outage in Box 6.1 illustrate the concept of "active touch"? Lederman and Klatzky (1987) described the touch behaviors that they observed as "exploratory procedures". Why do you think that they chose this description?

Skin

Your skin has a lot of jobs. It keeps bacteria and other bad stuff out and keeps your organs and other you-stuff in. It protects your organs from ultraviolet radiation (which would burn them up) and generates vitamin D when stimulated by sunlight (which you need for a lot of reasons, so go outside more often!). Skin is the largest organ in the body, weighing an average of 4 lbs (or 1.8 Kg) and covering 2 square meters of space—the size of a standard door! It is also the location of most (though, again, not all) of your somatosensory receptors.

Look at the back of your arm. Notice the little hairs? The vast majority of the skin on your body is covered in hair, although some of the hairs are so small as to be nearly invisible. This type of skin is (appropriately) called **hairy skin**. The only skin on your body that does *not* have hairs are parts of your face (lips, eyelids), the palms of your hands (including the palm-side of your fingers and your fingertips), and the bottoms of your feet. This kind of (non-hairy) skin is called **glabrous skin**. Glabrous skin also has different and more densely packed somatosensory receptors than hairy skin (more on this later).

> **Hairy skin** skin with hair follicles. Has less densely packed and different mechanoreceptors than glabrous skin.
>
> **Glabrous (non-hairy) skin** skin without hair follicles. Epidermis is thicker than hairy skin. Additionally, it has more densely packed and different mechanoreceptors than hairy skin.

> **Epidermis** outer layer of skin; thicker in glabrous skin.
>
> **Dermis** middle layer of skin.
>
> **Subcutis** innermost layer of skin, made of fat and connective tissue.

Skin (see Figure 6.1) has three layers, the **epidermis,** the **dermis**, and the **subcutis** (also called subcutaneous tissue). The epidermis is the outer layer of the skin (epi means top). It is the part of Fred's skin that got burned when he spent too much time in the sun in Chapter 2. Dermis is the middle layer. The innermost layer, the subcutis, connects the other layers of skin to the underlying muscles. The thickness of the patch of skin illustrated in Figure 6.1 varies across different parts of the body, but on average it is only 2mm thick (the thickness of a credit card or a contact lens!). Packed into this thin layer of tissue are several different types of somatosensory receptors. Which receptors and how densely packed those receptors are depends on the type of skin and location on the body.

> Socratic Question: This skin in the largest organ in the human body. What does this tell you about the importance of the touch system? Why do you think that so much less is known about the touch system than the visual system or the auditory system?

Somatosensory Receptors

As we have already mentioned, there are several different types of somatosensory receptors. The majority of those in the skin detect different kinds of mechanical disturbances to the tissue in which they are embedded. Different types are specialized to detect different types of

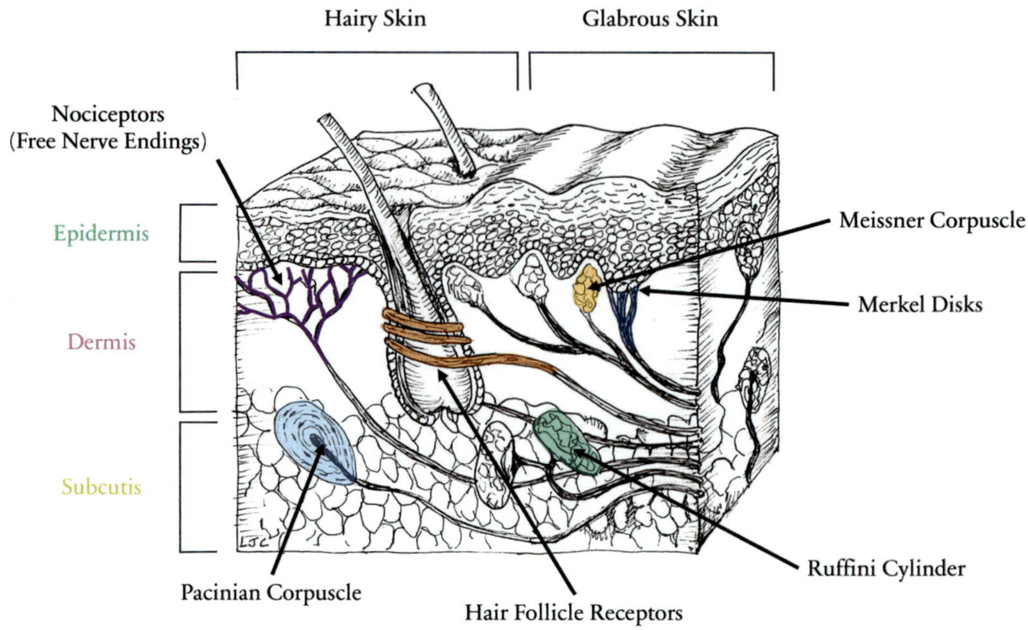

Figure 6.1 There are two types of skin, hairy skin and glabrous (non-hairy) skin. Both have three layers, epidermis, dermis, and subcutis. There are various somatosensory receptors in all layers of skin.

disturbances such as pressing, twisting, vibrating, and stretching. These cells are maximally stimulated when particular kinds of exploratory movements are performed on a given surface that bring about those kinds of disturbances (see Box 6.1). In addition to mechanoreceptors, your body also has cells that respond to many other types of stimulation such as heat or damage. In this section, we will describe each of these kinds of receptors in turn, along with the exploratory movements performed on a given surface that maximally stimulate that particular kind of cell, and what those movements and the response of the cells might reveal about the surface. In the next section, we will describe how these cells are connected to the brain.

Mechanoreceptors

In general, cells that respond to mechanical disturbances are called **mechanoreceptors**. Different kinds of mechanoreceptors differ from each other in several ways: their location in the skin, their shape, the type of mechanical disturbance that creates maximal stimulation, the size of their receptive field, and the type of nerve that carries the signal to the brain.

Mechanoreceptors specialized organs that respond to different types of mechanical disturbances of the skin.

Merkel disks (SA1) small receptors in the junction between the epidermis and the dermis. Are slowly adapting and have small receptive fields. Sensitive to pressure; aid in perceiving texture and shape.

Merkel Disks

Merkel disks (see Figure 6.2) are receptors found in glabrous skin (*not* hairy

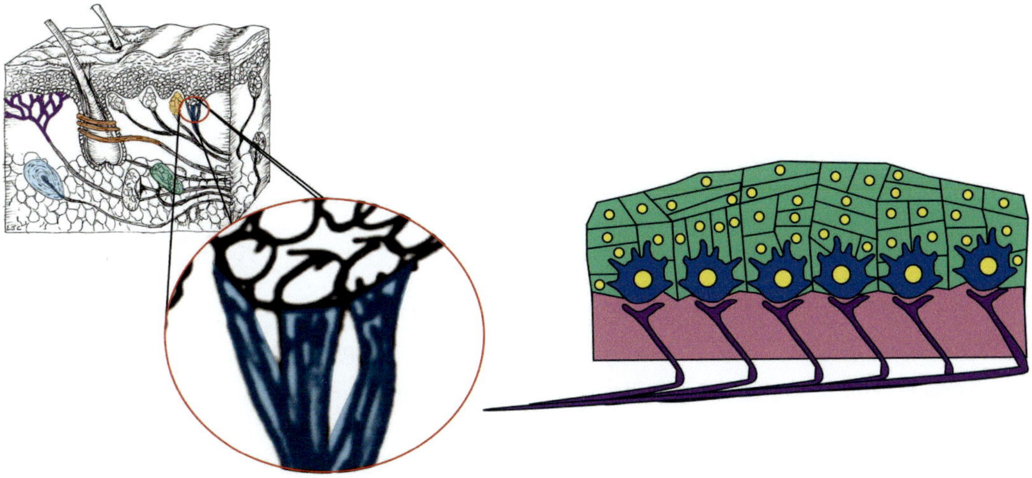

Figure 6.2 Merkel cells, also known as Merkel disks.

skin). They are small (like *really* small—*tiny fractions* of a mm) and are embedded in the junction between the epidermis and the dermis. They respond to pressure on the skin caused by surfaces that you touch or surfaces that touch you). As you might expect, given their size, they have small receptive fields. That is, they only respond to pressure in a very small area of the skin (roughly circular patches a few mm in diameter). Mechanoreceptors, like Merkel disks, that have small receptive fields are called **type 1 receptors** (see Figure 6.3, *top left*).

Type I receptors mechanoreceptors near the surface of the skin with small receptive fields.

Merkel disks are also part of the class of **slowly adapting (SA)** receptors. When pressure is first applied to the skin, they will fire rapidly. Then they will continue to fire so long as the pressure continues, but at a decreasing rate over time (see Figure 6.3, *bottom left*). They stop firing when the pressure stops. Merkel disks are densely packed, particularly in the fingertips. They are best suited to detecting small differences in texture and shape of a given object.

Slowly adapting receptors (SA receptors) respond continuously during the entire time a stimulus is applied. Response rate decreases over time, but does not go to baseline until the stimulus is removed.

When you explored this book through touch at the beginning of this chapter (you did do that, right?), Merkel disks were particularly stimulated when you felt the ridges of the edges of the paper and the sharp corners of the book because these parts created points or pressure on your skin. But they are useful for other things, too. Try this: take out a pad of paper on which you have written some notes. Close your eyes and feel the paper to see if you can tell where the writing is and where the page is blank. The impressions on the page also create points of pressure on your skin, though much more subtly. The Merkel receptors are specifically and maximally stimulated when surfaces are explored in these particular ways.

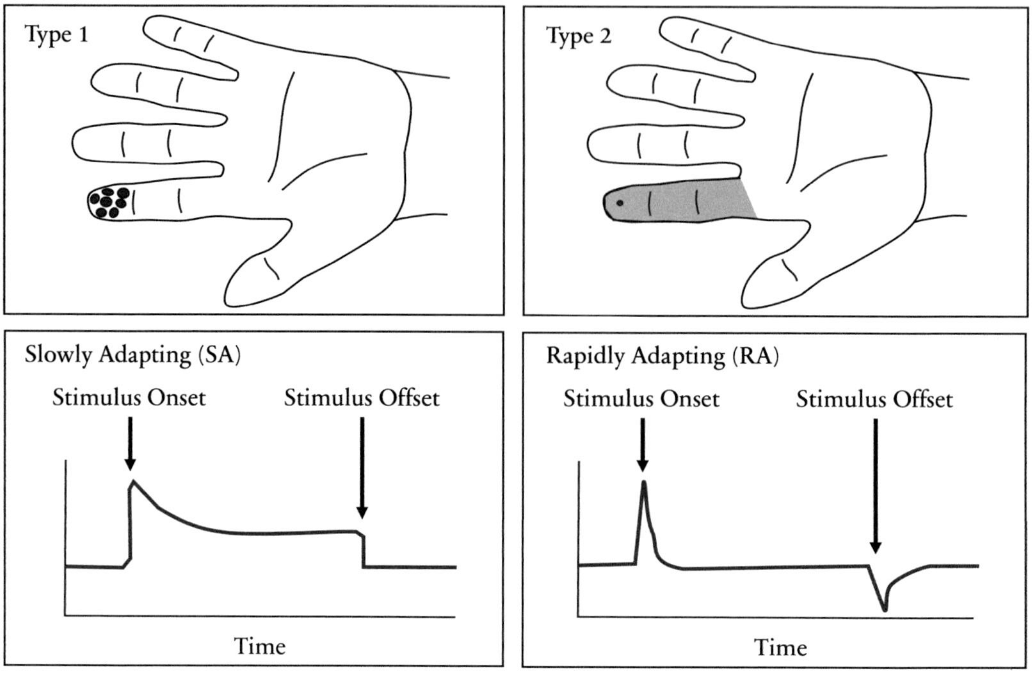

Figure 6.3 Top left, Type 1 receptors are near the surface of the skin and have relatively small receptive fields. Top right, Type 2 receptors are deeper in the skin and have relatively large receptive fields. Bottom left, the response of slowly adapting (SA) receptors. SA receptors respond the entire time the pressure is applied, but at a decreasing rate. Bottom right, the response of rapidly adapting (RA) receptors. RA receptors respond when the pressure is applied and when it is removed, but not during continuous pressure.

These receptors probably fired when Fred was trying to find the ridges on the side of the flashlight or the latch of the battery compartment on his flashlight.

Meissner Corpuscles

In glabrous skin, **Meissner corpuscles** (see Figure 6.4) are also at the junction between the epidermis and the dermis. These are larger cells (several times the size of Merkel disks), consisting of a nerve ending surrounded by a capsule. When there is pressure on that capsule, the fibers inside bend the nerve, causing a brief increase in the firing rate. When the force is removed, the *unbending* of the nerve creates a brief *decrease* in firing rate. Or in other words, the corpuscles respond at the onset of pressure and the offset of pressure, but not during continuous pressure. In this way, they belong to the class of receptors called **rapidly adapting (RA)** receptors (see Figure 6.3, *bottom right*).

Meissner corpuscles (RA1) receptors that are only found in the junction between the epidermis and the dermis in glabrous skin. Are rapidly adapting and have small receptive fields. Particularly sensitive to changes in pressure; aid in controlling grip.

Rapidly adapting (RA receptors) also called on/off cells. Respond with a brief spike of in action potentials when the stimulus begins and a brief decrease when the stimulus is removed, otherwise they remain at baseline firing.

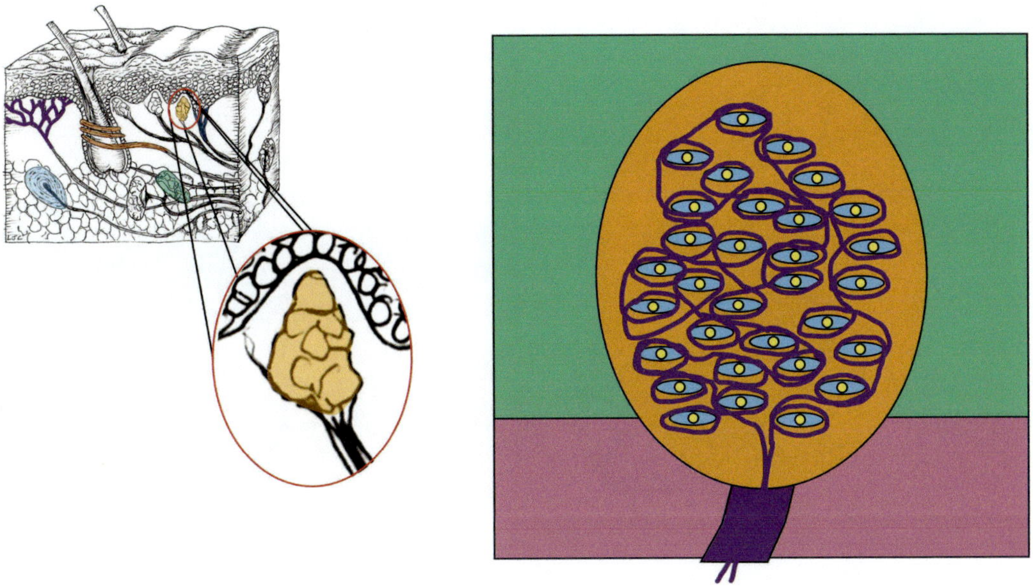

Figure 6.4 Meissner corpuscles.

Since Meissner corpuscles are sensitive to the onset and offset of pressure, movement of an object or surface across the skin will stimulate them in sequence along the direction of movement. This sequential stimulation of Meissner corpuscles is partly responsible for our awareness of whether we are holding an object firmly enough. Pick up a book and deliberately hold it loosely enough that it starts to slip out of your grip. But maybe don't use *this* book just in case you accidentally drop it—it's a really good book! Whichever book you choose, when it starts to slip, you can immediately tell that the book is falling and then quickly tighten your grip to keep from dropping it. This sliding that occurs between the book and your skin maximally stimulates the Meissner corpuscles. And this is an indication that you might not be holding the object firmly enough.

Ruffini Cylinders

Deeper in the dermis of the skin (both hairy and glabrous), are **Ruffini cylinders** (see Figure 6.5). They are also slowly adapting, but unlike the Merkel receptors, they have much larger (but still roughly circular) receptive fields. Mechanoreceptors with large receptive fields like these are called **Type 2 receptors** (see Figure 6.3, *top right*). Ruffini cylinders are shaped like a tube with a bulge in the middle—sort of looks like a cylinder, right? When the receptor is stretched, the nerve endings inside the bulge are squished, which increases their firing rate. In this way, they are responsible for conveying information about how your skin

Ruffini cylinders (SA2) receptors found in the dermis. Are slowly adapting and respond to being stretched; contribute to proprioception and some thermoreception.

Type 2 receptors mechanoreceptors deeper in the skin with larger receptive fields.

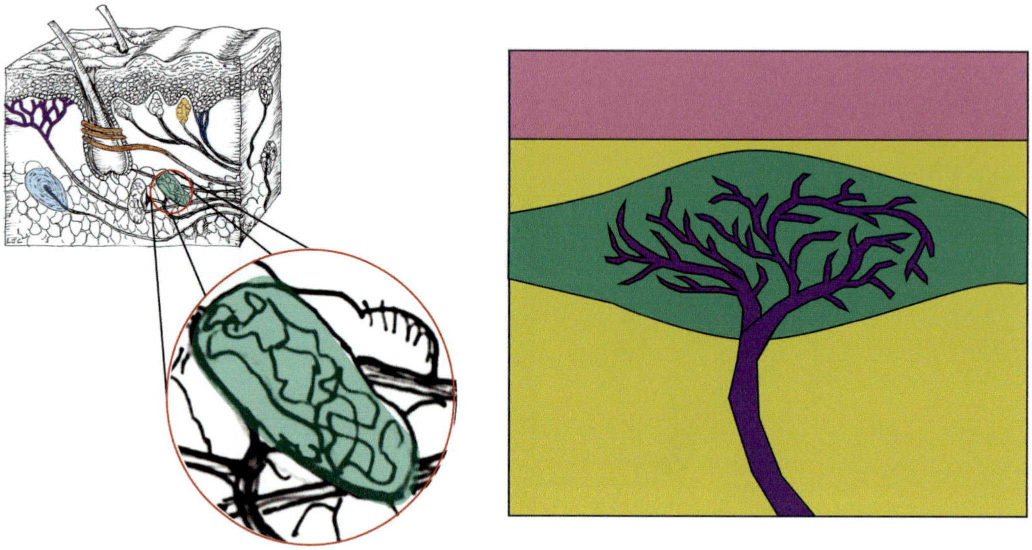

Figure 6.5 Ruffini cylinders.

is stretching. While they are located throughout the skin, they are more densely packed near joints. And this makes sense—the joints are where a lot of the stretching is taking place!

The closing number of *From Cockney to Yankee* was a dance sequence that required Fred to stretch out his fingers out wide (jazz hands!), then relax them; bring them to his face, then straighten his arms; kick his legs out straight, then bend his knees to his chest. Whew! Try it for yourself. When you do, pay attention to the feeling of stretching in your skin. The Ruffini cylinders respond to this stretching, but only in part. In this way, they contribute to **proprioception**—knowing where your body is and what position your limbs are in (we'll discuss more about proprioception and the role of Ruffini cylinders later in this chapter).

Proprioception the sense of the body's position.

Ruffini cylinders are also involved in the feeling of temperature, but in a less straightforward or well-understood way. They are responsible for the feeling of warmth that you get from a burn *after* the hot surface is removed. Once the skin is no longer being stimulated with the actual hot surface, burns still feel *hot*. While the mechanism of this is not entirely clear, scientists know that the Ruffini cylinders are responsible because when they are burned away by a particularly deep burn, that feeling disappears.

Pacinian Corpuscles

Pacinian corpuscles (RA2) receptors found in the subcutis. Are rapidly adapting and have large receptive fields. Particularly sensitive to vibration; contribute to perceiving texture.

Even *deeper* in the skin—well, relatively speaking anyway—in the subcutis, are **Pacinian corpuscles** (see Figure 6.6). They are rapidly adapting (like the Merkel disks) but have large receptive fields (type

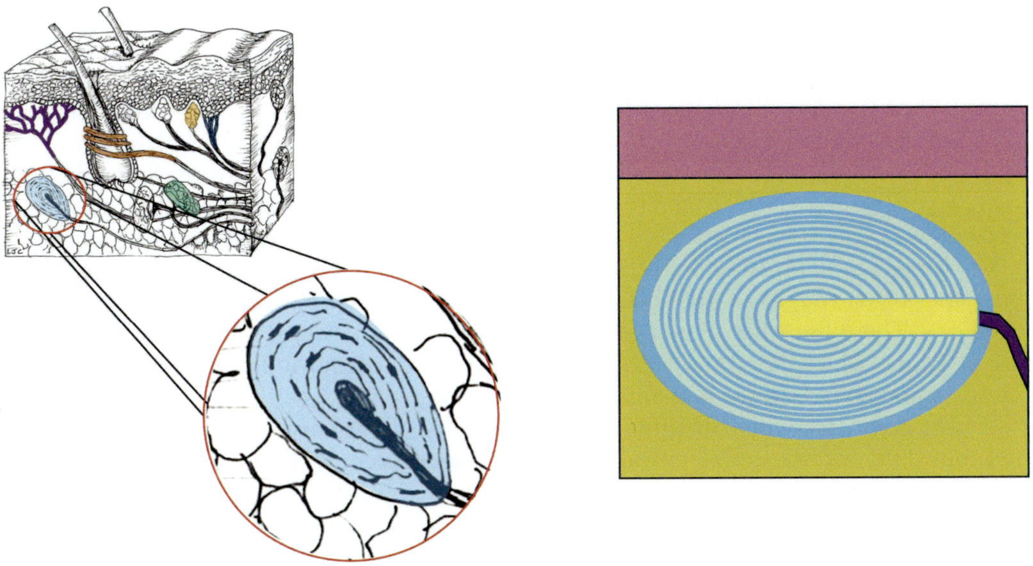

Figure 6.6 Pacinian corpuscles.

2, like the Ruffini cylinders). Pacinian corpuscles have an onion-like structure: a nerve ending surrounded by thin layers (called lamellae) separated by fluid. This structure contributes to their rapid adaptation. The onset of firm sustained pressure on this structure will disturb the embedded nerve, but will also cause the fluid to push out to the sides of the cell. Once the fluid is pushed out of the way, the nerve has room to return to its original position, which returns the receptor to its baseline rate of firing. When the pressure is *removed,* it once again disturbs the nerve in the opposite direction as the original push. This temporarily decreases the activity of the cell (see Figure 6.3, *bottom right*).

On the other hand, *vibrations* will cause a wave motion that maximally (and continuously) stimulates the embedded nerve. To understand why the ability to feel vibrations might be helpful, run your fingers across a smooth surface like a page in a book. Now run your fingers

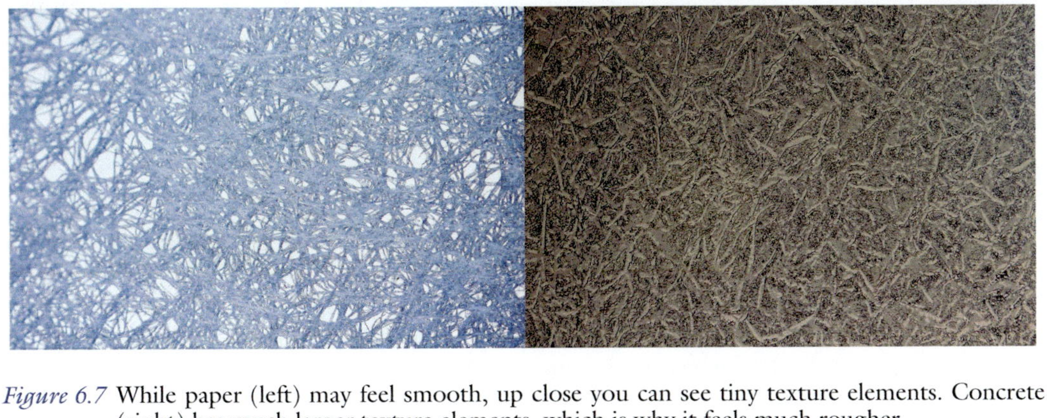

Figure 6.7 While paper (left) may feel smooth, up close you can see tiny texture elements. Concrete (right) has much larger texture elements, which is why it feels much rougher.

over a rough surface like a slab of concrete. During each of those movements, the skin of your fingers encountered the fine texture elements on each surface (see Figure 6.7) as a series of pressures on the skin. While it may seem completely smooth, paper has very tiny texture elements. When you run your finger across the paper, the very densely packed texture elements compress the corpuscles rapidly (i.e., it causes rapid vibration of the skin). A slab of concrete, on the other hand, has less dense, taller, and continuously changing texture elements. When you run your fingers across concrete, the sparsely packed texture elements compress the corpuscles less rapidly (i.e., it causes slower vibration of the skin).

The frequency of pressure on the skin (i.e., the rate of vibration) is an indication of the texture (smooth vs. rough) of the object. Pacinian corpuscles are particularly sensitive to these vibrations. These fire when Fred pets Topsy (elephants have rough skin) or a marble sculpture of Topsy (which does not), smooths down his silk or corduroy shirts, or feels around his (mostly smooth) face to see if he missed a spot shaving.

At this point, it's worth briefly recapping what we have covered. So far, we have covered four different types of mechanoreceptors: Merkel receptors (SA1), Meissner corpuscles (RA1), Ruffini cylinders (SA2), and Pacinian corpuscles (RA2). Notice two of these are rapidly adapting, and two are slowing adapting. And two of these are type 1 and two are type 2. Nice and symmetric that way, right? These (symmetric) four are the classic mechanoreceptors and older textbooks will list them as the complete set. They are not.

Hair Follicle Receptors

In hairy skin, there are receptors wrapped around the base of the hair follicles, called (predictably) **hair follicle receptors**. They respond to displacement of the hairs in the skin. In very hairy creatures (like cats and dogs), these receptors likely aid in proprioception. In less hairy creatures (like humans and Fred), the hairs are not densely packed enough to serve that function. So, when might you (or Fred) notice the activity of hair follicle receptors? Probably the most salient experience involving these cells is piloerection, otherwise known as "goosebumps". When this happens, the hair follicle is lifted enough to stimulate the hair follicle receptor—and for you to notice. But they also seem to be involved in the pleasant feeling we get from being touched (Jönsson et al., 2017). This is probably true for hairy animals as well. Of course, we cannot *ask* the hairy animals in our lives, but they certainly *seem* to also get pleasure from stimulation of the hair follicle receptors through petting.

> **Hair follicle receptors** nerve endings wrapped around the base of the hair follicle in hairy skin. Responsible for proprioception in very hairy animals. Likely involved in feelings of pleasure when pet.

Other Somatosensory Receptors

While some of the receptors we're going to discuss in this section do *sometimes* respond to mechanical disturbances, that is not the primary function of these receptors. Instead, they respond maximally to other types of stimulation such as temperature changes or damage to the body. And while some of these remaining receptors are in the skin, somatosensory receptors are found all over the body—in muscles, joints, and even in various digestive organs, etc.

Thermoreceptors—"Cold" and "Warm"

There are two different types of cells (called **thermoreceptors**) that respond to temperature changes. "Cold" thermoreceptors have ion channels that open in response to a *decrease* in temperature; "warm" thermoreceptors have ion channels that open in response to an *increase* in temperature. In either case, the change in temperature causes an increase in the rate of firing of the receptor. There are a *lot* more cold than warm receptors, with a ratio of about 30:1.

Thermoreceptors cells that respond to changes in temperature. One type ("cold") responds when the temperature goes down; one type ("warm") responds when the temperature goes up.

One thing to notice here is that these receptors respond to *changes* in temperature, not *absolute* temperature. Like when Fred walks inside his warm living room after being out in the snow—the room feels very hot! But after a while, it feels like a normal temperature. He noticed the *change* in temperature—from cold to hot—more than the temperature itself.

You can see this for yourself by trying this demonstration at home. Get three bowls of water—one cold (not *really* cold, just chilly—like refreshing drink cold); one room temperature; and one hot (not *really* hot, just nice and warm—like bathwater hot). Put your left hand into the cold bowl of water and your right hand into the hot bowl of water. Leave them there for a few moments, just long enough to "get used to it".

Then simultaneously move both hands to the room temperature bowl. The left hand (which was in the cold bowl) will feel the water as warm, maybe even hot. The right hand (which was in the hot bowl) will feel the water as cool, maybe even cold (see Figure 6.8). Weird, right? The lesson from this demonstration is that the thermoreceptors do not respond to absolute temperature. If they did, the room temperature water *would feel the same to both hands*. Instead, the thermoreceptors detect a change in temperature. The room-temperature water felt different to the two hands because the temperature changed in different ways for each hand.

Socratic Question: What does the experiment depicted in Figure 6.8 reveal about perceiving temperature? What does it reveal to us about perceiving *in general*?

Last summer, Fred went on vacation in Guadalajara, Mexico. It was a wonderful trip. He tried all the local cuisine, including *birria* and *jericalla*. But he went during summer and so it was really *hot!* However, the hotel he was staying in had marble floors, and he noticed something very strange—no matter how hot it got, the floors always felt cool under his feet. That wasn't true of other surfaces in his room. The wooden desk felt sort of room-temperature, and the fuzzy blankets always felt warm (particularly if he cuddled under them for a while). What is weird is that even though these surfaces all felt like they were different temperatures (especially the marble floor), they were all the *exact same temperature*—namely, room temperature. *Wait, what*? Yes! *No, really*? Yes, really.

These surfaces don't differ in temperature, but they do differ in what is called **thermal conduction efficiency**. To

Thermal conduction efficiency the relative speed with which a material diffuses heat energy.

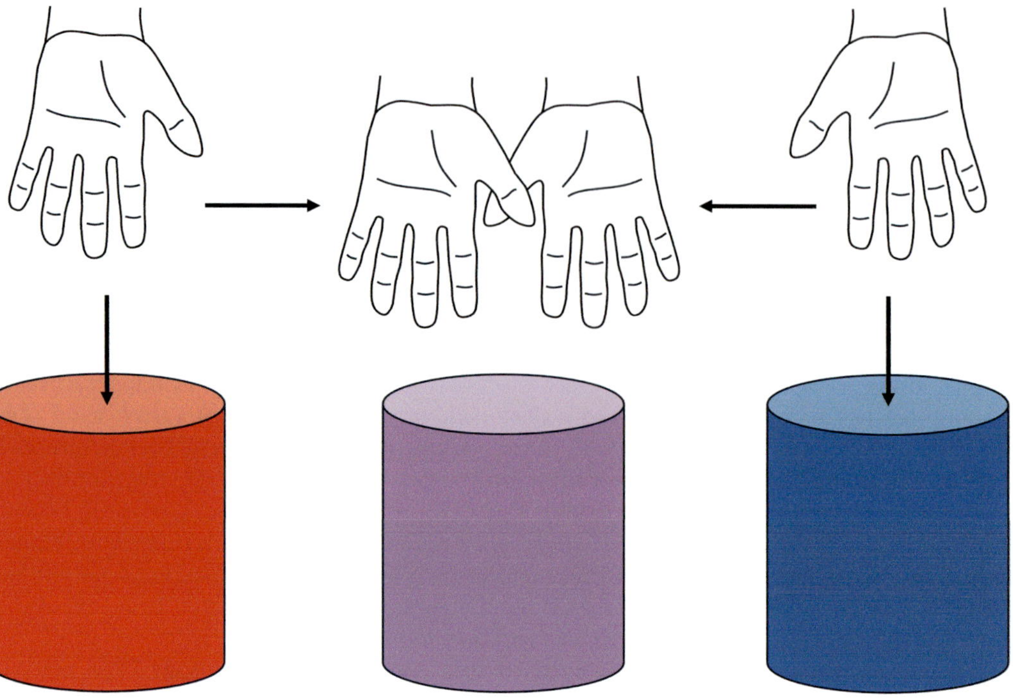

Figure 6.8 A demonstration of relative temperature sensing. A hand that has been in cool water will feel room-temperature water as warm. A hand that has been in warm water will feel room-temperature as cold.

understand what that means, you first have to know that cold is not really a thing. *Wait? What?* Fred surely thought cold was a thing that one winter he spent cross-country skiing across Norway. But it's true. *Heat* is a thing. Cold is not. *Cold* is just the absence of heat. Heat is energy. Your hand is warm because it has energy in it. Also, heat energy (like all energy, really) is always trying to even out. Heat will always move from areas of higher heat energy (like the *inside* of Fred's cabin in Norway) to areas of lower heat energy (like the *outside* of Fred's cabin) unless it is stopped (which is why people always told you to close the door during winter!). The movement of heat (or any other kind of energy) from areas of higher concentrations to areas of lower concentration is called diffusion.

Most surfaces in a room will be cooler than your hand because your hand is *well above* room temperature. So, when you touch one of these surfaces, the heat energy will leave your hand and enter the surface. The material of the surface will determine *how quickly* that transfer happens. If the material is something like tile or marble, that transfer will happen very quickly. Tile and marble are very efficient at conducting heat (they have high thermal conduction efficiency). This is why the marble floors always felt cool under Fred's feet. This is also why Fred really appreciated the heated tile floors in the bathroom in his cabin in Norway.

Other surfaces like wool and other fabrics transfer heat very slowly. In fact, they transfer heat so slowly that the air in between the wool and your skin might absorb more heat than the wool itself. Consequently, the wool or fabric will feel warm. This is why the blankets felt warm to Fred. This is also why Fred wore sweaters on his ski trip!

In this way, thermoreceptors are conveying information about the surface we are touching—namely, its material properties.

Muscle Spindles, Golgi Tendon Organs, and Joint Receptors

All of the receptors we have discussed so far are found exclusively in the skin. Skin, after all, is what makes contact with surfaces, so it makes sense that these somatosensory receptors would be there. But there are other receptors in other locations of our bodies—in particular, in locations that would provide information about where those body parts are.

To start, let's take some time to understand how the body moves, using the arm as an example. Your arm consists of several bones—one in the upper arm, two in the forearm, and a bunch more in your wrist, hands, and fingers. Muscles are connected to the bones by strong flexible tissue called tendons. When the muscles contract, they pull on the tendons which, in turn, pull on the bones, and move your arm. That movement happens around a pivot point called a joint (see Figure 6.9, *left*).

If you were to swing a tennis racket, you would need to contract some muscles and relax others. Gravity would pull your arm (and the racket) towards the ground. So, at minimum, your muscles would need to work to resist the pull of gravity. Contracting the muscles will pull the bones which will swing the racket. But swinging the racket also pulls on the muscles. Muscles are elastic—kind of like a rubber band—and so they automatically pull back against any stretching. Your awareness of all of those forces (both those you control and the reactive forces) is proprioception.

In every muscle, there are receptors called **muscle spindles** (see Figure 6.9, *top right*). When the muscle is contracted, it

> **Muscle spindles** receptors in the center of muscles. They are stimulated by the lengthening of the muscle.

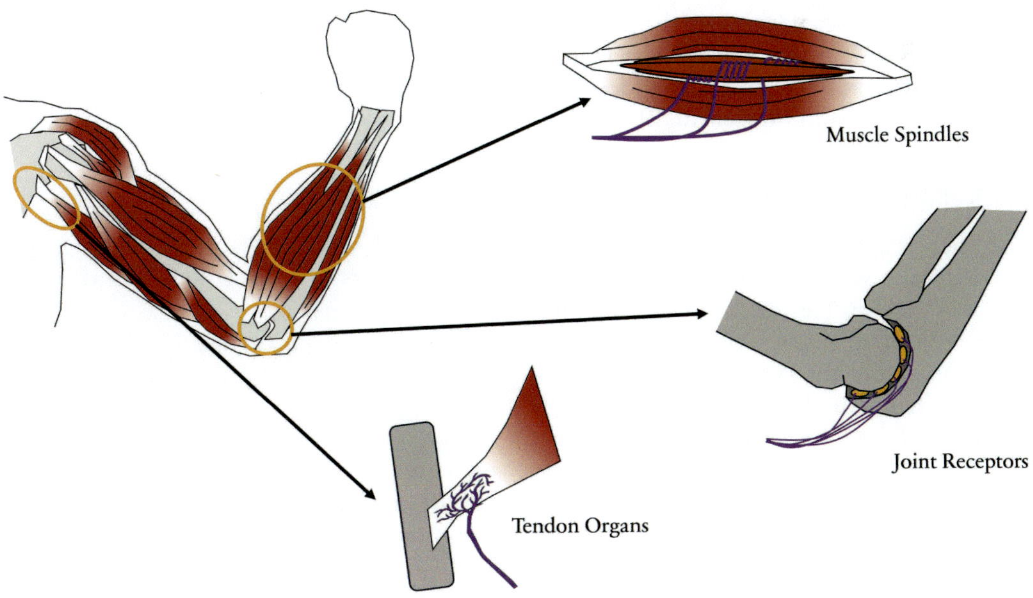

Figure 6.9 Left, muscles pull on bones to make your arm rotate around points called joints. Right, inside the joints are several different types of receptors that respond to changes in that joint.

gets shorter and fatter. When it is relaxed, it gets longer and thinner. The longer and thinner the muscle, the more the muscle presses down on the muscle spindles, causing an increase in its firing rate. In this way, the muscle spindles indicate muscle length (Macefield & Knellwolf, 2018).

In every tendon, there are receptors called **Golgi tendon organs** (named after Italian biologist named Camillo Golgi, who is perhaps best known for inventing a staining technique that allowed us to actually look at nerves for the first time).[1] These are branching structures that respond to the force with which a muscle is contracted (the more force, the higher the rate of firing; see Figure 6.9, *bottom right*). They will also respond to steady, sustained forces—if you are holding a heavy book, your muscles have to work to counter the weight of the book. Such forces pull on the tendons as well. In this way, the Golgi tendon organs provide information about muscle force (Schoultz & Swett, 1972).

Golgi tendon organs branching receptors in the tendons of the body. They are stimulated by the tendon changing shape during muscle contraction.

Finally, embedded in the space between bones at each joint are receptors called (predictably) **joint receptors** (see Figure 6.9, *middle right*). You might guess (as did most scientists for a long time) that these detect the exact angle of the joint, but you (and they) would be wrong. Don't feel bad, though. That's how science is supposed to work! Instead, joint receptors only seem to respond when the joint reaches the limit of its range of motion (Proske, 2023). For example, the joint receptors in your elbow respond when your arm is as straight as you can make it, or as bent as you can make it, but not really at any angle in between those two extremes.

Joint receptors receptors in the joints of the body. They are stimulated by the joint reaching its extreme positions.

Together with the Ruffini cylinders (the stretch organs in the skin), these three types of receptors detect position and movement of your limbs. It is generally understood that the muscle spindles do most of the work here; however, recent research also points to an additional role for the Ruffini cylinders in the skin, particularly in detecting limb *movement* (rather than position; Macefield, 2009).

Nociceptors (Free Nerve Endings)

The final receptor we are going to cover is probably one you wish you didn't have—the ones responsible for feeling pain. But while you might wish you didn't have them, as you'll see later, you should be grateful that you do! **Nociceptors** (also known as **Free Nerve Endings** because unlike most mechanoreceptors, they are not surrounded by other structures; see Figure 6.10) are located throughout much of our bodies.[2] They can be stimulated in a couple of ways, all of which indicate that the body is being—or is about to be—damaged.

Nociceptors (aka Free Nerve Endings) branching receptors found in various places in the body. They are stimulated by damage to (or threat of damage to) the body.

When cells are destroyed (or damaged) through force (by being cut, smashed, ripped, etc.) they release a chemical called cyclooxygenase which binds to the free nerve endings and causes them to send neurotransmitters called prostaglandins to the brain. Nociceptors are

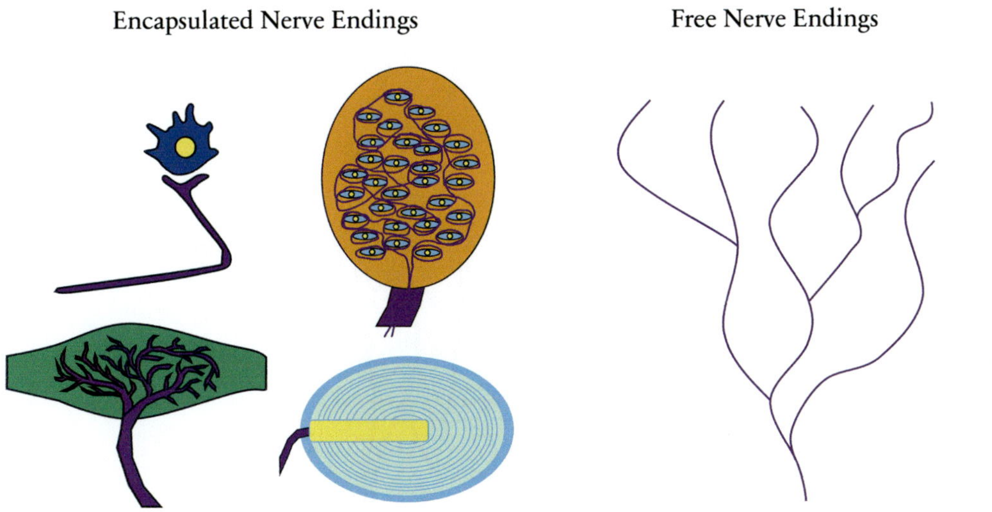

Figure 6.10 Nociceptors are also called "free nerve endings" because unlike other mechanoreceptors, they are not encapsulated.

also stimulated by pressure—they are deep enough in the skin that pressure stimulation at that depth is an indication that bodily damage is likely. Think about someone shaking your hand too tightly (ow!); it hurts because those nerve endings are being squished, and if they keep doing it, it will leave a bruise.

We'll talk about some of the other interesting ways that nociceptors can be stimulated in the next chapter, but even in those cases, pain is an indication of possible damage to the body. And this is ultimately why you do not want to be without this crucial sense—pain is a way of letting you know that your body is in danger and that you need to do something about it!

Pain insensitivity syndrome is a condition where the free nerve endings do not develop properly[3] and a person does not feel pain. Sadly, these people live very difficult lives. Many of them are blind, for example, because they did not learn to associate poking themselves in the eye with pain and as infants damaged their eyes beyond repair! They have dramatically reduced lifespans relative to the general population, largely because they do not experience the pain that indicates a life-threatening problem that needs to be fixed.

> **Pain Insensitivity Syndrome** a condition where the free nerve endings do not develop properly and the person cannot feel pain.

The type of pain we have been discussing is called **nociceptive pain** because it is pain caused by the stimulation of the pain receptors through damage to the tissues of the body. It can feel sharp, achy, throbbing, or stabbing, usually in a particular location. However, there are actually (at least) three different types of pain. **Neuropathic pain** is caused by damage to (and inflammation of) nerves. This kind of pain can feel like a burning, tingling, or stinging sensation. One common

> **Nociceptive pain** pain felt from the stimulation of the free nerve endings.
>
> **Neuropathic pain** pain felt from damage to and/or inflammation of nerves.

Figure 6.11 Sciatica is a common type of nerve pain. It is caused by a disk pressing on the sciatic nerve, which runs down the length of the leg.

example of this is sciatica. The sciatic nerve runs from the lower back down the length of the leg. A disk in the spine pressing on this nerve can cause it to become inflamed, causing pain down that entire pathway (see Figure 6.11).

Finally, there is **nociplastic pain**, caused by a general sensitization of the nervous system. This kind of pain can feel like a widespread dull aching or throbbing. This is a particularly complex type of pain, and also one that is notoriously difficult to treat (see Box 6.3). One example of this is fibromyalgia, a widespread sensitization of the nerves. Scientists aren't really sure why it happens, but it causes widespread pain, increased pain response to nociceptive and neuropathic pain, fatigue (probably from having a sustained sympathetic nervous system response!), and trouble sleeping. Sounds bad, and it is.

Nociplastic pain pain felt from a general oversensitization of the nervous system.

A subclass of nociceptors called pruriceptors are responsible for our feeling of "itchiness". They are sensitive to pruritogens (itch-causing substances like the chemical in a mosquito's bite) and small irritations of the skin (like a scratchy sweater). These signals travel the same neurological pathways as pain.

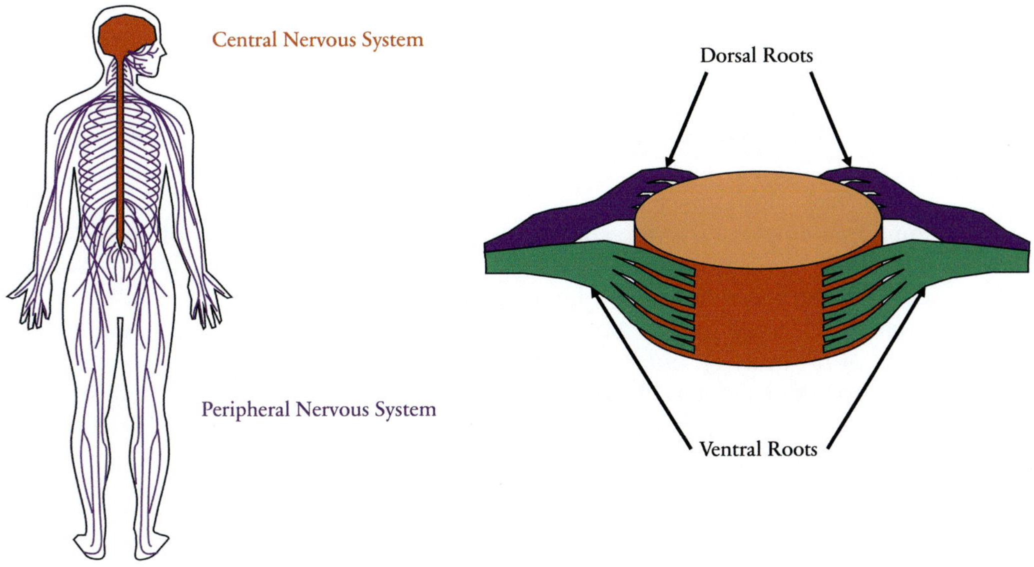

Figure 6.12 Anatomy of the central and peripheral nervous system (left) and the spine (right).

> Socratic Question: There are many kinds of somatosensory receptors—including mechanoreceptors, thermoreceptors, and nociceptors. How is this fact consistent with the historically popular idea of Specific Nerve Energies (from Chapter 1)?

Neurological Pathways for the Somatosensory System

All the neurons in the body are collectively called the nervous system. The brain and the spinal cord are the **central nervous system** and the branching neurons in the rest of the body are called the **peripheral nervous system** (see Figure 6.12, *left*). Nerves run from the somatosensory sense organs in the skin, muscles, tendons, and joints to the spine, then from the spine to the brain. The spine has 31 segments; each segment is a bony structure and the bones are separated (and cushioned in-between) by disks of cartilage.

> **Central nervous system** the brain and the spinal cord.
>
> **Peripheral nervous system** all neurons not part of the brain or the spinal cord.

Signals from the brain travel down the spine and leave a segment through the **ventral root**: a bundle of nerves that leaves the spine from the anterior (towards the belly) side.

> **Ventral root (of spine)** nerves that leave the spine from the anterior side, carry outgoing signals from the brain.

Box 6.2 Disruptions in Somatosensory Systems: The Case of Ian Waterman

One of the most famous case studies in the science of somatosensory systems is the story of Ian Waterman (Cole, 1995). In 1971, at the age of 19, Ian contracted a virus with flu-like symptoms. He cleared the virus in a few days, but while he slept his autoimmune system went haywire and attacked the ascending pathways of his nervous system. He woke up unable to feel anything below his neck. He was still able to move, but without proprioception found it intensely difficult.

He eventually learned how to move and walk by using his visual system to guide the movements of his body(!), but it required intense concentration and constant visual feedback. If someone turned off the lights or if he experienced an unexpected perturbation like sneezing or someone bumping into him, he would fall over! He eventually turned his experience into a positive: he made a career out of assessing various businesses (vacation spots, banks, hospitals, etc.) for their accessibility to people with disabilities.

While cases like Mr. Waterman's are rare, more common disruptions are possible. One condition, peripheral neuropathy, is a common side effect of badly managed diabetes. In that case, decreased blood flow damages the nerves in peripheral areas (most commonly the hands and feet), leading to numbness, pain, and so on. And damage to the dorsal root (through injury, infection, etc.) can cause partial or total numbness below the site of the injury.

Socratic Question: Think about Ian Waterman's predicament (Box 6.2). How easy or difficult is it to imagine being unable to use touch? Compare this to how easy or difficult it is to imagine being unable to see, hear, smell, or taste. What might this say about the touch system?

Signals from the somatosensory organs travel to the spine and enter a segment through the **dorsal root**: a bundle of nerves that enters the spine from the posterior (towards the back) side (see Figure 6.12, *right*).

Dorsal root (of spine) nerves that enter the spine on the posterior side, carrying signals from the body to the brain.

Two Ascending Pathways

The ascending somatosensory pathway (from sense organs to the brain) is really *two* pathways (see Figure 6.13): think of them like the express train and the local. In this metaphor, the express train is the **medial lemniscus** (ML) pathway. It is made of large fibers which allow faster transmission. These fibers are also **myelinated**; that is,

Medial Lemniscus (ML) pathway the faster, myelinated, ascending somatosensory pathway.

Myelination insulation of the nerves via a protein and lipid layer; speeds up neural transmission.

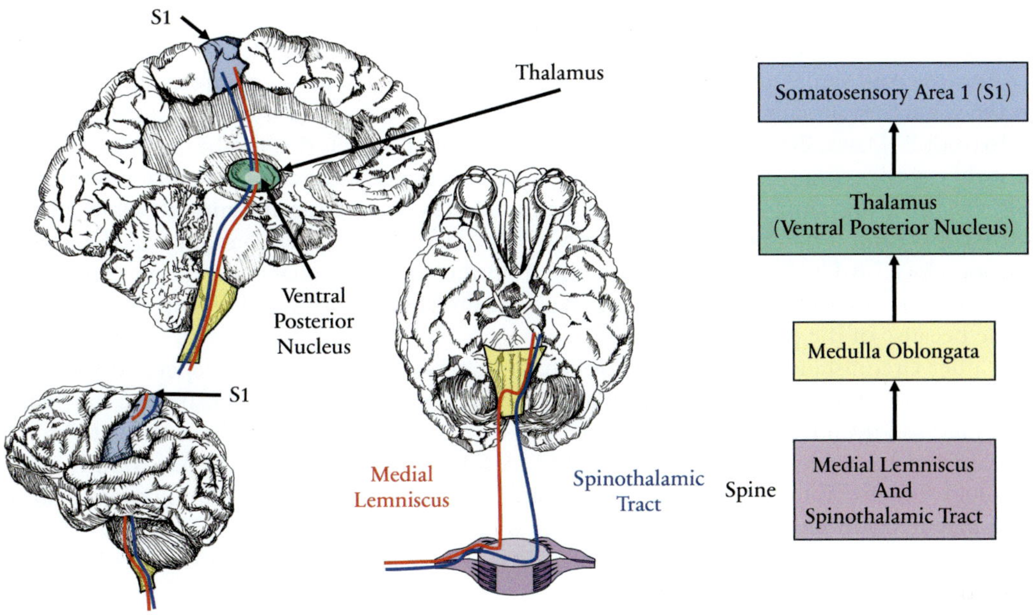

Figure 6.13 The neural pathways of the somatosensory system (only the pathway for the right side of the body is shown); see text for details.

they are covered in a protein and lipid (fatty) layer that acts as insulation. Think of an extension cord—yes, another metaphor—whose metal center is covered in a rubber coating. The metal wire carries the signal, the rubber coating ensures that the electricity stays in the wire and gets where it is going quickly. Myelinated fibers carry neural signals faster than non-myelinated in the same way. The ML pathway carries proprioceptive information to the brain and does so *very quickly*.

The local train is **spinothalamic pathway** (SP). It is made of smaller, non-myelinated fibers. Consequently, its transmission speed is noticeably slower than that of the ML pathway. The SP carries thermoreceptive information. That means that you will notice the forces that something generates on your skin more quickly that you will notice the temperature of that thing. Like when Topsy drooled on Fred's hand (ewwww!). He could feel the drop hit his hand (proprioceptive information) before he could feel that it was a bit warm (thermoreceptive information).

Spinothalamic (SP) pathway the slower, non-myelinated, ascending somatosensory pathway.

Pain signals travel along their own special pathways. Some pain information is sent via the ML pathway—specifically pain in response to burns and fast pressure (like when Fred hit his thumb with a hammer—*sharp pain*!). Some pain information is sent via the SP—specifically pain in response to slower pressure (like when Fred was teaching Topsy to shake hands with her trunk, and Topsy squeezed a little too hard—*discomfort*!), hot and cold, and toxic chemicals (like acid, or the chemical in a mosquito's bite—*itch*!). If intense enough, a pain signal can short-circuit the whole system. That is, the signal will travel to the appropriate spinal segment, but then—in addition to heading to the brain—the signal will travel to the ventral root of the spine. There, it will generate an unconscious (reflexive) movement. Like when

Fred accidentally touched a pot on the stove—*ouch!*—he began to jerk his hand away even before he was consciously aware that he was feeling pain. Weird, right?

And the pain signal gets even more complex than that! There is a complicated mechanism in the spine that actually *prevents* the pain signal from heading to the brain in a few situations (Moayedi & Davis, 2013). *Wait, what?* One situation in which this might occur is if you are already experiencing one kind of pain and then experience a different or more intense pain. For example, one time Fred had a sprained ankle (he wasn't careful enough while playing with Topsy) and it had been hurting for a while. Then when he was hanging up the antique cuckoo clock his Uncle Jimmy had given him on the wall, he managed to hit his thumb with the hammer—*sharp pain*! What was weird is that Fred actually stopped feeling the pain in the ankle because of the pain in his thumb!

Under circumstances like this, the mechanism acts like a "pain gatekeeper" to the brain. New pain or some other specific stimulation of the nerves (see Box 6.3) can close the "gate", keeping Fred from feeling that pain. The pain signal from his thumb "closes the gate" to the signal from his ankle pain. Not that we're recommending that you hit your thumb with a hammer the next time you have a sprained ankle—maybe try ice or acetaminophen instead? And maybe try to be more careful with your ankle, too.

Tickling and itching use same neural pathway as pain receptors. This is (probably one reason) why you can't tickle yourself: the expectation that the stimulation is coming sends a signal down the descending pathway and that closes the gate that would allow the signal of tickling through. This is also why scratching relieves itch—causing slight pain to the area closes the gate to the signal from the pruriceptors. When you scratch an itch, you are essentially doing the same thing Fred did with his hammer—but much more precisely—causing a new pain to make an old "pain" stop being noticeable!

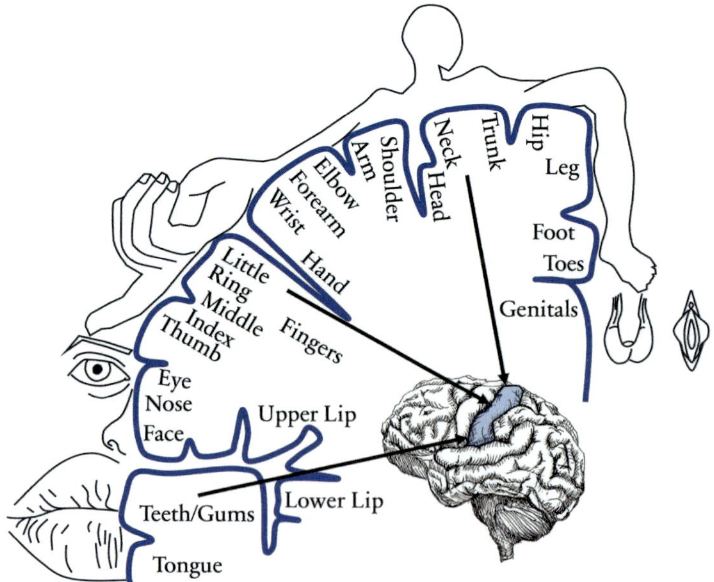

Figure 6.14 The somatosensory map of S1.

Neural Pathways

Imagine drawing a line down the center of your body, nose to lips to sternum to belly button all the way down to the ground. Stimulation that occurs on your body to the left of that line enters the spine through the left dorsal roots. Everything to the right of that line enters the spine through the right dorsal roots. Both the SP and ML pathways end up crossing sides (that is, signals from the right end up going over to the left side of the body and vice versa). The only difference is *where* they cross. The SP pathway crosses to the other side of the spine right away; the ML pathway crosses once it gets to the medulla oblongata. Either way, the signal from the right side of the body goes through the left side of the medulla oblongata before heading to the ventral posterior nucleus of the *left* thalamus. The signal from the left side of the body goes to the corresponding location of the *right* thalamus[4] (see Figure 6.13).

From the thalamus, the signal travels to S1 (for **S**omatosensory Area **1**; see Figure 6.14). The signals projected from various parts of the body project to specific areas of S1, creating a rough *somatotopic map* of the body. That is, signals that started next to each other in the world (say, a signal from the knee and a signal from the calf) end up next to each other in S1 (first discovered by Wilder Penfield in 1937 during brain surgery; see Figure 6.15).[5]

However, there is not a 1-to-1 correspondence between the size of the body part and the size of the brain region dedicated to that part. Just as we covered in Chapter 3, where there was cortical magnification for the fovea; here, there is cortical magnification for certain parts of the body.

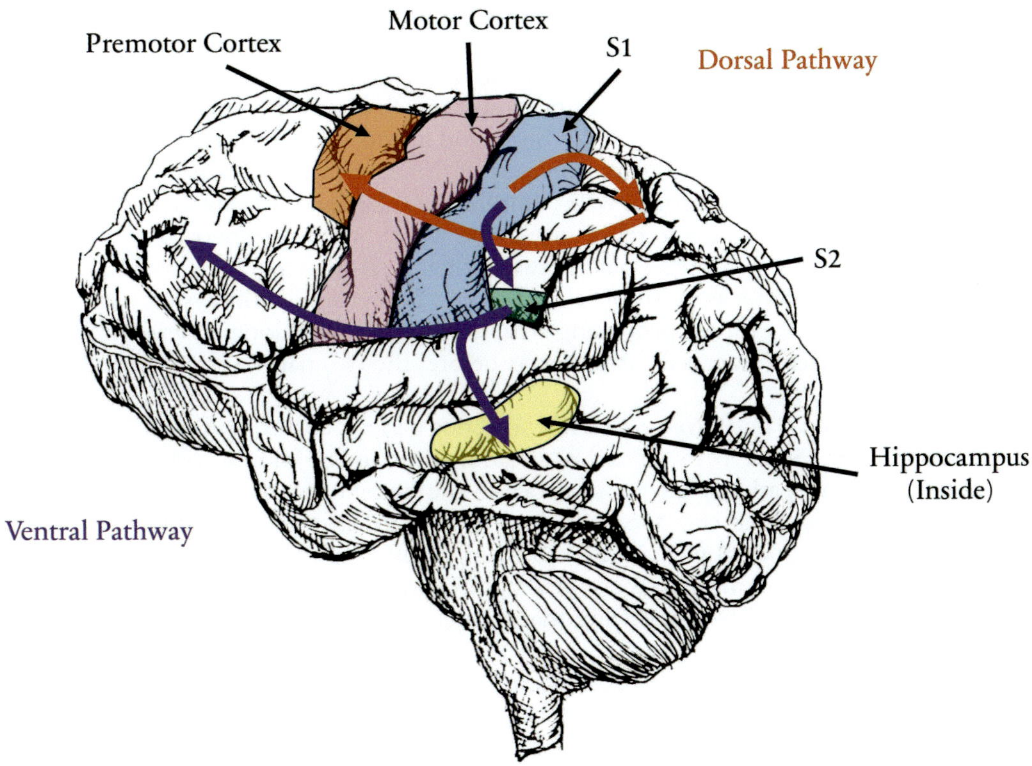

Figure 6.15 Dorsal and ventral pathways of the somatosensory systems.

The face, lips, and tongue, for example, take as much space as the entire leg! The hand (particularly the pointer finger) takes up as much space as the entire trunk. See how you can almost see a person with distorted limb sizes draped over the brain? This is called the **somatosensory homunculus** (homunculus comes from the Latin for "little man"; Penfield & Boldrey, 1937).

Somatosensory homunculus a visual representation of the body on the somatosensory cortex (S1). Areas are distorted relative to their actual size in accordance with how much sensory information is coming from which areas (e.g., the fingers take more space than the trunk).

Socratic Question: How is the somatosensory homunculus (Figure 6.14) consistent with the historically popular idea of the Specificity of Neurological Areas (from Chapter 1)?

The somatosensory receptors send their signals to S1, and these respond with an on-center/off-surround organization (similar to the ones in the visual system) that responds best to areas of contrast. Consequently, S1 plays a role in helping the touch system identify edges of felt surfaces, much like V1 helps the visual system identify edges of viewed surfaces. Areas of the body that are better at sensing fine details (like the hands and lips) have more densely packed somatosensory receptors and consequently more space in S1 dedicated to receiving the signal from those receptors.

Interestingly, at birth, this topographic map looks a little different. At birth, the lips and the tongue have disproportionate amount of brain space in S1, but the rest of the body is more evenly distributed. Makes sense, right? Newborns and infants know about the world largely by putting things in their mouth—it is the only part of their body capable of noticing all the tiny details! It isn't until the child starts to walk (thus freeing their hands to explore their surroundings) that the distribution starts to reorganize in the way shown in Figure 6.14.[6]

After leaving S1, the signal travels along two pathways. If you have been reading this book in order, this should come as no surprise! Just like all the sensory pathways we have covered so far, after leaving the primary processing area, the signals travel along a *dorsal pathway* and a *ventral pathway* (see Chapter 3). And just as before, the two pathways appear to have different specialties.

The dorsal pathway goes from S1 to the posterior parietal cortex, and then into the premotor cortex (see Figure 6.15). Both its location next to the motor cortex and the fact that damage to this pathway results in apraxia—the inability to plan or execute complex movements—suggests that the dorsal pathway is involved in touching as part of moving. The ventral pathway goes from S1 to S2 and then to both the prefrontal cortex and the hippocampus. Conversely, damage to the ventral pathway results in tactile agnosia—the inability to identify objects by touch—suggesting that the ventral pathway is involved in touching as a part of identification.

Just like nociception has its own pathways *to* the brain, it also has its own pathways *through* the brain. There are two different aspects to pain perception: the discriminative dimension (i.e., awareness of what is causing the nociceptive signal and where it is—needle poke on shoulder) and affective dimension (i.e., the unpleasant feeling of pain—*ouch*!). Each aspect has its own pathway within the brain. The discriminative pathway goes from the thalamus to S1 and S2 along with the typical somatosensory signals. The affective dimension, on the other hand travels from the thalamus to the anterior cingulate cortex and then to the amygdala and anterior insular cortex. These areas are responsible for the body's *reaction* to the signal.

Specifically, nociception causes a sympathetic nervous system response—increased heart rate, increased breathing rate, release of adrenaline, etc. *This* response is what we consider the psychological feeling of "pain"—the unpleasant response to the nociceptive signal. Some animals (such as octopuses) do not have a pain signal even though they have a nociceptive signal (Yong, 2022). That is, they will feel that damage is being done but will not feel the negative bodily reaction to that damage. As if octopi were not wonderfully strange enough already.

Box 6.3 Pain Relief

Fred decided that hitting his thumb with a hammer was not a good solution for managing the pain of his sprained ankle. So, he went to see his orthopedist—Dr. Chris—to discuss other options. Dr. Chris explains that because of the unpleasant nature of pain, scientists have spent a lot of time, energy, and money trying to find ways to reduce pain. Fred is grateful for them for doing it because now his thumb *and* his ankle hurt.

For better or worse, many pain treatments come in the form of medication taken to change the chemical response of the body in a way that reduces the feeling of pain. Fred was surprised to hear that many of these medications don't really affect that body part that is causing the pain in the first place. Instead, some medications work on the pain signal itself. For example, NSAIDs (non-steroidal anti-inflammatory drugs such as ibuprofen) reduce pain by blocking the receptors in the free nerve endings that would respond to cyclooxygenase (the chemical released by damaged cells), preventing them from sending the prostaglandins to the brain in response. Other, non-NSAID drugs (such as acetaminophen) work in the brain and keep it from *responding* to the prostaglandins, although the mechanism for that is not entirely clear.

Numbing agents that Dr. Chris and his colleagues use during certain procedures such as lidocaine or novocaine block not only the free nerve endings, but also several other of the mechanoreceptors (which is why the treated area feels numb to all stimulation, not just pain). Ice works in a similar way—it slows the transmission speed of the nerves, keeping them from sending the pain (or any other somatosensory) signal. Ice also constricts the blood vessels, reducing swelling and any pressure it was putting on the nerves.

Other pain-reduction methods work by influencing nociception *after* the initial response. After a surgical procedure, Dr. Chris and his colleagues might prescribe opioids (or another medication of this kind). These kinds of medications work not on the nociception itself, but on the sympathetic nervous system's *response* to that stimulus. These chemicals attach to the native opioid channels (the ones also stimulated by sleeping, meditation, and pleasurable feelings) and engage the body's parasympathetic response. The parasympathetic response is the *opposite* of the sympathetic response—it slows the heart rate, decreases the breathing rate, starts the filtering of the adrenaline

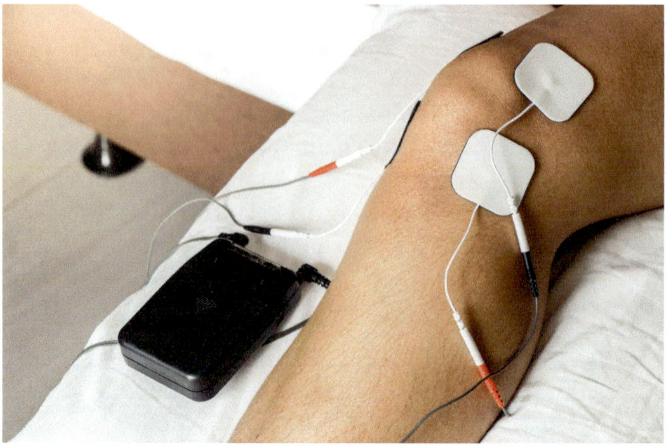

Figure 6.16 A TENS unit runs electrical current across an area experiencing pain. That current trips the "gate" and stops the signal, providing relief.

from the blood, etc. In other words, opioids don't actually stop pain, they stop you from *caring* about the pain.

For patients who have chronic pain, Dr. Chris sometimes recommends methods that take advantage of the gated nature of the pain response. A TENS (transcutaneous electrical nerve stimulation; see Figure 6.16) unit runs an electrical current across the nerves near the site of the pain. It's not enough stimulation to cause (much) pain to the person (it feels a bit like sustained muscle twitching), but it *is* enough stimulation to trip the "gate" in the spinal column and stop the signal from the painful area. This method works best for neuropathic pain, but can provide momentary relief for nociceptive pain.

For people in chronic pain, any risk might be worth trying. Doctors have attempted to remove the parts of the brain that receive the pain signal (specifically the areas of S1 to which the pain signal projects) but have had little success. This is likely because the pain signal is so widespread in its neural activation that removing all projection areas would be, if not impossible, certainly ill-advised.

Passive Touch

Up until this point of the chapter we have focused mostly[7] on *active touch*. In an active touch experiment, a participant is encouraged to explore an object by grasping, squeezing, and lifting it and reporting on what they feel (see Box 6.1). By contrast, in a passive touch experiment, the experimenter presses some type of surface onto the subject's skin and then asks them to report on what they feel. Interestingly, in active touch studies, participants tend to describe the *surface or object being explored* whereas in passive touch studies, participants tend to describe the *sensation being felt*. For example, in an active touch study they might report feeling "a sewing needle", whereas in a passive touch study they might report feeling "a sharp poke".

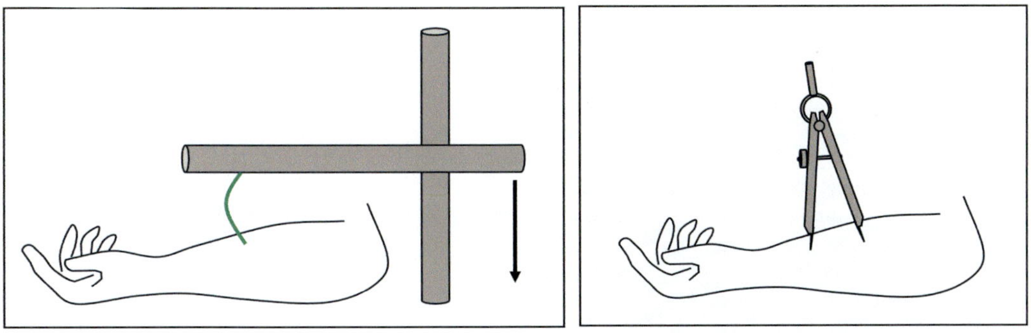

Figure 6.17 Left, a typical setup for measuring sensitivity. The fishing line is lowered (i.e., the amount of pressure on the skin is increased) until the participant says they can feel it. Right, a typical setup for measuring acuity. The points of the compass are moved closer together until the participant reports feeling one poke (instead of two).

Sensitivity

The early research on touch focused almost exclusively on passive touch. Psychophysicists (see Chapter 1) were particularly interested in mathematically describing the relationship between stimulation and experience. They might, for example, measure sensitivity by measuring the minimum threshold for pressure, heat, pain, etc.

A typical test of pressure sensitivity is illustrated in Figure 6.17 (*left*). In this test, a particular area of the body is poked with a thin probe, and the participant is asked to report if they feel the poke. The earliest studies in pressure sensitivity used horsehair as the probe (because it was sufficiently stiff and readily available) but current studies use fishing line with different diameters. The different diameters allow for different levels of stiffness (the thicker the line, the stiffer it is), which create different amounts of pressure on the skin. That way, the sensitivity to such pressure can be reliably measured.

As you might expect (and as depicted in Figure 6.14), the mouth and face have the highest pressure sensitivity on the body (as true for adults as it is for babies!). The next most sensitive are the trunk and upper extremities followed by the lower extremities. Pressure sensitivity is directly related to the density of the mechanoreceptors in that area. There are about the same number of receptors in the *entire trunk* as there are in a *single hand*. In addition, there is cortical magnification of stimulation occurring on the mouth, face, and hand (see Figure 6.14).

Our somatosensory systems are sensitive to remarkably tiny details. The smallest raised dot that can be felt with the fingertip is only one micrometer high (about the length of a typical bacterium!). No wonder raised bumps are used for Braille[8]—people are very sensitive to them! Meanwhile, we can feel temporal differences as small as 5 milliseconds (the time it takes for a single flap of a honeybee's wing!). That's faster than a similar measure in vision (where the smallest difference that can be seen is 25 ms) but slower than hearing (where the smallest difference that can be heard is a staggering 0.01ms!).

Acuity

A typical test of acuity is the **two-point (or difference) threshold**, which is the smallest separation between two points of stimulation that are still felt as two points instead of one single

Figure 6.18 The touch system shows greater acuity when tested with gratings (such as shown here) than when tested with two points (such as on a compass).

point.[9] You can perform a typical two-point threshold test at home—if you have a friend to help and an old-fashioned compass like the one in Figure 6.17 (*right*). You can also use a couple of sharp pencils if you don't happen to have a compass. Close your eyes and have your friend (gently!) press the points of the compass onto your cheek. Have them then decrease the distance between the points and try again, and again, and again until you can no longer feel them as two pokes but instead feel them as one. Have them repeat this procedure on your back. Likely, the distance at which you went from feeling two pokes to only feeling one was *very different* for the different areas.

Two-point (or difference) threshold smallest separation in stimulation (pressure points, differences in temperature, amount of pain, etc.) that can still be felt as two distinct things rather than one.

The two-point threshold varies dramatically across the body. The size of the two-point threshold is related to the size of the receptive fields involved. The same mechanoreceptors will have smaller receptive fields in areas of high acuity than in areas of low acuity.

Unsurprisingly, the areas with the smallest receptive fields are those typically used to explore the surroundings. The two-point threshold is the smallest on the fingertips—only 3–4mm (too small for you to do with your compass!). Other areas with very small two-point thresholds include the face (the cheek has a two-point threshold of 6–10mm) and the feet (the big toe's two-point threshold is 6–9mm). The back, arms, and legs all have much larger two-point thresholds (somewhere between 30mm and 50mm).

While the two-point threshold does a great job of providing an overall measure of acuity, it might actually underestimate the acuity of the skin. Participants can feel much smaller separations between ridges or gratings (see Figure 6.18) than they can small points like on the compass (Craig, 1999). This is particularly interesting because of the research on vision showing a similar preference for sine wave gratings (see Chapter 3). Even changing the *question* can have an effect on the size of the threshold. For example, asking "is there one point or two?" will result in a smaller measured acuity than "do you feel one point or two?" Nonetheless, two-point threshold measurements are useful for comparing the *relative* acuity across the body.

In vision, sensitivity and acuity were a tradeoff. Given how the receptors were connected to the next layer of cells, they *either* increased sensitivity *or* increased acuity, but not both. In the somatosensory system, however, that is not the case. In fact, areas that are very sensitive are usually (though not always) high in acuity and vice versa.

Socratic Question: One of the benefits of studying passive touch (as opposed to active touch) is that it is easier to investigate the sensitivity and acuity of passive touch. How might someone investigate sensitivity and acuity of active touch?

Box 6.4 Non-Human Somatosensory Senses

It would be a dramatic understatement to say that the world of somatosensory systems is vast and diverse. Tactile senses are found in nearly every living organism (even plants!) and come in such a variety that we simply do not have room for them all here (though, as we have mentioned elsewhere in this book, we recommend Ed Yong's book *An Immense World* to the interested reader).

Many animals have organs with mechanoreceptors like our own, which they also use to explore their surroundings. Famously, the star-nosed mole (which is named after its distinctively shaped and very sensitive snout) can barely see, but uses 11 pairs of fleshy appendages on its nose to feel the walls of its burrow by pressing on the wall repeatedly—up to 25 times a *second*.

The manatee has an *oral disk* (the flaps just above its mouth) that is as sensitive as our hands and as dexterous as an elephant's trunk. Exploring with this organ is delightfully called *oripulation*. Given that they can't see very well, manatees tend to explore all their surrounding by oripulating—see? delightful!. The bill of the duck-billed platypus (and the bills of other animals) is filled with more than 40,000 sense organs called *pushrods*. They are sensitive to mechanical pressure, but they are also sensitive to the movement and pressure of water, making them useful in hunting underwater prey.

And there are the *many* animals that use *vibrissal* systems—more commonly known as "whiskers"—stiff hairs that emerge from a bundle of mechanoreceptors in the skin. Sensing with whiskers, or "whisking" —also delightful!—is much like exploring the world with our hands, an active process that provides the animal with information about its surroundings.

Many birds use stiff bristles around the head (rather than whiskers) to detect changes in air flow. This is not unlike the hairs on hairy spiders' legs—they respond to almost unimaginably small changes in air.

Almost all fish (and some amphibians) have a line of receptors down their sides called the *lateral line*. It is a series of fluid-filled canals just below the surface of the skin that contain sense organs called neuromasts. Neuromasts are a hair cell embedded in a gelatinous cap, just like the ones in our inner ears (see Chapter 5). These are sensitive to very tiny changes in the water pressure around the fish—allowing them to navigate around obstacles, avoid predators, and swim in a group with other fish (called *schooling*) without bumping into each other.

Figure 6.19 Nonhuman organisms have different somatosensory receptors.

Many animals communicate using a sense of vibrations that *could* be considered a somatosensory sense, *or* it could be considered hearing depending on how you look at it. Insects invisible to the naked eye will use their abdomens to vibrate the leaf or blade of grass on which they are perched, and the leaf or blade of grass will carry those vibrations to another insect which senses the vibrations through its feet. In a similar way, elephants will grumble (think very low-pitched humming) and other elephants thousands of feet away will pause, lift their foot, and press the toe to the ground as if "listening" more carefully (see Figure 6.19).

Summary

The sense of "touch" (or more properly, the somatosensory systems) is actually several diverse and overlapping senses. There are many different types of somatosensory receptors that vary in the size of their receptive fields, the timing of their response to stimuli, and the way that they are connected to the brain. On the way to the brain, the signals from the left cross the midline to the right and vice versa. Once in the brain, the signal travels to a wide variety of areas. The sense of pain is also complex; there are (at least) three different types of pain that are experienced in (at least) two different ways, making pain relief complicated.

Notes

1 In fact, if you look back at Chapter 1, Figure 1.8 has a picture of Golgi-stained neurons.
2 There are no nociceptors in a few locations—the brain, for example. This is why you can perform brain surgery on someone who is awake and only need to numb the skin. A headache is actually stimulation of a nerve *entering* the brain, rather than a pain in the brain itself.
3 Specifically, they do not develop the sodium ion channels necessary for neurotransmission.
4 *Why* is the somatosensory system organized in this contralateral way? The short answer is it's complicated, there are a lot of guesses, and we don't really know.
5 This is just like how the signals in the visual cortex create a rough retinotopic map, and the signals in the auditory cortex create a rough tonotopic map.
6 Perhaps more interesting is how the brain might reorganize *across* modalities. In one study, participants wore a blindfold for five days, and during those days they trained on the use of Braille. By the end of the five days, exploring Braille no longer activated S1; it activated V1 instead!
7 The obvious exception is pain—which is not really part of active *or* passive touch research.
8 Another reason that raised dots are used for Braille is that their small size makes them less confusable than raised letters. Think about the Snellen charts in Figure 3.12.

7 Chemical Senses

Gustation and Olfaction

Recently Fred had a strange experience (see Figure 7.1). While out to lunch with his best friend Claudia, he ordered his favorite sandwich—tuna fish and pickles on toasted wheat—but when he ate it, it tasted very strange—more like kinda salty mush and kinda sour mush on sorta crunchy mush. Claudia tried it and insisted it tasted normal to her—*mmmm*, pickles! The next day, his favorite dessert—chocolate chip cookies—didn't taste like much at all. Two days (and a terrible cough) later, he was diagnosed with Covid. *Ugh*! When he recounted his experience with the sandwich and the cookies, his doctor told him that it was likely that he lost his sense of smell and that this that affected the taste of his sandwich and cookies. **Anosmia** and **ageusia**—loss of sense of smell and loss of sense of taste, respectively—are some of the most commonly reported symptoms of Covid. For Fred, it was clear evidence that these two senses are inextricably linked because the taste of the sandwich was so radically altered by the loss of his sense of smell. *Blech*.

> **Anosmia** lack of the sense of smell.
>
> **Ageusia** lack of the sense of taste.

Not only are taste and smell linked in our experience, but they are also (we are fairly certain) linked in the *functions they serve* as well. There is general agreement that, at least in part, these senses act as gatekeepers. That is, they are sensitive to the nutritional content and safety of the food we eat, and of our surroundings more generally. Carbohydrates and sodium are vital to our health—the former is our source of energy,

Figure 7.1 Fred and Claudia recently had lunch, and Fred's sandwich tasted strange.

DOI: 10.4324/9781032690964-8

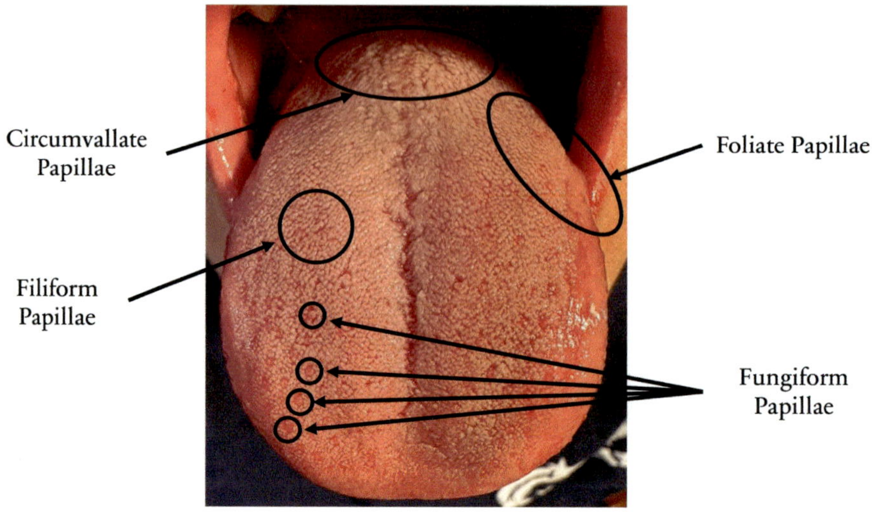

Figure 7.2 Papillae of the tongue.

and the latter is required for various chemical reactions as well as keeping our fluids and electrolytes balanced. Being able to taste sweet (the presence of carbohydrates) and salty (the presence of sodium) allows us to seek out foods that we need to survive. Being able to taste sour and bitter—and being able to smell rot—allows us to avoid food that has spoiled or contains toxins. Bacteria taste sour, toxins taste bitter, rot smells putrid. *Even more blech.* Both taste and smell are sensitive to chemicals in the air and in the food. This is why they are often combined into one chapter in textbooks (as they are here) and collectively called the *chemical senses.*

In this chapter, we will cover both the sense of taste and the sense of smell, as well as the experience of *flavor,* which is a sort of meta-sense, a combination of taste, smell, mouth feel, pain, and visual presentation. This is yet another area where drawing firm boundaries between the different senses doesn't do us any good. Having said that, there are distinct sets of sensory machinery as well as distinct neural pathways for smell and taste, and so this chapter will begin with those distinctions.

Gustation

The receptors for taste or **gustation** are largely (though not exclusively) on the tongue. No surprise there, right? Take a second and go check out your own tongue in the mirror. No, really. We'll wait. You'll notice that it's covered in tiny little bumps. These bumps are called **papillae** and there are several different kinds—filiform, fungiform, folate, and circumvallate (see Figure 7.2). All but the filiform papillae[1] contain the receptors responsible for taste. And since the very center of the tongue is entirely covered in filiform papillae you can place a **tastant**—that is, a thing that you can

Gustation formal name for the sense of taste; sensing of chemicals by taste buds.

Papillae small bumps on the tongue, the location of most taste buds.

Tastant a chemical that can be tasted.

taste—on the center of the tongue and it will not taste like anything. Try it sometime with a drop of vinegar or simple syrup—you will not taste the drop until it runs to one of the sides of your tongue.

Taste Buds

Inside the tissue of the papillae are **taste buds**, which get their name from the fact that they are shaped like flower buds—who knew? Each bud is made up of elongated receptor cells arranged like the segments in an orange (see Figure 7.3). The tips of the receptor cells have small hair-like structures called **microvilli** that are sensitive to the chemicals in the food. These microvilli protrude into a small hole in the surface of the papillae, called a **taste pore**. Saliva dissolves the chemicals in the food, and the tastants run into these pores and make contact with the **chemoreceptors**.

Taste buds a collection of taste receptors that gets its name from its shape—like a flower bud.

Microvilli small, hair-like protrusions on taste receptor cells. Respond to tastants.

Taste pore small holes in papillae that allow tastants to make contact with microvilli.

Chemoreceptors specialized cells that respond to chemicals.

Humans have about 5000 taste buds with approximately 50–150 taste receptors each. For those of you playing along at home, that means that humans have between 250,000 and 750,000 taste receptors. Because of the less-than-ideal conditions in the mouth, individual taste buds only last about 10 days (Beidler & Smallman, 1965). Every time you burn your mouth (*ouch*!), bite your tongue (*oof*!), eat something too acidic (*blech*!), or even

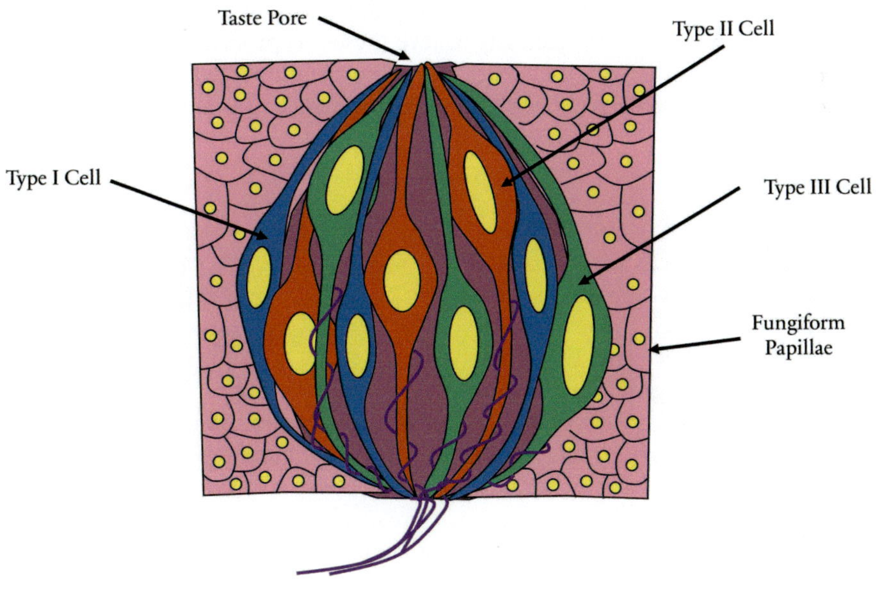

Figure 7.3 Taste buds are buried in the tissue of a papilla, a taste pore that allows tastants to make contact with the microvilli.

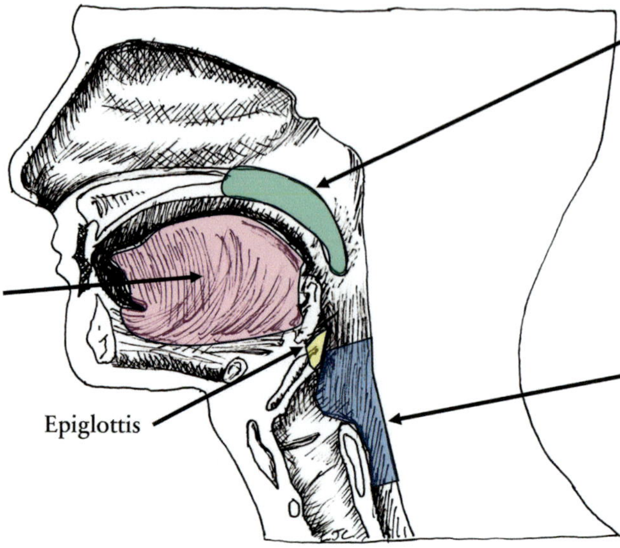

Figure 7.4 Cross-section of the face and neck showing the location of taste buds: tongue, soft palate, upper esophagus, and epiglottis.

just brush your tongue with particular vigor (*scrub*!), you damage taste buds, so they need to continually replenish themselves.

And the tongue isn't the only place that there are taste buds. *Wait, what? Yep.* We have taste buds on the soft palate,[2] the upper esophagus, and the epiglottis (see Figure 7.4). There is some recent research that strongly suggests that we also have taste receptors in the stomach and the gut (see Box 7.1; Finger & Kinnamon, 2011). There are even taste receptors in the *lungs* that are specific to sensing bitter and sour. Scientists believe these receptors are meant to sense toxins in the breathed-in air. When they do, they react by closing the lungs slightly to avoid absorption of possible toxins, as well as instigating coughing to remove any toxins already present.

Taste Receptors

> **Four basic tastes** The agreed-upon tastes that make up all other tastes—sweet, bitter, sour, and salty.

Taste buds are made of three different types of taste receptor cells that perform different functions. Type I cells are like the glial cells in the brain—their job is to maintain and support the other cells. Everyone needs a support system, right? Type II and Type III are the chemoreceptors that respond to the tastants. Before we go into how they work, however, it is necessary to talk about the **four basic tastes**. There is general consensus that there are at least four basic tastes:[3] *sweet*, *bitter*, *sour*, and *salty* (but there are probably more than this; see Box 7.1). Type II receptors are sensitive to sweet and bitter, and Type III receptors are sensitive to salty and sour. Finally, there is the taste of *spicy*, which for reasons that will become clear, should maybe be considered a somatosensory experience, rather than a taste per se.

Type II Receptors

On a molecular level, everything that tastes sweet to us—whether it is sugar or aspartame—has the same chemical structure. That is, those substances have the same physical shape at the molecular level. This includes, of course, the sugars in Fred's chocolate chip cookies—too bad he can't taste them! Everything that tastes bitter to us—whether it's arugula or coffee—*also* has the same chemical structure (but a different chemical structure than the sweet substances). Type II receptors work using a "key-in-lock" design—that is, the shape of the chemical fits the shape of the receptor site like a key going into a lock. Type II receptors come in (at least) two varieties: one that has receptor sites that match the shape of sweet-shaped molecules and one that has receptor sites that match the shape of bitter-shaped molecules.

Once the sweet or bitter chemical fits into the receptor site, it sets off a chemical cascade (just like in the photoreceptors; see Chapter 3) which sends a signal to a pre-synaptic neuron. These neurons are a bit like the bipolar cells in the retina in that they connect the receptors to the nerve that carries the signal to the brain. *Unlike* the bipolar cells in the eye, however, they do not appear to change the signal in any way; they just act as a conduit, sending the signal to the brain (see Figure 7.5).

Type III Receptors

What we taste as "salty" is the presence of an ion called sodium (Na+). Rather than a receptor site responding to the shape of the molecule, sodium acts as a neurotransmitter—entering the receptor cells through ion channels and setting off an action potential (see Chapter 3).

Sour tastants—like the pickles from Fred's sandwich—work in a similar way, except that not all sour things are made of the same molecule or have the same molecular shape. However, they are all *acidic*—like the brine or vinegar in the pickles—and all acids release hydrogen ions (H+). Just like Na+, H+ enters the receptor cell through an ion channel and sets off an action potential. Type III receptors connect directly to the nerves that carry the signals to the brain. Or in other words, they act as their own presynaptic neuron (see Figure 7.5).

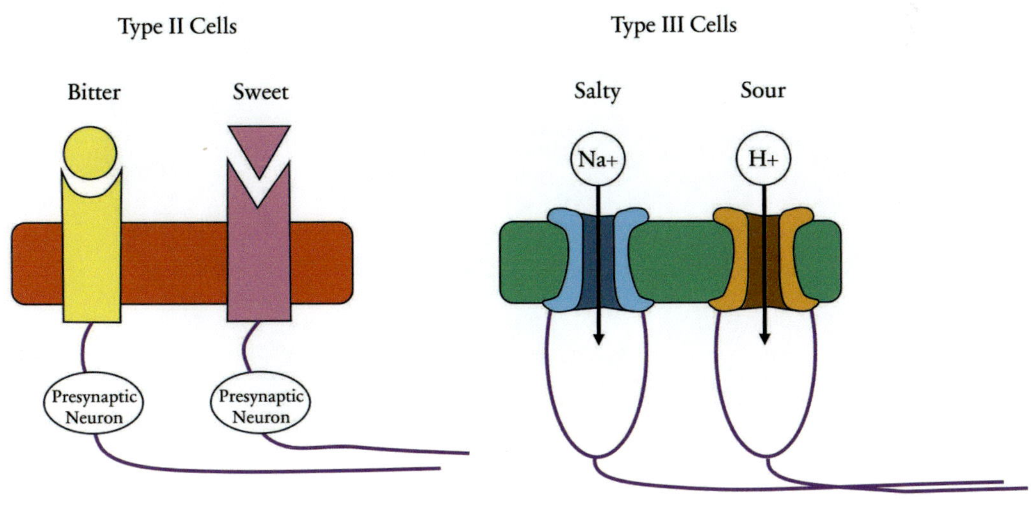

Figure 7.5 Schematic of Type II (left) and Type III (right) receptors and how they connect to the brain.

Free Nerve Endings

The vast majority of things we consider *spicy* contain a chemical called capsaicin. That chemical acts as an irritant to the free nerve endings in our mouths. But wait, you might be thinking, weren't free nerve endings what carried the nociceptive pain signals in Chapter 6? Yes! As it turns out, when we taste spicy things what we are sensing is actually *pain* (or nociceptive signals, anyway). Capsaicin (and other spicy-tasting chemicals) stimulates both free nerve endings and warm thermoreceptors (even if the food they are in is not *physically* hot, we will experience it as hot for this reason).

Spicy peppers are rated on the Scoville Heat Units (SHU) scale—developed by American chemist Wilbur Scoville in 1912. The scale rates how much dilution is needed before the spice can no longer be detected. For example, Jalapeño peppers rate 2,500 to 8,000 SHU (depending on how they are grown, see Figure 7.6). That means that a Jalapeno pepper requires 2,500 to 8,000 dilutions of sugar water before the spice can no longer be detected. There are worldwide competitions to create the hottest pepper—as of this publication, the current record holder is Pepper X, with a blistering 2.69 million SHU!

Fred's friend, Daniela (who loves spicy things), once dared Fred to eat a Habanero pepper (100,000–350,000 SHU) when they were out to eat one night. Not being one to pass up a dare, Fred complied. And boy, did he regret it! In response to his distress, the waiter rushed a glass of milk to the table. Fred experienced immediate relief upon drinking it—phew! As it turns out, milk (and other dairy products) contains a protein called casein, which has a strong affinity for capsaicin. When Fred drank the milk, the casein bonded with the capsaicin from the pepper and washed it away from the free nerve endings in his mouth. Ahhhhh!

Figure 7.6 Jalapeño peppers are a commonly eaten spicy pepper.

Pro tip: you can avoid the distress Fred felt! If you wait a moment after the first bite, the free nerve endings have time to *habituate* to the presence of capsaicin. That is, they will decrease their pain signal to your brain. Or in other words, if you just wait a bit after taking that first bite of a spicy meal until the spicy sensation subsides a bit, the subsequent bites will not taste as spicy (if you don't wait, repeated bites will irritate the nerve further and *increase* your sense of spicy). The habituation is relatively long-lasting, and as long as you eat something spicy once every 48 hours or so, you will have chronic desensitization and be able to eat even the spiciest of foods.

Since the nerves that carry the spicy signal are the same nerves that carry pain signals, scientists have figured out how to take advantage of the habituation effect to help people with painful mouth sores (typically cancer patients, given that mouth sores are a common side effect of chemotherapy; Caterina et al., 1997). They give them capsaicin-laced caramels which—after the initial spicy pain—significantly decreases the pain signal from the mouth, giving them some relief from the mouth sores.[4] Hooray for science!

Box 7.1 Other Candidate "Basic Tastes"

There is considerable debate about the possibility that there are other basic tastes (besides *sweet*, *bitter*, *sour*, and *salty*) that rely on other types of specific receptors. *Umami*,[5] or the taste of protein/savory—like the tuna in Fred's sandwich—is a frequent candidate for an additional basic taste, but there are some difficulties in figuring out how that would work. The protein molecules that are in our food are far too large to have a receptor site on our taste buds—the "key" would be too big for the "lock". We could have a Type II receptor site that responds to the amino acids which make up the protein. But the protein would need to be *digested* or broken down into amino acids first, and that doesn't happen until the food hits the stomach. As we have discussed, there are taste receptors in the stomach and gut, and the presence of umami-specific receptors in the stomach and gut would explain the "sated" feeling that eating protein gives us. The receptors send a signal to the hypothalamus in the brain, which releases hormones that make us feel full. However, the activity of these receptors wouldn't necessarily explain why we experience the taste of umami in our *mouths*. Hmmm.

One possible explanation for how we can taste umami comes from how the food additive monosodium glutamate (more commonly known as MSG) changes the taste of food. When added to food (most famously Chinese food), MSG increases the taste of umami/savory. Perhaps MSG is stimulating the same receptors that protein would stimulate more generally? MSG is made of two chemicals—sodium (for which we have a known receptor) and glutamate. Glutamate is a neurotransmitter present in most meat proteins, and there are known key-in-lock receptor sites for it in the brain. And it is possible (though not yet known for sure) that some of glutamate receptor sites are also present in the mouth. If this turns out to be the case, it is possible that it is the *combination* of sodium and glutamate that gives the flavor of umami/savory (which is why MSG works so effectively).

Another candidate basic taste is the taste of *fat*. Fat is indicated by the presence of lipid molecules, which much like proteins are far too big to have their own receptor sites. The far more likely scenario is that it is the *somatosensory* experience of fat that gives us the taste. This might be one reason by renowned cooks such as Julia Child and Gordon Ramsey have been quoted as saying "where there is fat, there is flavor". That is, the mouth-feel of things that contain fat are similar—they are thick, creamy, oily, and so on. Perhaps that mouth feel is what we are sensing, rather than a taste *as such.*

Socratic Question: How do Type II and Type III receptors reinforce the general consensus that there are four basic tastes? How does the experience of eating counter that consensus?

Tongue Map Myth

You might have heard that there are areas of the tongue specific to various taste experiences—like that the tip of the tongue tastes only salty things, while the sides taste only sour things (see Figure 7.7). This is not true. Well, mostly not true, anyway. The myth started because in 1942 an American scientist by the name of Edwin Boring[6] mistranslated a work by written by the German scientist D. P. Hänig in 1901. Hänig tested the sensitivity of the tongue to the four main tastes. He found that certain areas were more sensitive than others to specific tastes. For example, the tip of the tongue was the most sensitive to salt, *relative to the sensitivity of the other areas of the tongue to salt.* Or in other words, the whole tongue (minus the very center) can taste salt, but the tip is the best at it. But—and this is an important but—the differences are very small. The tip is only *marginally* better at tasting salt than the rest of the tongue.

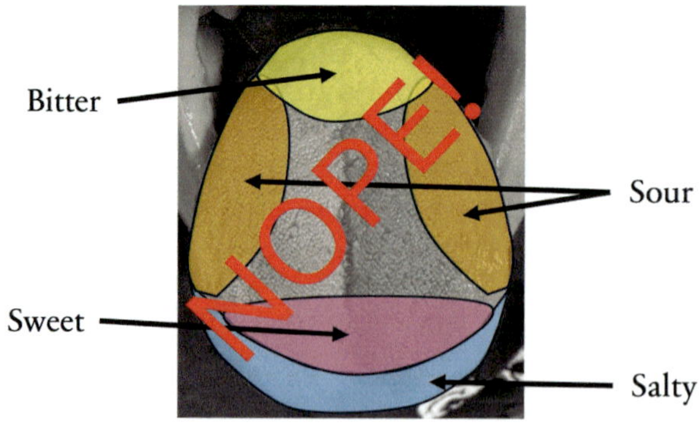

Figure 7.7 The "tongue map" is a myth.

Socratic Question: How is the myth of the tongue map comparable to the myth of the five senses?

Nontasters, Tasters, and Supertasters

In 1931, an American chemist named Arthur L. Fox was preparing a batch of a chemical compound called Phenylthiocarbamide (PTC) for an experiment he was performing. He was pouring the PTC powder into a bottle and some of the dust sprang up into the air. A nearby colleague, C. R. Noller, complained about the bitter taste in the air (blech!), which surprised Fox because he could not taste anything at all! Soon after that, Fox enlisted the help of American geneticist Albert F. Blakeslee to study the phenomenon. At that year's American Association for the Advancement of Sciences meeting, they asked 2500 people to taste the PTC crystals. Of those, 66% said the crystals were bitter, 28% said they were tasteless, and 6% said they tasted like something else. They described the 28% of people who could not taste PTC as "nontasters", although more recent research shows that it's not that "nontasters" cannot taste PTC—they just need it be in a higher concentration for them to taste it.

In addition to being dramatically less sensitive to PTC, nontasters also have fewer fungiform papillae and thus fewer tastebuds than the tasters. Armed with that knowledge, an American experimental psychologist named Linda Bartoshuk went in search of people who might have even *more* tastebuds than tasters. She found that about 25% of the population have far *more* fungiform papillae (and tastebuds to go with them) than tasters (see Figure 7.8; Bartoshuk, 1991). She called these people "supertasters".[7]

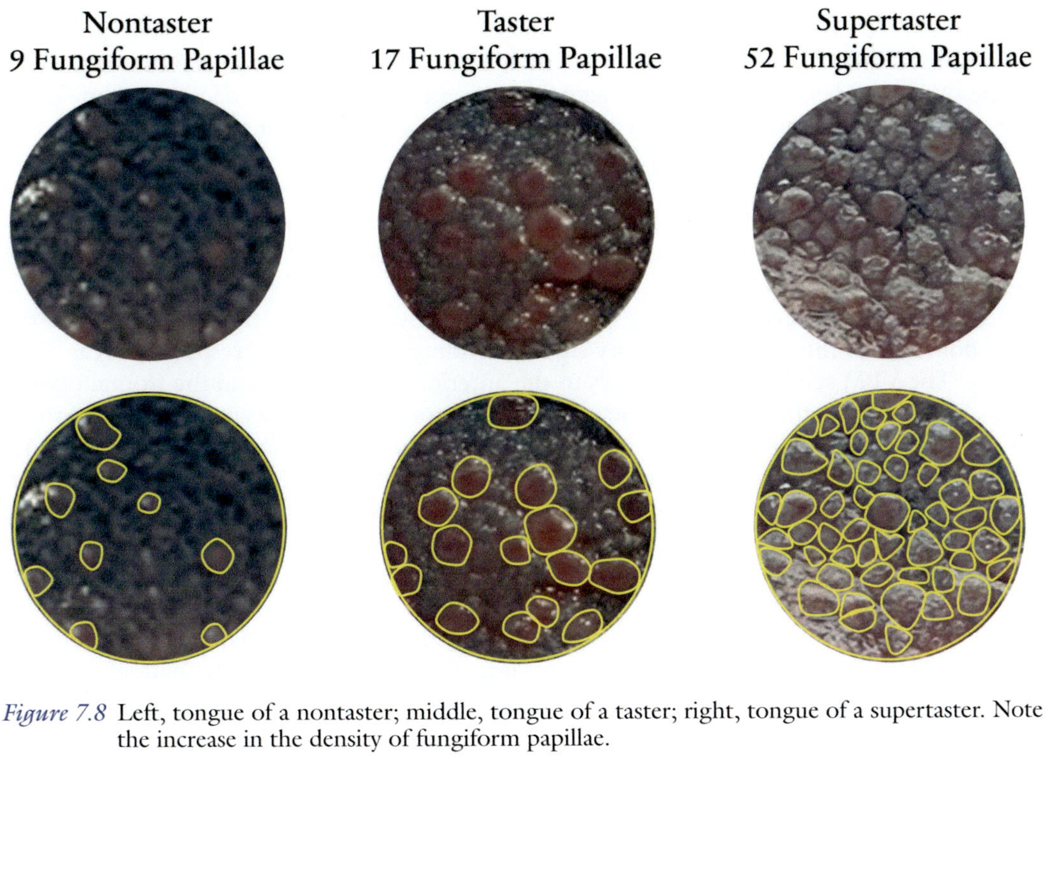

Figure 7.8 Left, tongue of a nontaster; middle, tongue of a taster; right, tongue of a supertaster. Note the increase in the density of fungiform papillae.

As you might expect, supertasters are more sensitive to the bitter taste of PTC, but that's not all! They are also better at discriminating between different tastes, have more pain receptors (both in the mouth and in the rest of the body), experience more intense mouth feel (from the texture of the food), and are more sensitive to the scent of food while eating. Given this pattern of differences, it might be that supertasters have more of the nerves that carry the signals from the various senses (or that the ones they have are more conductive) and that this is responsible for their heightened taste ability (rather than more tastebuds, per se).

Socratic Question: How are supertasters like tetrachromats (see Chapter 4)? How are they unlike tetrachromats?

Neural Pathways for Taste

The signal from the taste buds is carried to the brain via three cranial nerves—the 7th (facial), 9th (glossopharyngeal), and 10th (vagus). The taste buds on the front (anterior) two-thirds of the tongue send their signals via the facial nerve (specifically the *chorda tympani* branch). The taste buds on the back (posterior) third of the tongue send their signals via the glossopharyngeal nerve. The rest of the tastebuds (those on the soft palate, esophagus, and epiglottis) send their signals to the brain via the vagus nerve. Each of these three nerves send inhibitory signals to the other two nerves. You might wonder why there are *three* nerves, and why they all inhibit each other. You are very curious! Good for you! One possibility is that it is part of a redundancy system to make sure that the taste signals are not diminished in case any of them are damaged. If one of the three nerves is damaged, there are still two nerves left to send the signal to the brain. *And* the damaged nerve stops sending its inhibitory signal, so the other two nerves send *stronger* signals to the brain. Amazingly, damage to one of the nerves usually causes an overall *increase* in taste intensity (at least temporarily).

All three nerves project to the solitary nucleus in the medulla (part of the brainstem). The signal then projects to four different places: 1) the mouth—to control the activity of the salivary glands, 2) the Amygdala, 3) the Hypothalamus—which is responsible for the autonomic nervous system including regulating digestion—and 4) the Ventral Posterior Medial Nucleus (VPM) of the Thalamus (see Figure 7.9).

Just like it has for every other sense that we have covered so far, the thalamus acts like a relay point for all the incoming sensory signals, sending them to their respective areas of the cortex. The VPM sends the taste signals to the anterior insula cortex and the frontal operculum (AI/FO). Together, these are the primary gustatory areas of the cortex. Damage to the AI/FO will cause ageusia on the same side of the mouth as the damage (so a stroke in the left AI/FO areas will cause loss of taste on the left side of the mouth). The primary gustatory areas are also involved in the somatosensory aspects of food—such as mouth feel, texture, and bite quality.

The anterior insula sends its signal to the orbital frontal cortex (OFC). The role of the OFC is debated, but some research suggests it is responsible for the pleasant/unpleasant aspect of taste. For example, in rats, this area of the brain will be stimulated while eating, but only if the rat is hungry and the food is high value (for rats, the sweeter the better). If the rat has just eaten or if the food is low value, this area will be less active (O'Doherty et al., 2001).

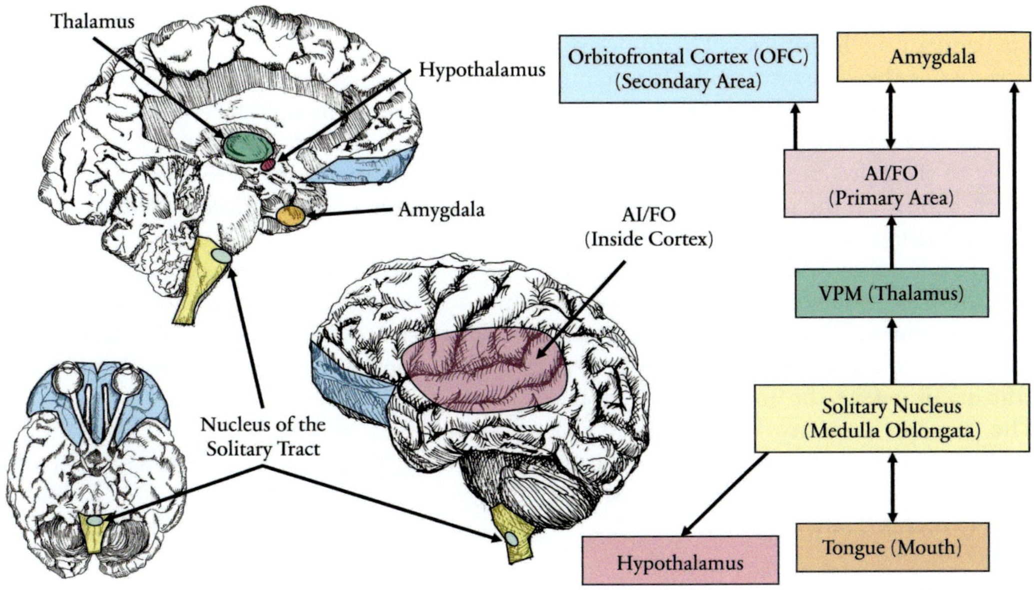

Figure 7.9 Neural pathways of gustation. Because of the complexity of the pathway, the brain drawings do not include the pathway, just the areas the pathway travels through.

Neural Coding

There is debate as to the exact nature of the neural coding of the signals from the tastebuds. The two main competing hypotheses are the **cross fiber** hypothesis and the **labeled line** hypothesis. There is evidence for both hypotheses, and both types of neural coding are exhibited by other sensory systems.

Cross-fiber coding the type of neural coding found in color perception; a few "primary" elements combine and the combination is sensed as a new unitary whole.

Labeled-line coding the type of neural coding found in hearing perception; there are many elements and their combination is sensed as many combined things rather than a unitary whole.

Cross-Fiber Hypothesis

The cross-fiber hypothesis suggests that the taste buds are responding *maximally* but not *exclusively* to their preferred taste, a pattern of response called **broad tuning**. In this case, there would be a graded response to say, a potato vs. a peach vs. a spoonful of sugar. The potato would elicit a small response from the sweet taste buds (because it contains complex carbohydrates, but not simple ones), while the peach would elicit a medium response (because it contains both complex carbohydrates and natural sugar), and sugar would elicit a maximal response (because it contains only simple carbohydrates).

Broad tuning responding maximally, but not exclusively to the preferred stimulus.

These graded responses would then be *compared* across taste bud types (*across fibers*, hence the name of the hypothesis. The response of the sweet taste buds would be compared to the response of the sour taste buds, for example, and the experienced flavor would be about the *overall pattern* of responses rather than the response of an individual taste bud. We saw this type of coding in color perception—individual cones responded maximally but not exclusively to their preferred wavelength, different areas of the spectrum were compared to each other, and it was the *comparison* that was sent to the brain. Combinations of colors are seen as a new color.

There is some evidence that supports this hypothesis. The receptors are quite specific, but there is (not very well understood) communication between the different types of receptors before the signal leaves the taste bud (Roper & Chaudhari, 2017). And, by the time the signal gets to the brain, there is even more evidence for broad tuning than for **specific tuning** (see the following section). The average response of a cortical cell leans more toward responding to all tastes than it does toward responding to a single taste (Scott & Plata-Salamán, 1999).

Specific tuning responding only to the preferred stimulus.

Labeled-Line Hypothesis

In contrast to the cross-fiber hypothesis, the labeled-line hypothesis suggests that the taste buds are *very* specific to their respective taste (i.e., they exhibit specific tuning). There is a graded response, but it is more about the *amount* of the tastant present rather than how well it matches the preferred stimulus of the cell. That is, it's about *how much* sugar is in the food, not about how close to the preferred stimulus the chemical is (as in the previous potato, peach, and sugar example).

The responses to the highly specific tastes are then each sent separately to the brain (so each "line" from the receptor to the brain could be "labeled" with the response to a particular taste, hence *labeled-line*). The taste of the food is a combination of the amount of each taste present, rather than a comparison of tastes. We have also seen this type of coding before—this time in hearing. The different areas of the Basilar membrane were specific to different pitches, and it was the combination of pitches (and how loud they were) that was heard.

The evidence more clearly supports the labeled line hypothesis. The receptors show a clear response curve to the *amount* of a tastant and seem to respond *exclusively* to that tastant. The neural pathways are specific, and as we mentioned earlier, there are studies showing a "gustatopic map" in the brains of mice. But it goes beyond that. You may never have thought about it this way, but our lived experience of taste is more like that of hearing sounds than that of seeing color. Let us explain. When two colors combine, we see a third color and the original colors are no longer visible—think red and green mixing to make yellow (remember this from Chapter 4?). On the other hand, when several sounds combine, we hear each individual sound but can also hear the combination of the sounds. Think of someone playing a chord on the piano or guitar—you can still hear each individual note while also hearing the combination as a chord. Tasting food is more like this: individual flavors are still discernable while appreciating the overall taste.

Finally, there is an evolutionary argument for the labeled line hypothesis and against the cross fiber. If the point of the gustatory sense is to be a gatekeeper (as we discussed at the beginning of this chapter), then it is important that the individual tastes be discernable even after combination! We cannot risk mixing tastes masking the sour of bacteria or the bitterness of a toxin.

Which Is Correct?

Truthfully, we don't know. This debate is ongoing, and taste perception is not as well understood as some of our other senses. It's also worth mentioning that it's possible *both* hypotheses are correct. Maybe the labeled-line hypotheses is correct for the experience of salty and sour—after all, experience of these tastes is more specifically tuned at the level of the receptors and more clearly represented at the level of the cortex. And maybe the cross-fiber hypothesis is correct for bitter and sweet—after all, experience of these tastes is far more broadly tuned at the level of the receptor, and sweet in particular is very broadly represented at the level of the cortex. More research is needed.

> Socratic Question: How is our lived experience of taste more like that of hearing sounds than that of seeing color? How is this evidence in favor of the labeled line hypothesis?

Olfaction

Fred's girlfriend, Carol, has a German shepherd named Frank (see Figure 7.10). Frank *loves* beef jerky. We mean *loves it*. Fred has to be careful not to eat or even handle beef jerky for a while before he hangs out with Carol and Frank, or Frank will pounce on him trying to find the source of that alluring scent—yum! (Carol has to be careful with peanuts around Fred's pet elephant for the same reason.) The first time this happened, Fred was very confused—after all, he couldn't smell the beef jerky himself, so how could Frank?

It's well-known that dogs (particularly German shepherds, bloodhounds, and Basset hounds) have a *very keen* sense of smell. That is, they have very *sensitive* olfaction. And while it's true that a human's olfaction is not nearly as sensitive as a dog's, it's still *awfully* sensitive, at least for some scents. For example, if you had two Olympic-sized pools filled with plain water and you put just three drops of ethyl mercaptan (the chemical that is added to propane

Figure 7.10 Fred and Frank—Frank can smell beef jerky on Fred for hours after he has eaten it.

to give it a distinct skunky or garlicky smell) into one of them, people could tell which pool had the chemical (Yeshurun & Sobel, 2010). And the human sense of smell is awfully acute as well. Humans can tell the difference between over 1 trillion olfactory stimuli—yes, that's *trillion*, with a '*t*'—making it our most acute sense (compare this to just 10 million different colors we can see and 350,000 different tones we can hear).

Despite this, the sense of smell (or **olfaction**) is the least understood of all the senses. There are several reasons for this. First, smell has always been the least appreciated or valued of the senses by everyday people.[8] If you asked everyone you know which sense they would choose to give up—if they had to give up one of them—most people would say their sense of smell. You'd probably make the same choice, right? And as you might expect, the lack of appreciation by everyday people can lead to a lack of investigations on the part of scientists. Second, even if the interest in studying olfaction were as strong as the interest in studying, say, vision, the *ability* to study it would still be limited by basic methodological problems. In order to scientifically study a sense system we have to be able to do two things: we have to be able to *manipulate the energy form* relevant for that sense (e.g., dimming the lights, changing the pitch of a sound), and we have to be able to *describe the effect of this manipulation on experience* (e.g., "it got darker in here", "the sound got higher-pitched"). Olfaction fails on both counts. We'll see why this is the case in the next two sections.

Olfaction formal name for the sense of smell; the ability to sense chemicals in the air.

Manipulating Smells

One of Fred's favorite things about visiting his friend, Richard, is that he *always* has coffee brewing at his house. Fred loves the smell of coffee (even if he doesn't love the taste) so he always takes a big *sniff* the moment he walks in the door. In this situation, the brewing coffee would be the **odor object**. It is the thing in the world that Fred is smelling. Given that Fred can smell the coffee brewing as soon as he walks in the door, smell is sometimes considered a *distance sense* (see Chapter 1), but given the way the receptors work (more on this later), it could *also* be considered a *near sense*.[9] Weird, right?

Odor object the thing in the world that has an odor.

In order for something to have an odor, molecules of the odor object (in this case, the coffee) need to be in gaseous form. That gas floats through the air and makes its way into Fred's nose—sometimes all on their own and sometimes after being deliberately sniffed in—to make physical contact with his receptors (see? Near sense!). In the case of coffee, there are about 600 different volatiles (floating molecules that stimulate the receptors) that make up the smell of *coffee*.[10] These volatiles are called **odorants**. Any one of these might have a smell all on its own, but the *combined* response is required for the particular **odor** of coffee.

Odorants floating chemicals, also called volatiles, that can be smelled.

Odor the experience the organism has of the odor object.

In order to manipulate the energy form relevant to the smell system, you would need to manipulate either the odor object itself or the odorants. Neither is particularly easy. You

Figure 7.11 Fred can smell the difference in Richard's different types of coffee.

could focus on changing the odor object: Richard likes to try out new kinds of coffee and Fred can tell the difference between a darker roast and a lighter one, between a caramel vanilla latte and a Black Cat fizz (a mix of espresso, orange bitters, and tonic water—yes, it's a thing) with that first big sniff (see Figure 7.11). In that case, different odor objects result in different experiences for Fred. But—and it's a big but—changing odor objects in a systematic way is very difficult. For example, while it's obvious that a caramel vanilla latte differs from a Black Cat fizz, it's not so obvious *on what dimensions* and *to what extent* they differ.

Most research in olfaction has focused on trying to manipulate the odorants, though, as you'll see, that isn't much easier! One of the biggest problems is that olfaction doesn't seem to follow the patterns that other senses do when it comes to having simple "primary" building blocks. For example, in color, we can appreciate over ten million different colors, but those are all made up of the same primary three (plus brightness and saturation). There are no similar simple building blocks for olfaction. Scientists have tried to identify "primary" smells[11] but were mostly unsuccessful.

The current understanding is that odorants are different chemical structures (just as in taste) but even manipulating those poses difficulties. How can you make sure, for example, that exactly the same number of molecules of gas make their way into a person's nose? Scientists have gotten around this with scratch and sniff stickers, smell pens, and enclosed spaces participants can stick their nose in, but it is still far more difficult than just dimming the lights.

Describing Smells

Despite the relatively high acuity people have when it comes to smells, they are spectacularly bad at describing or naming those smells. This may have something to do with the neurology of the olfactory system. Every other sense has a reciprocal connection between the primary projection area of the sense and the part of the brain thought to be involved in language, but smell does not.

Try this at home. Have a friend (even one who does a lot of cooking) close their eyes. Present different spices for them to sniff and ask them to name them. If your friend is anything like the participants in De Wijk and Cain's (1994) study, they won't do very well! The participants in that study guessed correctly only 40% of the time. However, if they were given a list of names to choose from, they guessed correctly 80% of the time! The problem wasn't in the ability to *identify* the smell, it was connecting that smell to a *name*. This is often called the tip-of-the-nose phenomenon (this is to relate it to the tip-of-the-tongue phenomenon, where you know you know the name, you just . . . can't . . . name . . . it).

Additionally, there's a strange phenomenon in which knowing the *name* of the smell radically alters the way it is experienced. If given a nice name to describe a smell (like pine trees), participants will report liking the scent more than if they are given a less nice name (like cleaning supplies) to describe the *same smell* (Djordjevic et al., 2008). And it's not just in the *experience*—changing the name given alongside the smell changes the way it is processed *at the level of the receptors* (more on this later), making it the sense most obviously affected by expectations.

Socratic Question: One of the reasons that smell is so poorly understood is that studying it in a systematic way is challenging. How so?

Structure and Function of the Olfactory System

You might think you smell with your nose, but you would be wrong! Or, at least, mostly wrong. The pointy bit of skin and cartilage on the front of your face is responsible for drawing air (filled with odorants) into the body, but it doesn't register anything about those odorants. That happens at the top of the **nasal cavity** (see Figure 7.12). Each

Nasal cavity open area in the head behind the nose, above the mouth, and below the brain. The olfactory epithelium is on the roof of the nasal cavity.

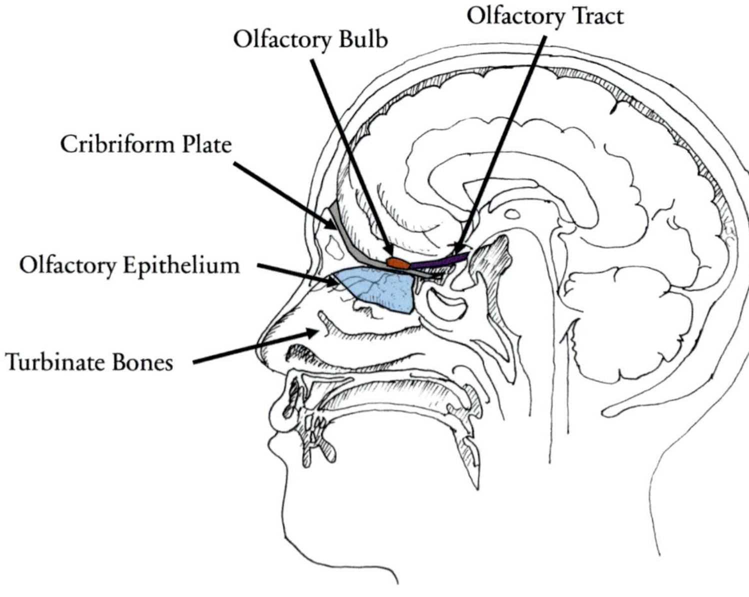

Figure 7.12 The nasal cavity. Turbinate bones direct the majority of the air to the lungs. Some of the air passing through the nasal cavity (and the odorants in it) contacts the olfactory epithelium. The signal from the olfactory epithelium is sent to the olfactory bulb.

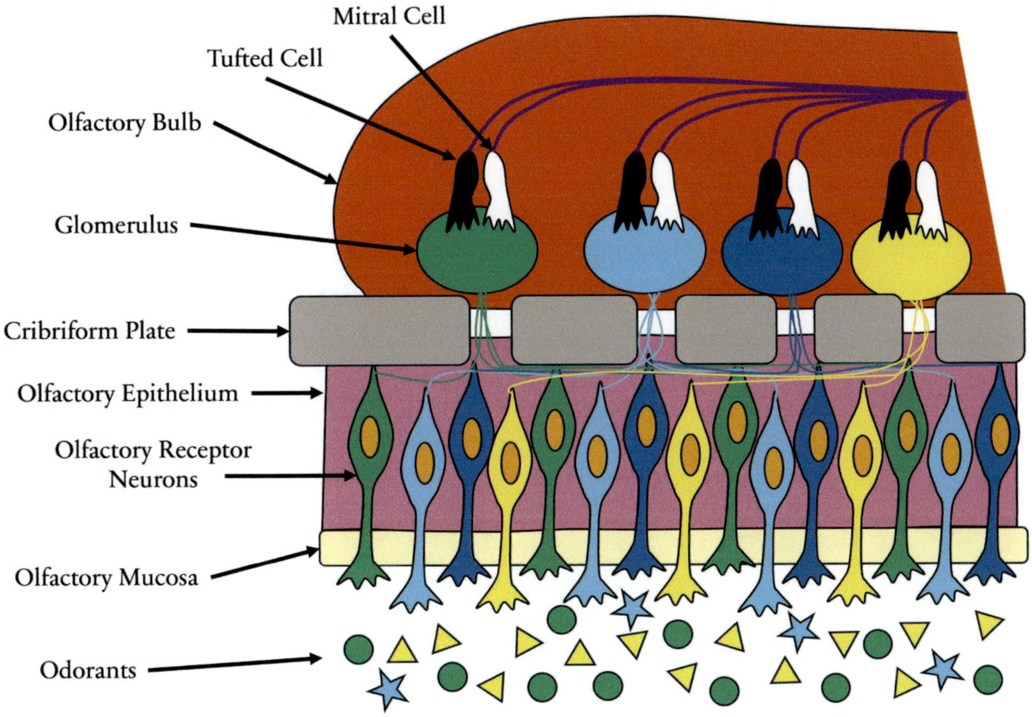

Figure 7.13 The olfactory epithelium and olfactory bulb. Receptor sites in the olfactory mucosa collect odorants. The olfactory receptor neurons send their signals through the cribriform plate to the olfactory bulb. In the bulb, the receptors synapse with mitral and tufted cells, which send the signal to the brain.

nostril leads to its own nasal cavity where the turbinate bones direct most of the air towards the back of the throat and (eventually) into the lungs. *Some* of the air floats upward into the **olfactory epithelium**. A big sniff (like the kind Fred does when he walks into Richard's house—*mmmm*, coffee!) forces extra air upward (which is probably why we do it!).

Olfactory epithelium skin-like organ that reacts to odorants.

Olfactory receptor neurons (ORNs) cells that respond to odorants.

Olfactory cilia hair-like receptor sites of the olfactory receptor neurons.

Olfactory mucosa mucus membrane that is the lowest layer of the olfactory epithelium, contains the olfactory cilia.

The olfactory epithelium is about the size of a US dime (about 1–2 cm across) and has two layers (see Figure 7.13). The upper layer (farther from the nasal opening) contains the cell bodies of the **olfactory receptor neurons** (ORNs; more on these later). The hair-like receptor sites (called **olfactory cilia**) project into the lower layer (closer to the nasal opening). This layer is a mucosal membrane called the **olfactory mucosa**. The olfactory epithelium also contains basal cells, which create new ORNs as needed. Just like the taste buds in the tongue, ORNs don't last very long—about a month on average—and so they need to be replaced often.

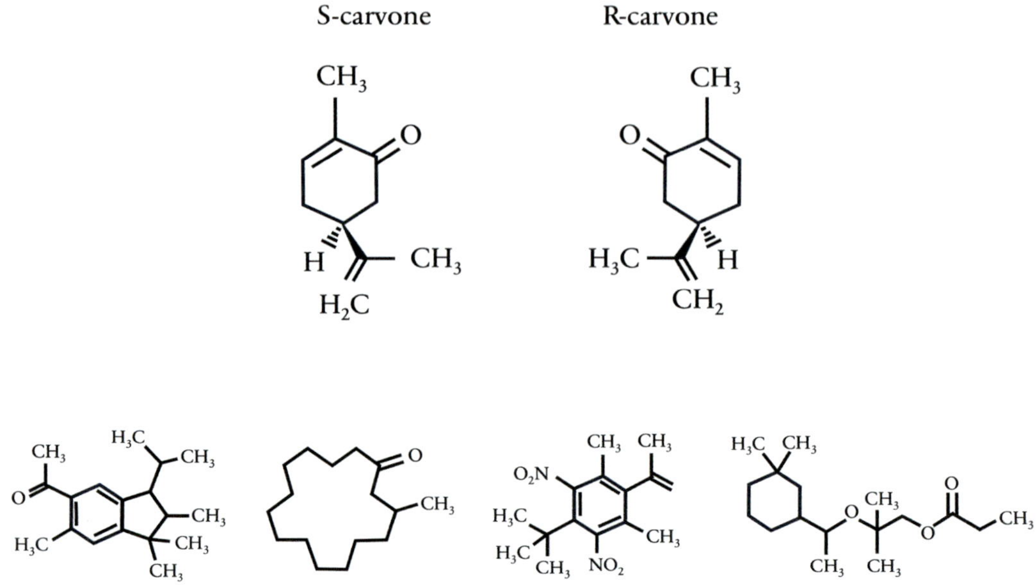

Figure 7.14 Top, two chemicals (S-carvone and R-carvone) that are nearly identical in shape but smell very different. Bottom, four chemicals that are radically different in shape but have the same musky smell (Genva et al., 2019).

Olfactory Receptor Neurons

Look, we're going to be honest with you here: the functioning of the ORNs is a bit *weird* (perhaps another reason why the sense of smell is not very well understood!). The receptor sites have a key-in-lock design (like the taste system), but the shape of the chemical doesn't seem to relate to the smell of the chemical *at all* (unlike in the taste system). Chemicals with nearly identical chemical structures (like S-carvone and R-carvone; see Figure 7.14, top) can have radically different smells (spearmint and caraway,[12] respectively). And chemicals with radically different chemical structures can smell exactly the same (like the four chemicals in Figure 7.14, bottom, which all smell musky despite being radically different in shape).

There are 5 to 10 million ORNs in each olfactory epithelium. There are between 350 and 400 different *types* of OFNs in the average human nose (Buck and Axel won the Nobel Prize for this finding in 2004). You read that right. We only have three different types of cones, but several *hundred* types of ORNs![13] ORNs are broadly tuned; each responds maximally—but not exclusively—to a particular chemical shape. Also, each odorant will activate multiple different types of ORNs—some weakly, some strongly. Recent research has suggested that odorants might activate different types of ORNs *in sequence* depending on their shape (see Figure 7.15) and that it is the specific *temporal* pattern that would give different odorants their different smells (we'll revisit a similar idea with Reichart detectors and motion perception; see Chapter 11).

How many and which types of ORNs you have depends on your genetics. Consequently, it is said that each person has a "unique nose". For example, about 20–40% of those with otherwise typical olfaction cannot smell androsterone (found in armpit sweat and pork), and those that *can* smell it either describe it as "urnious" (smelling like urine) or "sweet

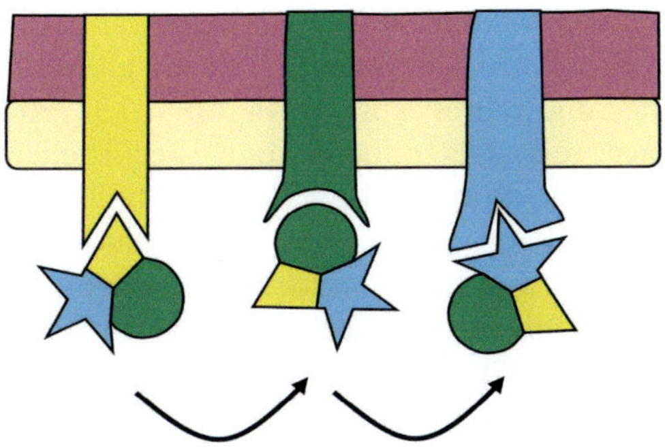

Figure 7.15 It is possible that odorants activate different olfactory receptor neurons in sequence and that cells farther along the pathway pick up on the timing of the activation as a way of identifying odorants.

musky-floral" because they have different types of ORNs that respond to the chemical. About 6% of the population cannot smell the chemical that makes your urine smell funny after eating asparagus; 10% cannot smell freesia flowers; and about 6% can't smell the sweaty-sock smell of isovaleric acid (Vockley & Ensenauer, 2006). If you are one of the 4–14% of people that say cilantro tastes like soap, you are likely missing the ORN responsible for detecting the floral notes of the herb, and so you only smell the soapy note. *Blech.*

By the way, just like in taste, there are some experiences that we describe as a "smell" that are actually a somatosensory reaction. For example, there are some scents that have a "burny" feeling (like ammonia) and some that convey a "soothing" feeling (like menthol). Those feelings are not related to particular odorants detected by ORNs. Instead, stimulation of free nerve endings (for burny smells) and "cold" thermoreceptors (for soothing smells) activates the 5th cranial nerve (the trigeminal nerve). Activation of the trigeminal nerve is also why we cry when cutting onions, sneeze with pepper, and "wake up" with smelling salts.

The axons of the ORN project upward through holes in a thin bone called the **cribriform plate** (technically part of the skull) which separates the olfactory epithelium from the **olfactory bulb** (technically part of the brain). As we continue our discussion of the olfactory system, keep in mind that there are two of each of these systems: one for the left nostril, and one for the right nostril.

Cribriform plate thin bone separating the olfactory epithelium from the olfactory bulb.

Olfactory bulb part of the brain lying directly on top of the nasal cavity, the olfactory receptor neurons project to this area.

Olfactory Bulb

Within the olfactory bulb, there are roughly spherical structures called **glomeruli** (singular: glomerulus). All ORN of a particular type (for example, all of the ORNs responsible for smelling androsterone) send their signal to two glomeruli

Glomeruli roughly spherical structures where the axons of the olfactory receptor neurons synapse with the mitral and tufted cells.

(two "anderosterone glomeruli")—one medial (more towards the center of the head) and one lateral (more towards the outside of the head). In the glomerulus, the axon terminals of the ORNs connect to tufted and mitral cells (see Figure 7.13). Each layer gets deeper in the olfactory bulb and each layer responds to increasingly specific chemical shapes.

The upshot of all these connections is that the olfactory bulb has a kind of chemotopic map (sometimes called an odortopic map). This means that specific chemical shapes end up stimulating specific parts of the olfactory bulb. But remember, changing the expectation of what the smell object is changes the overall pattern of excitation on the olfactory bulb. Also, for someone who has developed a particular taste aversion,[14] the smell of the offensive food activates a completely different part of the olfactory bulb than it did before the aversive event. And finally, remember that the chemical structure of the odorant is not a guarantee of what it will smell like!

Some (e.g., Barwich, 2020) have argued that in order for there to *be* an odortopic map, there would need to be a stable representation of scents and all of the data suggests that the olfactory system is just too dynamic for that. In other words, this is all very complicated! Scientists' best guess as to how chemical shape becomes experienced smell is that there is some transformation later in the processing chain—although it's not particularly well understood.[15]

Neural Pathways for Smell

Continuing to earn its reputation for being the weirdest sense, the olfactory neural pathways are unique in that they do *not* travel through the thalamus on the way to the primary projection area! The axons of the mitral and tufted cells of a particular olfactory bulb bundle together into the 1st cranial nerve (also known as the olfactory tract; see Figure 7.12). The olfactory tract projects to the brain on the same side as the sense organ (the olfactory epithelium); the right olfactory bulb projects to the right hemisphere and vice versa. This is also unusual—taste is the only other sense whose neural pathways do not cross over to the opposite side of the brain from the sense organ (the left side of the tongue projects to the left side of the brain and vice versa).[16]

The olfactory tract carries the signal directly to the primary olfactory cortex (the piriform cortex; see Figure 7.16). From there, the signal travels to four places: 1) the orbitofrontal cortex (the secondary olfactory cortex, likely responsible for the emotional/affective content of smells), 2) the entorhinal cortex (an area related to memory), 3) the hypothalamus (which regulates basic bodily needs), and 4) the thalamus. Yup, the thalamus! *After* the primary projection area! It's all backwards! Scientists think the projections to the thalamus likely regulate the incoming signals from other senses in some way. All four of these areas have reciprocal connections with the amygdala.

Neural Coding

The chemotopic map of the olfactory bulb is—more or less—preserved in the anterior (toward the front of the head) part of the piriform cortex, but any semblance of the chemotopic map vanishes once the signal travels to the posterior (towards the back of the head) piriform cortex. Here, all bets are off! Odorants that activated very specific areas in the olfactory bulb will cause widespread activation in the posterior piriform cortex. Two odorants that activated very different areas of the olfactory bulb will somehow activate the exact same areas in the posterior piriform cortex. The good news is that the activation in this part of the brain *does* reflect the experience of the smell. All things that smell "smoky" will activate the same area, all things that smell "sweet" will activate another area, and so on.

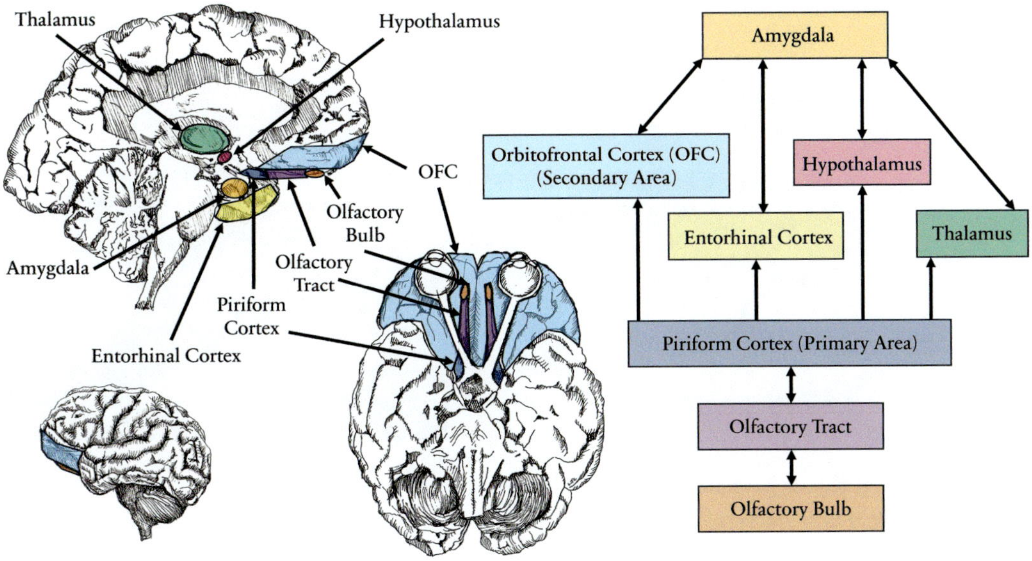

Figure 7.16 Neural pathways for olfaction. Because of the complexity of the pathway, the brain drawings do not include the pathway, just the areas the pathway travels through.

When we discussed taste earlier in this chapter, we talked about two ways the different sensory systems convey complex stimuli. Specifically, there is the *labeled-line* approach (like hearing) and the *cross-fiber* approach (like vision, particularly seeing color). Part of the reason we suggested that both might apply to taste is because both *definitely* apply in smell (and the two senses are very closely related). There is no question that overall patterns of multiple odorants (think the 600+ odorants involved in the smell of coffee—no wonder Fred enjoys going to Richard's house so much!) are sometimes experienced as one unitary smell, which is an experience associated with cross-fiber coding. However, when presented with two smells at once—for example, coffee and roses (the smell of roses is made up of more than 1000 odorants), the person will experience *both* coffee *and* roses (rather than some combination smell), which is an experience associated with labeled line coding.

Flavor

It is a very common experience to have the loss of the sense of smell profoundly affect the taste of food (like what happened to Fred during his bout with Covid). You might have noticed this yourself if you've had Covid, or even just a bad cold that stuffed up your nose. When we breathe out (even very small amounts) while eating, air from our mouths travels up the back of our throats into our nasal passages. The odorants in that air eventually make contact with the olfactory epithelium, a process called **retronasal olfaction**. (Sniffing the food before it's in your mouth is called **orthonasal olfaction**, in case you were wondering.)

> **Retronasal olfaction** traveling of odorants from the mouth to the nasal cavity via the back of the throat.
>
> **Orthonasal olfaction** odorants entering the nasal cavity through the nostrils.

Figure 7.17 Food that is presented in an aesthetically pleasing way (left) is rated as tastier than food that is not (right).

Our experience of food—what we commonly call flavor—is a combination of ortho and retronasal olfaction; gustation; somatosensory experiences (such as pain, trigeminal nerve stimulation, and mouth feel of the food); the sight of the food; and the way it sounds when we chew it (yes, really). And it *also* depends on what we think we are eating, and our past experience with whatever the food is. Change any one of those factors and it will radically change the experience of the food (see Rosenblum, 2011).

Earlier in this chapter we discussed how level of hunger or experience with food (like taste aversion) can change the way the brain responds to food. Those factors change the way people *rate* the flavor of the food as well. Hungrier people rate food as tasting better[17] (as you might expect), and taste aversion will cause people to refuse even foods that used to be their favorite (as you may have experienced).

Increasing the intensity of the scent of pear in a juice will increase its overall flavor, including making it taste sweeter. Similarly, simply adding sugar to the juice will increase the "pearness" of the juice (how much it tastes like pear). Actually, adding sugar to *any* food will increase how intense people perceive the flavor to be (which is probably why so many foods have added sugar). Likewise, changing the color of ice cream changes how it tastes—which is probably why mint ice cream often has added green food coloring. And there's a reason fancy restaurants spend time and effort on "plating" the food—arranging the different components of the meal just so on the plate (Michel et al., 2015). Research has shown that people rate food that is presented like Figure 7.17 (*left*) higher than food that is presented like Figure 7.17 (*right*).

Neurologically, there are clear reciprocal connections between the areas that respond to olfactory stimuli and those that respond to gustatory stimuli (see Figure 7.18). Changing any part of the eating experience (smell, taste, mouth feel, etc.) will change the pattern of activation. Finally, research has shown that (for Macaque monkeys, anyway) there is an area of the orbital frontal cortex that receives signals from the taste, smell, and vision primary projection areas (Rolls & Baylis, 1994). All of which is to say that flavor is clearly a multifaceted experience.

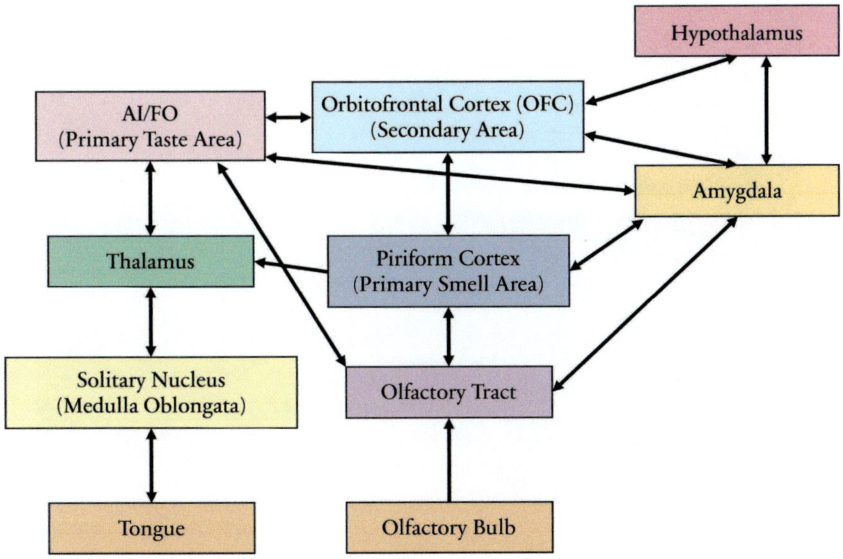

Figure 7.18 The interconnectedness of the (simplified) olfactory and gustatory neural pathways.

> Socratic Question: What is the difference between the experience of "taste" and the experience of "flavor"? Is there a comparable difference for visual, auditory, or touch experiences?

Gustation and Olfaction in Non-Humans

The chemical senses are perhaps the most fundamental of all of the senses. More than vision. More than hearing. More than touch. In fact, you would be hard-pressed to find a single living organism that does not sense chemical gradients of one kind or another. Even single-celled organisms like paramecia. And even plants! When a poplar tree is being attacked by caterpillars (read: when the caterpillars are eating its leaves), it will send out a wave of volatiles that attract wasps (who in turn eat the caterpillars). A nearby poplar tree will "smell" the volatiles and send out its own wave in response—even if there are no caterpillars on that tree (Dicke et al., 2009). Amazing!

The world of chemical senses is wild and diverse (see Yong, 2022). Many animals have two "smell" senses—one that acts much like our own, and a second that uses a different smell organ altogether (called a vomeronasal organ), but that sends the neural signal to the same places in the brain as the other smell organ. Snakes, for example, use their forked tongues to gather odorants from the air. When they retract their tongues, saliva washes the odorants into the vomeronasal organs. The forked tongue acts like our two-ear system—allowing directionality in smelling the air (see Chapter 12).

Taste organs appear in a variety of locations in a variety of animals (Yong, 2022). Most insects taste with their feet and legs (which makes sense for a bee landing on a flower or a fly landing on a piece of fruit). Several kinds of insects taste the air with antennae—both ants and moths use them to detect pheromones (species-specific chemical signals). Catfish are

Figure 7.19 The slits on the side of a dog's nose change the way air is circulated. Even when a dog is breathing out, the odorants are forced up into the olfactory epithelium.

literally covered in taste buds. They are like swimming tongues! Elephants have nostrils like we do, but their nose is very long and mobile—they can use their trunk to "smell around" just like we use our eyes to look around (and they have an astounding 2000+ ORN types, so they are *really good* at smelling around!). This is exactly what Fred's pet elephant, Topsy, does whenever Carol comes over—smelling for the peanuts in her pocket.

Frank's ability to smell the beef jerky on Fred is fairly common—dogs have an exceptionally keen sense of smell. That is partially because they have far more ORNs than humans, but it's also because of the way their *nose* is shaped. Check out the close-up in Figure 7.19. Those slits on the sides of the nostrils are functional. Unlike in humans, when dogs breathe out, it forces air *into* their nasal passages because of those slits. Or in other words, they are able to sample the surrounding odorants whether they are breathing in *or* out. No wonder they have been trained to detect any number of things like drugs, explosives, fluctuations in blood sugar, pregnant polar bears, and cancer (see Chapter 19). Yes, really—pregnant polar bears.

Socratic Question: Why might the chemical senses be the most fundamental of all the senses? Despite this, why do you think that the sense of vision is much more widely studied by scientists?

Disruptions in Smell and Taste

At the start of this chapter, we defined anosmia as the loss of the sense of smell and ageusia as the loss of sense of taste. These conditions are relatively rare, but probably more common than you think!

Anosmia

Congenital anosmia (that is, being born anosmic) is incredibly rare—affecting only about .01% of the population (although, fun fact, one of your authors has congenital anosmia; see Box 7.2!). However, partial loss of smell is relatively common. Even before Covid, about 1 in 100 people reported some period of total anosmia, while 1 in 20 reported some partial anosmia. That number has likely gone up since over half of the people who get Covid report anosmia as one of the symptoms, and a quarter of *those* people report either permanent loss or only partial recovery several months after recovering from the virus (Mitchell et al., 2023).

Partial or total anosmia is also a relatively common side effect of head trauma. The bony plate that separates the olfactory epithelium from the olfactory bulb is very thin. Breaking that plate can result in temporary or permanent loss because it tears the nerves that pass through it. Even when the bone *heals*, it often heals with scars that cover the holes that the nerves passed through, resulting in permanent loss.

Box 7.2 Temporary Recovery from Congenital Anosmia or That Time I Got My Smell Back for a Week.

I (Dr. Blau) am one of the very few people who was born with a total lack of sense of smell. Doctors think it is because I have chronic swelling in one of two possible locations: either in the cribriform plate or along the underside of my brain, where the olfactory tract passes through two tiny bony channels. In either case, swelling keeps the nerves from carrying the signals from my ORNs to my brain . . . except for one week when I was in my twenties.

I had an allergic reaction to something in my house (probably a new detergent, but we're not really sure) and had to have a shot of steroids as well as a series of oral steroids for about a week after the initial reaction. No problem. Unbeknownst to me, the steroids caused a widespread decrease in swelling—not only treating the allergic reaction, but also decreasing the swelling that blocked my olfactory signal. The next morning, I woke up and started noticing strange things. Making the coffee was suddenly a much more enjoyable experience (though I couldn't have told you why). Cleaning the kitty litter was suddenly a *much less* enjoyable experience (and here I was starting to suspect why). I could smell for the first time in my life!

My (very excited and scientifically minded) roommate took me through our spice collection. While I could tell that *something* was happening each time they handed me a jar, I couldn't distinguish between the spices in any meaningful way; it all just felt like *sensation*. Later, while visiting my parents, my (also excited and also scientifically minded) father similarly took me through *their* spice collection. This time, each time he handed me a jar, I knew I had smelled that smell before—in some cases, I could even guess which spice it was.

Food tasted *completely different*. Some things I had loved (like a tuna fish sandwich, just like Fred!) I now couldn't stand. Spices that had previously had no effect on the taste of food suddenly made it taste completely different after they were added. For that week, eating was an adventure (and not always a pleasant one). After I finished the course of the medication, my sense of smell slowly dwindled away again. For a few weeks afterwards, food tasted *so bland*; but eventually everything went back to how it was before.

Socratic Question: When Dr. Blau "got her smell back", things were a bit confusing. Suddenly some experiences were strangely pleasurable or unpleasurable and other things "just felt like sensation". Do you think that that experience of someone who is suddenly able to see, hear, or feel would be similar to hers?

Ageusia and Dysgeusia

Congenital ageusia and total ageusia later in life are relatively uncommon; however, *partial* loss of taste happens much more frequently. Because of the interaction between taste and smell, what some people report as loss of taste is actually an alteration in *flavor* due to the loss (either partial or total) of the sense of smell. However, various illnesses (such as salivary gland infections, gum disease, or diabetes) can impair the sense of taste. Far more common is **dysgeusia**—a "phantom", usually unpleasant, taste in the mouth. The most common cause of dysgeusia is certain medications. When Fred took Paxlovid for his Covid, he experienced dysgeusia—an unpleasant metallic taste in his mouth, a side effect so common it's called "Paxlovid mouth". *Blech.*

Dysgeusia a phantom, usually unpleasant, taste in the mouth.

Both anosmia and ageusia are common consequences of aging, but interestingly, it isn't an across-the-board loss in either sense. People lose their ability to taste bitterness with age, but not their ability to taste sweetness—probably better that way, right? People more quickly lose their ability to smell pleasant smells, but will retain their ability to smell unpleasant ones far longer—can't win 'em all, right?

Adaptation of Taste and Smell

Fred's friend, Pat, has a few cats. Actually, more than a few. Enough so that whenever Fred visits Pat, he can smell the litterbox the moment he walks into the house. *Pee-yew!* But after a short time in the house (really only a few minutes), he finds the smell hardly noticeable. After an hour or two, he can't smell it at all! The same thing happens to Pat when he visits Fred and his baby elephant. Smell habituation (also sometimes called adaptation) is at least partially due to the fatigue of the ORNs, but research has shown that's not the whole story. Participants who are told that a particular smell is benign will show adaptation to most smells. However, if they are told the smell is an indication of something dangerous, they will show no adaptation—no matter how pleasant or unpleasant the smell is (Dalton, 2002).

Some activities can actually *increase* your olfactory or gustatory abilities. For example, drinking a single alcoholic drink increases your olfactory abilities (although heavy drinking will decrease it). Going on a low-sodium diet will increase your ability to taste salt in a dish within only a week or so of being on the diet. Excessive and intense sniffing (you read that right) as well as smell training (a daily routine of smelling various essential oils) can improve a person's sense of smell. And if you're a smoker (or live with one), quitting smoking (or forcing your roommate to do so) will cause a dramatic improvement in both olfaction and gustation!

Summary

Taste and smell (olfaction and gustation, respectively) are inextricably linked. They are linked in function—both serve as "gatekeepers" for ingesting harmful substances. They are also linked in lived experience—the concept of "flavor" is an overlapping sense. But they do have different receptors. Taste buds are primarily on the tongue, and the (at least) four basic tastes are sweet, salty, bitter, and sour. Olfactory receptors are primarily in the nasal passage, and respond to hundreds of different scents. Congenital disruptions in taste and smell are relatively rare, but they do happen. Far more common are temporary disruptions like those you might have if you contracted Covid.

Notes

1 These are there for the somatosensory aspect of taste as well as increasing friction on the tongue to aid in food manipulation.
2 If you're not sure where that is, push the tip of your tongue onto the roof of your mouth and then slide it backwards until you find the part that feels softer (like there's no bone behind it); that is your soft palate.
3 At least for humans; cats and many other carnivores do not have the ability to taste sweetness, but are incredibly sensitive to the amino acids in meat protein.
4 Attempts to do the same with topical creams have failed—the free nerve endings in our mouths are *far* more sensitive than the free nerve endings in our skin. Capsaicin simply doesn't irritate the ones in the skin enough to help.
5 Japanese for "good flavor" or "delicious".
6 Remember that name—you'll encounter it again in Chapter 9. Boring was a prolific scholar.
7 Want to find out if you're a supertaster? Use a few drops of blue food dye to dye the tip of your tongue. The filiform papillae (and other tongue structures) will pick up the blue dye, but the fungiform papillae will not. Use a hole punch to cut a hole in a piece of paper and place it on the tip of your tongue just to the right (or left) of the midline (there are no fungiform papillae on the midline). Count the raised still-pink circles (this is easier if you take a photo and count them in the photo, like in Figure 7.8). If you have fewer than 15, you are probably a nontaster. If you have more than 30, you are probably a supertaster.
8 Although, arguably, people started caring a lot more in the wake of the Covid pandemic when many people temporarily or permanently lost their sense of smell!
9 Part of the reason why this distinction might not be helpful in the long run.
10 This is why there are coffee sommeliers, just like there are wine sommeliers.
11 For example, in 1916, Henning developed a "smell prism" with *fragrant*, *putrid*, *ethereal*, *burned*, *spicy*, and *resinous* as the corners.
12 A plant also known as meridian fennel which smells warm, spicy, and earthy—a bit like rye bread—and very much unlike spearmint.
13 That's nothing compared to the mouse, which has over 1000 different types!
14 Perhaps you have experienced this: you get sick right after eating something, and then you can no longer stand the taste or smell of that food.
15 It's also worth mentioning that the function of the olfactory bulb might not be as necessary to smell as once thought—one scientist (Weiss et al., 2020) identified several women who have no olfactory bulb and are nonetheless able to smell just fine.
16 Why? We have no idea!
17 Or in other words, there's truth to the phrase "hunger is the best flavoring"!

Part Two

The Traditional Approach

8 Limitations of a Biological Approach and Introduction to the Traditional Approach

The first seven chapters of this book have focused on the biological approach to sensation and perception. The primary assumption of that view was that all experiences—including the experience of knowing the world around us—are entirely biological. And that may be true! Or at minimum, it may be true that all experiences involve biological processes. But it does not necessarily follow that all experiences are best *understood* from a biological perspective. In other words, it does not necessarily follow that those experiences are *nothing more* than biological processes. In addition, it is certainly the case that taking an entirely biological approach to understanding sensation and perception leads to some unsolved (and possibly *unsolvable*) problems.

In the first part of this chapter, we will discuss some of the problems that are created or encountered when taking an entirely biological approach to understanding our experience of the world around us. It's not a fully comprehensive list (and it's not intended to be!); rather, it's supposed to give you a sense of the kinds of issues that crop up when taking such an approach. In the second part of the chapter, we will cover the assumptions of the traditional approach, which is the focus of Chapters 9-12.

Problem #1: Binding Problem

One day, Fred was cooking bacon on the stove (*mmmmm*, bacon). He watched as the color changed from vibrant pink and white to reddish-brown and dark brown; he heard the *crackle-pop* sound of the sizzling, smelled the smoky, savory, meaty aroma, felt the hard, metallic handle of the tongs in his hand, and jerked his hand away—*fast*—when the pan spat oil and burned him (*ouch*!). As we learned in the first seven chapters of this book, these experiences each involve different energy forms that stimulate different receptor cells in different organs—photoreceptors on the retina, cilia in the cochlea, olfactory receptor neurons in the olfactory epithelium in the nasal cavity, just to name a few. The signals generated by those receptor cells are processed by different parts of the brain—the occipital lobe, the parietal lobe, the orbitofrontal cortex, and so on. And those signals are sometimes processed at very different speeds—signals related to pain are processed faster than those related to sounds which are turn processed faster than those related to object recognition, for example. And yet, Fred experiences "cooking bacon" as *a singular event* rather than as a set of unrelated but equally real experiences (see Figure 8.1).

Fred's unitary experience of cooking bacon illustrates what is known as the **binding problem** (Burwick, 2014;

Binding problem how the brain links together the different energy patterns which generate stimulation in different organs and are processed at different speeds in different parts of the brain into a unitary experience

DOI: 10.4324/9781032690964-10

Figure 8.1 When Fred cooks bacon he experiences the event via several sense modalities, and yet he experiences the event as a unitary whole.

Treisman, 1996). That is, if the different energy patterns that are associated with a given event stimulate different receptors in different organs and are processed by different areas and at different speeds, how does the brain take all these very different streams of biological activity and connect them into a singular *experience*? This problem is particularly challenging if you believe either one (or both) of the historically popular ideas of the *Doctrine of Specific Nerve Energies* or *Hierarchical Processing* (see Chapter 1). First, if you believe that experience of the world is really awareness of the activity of nerves, and experiences of seeing, hearing, touching, tasting, and smelling are delivered to the brain along dedicated pathways, then it is absolutely necessary that to reunite these separate pathways and experiences at some point.

Second, if you believe that all processing happens in a stepwise fashion from simple to complex, then the binding problem can only be solved by having some part of the brain where all the different inputs come together to become one unitary complex whole and . . .*well* . . . that doesn't really happen. It turns out that there's no common "final destination" in the brain where all the different inputs come back together.

And yet . . . there *might* be a way out of this problem. As we pointed out in a few places in Chapters 2-7, there are reciprocal connections between all the different areas of the brain. This means that all the different processing areas communicate with each other at some point—even if there is no "final destination" in the brain. We don't fully understand how those connections work, but there are clear communication channels at every step of the processing. It is perhaps not a coincidence that most of the senses have dorsal and ventral pathways after the primary projection areas. Those dorsal and ventral streams communicate—both within *and* across senses. The ventral visual pathway communicates with the dorsal visual pathway and the ventral auditory pathway. So it's possible the binding problem can be "solved" by those reciprocal connections.

The binding problem is one of the (many) reasons why a strictly hierarchical processing model is no longer the dominant belief in neurological research. A more flexible view of the nervous system and brain in which different areas trade responsibilities and different pathways are possible resolves the location and timing problems of the binding problem (see Anderson, 2014; Favela, 2024). It doesn't matter if sound is processed in a different location than light—those areas talk to each other. It doesn't matter if pain gets to the brain before object recognition takes place; those experiences are being shared in the neural net over time.

Problem #2: Outness Problem

The fundamental assumption of the biological approach is that all experiences are, well, biological—no more and no less. That is, if Fred experiences the smell of cooking bacon (*mmmmm*, bacon), it is because of the activity of his olfactory receptor neurons coupled with the activity of his brain (in various areas). The problem here is that all of Fred's various sensory receptors and all of the various parts of brain (all his biological bits, really) are *in his body*, but his experience of the bacon is that it's *out there in the world*. If the biological activity that generates the experience of the bacon (or of anything really) is "in here", how does Fred experience those things as being "out there"? This is known as the **outness problem**—if all sensation is *internal*, how do we experience the world as *external*?

> **Outness problem** since all sensation is the activity of receptors and nerves that are inside the body, how is it that we experience the world as existing outside our bodies? Why don't we experience the world as an internal phenomenon?

Think about it like this: imagine you are inside of Fred's head (see Figure 8.2). It's round and roomy—kind of comfy, actually. Just go with it. *You* are the central executive—go, you! You notice that the photoreceptors in Fred's eyes are firing. You also notice that V1 is responding to those photoreceptors and that V2 is also, in turn, responding. All of this

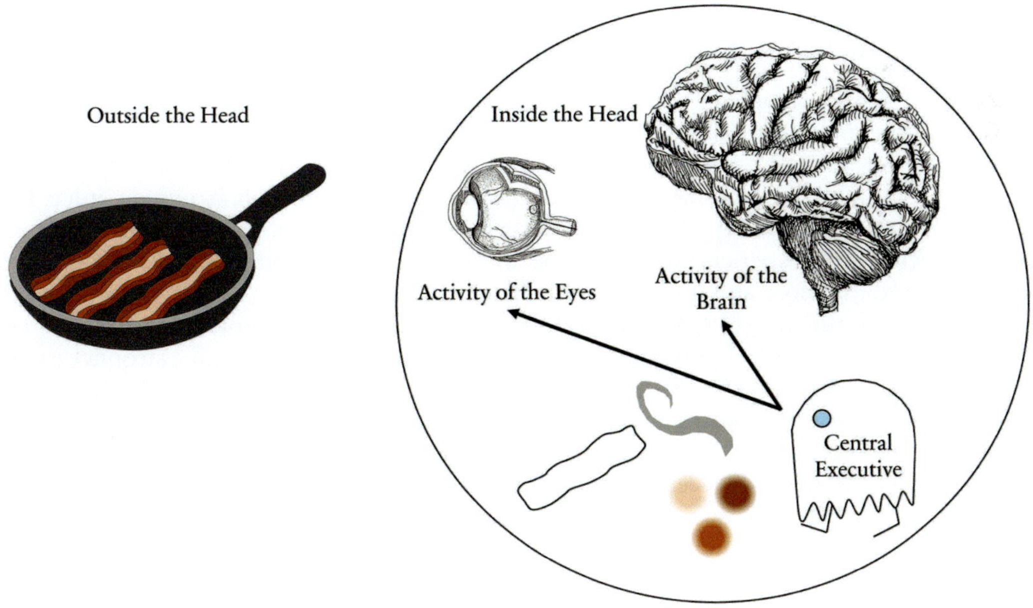

Figure 8.2 The outness problem. If you were the central executive and all the biological activity is happening inside *Fred's body*, why would you sense the world as being *out there*?

activity is in here with you. Why would you assume that the stimulus came from somewhere else? Isn't it more logical to assume that something is happening *in here* to cause it? If there were a commotion somewhere in your house, would you assume the source of that commotion was something outside, or would you more likely assume the source of the commotion was *inside with the commotion*?

What is particularly interesting about this problem is that there is at least some anecdotal evidence that the outness problem is overcome through experience—in particular, experience moving around in the world and learning to use cues. The most well-known of this anecdotal evidence involves one of the earliest cataract removal surgeries ever (back in 1728!). It was performed by English surgeon extraordinaire Dr. William Cheselden on a 13-year-old boy who had been blind (due to the cataracts) since birth. Although there is a great deal of controversy surrounding what exactly the patient could see after the cataracts were removed, Cheselden's notes indicate that "When (the patient) first saw, he was so far from making any judgment of distances, that he thought all objects whatever *touched his eyes* (as he expressed it)" (Cheselden, 1728, p. 448). Putting the controversy aside for the moment, the notes seem to indicate that the patient experienced what he saw as being *on* at least *very near* his eyes rather than being "out there". It is at least possible, then, that experience seeing and moving around in the world helps to shift experience from "in here" (or at least, "near here") to "out there".

> Socratic Question: Consider a visually impaired individual who uses a cane to explore their surroundings. How can this be described as another example of the "outness problem"? How might experience feeling and moving around help to "solve" this problem?

Problem #3: Biological Responses Are Not (Inherently) Meaningful

When Fred was cooking his bacon, he watched as it changed color (darker) and shape (smaller and wrinklier), waiting for the moment when it looked *just right* (dark, but not too dark; small but not too small; wrinkly but not too wrinkly—he likes it extra crispy) before he took it off the stove. The shape and color of the bacon is *meaningful* to Fred—it lets him know when to stop cooking the bacon and eat it—*mmmm*, bacon. And yet, in the biological approach, Fred's experience of the shape and color of the bacon is actually the firing of neurons—nothing more and nothing less—*mmmm*, neurons?

In processing the image of the bacon on Fred's retina, Fred's photoreceptors respond to patterns of light and dark. For the lighter parts of the bacon, they will send a stronger signal; for the darker parts (and the black of the pan) they will send a weaker signal. His ganglia respond to the photoreceptors and do so especially strongly to areas of contrast. That signal is sent to the cortex where simple, complex, and end-stopped cells respond to the activity of the ganglia and do so especially strongly at areas of contrast at particular angles, ends of edges, and movement. Those signals are sent along the dorsal and ventral streams where the cells respond to more and more complex shapes.

But the firing of a neuron doesn't *mean* an area of contrast (let alone bacon). It is firing *in response* to an area of contrast, but that is not the same thing! It's like saying that the word "elephant" and an actual elephant are the same thing. One can be used to *represent* the other, but only one of them will eat all your peanuts (see Figure 8.3).

Elephant

Figure 8.3 Only one of these two will eat all your peanuts.

The word "elephant" comes to represent this particular kind of animal because we associate the word with the idea of a large gray pachyderm with tusks and big floppy ears, but the word itself isn't *inherently* meaningful.[1] The same is true—more or less—of the firing of neurons. The firing of a set of neurons isn't *inherently* meaningful. Bacon is meaningful—especially to Fred. The neural response to bacon is not. So how does that set of neural firings come to *mean* bacon? Ultimately, that is a gap that needs to be crossed. This problem is known as the **grounding problem** (see Chapter 19; Taddeo & Floridi, 2005).

Grounding problem the challenge of reconnecting meaningless representations (e.g., symbols) with the meaningful things that they represent.

The biological approach attempts to solve the grounding problem through hierarchical processing. As the stimulation is processed hierarchically, areas of contrast become edges of a particular orientation, which become shapes, and so on. The problem is that there doesn't seem to be a part of the brain that takes shapes and turns them into *things with meaning*. At best, the biological approach can get a *representation* of bacon into the head,[2] but the image still isn't the same thing as what the meaning of that bacon might be.

Ultimately, the activity of the neurons might not be the right place to understand the way Fred perceives the meaning of his bacon. It might be the wrong level of analysis. In other words, neural activity might be necessary but not sufficient for perceptual experience. As an analogy, think about trying to understand how we get meaning from reading. You are reading this sentence and (hopefully) getting some meaning out of it. And while it's true that—at some level—a sentence consists of a sequence of individual letters, letters, on their own, have no meaning. Letters are the *wrong level* to try to understand reading. That is, they are necessary, but not sufficient. To understand reading, you minimally have to start at the level of words. But even that wouldn't fully capture it since the meaning of a sentence exists at the level of a sequence of words arranged according to rule (called grammar).

The argument here is that trying to understand visual perception at the level of the firing of neurons is a little like trying to understand reading at the level of letters. There's a *big gap* between the letters and the meaning. And you might not be able to get from one to the other. Nonetheless, the traditional approach (which we will talk about later in this chapter) tries to bridge that gap.

Problem #4: Ambiguity

Ambiguity (in perception) when identical physical situations result in different perceptual experiences OR when different physical situations result in identical perceptual experiences.

Another difficulty with the biological approach is the problem of **ambiguity**. Think about the black box logic in Figure 1.10—to figure out what's happening inside the box, we put in different inputs (here, different sensory stimulation patterns) and measure outputs (here, the resulting perceptual experience). One kind of ambiguity occurs when we provide the system with identical inputs, but it results in different outputs; another kind is when we provide the system with *different* inputs, but it results in identical outputs (like metamers; see Chapter 4). And unfortunately for the biological approach, this happens a lot—more than it should if experience is merely a biological process.

In Figure 4.14, we mentioned a picture of a dress—yes, *that* dress. Some people see the dress as white and gold, some as black and blue, and some people can see it both ways! In all cases, they are all looking at the exact same photograph and so the input to each person's visual system (and presumably the activity in each person's optic nerve and visual cortex) is identical. And yet . . . their visual experience of the dress differs. Figure 8.4 is another example called the Necker cube. You can see the box as if the orange square is closer to you (and you were looking at the box from below to the left). Or you can see the box as if the blue square is closer to you (and you were looking at it from above and to the right). This is an even thornier example, because we are not comparing your experience to anyone else's—just your experience *now* to your experience *later*. Presumably, the input to your person's visual system (and presumably the activity in your optic nerve and visual cortex) is the same now as it is later, and yet . . . your visual experience differs.

Another type of ambiguity is when we provided the system with *different* inputs, and nevertheless get *identical* perceptual experiences. One example we talked about in Chapter 4 (the chapter on color perception), color constancy, is when very different color profiles reach the eye, but we nevertheless view the object as having the same color. The apple always appears red even when we see it in blue light. The problem is the inverse of the one that we described earlier. The input to the visual system (and presumably the activity in the optic nerve and visual cortex) is different. And yet, the visual experience is the same.

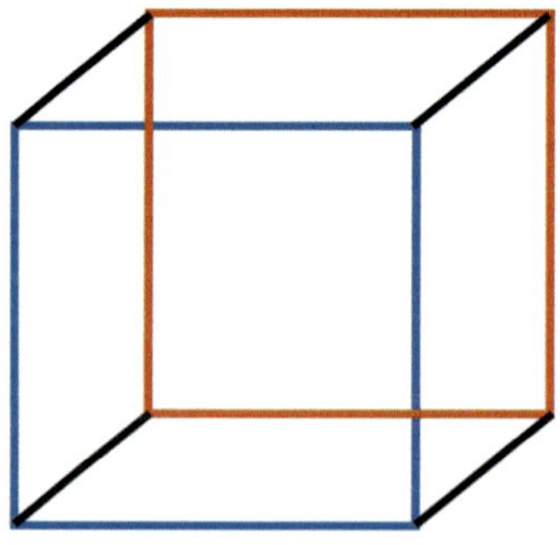

Figure 8.4 The Necker cube can be seen in multiple ways. For example, either the orange square or the blue square could be seen as the front face of the cube.

In other words, there are both "one-to-many" relationships (meaning one input resulting in many outputs) and "many-to-one" relationships (meaning many inputs resulting in one output) in perceptual experience. Explaining both kinds of experiences is one of the challenges facing the traditional approach.

Assumptions of the Traditional Approach

As we described in Chapter 1, all scientific investigations—and therefore all approaches to understanding sensing and perceiving—start with assumptions. These assumptions both inform and restrict the explanations provided by these approaches.

As we also discussed in Chapter 1, all three of the approaches that we describe in this book—the biological approach, the traditional approach, and the ecological approach—share a fundamental set of assumptions. These include the assumptions that the world really exists (realism), that we start with no knowledge (*tabula rasa*), that we gain all knowledge through our senses (empiricism), and that our senses are at least reasonably reliable so we *can* use them to learn about our environments. Now, we turn to an additional set of assumptions that underlie the traditional approach.

Traditional Assumption 1: All Causality Is Local

This might seem a bit off-topic at first, but we swear it's important, so just bear with us. The traditional approach (and to some extent, the biological approach) makes a particular assumption about the nature of science and causality. That assumption is going to dramatically alter not just *what* questions they ask but *how* they try to answer those questions. Traditional theorists assume all causality is *local* (see Box 8.1).

Box 8.1 Causality

Fred and his best friend, Claudia, are playing a game of pool. Claudia uses the pool stick to strike the cue ball, the cue ball moves and strikes the 8-ball, the 8-ball moves across the table and drops into the corner pocket (see Figure 8.4). A scientist might look at this situation and ask: what caused the 8-ball to go into the corner pocket?

Here are some (not mutually exclusive) hypotheses for why the 8-ball fell into the corner pocket:

1) The specific materials that form the pool stick, table, cue ball, 8-ball, and pocket change the way they interact with each other and consequently how the event happens (*material cause*).
2) The reason these objects exist is to facilitate a game in which the 8-ball eventually goes into the corner pocket. That reason for being will bring about this event (*final cause*).
3) The person who designed the objects designed them in such a way that this event would be possible, even inevitable (*formal cause*).
4) The player uses the pool stick to transfer momentum to the cue ball, the cue ball transfers momentum to the 8-ball and that momentum carries it into the pocket (*efficient cause, aka local cause*).

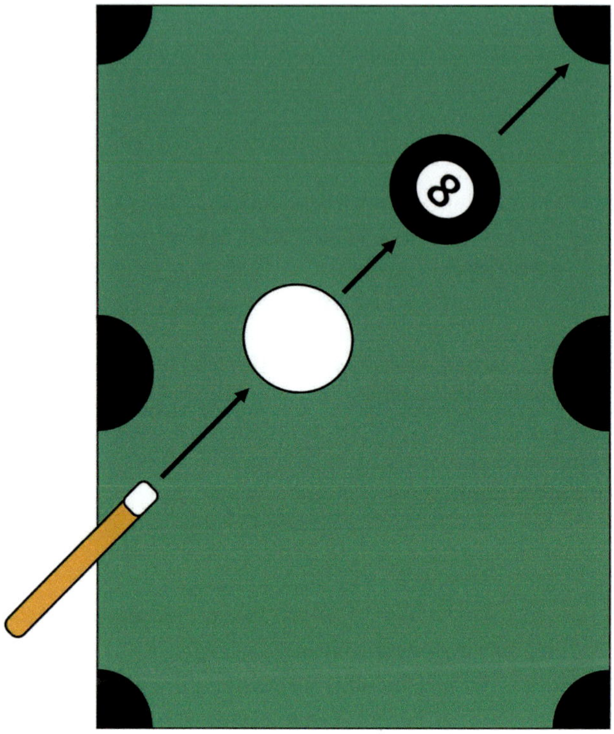

Figure 8.5 What is the cause of the 8-ball moving into the pocket?

5) God wants it this way (*metaphysical cause*).
6) Claudia was inspired by a Paul Newman movie and, after months of practice, managed to win a game against Fred (*psycho-social cause*).
7) Invisible mind-reading gnomes read the minds of the players and the balls and scurry about the table, making certain outcomes happen according to a moral system known only to them (*gnomic cause*).

If you have even a passing relationship with science, you might notice that number four seems the most reasonable, and number seven sounds downright silly. Yet, all of these (with the exception of number seven) have been used for an understanding of causality at some point. In fact, Aristotle (c. 350 BCE) thought that we needed *all* of the first four in order to truly understand the "why" of this situation. Even number seven is not illogical; it is just impossible to disprove and thus impossible to submit to the scientific method.

The type of causality used in number four is not the most logical one; it just *feels* that way because most of modern science is based on the assumption of efficient cause, also known as *local causality*.

Socratic Question: Can you imagine scenarios where the other kinds of causes described in Box 8.1 are just as important to understanding why a given outcome occurred?

Figure 8.6 Fred is not in direct contact with the tree, and yet his behavior is clearly influenced by it. This is a seeming violation of local causality known as the action-at-a-distance problem.

While science could proceed on any number of different types of causality, the traditional approaches—and most of modern science—assume *local causality.* Local causality suggests that in order for thing A to be the cause of thing B, thing A must be in direct contact with thing B.

Local Causality and the Problem of Action-at-a-Distance

While local causality certainly seems like the right way to go for understanding things like what causes a pool ball to move the way that it does (see Box 8.1), it almost immediately runs into problems for understanding things like how an animal—like Fred—perceives the world around them. In Chapter 1, we introduced you to Fred as he was trying to get an apple from an apple tree (see Figure 8.6). As Fred sees the apple on the tree and approaches it from across the field, Fred is clearly not touching or otherwise making physical contact with the apple on the tree, and yet his awareness and behavior are each affected by it. He moves in the direction of the tree, reaches out to grab the apple, closes his hand around it, and until that very last moment does not come into physical contact with any part of the apple or the tree.

In some sense, the cause of his behavior is clearly the apple on the tree and yet he is not in direct contact with it until the very end of the behavior. It seems to be in violation of the assumption of local causality! How could something *way over there* (the apple on the tree) cause something way over here (Fred walking to the tree)? And what more, how could something in the future (eating the apple) cause something now (approaching the apple)? This concern, called the **action-at-a-distance problem**, must be resolved in order to continue investigating how it is that animals—like Fred—perceive the world around them.

Action-at-a-distance problem perception appears to be in violation of local causality because we are not in direct contact with the things we see, and yet they affect our experience and our behavior.

Traditional Assumption 2A: Contact with the World is Mediated by a Representation.
Traditional Assumption 2B: That Representation Must Contain Geometric and Physical Information About the Environment.

One possibility for resolving the action-at-a-distance problem is to propose that there is *mediated* (i.e., indirect) contact between Fred and the (apple on the) tree. Continuing the earlier example (from Box 8.1) in local causality, the cue ball causes the 8-ball to move. In mediated local causality, the pool stick causes the cue ball to move, which in turn, causes the 8-ball to move. The pool stick is the ultimate cause of the 8-ball's behavior, but the cue ball *mediates* the contact between the pool stick and the 8-ball. Applying this to Fred's problem, we could propose that while he is not in contact with the tree, perhaps there is a third thing that goes between Fred and the tree and is in contact with both (see Figure 8.7). In fact, in order to maintain local causality, we have *no other choice* but to assume that something like this occurs.

There are a handful of options here, but they all boil down to the same idea. There is a *representation of the world* that goes between Fred and the world which allows him to experience that world despite not having direct contact with it. Or in other words, the tree gets represented (somehow) in Fred's mind, and the *representation* of the tree is what is in direct

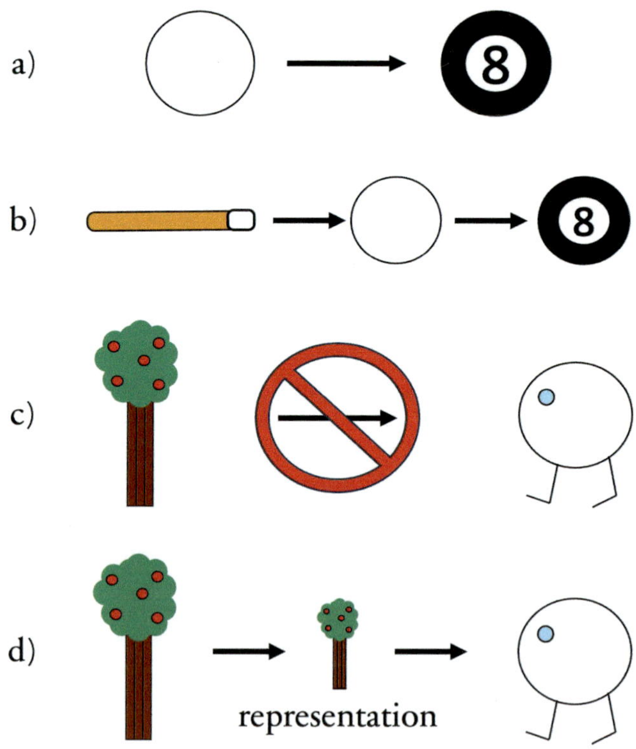

Figure 8.7 Different causal situations: a) local causality; the cue ball causes the 8-ball's movement, b) mediated local causality; the pool stick causes the 8-ball's movement, mediated by the cue ball, c) action-at-a-distance; the tree seems to cause Fred's behavior, but is not in contact with him, d) mediated local causality; the tree causes Fred's behavior, mediated by the representation.

contact with Fred. The representation is then able to influence his understanding of the world and inform his behavior.

As we have suggested, the assumption of local causality leads to the conclusion that a representation of the world must come into contact with Fred somewhere along the lines. But what kind of a representation? What kind of properties of the tree would the representation need to copy? Well, in general, the traditional approaches also assume that for Fred to successfully approach and eat the apple, he would need to have some sense of the geometric and physical properties of the environment. After all, the argument goes, geometry and physics provide a completely objective description of the world. They describe the world as it exists independently of any particular animal or that animal's experience. They are, in some sense, the one true description of the world and its contents. Therefore, geometry and physics provide the best (the most objective) basis for what any animal needs to know about the world.

The idea is that Fred will use this representation to know about the geometric and physical properties of the world—like how big the tree is, how far away it is, what shape the apples are, and so on. These properties will not only be used to generate Fred's experience of the tree and the apple but also to create and enact a plan for approaching, grabbing, and eating the apple. So not only must there be a representation of the world that comes into contact with Fred, but at least to some extent, this representation must inform him about the geometric and physical properties of the world around him.

Socratic Question: How does the historical separation of mind and body and the description of "body as machine" (see Chapter 1) contribute to the need for experience to be mediated by representations?

Traditional Assumption 3: The Representation Is Bad and Needs to Be Fixed

In Chapter 2, we introduced you to the concept of the retinal image (see Figure 8.8). At the time, we explained that for the traditional theorists, the retinal image is the starting point for vision. And the reason why is that it serves as the representation of the world that seems to be so badly needed to avoid the action-at-a-distance problem! But how good of a representation is the retinal image? Let's take a closer look at the retinal image that is formed and what its properties are.

Light travels from a light source (in Figure 8.8, that source is the sun, but the same would hold true if it were a candle, an LED light, or a cellphone screen). That light travels in straight lines, and that light hits all the various substances and surfaces in the environment (here, the tree). It bounces off those objects, also in straight lines. Some of that reflected (or *ambient*) light makes its way into Fred's eye. Notice that the light from the top of the tree ends up at the bottom of Fred's eye, and the light from the bottom of the tree ends up at the top of Fred's eye. Or in other words, once the light gets to the retina, the orientation of the tree is *upside down*. By the same logic, the light from the right side of the tree will end up on the left of Fred's eye, the light from the left side of the tree will end up on the right. Or in other words, the retinal image will be *reversed*.

Additionally, the back of the eye is like a flat but curved projector screen in a movie theater: the light reflected from the tree is projected onto this two-dimensional screen. Therefore, the image created is *flat*.

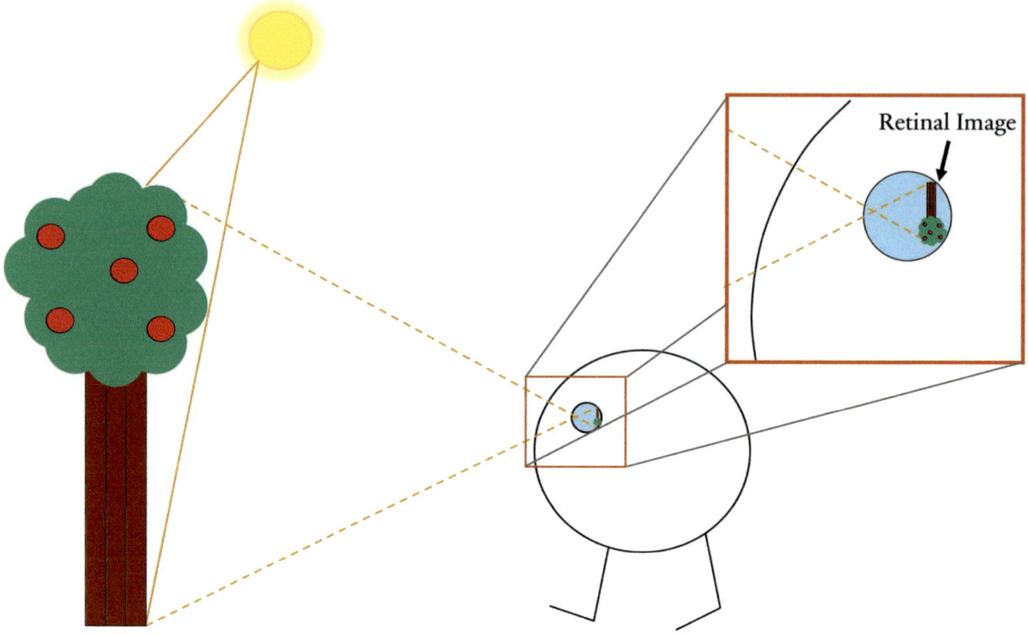

Figure 8.8 Light travels in straight lines and creates a retinal image that is upside down, reversed, and two-dimensional.

To sum up: the retinal image is upside down, reversed, and two-dimensional—but it's a representation of the world! It's a start. The problem, of course, is that this description of the retinal image does not match our experience and it doesn't match the stated requirements of a representation. We experience the world as right-side up, not reversed, and three-dimensional.

And these are mere distortions. This two-dimensional image is also lacking in the geometric and physical variables that Fred needs to successfully approach, grasp, and eat the apple. When it comes to those, the retinal image is *ambiguous*. Hopelessly so. Somehow, Fred (or his brain) must convert the pattern of stimulation on the retina (and the subsequent reaction of the photoreceptors and the rest of his visual system) not only into a perceptual experience but also a set of instructions to move his body.

While we have been discussing (and primarily will keep discussing) the problems with the retinal image, it's important to remember that the rest of the senses have similar distortions and ambiguities. For example, in Chapter 5, we talked about the ambiguity of the vestibular system—the otolith organs respond exactly the same way to looking down as they do to slowing down. If Fred's central executive is trying to figure out which is happening to Fred, the representation on the otolith organ does not carry that information. The same is true for when the skin responds to two pokes and one poke exactly the same way (i.e., below the two-point threshold discussed in Chapter 6), or when the exact same smell is experienced differently depending on the expectations of the sniffer (as we talked about in Chapter 7). In all those cases, the relationship between the representation made on the senses and the world out there is not fully straightforward. Our sense organs do not create an unambiguous representation of the world.

This assumption is also known as the **impoverished stimulus** (or sometimes the **poverty of the stimulus**; Berwick et al., 2011; see Blau & Wagman, 2022) because it says that the incoming representation (the stimulus) is poor (impoverished). There are distortions and ambiguities. The essential concern is that the identified representation (like the retinal image) does not offer clear, unambiguous, reliable information about the geometric and physical variables of the world. And given the assumption that those things are necessary, this is a problem! In order for Fred to use the representation of the world on his senses, he is going to need to *fix it* into something useful first.

Impoverished stimulus (aka poverty of the stimulus) the assumption that the representation of the world created by the sense organs is poor. In other words, the representation does not contain the necessary information for us to successfully experience or navigate our surroundings and does not match our experience.

Socratic Question: How do the anatomy and physiology of the eye (see Chapter 2, and especially Figure 2.22) contribute to the distortions and ambiguities that occur in the retinal image?

Unpacking the Impoverished Stimulus

Before we go much further it is worth asking the question: Just how challenging an issue is the impoverished stimulus for perception? Is it quickly and easily solved? Or is it more complicated? Let's examine just one of the issues in order to get an idea of the scope of the problem.

The retinal image is flat. Fred's only visual contact with the apple and the tree is a two-dimensional retinal image. Why might this cause problems for Fred? Well, for one thing, in a two-dimensional image, depth (i.e., distance between the perceiver and a depicted object) does not exist—all points are collapsed on a single surface and therefore depth cannot be perceived. That may seem like an extraordinary statement! After all, even in (similarly two-dimensional) photographs, we are able to understand depth to a certain extent. However, the fact that depth cannot be perceived in a two-dimensional image is easily demonstrated. In the top of Figure 8.8, we see that the four points (and indeed, any one of an infinite number of points along the same line) would project to precisely the same point on the retina (Molyneux, 1688). If all Fred has access to is the two-dimensional retinal image, how does he know which of the points is the cause of the stimulation? Or in other words, how does he know the *distance* of the point that is the cause of the stimulation?

But wait, that's asking about perceiving disconnected floating points! That's not at all like the environment Fred normally encounters. Normally he encounters objects, not just points. What about the tree? Surely a larger—and more complex—object such as a tree would not create same problem? Unfortunately, this is not the case. As you can see in the bottom of Figure 8.9 the four trees (and indeed any one of the infinite number of trees that would fit between the lines) all produce the exact same-sized retinal image. And this really does matter! If the tree in the world is one of the faraway large ones (say, A or B), then it might be a real, full-size, living tree and have apples to eat. If it is one of the small close ones (say, C or D), then it is more likely a small model, a toy, or a carving, and will provide no nourishment for Fred.

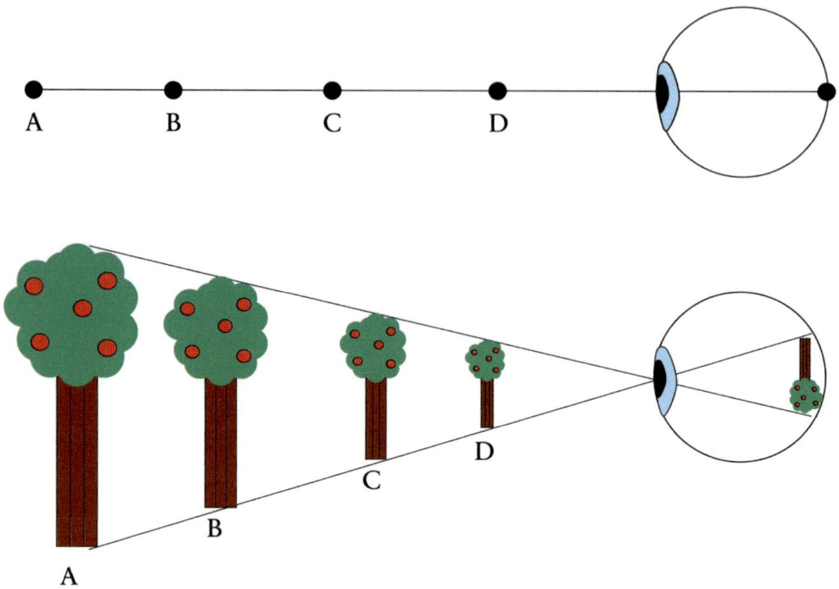

Figure 8.9 A problem of distance (from the perceiver, or depth) and size. Top, points A, B, C, and D, all project to the exact same place on the retina. Distance is indistinguishable. Bottom, trees A, B, C, and D, all project the exact same image on the retina. Size and distance are indistinguishable.

The inability to perceive size and distance from the perceiver is just *one* of the issues that results from the impoverished stimulus (and one we will cover in Chapter 9). To provide an explanation as to how Fred perceives the tree, we must also grapple with a number of other issues. For example, Fred must be able to identify what he is seeing (an issue we will grapple with in Chapter 10). To start to identify the tree (and its yummy apples), his visual system would first have to figure out where the tree stops and the world around it begins. It cannot be a simple matter of contrast. For example, in Figure 8.10, there is more contrast between the apple and the leaves surrounding it than between the leaves of the closest tree and the leaves of the tree right behind it.

And even if Fred solves the problem of separating the object from its surroundings, identifying the shape is not as straightforward as you might imagine. Different shapes can create the same-shaped retinal image depending on their orientation relative to the observer (ambiguity again!). For example, a cone, a cylinder, and a sphere all can result in a circular image on the retina (see Figure 8.11). Admittedly, that's a specialized case, but it highlights the issue: a two-dimensional retinal image is missing a lot of the information we need in order to properly understand our world. In our daily lives, we almost never mistake a sphere for a cylinder, so we must *somehow* solve this problem.

Traditional Assumption 4: Unconscious Inference Is Used to Fix the Bad Representation

While it may be possible to address each issue individually or come up with solutions that work in specific contexts (e.g. perhaps Fred knows the size of this particular apple tree, so the distance from him is derivable from that knowledge), it is unlikely that perception is based on

Figure 8.10 Contrast is not enough for form perception. There is more contrast within the tree than between the tree and its neighbors.

such ad hoc and unsystematic approaches. Knowing the size of *this* tree would not help Fred deal with the appearance of a *new* tree, and it just won't work for Fred to know about size only *after* he has come into contact with the specific object. We need a systematic approach that will help Fred with *all* the problems of the impoverished stimulus, for all the contexts in which they might be presented.

The most influential idea came from Helmholtz (yup, the same Helmholtz we talked about in Chapter 4!). He suggested that the flat retinal image was not completely meaningless. Impoverished doesn't mean useless or *worthless,* right? It just means it has less than it could have. So the retinal image still provides data—imperfect data—but data nonetheless. For example, the distance between Fred and the tree and its shape and form could be *inferred* from specific patterns (called cues) present in a two-dimensional image (see Chapters 9-11). Helmholtz suggested that we learned about these cues and abstracted rules for applying them during months and years of experience perceiving the world—especially as very young children. Our ability to apply those rules immediately and continuously without effort or confusion was based on that experience.

According to Helmholtz's theory, Fred is not consciously aware of this interpretation. He does not have to be (or want to be). In this way, seeing is like walking or talking—a behavior that is learned in childhood and applied situationally without conscious effort or interference (Fred's stride is adjusted for uneven ground without Fred having to consciously adjust his gait, and Fred's language use is adjusted similarly). Unlike walking or talking, however, Fred has no ability to consciously control or even be aware of how he makes inferences about the impoverished input. Fred's mind looks at the incoming bad stimulation, identifies the cues, identifies the relevant rules, and ***unconsciously infers*** what must be happening in the world in order to have created that particular stimulation on his senses. Fred's understanding of this scene can thus be illustrated like this:

Cue: In the stimulus	**Rule**: Learned from Experience ⇒ Understanding

In situations like Figure 8.11, where multiple circumstances in the world can cause the same pattern of stimulation on the retina, Helmholtz argued that the inference was aided by an understanding of the most likely situation. Or in other words, in the case of the ambiguous circle on the retinal image in Figure 8.11, if the rest of the field of view was a ball pit, then the sphere was the most likely shape. If the rest of the field of view was a pile of aluminum cans put aside for recycling, then the cylinder was the most likely shape. This is the so-called **Principle of Maximum Likelihood.** Helmholtz (1910/2000) suggested that every ambiguity in the retinal image could be solved by a combination of unconscious inference and the Principle of Maximum Likelihood. The result was a **mental representation** of the world that could be used to plan and execute behavior.

This suggestion proved so compelling that it was a very long time before anyone operated under any other supposition. The only debate was over *what* cues and *what* rules we learned during our experience.

Helmholtz's Principle of Maximum Likelihood in ambiguous situations, the retinal image will be interpreted via the most likely situation.

Mental representations in the traditional view, we have no access to the world. Instead, we build up (through cognitive computations) a representation of the world in our heads.

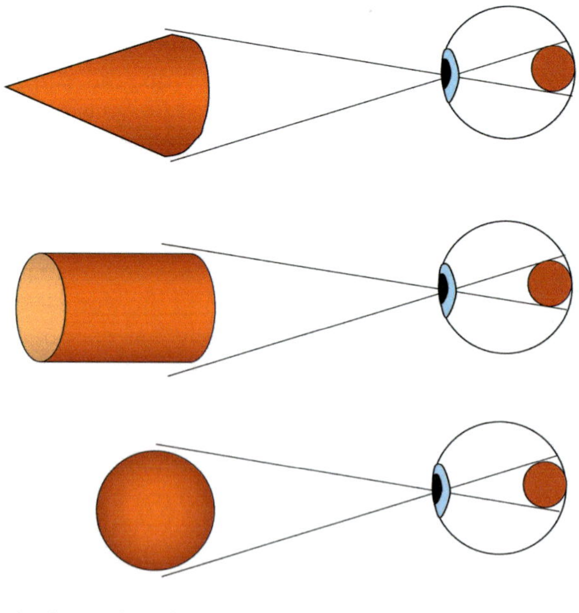

Figure 8.11 A cone, a cylinder, and a sphere could all produce a circular image on the retina.

Socratic Question: Mental representations play a central role in traditional approaches to understanding perception. Can you think of other psychological processes in which mental representations also seem to have a central role?

Traditional Assumption 5: Indirect Perception

In the traditional approaches, what people see, hear, feel, smell, and taste is not the world itself, but the world as represented in (or otherwise created in) the mind. In other words, they do not access the world directly, but rather an interpretation (or alteration) of a (bad) representation of the world. Fred is not aware of the tree directly; he is aware of the tree only through his *representation* of the tree. In this way, perception is **indirect**.

To sum up the situation so far: the world is out there, and it is being represented (imperfectly) by Fred's sense organs. Fred's mind does not have access to the world *out there* except through the representation from his senses *in here*. The representation *in here* is not great. Fred's mind (or brain) has to somehow figure out what is happening *out there* just by using the bad representation *in here*. As we discussed in Chapter 1, the world *out there* is called the distal stimulus and the energy that reaches Fred *in here* is called the proximal stimulus. So, another way of putting this is that Fred's mind needs to figure out what the distal stimulus is, but it (and he) only has access to a (crummy) proximal stimulus. What distal stimulus could have caused this proximal stimulus? To do that, Fred's mind will use unconscious inference (aided by the principle of maximum likelihood) to convert the (crummy) proximal stimulus into a (hopefully useful) representation of the tree. In traditional terms, the reaction of the sensory organs to the proximal stimulus is called **sensation** and the awareness of the representation is called **perception.**

Indirect perception the view that experience is not of the world itself, but rather of some representation of the world in the head.

One important thing to point out is the way this assumption separates the organism from the environment around them. We discussed the mind-body dualism in Chapter 1. This is another kind of a dualism, an *organism-environment dualism*—organism and environment are considered to be independent entities (see Turvey, 2019). Fred has no access to the world; he does not even have access to the stimulation on his sense organs (i.e., the representation of the world delivered to his brain). He only has access to his *unconscious interpretation* of this representation of that world. When proponents of the traditional approach talk of Fred's knowledge of the world, what they are really talking about is Fred's knowledge of *his representation of* that world. Because they assumed that our senses are at least reasonably reliable, they further assume that the representation resembles the world, but we don't really have any way of validating whether it is or not (more on this later). Or in other words, Fred's experience is *entirely* based on the internally constructed representation, *not* the stimulation that leads to the representation.

Sensation the stimulation of the sense organs by physical energy.

Perception (traditional) the meaningful awareness of the distal stimulus achieved by being aware of the representation of the world.

Traditional Assumption 6: Passive Perception, Static View

The historically popular idea of hierarchical processing assumes that to process an image (or a sound or a touch, etc.), our systems start with very simple elements in the most basic of circumstances and build them into complex wholes, piece by piece. A great deal of effort, then, has been put into figuring out what the "simple elements" and "most basic circumstances" might be. Both are assumed, for example, to be ones that have very few variables. The idea that vision starts with nothing but an area of contrast (and builds into a complex whole) is very much in keeping with this idea.

This is also consistent with the tried-and-true general scientific strategy of breaking any complex process down into simpler processes involving only the most basic components operating independently of the greater context. For example, when Fred wanted to understand how his antique cuckoo clock worked, he took it apart and examined how each part worked independently of the other parts. Only then could he understand how all the parts worked together. So, in order to understand *complex* perception, we must first understand the *simple case*. Complexity can be built from the addition of several simple units and the stepwise introduction of context into a given simple situation.

In service of this idea, traditional theorists often start with what might seem to be the most basic or general case of perceiving—the organism is still, the environment is still, and the environment is mostly bare except for an energy source and a thing to be perceived (the distal stimulus). Under these circumstances, energy of some kind makes contact with and stimulates the animal's sense organs. In this way, the organism's sense organs *passively* receive stimulation about the distal stimulus (and only the distal stimulus). Further, our understanding of physiology tells us that the sense organs respond to stimulation and send a signal to the brain in a fraction of a second.

The representation of the world on the senses is thus assumed to be essentially a basic (static, momentary, partial) glimpse of a larger and more complex world. Longer and more complex perceptual experiences must be built up out of this most basic case. Depth and motion, for example, cannot be seen directly and must be inferred. We discuss these issues in Chapters 9 and 11.

Traditional Assumption 7: The Central Executive

According to the traditional approaches, this is more or less the process by which Fred sees (or hears, or feels, or tastes, or smells) the world. The world exists at some distance away from Fred, and in order for Fred's experience and behavior to be affected by anything in the world, a representation of the world must be made in his head. That representation is bad, and so it needs to be fixed in order to be useful. What's more, in order to fix it, there are a series of cues to extract, rules to apply, and likelihoods to compute. Those computations must be performed by some kind of thinking entity—maybe Fred's brain or some part of Fred's brain—who is able to rationally apply all those principles. This rational entity is called a variety of things, but the most common in cognitive science is the **central executive**[3] (see Baddeley, 1996) (depicted as little ghost Fred within bigger Fred in Figure 8.2).

> **Central executive (aka homunculus, mind, unconscious, etc.)** a rational entity that performs the required computations to fix the impoverished input into a useful representation. Its actions are outside of the conscious awareness of the person.

It's worth noting that the central executive is different than consciousness itself—after all, the work done by the central executive is largely *unconscious*, Fred has no awareness of that work. Good thing, too—Fred's life is exhausting enough already! Moreover, the central executive is entirely dependent on input from Fred's sense organs for its (and therefore Fred's) awareness of the outside world (see Figure 8.2).

> Socratic Question: How does the historical separation of mind and body and the description of "body as machine" (see Chapter 1) reinforce the concept of a "central executive"?

So . . . What's Next?

In Chapters 9-12, we cover a few of the classic issues in perception as they are addressed by the traditional approach. You might notice that almost all of them (everything except Chapter 12) cover issues in visual perception. While it is certainly the case that the traditional approach has been applied to all the senses, the vast majority—and particularly the early, precedent-setting work—has been done in visual perception. Auditory perception is a distant second and the rest of the senses are well behind that.

Our goal in this section is to give the reader a sense for how the traditional approach deals with what it sees as the fundamental issues. To that end, we have included a chapter on each of the major issues in visual perception (Chapter 9 covers size and distance perception, Chapter 10 covers object recognition, and Chapter 11 covers perception of movement), as well as one chapter in auditory perception (Chapter 12). From these, the reader can get a sense for how the assumptions outlined here, as well as the strategies for addressing questions are applied.

Summary

A purely biological view of perception runs into problems such as the binding and outness problems, the lack of meaning in biological processes, and issues of sensory ambiguity. Particularly in response to the latter two issues, the traditional view assumes a cognitive process by which they can be solved. From the traditional view, then, the process by which perceiving occurs is as follows: Some object out there in the world affects some type of energy that our sense organs can detect. That energy makes contact with our sense organs and causes a reaction; that reaction is called sensation. This reaction of the sense organs is inherently meaningless and so it has to be converted (by unconscious inference) into a meaningful mental representation of the world (which is what we experience when we perceive).

Notes

1 This is why different languages can use different words for "elephant", like *elefante* (Spanish), *olifant* (Dutch), and *arewhana* (Maori).
2 Maybe by means of stimulating "bacon cells" in the brain. No, really—read about "grandmother cells" in Chapter 10.
3 Other names for the same idea are *the ghost in the machine*, *mind*, *spirit*, *soul*, *the man in the inner room*, and some theorists have derisively called it the *homunculus* (Latin for "little man").

9 Visual Perception of Depth and Size

As we discussed in Chapter 8, the retinal image is ambiguous about the various physical properties of surrounding objects and surfaces. In particular, it is ambiguous about the various distances,[1] depths, and sizes of those surfaces. In large part this is because the retina itself is flat and small (see Chapters 2 and 3). And so, the pattern of light falls on a small and flat surface.

Go get yourself a ping pong ball and a flea (see Figure 9.1). Yes, really. Trust us. Got both of them? Good. Now think about this: your eye is a little bit smaller than a ping pong ball (which is 4 cm in diameter). But for the sake of argument, let's assume they are the same size. We'll get to the flea shortly, but first, imagine cutting the ping pong pall in half. Now, imagine getting a (tiny) movie projector and setting it up so that the movie projects completely on the inside of one half of the ping pong ball. That would be one tiny screen! In fact, it would be about 1/15 the size of an average cell phone screen. It can sometimes be hard enough to get a sense of distances, depth, and sizes from images on a *regular* movie screen, let alone those on a cell phone screen. So, you can imagine how hard it would be to do so on a screen this size! The problem, of course, is not just that the screen is tiny—which it most definitely is—it is that the screen is flat. This means that the three dimensions of the events in the world are compressed down into the two dimensions of the events on a (tiny) screen. In other words, there is *no such thing* as depth on a flat screen. Images on that screen can vary in location (where on the screen?) and size (how big on the screen?) among other ways, but not in depth. So how do we perceive depth from the images on a flat surface?

But wait! You didn't forget about the flea, did you? Your fovea is about the same size as a flea (which is 1.5 mm in diameter). As you know, the clarity of the image on the fovea is what really matters for seeing detail (see Chapters 2 and 3). So, now imagine putting the flea on the back of the ping pong ball and resetting the movie projector so that the movie (or most of it, anyway) projects on to the surface of the flea—or perhaps a flat section of the inside of the ping pong ball that this the same size as a flea. World's. Smallest. Movie Screen. Ever. How hard would it be to get any sense of distance, depth, or size now?[2]

The point here is that the light that reflects from three-dimensional objects of various sizes located at various distances from you and enters the eye through the pupil is projected onto a small—like *really* small—two-dimensional surface. This retinal image is a small and flat—and therefore ambiguous—representation of a three-dimensional world. And so, from the traditional approach, the fundamental challenge of perceiving distance, depth, and size is *reconstructing* a three-dimensional world from this two-dimensional image. For people who study these processes, this means identifying the cues that are available about these properties and how those cues are used in reconstructing a three-dimensional world. In other words,

DOI: 10.4324/9781032690964-11

Figure 9.1 Fred examines a ping pong ball (which is about the same size as a human eye) and a flea (which is about the same size as a human fovea).

it requires understanding how ***unconscious inferences*** are made about such cues to generate mental representations of distance, depth, and size.

Fortunately, there are several different types of cues that could be used to make such unconscious inferences. We can (more or less) group these into three categories: (1) cues that are available in what the (muscles of the) eyes do—called *oculomotor cues*, (2) cues that are available in a *single* retinal image—called *monocular depth cues*, and (3) cues that are available by comparing *two* retinal images—called *binocular depth cues*. After we cover those three types of cues and discuss the possibility that cues about depth (and size) are combined, we'll introduce you to several common size illusions (see Shapiro & Todorović, 2017) and provide explanations of these illusions as unavoidable consequences of combining cues. So, let's get started.

Oculomotor Cues

> **Oculomotor cues**: cues about distance or depth that are available in the activity of eye muscles.

First, let's clarify. "Oculo" is a prefix meaning "eye", and (in this context, anyway) "motor" refers to muscle activity. So, **oculomotor cues** are cues that are available in the activity of eye muscles. We mentioned the various eye muscles and their functions in Chapter 2. There are two kinds of oculomotor cues to distance—accommodation and convergence.

Accommodation

One of the eye muscles that we mentioned in Chapter 2 is located inside the eye itself—the ciliary muscle that surrounds the lens. You can feel this muscle working just like you can feel the other muscles of your body working. And this muscle gets tired after a long day of staring at screens or pages, just like your other bodily muscles get tired from a long day hiking or playing tennis.

Imagine that Fred closes one eye and holds a pen (or any other object he has on hand, like a bowling ball, a flea, or his pet baby elephant) at arm's length. He slowly brings the object closer to him and tries to keep it in focus the entire time. As he brings the pen, the bowling ball, the flea, or his pet baby elephant closer and closer, his ciliary muscles will need to work harder and harder for the lens to keep the image of that object in focus on the retina—in particular, on the fovea. Try it yourself—except maybe just use a pen!

In other words, the ciliary muscle needs to do work to assist—or *accommodate*—the lens. The amount of **accommodation** provided by the ciliary muscles—the amount of contraction required to keep the image of the object in focus on the (fovea of the) retina—could be a *cue* to object distance (see Chapter 2 and see Figure 9.2, left). In particular, the rule to be applied by the central executive is that the more accommodation required to keep the image of an object in focus on the (fovea of the) retina, the closer that object is. Said another way, objects that require more accommodation to keep the image of that object in focus are closer than objects that require less accommodation to do so. There is (at least) one caveat here, though. Accommodation is only useful as a cue when looking at objects at distances of up to a few meters away. When looking at objects that are more than just a few meters away, the ciliary muscles are completely relaxed—good for them; they work hard!

Cue: Accommodation	**Rule**: More accommodation --> closer object; Less accommodation --> farther object (but only useful for distances up to a few meters)

Convergence

Other eye muscles that we mentioned in Chapter 2 are located outside of each eye. These include the six muscles that move each eye. Now imagine that Fred does the same thing that he did before with the with the pen, the bowling ball, flea, or his baby elephant, but this time leaves both eyes open. As he brings the object closer and closer, he will feel these muscles—in particular, the rectus muscles—working harder and harder to keep both eyes pointed at the object so that focused images of that object stay on the fovea of each eye. Again, you can try this yourself with the pen—you've still got the pen, right?

In other words, under these circumstances, the rectus muscles will need to work more and more so that both eyes (and both fovea) can *converge* on the object. The amount of **convergence** provided by the contraction of these muscles is another *possible cue* to distance (see Figure 9.2, right). In particular, the rule to be applied by the central executive is that the more convergence that is required to keep focused images on each fovea, the closer that object is. Said another way, objects that require more convergence to keep focused images on each fovea are closer than objects that require less convergence to do so. The same caveat applies for convergence as for accommodation, though—convergence is only useful as a cue for objects that are within a few meters (Schachar, 2006). When looking at objects at distances farther than that, the eyes are essentially pointing straight ahead and so the rectus muscles are completely relaxed as well—good for them, because they work hard, too!

Convergence the process by which the rectus muscles point the eyes inward so that images of a nearby object can be focused on the fovea.

Cue: Convergence	**Rule**: More convergence --> closer object; Less convergence --> farther object (but only useful for distances up to a few meters)

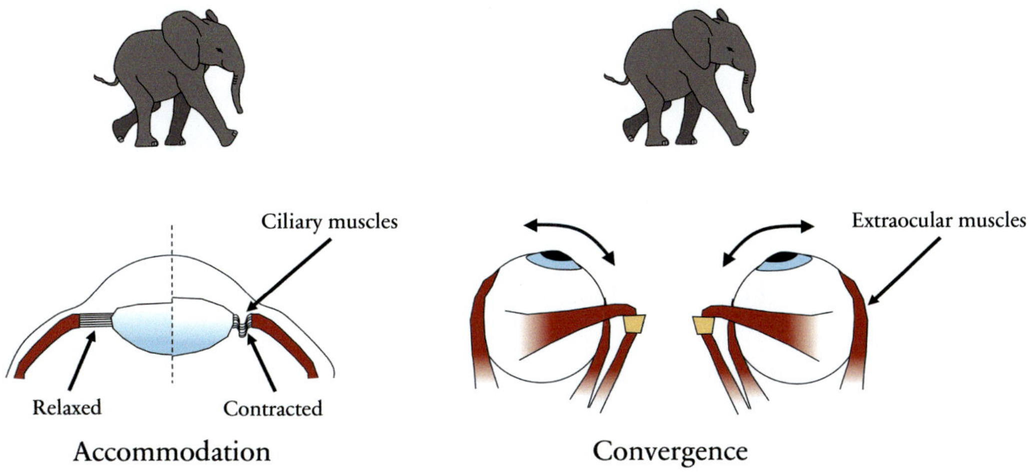

Figure 9.2 Left, accommodation is a monocular oculomotor cue to distance. Right, convergence is a binocular oculomotor cue to distance.

Socratic Question: Oculomotor cues only work as cues to depth for distances up to a few meters. Is this a feature or a bug of the visual system?

Monocular Depth Cues

As you might assume, **monocular ("one eye") cues** are cues that are available in a single retinal image. These are cues that would allow you to see depth even if you were limited to viewing surrounding objects with just one eye—like a Cyclops or a stereotypical pirate with an eye patch (ahoy, matey!). Fortunately for Cyclops, pirates, and everyone else, there are numerous monocular cues to depth. These are cues that artists can use as techniques for depicting depth in paintings, drawings, or films. Let's deal with the ones that can be used in paintings or drawings first because these cues do not involve movement. In other words, these cues are **static or pictorial depth cues**.

Monocular cues cues to depth that are available to a single eye.

Static or pictorial depth cues cues to depth that are available in the absence of movement of the image on the retina.

Size and Height

Imagine that Fred is back in first grade art class—yay! He puts on his smock, tries to resist the urge to eat paste (boo!), and gets out two baby elephants (good thing he didn't forget them at home like last time). The teacher—Mr. Raoul—instructs Fred to put one of the elephants farther away and one closer to him and then try to *draw* the scene. How would he—or even better, how would Mr. Raoul—draw the two baby elephants so that one looks farther away than the other?

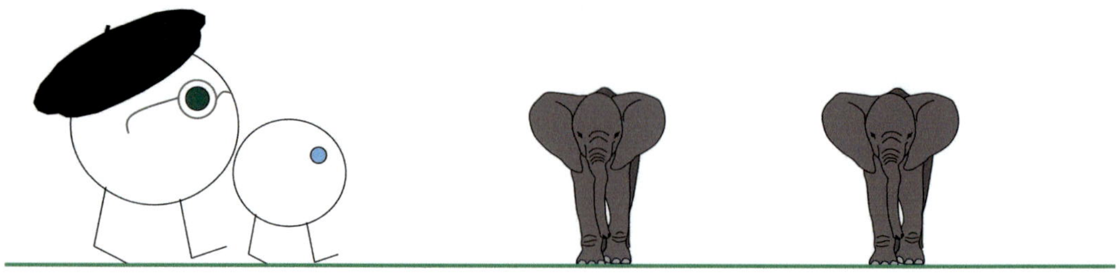

Figure 9.3 Fred and his art teacher, Mr. Raoul, admire baby elephants at two different distances.

retinal image size the amount of space that the image of an object takes up on the retinal surface.

Well, one thing that he might do is to draw the baby elephant that is farther away *smaller* than the one that is closer. Right? The farther away a given object is, the smaller the size of the retinal image of that object (see Figures 9.3 and 9.4). So, a baby elephant that was nose-to-nose (er . . . trunk-to-nose) with Fred would create a larger retinal image than one that was all the way on the other side of the classroom (or all the way on the other side of the African savanna). Consequently, **retinal image size** is a possible cue about the distance of an object[3] (see Figure 9.4). And the rule to be applied by the central executive is that the smaller the retinal image of an object, the farther away that object is. Said another way, objects with larger retinal images are closer than objects with smaller retinal images.

Cue: Retinal image size	**Rule:** smaller retinal image size --> farther away; larger retinal image size --> closer

Figure 9.4 Retinal image size is a monocular cue to object distance. The smaller elephant is seen as farther away.

But Mr. Raoul has even more tricks up his sleeve for drawing the elephants so that one baby elephant looks farther away than the other. Another thing he might do is to draw the baby elephant that is farther away *higher up on the page* than the one that is closer (see Figure 9.5, left). And so, the rule to be applied by the central executive is that the higher an object appears to be, the farther away that object is. But not so fast! Let's say Mr. Raoul wants to add a little bit of context to the drawing. So, he draws in a horizontal line representing the horizon (see Figure 9.5, center). And then—inspired by the incomparable Bob Ross—he adds a few happy little clouds that float around the sky and have fun (see Figure 9.5, right).

Once these details have been added, Fred sees that it is not necessarily *how high* objects appear to be the page that gives an impression of depth. Instead, it is where they appear to be relative to the horizon. So, **height relative to the horizon** is another possible cue to distance or depth (see Figure 9.5, center and right). And the rule to be applied by the central executive is the closer than an object is to the horizon, the farther away that object is. Said another way, the farther that an object is from the horizon—the farther above or below the horizon it is—the closer that object is.

Height relative to the horizon how far above or below the horizon an object appears to be.

Cue: Height relative to the horizon	**Rule:** Coser to the horizon--> farther away; Farther from the horizon (above or below) --> closer

Linear Perspective and Texture Gradient

But Mr. Raoul is not done yet! Not even close. Let's say that he wanted to fill in the drawing a bit. Maybe rather than just a horizon line, he wanted to draw a patch of ground in the African savanna that the baby elephants are standing on. After all, the elephants aren't just floating there, right? Let's say that he wants to draw the elephants standing on a rectangular patch of ground. Depicting this in a drawing is more complicated than merely drawing a

Figure 9.5 Height in the visual field and height relative to the horizon are both monocular cues to depth.

Figure 9.6 Linear perspective and texture gradients are monocular cues to distance.

rectangle around the elephants—that wouldn't look right at all. Instead, Mr. Raoul would need to draw something like a ***trapezoid*** to indicate that the rectangular patch of ground ***recedes into the distance*** (see Figure 9.6, left). This is because of the way that lines—in particular, parallel lines—look in two-dimensional images (like the retinal image). When two parallel lines recede into the distance, it will appear as if the two lines converge at a point way, way off into the distance. This is the case for any set of parallel lines including the left and right edges of the rectangular patch of ground but also railroad tracks, roads, and even a long hallway.

Linear perspective the fact that parallel lines appear to converge as they recede into the distance.

So, how lines look when viewed from a particular perspective—or **linear perspective**—is another possible cue to distance (see Figure 9.6, left and center). And the rule to be applied by the central executive is that on the retina, the closer an image of an object is to the point at which the lines appear to converge, the farther away that object is. Said another way, objects that appear to be closer to the apparent convergence point are farther away than objects that appear to be farther away from the apparent convergence point.

Cue: Linear perspective	**Rule**: Closer to apparent convergence point --> farther away; Farther from the apparent convergence point --> closer

Another thing that Mr. Raoul could do to fill in the drawing a little bit is to draw in some details—or *texture*—maybe in the form of grass on the patch of ground. But just like he would need to draw the elephant that is farther away smaller than one that is closer, he would need to draw the blades of grass that are farther away smaller than the ones that are closer (see Figure 9.6, right). And so, blades of grass that are meant to appear really close—like the ones right in front of Fred—would need to be drawn relatively large. These would probably be large enough that he could clearly see individual blades of grass. In other words, grass that is meant to appear close would need to have lots of texture. But blades of grass that are meant to appear farther away will need to be drawn smaller and smaller. And grass that is meant to appear farthest away would need to be drawn as a green blur. In other words, grass that is meant to appear farther away would need to be drawn with little (or even no) texture.

These progressive changes (or gradients) in texture—a **texture gradient**—are another possible cue to distance (Gibson, 1950). And the rule to be applied by the central executive is that texture gradients on the retinal image indicate that a surface recedes into the distance (see Figure 9.6, right). In particular, parts of the surface with more texture are closer that parts of the surface with less texture. And so, *objects on* part of a surface with less texture are farther away than *objects on* part of that surface with more texture.

Texture gradient the changes in texture that occur as a surface recedes into the distance.

Cue: Texture gradient	**Rule**: on part of surface with more texture --> closer; on part of surface with lese texture --> farther away

Superposition

One final technique that Fred's art teacher might use to make one baby elephant look farther away than the other is one that we will discuss in the next chapter in the context of object perception (see Chapter 10). In particular, he might draw one elephant so that part of it—or maybe even most of it—hides or blocks the view of the other elephant. In other words, he might draw one so that it appears to be "superpositioned" (positioned on top of) the other elephant (see Figure 9.7). So, **superposition** is a possible cue to distance as well. And the rule to be applied by the central executive is pretty is simple—when the image of one object on the retina overlaps or covers up an image of another object, the object that appears to do the overlapping or covering up is closer to the viewer, and the object that appears to be overlapped or covered up is farther away.

Superposition when one object appears to cover up or block another object.

Figure 9.7 Superposition is a monocular cue to depth.

Cue: superposition	**Rule:** image blocked by another object --> farther away; image blocking another object --> closer

As you can see by the examples that we used, most of the time, more than one cue to distance is available. For example, Figure 9.6 (*right*) not only has texture gradient cues but also linear perspective cues, and retinal image size cues (see the section "*A Note on Combining Cues*"). In general, the more cues, the better for the central executive (and for Cyclops and pirates, too!). The central executive needs all the help it can get to reconstruct a three-dimensional world from a two-dimensional retinal image. And most of the time (including in Figures 9.4, 9.5, 9.6, and 9.7), the cues all lead to the same conclusions about the distances of surrounding objects. Even better!

> Socratic Question: Look at the photo of the owl in Figure 1.4, the photo of the cats in Figure 2.24, and the photo of the apple tree in the left half of Figure 4.1. What monocular depth cues are available in each of these images?

Motion-Based Cues

All of the monocular cues that we just described are ones that can be used to depict depth or distance in drawings or paintings. But the thing about drawings and paintings is everything depicted in them is perfectly still. The surfaces and objects in those drawings and paintings don't move at all. And—just as important—neither does the viewer's perspective on those surfaces and objects. But this isn't the way the world works most of the time, is it? Things move. A lot. So does Fred and so do you. And so do Cyclops and pirates. So, now let's discuss cues to depth that apply when things—including the viewer—move. These are known as motion-based cues to depth. These kinds of cues cannot be used in drawings, but *can* be used in filmmaking, video game design, or animation. Of course, perceiving motion presents its own challenges (see Chapter 11), but assuming that can be worked out, then motion can be a cue to depth.

Motion Parallax

Imagine that Fred is in video game design class. He grabs his computer mouse, stops playing Minecraft, Fortnite, or Rocket League (boo!), and gets out his two baby elephants (good thing he didn't leave them in art class). He then puts one farther away than the other and animates a scene using them as models.

The game he is designing—*Homunculus 2: The Search for the Invariant*[4]—takes place on the African savanna. In this scene, the main character—Pablo Ángel—drives across the African savanna—from right to left on the screen—with the two elephants in the distance, one farther away than the other. Pablo Ángel glances at the elephants as he whizzes by in his Jeep. What would this look like from his point of view? How would Fred—or better yet, his animation teacher—animate this scene so that one baby elephant looks farther away than the other?

Well, the first thing that they would need to do is to animate the scene so that everything in Pablo Ángel's view (including both baby elephants) appears to move in the *opposite direction* on the screen—in this case, from left to right (see Figure 9.8). But hold on a minute. This will make it look like Pablo Ángel and the Jeep are moving from right to left, but it

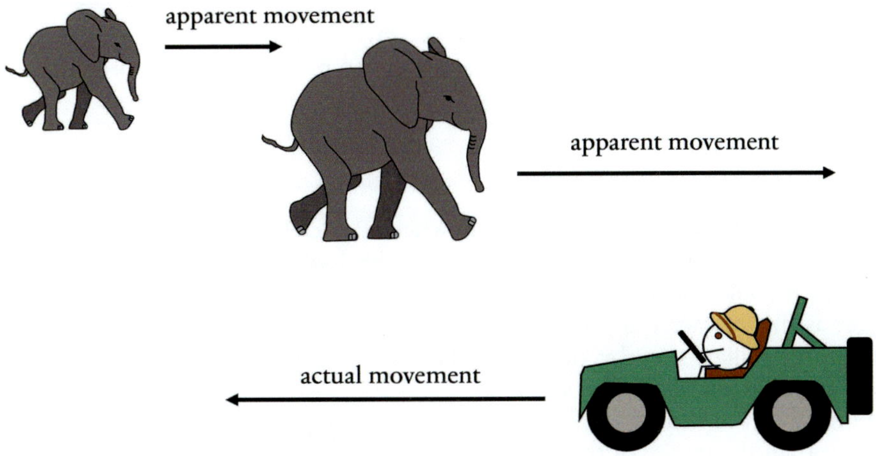

Figure 9.8 Motion parallax is a monocular movement-based cue to depth.

won't necessarily make it look like the baby elephants are at different distances. To do this, Fred's teacher would need to animate it so that the baby elephant that is closer appears to move from left to right *faster* than the one that is farther away. In other words, they would need to animate the scene so that when Pablo Ángel's view moves, the nearby baby elephant appears to move *more*, and the faraway baby elephant appears to move *less* (see Figure 9.8).

You can experience this even if you are not a character in a video game driving across the African savanna. The next time you are a passenger in car (or bus or a train) traveling at a steady rate of speed (especially on an open highway or country road), look out of the passenger side window. First, look down at the ground. It will appear to move very quickly in the opposite direction. In fact, you won't be able to look at any particular patch of ground very long before it zips by out of your field of view. Then look at something much farther away, maybe a tree or building on the horizon. It will also appear to move in the other direction, but this time, it will appear to do so more slowly. Depending on how far away it is (and how open the road is), you might be able to look at it for a few seconds—or even a few minutes—before it is completely out of your field of view. In other words, as you move, the nearby patch of ground will appear to move more, and the faraway object will appear to move less.

The difference in apparent movement of objects at different distances is called **motion parallax** (or just "parallax"), and it is a possible motion cue to distance. The rule to be applied by the central executive is that when the perceiver is moving, objects that appear to move more (or more quickly) in the other direction (based on the movement of images on the retina) are closer than objects that appear to move less (or less quickly) in the other direction. And the greater the difference in apparent movement between the two objects, the greater the distance between those objects.

Motion parallax the difference in apparent movement of objects at different distances.

Cue: Motion parallax	Rule: When the perceiver is moving . . . . . .objects that appear to move more --> closer . . .objects that appear to move less --> farther

Retinal Flow[5]

Let's say that Fred is now designing a scene where Pablo Ángel parks the Jeep and walks in the direction of the baby elephants. What would this look like from his point of view? Well, one thing Fred could do is to animate the scene so that the elephants appear to get bigger and bigger as the character approaches. But then he remembers the lessons that he learned about motion parallax—nearby objects appear to move more than faraway objects. So, it would be better to animate the scene so that the image of the nearby elephant got *bigger faster* than the image of the faraway elephant. The movement of the image on the retina is called **retinal flow** (but see Chapters 15 and 16). And the rule to be applied by the central executive is that faster retinal flow means that an object is closer.

Retinal flow movement of the image on the retina.

Cue: Retinal flow	Rule: object with faster retinal flow--> closer object with slower retinal flow --> farther

Binocular Depth Cues

All of the cues that we have covered so far (including convergence) could be of use to you if you were viewing the surrounding objects with just one eye. But—Cyclops and stereotypical pirates with eye patches aside—most people see the world with *both* eyes. And doing so might provide *additional* cues to depth—in addition to those provided by monocular cues. Earlier, we defined parallax as a perceived change in location with a change in viewpoint. So, when Fred views an object from two different viewpoints, that object might appear to change location. But parallax also occurs when he views an object with one eye or the other (because each eye is located at a slightly different viewpoint).

Retinal Disparity

Say he closes one eye while holding a pen (or any other object he has on hand, like a bowling ball or a baby elephant) at arm's length. He positions the pen so that it is *exactly aligned* with something across the room—maybe a doorknob, his bowling trophy, or another baby elephant. Now, he closes that eye and opens the other eye. The pen would no longer appear aligned with that object, would it? Now, he switches back. Now it's lined up again! Try it yourself with a pen and doorknob (see Figure 9.9). *What kind of sorcery is this!?* No kind, actually.

As we mentioned, Fred's two eyes (and your two eyes) have slightly different viewpoints in the world. We don't really know how far apart Fred's eyes are, but human eyes are about 5 cm apart on average. And while 5 cm isn't that much of a difference, it's enough that the eyes don't have identical views. In most cases, the two eyes will see the same set of objects, just slightly

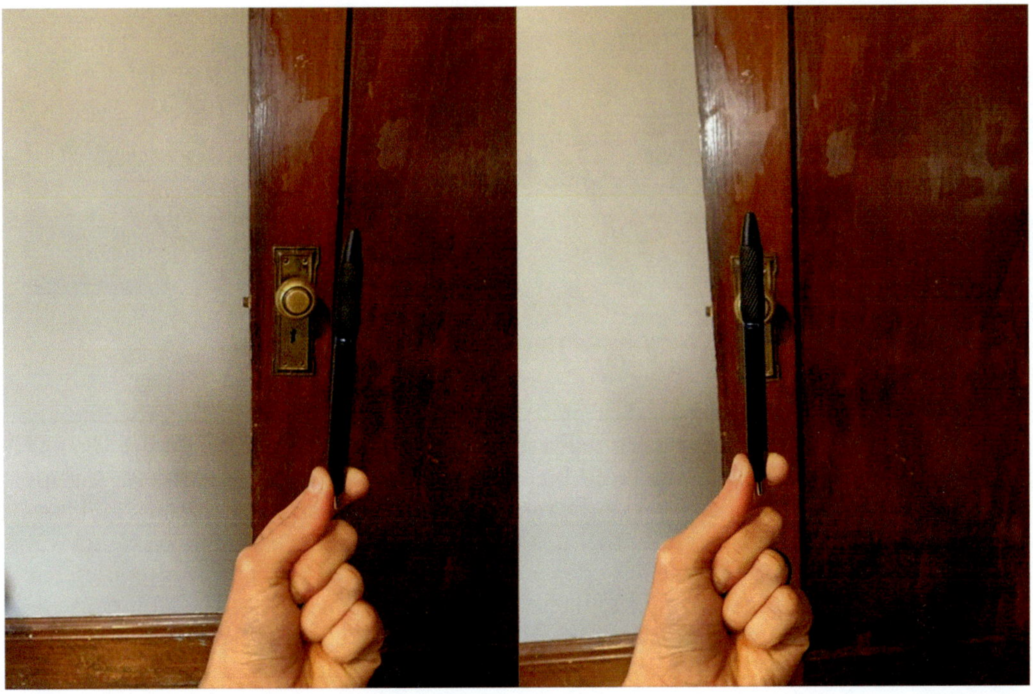

Figure 9.9 Retinal disparity is a binocular cue to depth. The photos above are meant to simulate the views from the left eye (left) and the right eye (right).

shifted in location (like how your pen moved on and off the doorknob when you viewed it with each eye). This is because the images of the objects in front of you will be on slightly different locations on the retina of each eye (see Figure 9.9). The slight difference in the retinal images of each eye is known as **retinal disparity**. And retinal disparity is a possible binocular cue to distance. The experience of depth from retinal disparity is known as **stereopsis**. You have experienced stereopsis if you have ever used a VR headset (like an Apple Vision Pro, a Meta Quest, or any number of others) or if you have ever watched a 3D movie with special glasses (see Box 9.1).

Retinal disparity the slight difference in the retinal images of each eye given their different locations and viewpoints.

Stereopsis the experience of depth from retinal disparity.

Box 9.1 How 3D Effects in Movies and VR Work

Fred went to go see a horror movie called "*The Purple Perils in 3D*". He was given a pair of glasses like those in Figure 9.10 (*left*) and when he put them on, the heroic quartet known as the Gang of Four seemed to jump off the screen at him!

In order to achieve this effect, the movie makers used a special camera that simultaneously filmed two versions of the movie, from just a few inches apart. If it was animated,

Figure 9.10 Left, typical 3D glasses used in movie theaters. Right, VR goggles.

they would draw (either by hand or by computer) two versions from slightly different perspectives. Either way, they essentially create a left-eye version and a right-eye version. As we discussed when we introduced binocular depth cues, the two eyes have slightly different views. The two versions of the movie are projected onto the screen simultaneously and the special glasses filter that image so just the right eye version makes its way to Fred's right eye and just the left eye version makes its way to the left eye. *Voila*! The battle between the Agents of Lawfulness and their arch nemesis—The Ghost in the Machine—is occurring both near and far!

Virtual reality (VR) goggles work in a very similar way. Instead of filtering light from a screen, each eye gets its own tiny screen to look at (see Figure 9.11, right). In addition to binocular disparity, VR adds the cue of motion parallax—as you move, the image in the screens moves with you, allowing your motion to reveal the depth of the scene (but see Box 16.2).

Admittedly, the specifics of how retinal disparity leads to stereopsis are a bit complicated, but (try to) bear with us. Essentially, it has to do with the *direction* of disparity and *amount* of the disparity. First, let's deal with direction. Imagine that Fred closes one eye, holds a pen at arm's length, and positions the pen so that it is exactly aligned with a doorknob. Then, he opens both eyes and focuses his gaze directly on the pen. He will see a double image of the doorknob *behind* the pen. Try it yourself. Now he refocuses his gaze directly on the doorknob. Now he will see a double image of the pen *in front* of the doorknob. Again, try it yourself. *What kind of sorcery is this!?* It's no kind of sorcery, but it is *two different kinds*—that is, two different directions—of retinal disparity (see Figure 9.11).

Crossed Disparity

Let's start with the case where Fred's gaze is focused on the doorknob (which is farther from him) and he sees a double image of the pen (which is closer to him). Given that both of his eyes are pointing directly at the doorknob, the images of the doorknob fall on corresponding places on each retina—pretty much right in the middle of each fovea of each retina. This means that if the left and right retinal images were overlayed right on top of one another, the images of the two doorknobs would—for the most part—coincide.

In contrast, the images of the pen *do not* fall on corresponding places on each retina. Specifically, on his right retina, the image of the pen would fall *to the right* of the image of the

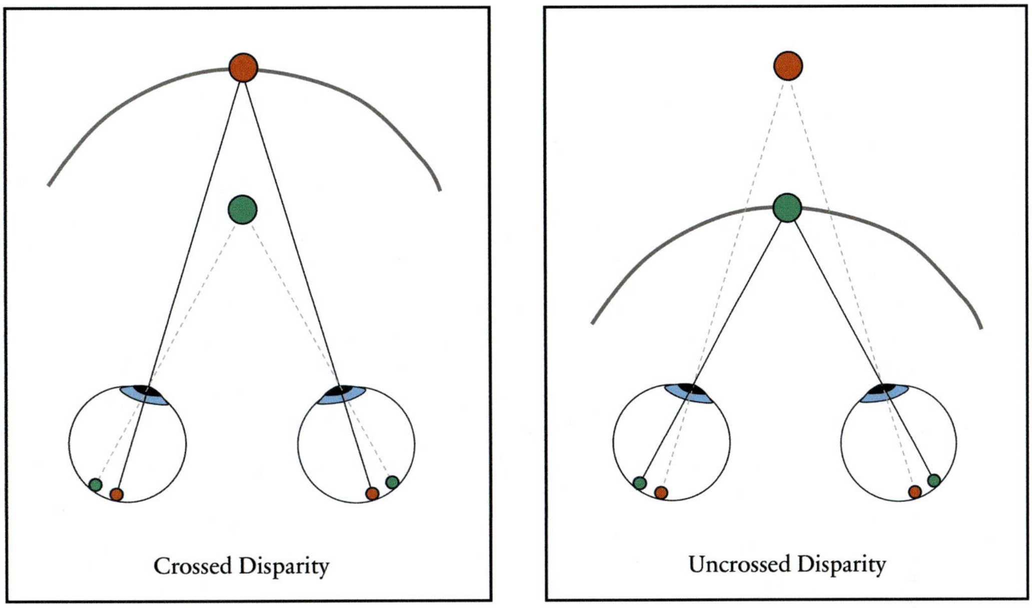

Figure 9.11 Left, crossed disparity occurs for an object that is closer than the distance at which gaze is focused. Right, uncrossed disparity occurs for an object that is farther away that the distance at which gaze is focused.

doorknob, and on his left retina, the image of the pen would fall *to the left* of the image of the doorknob. This means that if the left and right retinal images were overlaid right on top of one another, the images of the pen would not coincide at all. In fact, *there would be two of them*—one on either side of the image of the doorknob—which is why he sees a double image of the pen under such circumstances! The point here is that there would be *much more retinal disparity for the image of the pen* than for the image of the doorknob.

This is called **crossed disparity**[6] (see Figure 9.11, left), and it is a cue that the object generating more retinal disparity—in this case, the pen—is closer to you than where your gaze is focused—in this case, the doorknob. If you are using a VR headset or watching a 3D movie, for example, crossed disparity is what makes it look like an object is closer to you than the screen itself (see Box 9.1). And the more crossed disparity there is, the closer to you the object will appear to be (look out—a charging baby elephant!).

Crossed disparity retinal disparity that occurs for an object that is closer than where your gaze is focused.

Uncrossed Disparity

Now, let's move on to the other case where Fred's gaze is focused on the pen (which is closer to him) and he sees a double image of the doorknob (which is farther away). In this case, the images of the *pen* fall on corresponding places on each retina, but the images of the doorknob do not. This means that if the left and right retinal images were overlaid right on top of one another, the images of the two pens would—for the most part—coincide, but the images of the doorknobs would not. In fact, there would be two of them—one on either side of the image of the pen—which is why he sees a double image of the doorknob under such circumstances. The point here is that there would be ***much more retinal disparity for the image of the doorknob*** than for the image of the pen.

This is called **uncrossed disparity**[7] (see Figure 9.11, right), and it is a cue that the object generating the disparity—in this case, the doorknob—is farther away than where your gaze is focused. If you are using a VR headset or watching a 3D movie, for example, uncrossed disparity is what makes it look like an object is farther away than the screen itself (see Box 9.1). And the more crossed disparity there is, the farther away from the screen the object will appear to be (look at that baby elephant way off in the distance!)

Uncrossed disparity retinal disparity that occurs for an object that is farther than where your gaze is focused.

So, the rule to be applied by the central executive is that when there is crossed retinal disparity for a given object, that object is located closer than where your gaze is focused. And the more crossed disparity, the closer that object is. When there is uncrossed retinal disparity for a given object, that object is located farther away than where your gaze is focused. And the more uncrossed disparity, the farther away that object is.

There are (at least) two caveats here, though. Like accommodation and convergence, binocular disparity is most useful as a cue for objects at distances of up to 20 meters or so. For distances beyond that, there really isn't enough retinal disparity to make (too much of) a difference. Second, for retinal disparity to serve as a cue to depth, the central executive needs to figure out what differences there are between the two retinal images. This means that it needs to figure out what parts of the retinal image from the right eye match up with the parts of the retinal image from the left eye, and vice versa.[8] Only then can it figure what parts *do not* match up, figure out whether these differences indicate crossed or uncrossed disparities, and then generate the relevant experiences of depth. The challenge of figuring out what parts of each image match up with each other is known as the **correspondence** problem, and it is not trivial (see Chapter 11 for how this impacts the understanding of motion).

Correspondence problem the challenge of determining what parts of each retinal image match up with each other.

Cue: Retinal disparity	Rule: Crossed disparity -- > object nearer than where your gaze is focused; Uncrossed disparity --> object farther than where your gaze is focused

Socratic Question: Which cues to depth can be used in drawings, paintings, or photographs? Which can be used in standard (2D) movies or videos or video games? Which can be used in 3D (or VR) movies, videos, or video games?

A Note on Combining Cues

Of course, the central executive is not limited to making inferences about depth one cue at a time. Some cues are more useful in some situations than in others, and none of the cues are

100% reliable on their own. It's quite a challenge to reconstruct a three-dimensional world from a two-dimensional image! So, the central executive is generally better off using *multiple cues*—as many cues as possible, actually. The central executive could even combine several cues—maybe after weighting each cue based on how reliable it usually is in this particular situation—to generate an *even better* inference about depth.

Think about it this way—the central executive attempting to figure out the three-dimensional world from a set of cues in the retinal image is a lot like a detective trying to solve a crime based on the clues available at the scene (Gregory, 1980). Both can only make inferences to come up with a most likely scenario based on evidence that they have at the time. And neither one should be satisfied with a single piece of evidence. Instead, it is in their best interest to consider as much evidence as possible. It is also in their best interest to carefully weigh each piece of evidence depending on its value in any given situation.

So, in general, the central executive is better off combining *multiple cues* to generate the best possible guess about a given property than they are using a *single* cue to do so. Of course, there are always many different properties to be perceived. And so, the central executive may be *even better* off if they can combine multiple cues to generate the best possible guess about *multiple properties*—especially when those properties are related. This could be the case for properties such as distance and size, for example. The possibility that perceived size and perceived distance are related such that perceived size can be used to figure out perceived depth, and vice versa, is known as the **size-distance invariance hypothesis**. Before we discuss this possibility and introduce you to two well-known perceptual illusions that might result from combining cues about distance and size, we should briefly discuss size perception.

Size-distance invariance hypothesis the possibility that perceived size depends on perceived distance, and vice versa.

Size Perception

For the same reasons that the pattern of light on the retina is ambiguous about depth and distance, it is also ambiguous about size. The projected image not only makes it hard to figure out how far away objects in that projection are, it also makes it hard to figure out how big or small those objects are.

As we foreshadowed earlier, retinal image size is not only a cue about depth, but it is also a cue about size. Imagine that Fred is—once again—in first-grade art class. He takes out one of his baby elephants. He puts it right next to a toy baby elephant (Fred didn't need to worry about bringing this one—Mr. Raoul brought it for him). Now Mr. Raoul asks Fred to try to draw the scene. This is easy. When the two elephants are right next to each other, he would draw the actual baby elephant much (much) bigger than the toy baby elephant (see Figure 9.12). Easy, peasy.

Consequently, **retinal image size** is a possible cue about object size. And the rule to be applied by the central executive in this case is that the larger the retinal image of an object, the larger that object is. Said another way, objects with larger retinal images are larger than objects with smaller retinal images. But wait, there's more!

Cue: Retinal image size	Rule: smaller retinal image size --> smaller object; larger retinal image size --> larger object

Figure 9.12 When objects are at the same distance, retinal image size alone is a potential cue about object size.

Now, Mr. Raoul wants the class to try something else. He asks Fred to back the actual baby elephant up a bit so that it is farther away than the toy baby elephant. Mr. Raoul asks Fred to try to draw the scene again. Also easy. He would draw the actual baby elephant a little bit smaller this time. Now Mr. Raoul asks Fred to do the same thing a few more times. There will eventually come a point where the actual baby elephant is far enough away that Fred would need to draw it *exactly the same size* as the toy baby elephant (see Figure 9.13). And so, in the drawing, it might look like the two elephants are the same size even though they are vastly different in sizes. Well, that's weird.

The point here is that in the absence of additional information, retinal image size is completely ambiguous about actual object size. An object that creates a given retinal image size could be a smaller object that is closer or a larger object that is farther. Clever photographers and filmmakers sometimes take advantage of this ambiguity in so-called 'forced perspective' photography (see Figure 9.14).

Figure 9.13 When objects are not at the same distance, retinal image size alone is ambiguous about object size.

Figure 9.14 These are all examples of "forced perspective" photography. Creating such images requires carefully aligning objects of difference sizes at different distances from the camera.

So, how would Fred or you (or the central executive) ever know if an object that creates a given retinal image size is a smaller object that is closer or a larger object that is farther? This is where cue combination comes into play. There is evidence for exactly this sort of cue combination. In a classic study investigating this, participants viewed discs of different sizes placed at different distances (Holway & Boring, 1941). The experimenters carefully chose combinations of size and distance so that no matter the size or distance of the disc, the retinal image of the disc was always the same size—similar to how objects might be arranged in forced perspective photography.

In this experiment, the participant's job was to judge actual disc size. But . . . wait a minute. If retinal image size of the disc was the same in every case, how could the participants tell the difference? Well, they couldn't. At least they couldn't do so very well when there were very few (if any) cues to disc distance. For example, when participants stood completely still and looked through a peephole to remove motion parallax and only used one eye to remove convergence and binocular disparity, they were not very good at the task at all. Under these circumstances, larger discs looked larger, but only a little (see Figure 9.15). In other words, perceived disc size did not match actual disc size very much at all. However, when there were *many* cues to disc distance—for example, when participants could sway from side to side and could use both eyes—they were really good at the task. Not only did larger discs look larger, but perceived disc size nearly *perfectly matched* actual disc size. In other words, the more cues that were available about *disc distance*, the more accurate perceived *disc size* was. So maybe cue combination helps the perceiver disambiguate what might otherwise be an ambiguous cue.

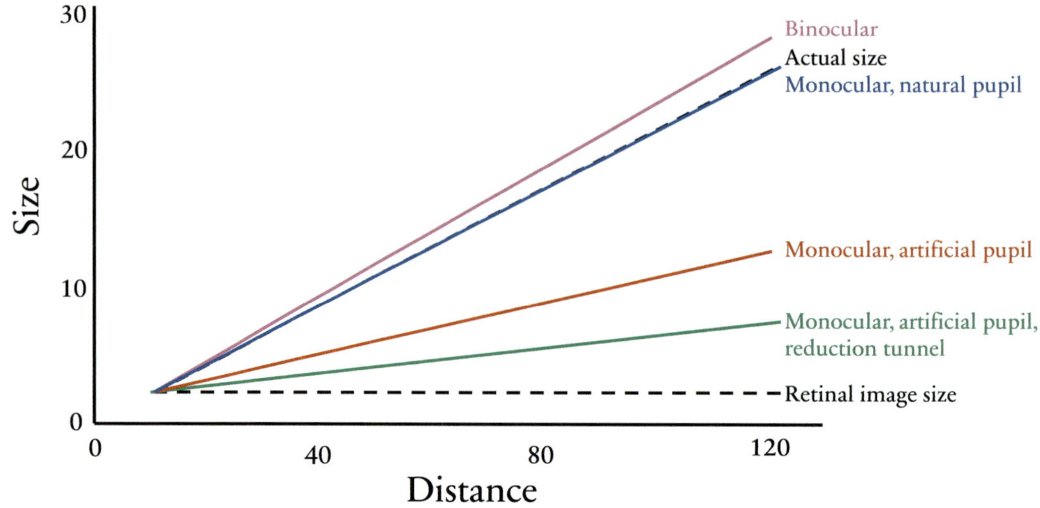

Figure 9.15 In the study by Holway and Boring (1941), people were better at perceiving object size when there were multiple cues to object distance.

Socratic Question: How do the results of the study by Holway and Boring (1941) suggest that cues are combined when perceiving size and depth?

Size Constancy and Illusions

And to the extent that this sort of cue combination process is how size and depth are perceived, most of the time, this process seems to go quite well. That is, most of the time, we experience **size constancy**—we perceive objects to remain the same (actual) size even when retinal image size changes. For example, when Fred watches his friend, Damian, approach from across the street, he perceives Damian to be getting closer, not bigger. This could be due to Fred's central executive deftly and correctly combining cues about size and depth to generate accurate perceptions of both properties.

Size constancy the fact that perceived object size remains unchanged despite changes in retinal image size.

But, if size constancies are what happen when cues about size and depth are combined correctly, then it could be that *size illusions* are what happen when these cues are combined incorrectly (Gillam, 1980; Gregory, 1980). In fact, it might be that—in general—perceptual illusions are a necessary but unfortunate byproduct of cue combination.

We will discuss how this might happen in two different illusions. But first, it might help to discuss how this process works when cues are combined correctly. Look at the picture in Figure 9.16. It should look like there is a person on the right with bows in her hair (let's call her 'Paula') close by and another person on the left dressed similarly —but without bows in her hair—farther away (let's call her 'Kerry'). Easy peasy.

Figure 9.16 These two children create very different retinal images sizes, but most likely this difference is due to a difference in distance, not size.

But how did your central executive come to this conclusion? Well, what cues are available to the central executive about size and depth? There are several of them, but let's start with retinal image size. The retinal image size of Paula (on the right, with the bows) is much larger than that of Kerry (on the left, without the bows). And so, based on this cue alone, the central executive would almost certainly (and incorrectly!) conclude that the two of them are very different sizes. But not so fast! As we have discussed, the central executive is better off combining cues—especially when retinal image size in involved.

So, what *other* cues are available? Well, there is also linear perspective[9] (see Figure 9.6). The sides of the hallway are parallel and so they seem to converge in the distance. Kerry (on the left, without the bows) is closer to this apparent convergence point. This suggests that Kerry (on the left, without the bows) is farther away than Paula (on the right, with the bows). So, if Kerry is farther away than Paula, then—in all likelihood— the difference in retinal image size is merely confirmation of this difference in distance. And so, the central executive can readily conclude that since they are located at different distances, Paula and Kerry are probably similar in size, despite the (large) difference in retinal image size. Easy peasy!

Ponzo Illusion

Figure 9.17 shows the three variations of the Ponzo illusion. Let's keep it simple and focus on the example on the left. In this example of the Ponzo illusion, the horizontal line at the top of the figure should appear larger (i.e., longer) than the horizontal line at the bottom of the figure. They are, of course, the same length.

Figure 9.17 Three variations of the Ponzo illusion. In all cases, the object at the top of the figure should appear larger than the object at the bottom of the figure.

So, why is this happening? How did your central executive come to this (this time, incorrect) conclusion? As before, let's consider what cues are available to the central executive about size and depth, starting with retinal image size. The two lines have the same retinal image size (because they are, in fact, the same size). Based on this cue alone, the central executive would almost certainly (and correctly!) conclude that the two lines are indeed the same length. But not so fast!

There are other cues to consider—in particular, linear perspective. The two angled lines look just like two parallel lines receding into the distance. The two horizontal lines are located at different distances from the point at which the angled lines appear to converge. The top line is closer to this apparent convergence point, which suggests that the top line is *farther away* than the bottom line.

Let's pause for a minute here. This creates a bit of conundrum for the central executive. If the top line is *farther away* than the bottom line, then what does it mean that there is *no difference* in retinal image size between the two lines? That's a little weird, right? And so, the central executive has some thinking to do. How could it be that two objects at different distances produce the same retinal image size? Hmm . . . it *must be the case* that the object that is farther away (in this case, the top line) is larger. It is the only way to make the geometry work (e.g., see Yildiz et al., 2022). And so, the central executive *has no choice but to conclude* that since they are located at different distances, the top line is longer than the bottom line, because there is no difference in retinal image size. Easy . . . peasy?

Ames Room

Figure 9.18 shows one version of the Ames room illusion. In this version, the person on the left should look much (much) bigger than the person on the right, even though the two are likely quite similar in size.

Clearly the person on the left is not much (much) bigger than the person on the right. So, what in the name of Hermann von Helmholtz is going on here?! How did your central executive come to this—seemingly outrageous—conclusion?

Before we explain this, we should tell you about the room and the viewing circumstances. As you might have guessed, there is something fishy about each one. The room is not an ordinary room. For one thing, it is shaped more like a trapezoid than a rectangle or square (see Figure 9.19). Therefore, the person on the left is *much closer* to the viewer than the

Figure 9.18 The Ames Room illusion.

person on the right. For another, the floor is slanted up to the left so that the person on the left is *closer to the ceiling* than the person on the right.

So why isn't this unusual geometry immediately obvious? Because the pattern on the floor, walls, and ceiling was specifically designed to disguise it. You can see that checkerboard pattern of the floor is stretched out in some parts and squished in in others. The same thing is also true of the ceiling and the walls. Clever. And sneaky.

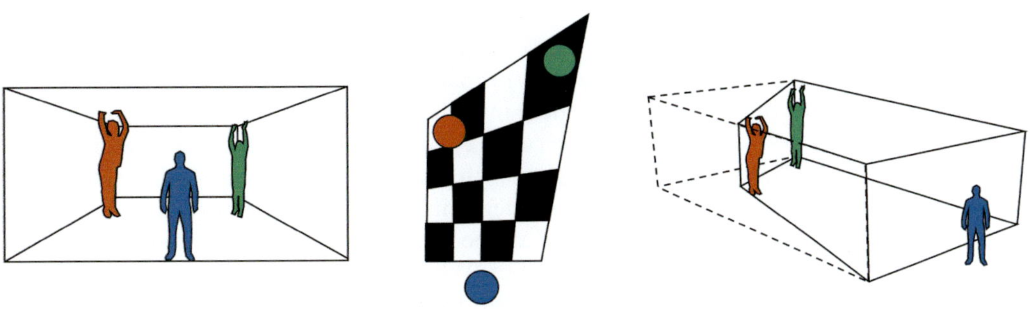

Figure 9.19 Left, the view seen by the observer. Center, a top-down schematic showing how one of the children is much farther away, and how the pattern on the floor is distorted. Right, a schematic showing how the height of the floor and the ceiling is also systematically varied to manipulate cues for distance and size.

And these are not ordinary viewing circumstances, either. Earlier, we briefly discussed forced perspective photography. By placing the camera in just the right place relative to two different objects, a photographer can give the impression that two objects at very different distances are at the same distance. And this can generate illusory differences in size. The exact same thing is happening here. The viewer (or photographer) can only see into the oddly shaped room through a small peephole (like in the Holway and Boring experiment described earlier). From this exact (and stationary) point of view, the room looks rectangular. And so, through a *conspiracy of geometry*, two people who are very different distances from the viewer appear to be at the same distance from the viewer.

Now, we can talk about how the illusion happens. Once again, let's consider what cues are available to the central executive about size and depth, starting with retinal image size. The retinal image of the person on the left is much larger than that of the person on the right (because they are much closer to the viewer!). Based on this cue alone, the central executive would almost certainly (and incorrectly!) conclude that the person on the left is much (much) larger than the person on the left.

Of course, as always, there are other cues to consider. But, given the unusual geometry of the room and the restricted viewpoint, all of these other cues—including linear perspective—suggest that the two people are located at the same distance.

Again, this creates a conundrum for the central executive. If the person on the left is at the *same distance* as the person on the right, what does it mean that the retinal image size of the person on the left is *much larger* than that of the person on the right? Hmm . . . it *must be the case* that the person on the left is much larger than the person on the right. There is no evidence to the contrary, right? And so, the central executive can readily conclude that since they are located at the same distance, the person on the left is much larger than the person on the right because of the (large) difference in retinal image size. Easy . . . peasy?

Socratic Question: What is the difference between a size constancy and a size illusion? Are there any reliable ways to figure out whether you are experiencing one or the other?

Summary

The retinal image is ambiguous about distance, depth, and size. In the traditional approach, cues available in what the eyes do and in the retinal image itself are used to make unconscious inferences about these properties. These include (1) cues that are available in what the (muscles of the) eyes do—called *oculomotor cues*, (2) cues that are available in a single retinal image—called *monocular depth cues*, and (3) cues that are available by comparing two retinal images—called *binocular depth cues*. In cases where multiple cues to distance, depth, and size are available (which is most of the time), cues can be weighted and *combined* to reach the best or most likely conclusion about these properties. Whereas combining cues correctly might lead to size constancies, doing so incorrectly might lead to *size illusions*, including the Ponzo illusion and the Ames room illusion.

Notes

1 When we use the term "distance", we really mean distance between the perceiver and a given object (or "egocentric" distance), not distance between two objects (or "allocentric" distance). In other words, we more or less use the terms "distance" and "depth" interchangeably.
2 And while we're at it, consider how the flea might perceive distance, depth, and size. It doesn't have any sort of screen on (or in) its eyes.
3 You might be thinking: "But isn't retinal image size also a possible cue to object size?" Hold that thought.
4 The long-awaited sequel to *Homunculus: The Infinite Regress.*
5 In the ecological approach, researchers are less concerned with flow of images on the retina and more concerned with flow of structured light around the animal. This is called optic flow. It is not a cue, but an *invariant*. We'll explain the difference in Part 3.
6 Because you'd have to "cross" your eyes to see a single image of the pen instead of a double image of the pen.
7 Because you'd have to "uncross" your eyes to see a single image of the doorknob instead of a double image of the doorknob.
8 Remember playing the "find the differences" game where you try to identify the 5 things that differ between two nearly identical pictures? It's like that—except the pictures are very complex and constantly changing!
9 Not to mention superposition and texture gradients!

10 Visual Perception and Recognition of Objects

As we have discussed in Chapter 9, the pattern of light on the retina is ambiguous about the various distances, depths, and sizes of surrounding objects and surfaces. But it is *also* ambiguous about the shape, connectedness, and identity of those objects and surfaces. In part, this is due to **projective geometry**—how three-dimensional objects create images on a two-dimensional surface. When Fred was younger, his friend Rob would sometimes entertain him by making shadow puppets on the wall (see Figure 10.1). Sometimes he would make a shadow of a swan or a rabbit. Other times, he would make one of a baby elephant—like Topsy! The skill in creating shadow puppets is knowing what kind of three-dimensional shape to make with your hands and arms to create a very particular two-dimensional shape (in this case, a shadow in the shape of a swan, rabbit, or baby elephant) on the wall.

Projective geometry the mapping between shapes and images of those shapes projected onto a flat surface.

Projective geometry comes into play in visual perception because the three dimensions of surrounding objects and surfaces are compressed down into two dimensions on the retina. Consequently, the shapes of objects projected on the retina are necessarily ambiguous. As we alluded to in Chapter 9, under typical viewing conditions, a rectangular patch of ground viewed from anywhere except directly above will create a trapezoid pattern on the surface of the retina (see Figure 9.6). Likewise, a circular object viewed from anywhere other than from a 90° angle will create an elliptical (oval) pattern on the surface of the retina. This creates a one-to-many relationship between properties of the retinal image of an object and properties of the object itself—a one-to-many relationship between physical states and mental states (see Chapter 8).

So, part of the job of the central executive is to undo the ambiguities created by projective geometry. But these ambiguities are made even worse (!) by a few basic facts about real-world objects and surfaces that surround us and how we tend to encounter those objects and surfaces in everyday life. As we'll see in the next section, these basic facts make the already difficult task of undoing the effects of projective geometry that much more difficult (see Box 10.1).

Fred is inspired by Rob to put on his own shadow puppet show. So, he goes to the junk drawer in his kitchen—everyone has one, right?—to see if there is a small flashlight in there, the same one he used during the blackout in Chapter 6. Humor us and go to your kitchen and look inside your own junk drawer (or take a look at 'Fred's' junk drawer

DOI: 10.4324/9781032690964-12

Figure 10.1 The creation of shadow puppets relies on projective geometry. So does the creation of the retinal image.

Box 10.1 "Select All Squares With . . ."

Fred has a problem. He has far too many online subscription services. But he also has another problem. Whenever he attempts to sign up for a new one, he is put through a (minor) ordeal. Sometimes, he is asked to re-type nonsense words in hard-to-read-text or pick all the squares that have a particular object in them—traffic lights? stairs? taxis? elephants? Frustrating? Yes. Relevant to a chapter on object perception and recognition? Also yes (see Figure 10.2). In general, these types of checks are called CAPTCHAs,[1] and at the time they were developed, they were meant to provide some degree of safeguarding that Fred (or whoever) was human and not an AI bot.

You might not think of them in this way, but the tasks that these types of CAPTCHAs ask users to do are all object perception tasks. Object perception tasks were used for this purpose because at the time that these types of CAPTCHAs were developed in the late 1990s and early 2000s, the human visual system was much better than AI bots at overcoming the challenges to object perception that come with these tasks—including clutter, object variety, and variable viewing conditions. As you most certainly know, there have been tremendous advancements in AI in the last few years. These advances have made it so that these types of CAPTCHAs are less effective, especially against more sophisticated AI bots. Nonetheless, they are still used, especially if other safeguards suggest that the user may be an AI bot.

Figure 10.2 Fred has to complete a CAPTCHA by clicking on all the squares with elephants in them. Although it might not seem like it, CAPTCHAs are object perception tasks.

in Figure 10.3). It's kind of a mess. It's a *junk* drawer, after all. There are lots of things in there, scattered all over the place with objects next to, on top of, and underneath other objects. In fact, many (if not most) of the objects in the drawer are at least partially covered by one or more other objects. This brings us to the first basic fact about real-world objects and surfaces. Like Fred's junk drawer, the real world is absolutely filled with objects and surfaces. As Fred looks around—not just in his junk drawer, but even in much tidier places like the rest of his kitchen—he sees objects and surfaces *everywhere*. In other words, real world objects and surfaces are *cluttered*. Therefore, the retinal image of objects and surfaces is similarly cluttered.

Fred looks once again in his junk drawer. Not only are there lots of things in there, there are lots of *different types* of things in there. There are bag clips, matches, a cheese grater, scissors, an ice cream scoop, a cherry pitter, chopsticks, box cutters, can openers, a potato masher, skewers, twist ties, and many, many—probably too many—other things. (But unfortunately for Fred, no LED flashlight!) All of these objects differ in size, shape, color, and material, among other properties. Making matters worse, there are many different kinds of bags clips, several different kinds of scissors, several different kinds of can openers, several different kinds of chopsticks, and so on. This brings us to the second basic fact about objects and surfaces. Like Fred's junk drawer, the world has many different types of objects in it. That is, there is a great deal of *object variety*. Therefore, the retinal image of objects and surfaces has similar variety of images.

Fred takes one more look in his junk drawer, but this time he squats down a bit before he does. Then he steps to the side of the drawer and looks at it again (see Figure 10.4, left and center). That flashlight has got to be in there somewhere! All of the same objects are in there, but now those objects look a little different. He can see more of some objects and less of others from the different viewpoints. And, given the projective geometry that we discussed

Figure 10.3 Real-world objects and surfaces are cluttered and have a great deal of variety, as evidenced by the objects in this junk drawer.

earlier, the very same object creates a retinal image of a different size or shape depending on his position relative to that object. Although this won't really help him find the flashlight, he turns out the lights and looks at the drawer again (see Figure 10.4, right). Now those objects will look different still (remember the Purkinje shift? see Chapter 4). This brings us to the third basic fact about objects and surfaces. We encounter objects and surfaces from different viewpoints and under different conditions. That is, there are *variable viewing conditions.* These variable viewing conditions create variable images on your retina—even for the very same object.

So, the objects that we encounter in everyday life are *cluttered*. There are many different *types* of objects, and there are many different *kinds* of a particular type of object. And we see these cluttered and varied objects under *variable viewing conditions.* These facts about real-world objects and surfaces and how we encounter them—coupled with projective geometry—make the retinal image *even more* ambiguous about the properties of these objects and surface. Nonetheless, for the most part, these challenges are not too much for the central

Figure 10.4 We tend to encounter objects under variable conditions and from variable viewpoints.

executive to overcome—even if it is sometimes hard for Fred find what he is looking for in his junk drawer (see Box 10.1)!

The point is that for lots of different reasons—including clutter, variable viewing conditions, and projective geometry—the retinal image is ambiguous about the properties of objects. And so, from the traditional approach, the fundamental challenge of perceiving objects is to ***disambiguate*** this two-dimensional retinal image (see Chapter 8 and 9). For people who study this process, this means identifying the cues that are available about the properties of objects and how those cues are used in representing those objects. In other words, it requires understanding how *unconscious inferences* are made about such cues to generate mental representations of objects (see Chapter 8). In principle, this is no different than the fundamental challenge of reconstructing a three-dimensional world from this very same two-dimensional image (see Chapter 9).

In this chapter, we will discuss how the central executive might do this. We'll start off with a description of cues that might be useful in performing several fundamental steps in perceiving objects and how they relate to one another. These steps include representing edges and regions, dividing regions into foreground and background, grouping regions that have similar properties, and then filling in any missing edges and regions.

But of course, *perceiving* an object is one thing. *Recognizing* an object is another. For example, Fred might be able to perceive that—in the upper right corner of the junk drawer in Figure 10.3—there are two red objects, each with three curved pointy extensions that kind of look like oversized combs or hair clips. However, he may or may not be able to *recognize* those objects as salad tongs. So, after we cover object *perception*, we'll turn to object *recognition*. Finally, we'll wrap up with *scene perception* which is about how the objects that are perceived and (hopefully recognized) fit together—in part, based on the context in which those objects are encountered. So, let's get started.

> Socratic Question: How do clutter, object variety, variable viewing conditions, and projective geometry make it so that the retinal image is ambiguous about the properties of objects?

Perceptual Organization

As we have mentioned, in the traditional approach, much of the work in perceiving and recognizing objects is trying to find a way to disambiguate—or *organize*—the ambiguous, cluttered, and variable retinal image. Look again at Fred's junk drawer in Figure 10.3. There are a few types of cues that would be awfully helpful in disambiguating the retinal image created by the mess of objects and surfaces in there. For one thing, it would be helpful to have cues about what *regions are bounded by edges*. These cues could indicate the *outer boundaries* of a given object, the *shape* of that object, and the *borders* between that object and other objects. As we discussed in Chapter 3, the activity of photoreceptors and (especially) ganglion cells could be instrumental in providing these cues.

These kinds of cues might help the central executive determine that there is a border between the bottom part of each tray and the drawer surface and consequently conclude that there is a separation between those two objects (see Figure 10.5). They also might help the central executive determine that there is a clear region bounded by edges around the cheese grater and consequently conclude that this is the outer boundary of this object.

Figure 10.5 In the traditional approach, perceiving and recognizing objects requires organizing the ambiguous, cluttered, and variable retinal image.

It would also be useful to have cues about which regions are in the foreground and which are in the background. These cues—perhaps the ones from Chapter 9 about size and distance—could indicate the *relative locations and distances* of several objects. For example, such cues help the central executive determine that the objects such as the cheese grater, matches, and purple bag clip are in the foreground, and the trays and drawers are in the background (see Figure 10.5).

It would also be useful to have cues—perhaps ones about brightness or color from Chapters 3 and 4—about what (parts of) objects go together and what (parts of) objects do not. These cues could indicate that one object is *connected to or belongs with* another object—even if other cues indicate otherwise. For example, these cues might help the central executive to figure out that the skewers at the top of the picture are all separate objects with separate edges and borders and regions, but they should be grouped together. Yet, they should be grouped separately from the ice cream scoop, which also has several parts that should all be grouped together (see Figure 10.5).

Figuring out what (parts of) objects go together is especially important when it is not possible to see every part of every object . . . which is just about all of the of the time. This means that it would also be helpful to have cues about *missing edges* and *surfaces.* These cues could help the central executive to figure out that one object should be represented as a *single object* even if other cues might indicate otherwise. For example, part of the yellow and grey handle of one of the pairs of scissors is hidden behind the green box cutter (superposition; see Chapter 8), but the scissors should be represented at a single continuous object. So, let's take these kinds of cues one at a time and in this order, even though the central executive might not use them in exactly this way.

Representing Edges and Regions

Edge boundary, border, or corner of an object or a part of an object.

What makes an **edge**? In terms of an actual solid object, an edge is what separates that object from another object or what separates some parts of that object from other parts of that object. In other words, an edge is a boundary, border, or corner of an object or a part of an object. But the real question here is what makes something *look like* an edge to the central executive. As we have seen in Chapters 3 and 4, this is often due to an abrupt change in color or brightness. Finding these abrupt changes in color or brightness is relatively straightforward in simple scenes with relatively few objects and sharp contrasts.

Consider Fred's white coffee mug on his back stovetop in Figure 10.6, top left. The edges of this object are clear enough, right? We have highlighted them for you using an image processing software program that determines what is and is not an "edge" based on where these abrupt changes in brightness occur (see Figure 10.6, *top right*). Note, however, that in addition to "correctly" highlighting the border of the mug, the program also "incorrectly" highlights 'edges' just above and just below the mug—which are merely reflections on the stovetop surface—and a tiny speck inside the mug as well.

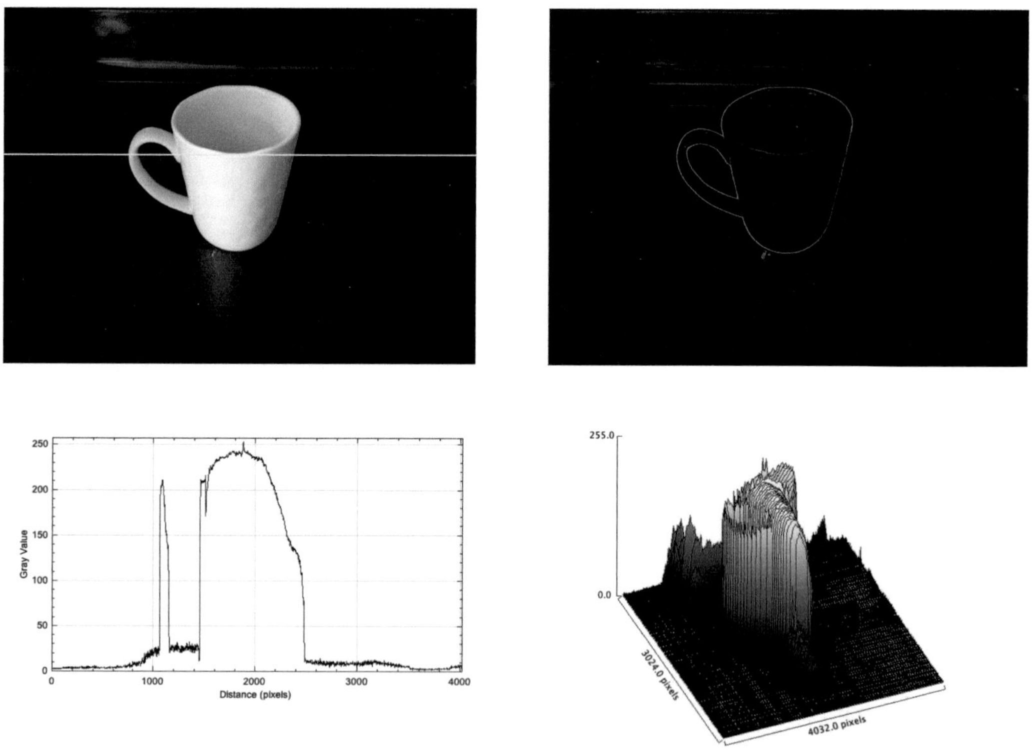

Figure 10.6 Top left, a white coffee mug on a black stovetop. Top right, with abrupt changes in brightness highlighted. Bottom left, a graph of the changes in brightness of the mug in one dimension (along the yellow line). Bottom right, a graph of the changes in brightness of the mug in two dimensions.

Perhaps the central executive does something similar and scans the retinal image of the object, keeping track of abrupt changes in brightness or color. Then, it can use these abrupt changes as cues to indicate the edges—the outer boundaries—of objects. For the sake of argument (and simplicity), imagine that the visual system scans the image of the mug from left to right along the yellow line (see Figure 10.6, *top left*) and keeps track of the changes in brightness that occur. We have graphed these changes (using the same image processing software program as before) in Figure 10.6 (*bottom left*). On the x (horizontal) axis is the distance from left to right across the image on the yellow line in pixels. On the y (vertical) axis is the brightness of the image at that location (a larger number means brighter; a smaller number means darker).

Remember that what makes something look like an edge to the central executive is an *abrupt change* in brightness. This graph shows four points at which this occurs. On the far left on the yellow line (at 0 pixels) the image is pretty dark—it is a *black stovetop*, after all. But then, at about 1100 pixels, there is a sudden, large *increase* in brightness. And what do you know, there is an edge right there! That's the *outside* (far left) edge of the handle of the mug. But it doesn't stay that bright for long. At about 1200 pixels, there is a sudden, large *decrease* in brightness which almost—but not quite—brings the brightness down to where it was when we started the scan. And there's an edge there, too! This is the *inside* (right) edge of the handle of the mug. It stays at that level of brightness for about 200 pixels and then there is another sudden, large increase in brightness at about 1400 pixels. And—wouldn't you know it—there's another edge right there, too! That's where the handle meets the mug.

Then the brightness stays (more or less) constant until about 2100 pixels, at which point it begins a steep (but slightly more gradual) decline. This is the *outside* (right) edge of the mug. Why *more or less* constant? And why *only slightly more* gradual? In other words, why aren't there the exact same abrupt changes in brightness on the right side of the mug as there were on the left side of the mug? Because when this photo was taken in Fred's kitchen, the light source was on the left and so (parts of) the right side of the coffee mug are more in shadow than the (parts of the) left side of the coffee mug. Nonetheless, the edges of the coffee mug are still very clearly indicated by the abrupt changes in brightness shown on the graph.

Region an area of space bounded by an edge.

What makes a **region**? An area bounded by an edge. So, the coffee mug itself is a region, but so is the portion of the stovetop surface encircled by the handle of coffee mug. In other words—for the most part, all objects are regions, but not all regions are objects. But of course, the visual system would need to scan the *entire* two-dimensional image for changes in brightness to represent regions, not just a one-dimensional section of that image (like along the yellow line). We have graphed these changes in brightness over the *entire two-dimensional image* in Figure 10.6 (*bottom right*). And it *sort of* looks like a mug, right?

As we have seen, finding and representing edges and regions is relatively straightforward in simple scenes with just a few objects and sharp contrasts. But the central executive has to do this for more complex scenes under variable viewing conditions. Let's consider one of the variable viewing conditions we mentioned earlier—lighting (see Chapters 3 and 4). Again, consider Fred's white coffee mug on his black stovetop, but this time, with different lighting—in particular artificial lighting coming from above rather than natural lighting coming from the left (compare Figure 10.7, *top left* with Figure 10.6, *top left*). The edges of this object are still pretty clear. Again, we have highlighted them for you using the image processing software program (see Figure 10.7, *top right*). Note, however, that in addition to

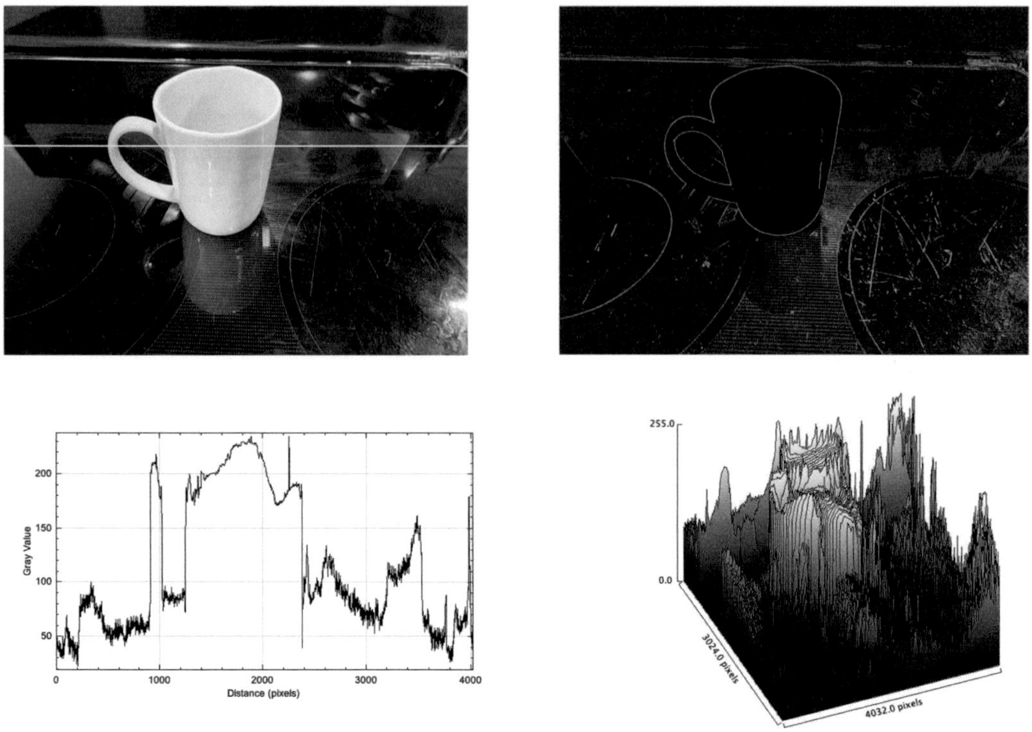

Figure 10.7 Top left, a white coffee mug on black stovetop, this time with different lighting. Top right, with abrupt changes in brightness highlighted. Bottom left, graph of the changes in brightness of the mug in one dimension (along the yellow line). Bottom right, a graph of the changes in brightness of the mug in two dimensions.

"correctly" highlighting the border of the mug, the program also "incorrectly" highlights edges that are really reflections, markings, or even scratches(!) on the stovetop surface.

So, again, for the sake of argument, imagine that the visual system scans the image of the mug from left to right along the yellow line (see Figure 10.7, *top left*) and keeps track of the changes in brightness that occur. We have graphed these changes in Figure 10.7 (*bottom left*). Once again, on the x (horizontal) axis is the distance from left right across the image on the yellow line in pixels. On the y (vertical) axis is the brightness of the image at that location (remember, a higher number means brighter). This graph shows the same four abrupt changes in brightness—one on each side of the handle and one on each side of the mug itself. Score!

But it also shows *a few other abrupt changes in brightness* as well. At about 200 pixels, there is a sudden, large decrease in brightness and about 400 pixels, there is a steep (but slightly more gradual) decline. And then, something similar happens at about 2600 pixels and again about 3200 pixels. These abrupt changes in brightness have nothing to do with edges on an object. Instead, these changes are due to the *reflection of the control panel* (the part with the knobs) on the stovetop surface.

Still, even under these lighting conditions, the edges of the coffee mug are pretty clearly indicated by the four abrupt changes in brightness (at 1100, 1200, 1400, and 2100 pixels).

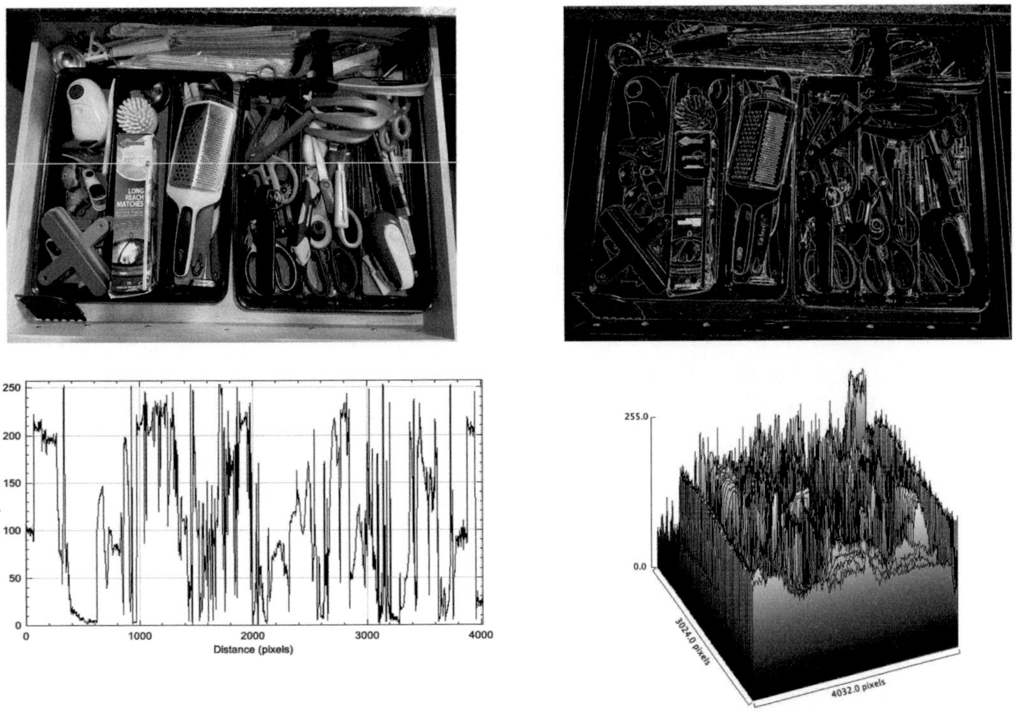

Figure 10.8 Top left, the junk drawer. Top right, with abrupt changes in brightness highlighted. Bottom left, graph of the changes in brightness of the items in the drawer in one dimension (along the yellow line). Bottom right, graph of the changes in brightness of the items in the junk drawer in two dimensions.

But the central executive would need to pay special attention to these edges and less so to the abrupt changes in brightness are due to reflections, markings, or scratches on the stovetop surface. This is especially so when scanning the entire two-dimensional image to represent regions and to figure out which regions are objects. As before, we have graphed the changes in brightness across the entire two-dimensional image in Figure 10.7 (*bottom right*). And *part of it* still sort of looks like a mug, right? Maybe just a teensy bit?

At long last, it's time to return to Fred's junk drawer in all of its beautiful real-life clutter (see Figure 10.8, *top left*). You don't need us to tell you that the images of Fred's junk drawer in Figures 10.3 and 10.4 are much more like the scenes that you encounter in your daily lives than the (staged) images of Fred's coffee mug in 10.5, top left and 10.6, top left. You also don't need us to tell you that this is because real life is cluttered, with lots of variety, and lots of variability. You heard it here first—life is more like a junk drawer than a white coffee mug on a black stovetop!

And, as you might expect, in this photo of the junk drawer, there are *lots* of edges. So. Many. Edges. Once again, we have highlighted them for you in Figure 10.8, top right. And while there are many cases in which the edges identified by the program clearly create regions that indicate objects—the bag clip, box of matches, the cheese grater—there are other cases where this isn't quite as clear. In fact, in many cases, there are far more edges *within* a given object than there are between that object and the next one.

And—one more time with feeling—let's imagine that visual system scans the image from left to right along the yellow line and keeps track of the changes in brightness that occur. We have graphed these changes Figure 10.8 (*bottom left*). So. Many. Abrupt changes in brightness. Too many to mention, actually. There are a few identifiable landmarks, though. The large and sudden increase in brightness followed by a large and sudden decrease in brightness at 400 pixels is the light reflecting from the far-left edge of the tray. A somewhat similar pattern at 600 pixels is the handle of the wooden spoon (turned on its side) just to the left of the box of matches. The large and sudden increase in brightness at 800 pixels is the box of matches itself. Then it starts to get messy. And then it starts to get *really* messy. Like, *really messy.*

Other than the landmarks we pointed out, it is really hard to figure out whether any of the abrupt changes in brightness correspond to edges, whether these edges form regions, and whether those regions indicate objects. And this is despite the fact that we know what the image of the junk drawer looks like in the first place! Maybe a graph of the changes in brightness across the entire two-dimensional image will help? See for yourself in Figure 10.8 (*bottom right*). So many peaks and valleys. It looks like a topographic map of the world's most treacherous mountain range. But wait! What about the tallest peak in the upper right corner of the graph? That must be something, right? It is, but it's not an object. That's the light reflecting from the lip of the countertop in the top right of the photo (see Figure 10.8, *top left*). Oh, well.

Socratic Question: What is an edge? What makes something *look like* an edge? What is a region? What makes something *look like* a region?

Dividing Regions into Foreground and Background

So, the central executive can use edges to determine the boundaries on regions. But as we have seen, not all regions are objects. Some regions are merely background. Look back at Figures 10.6 and 10.7. Fred's coffee mug is a region, but so is the portion of the stovetop surface encircled by the handle of the coffee mug. Granted, the entire stovetop surface (and the rest of the stove) is an object, but *this portion* of the stovetop is not. And regardless of how you classify it, this particular region is not in the foreground. Instead, the coffee mug is the object in the foreground (i.e., the "**figure**") and the stovetop is merely the background surface (i.e., the "**ground**").

> **Figure** the part of an image (usually an object) in the foreground.
>
> **Ground** the part of an image (usually a surface) in the background.

So how does the central executive figure out what region(s) of an image qualify as figure, and which region(s) qualify as ground? This may come down to how the central executive assigns **border ownership** (Williford & von der Heydt, 2013). In other words, when there is a border between two regions, the central executive needs to figure out which region actually

> **Border ownership** the assignment of a border between two regions as "belonging" to one region or the other by the central executive. The region that "owns" the border is perceived to be an object in the foreground.

"owns" that border (i.e. which region the edges actually "belong to"). Once it does so, then it can figure out what is figure and what is ground. In particular, the region that "owns" the border is the object in the foreground—that is, the figure. The region that does not "own" the border is the surface in the background—that is, the ground.

In the case of Fred's coffee mug, your central executive (correctly) decided that the borders between the handle of the coffee mug and the stovetop belonged to the handle and not the stovetop. That is, the handle of the coffee mug has (i.e., "owns") the edges that create the border. The stovetop does not. Consequently, you (correctly) see the entire mug (including the handle) as foreground and the stovetop as background.

But not all borders are so easily assigned. Ambiguous border ownership may lead to ambiguous figure-ground relationships. Look at Figure 10.9, left. Whether you see this as white cross on a black background or four black squares on white background might depend on how your central executive assigns border ownership to the borders that separate the black and white regions. If your central executive decides that the white region "owns" these borders—that they "belong" to the white region—then you'll see it as a white cross on a black background. If it decides that the black regions "own" the borders—that they "belong" to the black regions—then you'll see it as black squares on a white background. The same thing can be said for Figure 10.9, right (known as Rubin's vase; Rubin, 1921) which can be perceived as two white faces on black background or a black vase on a white background.

Fortunately, there are a number of cues that might help your central executive determine border ownership. None of these cues are foolproof—*no cues ever are*[2]—but they may help the central executive come to a decision and move on with its life—and yours. One of these is ***perceived depth*** (see Chapter 9). When there is a border between two regions, the central executive usually assigns border ownership to whichever region is perceived to be closer. So, if your central executive uses the depth cues discussed in Chapter 9 to determine the relative depth of two such regions, it will likely decide that the region that is closer owns border and should therefore be perceived as an object in the foreground—that is, the "figure".

Figure 10.9 Figures with ambiguous figure-ground relations. Whether you see the white or black regions as figure or ground may depend on how the central executive assigns border ownership.

Figure 10.10 Left and center, one cue to border ownership is surroundedness. The central executive usually decides that the surrounded region own the border. Right, under some circumstances, however, the central executive decides that the surrounded region owns the border.

Another cue to border ownership is *surroundedness*. When there is a border between two regions that completely surrounds one of those regions, the central executive usually decides that the surrounded region owns the border. That region should be perceived as the object in the foreground. For example, in Figure 10.10, left, the gray circle is completely surrounded by the border with the orange and white surface. The central executive is likely to decide that the gray circle 'owns' the border and that the image should be perceived as a gray circle on an orange and white background rather than as orange and white background with a hole in it (and a gray surface underneath). The same thing can be said for the sea star on the gray countertop in Figure 10.10, center. However, surroundedness doesn't quite work for the completely surrounded regions of the outdoor scene in Figure 10.10, right (seen *through* the completely surrounding borders of the window frames), nor does it work for the region of the countertop completely surrounded by the handle of Fred's coffee mug in Figure 10.7. Oh, well.

Another cue to border ownership is *meaningfulness*. When there is a border between two regions, the central executive usually assigns border ownership to whichever region is (more) meaningful—that is, which region has a more recognizable shape. The region with the more recognizable shape is perceived as the object in the foreground. Like using the cue of perceived depth, using the cue meaningfulness requires that the central executive first figure out the meaningfulness or recognizability of a particular region and then work backward to assign border ownership. We'll discuss object recognition a little bit later in the chapter, but for now consider the four images in Figure 10.11 (which are based on images created by Peterson & Gibson, 1993, 1994).

In Figure 10.11a and b, neither the black nor the white regions have recognizable shapes,[3] and so the central executive may have a harder time assigning border ownership and deciding which region should be perceived as figure and which should be perceived as ground. In Figure 10.11c and d, the white regions *do* have recognizable shapes[4] and so, in each case, the central executive is likely to decide that the white region 'owns' the border and that it should be perceived as the figure.

Other cues to border ownership also include *symmetry* and *convexity*. The central executive usually decides that a region with symmetric borders owns the border and should be perceived as the "figure". For example, in Figure 10.12 (*left*), the gray circle has symmetric borders and so the central executive is likely to decide that it 'owns' the border and that the image should be perceived as a gray square on a blue background rather than as blue

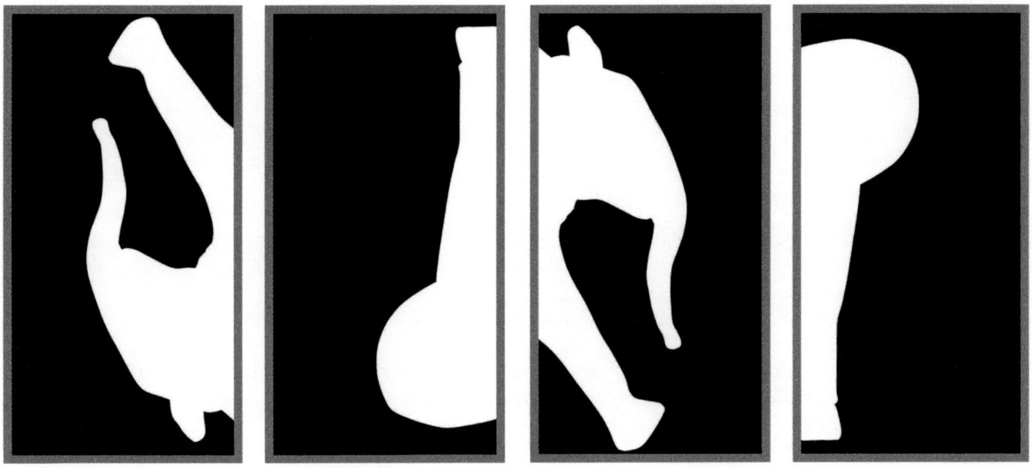

Figure 10.11 Another cue to border ownership is meaningfulness. The central executive usually decides that the more meaningful region owns the border. See text for details.

background with a gray (circle-shaped) hole in it. Conversely, in Figure 10.12 (*center*), the border of the white shape is asymmetric and so the central executive is more likely to decide that the gray shape should be perceived as the background—maybe an oddly shaped hole in a blue surface?

Likewise, the central executive usually decides that that a region with convex (i.e., bulging out) borders owns the border and should be perceived as the "figure". In Figure 10.12 (*right*), the border of the gray shape is convex, and so the central executive is once again more likely to decide that the gray shape should be perceived as the background—maybe an *even more* oddly shaped hole in a blue surface?

Socratic Question: How might ambiguous border ownership lead to ambiguous figure-ground relationships such as those depicted in Figure 10.9?

Group Regions Together

So, the central executive can use edges to determine boundaries on regions and then use border ownership to determine which regions are objects and which are not. But, of course, many—if not most—objects consist of multiple regions. Look back at Fred's junk drawer in Figure 10.3. In particular, look at the ice cream scoop in the upper left corner. That one object consists of several regions. *At minimum*, there is the silver round scoop on the far left, the thumb trigger mechanism in the middle, and the long white handle on the far right. Yet this is a single object, and the central executive must identify it as such.

So how does the central executive figure out what regions should be grouped together and which should not? How do we see surrounding objects and surfaces as *organized wholes* rather than merely as collections of unrelated component pieces? And how do we do this, given the beautiful real-life clutter of everyday life?

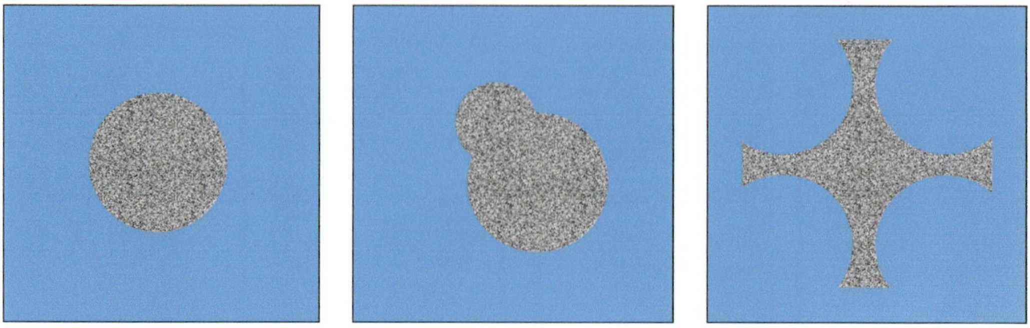

Figure 10.12 Two other cues to border ownership are symmetry and convexity. The central executive usually decides that a region with symmetric borders or with convex borders owns the border.

Understanding exactly how this occurs was the goal of a group of German psychologists working in the early-to-mid-20th century known as the Gestalt[5] psychologists. Over many decades of work, the Gestalt psychologists—in particular, Max Wertheimer, but also Kurt Koffka and Wolfgang Köhler—concluded that the visual system uses a set of grouping principles to organize regions into objects. We will discuss six of these principles here—proximity, similarity, symmetry, parallelism, continuity, and closure. You might think of these principles as a kind of "glue" that the visual system can apply to certain regions of an image so that those regions 'stick together' in your visual experience.

Proximity

> **Proximity** the Gestalt organizational principle that states that the visual system tends to group regions together if those regions are close together.

The principle of **proximity** states that the visual system tends to group regions together if those regions are close together. Look at Figure 10.13a. It might not seem this way to you, but this pattern of four shapes is completely ambiguous. *Wait . . . what? Yep.* You could see this particular arrangement of shapes in many different ways. It could be a single group of four squares (probably), two groups of two squares, or four individual squares (probably not). It could also be a group of three squares plus one individual square (*definitely* not). But we're still not done. If it *is* more than one group of squares, then which squares belong in which groups?

Despite this ambiguity and all of these possibilities, you and Fred and everyone else (almost certainly) see the four individual shapes in Figure 10.13a as a single group of four squares—maybe as a column or a rectangle. Full stop. Why do you see these four squares as "belonging together" in this way even though they are, in fact, four separate shapes? In part, it is because of their *proximity* to one another. If we spread them out a bit—like in Figure 10.13b—all the same ambiguities exist, but now they look *less* like a single grouping of four shapes and *more* like four individual shapes. And, if we move the top two and the bottom two closer together—like in Figure 10.13c—they look more like *two separate groupings* of two squares each.

Now look at Figure 10.13d. Here, different ambiguities exist, but you and Fred and everyone else (almost certainly) see two distinct groupings of shapes—a "column" on the

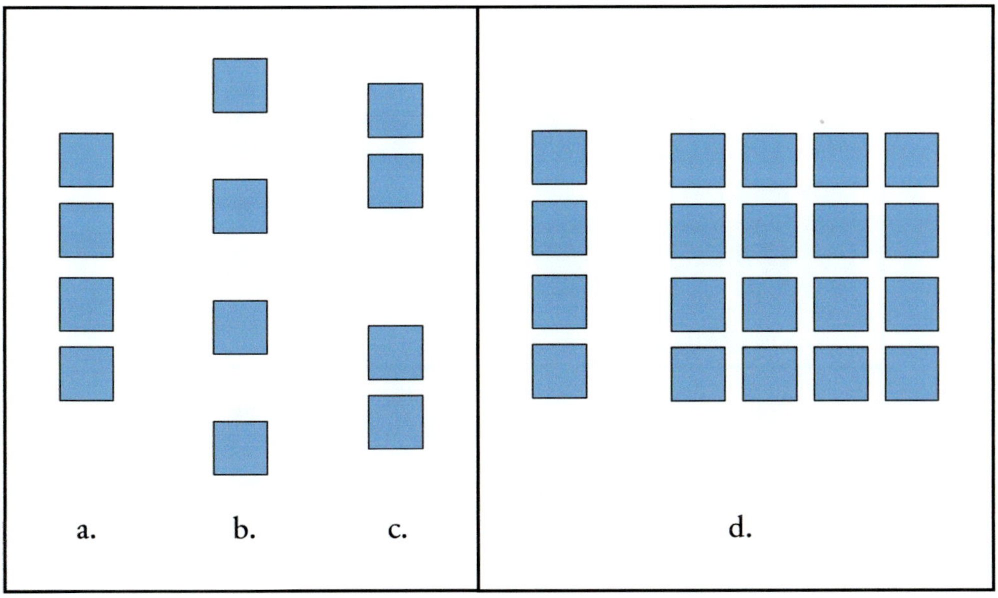

Figure 10.13 One Gestalt grouping principle is proximity. You will likely see the four squares in (a) as a single column, the four squares in (b) as four individual squares, and the four squares in (c) as two groups of two squares. You are likely to see the twenty squares in (d) as a column and a square.

left consisting of a group of 4 squares in a rectangle or column on the left and then another group of squares in larger (4 × 4) square on the right. The principle of proximity goes a long way toward explaining why you see the components of the ice cream scoop at the top of Figure 10.3 as "belonging together" as part of a single object and why you see the individual chopsticks on the right of Figure 10.3 as "belonging together" as a pair of objects.

Similarity

> **Similarity** the Gestalt organizational principle that states that the visual system tends to group regions together if those regions are similar in size, shape, color, orientation, or movement.

The principle of **similarity** states that the visual system tends to group regions together if those regions are similar in size, shape, color, orientation, or movement. Look at Figure 10.14. Like the patterns in Figure 10.13, each of these patterns is completely ambiguous. But of course, none of them look that way. You and Fred and everyone else (almost certainly) see the four smaller squares in Figure 10.14a as forming their own group. Same with the circles in Figure 10.14b, the orange squares in Figure 10.14c, and the tilted squares in Figure 10.14d.

Why do you see these particular groupings and not others? In part, it is because of similarity—in particular similarity of size (Figure 10.14a), shape (Figure 10.14b), color (Figure 10.14c), and orientation (Figure 10.14d). The principle of similarity goes a long way toward explaining why you see the skewers at the top of Figure 10.3 as "belonging together" as a single group of objects and the salad tongs at the top right as "belonging together" as a pair of objects.

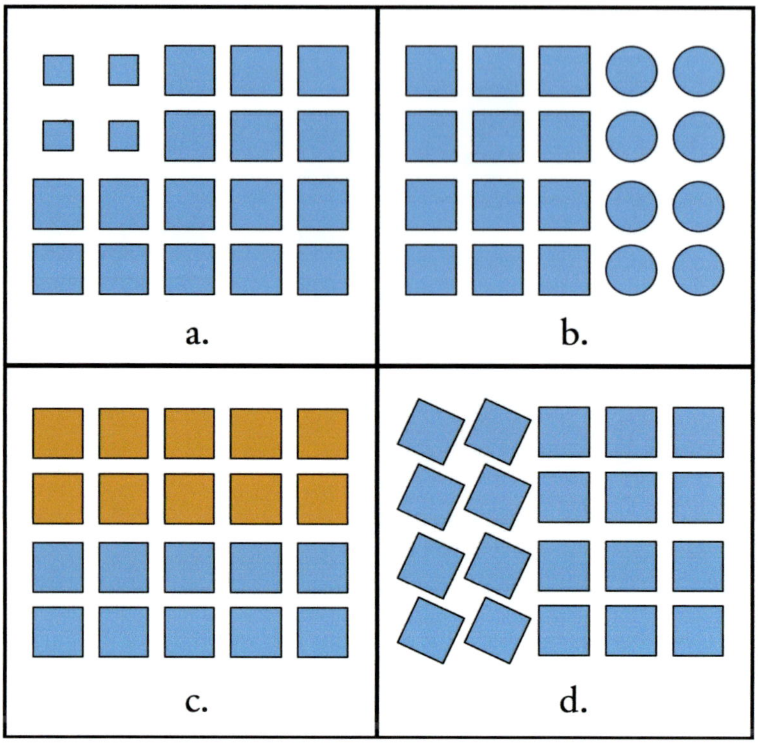

Figure 10.14 Another Gestalt grouping principle is similarity. You will likely see the four smaller squares in the top left belonging together, the eight circles in the top right as belonging together, the eight orange squares in the bottom left as belonging together, and the eight titled squared in the bottom right as belonging together.

Symmetry and Parallelism

Symmetry and parallelism the Gestalt organizational principles that state that the visual system tends to group regions together if those regions are symmetric or parallel.

The principles of **symmetry** and **parallelism** state that the visual system tends to group regions together if those regions are—you guessed it—symmetric or parallel. Look at Figure 10.15. Once again, each of these patterns is completely ambiguous. Nonetheless, you and Fred and everyone else (almost certainly) see the 10 squares in Figure 10.15a as forming a single group—maybe one that looks something like an "H". And you (probably) see the ten squares in Figure 10.15b as also forming a single group as well—maybe like a "8" with the very top missing. But you (probably) do not see the ten squares in Figure 10.15c as forming a single group—at least not as easily as for the patterns in a and b.

Why? Because the top and bottom halves of Figure 10.15a are symmetric, the top and bottom halves of Figure 10.15b are parallel, and the top and bottom halves of Figure 10.15c are . . . well . . . neither. The principle of parallelism goes a long way toward explaining why you see the multiple (parallel) pairs of scissors in the middle of Figure 10.3 as "belonging

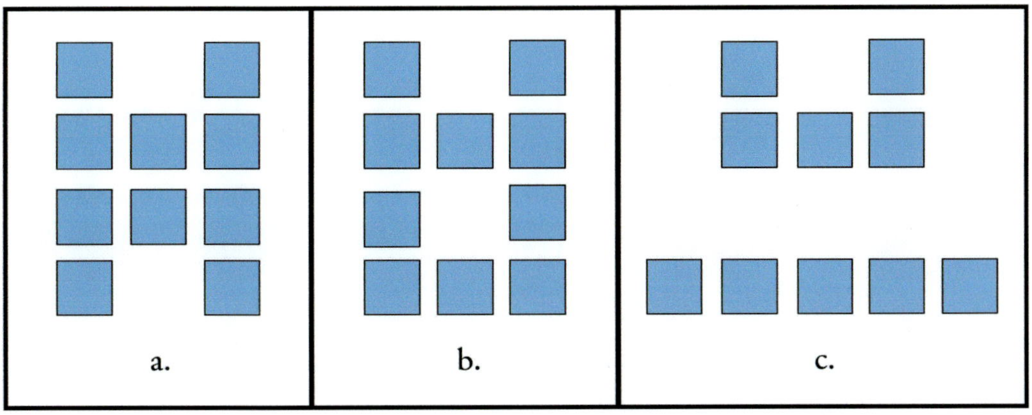

Figure 10.15 Two other Gestalt grouping principles are symmetry and parallelism. You will likely see the 10 squares in (a) and (b) as forming groups of 10 squares each. This is less likely to be the case with the ten squares in (c).

together" as a single group of objects and the two large (symmetric) bag clips in the lower left as 'belonging together' as a pair of objects.

Continuity and Closure

The next two principles—continuity and closure—are most relevant when some parts of some regions are not visible . . . which is almost all of the time! In these cases, your visual system can use these principles to decide where the edges between such (unseen) regions should go and therefore how to group those (unseen) regions into objects. Both of these principles might be how the visual system deals with the superposition of objects (see Chapter 9).

> **Continuity** the Gestalt organizational principle that states that the visual system tends to group (unseen) regions together when doing so would form a smooth or continuous shape.

The principle of **continuity** states that the visual system tends to group (unseen) regions together when doing so would form a smooth or continuous shape. Look at Figure 10.16a and b. By now, you don't need us to tell you that both of these patterns of shapes are ambiguous. But we'll do it anyway—both patterns of shapes are ambiguous! But . . . in Figure 10.16a, you and Fred and everyone else (almost certainly) see the two white regions on either side of the pink rectangle as being part of the very same object. That is, you see them as being the two ends of a white rectangle that is *underneath* the pink rectangle, even though they *could be* parts of entirely different objects. And in Figure 10.16b, you and Fred and everyone else (almost certainly) see the two white regions on either side of the pink rectangle as being part of different objects even though they could be two parts of the same—albeit oddly shaped—white object.

Why? Because the grouping of regions in Figure 10.16a creates two smooth or continuous shapes. The principle of continuity helps to explain why you see the red regions on either side of the potato masher in the upper right corner of Figure 10.2 as being part of the same object—the salad tongs.

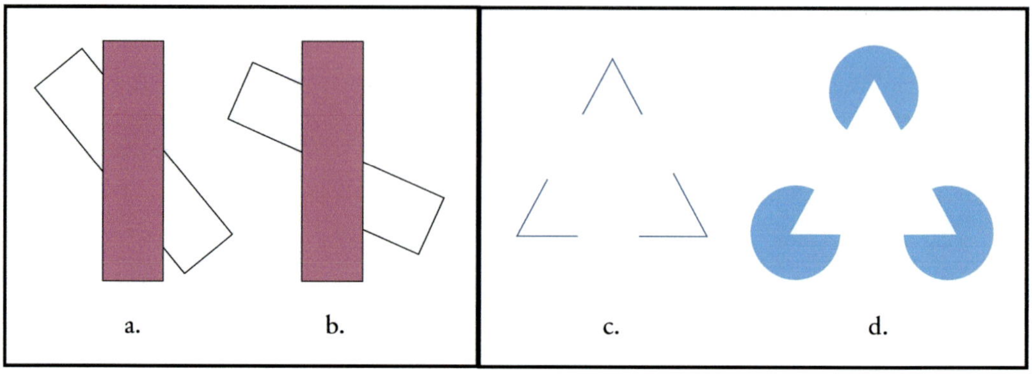

Figure 10.16 Two other Gestalt grouping principles are good continuation and closure. You will likely see two separate shapes in (a) but three separate shapes in (b). You are also likely to see a triangle in (c) and a triangle and three circles in (d).

Closure the Gestalt organizational principle that states that the visual system tends to group regions together when doing so would form a complete shape.

The principle of **closure** states that the visual system tends to group regions together when doing so would form a complete shape. As you might expect, Figures 10.16c and 10.16d are also each completely ambiguous. But in each case, you and Fred and everyone else (almost certainly) see a white triangle. Well, do we have news for you! In neither case is there a triangle present. *Wait . . . what? Yep.*

Look again. In Figure 10.16c, there are three *corners* present, but the line segments that connect those corners are not there. Of course, this means that there is no triangle there, either. But it sure looks like there is. In fact, it might even look as if there are *two* triangles present—one pointing up outlined in blue underneath (a very faint, almost ghostly) white one pointing down. *Weird.* Figure 10.16d is even more interesting because it sure looks like a white triangle is on top of three blue circles. But of course, *none* of those shapes (triangle *or* circles) are actually there. *Even weirder.* In both Figure 10.16c and 10.16d, you likely see *edges of the triangles* even though those edges are not actually present in the image. *Super weird.* Such edges are known as **illusory (or subjective) contours** (Kanizsa, 1976). And you might even see the surface of the illusory triangle as being "brighter" than that surface behind it. *Weirder still.*

Illusory or subjective contours edges that appear to separate one region or shape from another even though no edge is present.

Why? Because your visual system is grouping together regions that would form a complete shape. Closure is one reason why you see the silver bowl of the ice cream scoop in the top left of Figure 10.3 as circular or dome-shaped, even though you cannot see the entirety of the scoop.

Perhaps the best way to sum up how the Gestalt grouping principles—including proximity, similarity, symmetry, parallelism, continuity and closure—help the visual system to organize regions into objects is the **Principle of Prägnanz.**[6] This principle states that "Of several geometrically possible organizations, the one that will actually be perceived is the one that possesses the simplest and most stable shape" (Koffka, 1935). We should point out that for the Gestalt psychologists, what qualified as "the simplest and most stable shape" was not determined by the central executive so much as it was determined by the laws of nature (see Box 10.2).

Principle of Prägnanz the idea that the visual system organizes regions into in a way that reflects simplicity and stability.

Box 10.2 Were the Gestalt Psychologists Just Ahead of Their Time?

Most discussions of the Gestalt grouping principles (including ours above) describe them as rules that the central executive uses to organize the retinal image. But this is not how the Gestalt psychologists would have described them. As we have mentioned, they were interested in explaining why it is that perceptual experience consists of organized wholes (see Figures 10.13–10.16). And while the *principles* they developed get lots of attention, *the explanation of* those principles do not.

In part, this is because their explanation requires taking a scientific leap of faith. Here is the first part of their explanation: complex, natural systems each exhibit a particular kind of organization—think of the patterns that are formed in ripples in water, lightning bolts, a nautilus shell, or planets orbiting a star, such as our sun (see Figure 10.16). These patterns emerge because of the way that the laws of physics and chemistry affect how energy of various kind *flows through* these systems. In other words, the laws of physics and chemistry organize the energy that flows through these systems which produces these patterns. So far, so good, right?

Now for the leap—ready? In principle, *the nervous system and brain are the same kind of complex, natural system* and exhibit the same kind of organization. In particular, patterns in the nervous system and brain emerge because of the way that the laws of physics and chemistry affect the *stimulation patterns* flowing through this system. In other words, the laws of physics and chemistry organize the stimulation that flows through the nervous system and brain which produces the patterns that you (and Fred and everyone else) experience! And so why does perceptual experience consist of organized wholes? Because the laws of physics and chemistry acting on complex, natural systems make it so.

So, you can see why this explanation might not have caught on. Not everyone is willing to accept the idea that—in principle—the nervous system and the brain are no different than ripples in a pond, lightning bolts, nautilus shells, and the orbiting of planets around a star. For better or worse, though, this perspective has gained quite a bit of traction in the last several decades (see Kelso & Engstrøm, 2024; Mangalam & Kelty-Stephen, 2026; Spivey, 2008). Maybe the Gestalt psychologists were just ahead of their time.

Figure 10.17 In complex natural systems, patterns emerge because of how the laws of physics and chemistry affect the flow of energy through those systems.

Socratic Question: How do each of the Gestalt grouping principles exemplify the Principle of Prägnanz? How might the Gestalt psychologists have been 'ahead of their time'?

Recognizing Objects

So, after doing all of the things that we have described to this point in the chapter, Fred's central executive has gone a long way toward organizing the ambiguous, cluttered, and variable retinal image of his junk drawer in Figure 10.3. It has used cues like changes in color or brightness to figure out where edges between regions are. It has used cues about border ownership to figure out which regions are objects, and which regions are not. It has applied the Gestalt organizational principles—including similarity, proximity, symmetry, parallelism, continuity, and closure—to group regions and objects together, even in cases where some parts of some regions are not visible. If all goes well, these processes unfolded instantaneously, and he and you and everyone else were successfully able to perceive all of the various objects in there. Hooray! This is truly an impressive feat. Seriously. Just look at all the stuff in that drawer (Figure 10.3).

Now that Fred was able to do this, he can get on with the rest of his life. Except . . . maybe not just yet. As we mentioned earlier in the chapter, *perceiving* objects is one thing. *Recognizing* those objects is another. And *how exactly* Fred gets on with the rest of his life depends on his ability to recognize what those objects are. Is the roundish reddish thing with the white stripe down the middle the *flashlight* that he was looking for or something else?[7] Is the silver round bowl with the thumb trigger mechanism and long white handle an *ice cream scoop* or something else? Are the two red objects with three curved pointy extensions *salad tongs* or something else?

Recognizing an object means *knowing something about* the object that you are perceiving. So, recognizing objects means connecting *what you perceive* with *what you know*. But how does this happen? How do you know *what it is* that you are seeing? How does Fred know that the object that he sees in his junk drawer is, in fact, an ice cream scoop? How does he know that the person he sees in the doorway of his kitchen is, in fact, a person? And how does he know that the person that he sees is, in fact, his grandmother—Agnes?

Bottom-up Approaches

Many (if not most) approaches to object recognition are so-called **"bottom up" approaches**. These are based on the historically popular idea of hierarchical processing (see Chapter 1). In these approaches, the assumption is that the central executive "builds up" a representation of an object by identifying both the key features or components of that object and how those features or components fit together. To a large degree, this "building up" is proposed to occur as signals travel through the visual system from retina to visual cortex (i.e., from V1 to V4 to the IT cortex (for a refresher, see Chapter 3). Although many of the exact details of this process remain to be worked out, the resulting representation of the object can then be matched by the central executive to the one stored in memory. *Voilá!* Except . . . what are the key features or components of objects? And what is this matching process like? Let's deal with the first question for now.

> **Bottom-up approaches** approaches to understanding perceptual experience in which a representation is generated by combining pieces or components.

Most researchers have focused their investigations on basic two- or three-dimensional shapes—the same kinds of shapes that generate activity in the pathways that run from the retina to visual cortex (again, for a refresher see Chapter 3). One influential model of how representations of objects are formed is the **"recognition by components" model**, developed by American vision scientist Irving Biederman in the 1980s. He proposed that the key features or components of objects were a few dozen three-dimensional shapes that he called "geons". These included common three-dimensional shapes that look like bricks, spheres, wedges, and cones, but also less common ones that look like lemons,

> **Recognition by components model** model of object in which objects are recognized by the set of geons that comprise that object and how those geons fit together.

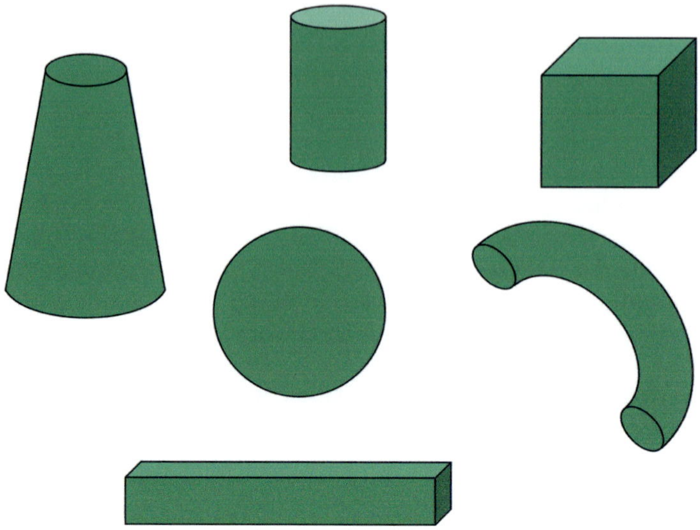

Figure 10.18 In the "recognition by components" model, the basic components of visual perception of objects are basic three-dimensional shapes called geons.

horns, and gourds—yes, gourds (see Figure 10.18). For him, the central executive recognized an object by the set of geons that comprise that object and how those geons fit together. An object could be recognized as a coffee mug—like the one in Figure 10.6, for example—if it consisted of a cylinder with a curved tube attached to the side.

Perhaps the biggest advantage of this model is that it produces a very general representation of a given object. This is helpful in dealing with the object variety and variable viewing conditions that we encounter in everyday life. For example, so long as the central executive can identify that a given object consists of a cylinder with a curved tube attached to the side, that object will be recognized as a coffee mug regardless of its size, color, orientation, and lighting, among other factors (see Figure 10.7).

However, the fact it produces a very general representation may also be the biggest *disadvantage* of this model. Fred's ability to recognize that an object is a coffee mug or that an object is a person is one thing. His ability to recognize that the object is *his* coffee mug or that the person is *his grandmother* is another. In other words, while Biederman's model does a reasonable job in explaining how Fred and you and everyone else recognizes *categories* of objects, it may not do such a great job in explaining how he and you and everyone else recognize *individual objects.* Now what?

The problem of recognizing individual objects is a challenging one because it would seem to require *very specific*—as opposed to very general—representations. But how specific can a representation get? Does Fred's central executive produce a representation that is specific to *his* coffee mug or *his* grandmother? Is there a "grandmother cell" in Fred's visual cortex or somewhere else in his brain? On the one hand, this sounds absurd because it would imply that somewhere in his brain there is a cell for every single object that he can recognize. There would not only need to be one for his grandmother, but also one for his grandfather, one for his cousin, and one for his cousin's baby elephant (named FloJo)!

As absurd as this may sound, there is (at least some) evidence that there are (something like) grandmother cells in the brain. Researchers (Quiroga et al., 2005) recorded the activity of single cells in the medial temporal lobes[8] of people—who were already undergoing brain surgery for other reasons—when those people were shown dozens of different images on a computer screen, one image at a time.

These images included photographs of famous landmarks—such as the Eiffel Tower, the Golden Gate Bridge, and the Sydney Opera House—and of famous people—including former basketball star Kobe Bryant, actress Jennifer Aniston, and former US President Bill Clinton. The researchers found individual cells that were specific to *particular places*. For example, cells that responded to a variety of photos of the Sydney Opera House did not respond to photos of the Eiffel Tower, and vice versa. And they also found individual cells that were specific to *particular people*. For example, cells that responded to a variety of photos of Jennifer Aniston did not respond to photos of Bill Clinton, and vice versa.

So, is there a "grandmother cell" (and a Jennifer Aniston cell and Sydney Opera House cell) in the brain? Well, maybe. But also, maybe not. There are a few reasons to be skeptical of what exactly these results mean. First, it is unclear how specific the responses of these particular cells are. Maybe the "Sydney Opera House cell" is really just an "opera house" cell or a "Sydney landmark" cell. Maybe the "Jennifer Aniston cell" is really a "cast of *Friends*" cell or a "multiple Emmy Award winner cell". Second, maybe these cells are involved in recognizing these specific *photographs* of landmarks and people but not necessarily in recognizing the specific landmarks and people themselves. And third, maybe we're just giving too much credit to a single cell out of the 86–100 billion in the brain.

> Socratic Question: What is the evidence for and against the possibility that there are "grandmother cells" in the brain?

Top-Down Approaches

Another reason to be skeptical of "grandmother cells" in the brain is that object recognition—like object perception—occurs in a context. Fred doesn't just recognize his coffee mug. He recognizes his coffee mug in a specific location in a specific setting at a specific time. He would be far more likely to recognize his coffee mug if it was on the stovetop in his kitchen than if it was on the Concert Hall stage at the Sydney Opera House. And he would be far more likely to recognize his grandmother if she was in the doorway of his kitchen than if she was on top of a bucking bronco at a rodeo.[9]

> **top-down approaches** approaches to understanding perceptual experience in which a representation is generated by applying knowledge or expectations.

So, another way to understand object recognition is through **top-down approaches**. In these approaches, the central executive generates a representation of the overall layout of the scene in which a given object appears. Then, this representation (along with the knowledge and expectations that come along with it) can aid object recognition (Olivia & Torralba,

2007). Such approaches are supported by evidence that all of the senses have both "ascending" and "descending streams". The "descending" streams could be sending information about the overall layout or the "**gist**" of the scene. When you get the "gist" of something, you understand the essentials or basics without necessarily understanding the details. That's exactly what it means here, except that we are talking about what is essential or basic to your visual system.

gist the essential or basic components of the layout of a scene.

One idea is that—almost immediately—the central executive calculates what are known as "ensemble statistics"—a rough average of the essential or basic properties of regions in that scene, such as orientation or color (Dandan, 2025). Take one last quick look at Fred's junk drawer in Figure 10.3. That quick glance is likely enough for your central executive to determine that the objects in that scene are mostly arranged in columns and are various colors including shades of red and purple. That's not a lot of information, but it's *something*. And it might be enough to form a representation of the overall layout that aids in object recognition. In particular, it might be enough for the central executive to use this information to make better unconscious inferences about what objects are most likely to be in that scene.

Of course, bottom-up and top-down approaches are not necessarily incompatible. In fact, it might be the case that the central executive builds up a representation of the object and a representation of the scene *simultaneously*, using one to reinforce the other (see ascending and descending pathways for all of the other senses, Chapters 3 to 7). Some studies have found evidence that this might be the case. In one of these studies (Davenport & Potter, 2004), people very briefly viewed images of scenes in which the foreground object (say, a charging bull or jogger) either was or was not consistent with the background scene (say, a bullfighting arena or a city park). In one condition, their task was to identify the object in the foreground. In another condition, their task was to identify the scene. In both cases, identification occurred faster when the object and scene were consistent than when they were not.

Socratic Question: How might the central executive use bottom-up and top down simultaneously during object recognition?

Summary

For multiple reasons—including clutter, variable viewing conditions, and projective geometry—the retinal image is ambiguous about the shape, connectedness, and identity of surrounding objects and surfaces. In the traditional approach, perceiving objects and how they relate to one another means using cues available in the retinal image to make unconscious inferences about these properties. These cues allow the central executive to organize the retinal image by—among other things—representing edges and regions, dividing regions into foreground and background, grouping regions that have similar properties, and filling in missing edges and regions. In the Gestalt approach, this organization is based on the laws of physics and chemistry. Taken as a whole, these processes generate the representations of objects that are used to both perceive and recognize objects.

Notes

1 Completely automated public Turing test—IYKYK.
2 Remember this for later, especially for Chapter 13.
3 Even though they are the same images as Figure 10.10a and 10.10b—just upside down!
4 Fred's elephant from the side and from the front.
5 Fittingly, the term "gestalt" is German for "whole" or "put together".
6 Prägnanz is a German word meaning "conciseness" or "precision".
7 It's something else—a battery-operated can opener.
8 In the ventral pathway; see Chapter 3.
9 We are, of course, making assumptions about grandmothers. Perhaps the opposite might be true for your particular grandmother.

11 Visual Perception of Motion

As we have discussed in Chapters 8-10, the pattern of light on the retina is ambiguous about many different properties of the world including the distances, depths, and sizes of surrounding objects as well as the shape, connectedness, and identity of those objects. And surely, if the patten of light on the retina is ambiguous about these properties when those objects are completely stationary, it is also ambiguous about these properties when those objects are *moving*, right? Movement just makes a hard problem even harder. Lassoing a fence post? Pretty hard. Lassoing a rampaging bull or even a rampaging baby elephant? Even harder. It was challenging enough for the central executive to undo the ambiguities created by projective geometry when the images on the retina were stationary. But now it has to do this when they are *moving*? Yikes!

In Chapter 9, we asked you to get yourself a ping pong ball and a flea. Well, take another ping pong ball (one that *isn't* cut in half, like the one from Chapter 9) and give it to Hugo Calderano, who is Fred's favorite table tennis player and one of the best players in the world. Give the flea to Wang Chuquin, who is Fred's *second favorite* table tennis player and *also* one of the best players in the world. Ask Wang Chuquin to put the flea in his pocket (just for safekeeping). Then give both of them a ride over to Fred's house so that they can play a match in Fred's rec room.

Now that everyone is in Fred's rec room, play begins. Fred is enthralled. The players send the ball flying back and forth across the table, sometimes with speeds up to 30 meters per second (almost 70 miles per hour) and other times in rallies of multiple shots per point, with delicately placed loops, drop shots, and lobs. He watches the action in awe (see Figure 11.1).

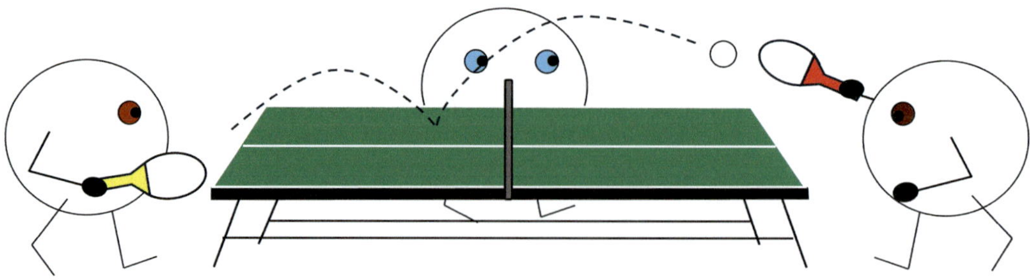

Figure 11.1 Fred watches a table tennis match.

DOI: 10.4324/9781032690964-13

As the ball flies across the table, light reflects from it and projects through his pupil and on to his retina. As we discussed in Chapters 9 and 10, the retina is not only small but flat. This, means, of course, that the three dimensions of objects in the world are compressed down into the two dimensions of the events of the match on a (tiny) surface—the size of a flea! This projective geometry (see Chapter 10) is one of the reasons why the pattern of light on the retina is ambiguous about properties of objects such as distance, size, and shape. And this is the case even when those objects are completely stationary. So, naturally, the pattern of light on the retina is *also* ambiguous about properties of objects that are zipping and dipping across Fred's field of view—thanks to the skilled paddle work of Hugo Calderano and Wang Chuquin!

But there is an even bigger problem. *Wait . . . what? Yep.* The pattern of light on the retina is not just ambiguous about properties of objects that are in motion, it is also ambiguous about *whether motion* is even occurring at all! Think about it this way—motion is defined as a change in position of an object over time. But the retinal image is ambiguous about the position of that object in the first place! So, figuring out whether a given object moved from one position to another is not so easy.

Let's break it down. To figure out whether an object moved, the first thing that the central executive would need to do is to compare the pattern of stimulation on the retina at a given moment in time to the pattern of stimulation on the retina at the very next moment in time. In particular, it would need to determine whether there is any *difference* in this pattern across these two moments in time. This would be a lot easier if the two stimulation patterns were both present at the same time—like one of those 'find the differences between these two pictures' games. But, of course, the stimulation pattern on the retina from just a moment ago is already gone. *Poof!* This means that this real-life 'find the differences' task is that much harder. In fact, it becomes something like a 'remember the differences' task (see Figure 11.2). But let's assume that the central executive can still manage to make this comparison despite the increased degree of difficulty.

Figure 11.2 The central executive needs to be able to compare differences in patterns across time in order to determine if there was any motion. In this image, the previous time is still there; but for the central executive, the previous image is already gone.

Next, it would need to determine whether any differences that were found between the two stimulation patterns are due changes in the *location* of stimulation. There are lots of ways that the pattern stimulation on the retina could change from one moment to the next—including location—but also size, shape, color, brightness, and so on. Then, it would need to determine if any changes in location in stimulation on the retina were due to motion of an object. Oh, did we forget to mention that not all changes in the location of stimulation on the retina are due to motion of objects? Well, the central executive will need to sort this out. And this, of course, will make the task that much harder, too. Did we *also* forget to mention that changes in location of stimulation on the retina that are *not* due to motion are sometimes *perceived as motion anyway* (see the section on real motion and apparent motion, as well as Box 11.1)? Well, there's that, too.

And of course, as we discussed in Chapter 10, the world is absolutely cluttered with objects so there will be lots of patterns of stimulation on the retina to keep track of. And there are lots of *moments of time* to keep track of, too. In fact, here comes one right now! And here's another. And another! They. Just. Keep. Coming. One after the other. So, whatever kind of comparison process the central executive uses to perceive motion must be both *comprehensive* and *fast*. And this would be challenging enough if the problems that we have described so far were the only ones to be solved in perceiving motion. But they're not. *Wait . . . they're not?* Unfortunately, no.

Back in Fred's rec room, Fred is desperately trying to keep up with the action in the match between Hugo Calderano and Wang Chuquin, his eyes are darting all over the place. In order for him to see the ball clearly, the light reflecting from it must project to his fovea, which is really small (see Chapter 3)—about the same size as the flea in Wang Chuquin's pocket! And so, as the ball flies back and forth, he has to move his eyes along with it—as best he can anyway—to keep the image of the ball on his fovea at all times. The problem is that moving his eyes creates changes in the location of stimulation on the retina from one moment to the next—even when none of the objects in his field of view are in motion. Say he is looking directly at the net in the middle of the table. This creates an image of the net on his fovea which is—more or less—at center of his retina. Then he moves his eyes to the right. When he does this, the image of the net will move from the center of his retina to the left side of his retina, even though the net has not moved at all.

But of course, when he is watching the match between Hugo Calderano and Wang Chuquin, *some* of the objects in his field of view *are* in motion—the ball, the players—and other objects in his field of view are *not* in motion—the table and the net. And his central executive has to be able to tell the difference. And fast. Did we mention that the very next moment in time is coming up right away? Like right now!

The point is that for lots of different reasons—including projective geometry but also eye movements—changes in patterns of stimulation on the retina over time are ambiguous about motion of objects. And so, from the traditional approach, the fundamental challenge of perceiving motion is to *disambiguate* these changes so that motion can be perceived. For people who study this process, this might require understanding how the central executive links together patterns of stimulation on the retina occurring at two different moments in time. It also might require understanding how the central executive differentiates changes in patterns of stimulation over time that are due to *object motion* from changes that are due to *eye movements*. In other words, it requires understanding how the central executive uses cues to make *unconscious inferences* about these ambiguous changing patterns of stimulation on the retina. We will cover each of these in turn. But first, we will return to an issue that we alluded to a few paragraphs ago—the difference between *real motion* and *apparent motion*.

Figure 11.3 Fred watches a table tennis match on a screen.

Real Motion and Apparent Motion

Real motion change in the physical position of an object over time.

Earlier, we defined motion as a change in the location of an object over time. This is **real motion**, meaning that a single object—say, the ball in the table tennis match—is continually changing location over time. As Fred watches the match, the changing location of the ball creates a changing pattern of stimulation on his retina. And if all goes well, he would perceive that the ball is moving from one place to another. Hooray!

But what if Fred was not able to be at the match in person and had to watch it online instead (see Figure 11.3)? Good thing that he renewed his on-demand table tennis subscription service! As play unfolds, the ball being hit back and forth by Hugo Calderano and Wang Chuquin still exhibits real motion. That is, it still continuously changes location over time. But on his screen, the *image* of the ball does not exhibit real motion. *Wait . . . what? Yep.* Fred's screen is made of millions of pixels—individual points of illumination. At any given moment in time, the ball will be represented by a subset of illuminated pixels. At the very next moment in time,[1] it will be represented by a *slightly different* subset of illuminated pixels. And so on. And so, the image of the ball that (appears to) move across his screen is neither a single object nor is it continuously changing location. Instead, it is many objects—many individual pixels—illuminating (and dimming) in sequence. And yet, if all goes well, he would *still* perceive that the (image of the) ball is moving from one place to another across (the image of) the table. Hooray! This is **apparent motion** (see Box 11.1). Thank goodness he (and you and everyone else) can perceive apparent motion. Otherwise, renewing his on-demand table tennis subscription service would have been a complete waste of money.

Apparent motion change in the perceived position of an object over time in the absence of actual motion of that object.

Box 11.1 The Many Different Kinds of Apparent Motion

As we mentioned, there is a difference between real motion and apparent motion. The name 'apparent motion' seems to imply that when we perceive apparent motion, our experience is not matching what is really happening. In other words, it makes it seem that perceiving apparent motion is an illusion of some sort. Maybe. Maybe not. But if it is an illusion, then there are lots of different ways that we experience that particular illusion (see Ramachandran & Anstis, 1986). We mention some of these here.

First, there is **beta motion**. Beta motion is when a series of still images is presented in sequence or when sets of pixels are illuminated and dimmed in sequence. This is the kind of apparent motion that allows you or Fred to watch anything on a screen—a social media video, a movie, or the online version of the table tennis match between Hugo Calderano and Wang Chuquin.

Beta motion a type of apparent motion that occurs when still images or objects are presented in sequence (or when pixels are illuminated and dimmed in sequence).

Then there is a related kind of apparent motion is called **Φ motion** (or **phi motion**). This is when lights flash on an off at multiple stationary locations. This is the kind of apparent motion that occurs in the phi phenomenon (see Figure 11.6) or in flashing neon signs, traffic warning lights, or other kinds of lighting displays. The differences between phi motion and beta motion are subtle, and there are often disagreements about the differences between the two. For what it's worth, beta motion is typically experienced as smooth and continuous movement from Point A to Point B, and phi motion is experienced as a kind of jumpy and discontinuous movement between Point A to Point B.

phi motion a type of apparent motion that occurs when two nearby images or objects appear and disappear in an alternating sequence.

There is also **induced motion**. This is where a stationary object appears to move because of how other objects move around it. This is the kind of apparent motion that occurs when the clouds pass in front of the moon and the moon appears to move in the opposite direction. It may also be the kind of apparent motion that makes it look like the sun is rising and setting every day.

induced motion a type of apparent motion that occurs when an object moves relative to an object that is stationary.

Another kind of apparent motion occurs in some kinds of *optical art* in which completely still images appear to move or oscillate back and forth. The following image is called the "rotating snakes" illusion (Kitaoka & Ashida, 2003; see Figure 11.4, *left*). As you move your eyes around the image, the spiral patterns might look like they are rotating (at least a little). Weird right? A similar phenomenon occurs with the second image (see Figure 11.4, *right*). This one might look like the blue circles ripple or wave as you move your eyes around.

Another kind of apparent motion is known as *motion aftereffect*. As you might guess, this kind of apparent motion occurs only after some other kind of motion has occurred. In

Figure 11.4 Left, the "rotating snakes" illusion. The circles should appear to rotate clockwise or counterclockwise, especially as you move your eyes around the image. Right, another example of optical art depicting apparent motion. This time, the circles should appear to ripple or wave.

particular, it occurs after you watch continual motion in a particular direction over a long enough period of time and then that motion stops or you look at a completely stationary object. When that happens, you are likely to see at least some motion in the opposite direction. This is often called "the waterfall illusion" because it can happen after watching a waterfall and then looking at a nearby rock or tree. Another compelling example occurs after watching a spiral pattern rotate or swirl in a particular direction for a while (see Figure 11.5). When that motion stops, you will most likely see rotation or swirling in the other direction. We describe possible explanations for some of these types of apparent motion—including the phi phenomenon and motion aftereffects—later on in the chapter.

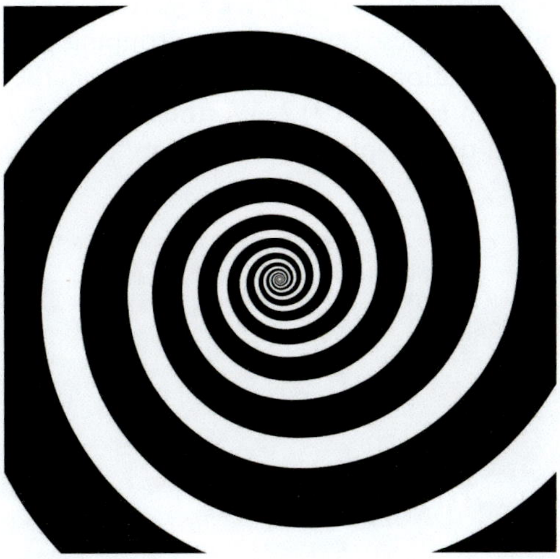

Figure 11.5 If this "hypnosis spiral pattern" were to rotate inward for a while and then stop, you might experience a motion aftereffect in which it briefly appears to rotate outward.

Socratic Question: What is the difference between real and apparent motion? How much does this difference matter?

You'll notice that—for both real and apparent motion—we said that you would only perceive motion "if all goes well". What did we mean by this? Well, as we have mentioned already, perceiving motion is complicated. One of the reasons that it is complicated is that the central executive has to be sensitive to changes in stimulation over successive moments in time. And, as we have already discussed, this is complicated!

But the central executive has an *even more fundamental* problem to solve. It has to be able to connect the stimulation occurring at one moment in time to the stimulation occurring at the very next moment in time. Let's say that at a given moment in time, there is a roughly circular pattern of stimulation on a particular spot on the retina. Maybe it's a ping-pong ball! At the very next moment, there is roughly circular pattern of stimulation *just next to* where the original pattern of stimulation was. Maybe the ping-ping ball *moved* from one place to another! But maybe not, right? After all, it could be a *completely different* ping pong ball. Maybe the first one appeared and disappeared, and then a second one just so happened to appear right next to where the first one disappeared. Unlikely? Sure. But it's *possible*, right?

The point is that in order for the central executive to conclude that changes in a pattern of stimulation on the retina across two moments in time are due to an object in motion, it must first conclude that the two patterns of stimulation were created by the *same object*. This is another version of the *correspondence problem* from Chapter 9, except that all of the stimulation is occurring on a single retina.

In Chapter 10, we discussed a set of grouping principles developed by the Gestalt psychologists—in particular, Max Wertheimer, but also Kurt Koffka and Wolfgang Köhler. As we described in that chapter, these principles serve as a kind of "glue" that the visual system can apply so that certain regions of an image "stick together" in your visual experience (see Figures 10.13-10.16). It might be these same sorts of grouping principles are applied so that two successive patterns of stimulation on the retina "stick together" as a way to overcome the correspondence problem. In fact, in 1912, Wertheimer discovered a particular form of apparent motion that he called the "Φ-phenomenon" (or "phi" phenomenon).

Figure 11.6 Many train crossing lights consist of two lights that flash on and off in an alternating sequence but that look like a single light moving back and forth.

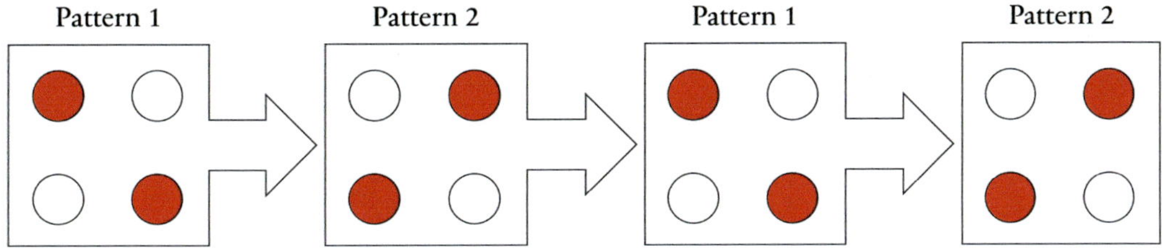

Figure 11.7 Fred could see this alternating pattern in several different ways—for example, as pairs of red dots moving side to side or as pairs of red dots moving up and down.

Fred always enjoys experiencing the phi phenomenon whenever he is at train crossing signal waiting for a train to pass.[2] Most train crossing signals consist of two lights that flash on and off in sequence (see Figure 11.6). One light turns on and off, and then the other one turns on and off. And Fred *could* see this pattern that way. After all, that is what's really happening. However, despite this possibility, Fred, you, and everyone else will (almost certainly) see it as a *single light moving back and forth.* In fact, the experience will likely be so compelling that it might be hard to see it the other way around—as two lights turning on and off in sequence!

As you might expect, the timing and spacing of the lights are both critical here. The Φ-phenomenon will not occur, for example, if there is too much of a delay between one light turning off and the other light turning on or if the two lights are too far apart. But with just the right timing and spacing, the visual system organizes the stimulation according to the Principle of Prägnanz (see Chapter 10) and groups together the two individual lights turning on and off in a sequence as a single light moving back and forth between the two locations.

Socratic Question: How is the "phi phenomenon" an example of the Principle of Prägnanz from Chapter 10?

The effect of the distance between the lights on perceived motion is especially clear when there are *multiple* pairs of lights flashing on and off in sequence (see Figure 11.7). Let's say that Fred happens upon a new kind of train crossing signal light. In this kind of signal, there are *four* lights arranged as if they were on the corners of a square. And when the train is about to pass, two of the lights on opposite corners—say, the top left and bottom right—turn on and then turn off at exactly the same time. Then, the lights on the other corners—the top right and bottom left—do the same thing. They turn on and then turn off at exactly the same time. This sequence repeats again and again, just like with the more typical train crossing signal lights.

There are several ways that Fred could see this pattern. He could see it as two lights turning on and off and then two more lights turning on and off. After all, that is what's really happening. But he is more likely to see *pairs of lights* moving back and forth.

But which way will he see the lights move? Up and down or side to side? Actually, it could be either one. And he might even see it spontaneously switch from one to the other. But we could change how likely he is to see movement in one direction than the other by changing the distances between the lights.

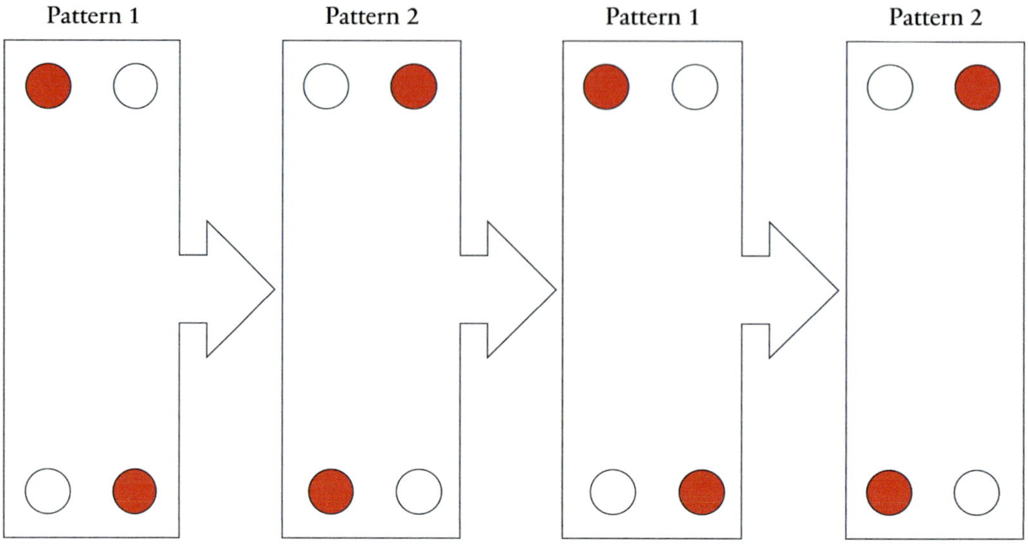

Figure 11.8 Fred could also see this alternating pattern in several different ways. However, given the distance between the upper and lower dots, he is more likely to see it as red dots moving from side to side than as pairs of red dots moving up and down.

Imagine that the square formed by the four lights is stretched out to become a rectangle (see Figure 11.8). If we stretch the square vertically so that the rectangle becomes taller and taller, then—all other things being equal—Fred will be more likely to see the lights moving side to side. Alternatively, if we stretch the square horizontally so that the rectangle becomes wider and wider, then—all other things being equal—Fred will be more likely to see the lights moving up and down (see Ramachandran & Anstis, 1986). In other words, the changing stimulation patterns are organized according to the principle of proximity (and similarity, symmetry, and parallelism; see Chapter 10; Figure 10.12) when it comes to perceiving motion.

Motion of Images on the Retina

Let's go back to the case where Fred is watching the match between Hugo Calderano and Wang Chuquin in person. Again, under these circumstances, he is experiencing real motion. That is, the ball really is changing location over time—zipping and dipping along the way—and he is doing his best to keep track of it. At any given moment, how would his central executive—let alone those of the two players themselves—know which way the ball is moving and how fast it is going?

Well, let's simplify matters a bit by making three assumptions. First, let's assume that Fred is not moving his eyes. We'll deal with this complication soon enough. Until then, however, let's say that he is looking straight ahead—maybe right at the net in the middle of the table. Second, let's assume that the ball is moving in a straight-line path. So, maybe it's doing more *zipping* and less *dipping*. In particular, let's say that the ball is moving straight across his field of view from (his) right to (his) left. Third, let's assume that the ball is moving at a constant speed, neither speeding up nor slowing down.

As the ball moves from his right to his left, light reflects from it and projects through his pupil and on to his retina (see Figure 11.9). The changing location of the ball creates a changing

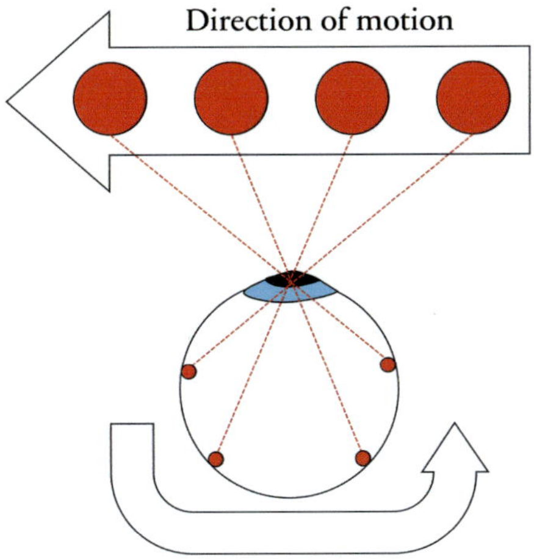

Figure 11.9 An object moves from Fred's right to his left, but the image of that object moves in the opposite *direction on his retina.*

pattern of stimulation on his retina. In particular, as the ball moves from his right to his left, the image of the ball moves in the *opposite* direction on his retina. This is nothing to worry about—it's just what happens to light that passes through a lens and projects onto a surface. As a reminder, the image on the retina is upside-down and left-right reversed (see Chapter 2).

So, with these assumptions (and left-right reversals) in place, how would Fred know which way the ball is moving and how fast it is going? We've already foreshadowed one possibility for how this happens. It sure seems likely that his central executive would need to compare the pattern of stimulation on the retina at given moment in time to the pattern of stimulation on the retina at the very next moment in time.

In particular, it would need to figure out which locations on the retina were stimulated, the order in which they were stimulated, how far apart those locations were, and how much time passed between the stimulation of each location. The central executive could then use the order in which the locations were stimulated as cues to help it determine *direction* (since we are assuming that the object is moving in a straight line). And then it could use the distance and time to determine *speed* (since we are assuming that the object is moving at a constant speed and since velocity = distance/time). *Voilà!*

Reichardt Detectors and Perceiving Real Motion

But what would the architecture of this kind of motion perception system be like? Given how complex the problem is, it might seem like it would need to be complicated system. This might come as a surprise, but—thanks to the three important assumptions that we made earlier—it might actually be quite simple. In fact, in its simplest form, what became known as a **Reichardt detector** would only need to consist of *three* connected components (see Figure 11.10).

> **Reichardt detector** a hypothetical system for detecting motion consisting of (at minimum) three components.

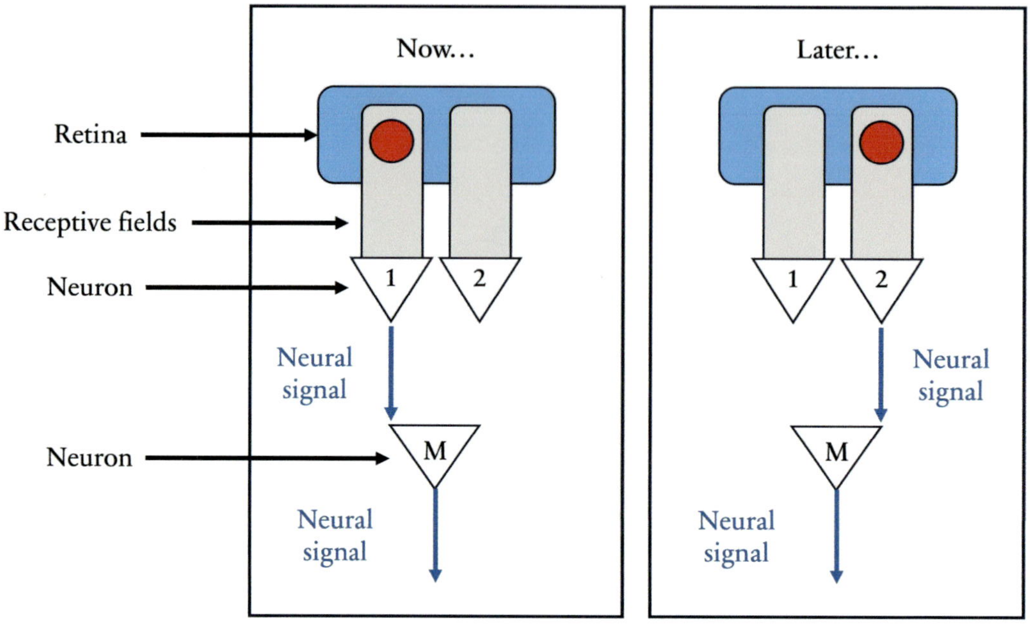

Figure 11.10 A simple Reichardt detector would not necessarily generate a strong signal (a rapid firing rate) in response to a moving pattern of stimulation on the retina.

Only *three*? Yep. Well, three for detecting (simplified) patterns of motion in a particular direction, anyway. And remember that these three components would be *part* of much larger and more complex neural networks of the kind that we described in Chapter 3.

The first component—call it "Neuron 1"; clever, right?—would monitor activity on a particular portion of the retina—its particular receptive field (see Chapter 3). The second component—you guessed it, "Neuron 2"—would monitor activity on a neighboring portion of the retina. And the third component—call it "Neuron M" (for Motion)—would monitor the activity of both Neuron 1 and Neuron 2. How's *that* for simple? Well, *sort of* simple, anyway, right?

So, what would happen in this simple system as the ping pong ball zips across Fred's field of view from his right to his left (from left to right on his retina)? Well, at a particular moment in time, the light reflecting from the ball will create a pattern of stimulation in the receptive field of Neuron 1. Neuron 1 will respond by generating a signal that is received by Neuron M. This will stimulate Neuron M, which will respond by generating its own signal. So far, so good, right?

Some (very short) amount of time later as the ball continues its path across his field of view, the light reflecting from the ball will generate a pattern of stimulation in the receptive field of Neuron 2. Just like Neuron 1 did, Neuron 2 will respond by generating a signal that is received by Neuron M. And just like before, this will stimulate Neuron M which will generate its own signal. And this sequence of events—Neuron 1 and Neuron 2 generating sequential signals each of which are received by Neuron M—should help the central executive figure out both the direction and speed of the moving object, right? Well, sort of. *Sort of*? Why only sort of?

Well, the problem is that Neuron M is only ever receiving a signal from *either* Neuron 1 *or* Neuron 2 at any given moment in time. By the time Neuron M receives the signal from Neuron 2, it has already stopped responding to Neuron 1. And so, the signal generated by Neuron M is never very strong—meaning its firing rate is not very high or not as high as it *could be*, anyway.

If, however, Neuron M received a signal from Neuron 1 and Neuron 2 *simultaneously*, things would be different. In that case, the signals form Neuron 1 and Neuron 2 could be *combined*, and this would maximize the firing rate of Neuron M. Hooray! Except . . . this scenario would only occur if the light reflecting from a given object stimulated the receptive fields of Neuron 1 and Neuron 2 *at the exact same time*. And if this were to happen, would this mean that the object is moving or not? It would be tough to know for sure. And there's the rub.

But there is a solution. The solution is to set up the system with a built-in delay between *when Neuron 1 is stimulated* and *when it generates the signal* that is received by Neuron M (see Figure 11.11). How in the name of Hermann von Helmholtz would this help? We're glad you asked. Again, assume that a ping pong ball zips across Fred's field of view from his right to his left (from left to right on his retina). At a particular moment in time, the light reflecting from the ball will generate stimulation in the receptive field of Neuron 1. But this time, Neuron 1 has a built-in delay, so it does not send a signal to Neuron M just yet. Instead, it waits *just long enough* for the light reflecting from the ball to stimulate the receptive field of Neuron 2. Unlike Neuron 1, Neuron 2 does not have a built-in delay. So, Neuron 2 sends its signal to Neuron M immediately. And this means that Neuron 1 and Neuron 2 send their signals to Neuron M at *exactly the same time.*

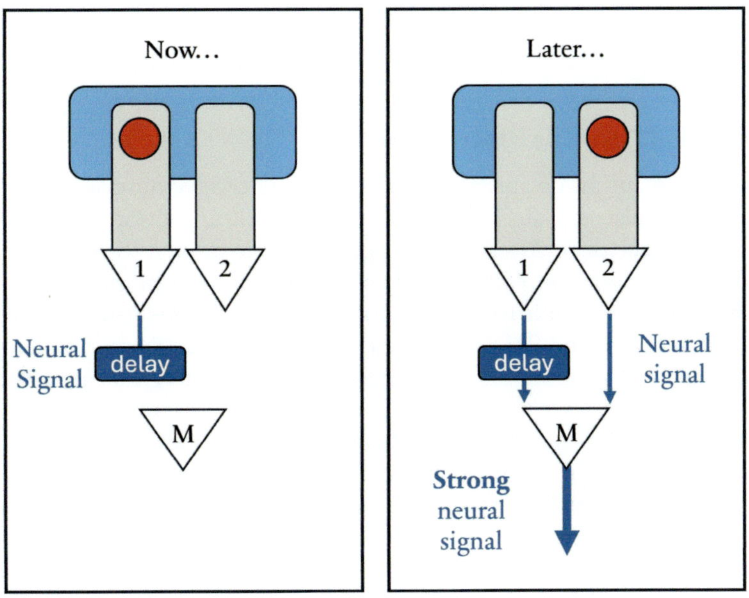

Figure 11.11 A modified Reichardt detector with a built-in delay would generate a strong signal (a rapid firing rate) in response to a moving pattern of stimulation on the retina.

Now, the signals from Neuron 1 and Neuron 2 can be combined which maximizes the signal produced by Neuron M. Hooray!

And so, building in this particular kind of delay in the system makes it so the signal produced by Neuron M is maximized when a pattern of stimulation moves from one receptive field to another, which is likely to happen when an object moves across Fred's field of view. Clever, huh? German neuroscientist Werner Reichardt probably thought so when he developed the idea in the mid-20th century (Reichardt, 1961). In fact, it was such a good idea that these sorts of motion detection systems became known as "Reichardt detectors". Except . . . building in this particular kind of delay means that each particular Reichardt detector system is only sensitive to motion in a *particular direction* and of a *particular speed*.

Sensitivity to direction is determined by which Neuron in the system has the built-in delay. If the pattern of stimulation moves from the receptive field of the neuron *with* the delay to that of the neuron *without* the delay—from Neuron 1 to Neuron 2 in our previous example—then the signal produced by Neuron M will be maximized. But if the pattern of stimulation moves in the other direction, then the signal generated by Neuron M will *not* be maximized—in fact, it will be the same strength (or weaker) as it was when there was no delay at all.

Sensitivity to speed is determined by the *length* of the delay. If the goal is to maximize the response of Neuron M, then the delay built into Neuron 1 must match the time that it takes for the stimulation pattern to move between the receptive fields of the two Neurons. If the delay is timed just right—like in our previous example—then Neuron 1 and Neuron 2 will send their signals to Neuron M at exactly the same time. This will maximize the signal generated by Neuron M. If the delay is too short or too long, then they won't send their signals at the exact same time, and the signal generated by Neuron M will not be maximized.

So, this means that there must be *a variety of Reichardt detectors* that are tuned to motion in different directions and at different speeds. And—luckily for Reichardt—neurons with these sorts of sensitivities have been discovered in particular parts of the visual system, including V1 (see Chapter 3).

Reichardt Detectors and Perceiving Apparent Motion

So Reichardt detectors might be able to explain how we perceive motion. And that's a pretty big deal. But can they also explain how we perceive *apparent* motion (see Box 11.1)? That would be an even bigger deal. After all, Fred paid all that money to renew his on-demand table tennis subscription service! Well, it turns out that, right out of the box, Reichart detectors can explain perception of at least one kind of apparent motion—the Φ-phenomenon (see Figure 11.5). And an upgraded Reichardt detector (Reichardt 2.0!) might be able to explain another kind of apparent motion—motion aftereffects (Mather & Harris, 1998). Let's take these one at a time.

Remember that in the Φ ("phi") phenomenon, a light turns on and off in one location and then shortly thereafter, a light turns on and off in a nearby location. With the right timing and spacing, Fred (and you and everyone else) would almost certainly experience this as the light *moving* from the first location to the second location. When the first light turns on, let's assume that it generates a pattern of stimulation on the retina in the receptive field of Neuron 1. Neuron 1 has a built-in delay, so it does not send a signal to Neuron M just yet. Then the first light turns off, there is a short delay, and the second light turns on.

With the right *spacing* between the two lights, the second light will generate a pattern of stimulation on the retina in the receptive field of Neuron 2, which will then send a signal to Neuron M. With the right *timing* between the two lights (so that it matches the built-in delay of Neuron 1), Neuron 1 and Neuron 2 will send their signals to Neuron M at *exactly the same time*. Now, the signals from Neuron 1 and Neuron 2 can be combined, which maximizes the signal produced by Neuron M indicating that movement has occurred. Easy peasy. Notice that this sequence of events is exactly the same as the one that occurs when an *actual object* exhibits *real motion* across Fred's field of view. No wonder the Φ-phenomenon is so compelling!

Socratic Question: Why is it critical to have a built-in delay in one of the neurons of a Reichardt detector? Why must there be *a variety of Reichardt detectors* that are tuned to motion in different directions and at different speeds?

So, now let's see how a Reichardt detector system might explain perception of motion *aftereffects* (see Anstis, 1997). Remember that motion aftereffects sometimes occur after someone watches continual motion in a particular direction over some amount of time. When that motion stops or when they look at some stationary object, they might see (slight) motion in the opposite direction. We mentioned that an even more upgraded Reichardt detector system might be able to explain this. So, what kind of upgrade are we talking about here?

Well, remember that a standard Reichardt detector system consisting of three basic components—Neuron 1, Neuron 2, and Neuron M—is only sensitive to motion in one direction. *Which direction* depends on whether Neuron 1 or Neuron 2 has the built-in delay. But a motion aftereffect involves perceiving motion in *two* directions—the direction of the actual motion and *then* the direction opposite direction the actual motion. So, one of the upgrades that we need to make is to combine two different Reichardt detectors—each sensitive to movement in opposite directions—into a single upgraded system. How might this work?

The upgraded system consists of two subsystems (see Figure 11.12). The first subsystem is sensitive to movement in one direction—say from left to right on the retina. It consists of three components—Neuron 1, Neuron 2, and Neuron M_R ("R" for "Right"). Neuron 1 is set up with a built-in delay in sending its signal to Neuron $M_{R,}$ which makes it sensitive to movement to the right. The other subsystem is sensitive to the movement in the opposite direction—from right to left on the retina. It also consists of three components Neuron 1 and Neuron 2 (which are shared with the first subsystem), and Neuron M_L ("L" for "Left"). In this subsystem, Neuron 2 is set up with a built-in delay in sending its signal to Neuron M_2, which makes it sensitive to movement to the left. So far, so good. But the upgrade isn't complete quite yet.

We need to add an additional component that monitors the activity of Neurons M_R and M_L and generates its own signal in response. Let's call this component Neuron D ("D" for "Direction"). Moreover, the upgraded system is set up so that signals from Neuron M_L have an *excitatory* effect on Neuron D (causing Neuron D to increase its firing rate) and signals from Neuron M_R have an *inhibitory* effect (causing Neuron D to decrease its firing rate; see Chapters 3 and 4). This means that the response of Neuron D will depend on the *difference between* the two incoming signals. If there is more excitatory signal than inhibitory signal, Neuron D will *increase* its firing rate, indicating motion from right to left. If there is

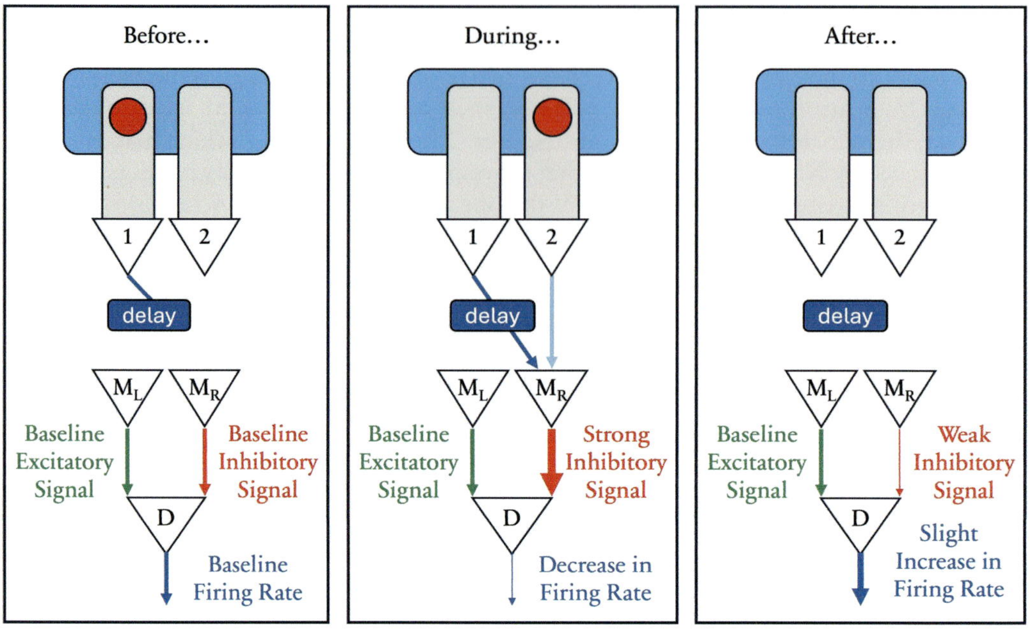

Figure 11.12 An upgraded Reichardt detector system can account for the motion aftereffect when the motion occurs long enough to fatigue either M_L or (as depicted here here) M_R.

less excitatory signal than inhibitory signal, Neuron D will *decrease* its firing rate, indicating motion from left to right. Got it? Maybe?

So, how might we explain motion aftereffects using this upgraded Reichardt detector system? Well, let's think about what happens before, during, and after motion from the left to right on the retina. *Before* any motion occurs, Neuron M_L will send a baseline excitatory signal to Neuron D, and Neuron M_R will send a baseline inhibitory signal to Neuron D (see Chapter 3). These baseline rates are (more or less) equivalent and so there is no difference in the amount of excitatory or inhibitory signal reaching Neuron D. Consequently, Neuron D will neither increase nor decrease its firing rate, indicating that no motion is occurring. Hooray!

When motion occurs, however, Neuron M_R will send a strong inhibitory signal to Neuron D, and Neuron M_L will (still) send its baseline excitatory signal to Neuron D. Now, there is more inhibitory signal than excitatory signal reaching Neuron D. Consequently, Neuron D will decrease its firing rate, indicating that motion is occurring from left to right. Also, hooray!

And now comes the key to understanding why we perceive the aftereffect. The longer the motion continues from left to right, the more fatigued Neuron M_R becomes. This is understandable—*you* trying sending a strong excitatory signal for an extended period of time. See how fatigued *you* get. The more fatigued that Neuron M_R becomes, the weaker (i.e., the slower) its baseline firing rate becomes. So, when the motion stops, M_R will only be able to send a weak baseline excitatory signal to Neuron D. At the same time, Neuron M_L will (still) send its typical baseline inhibitory signal to Neuron D. Now, there is (slightly) less excitatory signal than inhibitory signal reaching Neuron D. Consequently, Neuron D will (slightly) decrease its firing rate, indicating that (slight) motion is occurring from right to left.

This is the motion aftereffect![3] But as soon as Neuron M_R gets a chance to rest, its baseline rate returns to normal and there is (once again) is no difference in the amount of excitatory or inhibitory signal reaching Neuron D. The aftereffect goes away. Hooray, again!

Socratic Question: How can a modified Reichardt detector system explain motion aftereffects? How is this explanation like the explanation of color aftereffects in Chapter 4?

The Problem of (And Solution for) Eye Movements

As we discussed earlier, one challenge to visually perceiving motion is the ambiguity in the retinal image created by projective geometry. In particular, if the image formed on the retina is ambiguous about the properties of *stationary* objects, then it must also be ambiguous about properties of *moving* objects (including whether or not those objects are moving at all). But as we have already mentioned, an *additional challenge* comes from eye movements. Fred's eyes move. A lot. Like you, he moves his eyes 2-3 times *per second*. So, like you, he makes somewhere in the vicinity of 150,000 eye movements per day! This makes eye movements (among) the most commonly performed behaviors. Who knew?

We'll discuss the different kinds of eye movements later, but for now, we need to address the fact that when Fred moves his eyes, it creates changes in the location of stimulation on the retina from one moment to the next—even when none of the objects in his field of view are in motion. This makes it even harder to perceive which (if any) objects in his field of view of moving and which (if any) are not. This is why we assumed that Fred was *not* moving his eyes when we described the functioning of Reichart detectors in the previous section. But of course, if he is making 2-3 eye movements per second, this is not a safe assumption. Not even close.

Box 11.2 You Should Keep an Eye on That

As we have mentioned, eye movements are among the most commonly performed behaviors. On any given day, Fred's eyes move more than his heart beats (and it's not even close). But just like there are different kinds of arm movements (reaching, throwing, pulling) or leg movements (kicking, walking, jumping), there are different kind of eye movements.

We discussed one of these types of eye movements when we discussed binocular cues to depth in Chapter 9. *Convergence eye movements* occur when both eyes move toward or away from one another to keep the image of a nearby object in focus on the fovea of each eye. As we discussed in Chapter 9, the degree of convergence—that is, how much the eyes point toward one another—can be used as a cue to depth. Convergence movements are also important in creating crossed or uncrossed retinal disparity, which can be used as additional cue to depth (see Figure 9.11).

A second type of eye movements are **saccadic eye movements** or

Saccades quick, darting eye movements used to move from one location of focus in the visual field to another.

saccades. Saccades are the kind of jerky eye movements that Fred uses to quickly shift his focus from one part of the visual field to another. He makes saccades when reading, frantically searching for his keys on his cluttered desk, or when working on one of those "find the differences" puzzles that we mentioned earlier in the chapter. Saccades are fast. Like really fast. Each saccade takes about 50 ms, which means that he can make multiple saccades during a single heartbeat (which takes about 800 ms). When we mentioned that he (and you) make 2-3 eye movements per second, we were mostly referring to saccades. One of the interesting things about saccades is that during that during those 50 ms, visual sensitivity decreases—meaning you aren't able to detail as easily. Weird, right? This is a phenomenon known as saccadic suppression (see Matin, 1974). This may be one reason why you don't experience "blurriness" as you are reading this book (or any other time you are using saccades . . . which is almost all of the time!).

The saccades that occur as Fred is reading, frantically searching for his keys on his cluttered desk, or when working on one of those "find the differences" puzzles are voluntary in that he can control where, when, and how long he looks. There are also involuntary saccades that occur even when he is looking at a completely stationary object. These are called "*microsaccades*" because they are more like an eye 'jitter' than an eye movement. It could be that these kinds of eye movements—especially when they occur together with eye blinks—are responsible for the experience of the rotating snakes illusion mentioned in Box 11.1; see Otero-Millan et al., 2012). In short, the strong contrasts and repeating patterns may make it difficult for the central executive to figure out whether rapid moment-to-moment changes in the stimulation on the retina are due to motion of the snakes or microsaccades and blinks.

A third type of eye movements are **smooth pursuit** eye movements.

Smooth pursuit slower, more continuous eye movements used to follow a moving object across the visual field.

Figure 11.13 An "optokinetic drum" can be used as a basic test of visual acuity.

These are used when Fred follows a moving object or to keep a stationary object in view when he is moving. In contrast to saccadic eye movements, smooth pursuit eye movements are . . . well . . . smooth. Fred makes smooth pursuit movements when watching an airplane fly across the sky, when watching Topsy playfully run off with his keys, and when trying to follow the movements of the ping pong ball in the match between Hugo Calderano and Wang Chuquin.

A fourth type of eye movements are *reflexive eye movements.* As the name implies, these are involuntary eye movements that Fred neither plans nor controls. Reflexive eye movements include the vestibulo-ocular reflex (see Chapter 5) and the **optokinetic reflex**. As a reminder, the vestibulo-ocular reflex helps to stabilize Fred's eye movements when his head moves. When his head turns in a particular direction, his eyes turn the same amount in the opposite direction.

Optokinetic reflex the automatic movement of the eyes in the same direction as large-scale movements across the visual field.

In a similar way, the optokinetic reflex helps to do so when his head is stationary and the things he is looking at are moving. This is especially important when those things are all moving in the same direction and are taking up a large part of his visual field. Under these circumstances, the eyes tend to smoothly follow the moving objects and then make a "corrective" saccade back to where the motion started. Since these eye movements are reflexive, the optokinetic reflex can be used to test visual acuity in infants or people who may not be able to answer questions about what they can or can't see. This requires using an instrument called an "optokinetic drum"—a cylinder with vertical stripes that can be spun so that the stripes move across a person's field of view (see Figure 11.13). If their eyes automatically follow the stripes as they move across their field of view, it is a safe bet that they can see the individual stripes on the drum.

Socratic Question: What is the difference between a "saccade" and a "smooth pursuit eye movement"? What is the difference between a "saccade" and a "microsaccade"? What is the purpose of reflexive eye movements?

Efference Copy Theory

So, if Fred's eyes are darting all over the place when he is watching the match between Hugo Calderano and Wang Chuquin, how can he tell which (if any) of the objects in his field of view are moving and which (if any) are not? How can he tell which (if any) changes in the location of stimulation on his retina are due to motion of objects across his field of view and which (if any) are due to his own eye movements?

The answer might be that while Fred does not typically have advance knowledge about the movement of objects in his field of view, he *does* typically have advance knowledge about the movements of his own eyes. Right? Fred's eyes aren't moving *on their own,* are they? Someone is *making* them move. And that someone is *him* (or maybe his brain).

Motor command a signal sent from the brain to a specific set of muscles with instructions about how and when to contract to perform a specific movement.

As we described in Chapter 3, there are six muscles that control the movements of each eye. Let's assume that to make a particular eye movement, Fred's brain needs to send a particular set of instructions to theses muscles so that they know exactly what they need to do and when they need to do it. Let's call this set of instructions a **motor command** (or an "efference" signal). As a reminder, efference is the general term for "outbound" signals sent from his brain to his body (Chapter 3).[4] The fact that these instructions need to be generated ahead of time is what allows Fred to have advance knowledge about the movement of his eyes (or any other body part, for that matter).

Efference copy theory the proposal that the brain sends a copy of motor commands about eye movements to the visual system which then compares the actual and expected patterns movement on the retina.

But it's not quite enough for *Fred* to know that his eyes are about to move; his *central executive* needs to know this as well. Why? Well, if the central executive knows that his eyes are about to move, then it also knows to expect that there will be changes in the location of stimulation on his retina. And so, **efference copy theory** proposes that, in addition to sending a motor command to the muscles of his eyes, his brain sends a *copy of this command*—an "efference copy"—to his central executive (so maybe . . . **From**: Brain; **To**: Eye Muscles; **Cc**: Central Executive; **Re**: Eye movements) (see Figure 11.14).

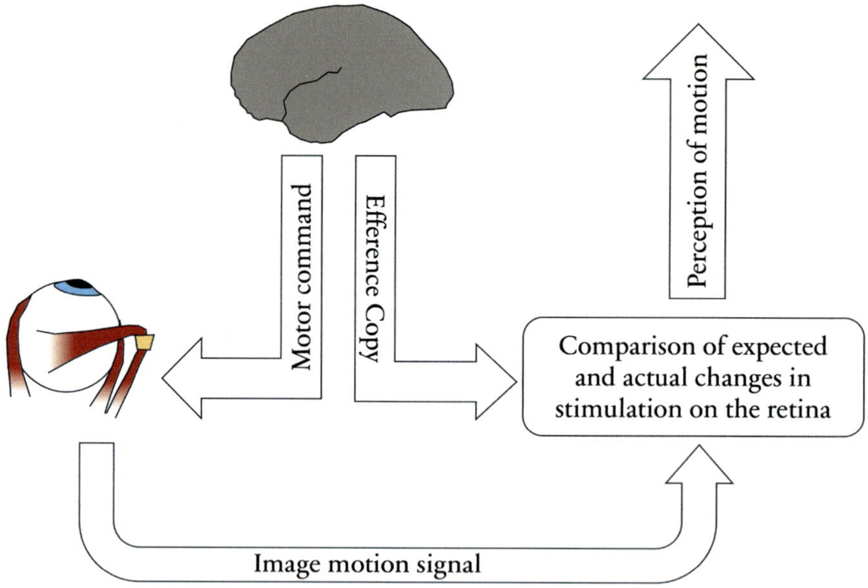

Figure 11.14 In efference copy theory, the brain sends a copy of eye movement commands to the visual system and to the central executive.

Fred's central executive can use the efference copy as a cue to figure out what changes in the location of stimulation to expect from the upcoming eye movement. It can compare the changes that it *expects* to occur with the changes that *actually* occur. Any *unexpected changes* in the location of stimulation can then be attributed to the motion of objects. Alternatively, if no efference copy is sent, then no comparison is made. In that case, any changes in the location of stimulation on the retina at all can be attributed to the motion of objects.

Let's see how this might work in a few different scenarios:

Scenario 1. Fred is watching the very start of the match between Hugo Calderano and Wang Chuquin. He is looking straight ahead at the net in the moment just before play begins. Everything is still. There are no moving objects, there are no changes in the location of stimulation on the retina, and there is no efference copy. So, Fred should not perceive any motion. And he doesn't. Hooray!

Scenario 2. Play begins unexpectedly while Fred is still looking straight ahead at the net. Now the ball *is* moving and there *are* changes in the location of stimulation on the retina, but there is no efference copy. So, changes in the location of stimulation on the retina can be attributed (only) to movement of an object (in this case, the ball). Hence, Fred should perceive that (only the) ball is moving. And he does. Hooray again!

Scenario 3. The ball hits the net and comes to rest on the table. The players stand motionless, having a (good-natured) stare-down over who is going to retrieve it. Fred nervously looks at the ball and then at each of the players, waiting. There are no moving objects, but there *are* changes in the location of stimulation on the retina, and there *is* an efference copy. So, changes in the location of stimulation on the retina can (only) be attributed to movement of his eyes. So, he should perceive that (only) his eyes are moving. And he does. One more time with feeling—Hooray!

Scenario 4. Play is furious. Fred follows the ball across the table as it flies from one side to the other. The ball is moving, there are changes in the location of stimulation on the retina, and there is an efference copy. Changes in the location of stimulation on the retina that cannot be attributed to movement of his eyes can be attributed to the movement of and object (in this case, the ball). So, he should perceive that *both* his eyes *and* the ball are moving. And he does. One last time with feeling—Hooray!

Bonus Scenario. Play has stopped for the moment. To amuse himself during the break, Fred gently presses on the outside corner of his eye and jiggles it up and down just a little. Well, THAT was weird. It sort of looked like *everything* was moving—up and down just a little. What in the name of Werner Reichardt is going on here!? In this situation, nothing is actually moving, of course. However, there are (large-scale) changes in the location of stimulation on retina, and—critically—there is no efference copy. Changes in the location of stimulation on the retina that cannot be attributed to movement of his eyes can be attributed to movement of an object (in this case, *all* objects). And so, he should perceive that everything is moving. And he does . . . Hooray? Weird, right?

Socratic Question: What is efference copy theory? How does it explain perception of motion (or the lack thereof) in each of the aforementioned scenarios?

Box 11.3 What Some People are Willing to Do in the Name of Science . . .

In the bonus scenario, we described a situation where no motor command was sent to Fred's eye, but his eye moved anyway. In that situation, there would be changes in the location of stimulation on the retina but no efference copy. This would create differences between the expected and actual changes of stimulation on the retina which would result in perceived movement. But what about a scenario where a motor command *was* sent to his eye, but his eye *did not move*? In that situation, there would be *no* changes in the location of stimulation on the retina but there *would* be an efference copy. This would *also* create differences between the expected and actual changes of stimulation on the retina which would *also* result in perceived movement. Too bad we'll never know for sure. Think about it. Under what circumstances could a person intend to make an eye movement yet be unable to actually make that eye movement?

Well, one way for this to happen is for a person to be administered medication that causes temporary paralysis but leaves them awake so that they could try to make an eye movement and (later) be able to report on what they experience. And, of course, this would never happen. This would be really, really dangerous. The temporary paralysis would mean that they couldn't breathe on their own and would need to be put on a ventilator and continuously monitored by qualified medical personnel . . . and that's exactly what happened. *Wait . . . what? Yep.* Several participants who were already undergoing temporary paralysis for some other reason agreed to do this (Whitham et al., 2011; see Matin et al., 1982)!

After the medication took effect, the lights were turned off and a small LED was illuminated 1m in front on the participant. The participants were then asked to attempt to look to the right and to left of the light (even though they couldn't actually move their eyes). Then, they were given a reversal medication. Once that medication took effect and they were able to breathe on their own (and talk) again, they reported what they saw earlier when they were instructed to look to each side of the LED light. Most of them experienced the light as moving *in the same direction* as the attempted eye movement. Why? Remember that in this situation, there is an efference copy and no eye movement. This means that the central executive was expecting there to be changes in the location of stimulation on the retina.[5] But there were none. Which is really weird . . . unless the light is moving in the same direction (kind of like what is happening in Scenario 4)!

Summary

For many different reasons, changes in patterns of stimulation on the retina over time are ambiguous about motion of objects. In the traditional approach, cues available in the sequence of stimulation patterns on the retina and cues about how the eyes themselves are moving are used to make unconscious inferences about the motion of objects. These cues are used to link together patterns of stimulation on the retina occurring at two different moments in time so that motion can be perceived. This process might be supported by a specialized—but simple—neural architecture called a Reichardt detector. These cues are also used to differentiate changes in patterns of stimulation over time that are due to *object motion* from changes in patterns of stimulation over time that are due to *eye movements*. The result is that in some cases, we perceive motion when objects really are changing location over time (i.e., real motion) and when they are not (i.e., apparent motion).

Notes

1 The time between moments on a screen is determined by the refresh rate of the device. This can range between 60Hz (60 refreshes per second) and 240 Hz (240 refreshes per second) or more. This is really fast, but it still does not qualify as "continuous".
2 In fact, Wertheimer discovered this phenomenon while on a train trip from Vienna to Frankfurt for a vacation. He became so fascinated with this phenomenon that when he arrived in Frankfurt, he decided to study it rather than continue with the vacation. Now that's a truly dedicated scientist!
3 In general, the explanation for motion aftereffects is roughly the same as the explanation for color aftereffects described in Chapter 4! Both are examples of "opponent processes". Opponent processes have been used to explain many different kinds of experiences and behaviors, including particular kinds of perceptual experiences in each of the so-called "five traditional senses".
4 In contrast, afference is the general term for "inbound" signals sent from the body to the brain (see Chapter 3).
5 Apparently unaware that the person had been temporarily paralyzed.

12 Auditory Perception

Just as the pattern of light on the retina is ambiguous about the various properties of surrounding objects and surfaces, so too is the pattern of vibrations on the eardrum. In fact, in some ways, the problem is *even worse* for the auditory system than it is for the visual system. *Wait, what? It can get . . . worse?* Maybe . . . let us explain.

Given the size and shape of the retina (small and flat) and the facts of projective geometry, properties such as distance, size, shape, connectedness, and identity just can't survive the journey from the world to the retina very well. But one property that *can* survive this journey—at least to some extent—is location. An object or surface in a *particular location* in the world will project an image on a *particular location* on the retina (see Chapters 2 and 3). And two objects that are located next to one another in the world will project images to locations that are next to one another on the retina.[1] In other words, it is possible for light to project on to *some* parts of the retina but not others. And this can be used as a cue to location (see Chapters 9 and 10) and movement (Chapter 11).

But location of a sound-producing object or surface will *not* survive the journey from the world to the eardrum. In fact, it is *impossible* for it to do so. This is because the pattern of vibrations reaching the ear are *not projected onto* the eardrum. In fact, they are not projected anywhere. At best, these vibrations are *funneled or directed toward* the eardrum by the pinna and ear canal (see Chapter 5). And, regardless of the location of the objects or surfaces that generate the vibrations, when those vibrations reach the eardrum, *the entire surface of the eardrum* vibrates.

The point is that all of the sounds that Fred hears—from the buzzing of a mosquito to animated conversation to distant thunderclaps—arise from the vibration of the eardrum, a small two-dimensional surface that is about the about the size of a pea (see Chapter 5). These vibrations are ambiguous about all of the various properties of those objects and surfaces, including location. And so, the fundamental challenge for the central executive is to undo these ambiguities and *reconstruct* the properties of sound-producing objects and surfaces from this pea-sized two-dimensional pattern of vibrations. In principle, this is no different than the challenge of overcoming the ambiguity in the stimulation reaching any of the sense organs (see Chapter 8)

But just like the ambiguities of the retinal image are made worse by everyday objects and how we tend to encounter them, the ambiguities of the vibrations on the eardrum are made worse by everyday sounds and how we encounter them. Consider what happens when Fred visits his favorite café—*Café do Duarte* (see Figure 12.1, top). He likes to go when it's busy—maybe on a weekend. Then he closes his eyes, sits there for a few minutes, and just *listens.*

What does Fred hear during these few minutes? Well, let's first consider what the sounds themselves are like. The graphs at the bottom of Figure 12.1 are from a recording that

DOI: 10.4324/9781032690964-14

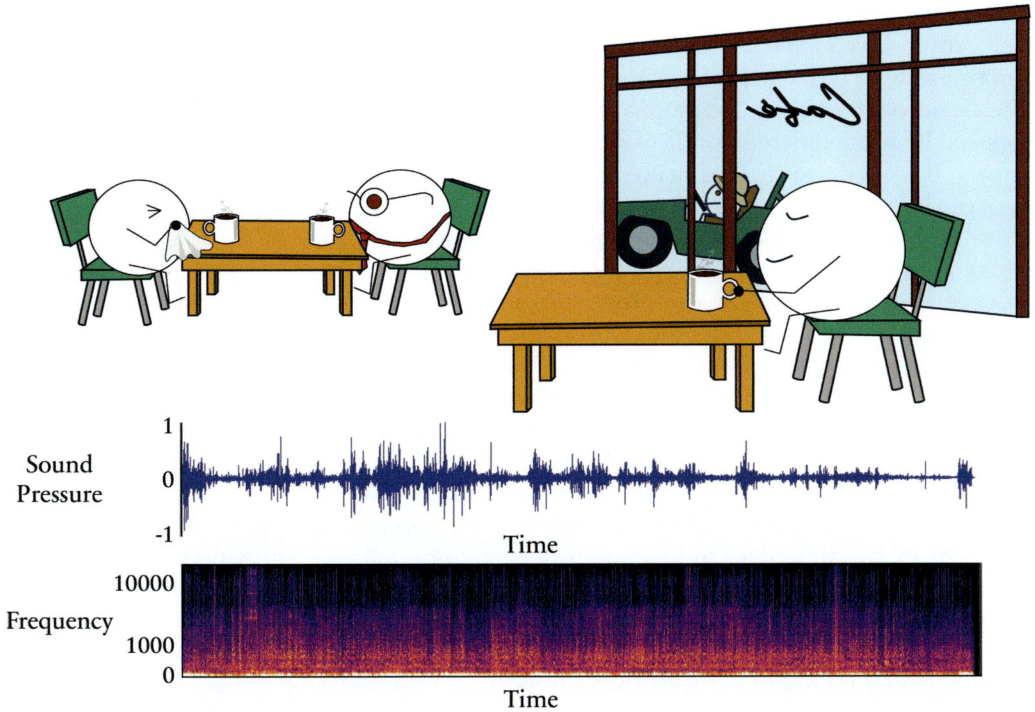

Figure 12.1 Top, Fred sits at a café and listens to the sounds around him. Middle, a waveform showing changes in amplitude of the sounds over time. Bottom, a spectrogram showing changes in frequencies of the sounds over time.

could have taken place at *Café do Duarte*. The first graph is the standard waveform introduced in Chapter 5 (see Figure 12.1, *middle*). It shows changes in amplitude (in dB) of the sound pressure over time. The second graph is a **spectrogram** (see Figure 12.1, *bottom*). It shows changes in frequency (in Hz) of the sound pressure over time. Both look like kind of a mess. The sounds that produced them are equally messy—just like the objects and patterns of edges in the junk drawer in Chapter 10 (see Figures 10.3 and 10.8).

Spectrogram a depiction of the changes in frequency of sound pressure over time.

What makes these graphs (and the sounds that produced them) so messy? Well, for one thing, the sounds *never stop*. There are times when it is louder or quieter, but there is no time when there is complete silence.[2] For another, the sound is *distributed unevenly* and *changes irregularly*. That is, not only does the sound never stop, but the sound *never stops changing*. Sounds come in bursts and so do changes in those sounds. In addition, there is no clear order of sounds or boundaries between sounds. Sounds occur before, after, and *at the same time as* other sounds. In fact, most (if not all) of the sounds occurring at *Café do Duarte* at least partially overlap with one or more other sounds. In other words, just like the objects in the junk drawer in Figure 10.3, the sounds at *Café do Duarte* are cluttered—in a manner of speaking, anyway. And so, the patterns of vibrations on the eardrum are just as cluttered.

But more than merely being cluttered, the sounds occurring at *Café do Duarte*—or anywhere, really—are *complex.* They consist of *many different frequency components* at *many different amplitudes* (see Chapter 5, Figure 5.3). This makes sense, of course. Although it's not quite clear from looking at the graphs, the sounds—the patterns of vibration in the air—were produced by many different kinds of objects interacting in many different kinds of ways. For example, there is the rattling of a cup on a saucer, the clinking of a spoon in a cup, the squeaking of the legs of a chair, the hum of many different people speaking, the swish of at least one person sniffing, the cackle of another person laughing, the drone of passing traffic, the zip and zoom of a Jeep approaching and then speeding off again, the squeal of brakes on a large truck, among others—maybe even the trumpet of a charging elephant! Actually, probably not the elephant—oh, well. In other words, just like the junk drawer depicted in Figure 10.3 has many different types of objects in it, *Café do Duarte* has *many different types of sounds* in it. That is, there is a great deal of *sound complexity* and *sound variety.* And so, there is a similar complexity and variety in the pattern vibrations on Fred's eardrum.

The point is that for lots of different reasons—including sound clutter, sound complexity and variability, and how vibrations are funneled toward the eardrum—the vibration of Fred's eardrum is ambiguous about the properties of sound-producing objects. And so, from the traditional approach, understanding auditory perception means identifying the cues that are available about the properties of sound-producing objects and discovering how those cues are used in reconstructing those properties from the vibrations on the eardrum. In other words, it requires understanding how *unconscious inferences* are made about such cues to generate mental representations of these properties. Fortunately, there are several different types of cues that Fred's central executive could use to make such unconscious inferences. In this chapter, we will focus on cues that can be used to make inferences about where a sound is coming from, which sounds "go together" (possibly because they are coming from the same source), and how to identify and understand sounds of speech. So, let's get started!

> Socratic Question: How do sound clutter, sound complexity and variability, as well as how vibrations are funneled toward the eardrum make it so that the vibration of the eardrum is ambiguous about the properties of sound producing objects?

Location

If vibrations are not projected onto particular locations on the eardrum, then how does Fred have any idea where those sounds are coming from and where these objects that produced those sounds are? How does he know where the clinking spoon or the zooming Jeep is relative to him? This is especially challenging considering that sounds come from *all around him*—in front of him (e.g., the birds outside of his window), to his right or left (e.g., his cell phone in the other room), and above him (e.g., his noisy upstairs neighbor). They even come from *inside* him (e.g., his own voice, his rumbling stomach). However—wherever a sound is coming from—its location relative to him can be described in terms of three parameters—distance, azimuth, and elevation (see Figure 12.2).

Distance should be pretty straightforward. It is the location of a sound source

> **Distance** the location of a sound source along an imaginary straight line that goes directly from perceiver to sound source.

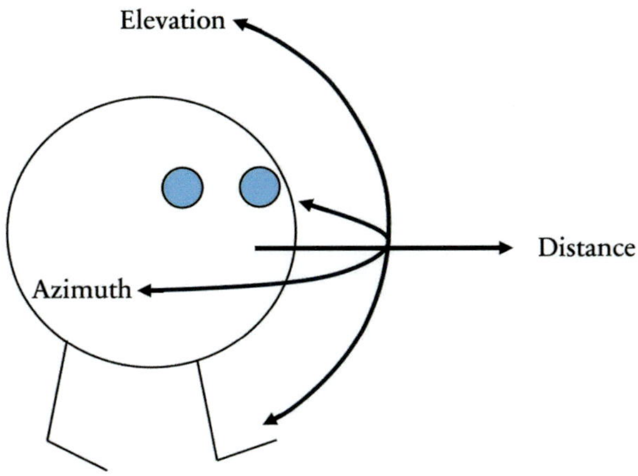

Figure 12.2 Any location in space can be defined relative to Fred in terms of elevation (up-down), azimuth (left-right), and distance.

Azimuth the location of a sound source on an imaginary horizontal circle with the perceiver at the center.

along an imaginary straight line that goes directly from Fred to the sound source. But what's **azimuth**? That's the location of a sound source on an imaginary horizontal circle with Fred at the center. Let's say that Fred points at something that is directly in front of him—maybe the birds outside of his window. Then he keeps his arm pointing in front of him and slowly turns to his right. He keeps turning all the way around until he is pointing at the bird again. His finger will trace a big horizonal circle with him at the center. That's azimuth. A sound can come from any angle along that imaginary circle.

Elevation the location of a sound source on an imaginary vertical circle with the perceiver at the center.

Elevation is similar. It is the location of a sound source on an imaginary *vertical* circle with Fred at the center. Let's say that Fred points at something that is directly above him—maybe his noisy upstairs neighbor. Then he brings his arm straight down in front of him to point at his feet (or his quiet downstairs neighbor) and then straight up behind him to point back up at the noisy upstairs neighbor again. His finger will trace a big vertical circle with him at the center. That's elevation. A sound can come from any angle along on that imaginary circle (see Figure 12.2).

Distance

So how does Fred know how far away a sound source is from him? One possible cue to the distance of a sound source is the intensity or amplitude of the sound wave produced by that object (see Chapter 5). The intensity (or amplitude) of a sound wave decreases with distance from the source because the energy in that sound wave is absorbed both by the medium (including the air) and surrounding surfaces[3] (see Figure 12.3). Given that sound waves with larger intensity (or amplitude) are generally perceived as louder, one cue to the distance of a sound source is the perceived loudness of the sound that it produces. And the rule to be

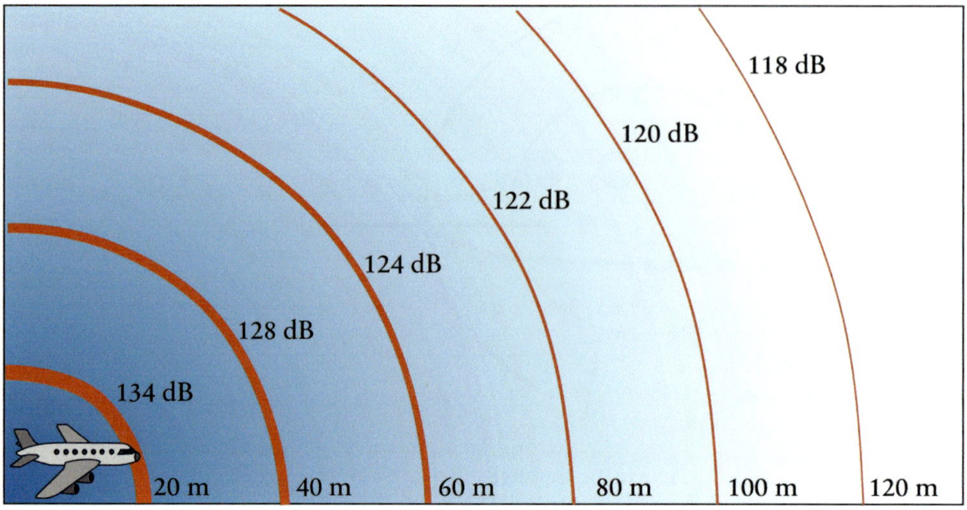

Figure 12.3 The farther away from the plane, the less sound pressure there is, and the quieter the sound gets.

applied by the central executive is that the louder a sound is, the closer the object that produced that sound is. For example, at *Café do Duarte*, the cackle of a person laughing nearby will likely be louder than the hum of the traffic in the distance.

Cue: Loudness	**Rule**: Louder sound --> closer sound source (especially for higher-pitched sounds); Softer sound --> farther sound source

While this might be true *in general*, it certainly isn't true all the time—just like it isn't true all the time that an object that creates a larger retinal image size is closer than an object that creates a smaller retinal image size (see Chapter 9). So, it would really help to be familiar with the sound source in the first place. But it's a start, right?

Except that . . . frequency of a sound wave *also* decreases with distance. That is, the decreases in intensity that occur with distance from the sound source affect high-frequency sounds more so than low-frequency sounds. This is because high-frequency energy patterns are absorbed by the medium and surrounding surfaces more easily. This is why Fred might only hear the bass of his noisy upstairs neighbor's music—*thump*, *thump*, *thump*. Annoying, right? Or why he might only hear adult elephants—and not higher-pitched baby elephants—trumpet in the distance. This creates a kind of "sound gradient" in which higher-frequency sounds are muffled more and more as they are farther and farther away. So, *perceived pitch* is also a cue to perceived distance. Of course, all of this is complicated by the fact that perceived loudness and perceived pitch change together, sometimes in strange ways (see Figures 5.11–5.12). For example, at *Café do Duarte*, the hum of the traffic will likely be lower-pitched than the clinking of the spoon in the cup.

Another possible cue to the distance of a sound source has to do with echoes. Echoes? Yes, echoes (. . .*echoes* . . . *echoes*). Some of the soundwaves that reach Fred's ears travel directly from a sound source. But others travel indirectly from a sound source and reach his ears only after bouncing off nearby surfaces (which creates an echo). For example, most of the sound-waves that come from his upstairs neighbor's music are reaching his ears *only after* bouncing off his ceiling and walls.

So, one cue to the distance of a sound source is *how much* of the soundwave reaching his ear comes directly from the sound source and how much comes indirectly from echoes. And the rule to be applied by the central executive is that the larger the ratio of direct to indirect sound, the closer the sound source is to Fred. For example, the ratio of direct to indirect sound will be larger for the squeak of the leg of the chair than for the squeal of the brakes on the truck. Of course, he'd need to be able to tell the difference between direct and indirect sound, but again, it's a start, right?

Cue: Ratio of direct to indirect sound	**Rule**: Larger ratio -> closer sound source; Smaller ratio -> farther sound source

Azimuth

So, how does Fred know whether a sound source is located to his left or to his right or somewhere in between? Well, just as there are binocular cues in vision, there are binaural (two-ear) cues in hearing (see Box 12.1). Having two eyes is handy for seeing depth because the two eyes have slightly different views on the world. Differences between the images on each eye can be used as cue to depth (see Chapter 9). Having two ears is handy for hearing where a sound source is along the azimuth for the same reason. That is, differences between the sounds reaching each ear—the interaural differences—can be used as a cue to azimuth.

Interaural Level Differences

Let's say that Fred again looks at the bird outside his window and moves into a position so that it is directly in front of him. He waits for it to chirp . . .*Chirp!* The soundwave reaching his left and his right ear will have identical properties—in particular, they will have identical intensity and frequency. Now he turns his head to the left so that the bird is located immediately to his right. He waits for it to chirp again . . . *Chirp!* This time, the soundwave will have *different* properties—in particular, different intensities and frequencies—when it reaches each ear. These are called **interaural level differences** (see Figure 12.4).

Interaural level differences differences in the properties of a sound wave produced by a given source when that sound wave reaches each ear.

In this case, interaural level differences emerge mostly because the soundwave has to travel farther to reach his left ear than his right ear. This extra distance isn't all that large—the width of a human head is only about 15 cm—but it's enough for there to be intensity differences, especially for high-frequency sounds. But interaural level differences *also* emerge because Fred's head gets in the way of the sound! That is, not only does the soundwave have to travel *farther* to reach to reach his left ear than his right ear, but it also has to travel *around* (and in some cases *through*) his head!

As it does, there is an *additional* reduction in intensity, especially for high-frequency sounds (see Box 12.1). Fred's head muffles the sound on one side of his head, kind of like how his ceiling muffles the sound of his upstairs neighbor's music. In other words, his head creates an

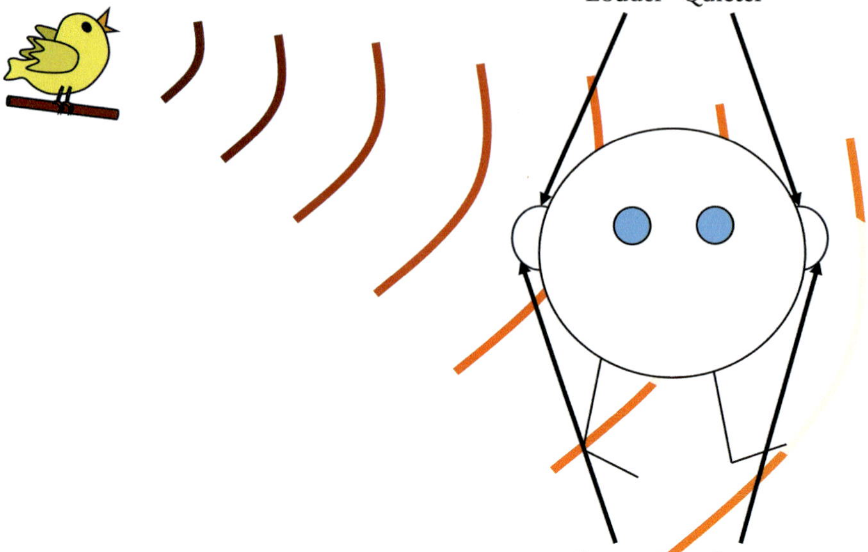

Figure 12.4 The sound of the bird chirping reaches Fred's right ear before his left. There is a time difference between ears. Because his head blocks some of the sound—that is, it creates an acoustic shadow—the sound of the bird chirping is louder in Fred's right ear than in his left. There is an amplitude difference between ears.

acoustic shadow (see Figure 12.4). These subtle interaural level differences are maximized for nearby high-frequency sounds located directly to one side of his head. Now we're getting somewhere! Right? *Right?*

acoustic shadow a region just behind an object where sound waves are blocked or altered by that object.

Cue: Interaural intensity difference	**Rule**: Sound located closer to ear receiving larger intensity soundwave (especially for high-frequency sounds)

Interaural Time Differences

Another consequence of the sound traveling farther to reach his left ear than his right ear is that it will reach his right ear *sooner*. That is, in addition to interaural level differences, there will be **interaural time differences** (see Figure 12.4). The additional time it takes for the sound to reach his left ear is not all that long. After all, the human head is relatively small—about 15 cm, remember?—and sound travels really, really fast.[4] Interaural time differences—like interaural intensity differences—are maximized for sounds

Interaural time differences differences in when a sound wave produced by a given source arrives at each ear.

located directly to one side of the head. But even then, the interaural time difference is only about 0.0007 sec (0.7 ms). For the sake of comparison, an eyeblink takes about 100ms! Still, people are sensitive to interaural time differences as small as 1ms, so there's still hope for Fred to locate that sound (for details, see Chapter 5). Right? *Right*?

Cue: Interaural time difference	**Rule**: Sound located closer to ear receives soundwave sooner; sound located farther from ear receives soundwave later

But wait! There is a problem. The problem occurs when sounds are not located exactly to one side of the head . . . which is pretty much most of the time. Under certain conditions, the pattern of interaural differences is potentially ambiguous about azimuth. Let's say that Fred is still standing so that the bird is directly to his right. He turns to his right just a little bit so that the bird is at a 45° angle—halfway between directly in front of him and directly to his right. He waits for it to chirp again . . . *Chirp!*

There will, of course, be interaural differences for the soundwave reaching his right ear and his left ear. But *the same exact pattern of differences* (down to the dB and the ms) would also occur if the bird was at a 135° angle—halfway between directly *behind* him and directly to his right. These same ambiguities occur for any two azimuth values on the so-called "cone of confusion" (see Figure 12.5).

So now what? After all of this, interaural differences are ambiguous about azimuth? But Fred isn't completely helpless here. There is something that he can do to disambiguate the location of this sound. He can move his head. Wait, what? Yep. Moving his head around moves the sound source off the cone of confusion (or at least to a different location on the cone of confusion). The changes in interaural differences with head movement help to disambiguate the location of a sound source (see Chapter 17).

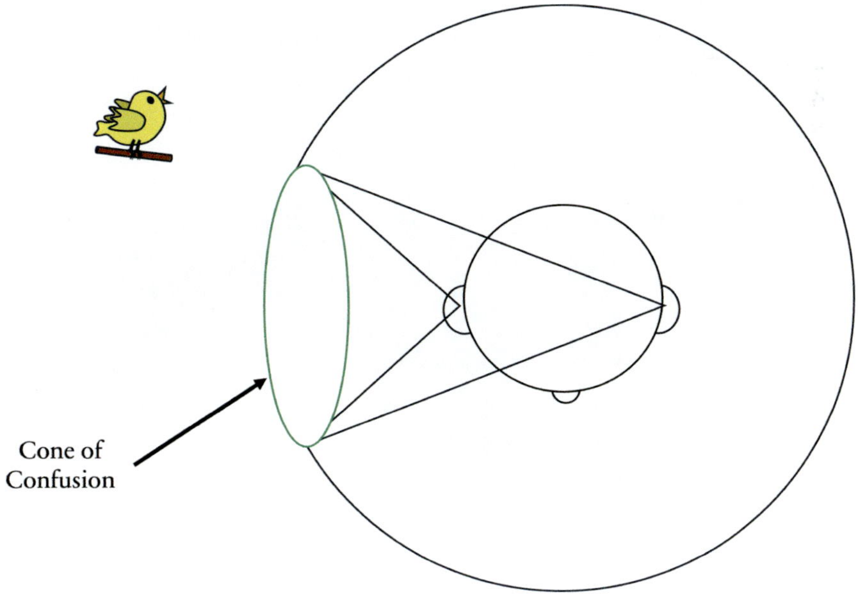

Figure 12.5 A sound source anywhere on the green circle would have the same interaural differences. This is why it is called the cone of confusion.

Box 12.1 You Could Learn a Lot from a Dummy (Head)

When Fred flew over to Australia and New Zealand to visit his friend Mike, he watched a movie to pass the time during the plane ride (maybe several movies—that's a long trip!). Being a considerate traveler, Fred wore headphones even though he knew that it would change the auditory experience. Specifically, it makes the experience really compact. After all, when he wears headphones, the sounds are coming from tiny speakers on (or in) his ears. With a good stereo recording (using two microphones) and good-quality headphones, he might experience a given sound as coming from a particular *direction*—to his left or to his right. But that would be pretty much it. He would not have the convincing *immersive* experience that a given sound was coming from a *particular location in space*—that is, from a particular distance, azimuth, and elevation. Enter binaural recordings.

Binaural recordings are also made by using two microphones, but these microphones are placed inside ear-shaped molds on a "dummy head" (which is sometimes even attached to a "dummy neck and torso"). Recording the sound like this preserves the particular way that the pinnae and the head (and even the neck and torso) change the soundwave as it enters the ear—think acoustic shadow cues for azimuth and spectral shape cues for elevation. Go online, put on headphones, and listen to some recordings that are made using this technique. Some of them are amazing. Like, really amazing. Many of them provide absolutely convincing immersive experiences that the sounds—including thunderstorms, the hustle and bustle of big cities, and even someone giving you a haircut!—are coming from very specific locations in space all around you.

Figure 12.6 A "dummy head" used to create binaural recordings that preserve how the pinna and the head itself affect sound.

Elevation

So, how does Fred know whether a sound source is located way up high (like his noisy upstairs neighbor), way down low, or somewhere in between? This may have something to do with what makes the odd-looking fleshy bits on the side of his head (and your head) so odd-looking and fleshy. The pinnae are not just openings on the side of the head. They are not shaped like smooth and symmetric funnels, either. They have bumps and ridges, most of which can be pierced (see Box 12.2).

Consequently, the pinnae do more than just collect and funnel sound toward the ear canal. They *change the properties of that sound*—in particular, they change the pattern of frequencies at different amplitudes. We invited you to experience the effect that the pinnae have on sound intensity in Chapter 5 by cupping your hand behind your ears. Now, we'd like to invite you to do something a little more . . . active. Grab your ears and—*gently!*—stretch, twist, or fold them. You might notice changes in loudness, but you also might notice changes in pitch. In particular, you might notice that certain pitches get louder and certain pitches get softer. Just like soundwaves bounce off surfaces before reaching your pinnae, they bounce off the bumps and ridges of your pinnae before reaching the ear canal and eardrum. That's right—your ear creates its own echoes!

As the soundwave bounces around the bumps and ridges of the pinnae, certain frequencies of the soundwave get amplified, and others get dampened. In other words, the frequency spectrum (or spectral shape) of the soundwave changes. How exactly the bumps and ridges of the pinnae change the frequency spectrum depends on *where exactly the sound is coming from*—in particular, its elevation. This changes which specific bumps and ridges it bounces off of and which ones of these it bounces off first.

Admittedly, the relationship between intensity, frequency, and elevation is complex. However, in general, there is a range of frequencies (roughly between 4–8 kHz) that are amplified more as the sound source is located at *higher elevation* (i.e., above ear height). And there is another range of frequencies (roughly between 8–16 kHz) that are amplified more as the sound source is located at *lower elevation* (i.e., below ear height) (Hofman et al., 1998; Zonooz et al., 2019). So, the pattern of changes in frequencies at different intensities can provide cues to elevation of a sound source (see Box 12.2). Of course, this cue is most effective for sound sources that produce a soundwave with a wide frequency spectrum—that is, broadband sounds. But still, it's a start, right?

Cue: Spectral shape	**Rule**: Particular range of frequencies amplified --> sound source located below ear height; different range of frequencies amplified --> sound source located above ear height

Auditory Scene Analysis

As we have discussed, in most everyday situations, sounds come from *all around Fred*—in front of him, to his right, to his left, above him, behind him, and even inside him. And cues like loudness and interaural differences can be used by the central executive to figure out where any one of those sounds is coming from at any given moment (see Figure 12.5). The problem, of course, is that—just like objects don't appear one at a time—sounds don't occur one at a time, either. On the contrary, sounds from

Box 12.2 An Ear-Piercing Sound

As we mentioned (and as you are surely aware), many of the bumps and ridges on the pinna are pierceable. But if the pinnae are useful in perceiving the elevation of a sound source because of how they reflect sound into the ear canal and on to the eardrum, might some extreme piercing—or maybe even some not-so-extreme piercings—affect this ability? The answer is yes, but probably not for long.

A study conducted in the late 1990s (Hofman et al., 1998) assessed perception of elevation of a sound source when people wore an "artificial pinna" (really just a molded pinna insert). They found that people who wore the artificial pinna were initially unable to perceive the elevation of sound sources very well. However, this ability improved over the course of several weeks (at which point it more or less returned to normal). Good to know. Now Fred won't let the possibility of modified resonant frequencies of his pinna stop him from getting that ear piercing he has always wanted.

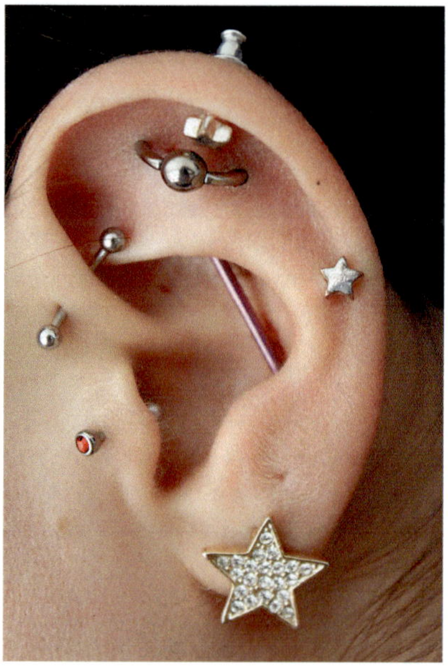

Figure 12.7 Extreme ear piercings may affect your ability to perceive elevation of sound sources, but not for very long.

Socratic Question: What is the cone of confusion? How can you eliminate ambiguities created by the cone of confusion?

multiple sound sources occur *simultaneously*. The soundwaves from those multiple sound sources combine in the air on the way to his ear (see Chapter 5 and Figure 12.1). And—as we discussed at the very beginning of the chapter—when the pinna and ear canal funnel those combined vibrations to the eardrum, the entire surface of the eardrum vibrates. So, just like sounds in *different locations* do not cause vibrations in different places on the eardrum, sounds from *different sound sources* do not do so, either. This was one of the biggest challenges facing Fred when he was listening to the sounds at *Café do Duarte* at the beginning of the chapter.

So, how does the central executive figure out which sounds come from which sources? How does the central executive figure out which sounds should be grouped together, and which should not? How does Fred hear the sounds from all around him as coming from distinct sources (an elephant *and* a bird) rather than as a collection of unrelated random noises (a hybrid birdelephant, see Figure 12.8)? In Chapter 10, we discussed the problem of how we *see* surrounding objects and surfaces as *organized wholes* rather than merely as collections of unrelated component pieces. This is exactly the same kind of problem, except that it is a problem for the auditory system. Fortunately, this means that it may have exactly the same kind of solution.

As we discussed in Chapter 10, the Gestalt psychologists developed a set of grouping principles that the visual system could use to organize regions of an image into distinct objects. These included proximity, similarity, symmetry, parallelism, continuity, and closure. Inspired by this approach, Canadian perceptual scientist Albert Bregman

Figure 12.8 If both Fred's baby elephant, Topsy, and the bird in his yard are making noise at the same time, how does he hear them as two distinct sounds instead of one combined sound?

developed a similar set of grouping principles that the auditory system could use to organize sounds into distinct auditory streams—what he called **auditory stream segregation** (Bregman, 1990, 2005). Next, we will discuss these auditory organizational principles—in particular, proximity, similarity, and continuity and closure.

Auditory stream segregation the perceptual process of organizing a mix of sounds into distinct auditory streams.

Proximity

In the context of visual perception, the principle of **proximity** states that the visual system tends to group regions together if those regions are close together (see Chapter 10). Given that this principle was being applied by the visual system, "close together" meant close together in *space* (see Figure 10.13). We can say the same thing about the auditory system, except that the "regions" are *sounds* and "close together" means close together in *time.*

Fred is at home practicing his guitar when he hears four knocks on his front door each separated by a very short delay—maybe it's his noisy upstairs neighbor . . . or his quiet downstairs neighbor (see Figure 12.9). Either way, there are four knocks in rapid succession over the course of a second or less: *knock-knock-knock-knock* (see Figure 12.10, *top left*). Not very

Figure 12.9 Fred hears four knocks on his front door. Will he hear it as four separate knocks, two sets of two, or some other pattern?

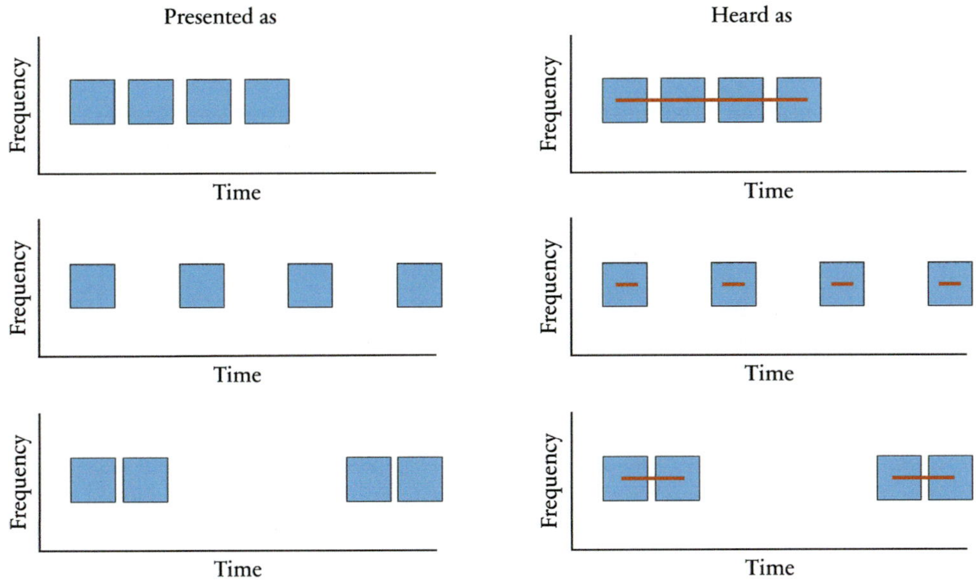

Figure 12.10 Auditory proximity (in this case, closeness to together in time). Fred will likely hear the four sounds at the top as a single group of four sounds, the four sounds in the middle as four individual sounds, and the four sounds at the bottom as two groups of two sounds each.

exciting—we know. But humor us and think about what it would *sound like* to Fred. Believe it or not, just like the pattern of shapes in Figure 10.13, this pattern of *sounds* is completely ambiguous. He could hear it as *sequence* of four sounds (probably), two sequences of two sounds each (probably not), or four isolated individual sounds (maybe). He could also hear it as a sequence of three sounds plus one unrelated isolated sound (*definitely* not). But we're still not done. If it *is* more than one sequence of sounds, then which ones belong in which sequences?

Despite this ambiguity and all of these possibilities, Fred would (almost certainly) hear the knocks in this example as a *sequence* of four sounds (that is, *knock-knock-knock-knock*; see Figure 12.10, *top right*). Full stop. Why would he hear these four sounds as "belonging together" in this particular way? In part, it is because of their *proximity* to one another (see Chapter 10, in particular Figure 10.13). Their closeness together in time allows the auditory system to group them together as a unit—a *sequence* rather than as four isolated sounds.

Let's say that whoever was at the door increased the delay between each knock so they were spread out over several seconds: *knock-—-knock-—-knock-—-knock* (see Figure 12.10, *left middle*). All the same ambiguities exist, but Fred might be less likely to hear the sounds as a sequence of four sounds and more likely to hear them as four isolated individual sounds (see Figure 12.10, *right middle*). And if whoever was knocking *decreased* the delay between the first and second knocks and between the third and fourth knocks and *increased* the delay between the second and third knocks: *knock—knock————knock—knock* (like in Figure 12.10, *bottom left*), he would be more likely to hear them as *two separate sequences* of two sounds each (see Figure 12.10, *bottom right*). Makes sense, right? Sounds that occur closer together in time are more likely to be related (in a sequence) than sounds that occur farther apart in time.

In the example that we just described, each sound in the sequence was identical. Each knock created a sound with the same set of frequencies and the same amplitude profile. No wonder it wasn't very exciting! Does the principle of proximity apply with sounds that were *less* boring, like ones that were *different* frequencies? Yes, it does. Might this lead to the auditory system grouping sounds of different frequencies together? Yes, it might.

Instead of knocking, maybe Fred hears tones or beeps—like the sound that a truck makes when it is backing up. Except the sound that this particular truck makes is a high-frequency tone ("*beep*"), followed by a short delay, then a lower-frequency tone ("*boop*"), followed by the same short delay. This cycle repeats until there are eight alternating tones over the course of a few seconds: *beep- -boop- -beep- -boop- -beep- -boop- -beep- -boop* (see Figure 12.11). At least a little more exciting, right? Exciting or not, this pattern of sounds is *also* ambiguous.

However, with just the right delay between tones—not too long but not too short—Fred would most likely hear it as *a single stream of tones* that *changes pitch* between high and low (see Figure 12.11, *top*). Given what we discussed in the previous example, it should be pretty clear why it matters if the delay between tones is too long. With too long of a delay, the auditory system would no longer group the individual tones together as a unit. In that case, Fred might be more likely to hear them as *four isolated tones* that happen to *alternate* pitch rather than a sequence of tones that *changes* pitch.

But why does it matter if the delay between tones is *too short*? Because with too short of a delay, tones of the *same pitch* would occur closer together in time than tones of *alternating pitch*. Therefore, the auditory system would group the high-pitched tones together as one unit and the low-pitched tones together as another unit. In that case, Fred might be more

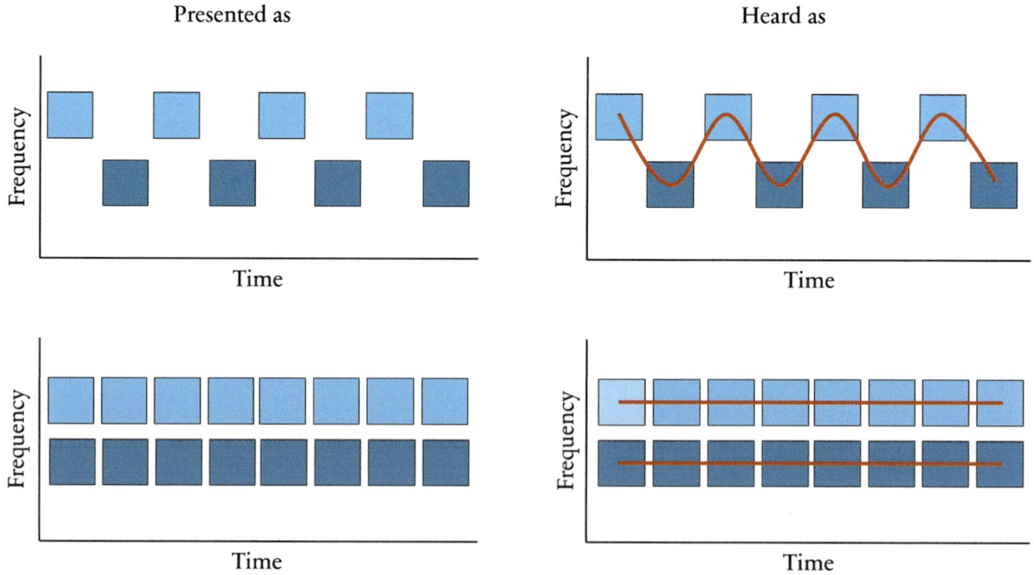

Figure 12.11 Auditory proximity (again, closeness to together in time). Fred will likely hear the tones at the top as a single stream of tones that changes pitch and the tones at the bottom as two continuous streams of tones.

likely to hear *two continuous streams of tones*—one high-pitched and one low-pitched (See Figure 12.11, *bottom*).

Similarity

In the context of visual perception, the principle of **similarity** states that the visual system tends to group regions together if those regions are similar in size, shape, color, orientation, or movement (see Chapter 10, in particular Figure 10.14). We can say the same thing about the auditory system, except that that "similar" would refer to properties of sounds like amplitude or frequency.

Let's go back to the previous example—a high-frequency tone, followed by a short delay, followed by a lower-frequency tone, followed by the same short delay and so on—producing eight tones that alternate in frequency over the course of a few seconds (*beep- -boop- -beep- -boop- -beep- -boop- -beep- -boop*, see Figure 12.12, *top left*). As we have already discussed, one of the factors that will influence how Fred hears these alternating tones is their proximity to one another in time. But another factor is their similarity to one another in frequency.

If there is a small enough difference in frequency between the alternating tones (as in the examples so far), then the auditory system might group those tones together as a unit. In that case, Fred would hear them as *a single stream of tones* that *changes pitch* between high and low (see Figure 12.12, *top right*). But if there is too much of a difference in frequency between the alternating tones, then the auditory system might not group the alternating tones as a unit. In that case, Fred might hear them as *two continuous streams of tones*—one high-pitched and one (much) lower-pitched (see Figure 12.12, *bottom*).

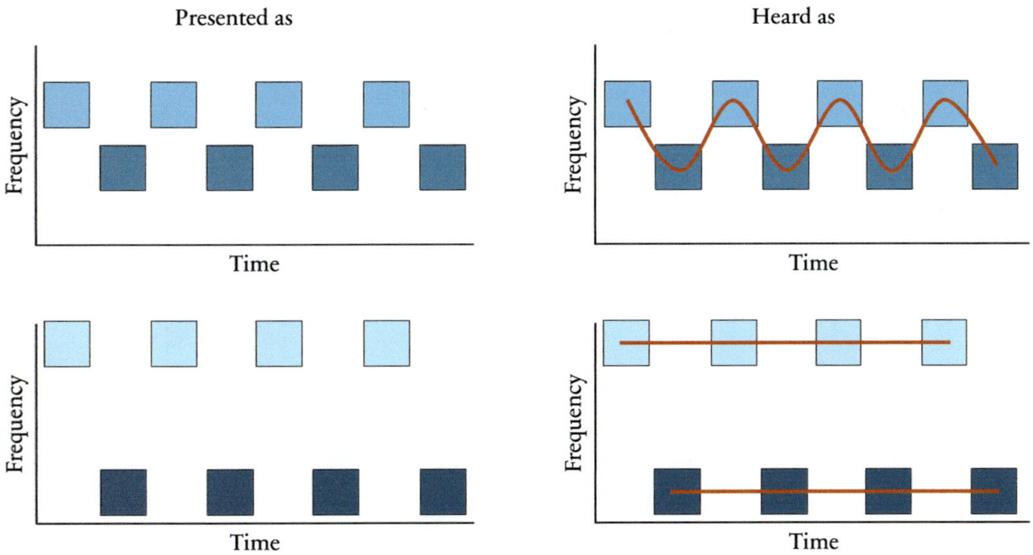

Figure 12.12 Auditory proximity (in this case, closeness to together in frequency). Fred will likely hear the tones at the top as a single stream of tones that changes pitch and the tones at the bottom as two continuous streams of tones.

Continuity and Closure

In the context of visual perception, the principle of **continuity** states that the visual system tends to group (unseen) regions together when doing so would form a smooth or continuous shape than when it would not (see Chapter 10, in particular Figure 10.16a and b). Likewise, the principle of **closure** states that the visual system tends to group regions together when doing so would form a complete shape than when it would not (see Chapter 10, in particular Figures 10.16c and d). We can say the same thing about the auditory system, except that "smooth or continuous" and "complete" would all refer to sequences of (unheard) sounds.

Now the knocking has stopped and Fred hears a tone that continuously increases in frequency from low-to-high *("boooooeeeeep")*, then a short delay, and then a tone that continuously decreases in frequency from high-to-low *("beeeeeoooop")*, and then another delay (see Figure 12.13, *top left*). Maybe his noisy neighbor went back upstairs and started playing (very) minimalist electronic music. Regardless, even with a relatively short delay between the tones, Fred would (almost certainly) hear it as *multiple separate streams*—a tone that is increasing in pitch followed by another tone that decreases in pitch (see Figure 12.13, *top right*).

But what if instead of silence during each delay, there was a burst of white noise (static)? More exciting, maybe? In this case, instead of hearing a tone that is increasing in frequency and then silence and then a tone that is decreasing in frequency, Fred heard a tone that is increasing in frequency and then static and then a tone that is decreasing in frequency (*"beeeeeooooo-shhhh-oooooeeeeep-shhhh-eeeeeooooop"*; see Figure 12.13, *bottom left*). Would he still hear it as multiple separate streams of tones? Probably not. Instead, he would (almost certainly) hear it as *a continuous tone* that is *interrupted by* white noise just as it is reaching

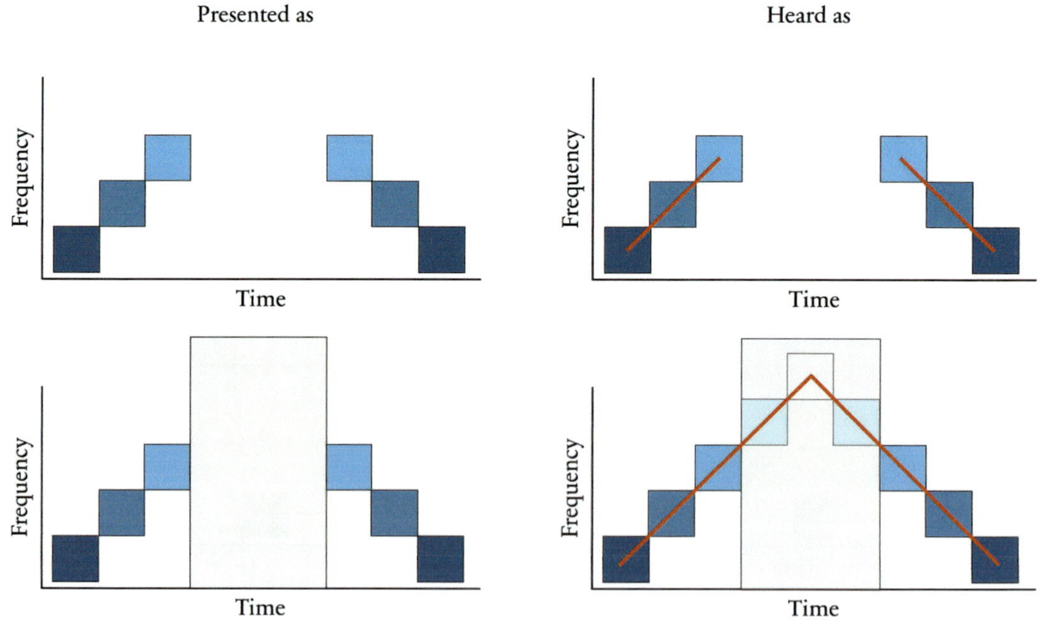

Figure 12.13 Auditory continuity and closure. Fred will likely hear the tones at the top as two separate streams and the tones at the bottom as a continuous tone interrupted by noise.

its maximum pitch (see Figure 12.13, *bottom right*). The important point here is that the delay—the time between hearing tones—is the same in each case. But filling that delay with another sound—in this case, white noise instead of silence—makes it easier for the auditory system to group the rising tone and falling tones into a smooth and continuous sound.

> Socratic Question: How can the Gestalt grouping principles such as proximity, similarity, and continuity and closure be applied to hearing sounds?

Speech Perception

As we have been discussing, sounds come from all around Fred. Some sounds, of course, come from other people. And some of those sounds come from the vocal tracts of those people in the form of the sounds of speech—like the hum of different people speaking at *Café do Duarte*. And the same ambiguities in the vibration on the eardrum that make it a challenge to perceive sounds in general also make it a challenge to perceive the sounds of speech.

In some ways, the sounds of speech are no different than any other sounds. After all, all sounds are patterns of vibration in air produced by different kinds of materials interacting in different kinds of ways. However, in other ways, the sounds of speech are quite special. One thing that makes them special is that they are produced by a speaker for the specific purpose of communicating with a listener.

Another thing that makes them special is that they are produced using a sequence of coordinated movements of the speaker's vocal tract—which includes, among other components: the trachea (or "windpipe"), the larynx (or "voice box"), the pharynx (the "back of the throat") as well as the mouth, lips, teeth, tongue, and nose.

> **Phonemes** the speech sounds of a given language.

Producing speech is like conducting a symphony performed by vocal tract! And so, to understand how the sounds of speech are perceived, we first need to understand a bit about this symphony is performed—that is, how the sounds of speech—called **phonemes**—are produced.

The Sounds of Speech

Fred can make lots of sounds with his vocal tract. But not all of them are the sounds of speech. Some of them are just the sounds of the body doing what it does—coughing, hiccupping, or chewing, for example. However, the sounds produced by the vocal tract that *are* sounds of speech are called phonemes. Phonemes are like the musical notes played by the symphony. Importantly, phonemes differ by language. That is, phonemes of one language are not necessarily phonemes of another language. This is one reason why learning a new language can be challenging.[5] English, for example, has about 40 phonemes (depending on how you count). But other languages have more than 70 (e.g., Lithuanian) and some have fewer than 30 (e.g., Greek).[6] In many cases, words that have accent marks—like the word "café" in *Café do Duarte*—are marking non-English phonemes. The important thing to note is that phonemes are *sounds*, not letters.[7] And *sounds*—or at least the vibrations in air that generate those sounds—are the stimulation pattern of relevance to the auditory system.

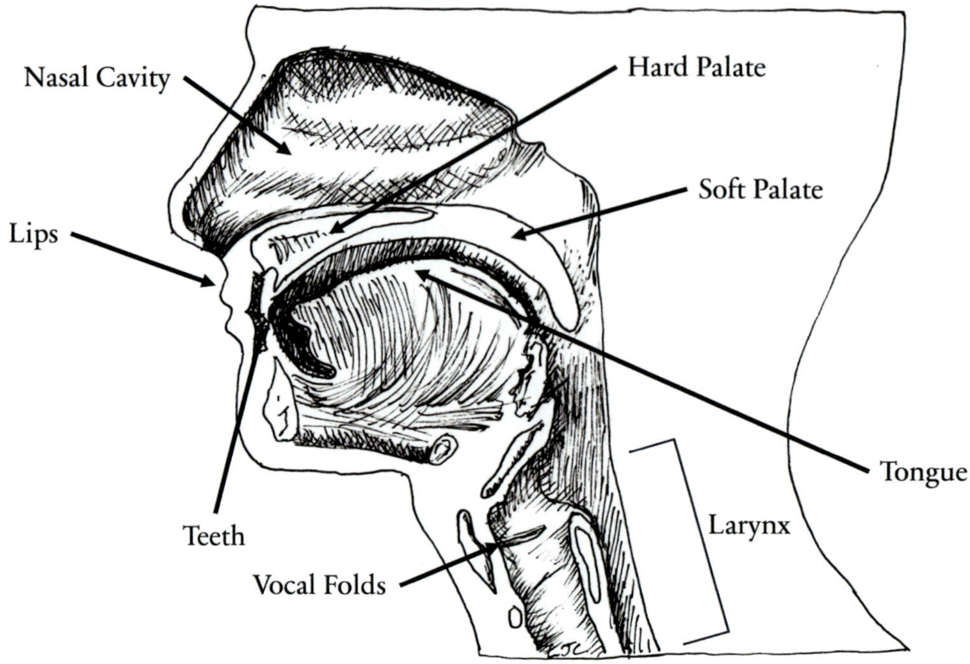

Figure 12.14 Vocalizations are produced by coordinated movements of the vocal tract, including the lips, teeth, mouth, tongue, and throat. The structure in the acoustic array is lawfully related to how those sounds were produced in the vocal tract.

As we mentioned earlier, producing speech—even a single phoneme—is complicated. All symphonies are. We'll only cover the (very) basics here. So, take a deep breath. No, really. Producing most speech sounds starts with breathing. That is, speaking requires inhaling and then exhaling *in a very particular way*. Air that is exhaled from the lungs passes through the many of the structures of the vocal tract on its way out of the mouth and nose. By controlling these structures in *just the right way*, Fred can create a particular pattern of vibrations in the air and generate a phoneme or—even better—a *sequence* of phonemes (see Figure 12.14).

Producing Vowels and Consonants

Air that is exhaled from the lungs travels through the trachea and into the larynx. The larynx contains the vocal folds, which are two membranes on either side of the larynx that create an opening for air to pass through.[8] When the vocal folds are completely relaxed and open, they don't vibrate at all when air passes between them—like when Fred exhales without speaking. However, when the vocal folds are tensed, they *do* vibrate—at least a little—when air passes between them. The size and thickness of the vocal folds will influence the fundamental frequency of these vibrations (see Chapter 5) and consequently go a long way toward determining the sound (or at least the pitch) of his voice. When Fred puts his hand gently around his throat and hums, the vibrations he feels are occurring at—more or less—the fundamental frequency of his vocal folds. Try it yourself.

Figure 12.15 Try saying "Ahhhhh", then say "Eeeeee"; you will notice that your mouth changes shape to make the different sounds.

This brings us to the first way that Fred can control the structures of the vocal tract to create a particular speech sound. He can control the *amount of tension* in the vocal folds. The more tension in the vocal folds, the more that they are pulled together, and the higher the frequency of the vibration created when air passes between them. If Fred were to put his hand gently around his throat and hum progressively higher notes—maybe Do-Re-Mi-Fa-So-La-Ti-Do—he'd feel this happening too. Try it yourself.

After air passes through the vocal folds, it moves into the throat and mouth. And this brings us to the second way that Fred can control the structures of the vocal tract to create a particular speech sound. He can change the *size and shape of his throat and mouth*. Doing this in just the right way will modify the vibrations enough to make a particular kind of speech sound—a **vowel** sound.

Vowel sound a particular kind of speech sound produced with a relatively unrestricted flow of air through the vocal tract.

Maybe instead of merely humming, Fred says "ahhh". In this case, not only are his vocal folds vibrating but his throat and mouth are open in a very particular way—both are wide open. Now he tries a different vowel and says "eeee". Now his throat and mouth are open in a very different way—wide but flat with his teeth exposed. No wonder doctors ask you to say "ahh" when they are trying to examine the structures of your throat, and photographers ask you to say "cheese" when they are trying to get you to smile! As this example shows, vowel sounds differ in the subtle ways that the shape of the throat and mouth change the vibrations in the air—in particular, the harmonic frequencies of those vibrations (see Chapter 5)—created by the vocal folds.

There are still other ways that Fred can control the structures of his vocal tract to create a particular speech sound. He can use his tongue, teeth, lips, and nose—really the nasal cavity—to restrict how the air flows through his vocal tract. The movements of these additional components of the vocal tract are called "articulations". Making these articulations in just the right way will modify the vibrations enough to create a different kind of speech sound—a **consonant** sound.

Consonant sound a particular kind of speech sound produced by restricting the flow of air through the vocal tract.

Now Fred tries saying "ahhh" again but adds a /b/ sound at the beginning (/ba/). One that of the things that happens is that his *lips briefly come together* just before the air passes completely out of his mouth. Now he swaps out the /b/ sound and swaps in a /d/ sound (/da/). When he does this, lips *don't come together at all.* Instead, the *tip of his tongue* briefly *touches the roof of his mouth* and does so *near his front teeth.* Now he swaps out the /d/ sound and swaps in a /n/ sound (/na/). When he does this, his tongue still briefly touches the roof of his mouth in the same spot. But this time, he is forcing some of the air to travel out of his nose. Don't believe us? Pinch your nose closed and try to say /da/. Easy peasy, right? Keep pinching and try to say /na/. Doesn't work as well, does it? Now, he swaps out the /n/ sound and swaps in a /p/ sound (/pa/). Just like when he made the /b/ sound, his lips briefly come together just before the air passes completely through his mouth. But this time, *his vocal folds don't vibrate at all* until he get past the /p/ and on to the to "ahhh" sound.

As you can see (and hear and feel), consonant sounds differ in sometimes very subtle ways based on things like *where* in the vocal tract the restriction of air flow occurs—called **place of articulation**—*how* the restriction of air occurs—called **manner of articulation**—and *whether or not* the vocal folds are vibrating—called **voicing**. Things can get pretty complicated pretty quickly given that—in English, anyway—there are seven different places of articulation, five or six manners of articulation (depending on how you count), and two different voicings. Nonetheless, in the previous examples, the sounds /b/ and /d/ differ in terms of place of articulation (lips vs. just behind the top teeth); the sounds /d/ and /n/ differ in manner of articulation (whether or not air is forced through the nose), and the sounds /b/ and /p/ differ in voicing (whether or not the vocal folds vibrate).

Place of articulation where the restriction of air flow occurs when producing a consonant sound.

Manner of articulation how the restriction of air flow occurs when producing a consonant sound.

Voicing whether the vocal folds are vibrating when producing a consonant sound.

Socratic Question: How do vowel sounds differ from consonant sounds? How might this explain why babies usually learn to produce vowel sounds before they learn to produce consonant sounds?

Perceiving the Sounds of Speech

So, perceiving speech should just be a matter of matching the sound produced by the vocal tract (the notes of the symphony) to a particular phoneme. Do that for a few successive phonemes and you've got a word! Do that for a few words and you've got a whole sentence! Case closed (mic drop). Except . . . it's not that easy. It turns out that there is not a straightforward relationship between the acoustic signal produced by the vocal tract and a particular phoneme. *Wait, what? Yep.* Let us explain (while you pick up the mic).

As we discussed very early in the chapter, everyday sounds are messy—they are cluttered, complex, and variable. Everyday speech sounds are no different. For one thing, everyday speech sounds—like other everyday sounds—come in messy bursts with no clear boundaries between sounds—just like the speech sounds at *Café do Duarte (see* Figure 12.1). Speaking

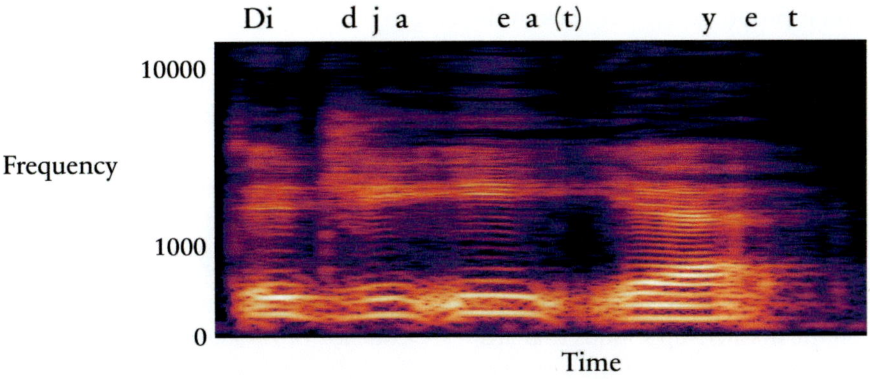

Figure 12.16 A spectrogram of one of your authors saying the phrase "Did you eat yet?" The approximate location of each sound is marked on top. Since the speaker is from Connecticut, the "t" in "eat" is more implied than voiced. Note that the breaks between sound do not necessarily line up with the breaks between phonemes.

rate varies by person and by situation, but the average speaking rate is about 150 words per minute—that's 2.5 words per second![9] This means that there just isn't time to produce each and every phoneme perfectly before moving on to the next one. Messy bursts, indeed!

This means that, like other everyday sounds, phonemes flow from one to the next in a continuous stream without clear breaks or boundaries. In reading this book, you can easily see where the breaks or boundaries are between the letters, words, sentences, and paragraphs. But if you are *listening* to this book, you would not be able to hear where the breaks are so easily. Remember, phonemes are *sounds*, not letters. It is up to the central executive of the listener to figure out where those breaks or boundaries should go. This is called the **segmentation problem** (see Figure 12.16). The segmentation problem is one reason why speech in a given language sounds so fast to a non-native speaker. One of the things that happen when you learn a language is that you learn to hear where the breaks between phonemes occur.

Segmentation problem the challenge that a listener faces in determining where the breaks between phonemes and words occur in the continuous stream of sounds produced by the vocal tract.

But the speed of everyday speech creates a different challenge for the listener, too. Since there isn't time for a speaker to produce each and every phoneme perfectly before moving on to the next one, they are forced to take short cuts. Think about how Fred might say something like "Did you eat yet?" This is a fairly complicated symphonic piece for his vocal tract. In particular, the first and last /d/ in the word "did" are each produced way in the front of his mouth with his tongue right behind his upper teeth and his mouth open flat and wide. The /i/ sound in the middle is produced more in the middle of his mouth with his mouth open a little more. And then the /y/ in "you" is produced a little farther back in his mouth with his lips more rounded. And then the /e/ in "eat" is produced with his mouth open flat and wide again. Whew! Coordinating all of this is complicated, especially considering he would likely produce all 11 phonemes of the question ("Did you eat yet?") in just a few seconds.

It would be so much easier if the multiple transitions between the first /d/ sound in "did" and the /e/ sound in "eat" were less challenging. One way to make them so is to take a shortcut by mashing all of these various sounds together into something like a /j/ sound.

A /j/ sound is produced farther back in the mouth with the mouth open flat and wide. This makes the transition to the /e/ sound—which uses the same mouth shape—much easier.

And in general, this is exactly what speakers do. When producing the phonemes of the question "Did you eat?," the vocal tract is already preparing to make the /e/ sound in "eat" while it is forming the /d/ sounds in "did". So, when Fred asks this question, the sound that comes out is more like "Jeetjet?". In other words, rather than being produced (or articulated) in a clean sequence one phoneme at a time, phonemes are *coarticulated*. It is up to the central executive of the listener to figure out what the phonemes were supposed to be based on the mashed-up sounds that are produced by the vocal tract of the speaker. This is called the **coarticulation problem.**

Coarticulation problem the challenge that a listener faces in determining what sequence of phonemes a speaker intended to produce given that speech sounds are not typically produced one phoneme at a time.

There is one final challenge facing the listener. There is a great deal of variety in everyday sounds and how we encounter them. The same is true for everyday speech sounds.

Every person you know (and every person you *don't know*) has a different voice. That means that everyone you hear speak makes different sounds with their vocal tract, even when they are producing the exact same phoneme or sequence of phonemes.

Go ahead—ask the next 10 people you see today to say the word "water". It will sound different every single time. And it's not just *voices* that differ among people. It is also other peculiarities of speech, like regional accents. One of your authors grew up outside of Philadelphia. In that part of the US, people say "water" more like "wooder". Your other author grew up in Connecticut. In *that* part of the US, people say "wahder". Fred's friend Mike grew up in New Zealand. In that part of the world, people might say (something like) "warder".

Complicating matters even further, the same person's voice will sound different in different circumstances—a person might shout now but whisper later. They might explode with happiness now but shrivel with sadness later. It is up to the central executive of the listener to figure out what phonemes are being produced despite this variability across speakers and across circumstances. This is called the **variability problem.**

Variability problem the challenge that a listener faces in determining what phonemes a given speaker is producing given that speech sounds differ across people and circumstance.

The point is that for lots of different reasons—including the segmentation problem, the coarticulation problem, and the variability problem, sounds produced by the vocal tract *are ambiguous about phonemes*. And so, from the traditional approach, the fundamental challenge of perceiving speech is to *disambiguate* this relationship. For people who study this process, this means identifying the cues that are available in the speech signal and how those cues are used in representing phonemes. In other words, it requires understanding how *unconscious inferences* are made about such cues to generate mental representations of phonemes. We discuss two general classes of theories of speech perception—general-mechanism and special-mechanism theories—next.

Socratic Question: How do the segmentation, coarticulation, and variability problems make it so the sounds produced by the vocal tract are ambiguous about phonemes? How have you encountered these problems in listening to others speak?

Theories of Speech Perception

We began the section on speech perception by noting that in some ways, speech sounds are no different than any other kinds of sounds, but in other ways they are quite special. The tension generated by this statement is reflected in two general classes of theories about how we perceive speech. In **general-mechanism theories**, perceiving speech occurs by the *very same processes* that are used to perceive other sounds. In **special-mechanism theories**, perceiving speech occurs by a distinct set of processes that are only used to perceive speech and are not used to perceive other sounds. For historical reasons, we'll discuss special-mechanism theories first.

General mechanism theories of speech perception theories of speech perception in which perceiving speech occurs by the same processes that are used to perceive other sounds.

Special mechanism theories of speech perception theories of speech perception in which perceiving speech occurs by a distinct set of processes that are not used to perceive other sounds.

Special Mechanism Theories

In the mid-20th century, researchers were working on developing a primitive speech synthesizer—a machine that could produce speech sounds. This doesn't seem like a big deal now with the proliferation of AI and digital assistants like Alexa and Siri, but in the 1950s this was a *really* big deal. When testing this device on listeners, they discovered that very subtle and continuous changes in the properties of an acoustic signal could result in abrupt shifts between two completely different perceived phonemes. For example, subtle and continuous changes in the harmonic frequencies resulted in abrupt shifts between perceiving /ba/ and /da/ (Liberman et al., 1957). Similarly, subtle and continuous changes in the onset of the vibration of the vocal folds (called **voice onset time**) resulted in dramatic shifts between perceiving /ta/ and /da/ (Eimas & Corbit, 1973; see Figure 12.17).

Voice onset time the onset of the vibration of the vocal folds when producing a phoneme.

This is a phenomenon known as **categorical perception**. This is a specific example of the more general phenomenon that people tend to perceive speech clearly, quickly, and easily despite the lack of a straightforward relationship between the acoustic signal and a particular phoneme. Some of these researchers concluded that the only way to explain this ability was to assume that there is a *special process* used to perceive speech that is not used for any other purpose (see Liberman, 1996).

Categorical perception When applied to speech perception, the phenomenon that subtle and continuous changes in the properties of an acoustic signal can result in abrupt shifts between two completely different perceived phonemes.

One of the best well-known and most influential special-mechanism theories of speech perception is the **motor theory of speech perception** (see Galantucci et al.,

Motor theory of speech perception the theory that perceiving speech is based on perceiving the movements of the speaker's vocal tract.

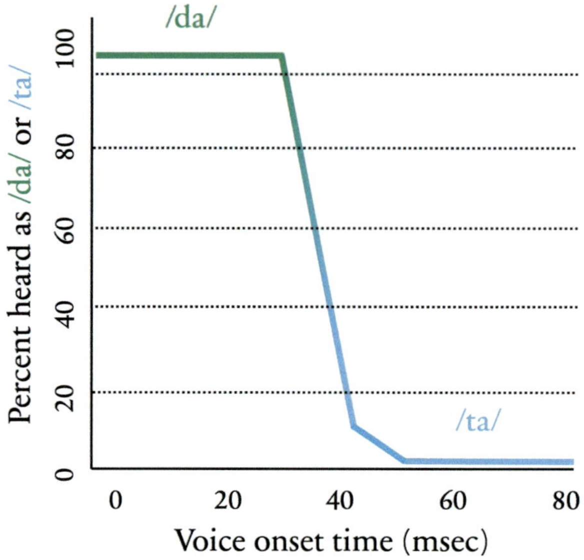

Figure 12.17 Categorical perception of the phonemes /da/ and /ta/. Subtle and continuous changes in voice onset time results in dramatic shifts between perceiving /ta/ and /da/.

2006; Liberman & Mattingly, 1985). In this theory, the lack of a straightforward relationship between the acoustic signal and the phoneme produced by the speaker is not a problem because perceiving speech does not depend on perceiving the acoustic signal. *Wait . . . what?* Perceiving speech does not depend on perceiving the acoustic signal? Yep. Let us explain.

Instead, perceiving speech depends on perceiving the *movements that the speaker is performing with the components of their vocal tract*—the vocal articulations. These researchers argued that if a listener could perceive what movements the speaker was making with their vocal tract, they could determine what phonemes they were saying *despite the ambiguity in the acoustic signal.* This means that *seeing* someone talk should influence what you hear them say, and it does (see Box 12.3).

Box 12.3 When it Comes to Perceiving Speech, Is *Seeing* Believing?

In most everyday circumstances, we see the people who are speaking to us. And in these situations, the sounds that the speaker is making perfectly match the movements of their vocal tract. In other words, when Fred's friend Riley says words "baby elephant", the /b/ sound occurs at the same time that he sees Riley's lips move together and then apart again. It would be really weird if it didn't, right? It would be like a badly dubbed movie in which the audio and the video don't quite match. And nobody likes that. But weirdness often makes for good experiments, and this particular weirdness is no exception. Researchers (McGurk & MacDonald, 1976) wanted to know what phoneme a listener would *hear* if the sound of that phoneme did not match the movements that they saw the speaker make with their vocal tract.

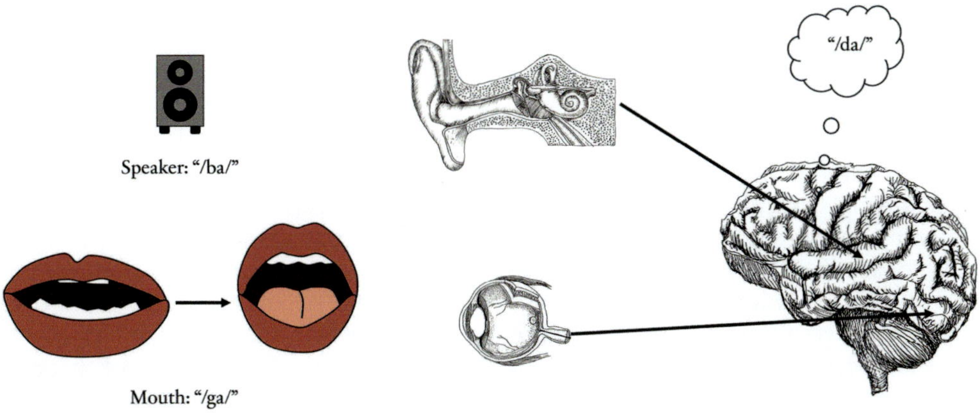

Figure 12.18 The McGurk Effect. Viewing the face from one sound and the audio from a second sound results in the perception of a third sound.

The researchers recorded video and audio clips of a person saying different syllables (e.g., /ba/ or /da/ or /ga/). Then they mixed and matched the video and the audio clips so that sometimes the video and audio were consistent (e.g., both the audio and the video were of the person saying /ba/) and sometimes they were inconsistent (e.g., the video was of the person saying /ga/ but the audio was of the person saying /ba/, or vice versa; see Figure 12.18).

On a given trial, the participant watched (and listened) to a given clip and reported the syllable that they *heard* the speaker say. As you might expect, when the video and the audio were consistent, the participant heard the syllable that was in both clips. For example, if the video and audio were of the person saying /ga/, the participant reported hearing /ga/. Not surprising, right? But when the video and the audio were *inconsistent*, that's when things got weird. In some cases, the participant reported hearing the phoneme that was in the *video clip*. Weird, right?

But other times, they reported hearing a phoneme that wasn't in *either* the video or the audio. *Even weirder.* Importantly, in these cases, the syllable that they reported hearing wasn't random. Instead, it was a syllable that was *in between* the one that was in the video and the one that was in the audio in terms of how those syllables are produced. For example, if the syllable in the video was /ga/ (which is produced in the *back* of the mouth) and the syllable in the audio was /ba/ (which is produced in the *front* of the mouth), participants would report hearing /da/ (which is produced in the *middle* of the mouth). This phenomenon—called the **McGurk effect**—suggests that people perceive speech, in part, by perceiving the movements of the speaker's vocal tract. These movements, of course, can be seen as well as heard.

McGurk Effect the phenomenon in which inconsistencies between the audio and video of a speaker producing a syllable affect what syllable the listener hears.

General Mechanism Theories

Other researchers claim that it is a mistake to assume that there is a special mechanism to explain speech perception. Instead, they argue that that perception of speech occurs by the same general-mechanism processes as auditory perception of any other properties of surrounding objects and surfaces. These processes include identifying and categorizing speech sounds, but without any specialized mechanisms dedicated to doing so. They point to evidence that people exhibit categorical perception of other kinds of sounds (like musical intervals), not just speech sounds. Likewise, they point to evidence that animals such as birds (e.g., Japanese quail) and rodents (e.g., chinchillas) *also* exhibit categorical perception of human speech sounds (Kluender et al., 2005; see Holt & Lotto, 2010). And these animals can't possibly be using special human speech perception mechanisms, can they?

Whether special-mechanism or general-mechanism, however, the challenge of theories of speech perception is not only in explaining how it is that we identify and categorize speech sounds but also how we do so despite the ambiguity in the pattern of vibration in the air and on the eardrum.

> Socratic Question: How is categorical perception used as evidence supporting special-mechanism theories of speech perception? How is categorical perception used as evidence supporting general-mechanism theories of speech perception?

Summary

In some ways, the challenge of hearing properties of surrounding objects and surfaces is more difficult than the challenge of seeing those properties. In the traditional approach, perceiving where a sound is coming from, determining which sounds "go together", and identifying and understanding the sounds of speech means using cues available in the vibrations in the air that are funneled toward the eardrum. These cues allow the auditory system to disambiguate and organize these vibrations by—among other things—comparing these vibration patterns across the two ears, grouping patterns of vibration that have similar properties or create a particular pattern, and identifying and categorizing those patterns of vibration that are sounds of speech.

Notes

1 Location in the world is even preserved in parts of the visual cortex (see Chapter 3).
2 In fact, there is almost never complete silence *anywhere*—unless you are in a special room called an anechoic chamber.
3 This is known as the "inverse square law" because intensity decreases in proportion to the inverse square of distance ($I \propto d^2$).
4 343 meters per second (or approximately 2300 times the width of your head per second).
5 It is also one reason why learners of new languages often have a discernable accent.
6 There are between 800 and 900 different phonemes used across languages.
7 This is why there are different numbers of phonemes (about 40) and letters (exactly 26) in English. The English word "ship", for example has *four* letters (s, h, i, p) but *three* phonemes (/sh/, /i/, and /p/).
8 The vocal folds are sometimes called "vocal cords", but they are more like folds than cords.
9 150 beats per minute is a common tempo for upbeat pop or rock songs like "Don't Stop Believin'" by Journey, "The Anthem" by Good Charlotte, and "All the Small Things" by Blink-182.

Part Three

The Ecological Approach

13 Limitations of the Traditional Approach and Introduction to the Ecological Approach

Chapters 8–11 of this book explored the traditional approaches to perception, which have been the dominant approaches to understanding "how we know stuff and how we do stuff" for several centuries. Most of the research and theorizing in perceptual science has focused on finding different ways to answer the same basic set of questions about what cues are available to the central executive and how rules can be applied to those cues to generate the best representation based on the most likely scenarios. And yet . . . these approaches run into a set of very thorny problems that do not have easy solutions—and may not have *any* solutions!

In the first part of this chapter, we will outline those problems. In the second part of the chapter, we will argue that the problem may not be so much with the answers to those questions, but rather with the *questions themselves.* In particular, the problem may be that the questions asked by the traditional approach were based on (often centuries-old) assumptions that were flawed in one way or another. This means that the answers were *guaranteed* to run into problems that do not have easy solutions! The third part of this chapter will introduce the assumptions of the ecological approach, which was developed explicitly to avoid running into the very same sets of (solution-less) problems. As we will see, developing the ecological approach required making different assumptions and asking an entirely different set of questions. First, let's explore the set of thorny problems without easy solutions.

Problem #1: The Loan of Intelligence

Like all three of the approaches that we cover in this book, the traditional approach assumes that we start with no information about the world, and that we learn everything about the world through our senses. What makes the traditional approach unique from the other two, however, is insisting that the stimulation reaching the sense organs and the resulting proximal stimulus is not very useful. This leads to the additional assumption that generating an accurate representation of the world cannot be accomplished without fixing the input using knowledge gained from our previous experience with the world.

That set of assumptions can be diagrammed like Figure 13.1. This triangle highlights an (unsolvable) problem: If all knowledge comes from experience *and* all experience comes from perception, then it's a problem if perception requires knowledge—there's no way to get what you need unless you already have it! It's like the old conundrum of not being able to get the job without the right experience but not being able to get the right experience without the job! There's no way to get started in this process!

DOI: 10.4324/9781032690964-16

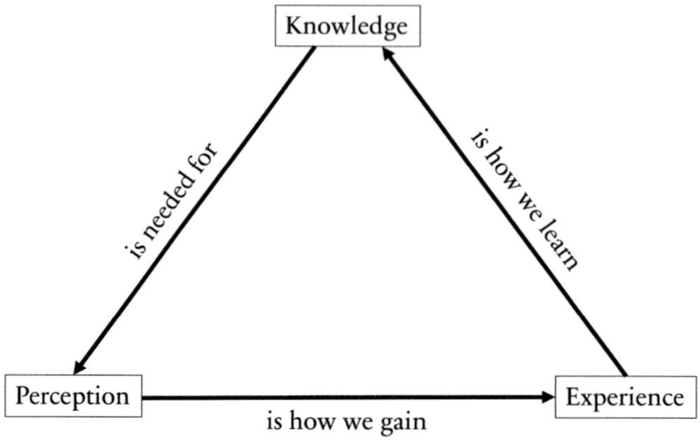

Figure 13.1 The traditional approaches assume that all knowledge comes from experience, all experience comes from perception, and that knowledge is needed for perception. This leads into a logical trap: how do you ever get started in this triangle?

The Plight of the Central Executive

In order to understand the difficulty depicted in Figure 13.1, let's work through a thought experiment. As we did in Chapter 8, let's imagine that *you* are the central executive—again, go, you! So, you are the ghost in Figure 13.2 being presented with stimulation on Fred's senses while he is looking for an apple to eat. You start with no known information about the world. The only information you have is the stimulation that comes in through senses, but as we have already described, that stimulation is assumed to be not particularly useful. For example, in the case of vision, you—as the central executive—are given a pattern of light projecting on to the retina and are tasked with trying to figure out what caused the stimulation.

In Chapter 8, we introduced the outness problem. In this thought experiment, the first thing you will have to do as the central executive is to solve the outness problem; you have to figure out that the stimulation on the retina is coming from the world *out there* rather than the world in here. So, it turns out that, before you even really get started figuring out what the pattern of stimulation is, you'll need some information about where that stimulation is coming from. So, you can do what many people do when they need something but don't have a way to get it. They take out a loan. But in this case, it's not a loan of money—it's a *loan of intelligence* (Dennett, 2010).

Socratic Question: Which assumptions of the traditional approach (see Chapter 8) necessitate a loan of intelligence? Which assumptions of the traditional approach are *violated by* a loan of intelligence?

So, we'll loan you that information—the world is actually at some distance rather than in here with you. Fine. With that in mind, let's take a look at the kind of incoming stimulation you have to work with: In the case of vision, the pattern of light on the retina is a flat and inverted and left-right reversed image. Why would you assume that this is *not* an accurate

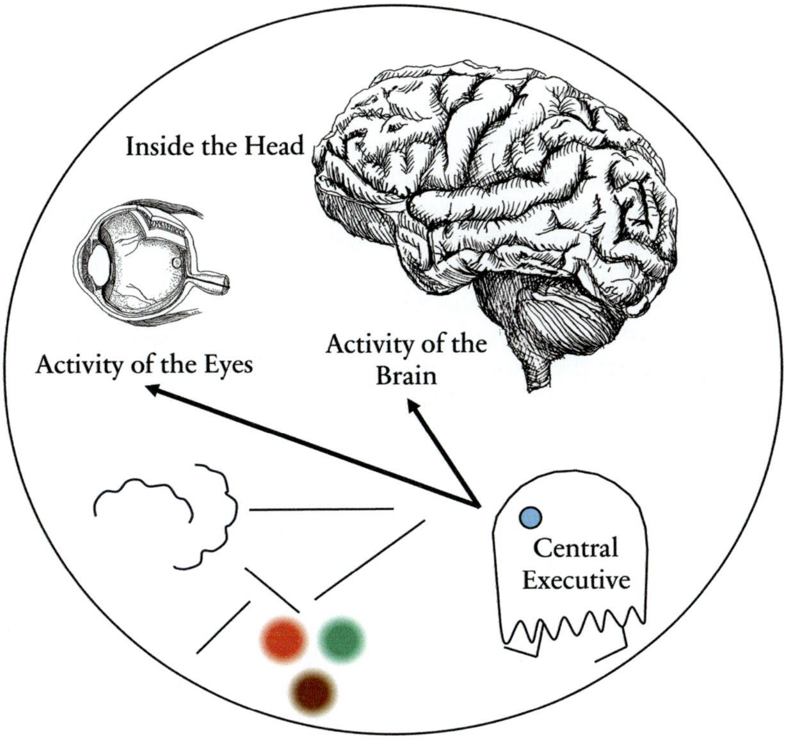

Figure 13.2 Fred's central executive has no access to the outside world. Without that access, he is unable to guess what distal stimulus could have caused these sensations.

representation of the world? How would you know this needs fixing at all? The image is *always* two-dimensional, *always* inverted, so why wouldn't you assume that the world could simply *be* flat, *be* upside down?

The problem is that you have no access to the world that does not come in through the same sensory system that gave you this image in the first place. So, where does the knowledge come from that this representation is *bad*? In order to begin the process of generating a representation, you'll need to have one other critical bit of information as well. So, you might need to take out another loan. This time, you need the knowledge that world is actually three-dimensional and that the sky is up and the ground is down. So, if the retinal image says otherwise, it will need fixing so that you can experience the world as it really is.

Next, you will need to use cues and rules and most likely scenarios in order to interpret this bad retinal image. Essentially, you need to look at the current pattern of stimulation and compare it to stored knowledge about previously encountered trees. You need to figure out which parts of *the current* stimulation match which parts of *the stored knowledge about trees* so we can figure out how to construct *the current* representation based on the stored knowledge (*the previous* representation). Except, how did you get this stored knowledge? If all current representations are generated based on comparisons to *previous* representations, where did *previous* ones come from (see Figure 13.1)? Or do you need still more information to get started (see Box 13.1)?

Box 13.1 What About the Other Senses?

In Chapter 1, we talked about the historically popular idea (introduced by Berkeley, 1709) that there are some senses that are *distance* senses (like sight) and some senses that are *near* senses (like touch). He suggested that stimulation reaching the near senses was *unambiguous*, which meant that there was no need to provide any loans of intelligence. In other words, when it came to the near senses, there was no need to provide any prior knowledge or information to the central executive about where a given pattern of stimulation was coming from or what that pattern of stimulation might mean. Given that the stimulation reaching them was *already unambiguous*, the near senses could be used to generate the prior knowledge or information that was needed to disambiguate the ambiguous stimulation reaching the distance senses. In other words, the near senses provided a way of getting started on the triangle in Figure 13.1. Hooray!

Fred might, for example, notice that when he is holding an apple in his hand very close to his face, his arm is bent and his hand is positioned close to him (unambiguous stimulation for the near sense of touch!) and the apple creates a large retinal image (ambiguous stimulation for distance sense of vision). When he holds that same apple farther away from his face, his arm feels less bent and his hand feels less close and the apple creates a smaller retinal image (see Figure 13.3). In this way, over time, retinal image size is associated with felt distance. While most modern traditional theories try to find ways to disambiguate stimulation used by a given sense without necessarily relying on other senses, Berkeley's idea of touch (or other senses more generally) being used to disambiguate vision persists in the use of oculomotor cues to explain depth perception (see Chapter 9), in the use of efference copies to explain motion perception (see Chapter 11), and in the use of cues to depth more generally.

Figure 13.3 If touch is unambiguous, it can be used to disambiguate vision. For example, the feeling of a bent arm (closer apple) can be associated with a larger retinal image, and the feeling of a straightened arm (farther apple) can be associated with a smaller retinal image.

However, this plan has problems: If touch is used to inform vision, how do we interpret visual cues for things that haven't touched (like apple tree on the other side of the field) or can never touch (like the moon)? Also, despite being historically popular, the distinction between unambiguous stimulation reaching the near senses and ambiguous stimulation reaching the distance senses may not be correct. Remember—what is popular is not always right, and what is right is not always popular (see Chapter 1).

Let's give you (as Fred's central executive) a bit more information to get started. We'll loan you the (stored) knowledge of a previously encountered apple tree. How can you compare the stimulation on the retinal image to this stored knowledge? Let's imagine what this might be like. Let's say that the stored knowledge is of an apple tree with a birdhouse on it and six other apple trees nearby. How do you know which parts of this stored knowledge are important to the formation of the accurate representation of an apple tree? If you do not know which parts were important, how do you know which parts we can safely ignore? For example: if the first apple tree had a birdhouse on it and this one doesn't, is it still an apple tree? Can Fred still eat its apples? If the first tree was surrounded by six others, and this one only has three neighboring trees, is it also approachable? How do you know?

We would have to give you *a lot* of information to get out of this one: information about birdhouses, what makes an apple tree an apple tree, and that having a birdhouse does not affect the identity of a tree, nor does the position or number of the surrounding trees. And it wouldn't just be about the birdhouse and nearby trees! What if there was a ribbon around the current tree? Or if it was a cloudy day vs. a sunny one? Or if you had come to this tree from the west and the other tree from the east? Does it matter? How do we know what does and does not matter before we ever encounter the situation? And one more time with feeling, when we encounter it the *first* time, how can we gain the necessary knowledge without having any ability to interpret the current situation without *past* situations that were similar?

As we discussed in Chapter 8, Helmholtz (1910/2000) attempted to get out of this puzzle by suggesting that the central executive uses the *Principle of Maximum Likelihood* to interpret the stimulation when it is ambiguous. If we are not sure whether the presence of a birdhouse matters, we simply need to ask ourselves: of all the times we have seen an apple tree with some sort of hanging structure on it, did it affect the edibleness of the apple?

He imagined this principle as a sort of internal tally: each time you encounter the situation, add a mark next to the eventual outcome. Then, when you have an uncertain situation, compare it to the tally and interpret the situation based on which outcome had the most tally marks.[1]

Let's return to the simpler situation that we presented in Chapter 8 (see Figure 8.11) in order to understand this fully: you are the central executive trying to guess what caused the circular pattern on our retina (see Figure 13.4). From experience, you know that it could be several things including a sphere (viewed from any direction) and a cylinder (viewed from one end). Without considering context, your internal tally for this situation is that spheres are the most common source of a circular pattern on the retina. However, if circumstances *outside* the circle are taken into consideration, you have a different tally. For example, if the circle is in the center of a bowl full of wooden balls, the sphere is still the most likely; however, if

Figure 13.4 Since many objects could produce a circular retinal image, the central executive must use other contextual cues to figure out the correct shape.

the circle is in the center of a bowl full of wooden cylinders, then a cylinder is the most common outcome.

How would you know which tally to use? When do you need to take the entire context into account, and when can you isolate certain aspects? And, if the answer is to *always* take the surroundings into account, then how do you interpret *the surroundings*? After all, the only reason you knew it was a bowl of balls vs. a bowl of cylinders was because you interpreted the shapes surrounding the circle on the retinal image. Where did that interpretation come from? And one more time with even *more* feeling, where did the tally come from? How did you interpret all of those images in order to build up a statistical awareness of the world? How do you know what's likely if you don't *already know what's likely*? That's a lot of information we have to give ourselves just to get started!

As we have already suggested, this requires what Dennett (2010) called *The Loan of Intelligence*. The central executive needs a lot of information just to get started, and there seems to be no way to get *any* of that information, let alone all of it. Once the central executive *has* that information, it might be possible to build a reasonably reliable system capable of using a set of rules to interpret cues and ultimately come to a conclusion about a most likely set of circumstances. These techniques have been used to some success, for example, in building robots that can move around grocery stores looking for spills and alerting the staff when they find one (e.g., Gutta & Philomin, 2004). But the difference here, of course, is that the robot must be programmed; that is, it must be given prerequisite information by an outside entity (the programmer). What about humans? Are we going to have to assume some kind of all-powerful entity interpreting our senses for us? Or programming us with the prerequisite information in violation of the tabula rasa?

Problem #2: Lack of Accurate Feedback

Another advantage the grocery store cleaning robot has over our naive central executive is the ability to get accurate feedback. Programmers can "train" these learning robots by carefully choosing the training situations and providing feedback on repeated trials. The robot uses the feedback to update the programming: If it correctly identified the spill, it will use that type of identification to identify spills in the future. If it incorrectly identified the spill, it will be less likely to use that type of identification to identify spills in the future.

This is not unlike Helmholtz's approach, which requires comparing new situations to old situations based on the "eventual outcome". But (and it's a big but!) this approach presumes that, at some point, the central executive finds out what really was going on. That is, it assumes that the central executive was able (somehow) to find out if their interpretation of the retinal image was correct. Remember: the central executive only has access to (presumed bad) information that comes in through the senses—where did this *accurate* feedback come from? How was the central executive able to access an uninterpreted (and thus trustworthy) version of the world? And if they had access to a version of the world that did not need interpretation, why are we going through all the trouble of interpreting a bad input in the first place? That would have been a huge waste of time, right?

The truth is that you, as the central executive, will never be able to get out of this tangle. Like asking "How do you get from California to New York?" this is a problem without enough constraints. In a typical logical problem-solving task, a person is asked to infer effect from cause—what outcome would result if a given event occurs. For example, if you ask Fred what will happen if someone were to strike a wineglass with a hammer, he will tell you that the glass will almost certainly break.

However, this is not the kind of logical problem-solving task faced by the central executive. Instead of being asked to infer effect from cause, the central executive is being asked to do the much more difficult task of *inferring cause from effect* (see Turvey, 2019). In particular, they are being given a pattern of stimulation on a receptor surface (an effect) and being asked to figure out what the object or event in the world is (the cause). So instead of asking Fred what will happen if a hammer strikes a wine glass, you bring him to a room where there is both a broken wineglass and a hammer present and ask him what caused the wine glass to break? He can't be so confident in his answer this time. This situation is *always* uncertain. There is a *most likely* scenario: the hammer caused the wineglass to break. But there are *other possible* scenarios as well: a different hammer caused the wine glass to break; the wine glass was broken by Topsy, who stepped on it and then fled the scene; the wine glass was shattered by Dio D. Vicen hitting a high C; and so on. And if Fred's central executive had *never* encountered a hammer or wine glass before, what possible reason would they have for assuming the event was "hammer smashed wine glass"?

Socratic Question: In the traditional approach, the central executive is a little bit like a detective solving a crime. What strategies does the central executive use to generate awareness of the outside world that might also be used by a detective in solving a crime?

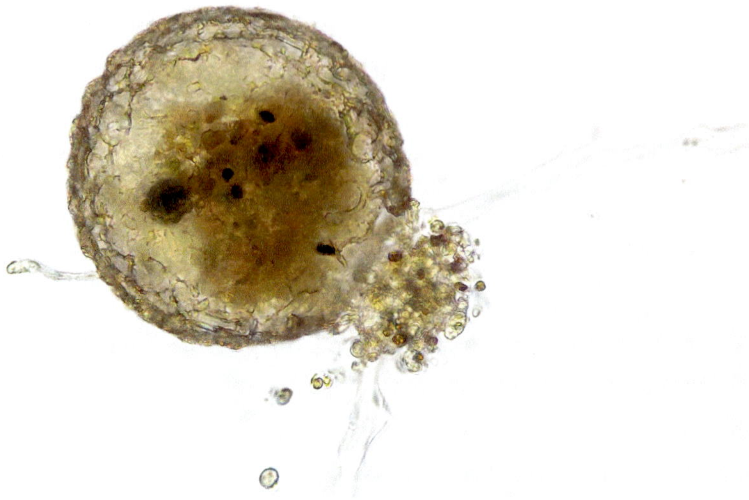

Figure 13.5 The single-celled organism *difflugia* will build itself a suit of armor out of the silt from the ponds in which they live.

Problem #3: Evolution Wouldn't Do This

The plight of the central executive ultimately feels like bad engineering. Why design—if evolution can be considered to be designing living things—an organism that cannot perceive its world without intervention? To our knowledge, very few organisms (if any) have the higher cognitive reasoning abilities that the traditional approach seems to require, but *every* organism has the ability to perform everyday behaviors (Reed, 1996; Segundo-Ortin et al., 2026). Those organisms successfully obtain food, avoid danger, find shelter, locate mates, and so on. If only those organisms with the ability to reason (even unconsciously) were able to successfully perceive well enough to perform everyday behaviors, such organisms could never have evolved because their predecessors would have died without the ability to eat, drink, and procreate! Distant past aside, we *know* this can't be the case—there are single celled organisms called *difflugia* that can build suits of armor around themselves out of the silt in the ponds where they live (see Figure 13.5). If you need a sophisticated cognitive process in order to understand your surroundings, how are these single-celled organisms able to do this?

And if organisms—*past and present*—without sophisticated reasoning abilities seem to know their surroundings well enough to perform everyday behaviors, then why introduce these sorts of processes into the perceptual process *at all*? Why would evolution go backwards, as it were, and create an organism whose sensory contact with the world is ultimately not very good (and thus in need of interpretation requiring sophisticated reasoning abilities)? Would it not make more sense that evolution had, instead, equipped every organism from the very first single-celled creature to modern-day dogs and cats and baby elephants (and Freds) with the ability to "know stuff" and "do stuff" directly—without cues, without rules, without unconscious inference? Wouldn't it make more sense to have an approach to perceiving that did not require such elaborate reasoning merely to allow the animal to perform everyday behaviors?

Where Does the Traditional Approach Go Wrong?

In Chapter 8, we outlined the key assumptions of the traditional approaches. So far, in this chapter, we have argued that these assumptions lead to problems without solutions. In other words, taking these assumptions to their logical conclusion leads to a theoretical dead end. In particular, Fred's central executive is starved for accurate, meaningful information about the outside world. So how did we end up here? Will we *always* end up here? Or put it another way, if we just modified *one* or *two* of the assumptions of the traditional approach, would that solve the problem? The ecological approach argues that there is no way to merely make one or two minor adjustments to assumptions and solve these problems. This is because proponents of the ecological approach claim that there are (at least) three ways in which assumptions of the traditional approach are fatally flawed.[2]

Fatal Flaw #1: Assumption That All Causality Is Local and Direct

The assumption of local causality originated so long ago it's hard to imagine questioning it, but we should. And we will! As hard as it might be to believe, causality is not necessarily limited to interactions that are close together in space and time. *Wait . . . what? Yep.*

Let's return to the question of what caused the 8-ball to fall into the corner pocket of the pool table from Chapter 8 (see Box 8.1). The traditional approach generally restricts their investigations of perceptual processes to *efficient* causality (in the case of the pool table, that was the transfer of momentum from the cue stick to the cue ball to the 8-ball until the ball fell in the pocket). However, like all events, the event "the 8-ball falls into the corner pocket" is an event that is *multi-causal.*

In fact, it is much easier to provide a straightforward answer to the question like "what stops the ball from falling into the pocket?" than it is to answer the question of "what caused the 8-ball to fall into the corner pocket?" because while many ongoing causes are often necessary for a successful event to occur and continue, only one cause is necessary to interrupt this process. For example, the 8-ball might not go into the corner pocket because it struck another ball that was blocking its path or because Topsy sneezed and changed its trajectory.

But what about the scenario where everything goes right and the 8-ball falls into the corner pocket? While it is true that momentum must have been transferred from the cue stick to the cue ball to the 8-ball for the 8-ball to go into the corner pocket, many other things must *also* have happened for this event to have occurred. It sounds strange, but it's true. To make our point, we'll just list some of these things. Gravity has to exist and work exactly the way that it does; the felt had to be smooth enough for the balls to roll predictably, but rough enough that the balls lost momentum as they continued to roll; the evolution of pool as a form of entertainment had to have happened just as it did; Claudia must have hit the cue ball squarely and with just the right amount of force; Fred and Claudia must have agreed to play against each other on this particular occasion; the table legs must not have broken in the middle of the game; Topsy must not have sneezed just after Claudia's shot. We could go on! And on! Causes both local and distant, obvious and non-obvious, all constrain this event.[3]

Not only does constraining ourselves to only local and direct causality not reflect the reality of complex causality, but it also forces us to solve the action-at-a-distance problem when explaining perception. This, in turn, leads to the need for a representation of the world that

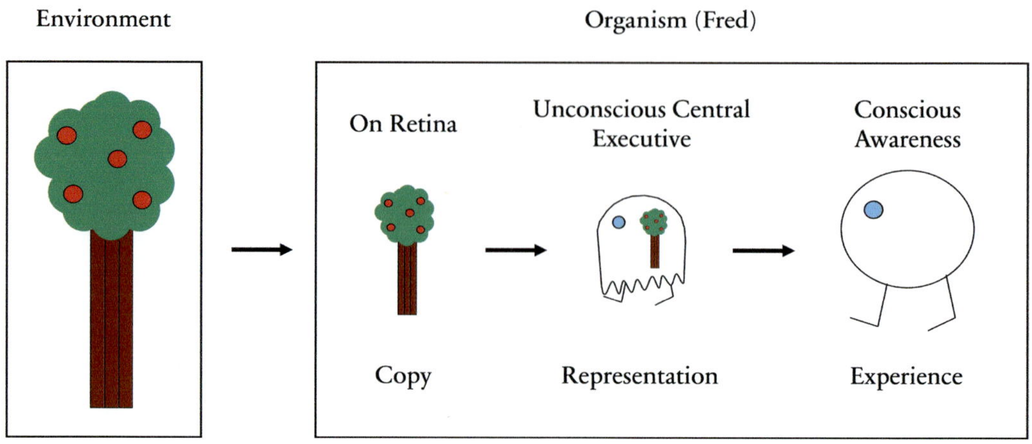

Figure 13.6 In the traditional view, perception is indirect, organism and environment are logically separated. Perception is of the central executive's interpretation (representation) of the world.

provides the bridge between the world and the perceiver. That representation and all that it entails is the source of the problems we listed earlier.

Fatal Flaw #2: Assumption of (Flawed) Representations

Assumption 2A—that our perceptual interactions with the world are mediated by a representation (see Figure 13.6)—was a huge part of what led us to our theoretical dead end. If the process of perception either uses or generates a *bad* representation, then some intelligent process or set of processes will need to fix or interpret that representation, which brings us back to the problem of to an information-starved but intelligent central executive.

We needed to assume the existence of representations in the first place because we needed to avoid action-at-a-distance, but our commitment to look beyond local causality makes that concern moot. We can allow Fred to know the world sufficiently to guide his behavior without needing any representation (or any other mediator) to preserve local causality.

Box 13.2 The Problem of the Retinal Image

Doing away with the representation as a starting point will also help with another difficulty encountered when trying to generalize our explanations of perception from humans to other animals. More specifically, starting with a representation in the form of the retinal image put perceptual theorists in a tangle when they considered organisms that do not have chambered eyes like Fred does (see Chapter 2 for some examples). Many organisms such as cats, dogs, snakes, elephants, and other primates have chambered eyes—which results in *what might be interpreted as* an actual *picture* being projected onto the back of the eye. But many (in fact, most!) organisms do not have a chambered eye. In actuality, most animals have compound eyes (like flies; see Figure 2.15), and compound eyes do not have a retina and cannot make an image.

Other animals have eye cups (like hagfish; see Figure 2.15), and those don't produce images either. And yet, these animals seem to see just fine, certainly well enough to perform everyday behaviors. Just ask any hagfish!

And it is worth noting that while chambered eyes *do* have a retina, they might not actually produce an image (Carello & Turvey, 2020). In other words, the retinal image may very well be a myth! The back of the chambered eye is *not* really a flat projection screen as it was assumed to be when the eye was first being dissected. In fact, the back of the eye may have only looked like a screen to the first scientists investigating it because of the *way* they were dissecting it. The scientists literally cut off the back of the eye and *replaced* it with a screen-like membrane. The image that formed on that screen may have had more to do with the optics of the front of the eye then the anatomy or typical functioning of the retina itself.

In actuality, there are multiple layers of retinal cells and blood vessels that more closely resemble a "folded fishing net" (Swanson, 2015) than an opaque screen. At best, we can say that certain spatial relationships in the world are preserved in patterns of stimulation that move through the chambered eye, but that is not the same as starting with an *image*.

When faced with the evidence of (at least) three types of eyes that have very different ways of interacting with light, we have a choice to make: either assume that the processes by which Fred, the fly, and the hagfish see the world are categorically different, or assume that we misunderstood how visual perception works in organisms with chambered eyes—eyes that theoretically could (but might not) form an image. If Fred, the fly, and the hagfish have *similar* visual perceptual processes, then we cannot think of the retinal image as a copy of the world *as such*. And it cannot be the starting point for visual perception either. Instead, it might be better to think of it as a side effect that is incidental to the perceptual process and shift our focus to what *similarities* exist between the fly's contact with the world and Fred's.

Socratic Question: Way back in Chapter 2, we said, "For the traditional approach . . . [the] retinal image is the starting point for vision". But in Box 13.2, we said, "the retinal image may very well be a myth!" What does this mean for traditional approaches to vision?

Whether or not the stimulation reaching the sense organs generates a representation inside of the perceiver, we still need to address the idea that this stimulation is *bad*. The Poverty of the Stimulus is the bedrock on which all the traditional theories of perception are built. Without this notion, all the assumptions that come after it are completely unnecessary. After all, if the stimulation reaching the sense organs and brain is *good*, then there is no need to rely on cues or to interpret or compute anything, unconsciously or otherwise. Having said that, the notion that the incoming stimulation is bad is compelling and has the support of Euclidian geometry (remember projective geometry from Chapter 10?). Let's examine just the notions of visually perceived size and distance as discussed in Chapter 8. It seems pretty clear that Fred cannot know the size and distance of the tree because the light (traveling in straight

Figure 13.7 The Beuchet chair illusion distorts size and distance when viewed from the "proper" location (left), but not when viewed from a slightly different location (right). This photograph of the author (5'3") and her husband (6'2") was taken at the Museum of Illusions in New York City.

lines from source to object to retina) forms a flat image on the back of his eye (although that's not really true; see Box 13.2). In a flat image, neither size nor distance from the viewer are perceivable and so they must instead be *computed* through the use of cues and inference.

Together with the assumption of static views, the use of cues and inference to compute size and distance is the premise of the Beuchet chair illusion (see Figure 13.7, *left*). This arrangement is carefully constructed specifically to capitalize on the size and distance problems caused by the flat retinal image. The figure on the left (one of your authors) seems much larger than the figure on the right (her husband) because the figure on the right is actually much farther away. Proponents of the traditional approach take this as evidence that the flat retinal image is interpreted via cues because the "chair" is specifically designed to make the cues contradict reality—the seat is on the floor, the legs are just posts at a much closer distance and oddly arranged, etc.—which is what leads to the illusion.

There is, however, another possibility. The Beuchet chair illusion only works if you look at the room from *one specific location*. It only works if you don't move your head, if you close one eye, if you don't sway, and if you don't shift forward or backward. It only works when the view is *static*. Honestly, it hardly works at all when you see it in person and only *really* works when you see pictures taken of it, like the ones in Figure 13.7. If you are in person and you lean to the side or move one step to the right, the entire illusion is dispelled and everything looks as it actually is (see Figure 13.7, *right*). The odd configuration of the posts and the cushion becomes clear, the relative size of the figures is easily discerned, and the illusion is revealed as a conspiracy of geometry (see Runeson, 1988).

In other words, another way to look at the Poverty of the Stimulus assumption is that the stimulation is only bad *if we make it so*—if, for example, we remove all the rich information available through movement and exploration. But movement and exploration are essential features of everyday life! As Gibson (1966) said (paraphrased): The animal that does not move is either asleep or dead (p. 10). But, in the traditional approach, the static retinal image is the generic case. It's the starting point. Movement should only make perceiving harder. In the ecological approach, the retinal image does not exist, and a moving animal is the generic case. Movement is what makes it possible to perceive! In addition to the dependence on an improbably static view, the traditional approach also has a reliance on the wrong *variables*.

Fatal Flaw #3: Assumption of Geometric and Physics Variables

When perceptual theorists were first grappling with the notion of the retinal image, they expected it to be making an exact representation of the world. But this carries a contradiction at its core: there can be no *exact* representation of the world. Representations (however conceived) will never have the same inherent meaning at the world itself. Fred can eat an apple but not a painting of an apple.

The images created on the retina (however conceived) do not have mass, are not three-dimensional, are greatly reduced in size from the object itself (they're smaller than a flea!). The representation is not—cannot be—exact; it's not even close. If the representation is not exact, then the necessary conclusion is that the representation must be preserving *some* of the structure of the world, presumably the kind that would be of some use to the organism. So, the key question then becomes what structure of the world—that might be preserved in the retinal image—would be of most use to organisms? For the traditional approach, the answer to this question is really about what description of the world is most *objective*. These theorists were looking for properties of that object—or, more often, in the light reflected from that object—independent of any observer. They reasoned that the perceptual systems *must* use those properties for exactly that reason—objective properties would exist regardless of any changes in context that might occur.

With that in mind, they borrowed variables from Euclidian geometry and Newtonian physics since they provided tried and true descriptions of those objective properties. If properties like length, width, depth, mass, and shape provided the most objective description of the objects and surfaces that animals might perceive, then it would make sense that these properties were somehow being represented in the stimulation and in the organism itself.

Having made that decision, they examined the (static) retinal image and found it wanting. Length, width, depth, and shape on the retina were all ambiguous! Of course they believed the stimulation was bad! By that reckoning, it absolutely is! If we assume that Euclidean and Newtonian properties are necessary for perceiving anything, and the image on the retina does not preserve those properties, then we have no choice but to also assume that those properties are somehow added back in. On the other hand, if we do away with these as the variables of importance, the problems raised at the beginning of this chapter simply disappear. One of the moves we will make later in this chapter is to reconsider whether the variables of Euclidian geometry and Newtonian physics are the right ones for understanding how animals know stuff and how they do stuff.

> Socratic Question: Why did the traditional approach borrow variables from Euclidian geometry and Newtonian physics in attempting to understand the process of perceiving? Why might this have been a mistake?

Where Are We?

The traditional approach sought answers to questions raised by a series of assumptions made about the nature of the relationship between the organism and its environment. However, those answers always ran into the same difficulties. In other words, it created unsolvable mysteries. And finding a coherent solution to those difficulties proved problematic at best, impossible at worst. The argument we are making here is that the problem lies not in the answers, per se, but rather in the questions themselves—and more accurately, in the *assumptions* that generated those questions in the first place.

The ecological approach makes the radical claim that all attempts to investigate the perceptual processes from a traditional approach are doomed to fail because they are attempts to answer questions that are based on fatally flawed assumptions (Gibson, 1979/2015). In other words, it is not possible to merely *modify* the traditional approach to overcome the theoretical shortfalls. Instead, we have to *start over.* The good news is that we are not starting from *nothing.* Not *all* of the assumptions that underlie the biological and traditional approaches are problematic. And exploring the biological and traditional perspectives at the very least highlighted which approaches *won't* work!

Given that we have discarded many of the assumptions of the traditional approach as fatally flawed, we need to start over—more or less—with a new set of assumptions. That is, we need a series of assumptions, explicitly stated, that will form the foundation for the ecological approach. That is the focus of the next section.

Assumptions of the Ecological Approach

The first assumption that ecological approach rejects is the assumption of local or direct causality. Local causality led to the problem of action-at-a-distance, action-at-a-distance led to the assumption of a representation of the world in the head, the assumption of a representation in the head led to the poverty of the stimulus, poverty of the stimulus led us to the need to fix a bad representation, and trying to fix a bad representation led us to the loan of intelligence for an information-starved but nonetheless intelligent central executive! Whew! The ecological approach starts with very different assumptions about the nature of causality, which ends up avoiding this entire set of problems.

Assumption 1: Non-local and Non-Linear Causality

The classical concept of causality is not just local but *linear.* Event A causes event B, which causes event C, which causes event D and so on (see Figure 13.8, *top*). The causality moves stepwise from one event to the next, like a sequence of falling dominos or links on a chain. But as we've already discussed, linear causality is an impossibly narrow perspective on why an event occurred. Even an event as seemingly straightforward as a ball falling into pocket on a pool table has a complex network of causes underlying it. You can imagine how complex the network are causes are that support complex behaviors—like walking across a field to pluck an apple from a tree—or complex situations— like the weather on any given day.

Ecological psychologists embrace Argentinian-Canadian philosopher and physicist Mario Bunge's (1979, see Figure 13.8, *bottom*) notion of causality. That is, that it should be thought of as being more like the legs of a table than like links in a chain. In this view, a great many things *support* the events happening as they do, but none of them are individually responsible for those events. In other words, many things are *necessary* for a given event to occur—all of

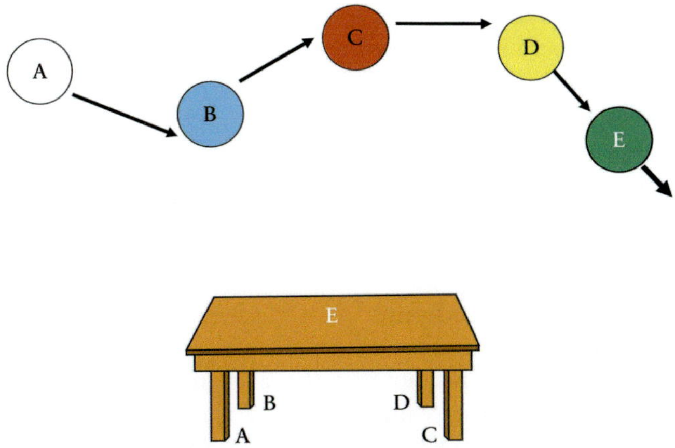

Figure 13.8 The classical view of causality is that is it like one ball hitting the next and so on in an unbroken, though not necessarily straight, line (i.e., it is linear). In this view, A causes B which causes C and so on (top). The ecological view embraces the idea that causality is better thought of as legs of a table. Each of (many) events (A, B, C, D, etc.) supports the event in question, E (bottom).

them play a particular role in the event occurring. But none of those things are *sufficient*—because none of them are enough *on their own*.

The linear version of causality makes sense in a science based on a foundation of Newtonian physics and Euclidian geometry (in which the context of events is explicitly removed). The mathematical formulas used to calculate the direction and speed of two objects after a collision include variables related to mass, velocity, and angle, but none of these variables have anything to do with the *context* in which the collision is occurring (a game of pool). But when we're talking about perceiving and behaving (in which context is absolutely key), is it safe to assume a linear version of causality? Fred's behavior is so much more complex than a ball rolling down a frictionless plane! Consider the simple fact that a ball on an inclined plane does not move itself anywhere—certainly not *up* the inclined plane. But Fred moves himself *everywhere*—including up hills and stairs all the time! Consequently, the *explanations* of his behavior need to be just as complex. The "legs of a table" type of causality is what we will call **nonlinear** because it is not a straight line. The causality is "spread out" both in space and in time.

Nonlocal, nonlinear causality complex causality, causes of a particular event might be near or far; recent, in the distant past, or in the future; obvious or nonobvious. Events are always multicausal and emerge out of a given set of causes.

The concept of causality in an ecological view borrows from the language of a *different* kind of physics—nonlinear dynamics (Strogatz, 2012). In brief, instead of thinking of causality as a singular straight and unbroken line, nonlinear dynamics describes events as emerging from the interactions occurring across an entire **system**. Think of how the weather on any given day is not really

System a group of independent and interacting parts that act as one unit.

caused by any one event but rather by many events, some of which were spread out in both distance and time. Every system has rules or boundaries (gravity is one of the boundaries for the pool table example, and geographical features like mountains and bodies of water are some of the boundaries for the weather), which are called **constraints**. Under a given set of constraints, certain behaviors might become more likely, some might become inevitable, and some are ruled out entirely. To understand the effect the apple tree has on Fred and his behavior, we have to look beyond the notion that the tree (or a representation of the tree) must somehow come in *contact* with Fred and instead consider that the existence of the tree is one of the *constraints* that influence Fred's behavior without causing it directly. To give a weather-related example of the same idea, snow might be more likely if you live on top of a mountain than if you live in the valley, but the mountain does not cause the snow to fall. It is merely one constraint that shapes where and how much snow falls.

Constraints rules and/or boundaries that govern the behavior of a particular system.

Once we have assumed nonlocal and nonlinear causality, the rest of the concerns raised by the classical perspectives simply fall away. Because we do not have to worry about an effect being in contact with the cause, the issue of perception being action-at-a-distance goes away. Effects can instead be constrained by (and emerge from) multiple near and distant causes, so the environment can constrain the behavior of the organism even if it does not directly contact the organism or directly cause the behavior. Without that concern, there is no need for a representation to reach or be generated by the perceiver. Without making the assumption that we need a representation of the world in the head, there's no concern about the poverty of the stimulus or how to overcome that poverty. Therefore, there is no need for interpreting (or otherwise fixing) representations.

Assumption 2: Organism-Environment as Fundamental Unit of Analysis

The ecological perspective holds an entirely different view of perceiving and of the relationship between the organism and the environment (see Figure 13.9). As implied by the name of the field, ecological psychologists assume that the environment and the organism cannot be so easily separated (note: ecology is the study of the fit between animals and their environments).

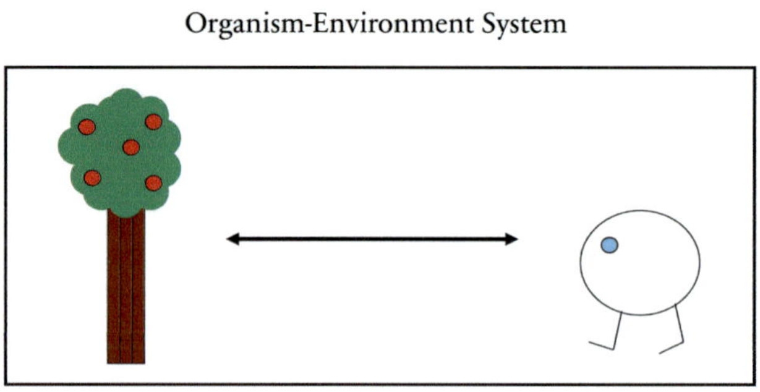

Figure 13.9 Direct perception: organism and environment are part of the same system. Perception is of the world.

In the traditional approaches, studying the organism or how it does anything—like perceive or think or move—starts with the assumption that the organism is a context-independent machine. The ecological approach argues that it is just not possible to understand anything about organisms—*especially* the performance of everyday behavior—this way. Organisms are not machines, and the behavior of organisms cannot be separated from the context in which that behavior occurs. It would be like trying to understand why someone might take a Sensation and Perception course in college without understanding the department's required courses, the motivations that brought them to getting a college degree in the first place, and the socio-economic forces that make getting a degree important for them!

Just as the fundamental unit of analysis for understanding the decision to take a Sensation and Perception class should be the *entire economy*, the fundamental unit of analysis for the understanding the behavior of any given organism should be the *organism-environment system* (Favela & Chemero, 2016). Moreover, when we (as scientists) strive to understand that system, we should choose variables (more about this in the next section) that are related to that relationship.

Socratic Question: Where does the term "ecological" in "ecological psychology" come from? How is this different than the "body as machine" metaphor described in Chapter 1? What is the difference between a machine and system?

Assumption 3: Action-Relevant Variables

Historically, one of the first fundamental ecological insights was that variables and properties borrowed from Euclidean geometry and Newtonian physics are useless for understanding perceiving and behaving precisely *because* they exclude the organism and the activity of that organism. Instead, we need properties that include the organism *and* the activity of that organism. We need *relational* variables and properties, not objective variables and properties (Turvey, 2019). The ecological approach suggests that we should not be providing different answers to the same question (e.g., "How does the retinal image copy objective environmental properties?" or "How does the visual system make inferences about depth from cues?"). Rather, we should be asking different questions entirely!

The traditional approach is built on the foundation that the retinal image and all other patterns of stimulation reaching the sense organs are ambiguous about properties of the world described in terms of Euclidean geometry and Newtonian physics. As we have mentioned, a big part of why the input seemed to be ambiguous or otherwise impoverished was that the variables that had been chosen were relevant to mathematics or physics, but perhaps not relevant to *organisms* or to *behavior*. To paraphrase (Nobel laureate in Physics) Steven Weinberg (1983, p. 16): you can choose whatever variables you like, but if you use the wrong ones, you'll be sorry!

As we discussed in Chapter 1, the historical predecessor to the traditional approach to perception was the psychophysics of 19th-century German psychologists Gustav Fechner and Ernst Weber. Their research attempted to objectively describe the relationship between stimulation patterns (borrowed from Euclidean mathematics and Newtonian physics) and the sensory experience of the perceiver.

For example, they investigated *thresholds* (how much light is needed before we can sense it?) and *just noticeable differences* (how much of a *change* in light does there need to be before we notice it?), both of which focused on properties of light (e.g., wavelength or amplitude) that were meaningful to *physics*, but not necessarily meaningful to their *participants*. And that's fine if we're just trying to understand the limits of our sensory physiology! But if we are trying to understand meaningful perceptual *experience* like Fred's awareness of an available snack, then using variables and properties that are *unrelated* to that experience is probably shortsighted. Nevertheless, by the time the traditional approach got its boots on, the language of perception was being conceived of entirely in terms of Newtonian physics and Euclidian geometry.

To understand how the variables of Newtonian physics and Euclidian geometry may be inappropriate for understanding the everyday experience of animals, let's join Fred and his physicist friend, Bob, as they examine an ice cube melting on the counter (see Figure 13.10). To Bob, when the block of ice melts, there is a story of conservation to be told. The water in the ice did not cease to exist—because matter can neither be created nor destroyed—but instead is just converted to a liquid state. Bob might even talk to Fred about heat energy, possibly even diffusion.

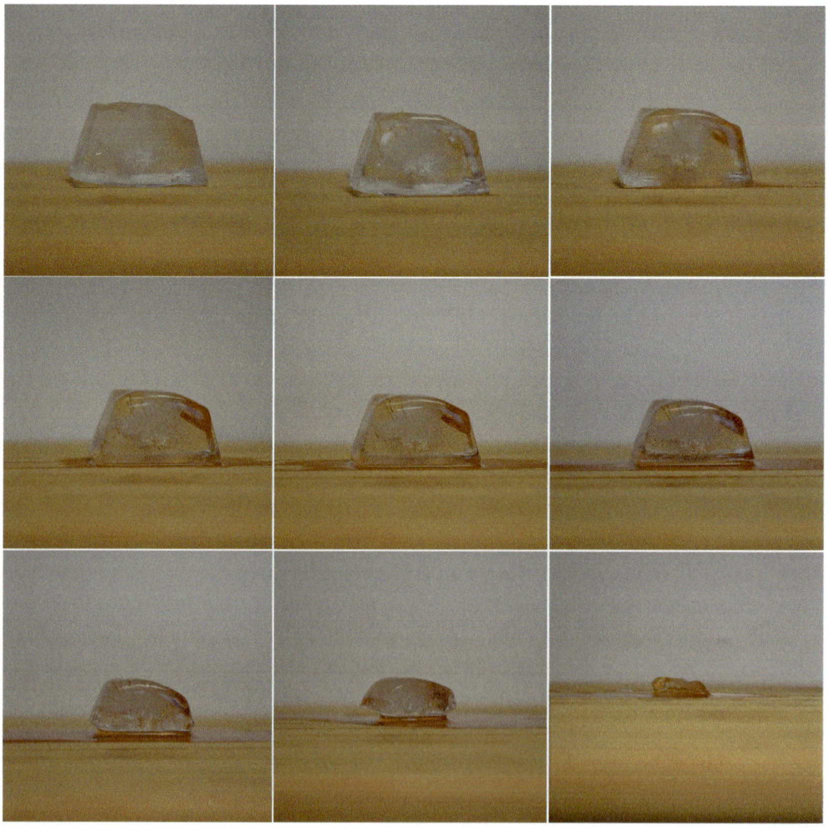

Figure 13.10 When an ice cube melts, the physicist sees a story of conservation of matter, but the average person just sees a mess.

While Fred might find those lessons in physics interesting, they are not related to the experience he is having. For Fred, the ice cube is gone. He can grasp the ice cube, but not the water, and certainly not the water vapor. He can no longer use the ice cube to cool his drink, and now he has to clean his counter. Do you see the problem? Fred sure does—it's all over his counter! There is no way for the language of Bob's Newtonian physics to be translated into the language of Fred's everyday experience. The ecological approach argues that we need to stop using the language of physicists and mathematicians and start using the language of organisms!

From the ecological approach, a focus on the wrong properties and the wrong variables is largely responsible for the mischaracterization of the stimulation reaching the sense organs as ambiguous. If we persist in treating *light as such* (e.g., light as wave, particle, or ray) as the stimulus, we will never be able to understand how Fred and other animals succeed in performing everyday behaviors without resorting to representations, computations, and the activity of a central executive.

Properties of light such as wavelength and amplitude are what the ecological approach calls "lower-order" variables in that they are the basic measurable units used to describe the physical properties of light. However, while such variables are of tremendous value to scientists, they may not be of everyday use to perceivers. What perceivers really need might be described as "higher-order" variables—variables that are of use to performing everyday behaviors, like how a perceiver might get from one place to another most easily. In the traditional approach, the goal is to figure out how the perceiver computes a higher-order perceptual experience from these lower-order variables by using the right set of rules to combine them and transform them in just the right way. This is not all that different from how someone might compute the (higher-order) area of a rectangle by applying the right set of rules (Area = Length × Width) to combine and transform a set of lower-order variables (Length and Width) in just the right way.

From the (meaningless) lower-order variables of wavelength and amplitude, Fred is somehow supposed to compute (meaningful) information about the existence of his snack, where it is, where he is, and how he might be able to move himself from here to there. The problem is that the lower-order variables bear no resemblance to the higher-order variables that Fred actually cares about! They are not the same language. And unlike the geometry problem described earlier, there may not be a way to get one from the other.

The ecological approach proposes a somewhat radical solution—*ignore* the lower-order variables and assume that the higher-order variables are the *starting point* in the perceptual process. That is, assume that the perceiver is able to perceive meaning directly because they are sensitive to higher-order variables from the get-go. This is a difficult concept to get one's head around when the focus has been on lower-order variables for so long. After all, how would you perceive something meaningful without computing it by applying rules to clues? How would we measure the area of a rectangle if not by measuring the length and width and then multiplying?

As it turns out, there is an elegant solution for measuring the area of *any shape*—not just rectangles—without calculating. In 1854,[4] the Swiss mathematician Jacob Amsler invented a tool called a polar planimeter (Eggers, 2020). It is an entirely mechanical (meaning no electricity, no internal computer—just gears and wheels and dials) tool for measuring the area of any shape at all—even ones that are irregular and squiggly (see Figure 13.11). To use the planimeter, the fixed pole is kept stationary, and the index is moved around the perimeter of the shape. The measuring roller mechanically responds to the movement over the surface

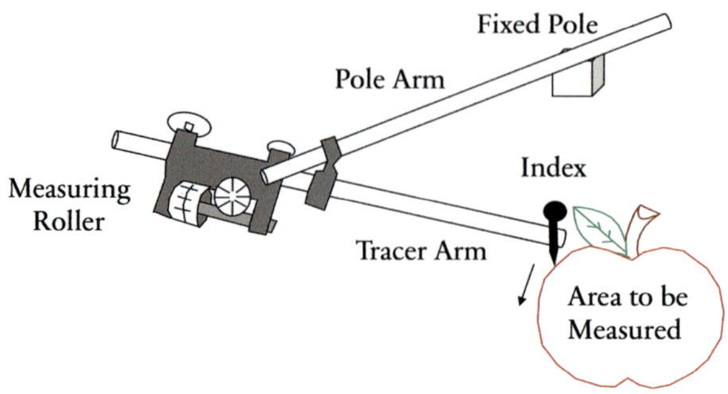

Figure 13.11 The polar planimeter: the index is used to tract around shapes and the measuring roller directly measures the area of the shape.

as well as the angle of the tracer arm to the pole arm. Together, these two mechanisms turn the gears, and—*poof!*—the area of the shape is displayed on the roller. Or in other words, by virtue of its construction and its use, the tool measures area directly, *not* by computing it out of other measurements.

The polar planimeter does not and *cannot measure length and width.* Appreciate that for a moment! This tool, which directly measures area, is *not capable* of measuring the lower-order variables that we would use to *compute* area. If we apply this metaphor to Fred and his tree, the ecological approach maintains that Fred is like the polar planimeter. He is capable of detecting, using, or measuring higher-order variables directly without calculating and without relying on or *even being able to* detect lower-order variables (see Runeson, 1977).

In fact, if you were to *try* to use a polar planimeter to measure lower-order variables, you would discover quite quickly that it was terrible at doing so—much like Fred proves to be terrible at perceiving the lower-order variables used by the traditional approach.

So what should the variables and properties of relevance to perception be? What is the "area" equivalent in perception? The ecological approach maintains that the variables should be rooted in **acting**—after all, acting is why we perceive in the first place! When we talk about Fred and the tree, we should not be focused on the wavelength of the light or the height of the tree or the exact shape of the apple. We should instead ask: can Fred perceive whether he can walk across this field? Can he perceive that the field *affords walking on*? Can Fred perceive that he can reach the apple? Can he perceive that the apple *affords reaching*? Can Fred perceive that he can grasp the apple? Does he perceive that the apple *affords grasping*? In short, we should be asking about perceiving whether surfaces are *walk-on-able* and whether objects are *reachable* and *graspable.* Gibson (1979/2015) called these opportunities for behavior **affordances** and argued that they should be the primary variables of perception (see Figure 13.12).

> **Acting** movement of an organism in an environment in order to achieve a goal.
>
> **Affordances** opportunities or possibilities for behavior given the fit between an animal and the environment—in particular, between the animal's action capabilities and environmental properties.

Chapter 14 goes into detail on the concept of affordances and Chapters 15–18 describe how animals can perceive these affordances directly by detecting particular patterns of

Figure 13.12 Rather than investigate how the micro-level properties of light convey the geometrical properties of objects, the ecological approach proposes we should investigate perception of action-relevant variables called affordances.

stimulation available in light, vibration patterns in the air, and pressure on the skin and muscles, so we won't go into too much detail here. However, there is one more important point that needs to be made explicit regarding the variables of perception: *the medium is not the message*. Or in other words, what we perceive is *not light*; it is whether the apple can be grasped. What we perceive is *not sound*; it is the layout of surfaces. What we perceive is *not pressure on the skin or muscles*; it is the usability of a tool. Focusing on light, sound, and skin pressure distracts from the relevant information which does not depend on a particular energy form.

Right now, you are reading this book. Whether you are reading it on paper or on a screen, what you are attending to is not paper, ink, pixels, or light waves. You are reading the *content* and (we hope) gaining new information about the world of perceptual theory. Understanding perception by looking at light waves would be roughly equivalent to trying to understand your reading experience by looking at the chemical makeup of the ink. *The medium is not the message.*

> Socratic Question: One way to describe what the polar planimeter does is that it "measures without calculating". How is this a good metaphor for the ecological approach to the process of perceiving one's surroundings?

Assumption 4: Unambiguous Information

At the risk of sounding redundant, a big part of why the stimulation was presumed to be bad (i.e., the poverty of the stimulus) in the traditional approach was because of the focus on lower-order variables, in particular the variables of Euclidean geometry and Newtonian physics. Once we made the ecological assumption that the focus ought to be on a different set of variables, we need to reconsider the assumption that the stimulation is bad.

The "poverty" in the stimulus was based—in part—on the idea that more than one distal stimulus world could result in a given proximal stimulus, and that a given distal stimulus could result in more than one proximal stimulus. Or in other words, the stimulation was

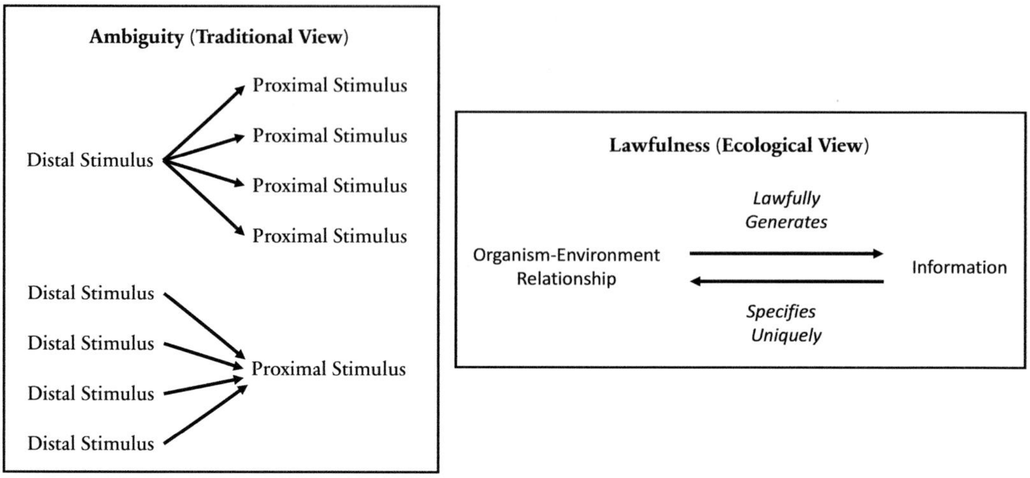

Figure 13.13 Left, in the traditional view, there are many-to-one and one-to-many relationships that need to be resolved (by a central executive). Right, in the ecological view there are only one-to-one relationships, so no interpretation is needed.

necessarily *ambiguous* (see Chapter 8 and Figure 13.13, *left*). The ecological approach is going to make the opposite assumption. That is, the ecological approach assumes that—properly described—the pattern of stimulation encountered by an organism is *unambiguous.* There is quite a bit to be unpacked here, and we'll do so more completely in the next few chapters. But the short story is that in the ecological approach, the pattern of stimulation that a given organism encounters is completely determined by its relationship to the surroundings. In other words, there is *one-to-one* relationship between the pattern of stimulation encountered by the organism and its relationship to the surroundings.

This means that when an organism has *this particular* relationship to its surroundings, it will *always* encounter *this particular* pattern of stimulation. And when it encounters *this particular* pattern of stimulation, the organism will always be *in this particular relationship* to its surroundings. Organisms who are sensitive to this pattern of stimulation will know about this relationship merely by detecting this pattern—no elaboration, fixing, or inferring required. This pattern will be "information about" this relationship (see Figure 13.13, *right*).

Assumption 5: Direct Perceiving

If we assume that—when properly described—the stimulation patterns are *good* and *useful* without any elaboration or input, then we do not need a representation of the world in the head or a central executive to generate or interpret that representation. In traditional approaches, perception is necessarily *indirect* because the representation of the world is what the organism experiences—not the world itself. The process of knowing the surroundings is always mediated by representations. However, if the information is good, there is no need for interpretation, elaboration, or representations of any kind. Perception can be **direct**. Instead of a representation in need of interpretation, the relevant

> **Direct perceiving** perceiving is of the world, not of (or by means of) a representation of the world.

information about its relationship to its surrounding is detected directly by the organism. No mediation and no representations are required (Blau & Wagman, 2022).

Assumption 6: No Central Executive

The first five assumptions of the ecological approach eliminate the *need* for a central executive. More than this, however, the ecological approach explicitly *rejects* a central executive of any kind. As was illustrated when you imagined yourself as Fred's central executive earlier in this chapter, any such entity will be completely unable to accomplish anything due to its isolation and naiveté. Rather than helping to provide a scientific explanation of how perceiving occurs, a central executive provides a *barrier* to such scientific understanding (Turvey, 2019). So while it is often tempting to suggest that there is some entity within us that receives and decodes messages from the world and moves our limbs, it is disallowed as an explanation in the ecological approach.

For various reasons, some of them religious rather than theoretical, the traditional approaches committed to dualism—the idea that the mind (soul) and body were separate entities (see Chapter 1). Like the modern biological approach, however, the ecological approach commits to monism, the idea that we are entirely physical beings, through and through (see Chapter 1). That which we call the mind is an ***emergent*** property of the animal-environment system, rather than as something separate from it.

> **Emergent** complex phenomenon that arises due to relationships among component parts or processes but that is not contained within the component parts or processes.

From the ecological view, then, the process of perceiving is an ongoing, active relationship between an organism and an environment. To understand perceiving, we have to ask entirely different questions:

1) What is perception for, and what does that mean for the variables of relevance to perceiving?
2) How is information about the world unambiguously structured?
3) How do organisms detect information about the world?
4) How do organisms use information about the world?

These are the questions that are addressed in Chapters 14–19.

Summary

The traditional approach assumes that organisms start with no knowledge, gain knowledge through experience, perception is required for experience, *and* knowledge is needed for perception. Given this triangle, there is no way to start learning information. This leads to unsolvable problems like the loan of intelligence, a lack of accurate feedback, and an inability to explain how evolution would have created such problematic perceptual systems in the first place. The ecological approach starts over with assumptions of complex causality (eliminating the need for representations), good input (eliminating the need for "fixing" and so the need for a central executive), and a focus on action-relevant variables (which allows for the input to be good in the first place). This leads to new questions and new avenues for research.

Notes

1 The popular and more modern-day version of this is called Bayesian modeling, but it's basically the same idea with fancier math.
2 In science, a "fatal flaw" is one where the assumption or logical step dooms the overall conclusion to be false. It's also one that cannot be fixed by small adjustments; you have to start over.
3 You may have heard about the "butterfly effect"—that a butterfly flapping its wings in one part of the world can cause a tornado in another part of the world. The butterfly effect is an acknowledgment of both non-local and non-linear causality.
4 Although Johann Martin Hermann invented the *first* mechanical planimeter in 1814, Amsler's invention was the first that was practical and accurate.

14 Perceiving Events and Affordances

As we have seen, the ecological approach requires a fundamental rethinking of what it is that perceivers perceive. In large part, this is because it requires a fundamental rethinking of *what exists to perceive*—of what the world of animals is like. In traditional approaches, it is assumed that the world of animals is really no different than the world *in the absence of* animals.

In the absence of animals, the world is often best described using the tools of Newtonian physics and Euclidean geometry. To be sure, they provide invaluable frameworks for understanding the world. They got us (well, not *us*—but *other people*) to the moon and back! What makes Newtonian physics and Euclidean geometry so powerful is that they are *completely objective*. The laws of physics and geometry are true even in an animal-independent world. For example, objects fall toward earth at $-9.8\ m/s^2$, and the interior angles of a triangle add up to 180° regardless of whether animals exist. Fred learned all about these facts in his physics and math classes in school. In the ecological approach, however, it is a mistake to use an animal-independent description of the world to understand how animals do the things they do, including how they perceive the world. Learning those facts in school doesn't help Fred cross a field and get an apple off a tree!

To be clear, the ecological approach does not suggest that Newtonian physics and Euclidean geometry are invalid for understanding the *world*, only that they are inappropriate for understanding the *world in which animals perform everyday behaviors*. In other words, they are most certainly appropriate for understanding how an object moves toward Fred but not for how Fred moves toward that object with the goal of catching it. Understanding this requires an *animal-dependent* description of the world. It requires an **ecological physics** and an **ecological geometry**. Whereas Newtonian physics and Euclidean geometry describe properties of the world in the abstract, ecological physics and ecological geometry describe properties of the world in which animals live, perceive, and behave. The goal of ecological physics and ecological geometry is to describe what exists to be perceived (and acted on) by animals. Two fundamental categories of such things are *events* and *affordances*.

Ecological physics and geometry a description of the properties of the world in which animals perform everyday behaviors (as opposed to a description of the properties of the world independent of any animal).

Socratic Question: How are ecological physics and ecological geometry different than Newtonian physics and Euclidean geometry?

DOI: 10.4324/9781032690964-17

Ecological Events

> **Ecological Events** changes in the properties of the world in which animals perform everyday behaviors. Ecological events can be as short as seconds or as long as days, weeks, or even years.

Ecological events occur over time scales that are relevant to the everyday behaviors of animals—seconds, minutes, hours, and days, but also, weeks, months, or even years. And the events that occur over these time scales involve *changes* to an animal's environment or to the animal's relationship to it. There are a few important things to point out here about these kinds of events. First, almost all of the time, these kinds of events involve changes in some things relative to other things. In other words, almost all of the time, some things change but other things do not. A strong breeze might change the location or orientation of a stray piece of paper on Fred's desk but would not change the location or orientation of the desk itself. Or possibly, *some* aspects of a given thing might change but not *other* aspects of that thing. The strong breeze would not change what is written on that piece of paper. And so on.

Second, these kinds of events involve changes that *necessarily* unfold over time. Pressing the pause button while watching a video stops the events on the screen from unfolding because it prevents any changes from taking place. But there is no pause button for the events of everyday life. And until there is, there is no way to stop everyday events from unfolding.

Third, different events unfold over different time scales. Said a different way, different events have different *durations*. Some events—a single footstep, the onset of darkness when lights are turned off in a room, a penalty kick in a soccer game—occur over short durations. Other events—walking to a nearby park, the onset of darkness as the sun sets, a team moving the ball downfield during a soccer game—occur over longer durations. Still other events—an afternoon hike, the changing patterns of light and dark over the course of a day, an entire soccer game (especially if the game goes into extra time!), an entire soccer season—occur over even longer durations.

Fourth, shorter events are *nested* within longer events. That is, events occur at multiple time scales *simultaneously*. A single footstep is embedded within a short walk to a nearby stream which is embedded within an afternoon hike. A sunset is nested within the events of an entire day, which are nested within the events of several days (see Figure 14.1). A penalty kick is nested within the events of an entire soccer game which are nested in the events of an entire soccer tournament.

Perceiving Ecological Events

There are also a few important things to point out here about *perceiving* events. First, perceiving an event is not the same as being sensitive to change. Rather, perceiving an event requires being sensitive to what *is* changing relative to what *is not* changing. Sensitivity to change will bring about an awareness that *something* is happening. Sensitivity to the relationship between what is changing and what is not changing will bring about an awareness of *an unfolding event*.

Second, perceiving an event is not the same thing as perceiving motion. Some events—like the change in brightness when a light is turned on or off—occur without any motion at all. Likewise, perceiving events is not the same as perceiving time passing. Durations of time are

Figure 14.1 A sunset is an event nested within the events of a day, which is nested within the events of a week and so on.

fixed and absolute. One hour is always 60 minutes and one minute is always 60 seconds, no matter what. Durations of events are variable and relative. They can be long, or they can be short. And it's the duration of the event—and not necessarily the time that passes during the event—that matters in the behavior of animals. As an example, consider the joke about the Canadian prairieland (though it might also apply to parts of the American Midwest): "The land is so flat that you can watch your dog run away for three days". The point here is that the very same event—witnessing your dog running away—can unfold over different durations depending on where the event takes place (e.g., a Canadian prairie vs. a New England forest).

Socratic Question: How is perceiving an event different than noticing change? How is perceiving an event different than noticing motion?

How to Investigate Perceiving Events

While it is the case that some events occur without any motion at all, for many events, it is a specific pattern of motion that *defines* that particular event. Consider events such an ice cube melting, waves crashing on the beach, or leaves being blown by a strong breeze (see Figure 13.10 and Figure 14.2). Likewise, it is a specific pattern of motion—no more and no less—that enables someone to *perceive* such events.

One way that researchers have investigated this is by using so-called **"point-light"** (or sometimes **"patch-light") displays**. Such displays are made by placing small light bulbs or reflective markers on the various parts of an object and then making a video of a particular event involving that object. The video is recorded, edited, or played back in such a way that only the lights (hence "point-lights") are visible.

Point-light (or patch-light) displays recordings of a moving object made by placing lights or reflective markers on parts of that object, showing (only) the movements of those points over time. Point-light displays of humans are usually made by putting such markers or reflectors on the major joints of the body.

Figure 14.2 Examples of events. Ice cube melting (left), waves crashing on the beach (middle), or leaves being blown by a strong breeze (right).

While early versions of these videos used inanimate moving objects (such a rolling wheel), the most impressive examples used *animate* moving objects—in particular, people (Johansson, 1973). In these studies, the lights or markers are placed on the major joints of a person's body—typically the shoulders, elbows, wrists, hips, knees, and ankles (see Figure 14.3). Then that person is video recorded performing various activities—say, walking or doing jumping jacks. When these studies were first done in the 1970s, the videos were recorded in the dark or in very dim lighting and the video was played back with high contrast. Neither of these techniques would be necessary today since these kinds of videos can be computer generated or computer enhanced. These computer-aided motion-capture techniques are how animations are created for realistic-looking video games—perhaps even *Homunculus 2: The Search for the Invariant.* But this was the early 1970s, well before computers (and even video cameras) were widely available. Regardless of how the videos themselves are made, however, the effect on the viewer is always the same.

When the video is paused, it just looks like a bunch of dots or lights (see Figure 14.3) . . . *maybe* a constellation of stars, but not really. But when the video plays, that bunch of dots *immediately* and *vividly* becomes a person walking or doing jumping jacks. And not in a "hey, that cloud looks a little bit like a dragon" sort of way, but in an "oh my gosh, that's a person walking or doing jumping jacks!" sort of way. The effect is immediate, and the impression is unmistakable. Go see for yourself. There are many of these kinds of videos posted online.

Now, pick your jaw up off the floor and think about what is happening here. The person viewing the video is watching 10–12 dots moving around on a screen for just a few seconds (or less!) but is *immediately* and *vividly* aware of a person walking or doing jumping jacks. It sounds a little hard to believe. For one thing, you might think that it would be *easier* to see what is going on when the video is paused and the dots are not moving all around. After all, movement should make a hard problem even harder, right (see Chapter 11)? Nope. On the contrary, the movement of the dots *is what provides information about the event.* But let's be careful here. It is not just that the dots are moving. It is that they are moving *in a particular way relative to each other.* Some are moving a lot, some less so. Some are moving *together*, some less so. And this pattern, unfolding over time, provides information about the event, which is also unfolding over time.

When the video is paused, this pattern no longer unfolds over time and does not provide information about the event. And, if the video is altered so that the dots move around completely randomly, no particular pattern unfolds over time. Consequently, people don't generally report seeing anything in particular as the dots move around (or if they do, it's in a "hey, that cloud looks a little bit like a dragon" sort of way).

Figure 14.3 Point-light displays: lights are placed on the major joints of an actor and video recorded in high contrast. The figures are unidentifiable when they are not moving, but clearly identifiable as people when they are moving.

Decades of research have shown that people watching these sorts of point-light videos can tell what the person in the video is doing—including walking, running, dancing, doing push-ups, or riding a bike—despite the fact that so much of the detail has been removed from these behaviors (Johansson, 1973). They can also tell whether the person in the video is a man or a woman, what emotions that person is feeling, and even whether the person is someone that they know—Fred could recognize Claudia, and vice versa (see Loula et al., 2005)! And the ability to perceive events in point-light displays showing human behaviors seems to develop relatively early in life. Newborn babies can tell the difference between point-light videos depicting randomly moving dots and a person walking (Bidet-Ildei et al., 2014).

And it's not just humans, either. Cats can (be operantly conditioned to) tell the difference between point-light videos depicting a cat walking and randomly moving dots and even an inverted walking cat (Blake, 1993). Spiders turn toward point-light videos depicting a spider walking and less so toward scrambled point-light displays without any structure (De Agrò et al., 2021)! And fish attempt to socially interact with point-light depictions of movements of a small group of fish and less so with point-light depictions of a person walking (Nakayasu & Watanabe, 2014).

One of the benefits of creating point-light displays is that it reduces a given event down to its most basic form (or at least a *more* basic form)—a pattern of relative movements unfolding over different durations. As we have seen, people (and animals) can perceive many different kinds of events occurring in point-light displays, even when viewing just a few seconds of video. Needless to say, however, the events depicted by means of point-light displays are very much unlike the events of everyday life. By design, they lack almost all of the glorious detail

Figure 14.4 The event recorders used by participants in Blau and Carello (2020) and Blau et al. (2013).

of the actual event, they occur over very short time scales (just a few seconds), and perhaps most importantly, they are isolated from other events, in particular those occurring at larger and smaller time scales. *Why* is that person walking or doing jumping jacks, anyway? What were they doing *beforehand* and *afterwards*?

Socratic Question: How can "point-light" or "patch light" displays be used to investigate perception of events?

For these reasons, researchers have also investigated how people perceive events under more naturalistic circumstances. For example, participants might be asked to watch a movie or listen to a narrative and indicate each time they notice that an event has occurred. However, the events that occur in the most naturalistic circumstances of all—and those that truly deserve the label "ecological"—are those that occur in the hustle and bustle of everyday life.

In some of these studies (Blau & Carello, 2020; Blau et al., 2013), participants carried "event recorders"—a small box with a button that was connected to a digital recorder (see Figure 14.4)—while hanging out in everyday locations on a university campus—an open field, a university plaza, a library entranceway, a student union building, a cafeteria, a dormitory entryway, or a basketball arena (during a game!). The participants stayed in that location between 30 minutes and 2 hours. Their job was to tap the button every time they "saw something change" (which was used as a proxy for "every time you see an event"). Remember, there is no pause button for the events of everyday life. There are *always* events occurring wherever you are. You just need to look for them. And that's what these participants were doing.

Consider a participant—Fred, for example—observing events in an open field. Over the course of a minute or so, he sees another person—his friend Vero!—walk into the field ("tap"), take three steps ("tap, tap, tap"), bend over to smell a flower ("tap"), sneeze ("tap") . . . twice ("tap"), pull out her phone ("tap"), take a photo of the flower ("tap"), text the photo ("tap") to a friend, sit down ("tap"), pull out a book ("tap") and begin to read ("tap").

Regardless of what location they were in, participants—like Fred—did quite a bit of tapping (as many as 5600 taps, but on average about 1800). But the researchers weren't necessarily interested in *how often* the participants tapped the button (that is, in the number of events they observed). *Wait, what? They weren't?* No. Not really. Instead, they were interested in the *intervals between* button taps—the intervals between observed events. Specifically, they were interested in how those intervals change from one tap to the next (i.e., the tap-to-tap variability). In particular, they were interested in whether the tap-to-tap variability over *shorter time scales* (just a few taps) was related to the tap-to-tap variability over *longer time scales* (many, many taps).

When they analyzed the tap-to-tap variability, they found that it had a particular kind of structure. The changes in the intervals between taps were not quite random, but they were not completely correlated, either. They also found that the tap-to-tap variability over shorter time scales was similar to the tap-to-tap variability over longer time scales. In particular, they found that the smaller patterns of change occurring over shorter time scales were similar (both visually and mathematically) to the larger patterns of change occurring over longer time scales (called "self-similarity").

Self-similarity a property of an object or process in which smaller micro-patterns are similar to larger macro-patterns. In other words, the object or pattern has the same properties at small and large scales.

What is so interesting about these findings is that this same kind of structure is also observed in the patterning of natural events such as heartbeats, earthquakes, and thunderstorms. In other words, the flow of events in everyday settings—an open field, a university plaza, a library entranceway, a student union building, a cafeteria, a dormitory entryway, or a basketball arena—may have deep commonalities with the flow of events in the natural world (see Box 14.1 and Box 10.2 in Chapter 10).

Box 14.1 Real and Reel Events

Events occur naturally in the context of everyday life, but they can also be depicted by design in the context of filmmaking and film editing. The events that are depicted in a finished film are, of course, determined by what is recorded by the cameras, but also by how the various recordings are edited together. One particularly important consideration is when and how frequently there should be "edit points" (cuts between scenes or cuts within a scene that go from a character's face to what they are seeing or from one character's point of observation to another; for example, see Figure 14.5).

Hollywood-style films have hundreds, if not thousands, of edit points. In almost all cases, these edit points are meant to be invisible to the viewer, who is supposed to notice the story but not necessarily how that story is being told. So, for a movie to be effective in telling a good story, the flow of events depicted on screen—both in what is recorded and how those recordings are edited—must be coherent. That is, the flow of events depicted on screen must approximate the flow of events in real life.

To investigate the extent to which this was the case, researchers identified the edit points in 15 professional (Hollywood) movies and 15 amateur movies (Blau & Carello, 2020). For each film, they analyzed how the intervals between edit points changed from one edit point to the next edit—the edit-to-edit variability. If this sounds familiar, it's because these studies were completed by the same researchers who analyzed the tap-to-tap variability in perceiving everyday events. They found that the structure in the edit-to-edit intervals in the professional films more closely reflected the structure in the tap-to-tap interval in real-life events. In other words, they found—whether they are aware of it or not—filmmakers demonstrate an understanding of how to depict events on screen in a way that is consistent with the flow of events in everyday life. The professional filmmakers were just a little bit more successful in doing so.

Figure 14.5 Typical editing structure. Two-shot (also known as an establishing shot, left), over-the-shoulder from the villain's perspective (center), over-the-shoulder from the heroine's perspective (right). The camera does not move continuously from one position to the next, but rather makes a discontinuous jump (at the edit point).

Affordances

The studies described to this point in the chapter show that people and other animals can perceive unfolding events—that is, they are able to perceive what *has been* happening and what *continues to* happen. But animals need to do more than this. They also need to perceive what *could happen* in the future. In particular, they need to perceive *what they could do*—what behaviors they could perform. And they need to perceive whether, when, and how to perform those behaviors.

As we have discussed, events are continually unfolding all around you—no pause button, right? Well, some of those events involve *you*. In particular, some of those events are behaviors *performed by you*. At any given moment, you could perform any number of behaviors. Consider Fred sitting at his desk working on a book manuscript on his laptop (see Figure 14.6). He could reach for the coffee mug on the desk, he could stand up and step over the pile of books on the floor, or he could (try to, anyway) squeeze under the desk to pick up the pen that has fallen on the floor. All of these are behaviors that Fred *could* perform (but may or may not actually perform). In other words, they are all *opportunities for behavior*. Such opportunities for behavior are known as *affordances* (see Chapter 13; Gibson, 1979/2015).

Figure 14.6 Sitting at his desk, there are many affordances—opportunities for behavior—for Fred.

Performing any of these behaviors requires *perceiving affordances* for that behavior. It requires perceiving *whether* the behavior is possible, and if so, *when* and *how* the behavior should be performed. Successfully stepping over the books, for example, requires that Fred perceive whether the books are "step-over-able" and if so, when the step should be initiated, how high the step should be, how long the step should be, and how the movements of the foot, leg, and torso should be controlled in performing this behavior.

But—and there's always a but—by definition, *opportunities* are things that *could* happen but have not happened yet (and may not *ever* happen). So perceiving affordances means *perceiving the future*—specifically, whether, when, and how a given behavior could be performed *before* that behavior is ever attempted. This might sound impossible, but don't get out your crystal ball or tarot cards just yet. You won't need them. What you'll need instead is a law-based explanation of perceiving that does not rely on the problematic assumptions that got us into this mess—in particular, local causality (see Chapter 1, Chapter 8, and Chapter 13). With this kind of explanation, it becomes possible to explain how you (and Fred and everyone else) can *perceive* opportunities for behavior, rather than *predict* them (see the section titled "How Are Affordances Perceived?").

When you think about it, you'll realize that you (and Fred and everyone else) perceive the future—that is, you (and Fred and everyone else) perceive affordances—*all the time.* Catching a ball requires that Fred put his hands where the ball *will be*, not where it was, or even where it *is*. And so, perceiving affordances for catching a ball means perceiving whether, when, and how this is possible (see Figure 14.6; see Chapter 15 and 16; Fink et al., 2009). Stopping a car at a stop sign requires that Fred start stepping on the brake *before* he gets to the sign, not *after* he gets there, or even *exactly when* he gets there (unless he is trying to test both the working order of his seatbelts and the heart health of his passengers). And so, perceiving affordances for stopping a car at a red light means perceiving whether, when, and how this is possible (see Figure 14.7).

Affordances are strange in another way, too. They are not quite properties of the environment but not quite properties of the perceiver, either. Instead, they *emerge* from the relationship between these two sets of things. Weird, right? It makes it sound as if affordances

Figure 14.7 Stopping a car at a stop sign requires stepping on the brake well before you get there. Catching a ball requires putting your hands where the ball will be, not where it is.

are not quite . . . real. Like they exist only in the head of the perceiver—like unicorns and leprechauns, and for some researchers, color (see Chapter 4).

But affordances—like other emergent relationships (including color)—are indeed quite real. Consider friction. The friction between the tires on Fred's car (or bike) and the road is not a property of the tires or of the road. Instead, it *emerges* from the relationship between these two things (see Chapter 13 for more on emergent phenomena). And friction is a real thing. And it would be silly to suggest that friction only exists in the head of the perceiver. We think that it is equally silly to make that suggestion about affordances (or color for that matter; see Chapter 4).

There are many different (and sometimes competing) ways to define affordances (see Heras-Escribano, 2019). The one that we think is best is one that we have alluded to already—affordances are *opportunities for behavior* that emerge from the relationship between animal and environment. More specifically, affordances are what an animal can (or could) do in a particular circumstance given the fit between its action capabilities and environmental properties. Common affordances that animals perceive and act on include avoid-able, catch-able, cross-able, move-able, pass-through-able, reach-able, grasp-able, sit-on-able, and step-on-able (see Figure 14.8).

Action capabilities the abilities of an animal relative to surrounding surfaces and substances. An animal's action capabilities are determined in part by its body size and shape, mass, strength, dexterity, and flexibility as well as how it moves itself through the world.

The term "**action capabilities**" requires some unpacking. In part, action

Figure 14.8 Common affordances—crawling under (top right), reaching (top left), grasping (bottom left), leaping over (bottom right).

Box 14.2 How Many Fits Make an Affordance?

We have described affordances as "opportunities for behavior that emerge from the relationship between animal and environment". This might give you the impression that affordances emerge from the fit between *one individual property* of the animal and *one individual property* of the environment. But this is almost never the case. Instead, affordances almost always emerge from a *simultaneous fit* among *multiple properties* of the animal and *multiple properties* of the environment. For a surface to afford walking on by Fred, for example, that surface must be sufficiently horizontal and flat (relative to Fred's ability to balance), sufficiently extended (relative to Fred's size), and sufficiently rigid (relative to Fred's mass), among others. If any one of these criteria does not hold, the surface does not afford standing on. Each one is necessary, but none of them alone are sufficient. The surface must meet all of these criteria, or it does not afford that particular behavior—much like a jigsaw puzzle piece must be "fully interlocked" with all of the surrounding pieces to fit appropriately and snugly in a given space (see Figure 14.9).

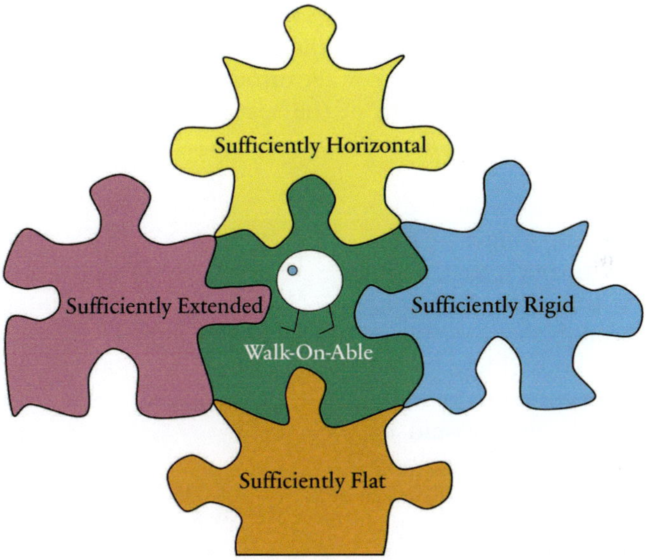

Figure 14.9 For a surface to afford walking on for Fred, several conditions must be met simultaneously—the surface must be sufficiently horizontal, extended, rigid, and flat. If any of these conditions are not met, the surface will not afford walking on.

Socratic Question: What are affordances? How does perceiving an affordance mean "perceiving the future"?

capabilities are determined by an animal's size and shape. Affordances for reaching differ between Victor Wembanyama—a 7'4" (2.22m) basketball player for the San Antonio Spurs—and Fred or either of the authors of this book (who are . . . um . . . shorter than that). But action capabilities are also determined by an animal's mass, strength, dexterity, and flexibility, as well as how it moves itself through the world. Affordances for dashing through an airport terminal differ between Sha'Carri Richardson—a world-champion sprinter who has run 100m in 10.65s—and Fred or either of the authors of this book (who are . . . um . . . slower than that).

How to Investigate Affordances

James Gibson described the concept of affordances in the 1960s (Gibson, 1966) and developed the concept in the late 1970s (Gibson, 1979/2015). However, an empirical method for studying affordances was not developed until the mid-1980s. American psychologist Bill Warren and others pioneered this method in several highly influential studies. These included investigations of perceiving affordances for climbing stairs, sitting on surfaces and walking through doorways (see Wagman, 2020). Partly because of the diversity of research that has followed in the subsequent decades, we'd like to focus on perceiving affordances for walking through doorways.

Consider what would be required for Fred to move through a space such as a doorway, hallway, walkway, or passageway. In part, doing so requires that he be able to fit the widest part of his body between the objects that form the outer boundaries of that space. This means that a primary constraint on the ability to walk through a doorway is neither an objective property of the environment—the width of the space—nor is it an objective property of Fred—his body width. Rather, it is *a relationship between* the two—the width of the space *relative to Fred's body width.*

So, at a certain ratio of doorway-width-to-Fred-width, it would no longer be possible for Fred to walk through that doorway. At values *below* this ratio, he might still be able to fit through the doorway—perhaps by turning his body sideways and shimmying or wriggling—just not by walking. At lower values still, Fred would be completely unable to fit through the doorway by *any* means—or at least not without *additional* means, like tools to widen the space (see Figure 14.10). In other words, different **modes of behavior**—passing through the doorway by different means—would be required at different values of this ratio.

Warren and Whang (1987) borrowed some terminology from physics and described the ratio of doorway-width-to-person-width at which walking through a doorway would be impossible (without turning the shoulders) as a **critical pi (π) value**. Then they conducted an experiment to determine what the critical π value for walking through a doorway is.

Modes of behavior the different means by which to act on a given affordance. Walking through, shimmying sideways, and wriggling are all different modes of behavior for acting on the affordance of pass-through-able.

Critical π (pi) value in the context of acting on affordances, the ratio between (some aspect of) action capabilities and (some aspect) of environmental properties at which a given behavior transitions from being impossible to being possible, or vice versa.

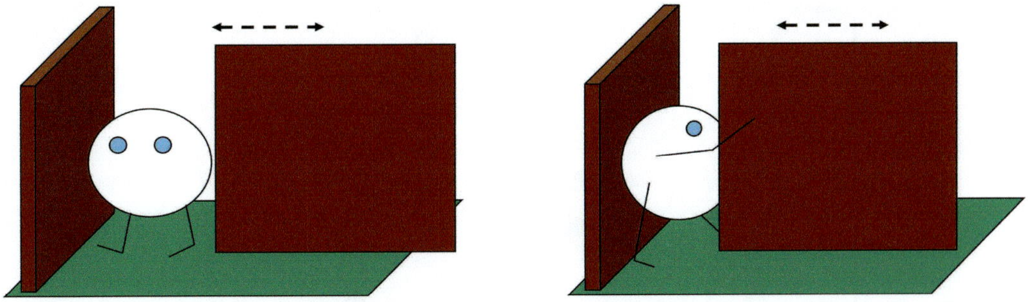

Figure 14.10 Left, when the gap is wide enough, it affords walking through for Fred. Right, when the gap is narrower, it only affords passing through by turning his body and squeezing through.

For most people (though probably not for Fred, who is sphere-shaped), the widest part of their bodies is their shoulders. So, the researchers recruited a group of people with wider shoulders—with an average shoulder width of 48.4 cm, approximately 19"—and a group of people with narrower shoulders—with an average shoulder width of 40.4 cm, approximately 16". This might not seem like a much of a difference in shoulder width, but trust us, it is. Each participant was asked to stand a few meters away from an adjustable doorway and then walk through the doorway. Then, the width of the doorway was adjusted, and they walked through it again. Sometimes the doorway started out really narrow (35 cm,[1] or 13.78") and was made wider on each subsequent trial. Other times, the doorway started out really wide (90 cm, or 35.43") and was made narrower on each subsequent trial.

The researchers then watched video recordings of each participant walking through each doorway width. They determined the doorway width at which the participant switched from walking through without turning their shoulders to walking through while turning their shoulders.

Not surprisingly, this value occurred at a wider doorway width for people with wide shoulders—53 cm, or approximately 21"—than for people with narrow shoulders—62 cm, or approximately 24.5". But here's the really cool part—the critical π value occurred at the *same ratio of doorway-width-to-shoulder-width for both groups* (approximately 1.3). This means that people with narrow shoulders were able to walk through narrower doorways than people with wider shoulders. However, the boundary between doorways that are "walk-through-able" without turning the shoulders and those that are not occurred at the same ratio of doorway-width-to-shoulder-width for *both groups.* Moreover, this ratio is little bit wider than shoulder width. Why not *exactly* shoulder width? Well, for one thing, if a person tried to walk straight through a doorway that was exactly as wide as their shoulders, that person would (probably) get stuck. For another, people generally sway from side to side a little bit while walking (more on this later).

In the next experiment, the researchers investigated whether they would find a similar pattern for the **perceived critical π value** for this behavior. As before, they recruited people with wide shoulders and

Perceived critical π (pi) value in the context of acting on affordances, the ratio between (some aspect of) action capabilities and (some aspect) of environmental properties at which a given behavior is perceived to transition from being impossible to being possible, or vice versa.

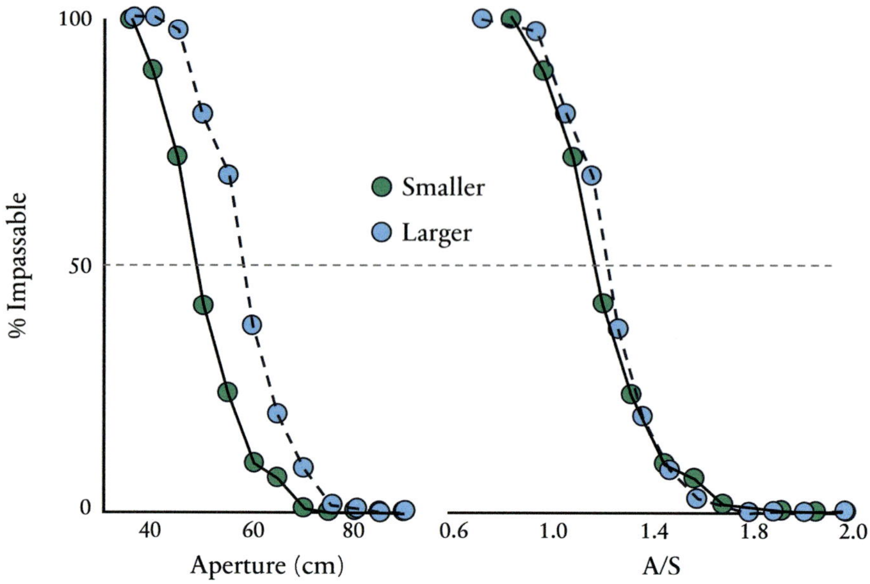

Figure 14.11 Using objective properties like doorway width results in different curves for people with different body sizes. Using a relational property like doorway width/shoulder width reveals a single curve. (Adapted from Warren & Whang, 1987.)

people with narrow shoulders. And as before, participants were asked to stand a few meters away from an adjustable doorway. But this time, rather than *walk* through the doorway, the participants simply reported *whether they would be able to do so*—that is, "whether they could walk straight through the opening without turning their shoulders". Then the width of the doorway was adjusted—again, from really wide to really narrow, or vice versa—and the participant made the same report again.

Let's look at a graph of the percentage of "no" responses at each doorway width for both groups of participants (see Figure 14.11). You can see that—for the narrowest doorway width (35 cm)—both groups of people said "no" on every trial. As width increased, both groups said "no" less often, but the curve for the people with wide shoulders is shifted to the right of the curve for the people with narrow shoulders. This means that, for most of the doorway widths, people with wider shoulders said "no" more often than those with narrower shoulders. Eventually, at the two widest doorway widths—90 and 95 cm (about 3')—both groups of people said "yes" on *every* trial.

The researchers then determined the *perceived critical π value* for each group of people—the doorway width at which each group switches their answer from "no" to "yes" or vice versa. This is the boundary between doorway widths that are perceived to be "walk-through-able" and those that are not. One way to figure this out is to determine the doorway width at which each group says "no" 50% of the time.

Notice where the horizontal line in the middle of each graph intersects the curve for each group—people with narrower shoulders or people with wider shoulders. At doorway widths narrower than this, people in that group are more likely to say "no" than "yes". At doorway widths wider than this, people in that group are more likely to say "yes" than "no". The perceptual boundary can then be derived by tracing down from each intersection point to the corresponding value on the horizontal axis. Just like the *critical π value,* the *perceived critical*

π value occurred at a wider doorway width for participants with wider shoulders—47 cm, or approximately 18.5"—than for those with narrower shoulders—56 cm, or approximately 22".

But look at what happens when we plot the data differently. Let's divide the doorway widths by the average shoulder width (doorway width/shoulder width) of each group of people and plot the percentage of "no" responses at each ratio. What does the graph look like now? The curves for the people with wide shoulders and people with narrow shoulders overlap almost completely! You can see that—for the smallest ratios of doorway width to shoulder width—both groups of people said "no" on every trial. As this ratio increased, both groups of people said "no" less often, and at the largest ratios, both groups said "yes" on every trial. The overlap of the curves shows that people with wide shoulders and those with narrow shoulders are perceiving whether the doorway is "walk-through-able" *in exactly the same way*—both groups do so relative to their shoulder width.

Warren and Whang then determined the *perceived critical π value* (this time in terms of doorway width/shoulder width ratio) for each group of people. And—just like the critical π value—the perceived critical π value occurred at the *same ratio of doorway-width-to-shoulder-width for both groups*. Moreover, this value—approximately 1.16—was not all that different from the critical π value—the ratio at which people transition between walking through with and without turning their shoulders—1.30. This means that people were perceiving whether they could walk through the doorway in relation to their shoulder width. In other words, they were sensitive to how the width of their bodies—and in particular, the width of the doorway *relative to the width of their bodies*—places limits on their ability to walk through doorways. Of course, other relationships also influence the ability to pass through openings like doorways, and people are sensitive to these as well. We'll explore these a little bit later on.

Socratic Question: Explain the pattern of results depicted in Figure 14.11 (right).

How Are Affordances Perceived?

As we have seen, the ecological approach requires that we rethink both what the relevant stimulation variables are and how those variables are used in the process of perceiving. In traditional approaches, it is taken for granted that the stimulation patterns are variables that have been useful in Newtonian mechanics and Euclidian geometry (e.g., light described as particles or rays traveling in a straight line) and that the animal passively receives this stimulation (e.g., these particles or rays enter the eye and strike the retina).

But these variables are (hopelessly) *ambiguously* related to environmental properties and require extensive fixing, interpreting, or processing to convey any meaning whatsoever to the animal. For example, the image on the retina is ambiguous about size and depth, and perceiving these properties requires the unconscious learning of cues and application of rules (see Chapter 9).

In the ecological approach, researchers instead seek stimulation variables that are *unambiguously (i.e., lawfully) related to relationships between animal and environment*. These variables *don't need to be processed* (see Chapter 13). They need only be *detected* to provide **information** about affordances (Wagman, 2020)—just like a particular pattern of dots moving relative

Information in the context of ecological psychology, patterns in structured energy that are lawfully related to relationships between animals and their environments (affordances).

to each other in a particular way provides information about a given event such as in the point-light displays described earlier.

These patterns are informative about affordances because substance and surface properties *lawfully structure* energy patterns such as reflected light (see Chapters 15 and 16). In other words, the properties of substances and surfaces that surround a given animal unambiguously structure the properties of the energy patterns that (also) surround that animal. These structured energy patterns are unique at every single point of observation at which an animal might encounter them. The point of observation that an animal occupies at any given moment and how this point of observation changes over time are determined by an animal's size and shape, its mass, strength, dexterity and skill, and how it moves itself through the world. Therefore, the structured energy patterns encountered at a given point of observation (and how these patterns change over time as the points of observation change over time) are informative about its *possible relationships to the surrounding substances and surfaces*. They are informative about *affordances*!

Perceiving Affordances for Fitting Through

We have alluded to the diversity of research on perceiving affordances for passing through openings that has occurred since the groundbreaking study by Warren and Whang (1987). In the next section, we cover this body of research in more detail. We could have just as easily covered the sizable body of research on perceiving affordances for other behaviors including reaching, stepping on or over, jumping, or throwing. The sad truth is that we just don't have the space to do this (but we invite the interested reader to read Chapter 5 of Blau & Wagman, 2022 or Wagman, 2020). The good news is that the general lessons to be learned—summed up in the following section headers—apply to perceiving affordances for these (and all other) behaviors.

Affordances for Fitting Through Depend on More Than Just Body Size

As we described earlier, Warren and Whang (1987) found that people are sensitive to how the width of their bodies—in particular, the width of the doorway *relative to the width of their bodies*—places limits on their ability to walk through openings like doorways. This makes sense, of course. Affordances are determined by the fit between an animal's action capabilities and environmental properties. And action capabilities are determined, in part, by an animal's size and shape.

But action capabilities are *also* determined by an animal's mass, strength, dexterity, and flexibility, as well as how it moves itself through the world. Therefore, these factors—in particular, how an animal moves and its ability to compress or contort its body—influence affordances for fitting through an opening. In particular, they influence affordances for both walking through openings and for *squeezing* or *wriggling* through particularly narrow openings. More recent research has investigated the extent to which people are sensitive to how these particular action capabilities influence affordances for these behaviors.

When Fred walks, he doesn't just move forward. He also sways from side to side and bobs up and down. So, his body takes up *more space* when he is walking (and even more when he is running) than when he is standing still. Accordingly, researchers have found that that people are sensitive to how the *size of their body in motion* (i.e., standing height + vertical bob or standing width + horizontal sway) affects affordances for walking through an opening

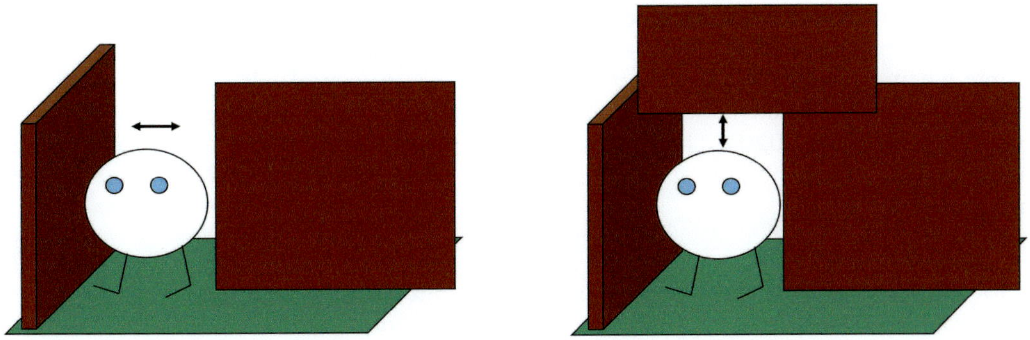

Figure 14.12 The size of the body in motion determines affordances for fitting through.

or under an obstacle. In fact, the size of the body in motion has more of an influence on perceiving affordances for performing these behaviors than does static body size alone (see Figure 14.12; Franchak et al., 2012).

When the width of an opening is narrower than Fred's shoulder width, he might not be able to *walk* through that opening. But he might still be able to *squeeze* or *wriggle* through the opening, depending on his ability to compress his body. Accordingly, people can perceive affordances for performing these behaviors as well. But since squeezing or wriggling an opening are both relatively complex and relatively unfamiliar behaviors, people are initially not quite as good at perceiving affordances for these behaviors as they are for perceiving affordances for other (less complex and more familiar) behaviors. However, they quickly get better at perceiving affordances for squeezing and wriggling when they repeatedly attempt—and repeatedly fail—to perform such behaviors (Franchak & Somoano, 2018).

Affordances for Fitting Through Depend on More Than Just the Body

Body size, how an animal moves through the world, and the ability to compress the body are all affected when an object is carried by or attached to the body. Think about something as mundane as when Fred carries groceries or something as unusual as when he wears medieval-style body armor. Or something not quite as mundane or quite as unusual as either of these, such as when his friend Andrew goes about his everyday activities in his wheelchair. In all of these cases, affordances for fitting through an opening—or for performing any other behavior, for that matter—are determined by a relationship between the **animal-plus-object** and the environment (see Vauclin et al., 2023).

Animal-plus-object system a system formed when an object is held by, worn, or attached to an animal. An animal-plus-object system has different action capabilities than the animal itself, so there are different affordances for the animal-plus-object system than for the animal-itself.

Just as people can perceive affordances for passing through an opening—by walking, squeezing, or wriggling—when *not* carrying or wearing an object, they can also perceive affordances for these behaviors when they *are* doing so (see Figure 14.13). In particular, they are sensitive to how affordances for walking or squeezing through openings change when carrying objects or wearing backpacks (Ishak et al., 2019), (non-medieval) protective equipment like shoulder pads, and when using (and learning to use) a wheelchair (Lucaites et al., 2020). They are also sensitive to how affordances for these behaviors change (slowly) over the course of pregnancy and then (less slowly) after delivery (Franchak & Adolph, 2014).

Socratic Question: How do studies on perceiving affordances for fitting through demonstrate that affordances "depend on more than just body size"?

Ability to Perceive Affordances for Fitting Through Develops Over the Lifespan

We foreshadowed this earlier, but affordances change over time. They change as the relationship between a person's action capabilities and the environment changes. These changes can occur quickly—like when a person puts on or takes off a backpack, high-heeled shoes, or medieval-style body armor (see Figure 14.13). But they can also occur more slowly—like when a person undergoes developmental changes in action capabilities over their lifespan (Adolph & Hoch, 2019; E. Gibson & Pick, 2000).

Of course, the most dramatic changes in action capabilities occur during the first few years of life. For example, in the first two or so years of a person's life, body weight quadruples and height doubles. Similarly, strength, balance, and coordination improve dramatically. And typically developing infants and toddlers will learn to roll over, sit, crawl, stand, walk, and so on. But these changes in action capabilities don't just stop as the person reaches adulthood.

Figure 14.13 People are able to perceive affordances for fitting through even when the size of their body changes.

Figure 14.14 Infants (left) are willing to squeeze through smaller gaps than younger adults (middle), who are in turn willing to squeeze through smaller openings than older adults (right).

They merely slow down. And then they speed up again in a different way as person reaches older adulthood. It's well-known that older adults just can't do (some) of the things that they used to do when they were younger adults (of course, they might not *want* to do many of those things anymore). Or maybe they *can* do the same things that they used to do, but just a bit more slowly.

And research has shown that people are sensitive to how developmental changes in body size or ability to move and compress the body affect affordances for fitting through (or squeezing or wriggling through) openings. For example, given their smaller body sizes, infants are willing to attempt to pass through smaller openings than are younger adults, and given their greater flexibility and balance, younger adults are willing to attempt to pass through smaller openings than are older adults (see Figure 14.14; Comalli et al., 2013).

People can Perceive Social Affordances for Fitting Through

The world is not a solitary place. Or, at least, it is not a solitary place very often. There are lots (billions!) of other people out there. And so, people often perform all sorts of behaviors—reaching, stepping on or over, jumping, throwing, and yes, even walking through openings—in the context of other people. Sometimes people perform these behaviors *with* other people—like when Fred and his friend Louie are walking side by side as they approach a doorway—and other times, people perform behaviors *with respect to* other people—like when Fred and Louie are both walking through a small crowd of people.

Consider the first case: Fred and Louie walking side by side as they approach a doorway (see Figure 14.15). Unless the doorway is really wide, they won't be able to fit through it if they keep walking side by side. They could *definitely* fit through it if they walked through one

Figure 14.15 Fred and Louie can perceive affordances for walking through a doorway together.

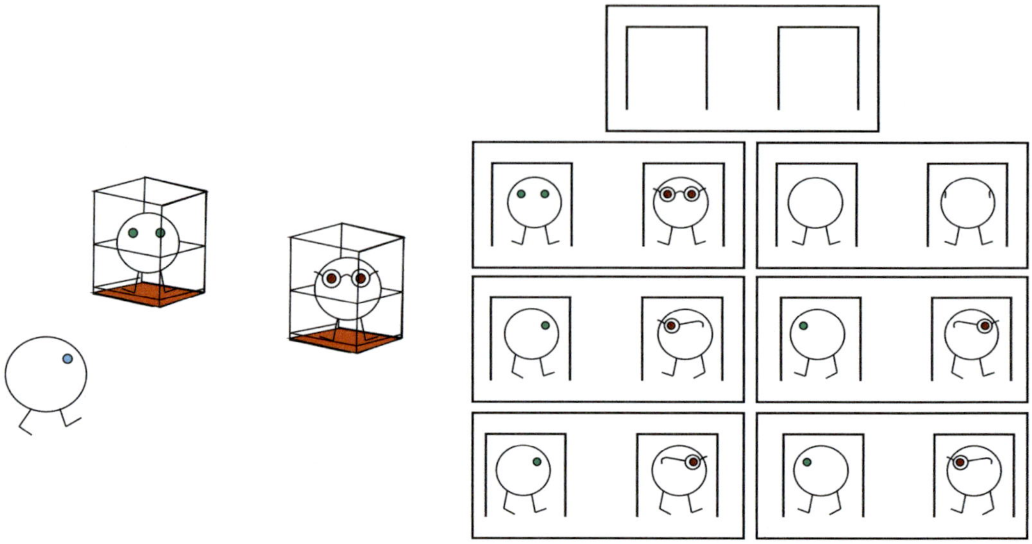

Figure 14.16 In an experiment by Tomono and colleagues (2019), participants were asked to walk between two box-shaped frames (left). In one condition, the frames were empty (right, top). In the other conditions, two people stood in the fames in one of six configurations (right).

at a time. But they also *might* be able to fit through at the same time if they each turned their shoulders and squished together just a little bit. This would mean giving up some of the space each of them would ordinarily have if they were walking through doorway one at a time. And this is exactly what happens when people walk through a doorway with another person.

As we have already seen, when people walk through a doorway by themselves, the transition between walking through with and without turning the shoulders occurs when the doorway is approximately 1.30 times their shoulder width. But when they walk through a doorway together with another person, this transition occurs when the doorway is approximately 1.15 times the combined shoulder widths of both people (Davis et al., 2010)

Now consider the second case: Fred walking through a small crowd of people. Walking between people is very different than walking between inanimate objects. If Fred were to move too close to another person it might be a little awkward at best, rude or even threatening at worst. If Fred were to move too close to an inanimate object, it wouldn't be awkward, rude, or threatening at all. And research has shown that people are sensitive to these differences.

When a person is walking between two other people who are facing one another (as they would be if they were having a conversation), the transition between walking through with and without turning the shoulders occurs when the space between the people is 1.70 times that person's shoulder width (see Figure 14.16; Tomono et al., 2019). The fact that this is much larger than the more typical ratio of 1.30 shows that person walking is trying to avoid getting too close to either of the other people as they pass between them.

People Can Hear and Feel Affordances for Fitting Through

In the ecological approach, people perceive affordances by detecting lawfully structured energy patterns at given point of observation. What makes something lawful is that it occurs the same way regardless of circumstance (see Chapter 8). For example, gravitational laws apply regardless

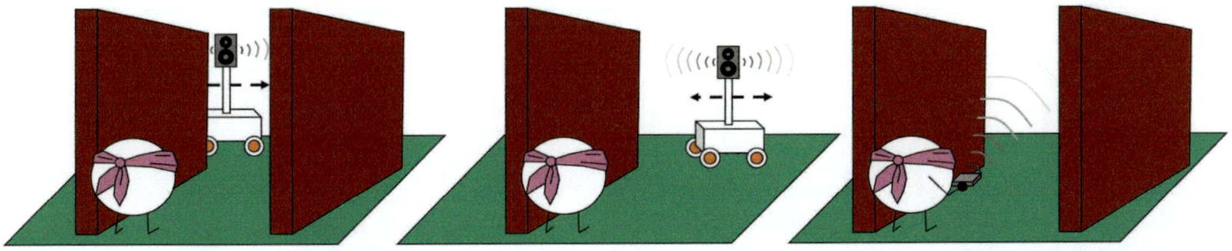

Figure 14.17 Left, people can hear an opening when the sound is projected through it. Middle, people can hear an opening when the sound is one of the sides of the opening. Right, people can feel an opening when they use an "enactive torch", a device that converts reflected light to vibrations.

of where Fred is—at his house, at Claudia's house, outdoors, and even on the moon.[2] In the same way, substance and surface properties lawfully structure *all* of the various energy patterns that surround a given animal—regardless of the specific form of that energy. Fred is not only surrounded by light, but also by sound (and forces and even odors). All of these energy patterns are lawfully structured by substance and surface properties. This means that people ought to be able to *hear* or *feel* whether they can fit through a given opening. And *they can* (see Figure 14.17).

People can *hear* whether an opening affords passing through by listening to sounds being projected *through* that opening (Gordon & Rosenblum, 2004)—that is, when the surfaces that form the opening block some of the sound from coming through the opening. They can also do so by listening to sound being produced by the objects that *form* the opening—that is, when sounds are played through speakers that are placed on the outer edges of that opening (Riehm et al., 2019). People can also *feel* whether an opening affords passing through by exploring that opening with a handheld rod. And they can do so when exploring that opening with an "enactive torch"—a handheld device that emits infrared light and converts distance information into vibrations that are felt on the wrist (Favela et al., 2018).

Other Animals can Perceive Affordances for Fitting Through

Lawfully structured energy patterns need only be detected—and not processed—to provide information about affordances. This means that *all sorts of animals* ought to be able to perceive affordances so long as they are capable of detecting the structure in a given energy pattern that provides information about those affordances. And *they can*.

Dogs choose whether and how to pass through an opening based on the relationship between the size of that opening and their body size (Horowitz et al., 2021). Frogs choose whether and how to jump through openings based on the relationship between the width of that opening and their body shape. In particular, they make these choices based on the shape that their body *will be* when they are in mid-jump (flat with legs splayed out), rather than the shape that their body is when sitting and viewing the opening (rounded with legs tucked under; Ingle, 1973). Hermit crabs choose whether and how to pass through narrow openings depending on the relationship between the size of the opening and the size of their shells. And they make different choices when an artificial extension is glued to their shell (Sonoda et al., 2012).

Socratic Question: What does the fact that other animals (such dogs, frogs, and hermit crabs) can perceive affordances for fitting through suggest about how affordances are perceived?

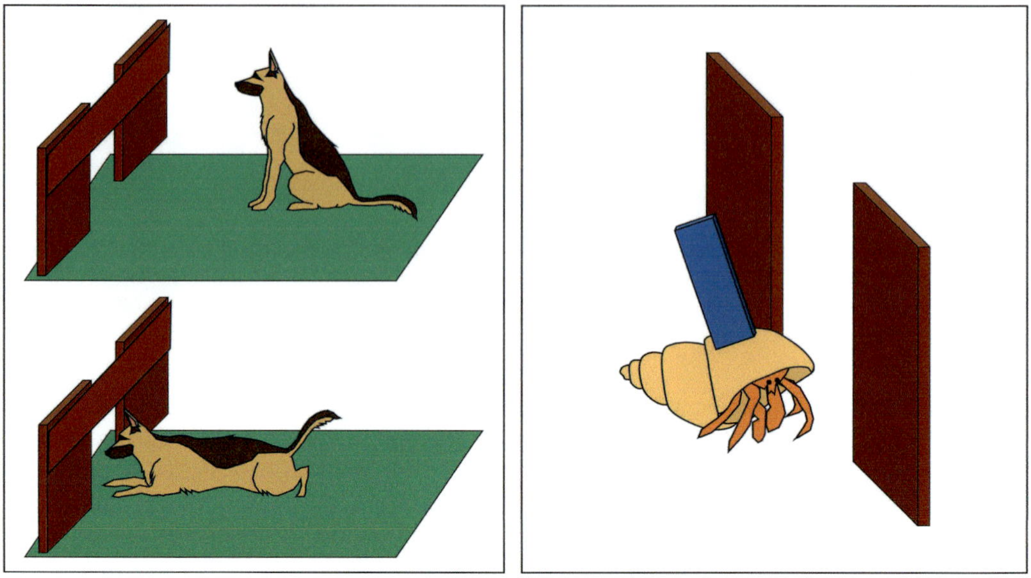

Figure 14.18 Dogs can perceive affordances for fitting through an opening, and hermit crabs can do so even when an artificial extension has been glued on to their shell.

Summary

As we have seen, the ecological approach requires a fundamental rethinking of what it is that animals perceive and act on. Two fundamental categories of such things are *events* and *affordances*. Ecological events are changes to the environment or the animal's relationship to it. Perceiving events requires being sensitive to what is changing relative to what is not changing. We have seen that people (and in some cases, other kinds of animals) can perceive a variety of events in real life, in films, and even in scaled-down displays (such as point-light displays).

But animals must not only be able to perceive what is happening in the present moment; they must also be able to perceive what could (and what will) happen at some point in the future. And we have seen that people (and other animals, too) can perceive whether, when, and how they could perform a given behavior. That is, they can perceive affordances—possibilities for behavior given the fit between action capabilities and environmental properties.

Perceiving affordances requires being sensitive to the lawfully structured energy patterns at a given point of observation. We have seen that people (and other animals) can use such energy patterns to perceive affordances for lots of different behaviors under lots of different circumstances.

Notes

1 For comparison's sake, a typical doorway width in a US home is 81 cm (approximately 32").
2 But, because the moon is much (much) less massive than the Earth, on the moon, objects fall at only 1.62 m/s^2 (compared to 9.8 m/s^2 on Earth).

15 Ecological Optics and Seeing

As we have discussed, the traditional approaches and the ecological approach start with different assumptions. These different assumptions lead to asking different sets of questions that generate very different sets of answers about what the stimulation patterns of relevance are and how the process of perceiving works.

In traditional approaches, it is assumed that the best way to describe (1) the properties to be perceived and (2) the stimulation variables by which such properties are perceived is by using concepts borrowed from Newtonian physics and Euclidian geometry (see Part II). In the context of visual perception, the properties of the world to be perceived are ones like height, width, depth, shape, motion, and color, among others. And the light that strikes (and copies) these properties consists of photons traveling in a straight line from light source to object and then from object to retina. The retina passively receives this light when it is struck by the photons the same way that the 8-ball passively receives forces when it is struck by the cue ball (see Chapter 1).

Of course, given that the retinal image is *ambiguously related* to the properties of the world, the retinal image must be "fixed" or "interpreted" by some process to generate a mental representation that allows the animal to visually perceive those properties (again, see Part II). Consequently, one way to describe the fundamental question to be answered in the traditional approaches to visual perception is: how does light get into and fixed by the brain? (See Figure 15.1.)

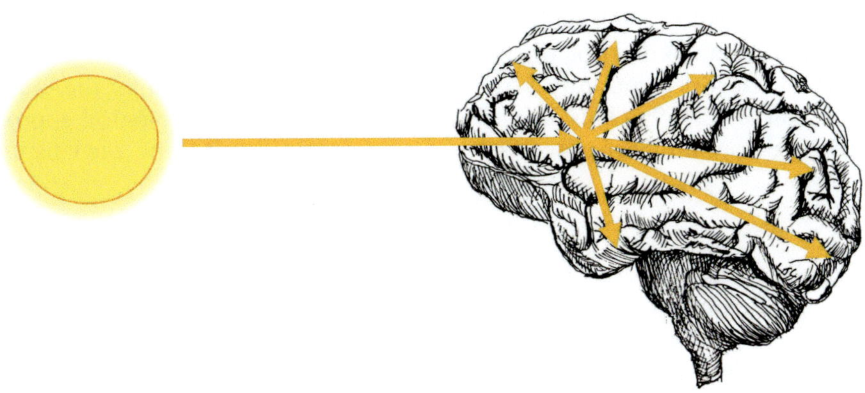

Figure 15.1 One way to describe the fundamental question in traditional approaches to visual perception is: how does light get into and fixed by the brain?

DOI: 10.4324/9781032690964-18

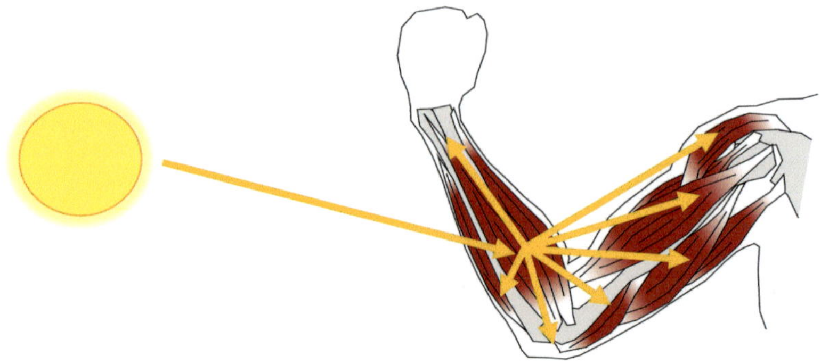

Figure 15.2 One way to describe the fundamental question in ecological approaches to visual perception is: how does light get into the muscle?

In contrast, in the ecological approach, the description of the properties to be perceived and the stimulation variables by which such properties are perceived are not borrowed from anywhere. Rather, this description is developed for the sole purpose of understanding how people and other animals perform everyday behaviors. As we described in the two previous chapters, this animal-dependent description of the world is known as ecological physics and ecological geometry (see Chapters 13 and 14).

Remember that the goal of ecological physics and ecological geometry is to describe the world in which animals live and behave—the world that is perceived and acted on by animals. And to a large extent, the world that is perceived and acted on by animals consists of the *various surfaces that surround that animal.* Wherever Fred goes, he is completely surrounded by surfaces. Let's assume that he is sitting in the comfiest chair he owns reading this book. There are surfaces *everywhere*—surfaces of the chair, of the book, of the floor, of the walls, and so on. And his relationship to those surfaces determines the affordances that exist for him (see Chapter 14).

As we will see, the light that reflects from those surfaces is lawfully (unambiguously) structured by those surfaces. And the structured light that an animal encounters at *a given point of observation* is unambiguously related to the animal's *relationship to* those substances and surfaces. In other words, the structured light that an animal actively encounters at a given point of observation is informative about affordances for that animal (see Chapter 14)! Consequently, one way to describe the fundamental question to be answered in the ecological approach to visual perception is: how does light get into and used by the muscles (see Figure 15.2; Turvey, 2019)? This is another example of how the ecological approach asks entirely new questions rather than seeking new answers to old questions (see Chapter 13).

Ecological Optics

Ecological optics a description of the properties of the light at the scale of the relationship between animals and their environments; in particular, a description of how light is affected by the surfaces and substances that surround an animal.

As we have discussed, the description of what exists to be perceived and acted on by animals is known as ecological physics and ecological geometry. The description of the *light* that animals use to perceive and act is known as **ecological optics**. There are three fundamental points to make

Figure 15.3 Left, radiant light is unstructured and uniform. Right, when looking at radiant light (like when looking directly into a spotlight), all that is seen is brightness.

about ecological optics. The first one is that animals—those that live above ground like Fred, anyway—are surrounded by light. They are *immersed* in light in the same way that fish or other animals that live in the ocean are immersed in water.

The second point is that the light that surrounds animals is *not uniform*. It differs in different directions. Wherever Fred happens to be, the light in front of him is different than the light behind him. And the light above him is different than the light below him. And so on. The third point is that the differences in the light that surrounds an animal do not come from the light itself. *Wait. What?* Instead, they come from the *surfaces that surround the animal*. When light reflects from these surfaces, it becomes *structured by* those surfaces. In other words, the surfaces that surround Fred unambiguously (lawfully) structure the light that surrounds him. This is the fundamental premise of ecological optics (Mace, 2020).

Let's back up a bit and go through each of these three points slowly and carefully. Let's again assume that Fred is sitting in the comfiest chair that he owns reading this book. There is a light source—say, a bright light bulb. The light bulb—like any light source—**radiates light.** And the light radiating from that bulb is both *unstructured and uniform* (see Figure 15.3, left)

> **Radiant light** the unstructured and uniform light produced by a light source.

Let's take these terms at a time. First, unstructured. The light coming from a light source—such as the sun or a light bulb—is pure brightness (see Figure 15.3, *left*). When Fred was performing in an off-Broadway production of *From Cockney to Yankee*, he made the mistake of looking directly into the spotlight that was shining on him. He saw nothing but brightness. It was *blindingly bright*, in the same way that a completely dark room is blindingly dark (see Figure 15.3, *right*).

Second, uniform. The light radiating from a light source is *equally unstructured* in all directions. The light radiating from one part of the light bulb is no different from the light radiating from any other part of light bulb. When Fred made the mistake of staring directly

Box 15.1 Light Is Invisible

Although it is going to seem radical to say so, particularly given lengthy discussions over the first few chapters of this book (see Chapters 2–4), we are now going to argue—as many ecological theorists have—that light, as such, is invisible. In other words, we never see light. Instead, we see illuminated surfaces (Gibson, 1979/2015).

Argument 1: Unstructured Light is Not Perceived

A few years ago, one of your authors took her four-year-old son to the movies; after the movie began, he looked up at the space between the projector and the screen and asked, "Where's the movie?" His question is simultaneously naïve and sophisticated. While the projector at the rear of the theater is visible, and the image on the screen opposite the projector is also visible, the space between the two appears dark. The light from the projector is streaming through that space, but it is not visible to four-year-old boys (or Fred or anyone else for that matter). In everyday circumstances, three things are necessary for seeing—a light source, the light itself, and a surface that reflects the light. But only two of these—the light source and the surface—are visible. The light itself is not, even though it completely fills the space between the other two. In fact, if you were to look directly into the beam of light coming from the movie projector—or a spotlight, like Fred—you would see *only* the light source.

Here is another example, borrowed from Carello and Turvey (2020)—imagine two astronauts in outer space. Space is *absolutely filled* with light—there are trillions of stars in addition to our own (the sun), producing light which travels in all directions through space until it hits an object. In other words, the two astronauts are *swimming* in a sea of light that surrounds them in all directions. But space appears dark. It is only when the astronauts look at a surface—each other, their spacecraft, the Earth, or the moon, for example—that they are able to see anything at all. They can see the *source* of the light (the stars) and the *surfaces* the light reflects off of (each other, their spacecraft, the Earth, or the moon) but not the light itself. And if they were to stare directly at a star, they see *only* the light source.

If we were able to see light *as such,* then the light above the four-year-old in the theater (or the light the astronauts are swimming in) should be visible to those observers. But it is not. As Carello and Turvey (2020) put it, "with regard to the triad of *that which illuminates, that which is illuminated,* and *illumination as such* . . . they did not see *illumination as such*" (p. 60).

Argument 2: Stimulation Does Not Necessarily Lead to Perception

No one is making the argument that light is not necessary for visual perception. This is obviously false. After all, you can't see a damn thing in the dark![1] The argument being made is that light *in and of itself* is not what is *perceived.* There is a difference between the response of rod and cone cells and the perceptual experience of the organism. It is entirely possible for the cells of the retina to be maximally stimulated and for the organism to see nothing at all.

The last time Fred went sailing, he did so in a dense fog. There was enough light coming through the fog that he was able to see the deck of the boat beneath his feet—sort of, anyway. However, the only thing that he could see when he looked out across the water was homogenous whiteness. He was not able see the shore, the water, anything! In that case, his retinas were stimulated—maybe even maximally so—but he was unable to perceive much of anything. Seeing requires not just light, but structured light. It turns out that you can't see a damn thing in the bright, either![2]

The story of Fred in the fog is an example of a Metzger's (1930) *Ganzfeld,*[3] a state of unstructured uniform stimulation. The same effect can be produced by cutting a ping pong ball in half (like we asked you to do in Chapter 9) and attaching it in front of the eye—the illumination becomes uniform and perception becomes impossible. To put it plainly, as we did in Chapter 13: *the medium is not the message*. Just because the rods and cones are stimulated by light does not mean that what the organism attends to is the light *as such*.

into the spotlight, the light was equally bright in all directions. Even when he leaned his head a little bit to the left or the right, there *still* weren't any differences in any direction. Looking into complete brightness is just as disorienting as looking into complete darkness!

Now imagine that Fred is no longer onstage and is—once again—back in his comfy chair reading this book. After a while, he gets bored of reading it (perish the thought!) and while standing up to stretch, he turns around and looks at the wall behind him. Now the light that reaches him (and his visual system) is no longer coming directly from the light source. Instead, it is coming *indirectly from the light source* because it is reflecting off of the wall—and other surfaces in the room—and *then* reaching him (and his visual system). After all, the light source is now *behind* him. He can no longer see it or the light radiating from it. The wall is in front of him. He can see the wall—but only because of the light reflecting from it.

Let's pause here to make a point that is so obvious that it is easy to overlook. Almost all of the time, animals see the things that surround them because of the light that *reflects from* those things, not the light that is *produced by* those things.[4] In other words, the light that is important for visually perceiving surrounding surfaces is **reflected (or ambient) light**, not radiant light (see Figure 15.4). The reason that this is such an important point is that when light strikes a surface, it becomes *structured by* that surface. And not in a uniform way. Instead, there are differences in the structured light in different directions. Let's now discuss how this occurs.

Ambient light the differentiated and structured light that reflects from surfaces and surrounds an animal.

When the light radiating from a light source strikes a surface, there are only a few things that can happen to it. In most cases, some of the light is absorbed by that surface, and some of the light is reflected by that surface. How much of the light is absorbed and how much is reflected is lawfully related to the properties of that surface. More light will be reflected if a surface is wet than if it is dry[5] or if it is glossy, rather than dull. How the light is reflected is *also* lawfully related

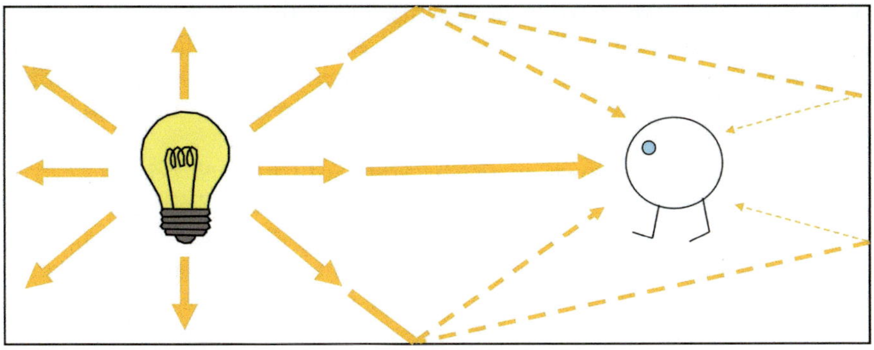

Figure 15.4 Ambient light encountered at a point of observation is both differentiated and structured.

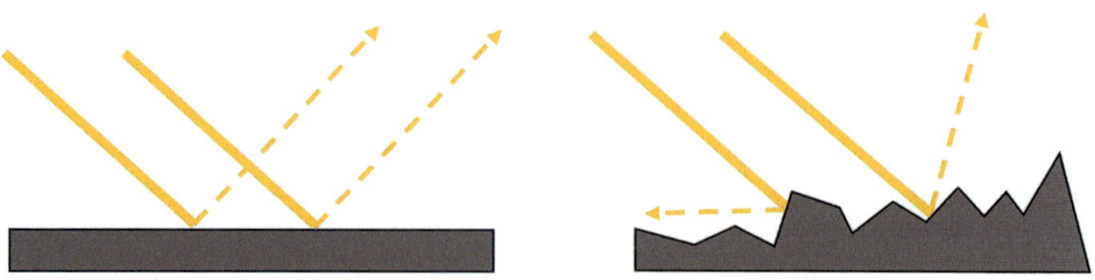

Figure 15.5 Differences in surface properties give reflected light optical texture.

Optical texture the patterns created when surrounding substances and surfaces lawfully structure reflected light.

to the properties of that surface. Light will be scattered more if a surface is bumpy than if it is smooth. And so, as we previewed in Chapters 2 and 3, the light reflecting from a surface will have differences in different directions depending on the properties of that surface (see Figure 2.12). These differences give reflected light structure—that is, they create **optical texture**. And this structure is lawfully related to the properties of the surface (see Figure 15.5).

But of course, there's more to the story than this. In all likelihood, the light that radiates from a light source and reflects off of a given surface will then reflect off of *another surface*. And so on. And so on. So, some of the light that reaches Fred while he is looking at the wall will be light that radiates from the light bulb and reflects from the wall. This light will be lawfully structured by the properties of the wall.

But some of the light that radiates from the light bulb and reflects off of the wall will then reflect off of the floor. This light will be lawfully structured by the properties of the wall *and* the properties of the floor. And of course, some of the light that reflects off the floor will reflect off other surfaces in the room. Soon—at the speed of light, in fact!—the room is filled with light reflecting from light source to surface to surface to surface, continuously filling the room with multiply reflected—and multiply structured—light. Since the light that strikes a given surface is lawfully structured by properties of that surface, the reflected light that fills the room is structured in ways that are lawfully related to the *entire set* of surfaces in that room.

Let's go back to Fred facing the wall in his house—not very exciting, we know. In this location, facing this direction, he will encounter a small portion of the structured light that fills the room. Nonetheless, the portion of structured light that he encounters will consist of light reflected from—and structured by—many sources. Most of the light that he encounters will reflect from the wall immediately after being radiated by the light source. But some of the structured light that he encounters will reflect from the wall only after being reflected by the floor, or vice versa.

Now imagine Fred looking down at his checkerboard-patterned floor instead of at the wall—still not very exciting, we know. Now, he will encounter a *different* pattern of structured light (see Figure 15.6). In particular, most of the light that he encounters will reflect from the floor immediately after radiating from the light source. Some of the light that he encounters will reflect from the floor only after being reflected by the wall, or vice versa.

But wait, there's more. Imagine that Fred faces the wall and then looks to his left or to his right—at least a little more exciting, right? In either case, he will encounter yet another different pattern of structured light. In other words, the pattern of structured light differs in

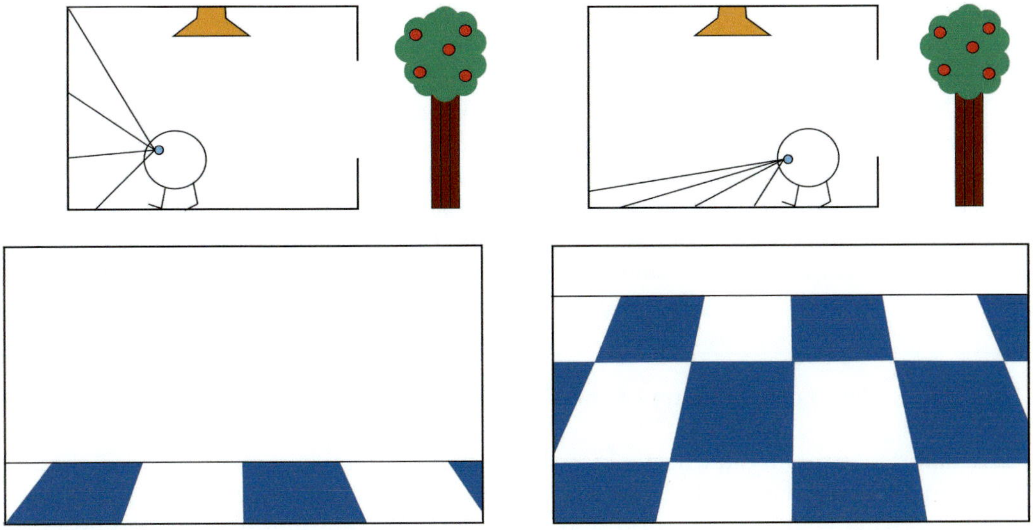

Figure 15.6 Top, Fred's actions. Bottom, his view during those actions The pattern of structured light encountered will be different when he looks at the wall (left) than when he looks at the floor (right).

different directions. And these differences emerge because of differences in how light reflects to that location from the various surfaces in that room.

> Socratic Question: What is the difference between radiant light and ambient light? What is the difference between "seeing light" and "seeing illuminated surfaces"?

The Ambient Optic Array

> **Ambient optic array** the structured light available at a given point of observation (at a location that an animal might be).

In fact, the pattern of structured light at *every location in the room that Fred could occupy* is unique (meaning one of a kind). At every possible point of observation, there is a unique distribution of structured light—a unique set of differences in different directions. This is another fundamental premise of ecological optics.

The structured light that fills the room and that is unique at every location that Fred (or any other animal) might occupy is called the **ambient** (meaning "surrounding") **optic** (meaning "light") **array** (meaning "distribution"). Let's stop for a minute (or maybe more) to think about what this means.

In the traditional approaches, the light that is important for seeing is the light that enters the eye and forms the retinal image—an ambiguous copy or representation of the properties of the world made inside of the animal (see Chapters 2 and 3). But the ambient optic array is *none of these things.* First, it is not an image, a copy, or a representation. An image is a depiction. A copy is a reproduction. A representation is a symbolic depiction. The ambient optic array *does not copy or depict depict anything, symbolically or otherwise.* Second, it is not ambiguous. On the contrary, the ambient optic array is unambiguously structured by the surfaces that surround the animal. The laws of optics make it so. And third, the ambient optic array is not inside of the animal. In fact, the animal is inside of it! It surrounds the animal just as the surfaces that structure it do.

Given all of this, seeing is not a matter of fixing the ambiguous representation of the surfaces on the retinal image. Instead, it is a matter of *actively encountering* the *unambiguous structure* in the ambient optic array. This requires a *visual system*, but it does not require a particular *type* of visual system (see Box 15.2 and Box 15.3). And as we'll see later, this structure is always detected at given a point of observation—that's where the animal is, after all. The structure at this point of observation provides information about the relations between the surrounding surfaces and the animal. It provides information about affordances! This is how we begin to answer the question of how the light gets into and used by the muscles!

Box 15.2 The Legs Are Part of the Visual System. Wait . . . What?

It is important to point out what we mean by the visual system. In traditional approaches, the visual system consists of the anatomical components that serve the animal in passively receiving light as stimulation, and then translating, transmitting, and processing the stimulation received by the retina. In a chambered eye, these components include the lens, the retina, the optic nerve, and the visual cortex, among others (see Chapters 2 and 3). Moreover, the set of components that define the visual system do not (and cannot) ever change. The set of components is what it is. Full stop.

In the ecological approach, however, the visual system is defined *functionally*. It consists of components that serve the animal in *exploring the structure in the optic array*. Seeing is an *activity*. It is something you do, not something that happens to you or inside of you. And seeing involves looking around. And not just by moving your eyes, but by moving your entire head. Doing so allows you to explore structure in the optic array. Does this mean that your *head and neck* are part of your visual system? Yes, yes, it does.

But if this surprises you, do we have news for you! You also look around by moving *your entire body* from place to place. What would you do if you wanted to see something across the room a little better? You might lean forward a little if it wasn't too far away, but you might also just walk over there. Doing these things also allows you to explore structure in the optic array. This makes your *torso and legs* part of the visual system, too. But that's not all. You also look around (in a manner of speaking) with your hands. What would you do if you wanted to see a small nearby object more closely? You might pick it up and manipulate it with your hands. This makes your *hands* part of the visual system too.

Unlike the components of your sense organs, the components of your visual system can change depending on what you are doing. Your legs are not really part of your visual system when you are lying flat on your back, but they are when you are standing up. And if that's not surprising enough, then consider that *inanimate objects* can also be (or become) part of the visual system—at least temporarily. Objects like glasses, a sun hat, or a telescope *also* allow you to explore structure in the optic array, making them part of the visual system—at least while you are using them for this purpose. Similarly, transportation devices such as cars, bicycles, roller skates, and assistive mobility devices like wheelchairs, walkers, and canes can also become part of the visual system for the same reasons.

Socratic Question: How is the ambient optic array different than the retinal image? How can the head, hand, legs, and objects like a hat be considered part of the visual system?

Information About Surfaces

So now, Fred gets bored of staring at the wall (who can blame him?!), and he sits back down in his comfy chair. There is a table in front of him and a window on the opposite wall through which he can see part of a tree (see Figure 15.7)—so much more interesting than the empty wall! The reflected light that he encounters at this point of observation is unambiguously structured by the properties of the surfaces that surround him—including the table, the wall, the window frame, and the tree. In this way, the structured light that he encounters at this point of observation provides information about the properties of these surfaces—including what those surfaces are like, how they are oriented, and how they are situated among other surfaces.

A *bumpy* surface—like the tree trunk—will structure light differently than a *smooth* surface—like the floor. A *vertical* surface—like the wall—will structure light differently than a *horizontal* surface—like the top of the table. A *continuous* surface—like the wall—will structure light differently than *a gap between two surfaces*—like the frame around the window. A relatively *nearby* surface—like the portion of the floor under his feet—will structure light differently than a relatively faraway surface—like the portion of the floor on the other side of room.

Something very particular happens if a nearby surface—like one of the legs of the table—is *between* Fred and a surface that is farther away—like the wall. In this case, some of the structured light reflecting from the farther away surface—some of the optical texture—will be blocked by the nearby surface and will not reach his point of observation (see Figure 15.8).

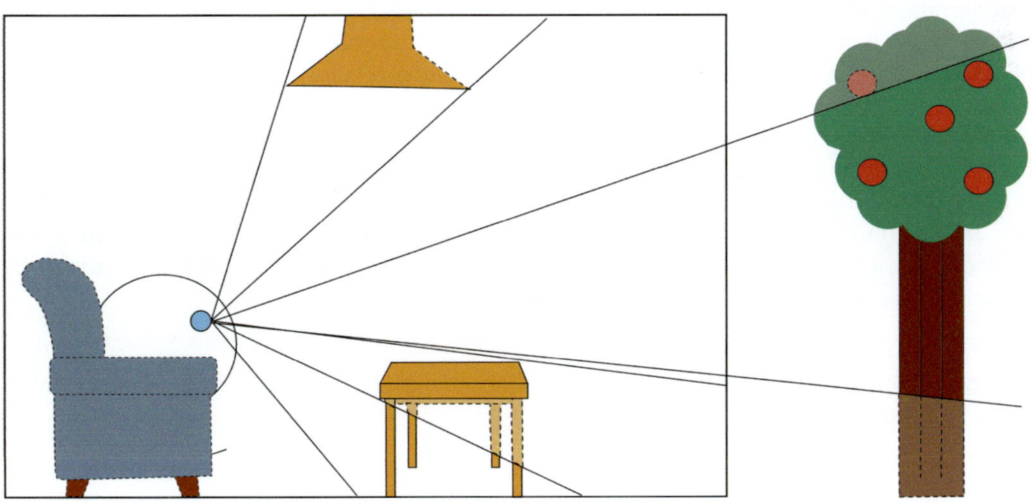

Figure 15.7 The structured light at Fred's point of observation is informative about the layout of surfaces.

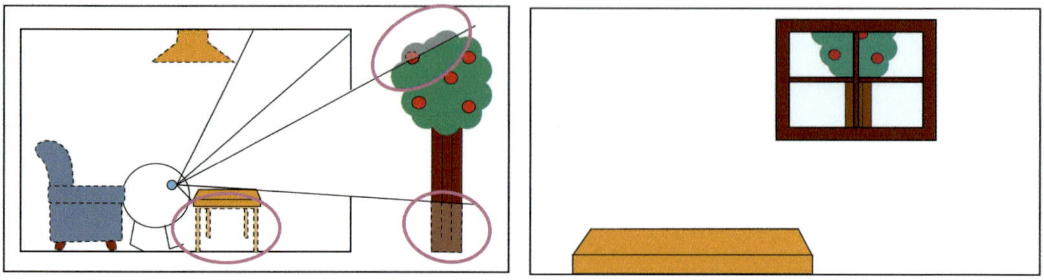

Figure 15.8 Left, from Fred's perspective, several surfaces (circled) are occluded. Right, his view (notice the occluded surfaces are not available at his point of observation). When one surface occludes another, there is a change in the structured reflected light at the outer edges of the occluding object.

The more technical way to put this is that the nearby surface will *occlude* the structured light reflected from (part of) the farther away surface (Gibson, 1979/2015; Heft, 2020). This creates a change in the structured reflected light at the outer edges—the "occluding edges"—of the nearby object. Such differences provide information about how the surfaces of these two objects are situated with respect to one another—in other words, the occlud*ing* surface is between Fred and the occlud*ed* surface.

> **Occlusion** the pattern in structured light that occurs when one surface is situated (the occluding surface) or moves in front of another surface (the occluded surface).

Occlusion might seem similar—or even identical—to one of the traditional approach's cues to depth that we discussed in Chapter 9—namely, superposition. However, the two are quite different. In the traditional approach, superposition refers to a relationship between *images on the retina*. This relationship provides cues about the relative depth of the surfaces represented in those images. In the ecological approach, occlusion refers to a pattern in structured reflected light that is lawfully related to the *relationship between two surfaces.* Given this lawful relationship—and unlike superposition—occlusion provides unambiguous information about the relative position of surrounding surfaces.

So, let's sum up. In the ecological approach, the relevant stimulation pattern is the structured light actively encountered by an animal, not the unstructured light passively received by the eye and projected on to the retina. Animals are surrounded by surfaces. Consequently, they are surrounded by the structured light reflecting from those surfaces, known as the ambient optic array. And the portion of structured light encountered is informative about the layout of those surrounding surfaces.

> Socratic Question: How is the ecological phenomenon of occlusion different than the cue of superposition?

Perception of Depth vs. Perceiving Surface Layout

With these basics of ecological optics in mind, we are ready to reconsider perception of depth. Perception of "depth" across "space" is one of the fundamental problems—perhaps

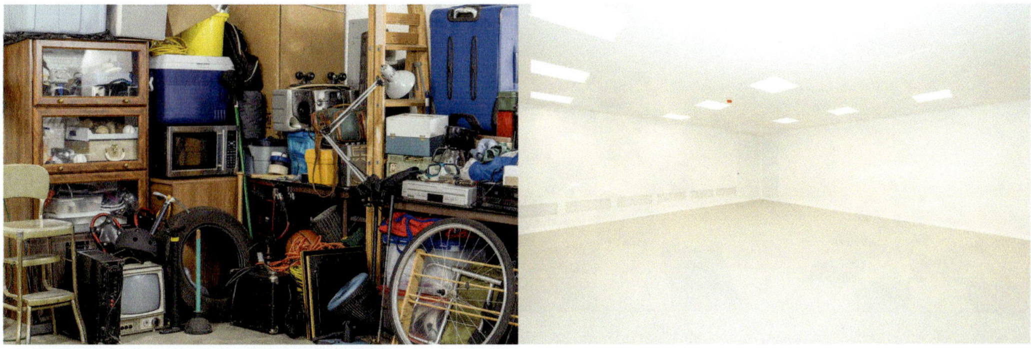

Figure 15.9 Left, Fred's attic has many surfaces and objects, but almost no space. Right, Fred's basement has a lot of space, but almost no surfaces or objects.

the fundamental problem—of the traditional approach to visual perception (see Chapter 9). But from the ecological perspective, this is a completely *unsolvable* problem. And here's why: both depth and space are abstract, geometrical concepts. They exist only *in the absence of objects.* Depth and space are the invisible expanses between objects. These terms are used to describe the imaginary "container" in which objects exist—not the objects themselves.

To see what we mean, have a look in Fred's attic. He uses it as a gigantic storage closet so it is *completely full* of objects—packed from wall to wall and floor to ceiling. Lots of objects, but no depth or space (see Figure 15.9, *left*). Now, have a look in Fred's completely empty basement. Lots of depth and lots of space, but no objects (see Figure 15.9, *right*). So, the question of how *depth* is perceived across *space* is really a question about how *empty space* is perceived (Carello & Turvey, 2020). That truly is an unsolvable problem!

Unsolvable problems just like this one show up all the time when concepts that are imported from Newtonian physics and Euclidean geometry are used to understand how animals perceive and act when performing everyday behaviors (see Chapters 13 and 14). When we instead use concepts from *ecological geometry* and *ecological physics* to understand how animals perceive and act when doing so, we are no longer faced with the unsolvable problem of how depth is perceived across space. Instead, we are faced with the solvable (but still challenging) problem of how animals perceive distances across surfaces—or more generally, *how animals perceive surface layout.*

Once again, imagine that Fred is looking down at his checkerboard-patterned floor. As he does so, he will encounter a particular pattern of structured light (see Figure 15.10, *left*). In particular, the light reflecting from the portion of the floor right under his feet will be more densely structured—it will have a more densely packed optical texture—than the light reflecting from portions of the floor that are farther away. This is information that the surface is oriented horizontally and extends away from him—just like a floor should.

Now imagine that he is standing at the bottom of a checkerboard-patterned *wheelchair ramp* that he installed at his front door for when his friend Andrew visits (see Figure 15.10, *center*). It will still be the case that the light reflecting from the portion of the ramp closest to his feet will be more densely structured than the light reflecting from portions of the ramp that are farther away. However, these changes will occur *more slowly* across the surface of the (inclined) ramp than across the surface of the (flat) floor. This is information that the ramp slopes *up*—just like a ramp should.

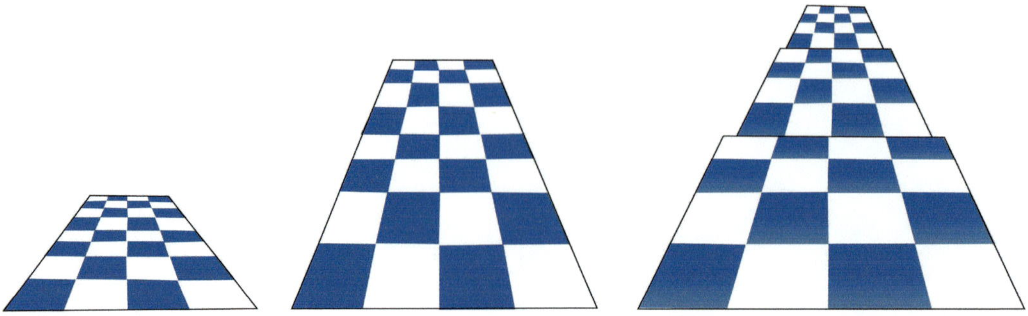

Figure 15.10 Optical structure differs based on surface layout: Left, a horizontal surface, and middle, an inclined surface each create a unique pattern of systematic differences in optical structure. Right, drop-offs between surfaces (like stairs) create dramatic differences in optical structure.

Finally, imagine that he is standing at the top of several steps—with the same checkerboard pattern (see Figure 15.10, *right*). Now, when he looks down at the steps, he will encounter yet another pattern of structured light. The structured light reflecting from the first step will be partially occluded by the floor. And the structured light reflecting from the second step will be partially occluded by the first step. This is information that there are vertical separations between these surfaces—just like steps should have.

Socratic Question: How does the ecological approach redescribe the problem of how depth is perceived across space?

Reconsidering the Size-Distance Invariance Hypothesis

In Chapter 9, we introduced you to the size-distance invariance hypothesis—the proposal that perceived size and perceived distance are related such that perceived size can be used to figure out perceived depth, and vice versa. In other words, not only are *cues about depth* used to make unconscious inferences about *depth*, cues about depth are *also* used to make unconscious inferences about *size*, and *cues about size* are also used to make unconscious inferences about *depth*. As you now know, this proposal is inconsistent with the ecological approach.

For one thing, the ecological approach might question whether geometric properties such as size and distance are really perceived at all. Putting that concern aside, however, from the ecological approach, visually perceiving a given property is a matter of detecting unambiguous structure—information about that property—in the ambient optic array. Perceiving size is a matter of detecting information about size, and perceiving distance is a matter of detecting information about distance. Full stop. Doing one should not depend on doing the other.

Researchers (Kim et al., 2016) attempted to investigate whether this is (or is not) the case by using a device called an "optical tunnel". Such a device is surprisingly simple to make . . . well, sort of. Get some white cardboard and cut it into 30cm x 30cm squares with a 20cm diameter circle cut out of the center of each one. Do the same thing with some black cardboard. Easy, right? Now comes the hard(er) part. Get a long wooden board and cut grooves in it every 4cm. Take one of the white pieces of cardboard and slide it into the groove nearest

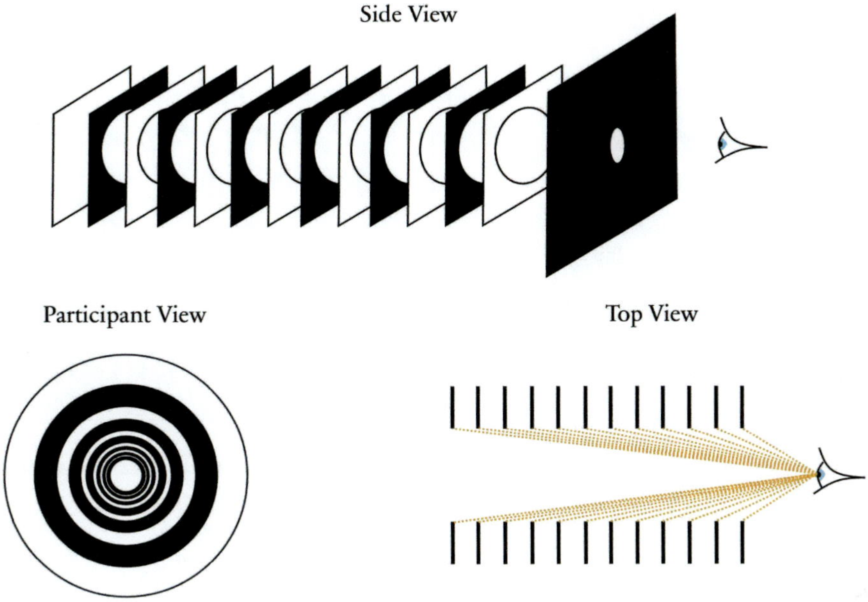

Figure 15.11 An optical tunnel (redrawn from Kim et al., 2016).

to you so that it is oriented vertically. Then take one of the black pieces of cardboard and slide into the next groove. Keep doing this until you run out of cardboard pieces (or grooves). Now look in one end of the tunnel (through the circles cut out of the cardboard pieces). Your setup should look like Figure 15.11. The alternating surfaces create a pattern of structured light that is information about the tunnel receding into the distance. Pretty cool, right?

So, what did these researchers do next? They placed small wooden rods of different lengths at different distances in the tunnel and asked people to report both the size (i.e., the length) and the distance of the rod. But they did one more thing. In one condition, when they placed the rod in the tunnel, it was attached to a regular piece of cardboard—one *without* a circular hole cut out of it. This made it so the tunnel abruptly stopped just behind the rod. In the other condition, the rod was attached to one of the pieces of cardboard that did have a circular hole cut out it. This made it so the tunnel continued beyond the rod (see Figure 15.12). Why did they do this?

Well, while the cues about size and depth—for example, retinal image size and linear perspective—are not different across these two circumstances, the pattern of structured light is *very different* across two circumstances. And so, if the size-distance invariance hypothesis is correct—and perceived rod size and perceived rod distance depend on one another—then this manipulation should *not* influence perceived rod size any differently than perceived rod distance (if at all).

However, if the ecological hypothesis is correct—and perceived size and perceived distance depend on detecting *different* patterns in the optic array— then this manipulation should influence perceived rod size differently than perceived rod distance. The results showed this manipulation did, indeed, influence perceived rod size differently than perceived rod distance. In particular, perceived rod size was larger when the tunnel abruptly stopped just behind the rod than when it continued behind the rod. However, perceived rod distance

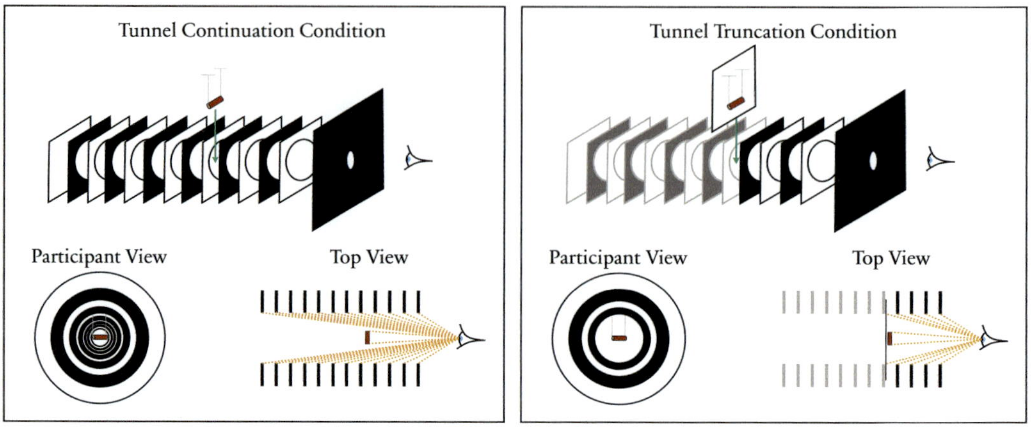

Figure 15.12 The experiment using an optical tunnel conducted by Kim et al. (2016, redrawn from original).

was no different in these two conditions. In addition, the results showed that perceiving size did not depend on perceiving distance, or vice versa. Instead, perceiving size and perceiving distance required detecting different patterns in the optical array.

Box 15.3 How Many Eyes Are Enough? And How Many Are Too Many?

Many animals—like Fred and his baby elephant, Topsy—have two eyes. And for some of these animals—again, like Fred and Topsy—those eyes are located on the front of the skull—so called "front-facing eyes". It is often proposed that having two front-facing eyes gives these animals an advantage in perceiving depth because it provides *binocular disparity* (see Chapter 9). To remind you, given that the visual fields of the right eye and the left eye overlap—at least to some degree—any differences in the retinal images on the left and the right eye can be used as cues to depth.

To some degree, the possibility that having two front-facing eyes with overlapping fields of view is advantageous because it enables (or enhances) the ability to perceive depth is consistent with lived experience. Try to go about your day (or a few minutes of your day, anyway) with one eye closed. Go ahead. Do it. We'll wait. You'll find that it is much more difficult to perform everyday behaviors with just one eye open than with both eyes open. And this may especially be so for behaviors that would seem to require "depth perception"—like walking through a cluttered room or catching a ball.

But is the benefit of having two eyes in these situations really because of enhanced "depth perception" from binocular disparity? Not necessarily. For one thing, in the ecological approach, animals don't perceive depth—they perceive surface layout. For another, the relevant stimulation pattern is not the ambiguous light that strikes the retina(s) but the ***unambiguous structure*** in the ambient optic array that ***surrounds*** an animal.

So then, why is it more difficult to perform everyday behaviors like the ones described here with only one eye open than with both eyes open? One simple answer is that you are just less able to explore the structure in the optic array with one eye than with two eyes. Your field of view is smaller. In fact, you would likely have the same difficulty performing these behaviors with both eyes open if you wore goggles (maybe made of two paper towel tubes taped together) that restricted your field of view by the same amount.

Besides, most animals on the planet do not have front-facing chambered eyes (eyes with retinas; see Chapters 2 and 3). Some have side-facing chambered eyes—like rabbits, horses, and parrots. Most have compound eyes that cannot form retinal images—like many species of insects. And some animals have *more than two eyes*—including some species of mollusks, arachnids, insects, amphibians, and fish. All of these situations pose a challenge to explanations of depth perception that are based on binocular disparity. But they do not pose the same challenge to explanations of perception of surface layout that are based entirely on encountering structure in the optic array.

Information About *Relationships Between* Animals and Surfaces

Back in his comfy chair, looking out the window at the tree, Fred's view is very different than when he was standing facing the wall—thank goodness! Sitting in the chair, he encounters structured light that directly reflects from the surfaces of the table and the tree (through the window), but not the structured light that directly reflects from the wall. This brings us to an obvious point, but one that must be made anyway. At any given moment, Fred encounters only the structured light in front of him and not the structured light behind him. This means that the structured light that a given animal encounters is information not just about the surrounding surfaces, but about its *orientation* to those surfaces.

Now imagine that Fred stands up from his comfy chair, still facing the window. The pattern of structured light he encounters is different than it was when he was sitting (see Figure 15.13). Now—when Fred is standing—he encounters *less* of the structured light reflecting from the floor in front of the table, *more* of the structured light reflecting from the surface of the table, and *none* of the structured light reflecting from the floor under the table (due to the table now occluding this surface).

The point is one that we've made before—the pattern of structured light at each and every point in the room—at each and every possible point of observation—is unique (meaning one of a kind). In this way, the structured light that Fred encounters is information about his *relationship to* surrounding surfaces.

But it's not just that the structured light encountered by someone who is *standing* is different than that encountered when they are sitting. It is that the light encountered by someone who is *taller* (say, Victor Wembanyama) is different than by someone who is *shorter* (say, Fred or one of your authors). This means that the structured light encountered at a given point of observation provides information about an animal's body size and location *relative* to surrounding surfaces. It is **body-scaled**!

Body-scaling information about surrounding surfaces and substances in relation to an animal's body size and shape.

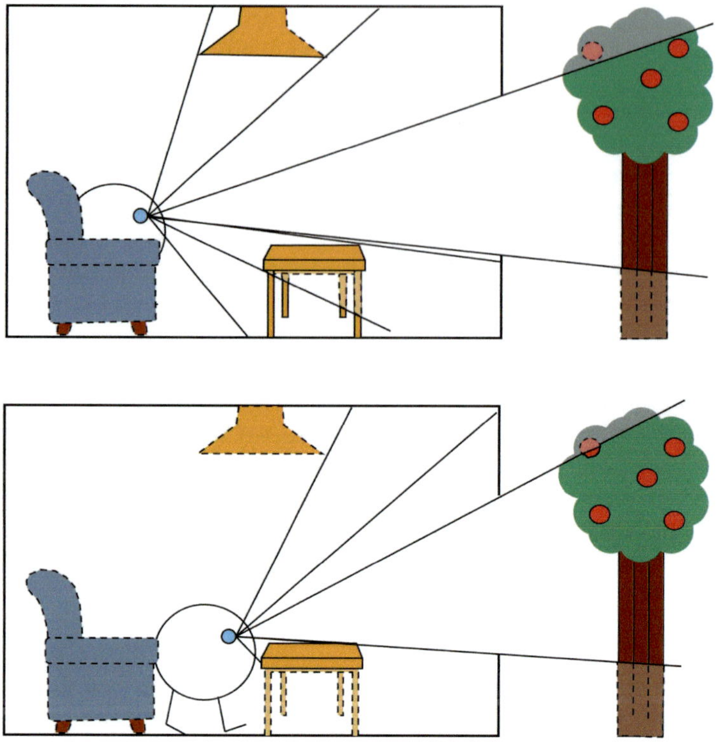

Figure 15.13 When Fred changes his point of observation, he encounters different patterns of structured light. These patterns are informative about his relationship to the layout of surfaces that the light strikes.

This is a critical point. This allows for the possibility that perceiving affordances for behaviors such as *fitting through, getting across or over, or reaching* (see Chapter 14) may (merely) be a matter of detecting the structured light at a given point of observation. This does not mean that perception of affordances occurs automatically or that animals are always successful when attempting to perceive affordances[6] (see Chapter 19).

What it does mean, however, is that the focus in attempting to understand how affordances are perceived shifts from understanding how representations are *fixed* to understanding how patterns in structured energy arrays (like the optic array) are *detected*. And experiments have shown that changing the structured light that a person encounters changes what affordances they perceive. For example, if a person's point of observation is raised relative to a particular surface layout (e.g., by standing on blocks attached to their shoes or by lowering the floor in front of them), they will—at least at first—perceive affordances as if they were taller (Mark, 1987; Warren & Whang, 1987)!

But there is an equally important point. So far, our description of ecological optics has focused on the structured light encountered at a *stationary* point of observation among *stationary* surrounding surfaces. But animals are almost never stationary, at least not for very long. On the contrary, animals move. A lot. And surrounding surfaces move too, though perhaps less often. What if—instead of merely standing and facing the

Figure 15.14 Top, Fred walks across the room. Bottom, the optical structure that he encounters changes as he moves.

Optic flow changing patterns of structure light that occur as surfaces move relative to an animal or an animal moves relative to surfaces.

window—Fred walked toward the window? He would encounter a continually *changing pattern* of structured light as he moved along this path. For example, he would progressively encounter *more* of the structured light reflecting from the tree through the window and *less* of the structured light reflecting off the other surfaces in the room—like the wall or the floor or the table. This changing pattern is called **optic flow** (see Figure 15.14; more on this in Chapter 16).

The word "flow" here is important. The changing pattern of structured light emerges not by a stitching together of static snapshots, but rather by a continuously unfolding optical event from start to finish (see Chapters 14 and 16). And just like the pattern of structured light is information about where an animal is relative to surrounding surfaces, the pattern of optic flow is information about *how* the animal is moving and *where* it is going relative to those surfaces as well as *when* it will get there.

And the optic flow pattern encountered by someone who is taller—say Victor Wembanyama—will be different than that encountered by someone who is shorter—say Fred or one of your authors. The optic flow pattern encountered by someone who is running—say, Sha'Carri Richardson—will be different than that encountered by someone walking. And even if both are walking at the same pace, the optic flow pattern encountered by a more massive person—say, champion sumo wrestler Takakeishō Takanobu—will be different than that experienced by a less massive person—say, champion marathon runner

Tamirat Tola. So, the changing pattern of structured light encountered by an animal not only depends on its size and shape, but also its mass, strength, dexterity and skill, and how it moves itself through the world. Therefore, the optic flow pattern encountered by an animal is not just body-scaled—it is also **action-scaled.**

Action-scaling information about surrounding surfaces and substances in relation to an animal's action capabilities.

Socratic Question: How does the structure encountered at a point of observation provide information about a perceiver's relationship to surfaces? What does it mean that optic flow patterns are action-scaled?

Reconsidering the Visual Cliff Studies

The fact that the optic flow patterns differ at different points of observation and for different ways of moving invite a reconsideration of the results of studies using one of the most famous pieces of apparatus in all of psychology—the visual cliff (Adolph & Kretch, 2012; E. Gibson & Walk, 1960; see Figure 15.15).

In studies using this apparatus, a baby is placed in the center of a clear Plexiglass table. One half of the table—the "shallow" side—has a checkerboard pattern right under the Plexiglass,

Figure 15.15 In the visual cliff paradigm, a baby is placed on the "shallow" side of the cliff and a caregiver encourages the baby to crawl to the "deep" side of the cliff. The tabletop is Plexiglas, so both sides are safe to crawl on.

and the other half—the "deep" side—has the checkerboard pattern on the floor. Both sides are perfectly safe for the baby to crawl on, but the question is whether the "deep" side *looks unsafe* to the baby. Does the baby avoid the "deep side" of the table? If so, when does the baby do so and why?

Results have shown that—in general—younger babies crawl right "over" the cliff and on to the "deep side" of the table. Older babies avoid doing so. These results are typically interpreted in terms of the development of "depth perception". Interpreted in this context, the results suggest that older infants are better at using cues to depth than younger infants, or—perhaps—that older infants have developed a more acute fear of heights than younger infants. However, neither interpretation has stood up to scrutiny. In the past several decades, it has become clear that what determines whether the babies crawl over the visual cliff is not age, but *crawling experience*. And what develops is not the ability to use cues to depth or a fear of heights but the *ability to perceive action-scaled affordances* from optic flow patterns at a given point of observation.

The studies that provided this evidence are ones that have used—more or less—the same basic methodology of the studies on perceiving affordances that we described in Chapter 14. In particular, researchers placed babies on the edge of *real drop-offs* or at the top of *real slopes*. They varied how deep the drop-offs were and how steep the slopes were. And they watched which drop-offs or slopes the babies attempted to descend (see Figure 15.16; Adolph & Hoch, 2019). And they caught the babies when they fell. Which they did. A lot.

Overall, these studies showed an interesting pattern of results. Consider babies who have just learned to crawl, who are placed at the top of a real slope, and who are encouraged by caregivers and researchers to crawl down that slope (see Figure 15.16, *right*). You might guess that since these babies have just learned to crawl, they would not be very good at telling the difference between slopes that they could safely crawl down and those that they could not. And you would be right.

Many new crawlers attempted to crawl down slopes that were *way* too steep and had to be quickly rescued by alert and agile researchers. You might also expect that as the babies became more experienced with crawling over weeks and weeks, they would *become better* at determining which slopes afforded safely crawling down and which did not. And again, you would be right—just like the babies were about the slopes! Experienced crawlers generally

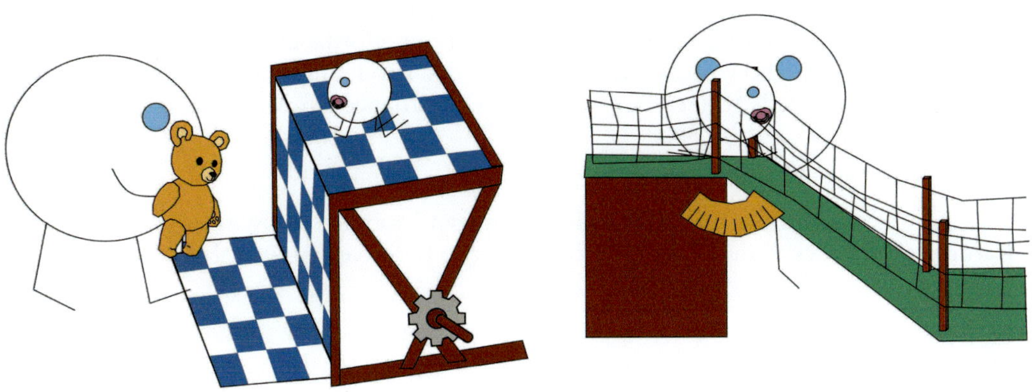

Figure 15.16 Studies on the development of perceiving-acting skills such crawling up to a brink, and crawling or walking down a slope have shown that infants learn specific affordances, not general facts about the world.

chose to crawl down safe slopes and refused to crawl down risky ones—and they were accurate to within 2° of their actual crawling abilities!

But what do you think happened when these *very same babies* returned to *the very same lab* a few months later after they had just learned how to walk? You might think that since these babies have *already learned to tell the difference* between slopes that afford safely *crawling* down and which do not, they would also be pretty good at telling the difference between slopes that afford safely *walking* down and those that did not. Cues to depth for one should work for the other, right?

But this time you would be wrong. Many of these same babies—quite happily—attempted to walk down slopes that were *way too ste*ep and had to be even more quickly rescued by alert and agile researchers. After weeks of walking experience, however, they became better at determining which slopes afforded safely walking down and which did not.

An analogous pattern occurred in tasks in which babies attempted to climb down from a drop-off before and after learning how to crawl or walk (Adolph, 2019). In all of these cases, the babies seemingly had to *start over from zero* after learning to crawl or to walk. And learning was no faster the second time around. In other words, what they learned about perceiving affordances for *crawling* did not seem to help in any way whatsoever when they were learning to perceive affordances for *walking*.

This does not make sense from the traditional approach in which the baby is learning to use cues to perceive geometric properties—like depth of the drop-off or angle of the slope. Previous experience should *always help* the central executive—even a baby central executive—in doing so, right? Figuring out what cues are useful now should help the baby later, right? At least a little?

But it *does* make sense from an ecological perspective. The relationship between the animal and the environment is *completely different* in crawling than in walking. Different limbs are involved, different coordination patterns are required, different postures are used, and different balance skills are required. And—here is the key point for our purposes—a crawling baby and a walking baby occupy very different points of observation in the optic array and therefore encounter very different patterns of optic flow (Adolph & Hoch, 2019).

As we foreshadowed at the beginning of the chapter, the optic flow patterns an animal encounters at a given point of observation are unambiguously related to the animal's *relationship to* those substances and surfaces. They are informative about affordances for that animal. And the optic flow pattern that is informative about affordances for *crawling* is entirely different from the optic flow pattern that is informative about affordances for *walking*. Consequently, the baby needs to (re)learn to perceive affordances in each case (see Adolph & Hoch, 2019).

> Socratic Question: How do studies with infants and toddlers show that—rather than learning about cues to depth—they are learning to perceive action-scaled affordances?

Summary

In the ecological approach to visually perceiving, the seemingly unsolvable problem of how empty space is perceived is replaced by the solvable (but still challenging) problem of how surface layout is perceived. Solving this problem requires a scientific understanding of how the structured light encountered by an animal at a given point of observation is informative not only about the layout of surrounding surfaces but also about *its relationship to* this layout—the affordances of those surfaces for the animal!

Notes

1 This is known as "Liebowitz's first law", named after the influential vision scientist Herschel Leibowitz (1925–2011).
2 Call this "Blau and Wagman's first law".
3 German for "whole field".
4 Exceptions, of course, include ever-present LED screens (like TVs, computers, tablets, and phones). LED screens *do* radiate light, and you are able to see what is on the screen, but only because of how the (depicted) text or objects on that screen change the properties of that radiated light. In this way, looking at text on an LED screen is like looking at a high-tech silhouette of an object in the "real" world.
5 This is one reason why wet dirt looks darker than dry dirt. When dirt is wet, the light bounces off of the surface of the water on the dirt and scatters; some of that scattered light is scattered in the direction of the dirt, so it gets a second chance to be *absorbed* by the dirt. This means that less light is reflected to the eye, making it look darker.
6 Just because structured light that provides information about an affordance is available to be detected doesn't mean that an animal wants to detect it, is capable of detecting it, or is capable of using it to perform the behavior.

16 Seeing Where to Go and How to Get There

With these basics of ecological optics in mind, we are now ready for an ecological redescription of visually perceiving motion. Most, if not all, traditional explanations of visual perception of motion—like most, if not all, traditional explanations of visual perception in general—are based on the pattern of light that strikes the retina. As a reminder, the basic idea is that when an object in your field of view moves, the light reflecting from it strikes a slightly different part of the retina than it did previously. So, as an object moves, there are corresponding patterns of stimulation on the retina over time. Cues available in this changing pattern of stimulation are used to perceive motion (see Chapter 11).

As you might expect, from the ecological perspective, perception of "motion" is yet another unsolvable problem (see Chapter 13). The fundamental issue is this—motion, like depth and space, is *an abstract concept.* Motion does not exist in the absence of a *moving object.* Therefore, motion itself—like depth and space—cannot be seen. In contrast, *moving objects* do exist and can be seen. In particular, movements of surfaces relative to an animal and of an animal relative to surfaces *can* each be seen. Let's discuss these in turn.

Movement of Surfaces Relative to the Perceiver

Imagine that Fred goes to sit down in his comfy chair to continue reading this book, which is sitting on the arm of the chair. But—whoops!—on his way to the chair, he stumbles and accidentally knocks the book off the arm of the chair and onto the floor right in front of the chair. As the book falls to the floor, it will create a continuously *changing pattern* of structured light. But this pattern will only occur in *a portion* of the ambient optic array. In other words, it creates a ***local***—as opposed to ***global***—**optic flow** pattern (see Chapter 15; see Figure 16.1).

When the book is sitting—undisturbed—on the arm of the chair, it will *occlude* part of the arm of the chair and the structure light reflecting from it (see Chapter 15). When the book begins to fall

Local optic flow a changing pattern of structured light in a particular location in the optic array. Such a pattern occurs when surfaces move relative to an animal.

Global optic flow a changing pattern of structured light across the entire optic array. Such a pattern occurs when an animal moves relative to surfaces.

DOI: 10.4324/9781032690964-19

Figure 16.1 Left, no optic flow specifies that neither the object nor the viewer are moving. Middle, global optic flow specifies that the observer is moving. Right, local optic flow specifies the object is moving.

to the floor, there will be a *continuously changing* pattern of occlusion. As it falls to the ground, the bottommost part of the book will progressively occlude the structured light reflecting from lower portions of the chair until it lands on the floor. In other words, while it is falling, the bottommost part of the book is an **occluding edge**, and the portion of the chair is an *occluded surface* (see Chapter 15; Figure 16.2, *middle*). At the same time, the upper edge of the book will progressively reveal the structured light reflecting from portions of the couch that had just been occluded. This pattern of progressive deletion of structured light at an occluding edge together with progressive revealing of structured light at the opposite (trailing) edge is information about one surface moving in front of

Occluding edge the part of a surface that blocks the structured light reflecting from another surface.

Figure 16.2 Left, when the book is sitting on the chair, it occludes part of the chair arm. Middle, when the book falls in front of the chair, the book progressively occludes lower parts of the chair and progressively reveals the chair. Right, when the book falls behind the chair, the chair progressively occludes the book until it is fully occluded.

another surface (see Figure 16.2, *middle*). In this case, it is information about the book falling to the floor in front of his comfy chair.

Now, imagine that Fred—somehow—knocks the book *up over* the chair so that it falls to the floor *behind* the chair. Under these circumstances, there will be a different continuously changing pattern of occlusion. As it falls behind the chair, more of the book and the structured light reflecting from it will be progressively occluded by the chair's surface. In this case, the topmost part of the chair will be the occluding edge, and the book will be the occluded surface. And this part of the chair will progressively occlude more of the structured light reflecting from the book until it completely disappears behind the chair (see Figure 16.2, *right*).

Unlike the case where the book falls in front of the chair, there will be no progressive revealing of—no structured light reflecting from—the chair or the book. This pattern of progressive deletion of optical texture at an occluding edge *without* progressive revealing of structured light at the opposite (trailing) edge is information about one surface moving *behind* another surface. In this case, the book falling *behind* the chair.

Humor us one more time and imagine that instead of sitting on the arm of the chair, the book is tucked away on the top shelf of a tall bookcase. But when Fred is on his way to the bookshelf, Topsy accidentally bumps into the bookcase, dislodging the book and sending it falling from the shelf (see Figure 16.3). Fred looks up and sees that—much to his dismay—the book is heading right for his face! As the book gets closer, it will progressively occlude the structured light reflecting from the surrounding surfaces—mostly the bookcase but also the ceiling. In this case, *the entire outer contour* of the book is an occluding edge.

In addition, as more structured light reflecting from the surrounding surfaces is occluded, more structured light reflecting from the book is revealed. That is, *the optical texture of the*

Figure 16.3 Top, a book falls off the top shelf towards Fred's face. Bottom, Fred's view as the book falls.

book will expand. In other words, there will be an **optical expansion** pattern. Moreover, it will appear to expand *symmetrically*. It will expand at the same rate in every direction, and the center of the expansion will be the center of the book. This pattern of *deletion* of optical texture at an object's outer edges plus *symmetric expansion* of that object's optical texture is information about that object moving *directly toward the perceiver*. In this case, it is information about the book falling directly toward his face (see Figure 16.3)!

Optical expansion the magnification or spreading out of the structured light reflecting from a surface or surfaces. This pattern occurs when a surface moves toward an animal or when an animal moves toward a surface.

Fred does not want the book to hit him in the face—or any part of him, really. He would much rather get out of the way—or better yet, catch it and read it (it is a really good book, after all). To do that, he needs to know *when* the book will get to him. From the traditional approach, this seems like a job that is tailor-made for the central executive. First, the central executive would need to use cues (from the ambiguous retinal image) to figure out (1) the distance between him and the book (d) and (2) the speed of the book (or velocity, v). Then it could calculate the time until the book hits him in the face based on the formula, $t = d/v$.

Even if the central executive could do all of this—and fast!—it would be completely unnecessary. It turns out that the time until the book arrives is available in changing patterns in the optic array—no cues or calculations needed! More specifically, it is available in *how quickly* the structured light reflecting from the book expands as it approaches. Said another way, it is available in how quickly the expanding structured light occludes the surrounding surfaces relative to how much it already does so (Lee et al., 2009; see Pepping & Grealy, 2007).

This relative rate of expansion is a variable called **tau (τ)** and it is information about *time to arrival*, assuming that current conditions continue. The variable τ reveals that there is potential for optical variables to provide information about when and where an object will arrive so that Fred can behave accordingly *before* it arrives. For example, the optical texture of the book will expand slowly at first and then expand more rapidly as the object gets closer. That is, the rate of optical expansion will increase. The bottom line, though, is that movements of objects relative to Fred—in front of other surfaces, behind other surfaces, toward an animal—lawfully generate patterns of change in the optic array.

Tau (τ) the rate of optical expansion of a surface relative to the background. Tau provides information about time to arrival of that surface (or to that surface).

But now imagine that when he looks up at the falling book, he sees that—rather than hitting him in the face—the book will pass by his right ear and land on the floor by his right foot. As the book falls, the right edge of the book will progressively occlude the structured light reflecting from surfaces located to the right. And the left edge of the book will progressively reveal the structured light reflecting from the surfaces located to the left. At the same time, there will be expansion of the optical texture of the book, but this expansion will be *asymmetric*, and the center of the expansion pattern will be shifted toward the right of the book. This means that the optical texture will expand more quickly on the right side of the book than on the left side (see Figure 16.4).

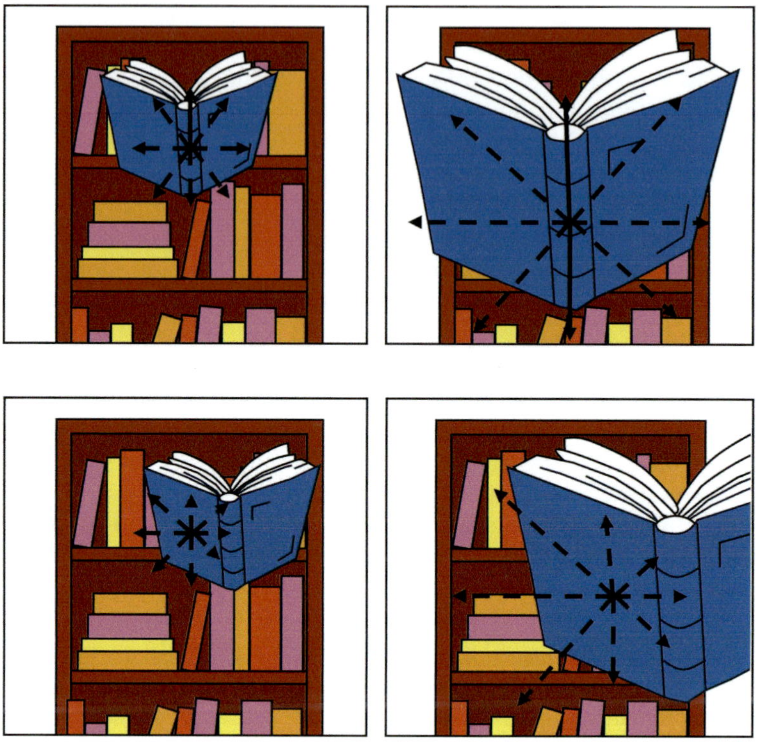

Figure 16.4 Top, symmetric expansion specifies that the book is falling directly towards Fred. Bottom, asymmetric expansion specifies that the book is falling to his right.

This pattern of progressive deletion of optical texture at an occluding edge and progressive *revealing* of optical texture at the opposite (trailing) edge *plus asymmetric expansion* of optical texture is information that the surface is moving *indirectly* toward Fred. In this case, it is information that the book is falling toward his right. How he can use such information to move into position to catch the book under these circumstances will be discussed later.

Socratic Question: What optical pattern will a perceiver experience if an object is moving directly toward them?

Movement of the Perceiver Relative to Surfaces of Objects

Fred manages to avoid getting hit in the face by the falling book—whew!—and now he walks over to pick it up from the floor (see Figure 16.5). As he approaches the book, he will encounter yet another continuously changing pattern of structured light. But this time, the pattern will occur across the *entire optic array*. That is, in contrast to a local optic flow pattern, this will be a *global* optic flow pattern (see Chapter 15; Gibson, 1979/2015). In particular, as Fred moves toward the book, he will encounter more of the structured light reflecting from surfaces in front of him. In particular, the optical texture of the surfaces in

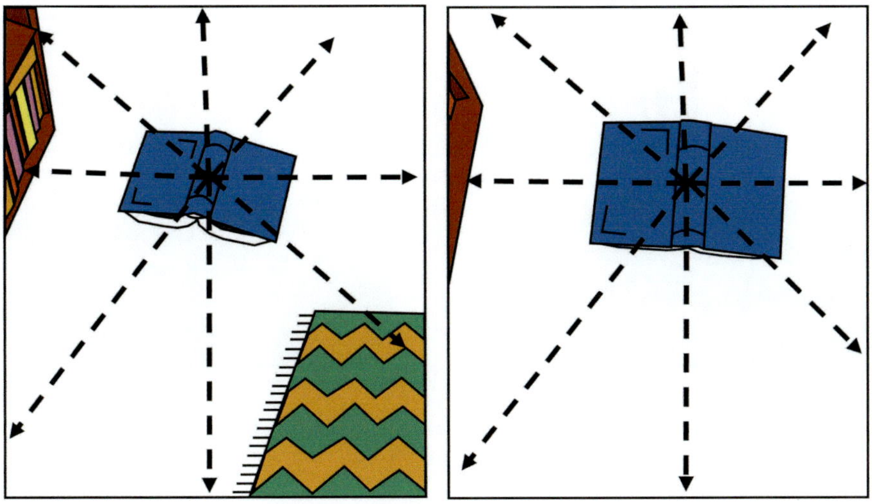

Figure 16.5 When walking toward an object on the ground, Fred's optic flow shows global expansion (specifying his forward movement); the outer contour of Fred's field of view is an occluding edge.

front of him will appear to expand, and the center of the expansion pattern will occur where he is heading—in this case, on the book itself. In addition, as he moves forward, he will see less of the structured light reflecting from surfaces behind him. Since Fred only has access to the structured light in front of him and not the structured light behind him, when he moves forward, the *entire outer contour* of his field of view is an occluding edge (see Figure 16.5).

This pattern of *deletion* of optical texture at the outer edges of the field of view plus *global expansion* of optical texture—and specifically the symmetric expansion of the optical texture of a given surface—is information that Fred is moving *directly toward that surface.* In this case, it is information that he is moving directly toward the book.

The specifics of the global optic flow patterns are informative about *how* an animal is moving, *where* it is moving, and *when* it will get there. The rate and direction of global optic flow are information about movement speed and direction, respectively. If Fred decides that he is not getting to the book fast enough—it *is* a really good book, after all—and he breaks into a run, the *rate* of global optic flow will increase. If he slows down again, the rate of optic flow will decrease. In particular, *how quickly* the optical texture of a given surface expands—that is, the rate of optical expansion or τ—is information about *time to arrival* (again, assuming that current conditions continue).

If he stops, the global optic flow will decrease to zero. If, for some reason, he decides to backpedal away from the book—*but wait! It's a really good book!*—the optic flow will *reverse.* This time, there will be a progressive revealing of structured light at the outer contours of his field of view plus a global contracting of optical texture—specifically a symmetric contracting of the optical texture of the book. This pattern is information about him moving directly away from the book.

If Fred turns his head or moves his body to the right, he will encounter yet another continuously changing pattern of structured light. Specifically, he will encounter more of the structured light reflecting from surfaces located to his right and less of the structure light reflecting from surfaces located to his left. In other words, optical structure will be progressively deleted at the outer left edge of his field of view and progressively revealed at the outer right edge of his field of view. The opposite pattern would occur if he were to turn his head

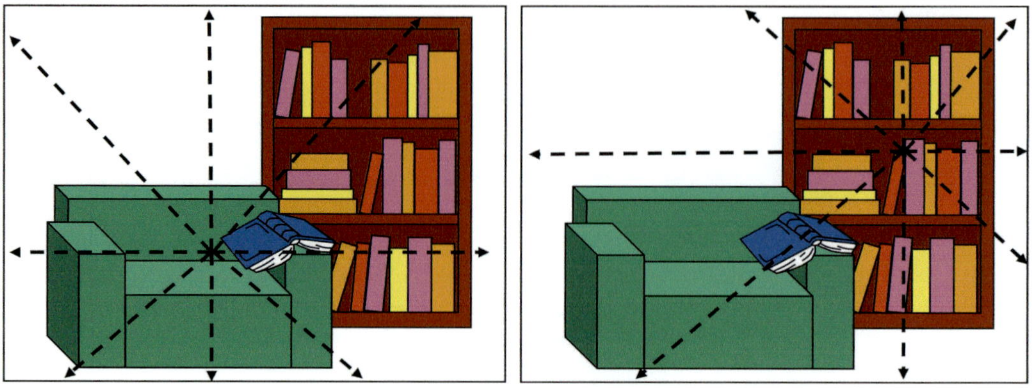

Figure 16.6 Left, the focus of expansion specifies that Fred is heading toward the chair. Right, the focus of expansion specifies that Fred is heading toward the bookcase.

to the right—optical structure will be progressively deleted at the outer right edge of his field of view and progressively revealed at the outer left edge of his field of view.

As we have mentioned, if Fred is moving toward the chair, there will be a symmetric global expansion of optical texture of the chair. In other words, the center of the expansion pattern—**the focus of expansion**—will be on the chair (see Figure 16.6). If he were to move toward some other object instead—the bookcase, perhaps—then the focus of expansion would be on the bookcase. So, the focus of expansion of optical texture is information about *where* he is going.

Focus of expansion the center of the magnification or spreading out of structured light reflecting from a surface. The location of the focus of expansion is information about direction of heading.

Box 16.1 The Ecological Solution for the Problem of Eye Movements

As we mentioned at the beginning of the chapter, traditional approaches to visual perception of motion are often based on motion of an image on the retina. As an object moves, it creates a corresponding pattern of motion of the image it creates on the retina. And in traditional approaches, this motion on the retina is used as a cue for perceiving motion of the object (see Chapter 11). For example, imagine that Fred is looking at Topsy, who is directly in front of him. If Topsy moves to Fred's left, the retinal image of Topsy on Fred's eye will move *to his right*. And Topsy moves to Fred's right, the retinal image of Topsy on Fred's eye will move *to his left*. So, maybe the cue is that movement of the retinal image is opposite that of a moving object. That sounds workable, right?

But, as we discussed in Chapter 11, there is a problem. Again, imagine that Fred is looking at Topsy who is directly in front of him. But this time, instead of Topsy moving, Fred moves his eyes or turns his head. Specifically, he moves his eyes or turns his head to the right. The retinal image of Topsy on Fred's eye will move to the *right*. This would ordinarily be a cue that Topsy moved to the left. But she didn't.

So how does the central executive know the difference? One proposed solution discussed in Chapter 11 is efference copy theory. As a reminder, this is the proposal that the brain sends a copy of motor commands about eye movements to the central executive, which then compares the actual and expected patterns movement on the retina. Any *unexpected changes* in the location of stimulation can then be attributed to the motion of objects. This sounds . . . complicated.

The ecological approach offers a simpler solution that doesn't involve cues or efference copies. In fact, we have already discussed it. Movements of objects in the world lawfully generate *local* optic flow patterns. Movements of the perceiver (including movements of their eyes or their heads)[1] lawfully generate *global* optic flow patterns. Movement of objects *and* the perceiver create *both* patterns. No cues, no efference copies. Just lawfully generated patterns that provide information about movement of surfaces relative to the self and movements of the self relative to surfaces.

Socratic Question: What optical pattern will a perceiver experience if they are moving directly toward an object? What about if an object is thrown towards them? What about if an object is thrown towards them *while* they are moving forward?

The Moving Room

As we described previously, when Fred moves, he lawfully generates global optic flow patterns. The specifics of these global optic flow patterns are informative about how he is moving, where he is moving, and when he will get there. What would happen if someone who was not moving somehow encountered a global optic flow pattern anyway? Would they feel like they were moving? Even though they are not moving? Yes, yes, they would.

This is not that uncommon an experience—especially with the advent of technologies such as virtual reality. But it can also happen in *actual* reality. Have you ever been parked at a red light when the car next to you pulled forward? You might have thought that you were somehow going *backwards*—even though your foot was firmly on the brake. Or maybe you have been to an immersive show at a venue like the Sphere in Las Vegas or an IMAX movie theater where you felt like you were moving—maybe even flying! —despite the fact that you were sitting still? Weird, huh?

In the 1970s—decades before virtual reality technology existed—researchers developed an apparatus called the moving (or gliding) room to investigate this phenomenon (Lishman & Lee, 1973). In the moving room, a participant stands inside of a small enclosure—consisting of three walls and a ceiling—inside of a larger room. Importantly, though, the walls of the moving room don't touch the floor (see Figure 16.7, *left*). Instead, they are suspended just above the floor and are connected to pulleys so that the entire enclosure can be moved back and forth—while the floor and the person standing on it both remain perfectly stationary—hence the name "moving room".

Moving the room creates patterns of global optic flow. These patterns are sufficient to make the person feel as if they are moving even though they are standing perfectly still. Imagine that Fred is a participant in one of these studies. He walks in and faces the back wall

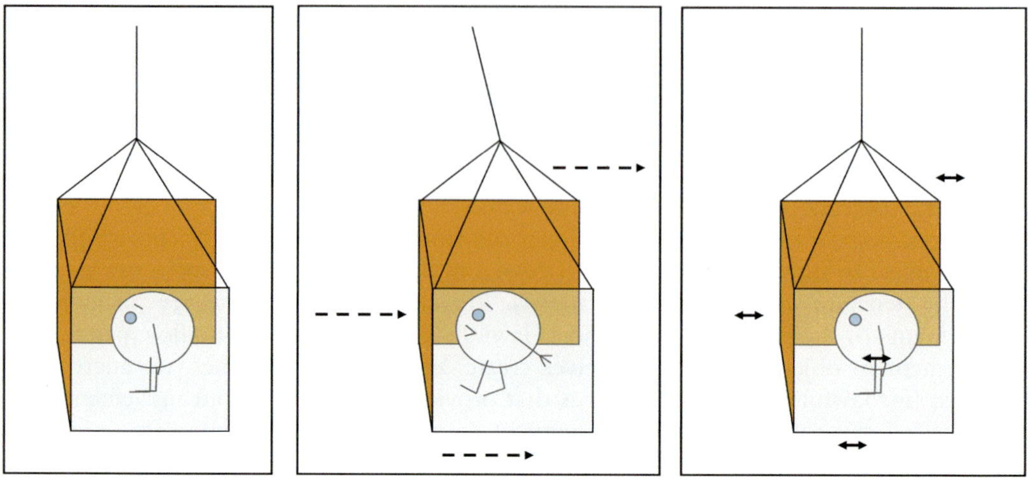

Figure 16.7 Left, in the moving room paradigm, the walls of a room can be slid toward or away from a person. Middle, if the room is moved a large distance, it will cause the person to lose their balance. Right, if the room is moved back and forth a small distance, it will cause them to sway.

of the moving room. At the moment, anyway, Fred has no reason to think that the room is anything but a regular (non-moving) room (see Figure 16.7, *left*).

Suddenly, the room is moved toward him approximately 50 cm (almost 2 feet)! This causes him to encounter a global optic flow pattern—specifically a global optic *expansion* pattern. In nearly every other set of circumstances, this pattern is information that he is moving forward—*and fast*! In this case, it might make him feel as if he has suddenly lost his balance and is falling forward. Most likely, he would lean or step backwards to steady himself—wouldn't you (see Figure 16.7, *middle*)? And this is exactly what participants (including Fred) do in the moving room under these circumstances.

If the room is moved *away* from him, he would also encounter a global optic flow pattern—this time a global optic *contraction* pattern. In this case, it might make him feel if he has suddenly lost his balance and is falling backwards. Most likely, he would lean or step forward to steady himself. And this is exactly what participants (including Fred) do under these circumstances.

In either of these cases, Fred might even fall down—especially if he was standing in an unusual or challenging posture—like on one foot or with his heels together and both feet pointed out—or if he was like Fred's baby niece Eleanor whose balance isn't quite so good just yet. And, under these circumstances, this sometimes happens to participants in the moving room (Lee & Aronson, 1974).

But wait, there's more! Now imagine that rather than suddenly being moved toward or away from Fred, the room is moved back and forth very subtly—maybe 5 mm (0.2 inches) instead of 50 cm (2 feet). This would create a global optic flow pattern, too. But it would be so subtle that he probably wouldn't even notice. Certainly, he wouldn't step forward or backward or fall over. However, he might start to sway back and forth in sync with the movements of the room, without even knowing that he is doing so (see Figure 16.7, *right*). And this is exactly what participants (including Fred) do under these circumstances (see Smart et al., 2020; see Box 16.2).

Box 16.2 Motion Sickness as an Inability to (Use Optic Flow to) Control Posture

If you've ever experienced motion sickness, you know that it can be terribly unpleasant. Like, *really* unpleasant. Something-that-you-would-not-wish-on-your-worst-enemy unpleasant. Symptoms include cold sweats, headache, dizziness, nausea, and vomiting. And it can last for hours or *even days*. Yuck.

People can experience motion sickness in moving vehicles such as cars, trains, airplanes, and especially boats (see Figure 16.8). But they can also experience motion sickness when using immersive technologies such as head-mounted virtual reality headsets (called "cybersickness"). The popularity of these devices is making this a bigger problem. The question is—why do motion sickness or cybersickness occur?

One traditional theory of motion sickness is that it has something to do with the brain getting conflicting cues about whether and how the body is moving. Here's how this might work: Imagine that Fred is taking a long boat ride on choppy seas. From the traditional approach, the up-and-down movement of the boat on the ocean creates a pattern of activity on his sense organs that provides cues that he is moving. These cues might include the up-and-down movement of the retinal image (see Chapter 11) and sloshing around of the fluid in the semicircular canals in his inner ear (see Chapter 5).

But . . . the central executive does not expect these patterns to occur. After all, no motor commands were issued that would generate these patterns. So, when Fred's eyes and other sense systems report to his brain that he is moving up and down, the central executive gets very confused—so much so that Fred feels sick. In other words, in these theories, motion sickness is the result of the central executive getting very confused about what exactly the body is doing because of conflict between expected and experienced movement patterns.

But this may not be what motion sickness is. Rather than being the result of a confused central executive, motion sickness may be the result of *unstable posture* (Stoffregen, 2011). In particular, motion sickness might occur when a person is unable to use optic flow *to stabilize* their posture. Some of the evidence supporting this idea has come from studies that used head-mounted virtual reality headsets to expose people to particular relationships between their own movements and optic flow patterns and also record their **postural sway** movements while this was happening (Smart et al., 2014).

Postural sway movements that a person's body makes for the purpose of maintaining upright posture and balance. Most of the time—but not always—these movements are small (millimeters in a given direction) and unintentional.

In these studies, people experienced motion sickness most often when—through the magic of VR—their postural sway movements generated a *reversed* optic flow pattern (i.e., when forward movement created a global optical contraction and backward movement created a global optical expansion). They experienced motion sickness less often when their movements generated a typical optic flow pattern (i.e., when forward movement created a global optical expansion and backward movement created a global optical contraction). And they experienced motion sickness least often when

Figure 16.8 Fred gets motion sickness in boats, as a passenger in a car, and when trying VR.

their movements were unrelated to a steady back-and-forth optic flow pattern (like in the oscillating moving room example described earlier).

In addition, people who experienced motion sickness *swayed differently* than people who did not. In particular, people who experienced motion sickness showed larger, more complex, and less flexible swaying patterns than people who did not. In other words, it seemed that people who experienced motion sickness were disrupted by—rather than stabilized by—the optic flow patterns they experienced. They were unable to discover how to use the optic flow patterns to stabilize their posture. Other research has shown that it is possible to predict who will experience symptoms of motion sickness based on subtle patterns in their postural sway—*even before that person is exposed to a situation in which they might get motion sickness*!

And so, preventing or reducing the symptoms of motion sickness might not require medications (which mostly work by making you drowsy, anyway). Instead, it might require learning to use optic flow patterns to help stabilize the body in an unusual context. This includes performing behaviors that help to stabilize posture *in general*. For example, motion sickness is less likely to occur when people *sit* than when they *stand*, and less likely to occur when they stand with *their feet farther apart* than with their *feet closer together* (see Stanney et al., 2020; Stoffregen, 2011).

Socratic Question: What might happen to a perceiver if a moving room is suddenly moved toward them? What might happen to a perceiver if a moving room is subtly moved toward and away from them?

Laws for Visually Controlling Movement

If patterns of optic flow provide information about how an animal is moving, where it is moving, and when it will get there, can Fred or any other animal use such patterns to control their movements? Yes. Yes, they can.

What makes optic flow and the other variables of ecological optics so powerful is that these patterns are available to be detected by any animal that has a visual system with appropriate sensitivity. This means that they have the potential to provide *a general explanation* for the visual control of behavior by *all* animal species.

The specific details of the animal's visual system do not matter. It does not matter, for example, if the animal has compound eyes or chambered eyes, nor does it matter how many eyes that animal has (see Boxes 15.3 and 15.4). Just as importantly, though, the specific details of the animal's movement system do not matter, either. It does not matter, for example, if the animal walks, hops, slithers, flies, or swims, nor does it matter if it has many legs, two legs, or no legs. It also does not matter how the parts of that movement system are coordinated at any given moment—crawling, walking, running, or even driving, for example (see Box 16.3).

Moving toward a surface in any of these ways will *always* generate a global optic flow pattern, and the specifics of that global optic flow pattern will *always* be informative about how that animal is moving, where it is moving, and when it will get there. This means that an animal can use these patterns to control its movements, regardless of the specific details of either its visual system or its movement system. These "laws for the visual control of movement" include the following (see Gibson, 2015/1979):

- To start moving, make the optic array flow
- To stop moving, make the optic array stop flowing
- To back up, make the optic array flow in the opposite direction
- To turn, shift the center of flow (the focus of expansion)
- To steer, keep the center of flow (the focus of expansion) away from obstacles and drop-offs

Note that it is not made clear how exactly how the animal is supposed to do these things (i.e., what limbs to use and how to coordinate them; see Box 16.3). What *is* made clear is what the optical consequences will be—what things will look like—if the animal is successful in doing those things. Next, we'll apply comparable laws to the visual control of two examples of everyday behaviors that require getting to the right place at the right time.

Box 16.3 The Birds and the Bees

We have tried to make the case that that the variables of ecological optics—especially optic flow—have the potential to provide *a general explanation* for how all animal species visually control behavior. Two examples of animal species that use optic flow patterns to perform complex behaviors are birds and bees.

Gannets are seabirds that hunt by diving from the air, plunging into the water, and pursuing fish. They can dive from heights of 30m (nearly 100 feet) and reach speeds of 100 km/h (over 60 mph). The problem for the gannets is this: they must keep their wings extended for as long as possible during their descent so that they can steer toward their moving prey. However, they also must retract their wings *before* entering the water so that they make a streamlined entry—and don't injure themselves . . . or worse! How do they know *when* to retract their wings? They don't start their dives from the same height every time so they can't simply "time" when to do so. Besides, they would need to know the height, velocity, and acceleration of a particular dive and then use these variables to *compute* time—all while hurtling toward the water at highway speeds (see Figure 16.9)!

Researchers analyzed video of gannets diving from different heights and found evidence that the birds were choosing when to retract their wings based on the optical expansion of a particular patch of water. In other words, they were using τ, which provides information about time to arrival (Lee & Reddish, 1981). Similar strategies

Figure 16.9 Left, gannets diving towards the water, and (right) bees navigating seem to use optical flow patterns to govern their behavior.

are used by insects attempting to land on (or avoid) a surface and may even be used to program wheeled, hovering, or flying robots to do the same (Serres & Ruffier, 2017).

You may already know that bees communicate the location of nectar sources to other members of their hive by dancing on the wall of the hive. A particular species of bee (*A. mellifera ligusta*) uses a "round dance" when a nectar source is near, and a "waggle dance" when a nectar source is "far". But how does a bee know how far it has flown so that it can communicate this information in its dance? One possibility is that they estimate distance based on the amount of energy they use when flying from the source to the hive. The more energy used, the greater distance they must have flown. Sounds reasonable, right?

But another possibility is that they use (the rate of) *global optic flow*. Researchers measured the duration of the "waggle portion" of the dance performed by bees who had flown through two different tunnels to a nectar source. The tunnels were the same length (6m) and the nectar source was the same distance away from the hive (35m). The only difference between them was what the tunnels *looked like on the inside*. One—the "line tunnel"—had a single black line running down the length of the tunnel. The other tunnel—the "ring tunnel"—had several black rings every few centimeters.

The bees that flew down the "line tunnel" were more likely to perform the round dance—indicating that the nectar was *near*—and the bees that flew down the "ring" tunnel were more likely to perform the waggle dance, indicating that the nectar was *far*—even though the distance flown was identical. Why? Flying through the ring tunnel generated *more optic flow* than flying through the line tunnel—which produced little to no optic flow—suggesting that the bees had used (the rate of) of optic flow and not the energy used to determine distance flown (Esch et al., 2001; Srinivasan et al., 2000).

Getting to the Right Place at the Right Time

The Outfielder Problem. One more time with feeling: imagine that Topsy playfully grabs Fred's book with her trunk and tosses it high up into the air, and it goes flying across the room. Fred is feeling particularly athletic—just like Victor Wembanyama or Sha'Carri Richardson!—and so he tries to run and catch it.

Where should Fred run? What route should he take? And how fast should he go? This is the challenge faced by athletes in sports such as baseball, softball, cricket, ultimate frisbee, soccer (what most of the world calls football), and football (what most of the world calls American football), among others. Athletes in these sports often need to get themselves to the place where a ball is going to land *before* it gets there so that they can make the appropriate play (e.g., catch it, deflect it, kick it). How do they—and how would Fred or you or anyone else—do this?

To get to the right place at the right time, the athlete would need to know where the ball is going to be and when it is going to be there. In other words, they would need to know what has been called the "current future"—what will happen in the immediate future if current conditions continue (see Bootsma, 2009). Again, this seems like a job tailor-made for the central executive. However, in this case, the central executive would really have their hands full. The time until the ball reaches the ground is much more complicated than $t = d/v$. It requires the math and the physics of projectile motion, and it requires knowing not just distance and velocity but *also* angle of launch, initial height, and maximum height—not to mention awareness of current weather conditions if the ball and the person are outside!

But even if the central executive is successful in calculating where the ball will land *and* when it will get there, they would still need to figure out what path along the ground the person should take to get to that place, when they should start taking that path, and how fast they should be going (see Figure 16.10). All of this seems . . . unlikely, especially given how quickly these decisions need to be made—not to mention that animals such as dogs, birds, and bats catch airborne objects on the regular. Do they have super-smart central executives, too?

Figure 16.10 Outfielders need to be able to catch fly balls, so they need to be able to synchronize their movements with the ball's trajectory.

So how might humans or other animals get to the right place at the right time if not by calculating? It turns out that information about how to do this is available in the optic array. Rather than applying the math and physics of projectile motion, people (or other animals) just need to follow a few simple rules based on information in the optic array. For example, if you want to catch an object—like a ball or a book—you only need to do two things (Zaal & Michaels, 2003):

- Move so that the object *does not appear to move* side-to-side
- Move so that the object *appears to move at a constant speed* up-and-down (move so to cancel or eliminate vertical acceleration)

Fred is standing in a triangular pattern with two other people, Brett and Kevin. Brett and Kevin are playing catch by throwing a ball to each other on a high arced path—like this ∩. When Brett throws the ball to Kevin, Fred will see it leave Brett's hand, go up, reach a peak at the top of the curve, and come back down as it lands in Kevin's hands. Part of this arced path is up-and-down, and part of this arced path is side-to-side. So, Fred will see the ball move in both directions.

Now Fred moves so that he positions himself directly *between* Brett and Kevin. They are now throwing the ball to each other in an arced path that goes directly over Fred's head. He is now *under* the arced path of the ball. So, when Brett throws the ball to Kevin, it will not look like this ∩ to Fred anymore. Instead, it will look more like a straight line, like this: |. Fred will see the ball move up-and-down, but he *will not* see it move from side to side. So, following Rule #1—moving so that the ball does not appear to move from side to side—will get Fred *aligned with the path of the ball*, but it won't necessarily put him in position to catch the ball (see Figure 16.11).

So how will Fred know where to go from here so that he can catch the ball? Given that Fred has already positioned himself directly *between* Brett and Kevin, when Brett throws the ball to Kevin, it will go up over Fred's head and land behind him—where Kevin is standing. So, when Fred watches the ball leave Brett's hand, it will appear to reach a *relatively high* peak and *do so faster* as it rises. In other words, it will *appear to speed up*—accelerate—as it rises. If this doesn't make sense to you, imagine standing at the end of a long runway and watching an airplane approach you, take off, and then fly directly over your head. If your gaze is fixed on the plane the entire way, your head will go up slowly at first as the plane begins to fly toward you, and then faster and faster as it flies directly overhead. The same thing will happen to Fred if his gaze is fixed on a ball that is thrown over his head. So, if he is trying to catch a ball and that ball appears to accelerate on its way up, he needs to back up.

Now imagine that Fred backs up way *too far* so that he ends up *behind* Kevin. Now when Brett throws the ball to Kevin, it will land in front of Fred. This time, when Fred watches the ball leave Brett's hand, it will appear to reach a relatively *low peak* and *do so slower* as it rises. In other words, it will *appear to slow down*—decelerate—as it rises. If this doesn't make sense to you, imagine watching that plane approach you, take off, start climbing, and then cut its engines so that it glides back down and lands in front of you. It will not get very high, and as it runs out of momentum on the way up, it will rise more slowly before it eventually starts to glide back down again. The same thing will happen to a thrown ball that runs out of momentum and lands in front of Fred. So, if Fred is trying to catch a ball and that ball appears to decelerate on its way up, he needs to move forward.

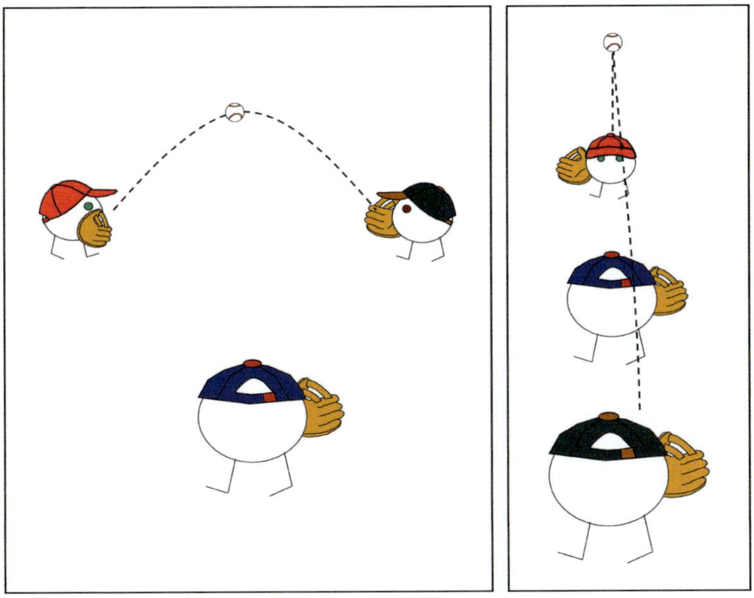

Figure 16.11 The shape of the trajectory of a ball is different depending on Fred's orientation to the game of catch.

Now imagine that Fred moves so that he is *exactly* where the ball will land. This time, when Fred watches the ball leave Brett's hand, it will appear to reach its peak *at a constant speed.* It will not appear to accelerate or decelerate as it rises. Following Rule #2—moving so that the ball appears to move at a constant speed up and down—or equivalently, moving to cancel or eliminate vertical acceleration—will put Fred in the specific location along the ball's trajectory where it will land and when it will land there. In other words, it will put Fred in the right place at the right time—no calculations required and no need to know in advance where or when the ball will get there (see Figure 16.12).

There is evidence that this is how baseball outfielders catch fly balls. In one experiment, participants (who were skilled baseball or softball players) put on a virtual reality headset and attempted to catch virtual balls launched from a virtual distance of about 35 m (about 164 feet) away (Fink et al., 2009). The researchers used sensors to record the position of the participant's head and glove as they attempted to move into position to catch the virtual ball. They then compared these movements to the side-to-side and up-and-down movement of the ball. They found that people seemed to follow both rules when catching the virtual balls—that is, they moved so that ball did not appear to move from side-to-side and appeared to move at a constant speed up and down.

Socratic Question: What are the two behavioral rules for getting into position to catch an object? Why do they work?

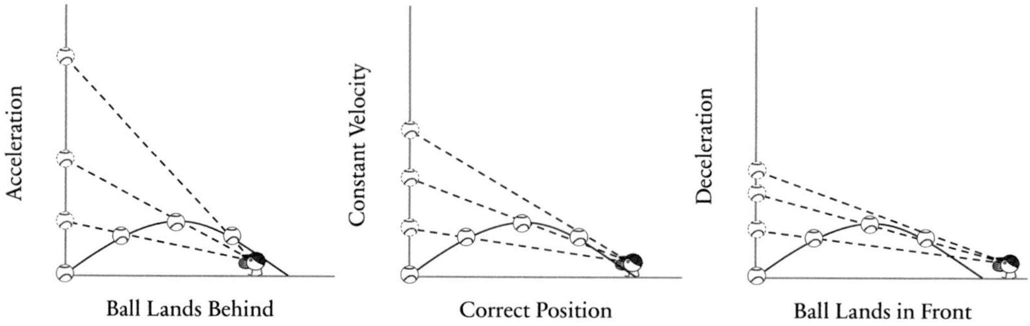

Figure 16.12 Left, if the ball is on track to land behind Fred, the visual angle of the ball (as shown as a projection on the vertical line in each panel) will accelerate. Middle, if the ball is on track to land directly at Fred's location, the visual angle of the ball will have a constant velocity. Right, if the ball is on track to land in front of Fred, the visual angle will decelerate.

Creating, Controlling, and Preventing Collisions

Earlier we defined τ as the rate of optical expansion of a surface relative to the background, and we said that the faster or slower the rate of optical expansion of a given object, the sooner or later that object or you will arrive. But just like you can move to change how fast an object appears to move up and down, like when attempting to catch a ball, you can move to change how fast an object appears to expand or contract, like when approaching or retreating from an object.

It turns out that moving to change the rate of optical expansion is how animals of all kinds—and even robots—control collisions with surfaces or avoid them altogether (see Box 16.3). Say Fred is moving toward his friend James (who goes by J). The slower the rate of optical expansion, the later Fred will arrive where J is. So, if Fred wants to approach J slowly but not necessarily collide with him—say, Fred is sneaking up on J to surprise him—then Fred will need to minimize the rate of optical expansion—the smaller the rate of optical expansion, the better. If Fred wants to approach J quickly and hit him as hard as possible—say, Fred is running toward J to tackle him hard!—then Fred will need to maximize the rate of optical expansion—the larger the rate of the optical expansion, the better. But if Fred wants to approach J collide and with him very gently—say, Fred wants to approach J and give him a hug or shake his hand—then Fred will want to keep the rate of optical expansion small and steady, but not too small.

There is evidence that this is how people and other animals control or prevent collisions. In one experiment, human participants performed a virtual driving task in which they had to decelerate and come to a stop at a virtual stop sign. The participants performed this task from various virtual distances and various virtual speeds and with stop signs of different virtual sizes. The results showed that participants controlled their braking based on the rate of optical expansion of the stop sign. And, in doing so, they attempted to maintain a constant rate of optical expansion (see Figure 14.7; Yilmaz & Warren, 1995). Other studies have found evidence that pigeons control decelerations when landing on perches and hummingbirds control "docking" with flowers by moving to maintain a particular rate of optical expansion (see Figure 16.13; Lee et al., 1991, 1993)

Figure 16.13 There is evidence that birds use tau to gently land (left) or to hover when feeding (right).

What is so critical about this is that the information for being in the right place at the right time is not on the retina or in the brain. It is in the structured light at a point of observation. And detecting this structured light does not require a particular kind of visual system. It only requires that the visual system be sufficiently sensitive to detect this structure. In other words, it has the potential to provide a general explanation for the visual control of pursuit, interception, and catching behaviors by a wide variety of animal species (see Boxes 15.4, 15.5, and 16.3).

Socratic Question: How can the rate of optical expansion be used to create, control, or prevent collisions?

The Development of Visually Controlling Movement

Patterns of occlusion and optic flow provide information about the movement of surfaces relative to an animal and the movement of the animal relative to surfaces. Therefore, animals can use these variables to visually control their behaviors. But animals—like Fred's baby niece, Eleanor—aren't born knowing how to do this. Why would they be? The womb is a pretty dark place. There are no optical patterns *at all* in there. Outside of the womb, however, there is an ambient optic array and lawful relationships between object movements and patterns of occlusion and optic flow. But babies still need to *experience* these lawful relationships to learn what these different patterns of changing optical texture mean. And this experience takes time.

At a few months of age, babies show that they are beginning to understand what different patterns of occlusion mean (E. Gibson & Pick, 2000). In particular, when babies who are a few months old watch a toy temporarily move behind a screen, they tend to look *where they expect the toy to reappear*—at the far end of the screen—rather than where it disappeared—at

Figure 16.14 At just a few months old, babies begin to understand what different patterns of occlusion mean. When a toy disappears behind a screen, they look for it where they expect it to reappear (rather than where it disappeared).

the near end of the screen (see Figure 16.14). At about a year of age, they tend to *put their hands* where they expect the toy to reappear as well (see van der Meer & van der Weel, 2020).

And while infants may not be coordinated enough to move out of the way of an object heading directly toward them—let alone *catch* the object—this doesn't mean that they can't do *anything* to prepare for the impending collision. One thing they *can* do is close their eyes—called defensive blinking. Studies have shown that when an object is heading right toward them, younger infants—closer to 5 months old—tend to blink based more on distance than on time. This sometimes causes them to blink too late, especially when an object is moving pretty quickly. But older infants—closer to 7 months old—tend to blink based on τ, which enabled them to blink appropriately regardless of how fast the object was moving. And when babies who are about a year old attempt to catch a toy that disappears behind a screen, they use τ to get their hands to the right location (where they expect the toy to reappear at the far end of the screen) at the right time (see van der Meer & van der Weel, 2020).

Babies also need to learn what patterns of optic flow mean about their own movements. As you might expect, babies learn this most easily once they have some experience moving themselves around (see Chapter 15). Younger infants with less crawling experience are generally unable to tell the difference among a global expansion pattern (information that they are moving forward), a global contraction pattern (information that they are moving backwards), and random motion (not informative about anything). Older infants with weeks of crawling experience are able to tell the difference among these patterns (Vilhelmsen et al., 2019). And this ability is likely related to why inexperienced and experienced crawling infants behave so differently on the visual cliff and when perceiving affordances of slopes and drop-offs (see Chapter 15, Adolph & Hoch, 2019).

But adults need to learn how to use optical variables like optic flow to visually control their movements, too—especially when they are learning to perform a new skill or when they are learning to perform an existing skill under new circumstances. In one study investigating this, participants wore a virtual reality headset and were asked to walk toward a (virtual) target that appeared at some (virtual) distance in front of them (Bruggeman & Warren, 2010). Except . . . as they walked straight toward the target, it looked to them—through the magic of VR—like they were drifting off at a slight angle from the target—say, off to their right. It was enough of a (virtual) drift that, fairly quickly, they made a correction in their walking path—by walking a little bit in the other direction, say to the left—but not enough that they noticed that they were doing this. In other words, without realizing they were doing so, they learned a subtly different way to use optic flow to visually control where they were walking.

And now comes the cool part. The participants were asked to walk toward the virtual target again, but this time the virtual drift was turned off. Now, they initially walked at a slight angle *in the other direction*—say *to the left*—and then had to make a correction by walking a little bit in the other direction—to the right. Makes sense, right? They had learned that they needed to walk slightly to the left to go straight. But now with the virtual drift turned off, they were off target because this caused them to drift to the left of the target.

Now for the *even cooler* part. The participants were then asked to *throw a ball* and *kick a ball* toward the (virtual) target. If they had learned a general fact about the (virtual) world (e.g., straight = slightly to the left), then they would throw and kick the ball slightly to the left as well. But they did not. What they learned about walking *did not transfer to* throwing or kicking. Why? Because what they had learned was not a fact about the world but a relationship between *optic flow and walking direction.*

The Promise of Getting Light into the Muscle

At the beginning of Chapter 15, we proposed that the fundamental question of the ecological approach to visual perception is "how does light get into and used by the muscles" (Turvey, 2019)? To this end, we introduced you to how the structured light at a point of observation changes when surfaces move relative to a perceiver—*local optic flow* including occlusion—and when a perceiver moves relative to surfaces—*global optic flow*. We also discussed how the structured light at a point of observation is informative about how that person must move in order to perform a given behavior, like catching a ball (or a book).

However, it might be that the person is just not capable of moving in the ways required to perform that behavior. Maybe they are not tall enough or fast enough or strong enough to do so. Not everyone is Victor Wembanyama, Sha'Carri Richardson, Takakeishō Takanobu, or Tamirat Tola. Therefore, the structured light at a point of observation must not only be informative about how an animal must move to perform a given behavior but also about how this compares to how an animal is capable of moving. It must provide information about the perceiver's ability to *do the required work*—it must be action-scaled.

This has been the focus of recent research on "affordance-based control" of visually guided action (Fajen, 2007). For example, Fajen (2005) found that the changes in optic flow that occurred when stepping on the brakes in a simulated driving task enabled drivers to adjust their braking behavior so that they were able to stop the car safely. In other words, these changes helped them learn to use the brake so that the time required to bring the car to a stop did not exceed their ability to do so (see Figure 16.15). This was the case even when the strength of the brake changed, as might happen if they were driving a different car—like a friend's car or a rental car.

Another, more recent study investigated how people perform a simulated drone-flying task that required them to fly the virtual drone through a series of three virtual gates (Jansen & Fajen, 2025). They set up the three virtual gates so that the first two were aligned but the third one was off to the side. The researchers found that when the drone was programmed to be more "sluggish", participants initially turned took a wide and less direct turn through the second gate. When the drone was programmed to be more "agile", they took a tighter and more direct turn through the second gate. Like the studies on braking, these results suggest that people are controlling their movements based on their action capabilities—in particular, based on their abilities to successfully perform the behavior given those action capabilities.

Figure 16.15 Left, optic flow patterns can be used to help drivers adjust braking behavior based on the strength of the brakes. Right, optic flow can also be used to help drone pilots adjust their turning behavior based on the agility of the drone.

Summary

In the ecological approach to visual perception, the seemingly unsolvable problem of how motion is perceived is replaced with the solvable (but still challenging) problem of how moving surfaces and movement of the animal is perceived. Solving this problem requires a scientific understanding of how the structured light encountered by a given animal changes as surfaces move or as the animal changes its point of observation. This is how we continue to make progress in understanding how light gets into the muscle!

Note

1 Of course, movements of the eyes and movements of the head lawfully generate subtly different patterns of global optic flow.

17 Ecological Acoustics and Hearing

In Chapter 14, we proposed that understanding how animals perform everyday behaviors requires developing an ecological physics and geometry—a description of what exists to be perceived and acted on by animals. In Chapters 15 and 16, we applied this approach to understanding how animals use light to perceive and act. This required developing an ecological optics. In this chapter, we will apply this approach to understanding how animals use sound to perceive and act. As you might expect, this will require developing an **ecological acoustics**.

Ecological acoustics a description of the properties of sound (most often in the form of vibrations in the air) at the scale of the relationship between animals and their environments; in particular, a description of how sound is affected by the surfaces and substances that surround an animal.

The energy form differs, of course, but the overall approach to ecological acoustics will be same as that to ecological optics. This is not just a matter of convenience. *It is a matter of necessity.* This is because—from the ecological perspective—the surfaces that surround a given animal don't just lawfully (unambiguously) structure the *light* surrounding that animal; they lawfully (unambiguously) structure *other energy patterns that surround that animal, too.* In other words, the different energy patterns that surround an animal are simultaneously and unambiguously structured by the surfaces that surround that animal.

Moreover, given that the same lawful processes apply across energy forms, then the surfaces and substances that surround a given animal ought to lawfully (unambiguously) structure these energy patterns in *exactly the same way.* The *details* will differ—light is not the same as sound, after all—but there will still be patterns in the structured energy that are lawfully related to the substances and surfaces that surround a given animal. Remember, the medium is not the message.

This means that structure in different energy forms (has the potential to) carry *the same information about* the surfaces that surround a given animal and relationships between that animal and those surfaces. Said differently, the structure in any given energy form (has the potential to) be informative about affordances for that animal. We say "has the potential to" because there may be situations in which theses surfaces or relationships don't structure a particular energy pattern or don't do sufficiently for an animal to detect that structure.

With respect to auditory perception, the sound that is generated by or reflected from the surfaces that surround a given animal is lawfully (unambiguously) structured by those surfaces. And the structured sound that an animal encounters at a given point of observation—*a given listening point*—is unambiguously related to the animal's relationship to those

DOI: 10.4324/9781032690964-20

substances and surfaces. In other words, the structured sound that an animal actively encounters at a given point of observation is (potentially) informative about affordances for that animal. So, the fundamental question in the ecological approach to auditory perception is whether the animal can use sounds to act on affordances. In other words, the fundamental question in the ecological approach to auditory perception is—how does sound get into and used by the muscles?

Ecological Acoustics

More or less, the same three fundamental points that we made about ecological optics in Chapter 15 also apply to ecological acoustics. The first point is that most animals are not just immersed in an ocean of light; they are also immersed in an *ocean of sound* (see Figure 17.1). To some extent, the ocean of sound surrounding animals is easier to imagine than the ocean of light surrounding animals. After all, by definition, sound-producing and sound-reflecting objects are noisy. By contrast, light-producing and light-reflecting objects are (often) silent!

The second point is that just like the ocean of light, the ocean of sound is not uniform. It differs in different locations and in different directions (at a particular listening location). However, *unlike the ocean of light*, the ocean of sound does not start out unstructured. Instead, it is structured by the (vibrations created by the) interacting materials that generate the sound. The third point is that the (already structured) sound becomes *differently* structured when those vibrations *reflect off* surrounding surfaces (see Figure 17.1). Together, these three points are the keys to ecological acoustics (Carello et al., 2005).

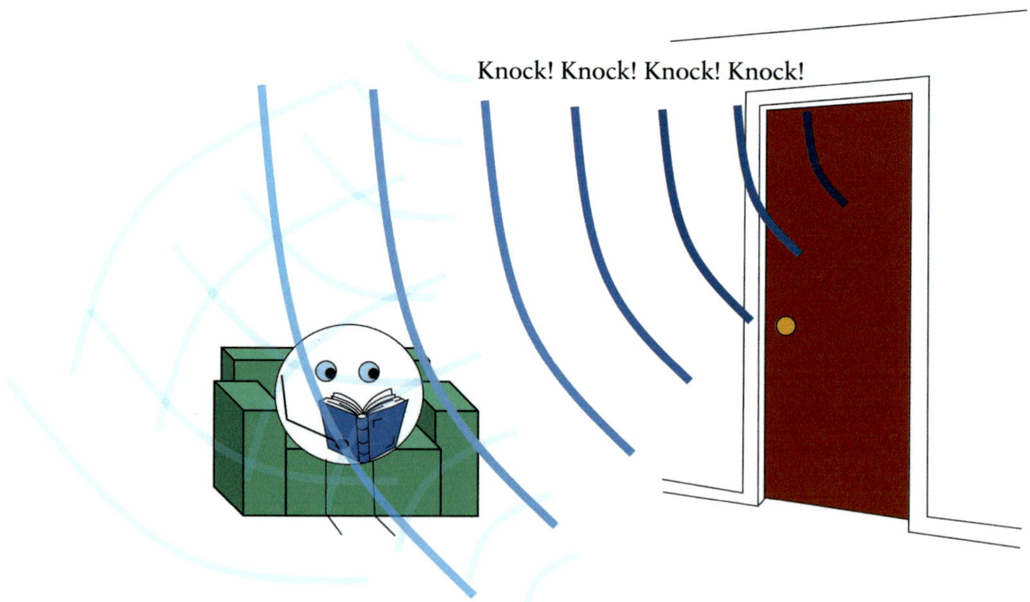

Figure 17.1 Sounds generated by a sound source are structured by the interacting materials that create the sound. The sound of the knock on the door bounces off the floor, furniture, ceiling, and walls. Fred encounters the sound directly from the door and reflected off all the surrounding surfaces. This ambient sound provides information about both the sound source and the surrounding surfaces.

Let's back up a bit and go through each of these points a little more slowly and carefully. Let's again assume that Fred is sitting in the comfiest chair he owns reading this book. Suddenly, there is a sound—say, a knock on his front door (see Figure 17.1).

Although it may seem strange, sound is caused when objects collide or interact in some other way, causing vibration in the air (see Chapter 5). In the ecological approach, the focus is on how these vibrations are lawfully structured by the properties of those objects as well as where and how those objects are interacting, among other factors (Gaver, 1993; Gibson, 1966). In other words, the focus is on how this *acoustic structure* is lawfully related to properties of the sound-producing object(s).

When the (mystery) person knocks on Fred's door, some of the structured sound that reaches him will come directly from (the vibration of) the door. This sound will be lawfully structured by the properties of the door (and the hand of the person knocking). For example, the knock will sound different depending on whether Fred has a wooden door or a metal door. And the knock might even sound different depending on *who* is knocking—sumo wrestler Takakeishō Takanobu or marathon runner Victor Kiplangat or his best friend Claudia, for example.

But some of the structured sound that Fred encounters will come *indirectly* from the door by reflecting off nearby surfaces in the room (e.g., the walls, the carpet, the window, the table). For example, the knock will sound different depending on whether the room is empty or if it is full of furniture. It will also sound different depending on whether the room has hardwood floors or carpet.[1] In fact, in most everyday situations, auditory perceiving typically occurs by means of **ambient sound**—structured sounds generated by a sound source and reflected from surrounding surfaces (Carello et al., 2005; Gaver, 1993; see Box 17.1).

Ambient sound the structured sound produced by sources and reflecting from surfaces that surround an animal.

Box 17.1 Musical Listening vs. Everyday Listening

As we mentioned earlier, it is not that difficult to imagine yourself surrounded by an ocean of sounds. But from the ecological perspective, you don't generally hear the sounds themselves. *Wait . . . what? Yep.* Instead, you hear the *sources* of those sounds—objects and events, surface layout, and affordances. This is not to say that you *can't* hear the sounds themselves. You certainly can. For example, you can describe properties of a given sound such as loudness, pitch, and timbre, among others (see Chapter 12). But doing so requires taking what some researchers have called a "musical attitude" (see Carello et al., 2005). This means specifically paying attention to the sounds themselves and not the *sources* of those sounds. While listening to music—maybe Fred's solo in *From Cockney to Yankee*—you might be aware of the sweeping ascending melody rather than what Fred is doing with his vocal tract or what the accompanying cellist is doing with her bow.

But in most everyday situations, you probably *don't* do this. Instead, most of the time, you take an "everyday listening attitude"—you pay specifically pay attention to the *sources* of the sound, not the sounds themselves (see Figure 17.2). In particular, you pay attention to your relationship to those sources and whether, how, and when you

Figure 17.2 As a musical listener, Fred would describe the noise from his window as loud, high-pitched, sudden. As an everyday listener, he realizes it's the raccoons in his garbage again!

might be able to perform everyday behaviors with respect to those sources. For example, if Fred heard clanging and crashing outside of his window at night, he might (want to) be aware of what caused those sounds (Topsy playing with her toys? Raccoons rummaging in the trash?) and what he might do about it (play with her? Shoo them away?), rather than the specific properties of the sounds themselves. In everyday auditory perceiving, we are generally aware of the sources of sounds and our relationship to those sources, but we can become aware of certain properties of the sounds themselves under certain circumstances. This is not all that different from everyday visual perceiving, where we are aware of the surfaces that structure the light and our relationship to those surfaces, but we can become aware of certain properties of the light itself (e.g., color, brightness, quality).

Socratic Question: How do the same three fundamental points about ecological optics apply to ecological acoustics? What is the difference between musical listening and everyday listening?

Like the light that reflects off surfaces, the sound that reflects off surfaces is structured by the properties of those surfaces. These surfaces create differences in structured reflected sound in different directions. Just like light, there are only a few things that can happen when sound—in the form of a vibration pattern in the air—strikes a surface. Some of the sound will be absorbed by the surface, and some of the sound will be reflected from it. *How much* is reflected and *how much* is absorbed is lawfully related to the properties of that surface. More sound will be reflected if the surface is *metallic*—like Fred's stainless-steel refrigerator—than if it is *plush*—like his couch. How the sound is reflected is also lawfully related to the properties of that surface. The sound will be scattered *more* if the surface is *textured*—like Fred's carpets—than if it is *smooth*—like his tile floors (see Figure 17.3).

Figure 17.3 Sound is lawfully structured by its contact with surfaces. More sound will be reflected by metal than by suede. Sound will be scattered more by carpet than by tile.

> **Acoustic structure (or texture)** patterns created when interacting and surrounding substances and surfaces lawfully structure sound.

So, just like reflected light will have different intensities in different directions depending on the surface(s) that it strikes, reflected sound will have different intensities in different directions depending on the surface(s) that it strikes. These differences give reflected sound *structure*—they create acoustic texture. And this **acoustic structure** *(or texture)* is lawfully related to the surface(s) that it strikes.

Like light, sounds reflect from surface to surface, reverberating in the room until the interacting materials creating the vibrations cease to interact. This *fills the room—at least temporarily—with structured sound*. And since sound is lawfully structured by properties of the surface(s) that it strikes, the reflected sound that fills the room is lawfully structured by the surfaces in that room.

And now we have reached a fundamental tenet of ecological acoustics. At any given point in the room, there will be differences in structured sound in different directions. This will be the case because of the specifics of the interacting materials that created that sound *and* how the reflected sound reaches that location from those directions (see Figure 17.4).

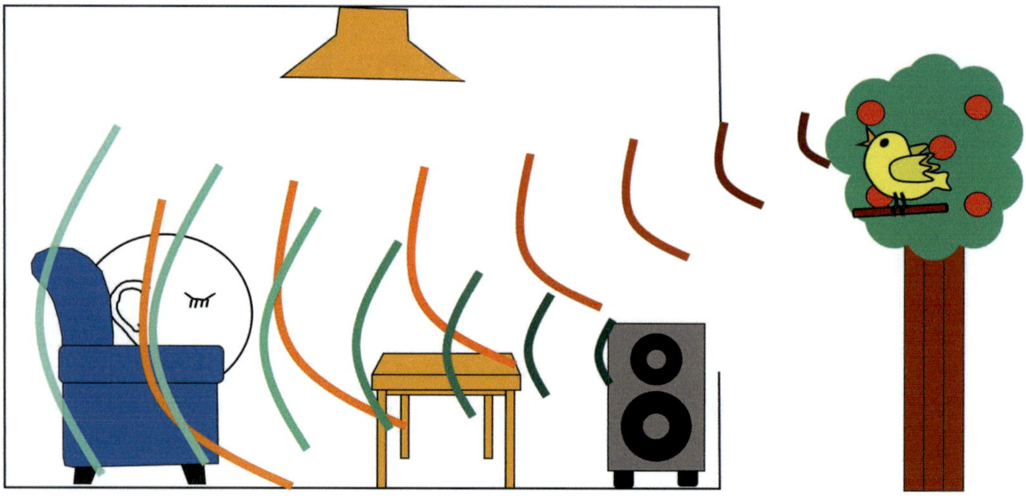

Figure 17.4 The acoustic structure converging at Fred's point of observation is informative about the layout of surfaces.

The Ambient Acoustic Array

The pattern of structured sound converging at *every location in that room that Fred could occupy* is unique (meaning one of a kind). At every possible listening point, there is a unique distribution of structured sound—a unique set of differences in different directions. This is yet another fundamental tenet of ecological acoustics (see Figure 17.4).

The totality of structured sound at each and every possible location in the room is the **ambient acoustic array**—the acoustic equivalent of the ambient optic array. In the ecological approach, the ambient acoustic array is the relevant stimulation pattern for auditory perceiving. And the ambient sound converging at a given listening point provides information about surfaces, their relationships to one another, and the listener's current relationship to these surfaces. It provides information about affordances! This is how the sound gets into the muscles!

Ambient acoustic array the structured sound available at a given point of observation (at a location that an animal might occupy).

Information About Surfaces

Imagine that Fred has finished reading this book for the afternoon and he is now setting the table for dinner for himself and some friends, including Claudia, who are set to arrive at any minute. He is carrying various plates, bowls, glasses, and silverware on a tray to the table when a loud knock on the door startles him so much that one of the items falls from the tray. He doesn't know which item it is, but he hears the object strike the ground. From the sound alone, however, he can tell quite a bit about the object, where it went, and what happened to it. For one thing, he knows that it is a ceramic object—a plate or bowl as opposed to silverware or glassware. For another, he knows that that it is flat, circular, and large—a dinner plate as opposed to a salad plate or a soup bowl. For another, he knows that it ended up on the floor by his feet and not under the table. And finally, he knows that it bounced and did not shatter—whew! The reason that he was able to know of these things just by listening is that each of these interactions among surfaces lawfully structure the ambient acoustic array.

Hearing Objects

Though it might not seem so, Fred's ability to know these things just by listening is fairly typical of everyday experience. In some ways, *hearing* properties of surfaces and relationships between surfaces and animals might seem to be an even bigger challenge than *seeing* such properties and relationships. In fact, strictly based on the complex Euclidean geometry, it should be difficult—if not impossible—to perceive geometric properties of objects based on sound alone. This is because for two-dimensional objects—which, strictly speaking, have no thickness and therefore only exist in the abstract—there is an ambiguous relationship between vibration frequency and shape.

A series of experiments conducted at the turn of the 21st century, however, demonstrated not only that people can people perceive geometric properties of objects based on sound alone, but that they can do it quite well (Kunkler-Peck & Turvey, 2000). Researchers built a rectangular wooden frame and used fishing line to suspend thin, flat objects of different sizes, shapes, and materials within that frame—one object at a time. A pendulum bob was attached by string to the top of the frame and was used to strike each object (see Figure 17.5, *left*). The pendulum bob was released from the same location—and therefore struck each object with the same amount of force—each time. Participants were on the other side of a screen and could not see the object or the pendulum, but they could hear the sound produced when the pendulum bob struck the object.

In one of these experiments, the objects were made of three different materials—wood, Plexiglas, and steel—and were three different shapes—a circle, square, and triangle. All the objects were the same thickness and had the same surface area. Of course, the steel objects weighed more than the wood objects which weighed more than the Plexiglas objects, but all shapes of a given material weighed the same amount (e.g., the wood triangle weighed the same as the wood square and the wood circle). On a given trial, one of the nine objects was

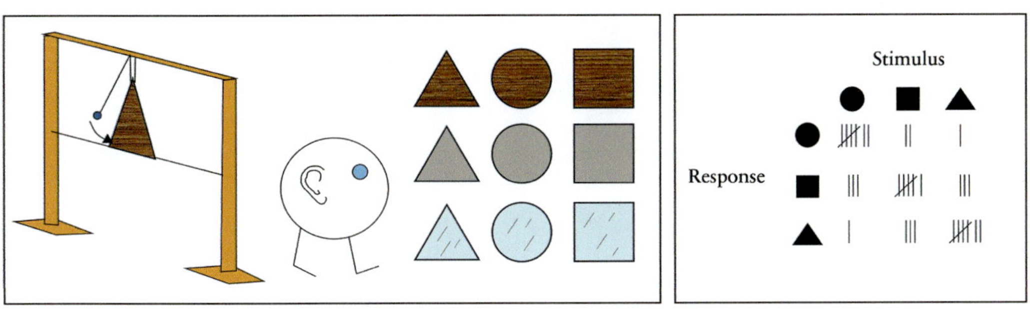

Figure 17.5 Left, the apparatus used by Kunkler-Peck and Turvey (2000). A pendulum bob was struck against suspended objects of different shapes and materials. Right, participants were able to hear material nearly perfectly and shape at a level above chance.

suspended from the frame, and the pendulum bob was released to strike the object three separate times. The participant listened to the sound produced by the pendulum bob striking the object and tried to identify both the material and the shape of the object by pointing to one of nine example objects.

Participants were pretty good at this task. As you might expect, they correctly identified the material on well over 99% of the trials—there was only one misidentification across all trials for all participants. And they correctly identified shape on 56% of the trials (see Figure 17.5, *right*). This doesn't sound so impressive—no pun intended!—until you consider that chance performance would have been 33%. In other words, reports of object shape were not perfectly accurate, but they were not random, either. As strange as it might seem, triangles sounded more or less like triangles, squares sounded more or less like squares, and circles sounded more or less like circles.

This is all well and good, but participants in this experiment were essentially completing a multiple-choice test. They knew ahead of time that there were only three options for material and three options for shape. Maybe this made the task too easy? What if all the objects were the *same* shape but were different *sizes*—maybe rectangles of different heights and widths? And, what if participants were not told how many different objects there were or how big or small they could be? And, what if participants had to report an *exact size*—height *and* width—of each object? This is precisely what happened in a different experiment. The objects were metal rectangles of three different sizes—one was over 3 times as tall as it was wide, one was about 1.5 times as tall as it was wide, and one was perfectly square.[2] All the objects were the same thickness, had the same surface area, and weighed the same amount.

On a given trial, one of the objects was suspended from the frame, and the pendulum bob was released to strike the object three separate times (see Figure 17.6, *left*). In one set of trials, the participant listened to the sound of the pendulum bob striking the object and then adjusted two movable markers on a horizontal track so that the distance between them was the same as the *width* of the struck object. In another set of trials, the participant adjusted two moveable markers on a vertical track so that the distance between them was the same as the *height* of the struck object.

So how did participants do? Perhaps surprisingly, they did remarkably well. Even though participants underestimated the overall sizes of each rectangle, they reported the relative heights and widths of the rectangles appropriately. As the rectangles got taller and thinner,

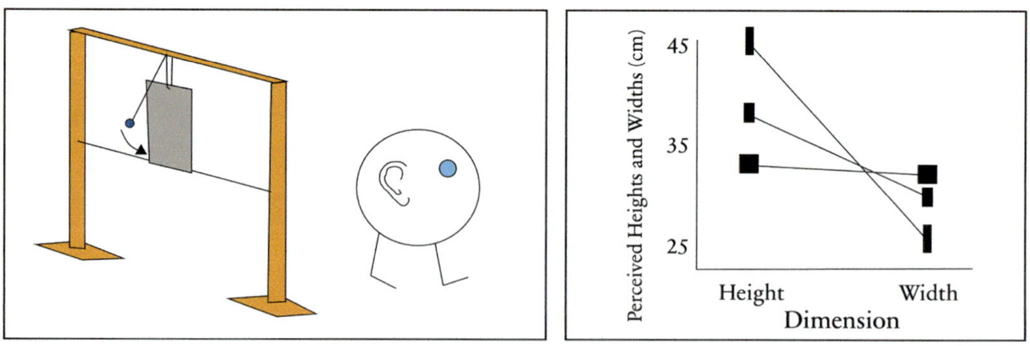

Figure 17.6 Left, the apparatus used by Kunkler-Peck and Turvey (2000). A pendulum bob was struck against suspended metal rectangles. Right, participants could hear whether the rectangle was taller than it was wide, as tall as it was wide, or wider than it was tall.

they were perceived to be taller and thinner. And as they got shorter and wider, they were perceived to be shorter and wider.

In addition, both the perceived heights and the perceived widths were in the approximate range of the actual heights and actual widths (see Figure 17.6, *right*). This is even more impressive when you consider that participants had no advance knowledge of how many objects there were or how big (or small) those objects could be. Rather, they were able to *hear* the approximate relative dimensions of each object when it was struck with the pendulum.

What was the structure in the acoustic array that could have provided information about the relative dimensions of the rectangle? The researchers proposed that such information was provided in the **vibrational dynamics** of the objects—how the material properties and shape of a given object influence how it vibrates differently along each of its axes when struck. In other words, the researchers proposed that for *real objects* made of *real materials* in a *real environment*—not two-dimensional objects that exist only in the abstract—there was an *unambiguous* relationship between sound and shape.

Vibrational dynamics how the material properties and shape of an object influences how it vibrates differently along each of its axes when struck.

Socratic Question: Mathematically speaking, it should be impossible to hear the shape of abstract two-dimensional surfaces. However, it turns out that people can hear the shape of real surfaces made of real materials. What is the difference between these scenarios in terms of ecological acoustics?

One potential objection to the research that we just described on hearing the shape of a struck object is how controlled the collision of the pendulum bob was. Remember that each object was suspended in a wooden frame so that its position was relatively stable, and the pendulum bob struck each object at the same location and with the same amount of force each time. Everyday auditory perceiving is much messier—and much less predictable—than this (see Chapters 5 and 12).[3] When Fred dropped what turned out to be a dinner plate, it likely tumbled unpredictably from the tray, striking the ground awkwardly, clattering and rolling until it came to a rest. Can participants still hear geometric properties of objects under these conditions? Yes, yes, they can.

In particular, people can hear how long a wooden rod is based on the sound it makes when it is dropped to the floor. Just as they did with the heights and widths of the struck plates, participants generally underestimated the lengths of the dropped rods. Nonetheless, as the actual length of the rod increased, so did the perceived length of the rod (Carello et al., 1998). What was the information about length in this scenario? The researchers proposed that—like the information about height and width of the struck objects—information about the length of the rods was in the vibrational dynamics of the rods—how the rod's material properties and shape influence how it vibrates along each of its axes.

An object's mass determines its inertia—its resistance to being moved. And inertia is one of the factors that influences the pattern of vibration when one object collides with another object. This is one reason why the knock will sound different if (the more sturdily built) Takakeishō Takanobu or (the more slightly built) Victor Kiplangat is the one knocking. But when a rod collides with the ground, it doesn't just land with a thud—it *clatters and rolls.* How much it clatters and rolls is determined by its *rotational inertia*—its resistance to rotation in different directions (see Chapter 18). And it turned out that rotational inertia did a better job at predicting perceived length than many traditional acoustical variables—such as signal duration, amplitude, and frequency (Carello et al., 1998).

Hearing Occluding Objects

And what about hearing whether the plate landed on the floor by his feet and not under the table? So far, we have been discussing cases in which a person hears the properties of a sound-producing object itself. What shape is it? What material is it? However, this particular task—hearing whether the plate rolled under the table—seems to require hearing a *silent* object (see Rosenblum, 2011). That is, it requires hearing where the clattering plate is relative to the silent table. Ponder this for a moment, but then remember that everyday auditory perceiving occurs by means of both sounds *generated by* a sound source and sounds *reflected from* surrounding surfaces. These reflecting surfaces typically don't make any sound at all, but they do change *how* the reflected sound is structured. In this case, the table is one of those surrounding surfaces. Also, keep in mind that this is no different than visually perceiving that one surface is behind—or occluded by—another object (see Chapters 15 and 16).

Accordingly, people can hear whether or not a surface occludes a sound-producing object. Moreover, they can hear whether the surface mostly or only partly occludes that object (Russell & Brown, 2020). In this experiment, a wooden board was placed completely in front of, mostly in front of, halfway in front of, only a little in front of, or not at all in front of, a loudspeaker (see Figure 17.7).

On a given trial, a blindfolded participant sat at a table, and the board was positioned at one of these five locations relative to the speaker. A sound was played through the speaker,

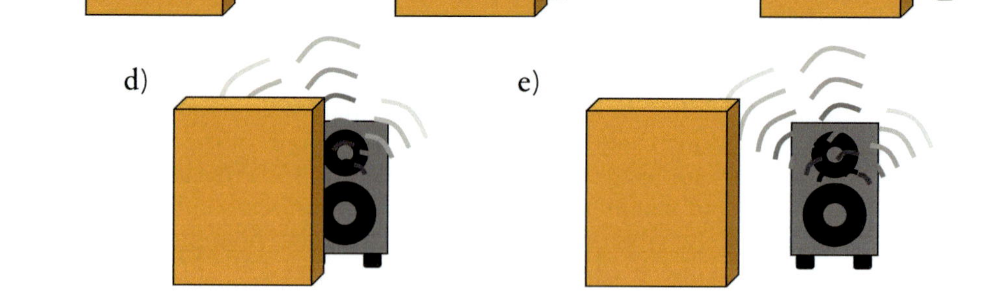

Figure 17.7 In the experiment by Russell and Brown (2020), participants could hear the extent to which a surface (a wooden board) blocked a sound source (a speaker). In their experiment, the surface was a) completely in front of the sound source, b) mostly in front of the sound source, c) and d) partly in front of the sound source, or e) not at all in front of the sound source.

Figure 17.8 Researchers hung shapes in front of speakers playing white noise. Participants were able to identify the shapes at a rate higher than chance.

and the participant was asked to report—yes or no—whether the board was blocking the speaker in any way whatsoever. In general, participants performed this task quite well. When the board was *completely* in front of the speaker, the participants correctly said "yes" approximately 90% of the time, and when the board was *not* in front of the speaker, the participants correctly said "no" approximately 85% of the time. Moreover, participants were more likely to say "yes" when the board was *mostly* in front of the speaker than when it was only *partly* in front of the speaker (Russell & Brown, 2020).

Amazingly, people not only can hear whether there is a surface between them and a sound producing object, they can hear *what shape that surface is* (see Figure 17.8; Rosenblum & Robart, 2007). In this experiment, foam shapes—a square, a circle, and a triangle, all with the same surface area—were positioned on a stand in front of loudspeakers. On a given trial, one of the shapes was placed on the support, and blindfolded participants stood with their ear next to the shape while a sound—in this case, white noise or static—was played through the speakers for 10 seconds. They listened to the sound and tried to identify which of the three shapes was positioned on the stand.

On average, participants correctly identified the shape on 43.2% of the trials. Specifically, they correctly identified the square 38.9% of the time, the circle 42.2% of the time, and the triangle, 49.2% of the time. Again, this doesn't sound so impressive—this time, pun absolutely intended!—until you consider that chance performance would have been 33%. Like the experiment in which participants listened to shapes that were struck by a pendulum bob, reports of object shape were not perfectly accurate, but they were not random, either. As strange as it may seem, silent triangles sounded more or less like triangles, silent squares sounded more or less like squares, and silent circles sounded more or less like circles!

Socratic Question: What is the evidence that people can hear the shapes of *occluded* objects (one that makes a sound) and of *occluding* objects (one that blocks a sound)?

Hearing Events—Bouncing vs. Breaking

What about hearing what happened to the plate—whether it bounced or broke? We know that people can *see* events (see Chapter 14). Given what we have already discussed, it would make sense that they can *hear* events, too. But can they hear the difference between these two different events? Yes, yes, they can.

In the first of several experiments investigating this ability, researchers recorded the sound that three different glass objects each made when they fell to the ground from a shorter height—resulting in the object bouncing—and from a taller height—resulting in the object breaking (Warren & Verbrugge, 1984, see Figure 17.9). They then played these recordings to people and asked them whether they thought that the object bounced or broke, or whether they were unsure. Participants were almost 100% accurate! And this is despite not having any information about what kind of object was dropped, the height from which the objects were dropped, the surface on which the objects were dropped, among many other factors.

The next two experiments in the study were geared toward understanding *how* participants were able to do this. In other words, the experiments were geared toward discovering what *information about bouncing or breaking* is available in the acoustic array. The researchers used a description of bouncing and breaking as ecological events as a guide. In particular, when an object bounces, there will be an initial impact with the ground that sets the *entire object* into vibration. The specifics of these vibrations will depend on the object's size, shape, and composition—like the struck metal objects or the knock on Fred's front door. The object will then fall back to ground and bounce again. As the object loses energy, each successive impact will occur more quickly until the object stops moving (and stops vibrating) altogether. How quickly these successive bounces occur will *also* depend on the object's size, shape, and composition. In other words, when an object bounces, it generates *a singular repeating pulse of energy* that decreases in strength over time—a single "damped" energy pulse (see Figure 17.9, *left*).

When an object *breaks*, however, there will be an initial impact that breaks the object into pieces and sets *each individual piece* into vibration. Each piece will vibrate (slightly) differently because each one is a (slightly) different size and shape. Then each piece will fall to the ground and bounce again. As each piece loses energy, each successive impact will occur more

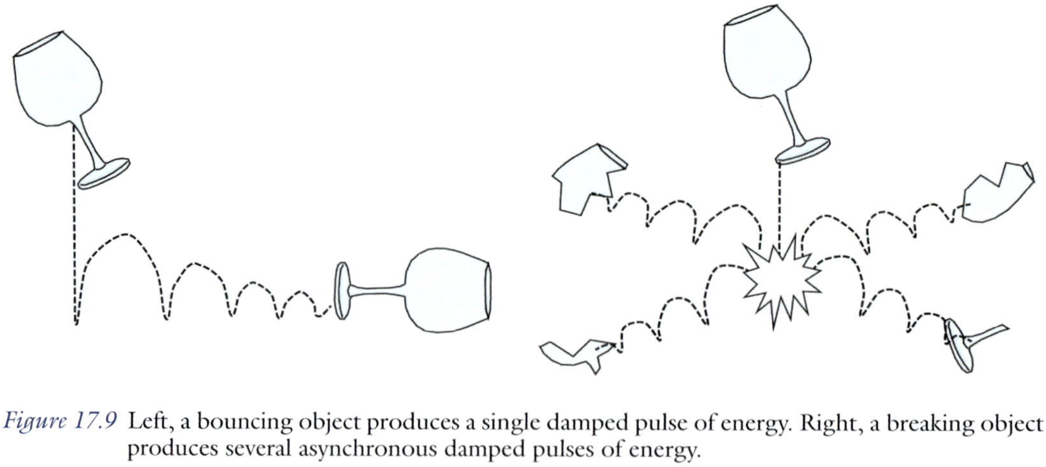

Figure 17.9 Left, a bouncing object produces a single damped pulse of energy. Right, a breaking object produces several asynchronous damped pulses of energy.

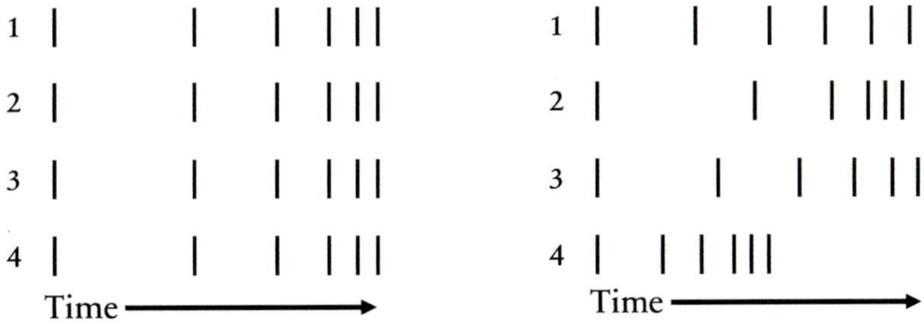

Figure 17.10 The timing of four separate acoustic energy pulses used by Warren and Verbrugge (1984). When the pulses were artificially put "in sync" (left), participants heard a bouncing object. When the pulses were artificially put "out of sync" (right), participants heard a breaking sound.

quickly until each piece stops moving (and stops vibrating) altogether. However, the timing of the successive impacts will differ for each piece because each piece will differ in size and shape. In other words, when an object breaks, it generates *multiple* repeating pulses of energy that decrease in strength over time, but these pulses will be "*out of sync*" with each other—*asynchronous* damped pulses of energy (see Figure 17.9, *right*).

To test this, researchers collected the four largest pieces of a broken glass bottle. They dropped each piece to the floor—one at a time—and recorded the (bouncing) sound that each piece made when it fell to ground. They then digitally manipulated these recordings to create an ***artificial breaking sound*** and an ***artificial bouncing sound***.

To create an artificial bouncing sound, the researchers adjusted the timing of the impacts to be the same across all four pieces. That is, they took four "out of sync" pulses of energy and artificially put them "in sync" (see Figure 17.10, *left*).

To create an ***artificial breaking sound***, they adjusted the timing of the impacts to be *different* across all four pieces. In other words, they ensured that the pulses of energy were "out of sync" (see Figure 17.10, *right*). When participants listened to these sounds, they identified the artificial breaking sound as a breaking object over 85% of the time, and they identified the artificial bouncing sound as a bouncing object over 90% of the time.

Information About *Relationships Between* Animals and Surfaces

Fred was able to know that the plate did not break just from the sound that it made when it struck the floor—*whew*! But what else could he know about it just by the sound it made? Could he hear whether the plate landed within reach? Likewise, what could he tell about the *door* based just on the knocking sound? Could he tell if it was open or closed? If the door was *partly* open, could he hear whether it was open wide enough for him to walk through? What if the door was *partly* open and—instead of knocking on the door—he heard traffic noises coming through the opening? Could he hear whether it was open wide enough for him to walk through it then? And if the traffic noise included the sound of a car driving toward his house, could he tell when that car might arrive? The answer to all of these questions is "yes".

Hearing What Is Reachable

A study investigating the ability to *hear* whether an object was within reach (Rosenblum et al., 1996) was based on studies that investigated the ability to see whether an object was within reach (see Chapter 14). The researchers recruited a group of taller participants and a group of shorter participants, under the assumption that taller people have longer arms than shorter people. Each participant was seated and blindfolded. A rattle consisting of paperclips in a small box was attached to a pole on a moveable cart. The cart was placed at a particular distance from the listener, and the rattle was shaken. The participant reported—yes or no—whether they would be able to reach the object (see Figure 17.11, *top*).

The researchers asked about two different types of reaches. When the object was within a range of *near* distances, the participant reported whether they could reach the object with their arm only (without bending forward at the waist). When the object was placed within a range of *far* distances, they reported whether they could reach the object with their arm if they were to bend forward at the waist.

In both cases, participants with long arms said yes more often than participants with short arms. And the perceptual boundary between objects that were and were not perceived to be reachable occurred at a farther distance for participants with long arms than for participants with short arms. However, this boundary occurred at the same perceived critical π value of object distance to arm length (or object distance to arm-plus-torso length) for each group. In short, participants could *hear* whether an object was within reach for two different styles of reaching, and perception was body-scaled (see Figure 17.11, *bottom*).

Hearing What Is Pass-Through-Able

We briefly mentioned two experiments that investigated the ability to hear whether an opening affords passing through in Chapter 14. We provide a little more detail here. Participants

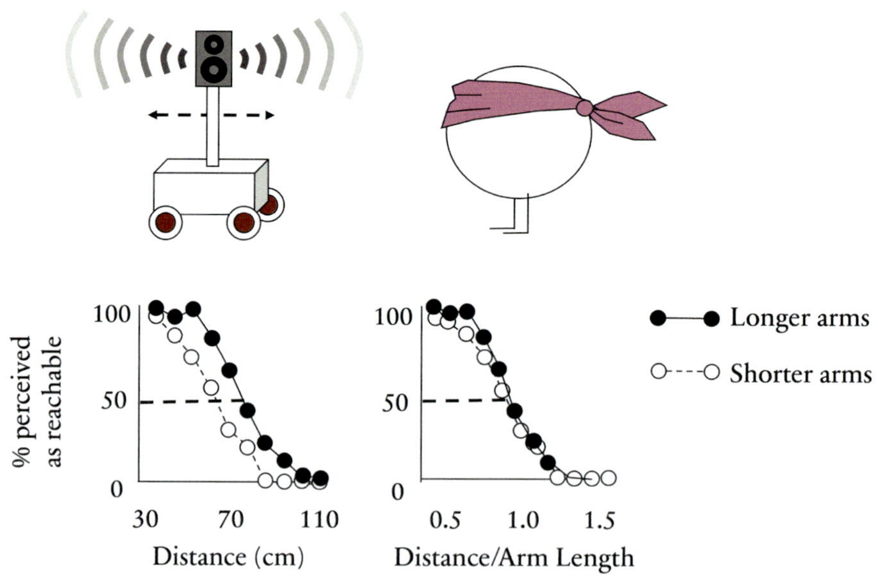

Figure 17.11 Top in a study by Rosenblum et al. (1996), blindfolded participants listened to a sound-producing object at different distances and reported whether they would be able to reach that object. The boundary between objects that were perceived to be reachable occurred at farther distances for people with long arms than those with short arms (bottom, left) but at the same ratio of object distance to arm length for both groups (bottom, right). Note the similarity between this graph and the one in Figure 14.10 showing results from an experiment on visually perceiving affordances for passing through a doorway.

were brought into a room and stood with one of their shoulders against a wall of the room and closed their eyes. A speaker was placed a few feet in front of them at different horizontal distances from the wall. A duck call[4]—consisting of eight distinct "notes" and lasting for approximately three seconds—was played over the speaker at each of these distances. Participants reported—yes or no—whether they would be able to pass through the space between the sound source and the wall without turning their shoulders (see Figure 17.12; Russell & Turvey, 1999).

The perceptual boundary—the perceived critical π value—between openings that afford walking through—without turning the body occurred at a ratio of opening-width-to-shoulder-width of 1.11, which is comparable to the value obtained for visually perceiving whether an opening could be walked through (1.16; see Chapter 14). More recently, researchers have investigated whether people can hear if they can *roller skate* between two sound-producing objects—yes, really (O'Neill & Russell, 2017). In this case, the perceptual boundary occurred at a ratio of opening-width-to-shoulder-width of 1.69, which was not much different than the perceptual boundary for *seeing* whether they can roller skate between two obstacles.

An experiment investigating whether people can hear if they can pass through an opening based on the sound passing through that opening was conducted by Gordon and Rosenblum (2004). In the first experiment, blindfolded participants stood on one side of two sliding panels on a horizontal track. When the panels were slid together, they formed a wall; when they were slid apart, they formed an opening—like a doorway. On the other side of the panels were six loudspeakers that played crowd noise,[5] recorded from a large lecture hall just before class started.

The panels were adjusted to form an opening of a particular size, and the crowd noise was played. The participants' job was to say whether or not they would be able to walk straight through the opening without turning their shoulders. The perceptual boundary (the

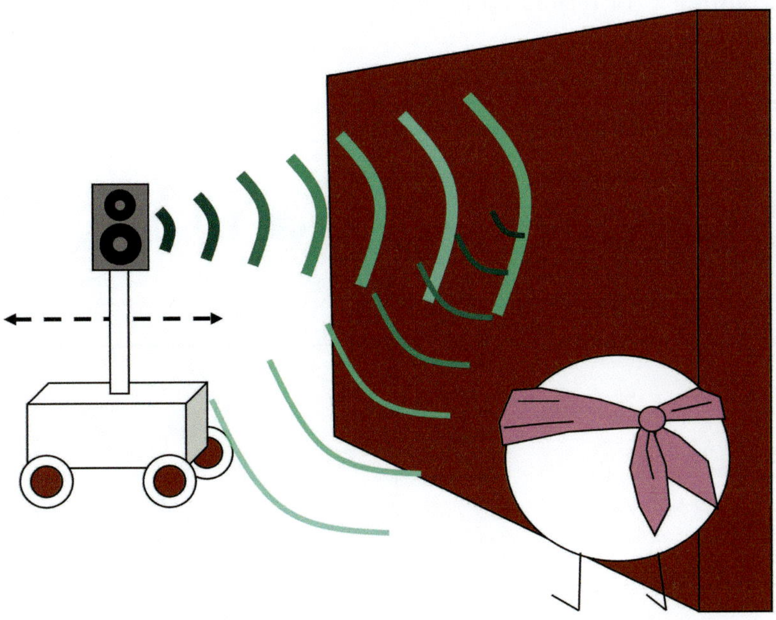

Figure 17.12 Blindfolded participants can hear whether they would be able to walk between a wall and a sound-producing object (a speaker).

perceived critical π value) for openings that afford walking through occurred at the same ratio of opening-width-to-shoulder-width for participants with narrow shoulders and participants with wide shoulders (on average about 1.06, again comparable to the experiments on visually perceiving of affordances for walking through an opening).

Socratic Question: How does the ability to hear affordances for behaviors such as reaching or passing through compare to the ability to see affordances for these behaviors?

Hearing Time to Contact

In Chapter 16, we discussed experiments showing that people can see when an object that is heading toward them will arrive based on a variable called tau (τ). As a reminder, τ describes how quickly the optical texture of the object expands as it approaches—the rate of optical expansion relative to the background. Can people *hear* when an object will arrive based on an acoustic equivalent of τ? Based on our claim that surfaces and substances that surround a given animal lawfully different energy forms in *exactly the same way*, then they ought to be able to do so.

As a sound source approaches, the acoustical structure created by the object will also "expand" as it approaches and will "occlude" background sounds. This will be experienced as the sound getting louder—and clearer—and progressively "drowning out" any other sounds. And, just as in the case where the person can *see* the approaching object, how *quickly* this structure expands as it approaches is information about its time to arrival. In this case, the sound will get louder and clearer slowly at first and then more rapidly as the object gets closer (like the time that a bee landed on Fred's nose; see Figure 17.13).

Accordingly, research has shown that both blind people and blindfolded sighted people can use acoustical τ (or related variables) to determine when an approaching vehicle or

Figure 17.13 As the bee approaches Fred, the acoustic structure produced by its vibrating wings will get progressively louder and progressively occlude background sounds. How quickly this occurs is information about time to arrival.

person will arrive or pass by their current location[6] (Rosenblum et al., 1993), bats can use acoustical τ (or related variables) to avoid obstacles while flying (Lee et al., 1992), and *hearing* a moving room move generates the same postural response as seeing a moving room move (Stoffregen et al., 2010, 2009; see Chapter 16).

Socratic Question: How does the acoustic information for time to contact compare to the optical information for time to contact?

Now imagine that Fred has retrieved the plate from the floor, answered the door, finished setting the table, and is currently pouring water into each glass on the table. Could he *hear* when he should stop pouring the water? Does acoustical τ provide information about the "time to arrival" of the liquid to the top of the glass? Yes, yes, it does.

Cabe and Pittenger (2000) investigated this in a series of experiments. In one of the experiments, participants were blindfolded and seated in front of a spigot. On a table below the spigot was a cylindrical plastic container—the size of a medium water glass. In one condition, the participants were asked to turn the spigot on, listen to sound of the container filling with water, and then turn the spigot off when the glass was *just full to the brim* without allowing it to overflow. In a different condition, participants were asked to do the same thing, except they were to turn the spigot off when the water was at a "preferred drinking level"—which would presumably be lower than all the way to the brim.

In the "full to the brim" condition, the participants filled the glass to 88% to the top on average, and in the preferred drinking level condition, the participants filled the glass to 70% to the top on average. Allowing participants to both see and hold the container as the water poured into it improved both accuracy and consistency of performance. Nonetheless, participants did not need to do either one to successfully perform the task. They could differentiate the two levels of fullness *just by listening*.

A follow-up study investigated whether participants were, in fact, using acoustical τ to perceive the time to arrival of the water to the top of the container. The researchers derived an acoustic variable that was analogous to optical τ. They investigated whether participants (could) use this variable to perceive when the water would reach the top of the container. Blindfolded participants listened to water flowing from a spigot into a cylindrical plastic container—this time, the size of a tall water glass—at three different fill rates. The researchers wanted to ensure that participants were not simply waiting for the water to overflow the container to make their response.[7] So, they only filled the glass partway (1/4, 1/2, or 3/4 full) and then turned the spigot off. The participant's job was to indicate when the container *would have been* completely filled if the water continued to pour in from the spigot. The researchers found that perceived time to fill tracked actual time to fill quite well. In fact, the results paralleled those investigating visual perception of time to contact—like the one on diving gannets (see Chapter 16; Box 16.3).

Box 17.2 Echolocation

From the ecological perspective, perceiving is an activity. In the case of auditory perceiving, for example, listeners move around and turn their heads to help orient to a sound source or cup their hand over their ear to better hear a sound source. This means

Figure 17.14 Bats echolocate—they produce sounds and use the reflected sounds to hear whether, when, and how to perform behaviors (left). People can do the same thing by making vocalizations (such as clicks, or by tapping with a tool such as a long cane) and listening to the reflected sound (right).

that—just like the legs and hands are part of the visual system (see Box 15.2)—they are also part of the auditory system! Behaviors like moving around or cupping the hand over the ear help the listener to explore the acoustic array by changing what structure they encounter or how much of that structure they encounter, respectively. But neither of these behaviors creates *new* structure in the acoustic array—they only help to reveal *existing* structure in the acoustic array.

However, auditory perceiving can be active in a way that *does* create new structure in the acoustic array. Echolocation is a process by which listeners use reflected acoustic structure (i.e., echoes) to perceive surface layout. But sometimes, there may not be enough existing reflected acoustic structure to provide the necessary information about surface layout. In these cases, listeners can (and do) purposefully create their own acoustic structure by making sounds (e.g., words or tongue clicks, claps, or taps of a cane) and then listening to how the reflected sound is structured by surrounding surfaces—much like bats. In this way, the listener purposefully performs behaviors (making the sounds) that create new structure in the acoustic array so that they can perceive surrounding surfaces more effectively (see Figure 17.14).

People who echolocate often move their bodies and heads while they are producing sounds and even change the sounds that they make to further explore the reflecting surface. Some blind individuals are able to use echolocation to perform everyday activities such as locating obstacles and doorways. Others are even able to perform not-so-everyday-activities such as hiking, mountain biking, skateboarding, and playing sports (Thaler & Goodale, 2016)!

Importantly, even people *without* visual impairment can learn to echolocate—with sufficient practice. In one study, after a brief familiarization task, sighted—but blindfolded—participants were asked to make a sound of their choice (e.g., a repeated word or a mouth click) to locate a wall placed at four different distances from them. Then the wall was removed, and they were asked to walk to where *the wall had been*. In general, participants were able to perform the task. They tended to walk farther when the wall had been farther away, though they overshot the target at the nearest distance and undershot it at the farthest two distances. Participants were slightly better at the task when they echolocated the surface while moving when they did so while stationary (Rosenblum et al., 2010).

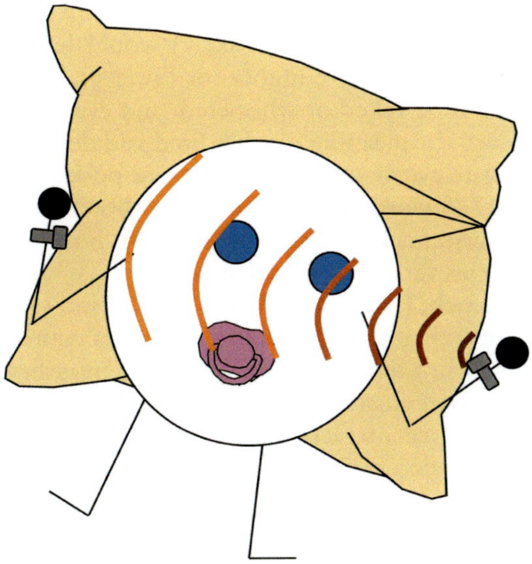

Figure 17.15 Studies have shown that very young infants with small speakers attached to their wrist learn to move their arms in a coordinated way to hear the sound better.

The Development of Auditory Perceiving of Surface Layout

Just like babies aren't born with the ability to use optical patterns to control their movements, they aren't born with the ability to do so with acoustic patterns, either. There *are* sounds in the womb, but there isn't all that much space to move around!

A few weeks after birth, however, infants are starting to learn how to control their movements based on sound. In one study, researchers put tiny speakers on the wrists of 3- to 6-week-old infants (van der Meer & van der Weel, 2011). The baby's mother was in another room and spoke or sang to the baby into a microphone. When her voice was played (in real time) through one of the wrist speakers, the baby was more likely to move that wrist toward them than away from them (see Figure 17.15). When no sound was played, that baby was just as likely to move their wrist toward them as they were to move it away from them.

So, newborn babies can use sound to control the movements of their arms. They know what to do so that they can hear something better. Do they know how to get to from one place to another by using sounds? In one study investigating this, researchers placed 6- to 9-month-old babies on their bellies in the middle of a circular mat (van der Meer et al., 2008). The mother was positioned at one of 10 different locations behind the baby on the perimeter of the circle and called out to the baby in whatever way seemed natural to her. Babies turned toward their mother using the shortest route almost 90% of the time. In other words, 6- to 9-month-old babies could hear how—and how quickly—to take the shortest route to their mother.

Perceiving Speech

Now dinner is underway, and Fred is conversing with each of his guests. At some point, he says, "Claudia, would you like more water?" Claudia not only *hears* the sounds that Fred makes with his vocal tract, but she also perceives the *meaning* of what he has said. How? Before we answer this, consider that Claudia (likely) would have perceived the meaning of what Fred said if even if his voice were higher- or lower-pitched, even if he spoke more quickly or more slowly, even if he yelled or whispered, and even if he spoke with an accent. In addition, Claudia perceived the meaning of what Fred said despite the fact that—like most people—he does not articulate every sound of every word perfectly. Instead, the sounds are "coarticulated" into a "blur" of words and sentences. In short, the acoustic signal itself varies greatly from person to person and situation to situation, but for the most part, speech is perceived independently of this variation (see Chapter 12).

From the ecological approach, Claudia's ability to understand what Fred said begins with what he *does* when speaking. What he does when speaking is coordinate the movements of his vocal tract—including but not limited to his lips, teeth, mouth, tongue, and throat (see Figure 12.14). This coordination creates vibrations in air that are lawfully structured by the nature of these parts, how they are interacting, and where they are interacting, among other factors. In other words, the structure in the acoustic array is lawfully related to *how these sounds were produced* by these movements of his vocal tract.

From the ecological approach, perceiving speech is not about perceiving sounds. Instead, it is about perceiving the *movements of the vocal tract* by means of the sound (Fowler, 2018). In principle, this is no different than any other instance of auditory event perception—like hearing whether an object bounced or broke—in which structure in the acoustic array provides information about an event, not the sound itself (see Box 17.1). To repeat, the medium is not the message.

To the extent that the movements of the vocal tract lawfully structure multiple energy patterns simultaneously, structure in any one of these patterns ought to carry the same information about such movements. The movements of the vocal tract *also* structure the optic array. Consequently, these movements can be *seen*. Research has shown that even people without hearing impairment read lips during everyday speech perception (though perhaps not as well as someone who is hearing impaired, Rosenblum, 2005). Along these lines, *watching* someone speak helps the listener understand what the speaker is saying—especially in noisy environments, and even when only parts of the speaker's face are visible (Bernstein et al., 2004; see Box 17.3).

Perhaps more impressively, the movements of the vocal tract *also* structure the bodily tissue of the speaker, especially their face, lips, and throat. Consequently, these movements can be *felt* by someone who places their hands on the speaker's face. And research has shown that *feeling* someone speak also aids in understanding what they are saying (Reed et al., 1985).

> Socratic Question: How is the ecological approach to speech perception (described in this chapter) like the motor theory of speech perception (described in Chapter 12)? How is it different?

Summary

In the ecological approach to hearing, researchers investigate how sound that is generated by or reflected from the surfaces that surround a given animal is lawfully (unambiguously) structured by those surfaces. They also investigate how the structured sound encountered

Box 17.3 Lipread Me Now, Hear Me Better Later?

From the ecological approach, the movements of the vocal tract simultaneously lawfully structure multiple energy patterns. This means that *simultaneously* watching someone speak and listening to them speak ought to help the listener better understand what that person is saying. And it does. But it also means that merely *watching* someone speak (i.e., lipreading them) *now* will help the listener better *hear* what that person says *later*. *Wait . . . what?* Yep.

It makes sense that lip reading someone *now* might help the listener *now*. After all—all other things being equal—watching *and* listening to an event will help you better understand what exactly is happening, right? But why would watching *now* help with listening *later*? That's just weird. Well, yes . . . but only a little.

Watching someone speak (i.e., lipreading them) will help you learn about the ways in which that particular person's vocal tract moves when they produce certain sounds. Just like different people coordinate the movements of their limbs in different ways when they walk, different people coordinate the movements of their vocal tract in different ways when they speak—even when saying the exact same thing. And just like you can identify people based on the way they walk (see Chapter 14), you can identify them based on the way they talk. And so, experience *seeing* the unique ways in which a given person coordinates their vocal tract to make certain sounds might help you *hear* the unique ways that they do so later. And this will help you understand them better. Not so weird anymore, right?

In a study investigating this, researchers gave participants about one hour of experience lipreading one of two different talkers (Rosenblum et al., 2007). Their task was to watch a video recording of the person saying simple sentences without sound (for example, "The football game is over") and then report (as best as they could) what the person said. They did this for a set of 100 simple sentences.

In the second part of the study, their task was to listen to an audio recording of one of the two talkers saying simple sentences and then report (as best they could) what the person said. Except . . . what the talker was saying was a little hard to hear because there was white noise (static) mixed into the audio—like a bad phone connection.

Figure 17.16 When participants had an opportunity to watch people speak (without sound), they were better able to understand them later (vs. other speakers).

Frustrating, right? Probably, yes. Nonetheless, participants performed this task for a set of 150 (probably frustrating) sentences.

The experimenters varied whether the participants listened to the same person that they lipread or a different person than they lipread. It turned out that people who listened to the same person that they lipread heard more of what was said than people who listened to a different person than they lipread. So, experience lipreading a particular person made it easier to hear what that person was saying later (see Figure 17.16).

by a given animal changes as surfaces move or as the animal changes its point of observation. These patterns can be used to acoustically control movement patterns. This is how sound gets into the muscle!

Notes

1 If you have ever been in a room specifically designed to reduce reflected sounds (like a recording studio or a room used for a hearing test), you know that things sound quite odd without (much) reflected sound.
2 Remember that all squares are rectangles, but not all rectangles are squares.
3 Remember the lesson from Chapter 10—life is more like a junk drawer than a white coffee mug on a black stovetop!
4 Yes, really. They used this sound because it is a naturally occurring sound with complex acoustic structure (as opposed to a computer-generated tone, for example).
5 Like a duck call, crowd noise is also a naturally occurring sound with complex acoustic structure. And crowd noise would likely be a familiar sound to students.
6 While the prevalence of hybrid and electric cars is great for the environment, it is not so great for blind pedestrians (or inattentive sighted pedestrians). This is because these cars are *so much quieter* than gas-powered cars. Consequently, blind pedestrians may have a harder time hearing whether hybrid or electric cars are approaching, and if so, how quickly the car might reach them (Robart & Rosenblum, 2009).
7 After all, this was a study about hearing when the glass would *become* full, not hearing when it *had already* become full.

18 Ecological Haptics and Touching

In Chapters 14, 15, 16, and 17, we developed an *ecological optics* and an *ecological acoustics*—a description of the properties of light and sound at the scale of the relationship between animals and their environments. In both cases, the stimulation patterns of relevance—the structured light and the structured sound—*surround* the animal. This structure carries information about properties of surrounding substances and surfaces. In particular, it carries information about the animal's *relationship to* those surrounding substances and surfaces—the affordances for that animal. In this chapter, we will develop an **ecological haptics**[1]—a description of the mechanical forces acting on bodily tissue at the scale of the relationship between animals and their environments.

Ecological haptics a description of the mechanical forces acting on bodily tissue at the scale of the relationship between animals and their environments.

When we introduced ecological optics and ecological acoustics, we made the point that animals exist in an ocean of light and ocean of sound. While it is certainly the case that animals likewise exist in an ocean of mechanical forces, it might be better to say it the other way around—*an ocean of mechanical forces exists in the animal*! This might seem like it makes the touch system or perceiving by touch an exception, or a special sense, but it is not (see Box 18.1 and Box 18.2).

Remember that understanding perceiving as a lawful process requires uncovering how properties of surfaces and relationships between animals and those surfaces unambiguously structure stimulation patterns. In the case of perceiving by touch, the stimulation patterns of relevance are the mechanical forces on the skin, muscles, tendons, and other bodily tissues when a person moves their body or manipulates an object. In part, this pattern of forces is produced by the animal. This is because manipulating objects and moving the body is *effortful*—it requires *applying* muscular forces. And the required muscular forces continually change—they are "*dynamic*". This is why perception of properties of the body itself or of objects manipulated by the body is called **effortful or dynamic touch** (J. Gibson, 1966; see Carello & Turvey, 2015).

Effortful or dynamic touch the subsystem of touch used to move the body or other objects by muscular effort.

Given that the same lawful processes apply across energy forms, the patterns of structured mechanical forces on bodily tissues will have the potential to carry *the same information about* surfaces and relationships between animals and those surfaces—the same information about affordances—as patterns of structured light or sound. The fundamental question of ecological haptics is how to best describe these forces so that they can serve the purpose of guiding goal-directed behavior.

DOI: 10.4324/9781032690964-21

Box 18.1 Is the Touch System Rebellious . . . Or Just Misunderstood?

From the traditional approach, touch seems to be very much *unlike* its close cousins—vision, hearing, smell, and taste. By all accounts, vision is the overachiever of the group. It receives nearly *all* the attention. In fact, many if not most *Sensation and Perception* textbooks have as many chapters dedicated to vision as they do to hearing, touching, smelling, and tasting *combined*. (And this book is no exception!) In part, this is because vision seems to play firmly by the traditional rules of how perceiving is supposed to work. For example, vision seems to have an easy-to-identify organ (the eye!) located in a particular place on the body (the head!) that passively receives stimulation (light rays!) on a ready-made surface capable of forming a copy (the retinal image!). Moreover, it is easy to describe vision as an "input" process of creating, delivering, and disambiguating that copy that is entirely separate from the "output" process of moving the body.

Touch, on the other hand, is a bit of a rebel, an outcast, or a misfit. It *doesn't* play by the traditional rules. Touch doesn't have an easy-to-identify organ located in a particular place on the body, and there is no ready-made surface on which a copy might be formed—the touch system spans the skin, muscles, and connective tissue of the entire body![2] Moreover, the touch system does not passively receive stimulation, and the process of touching cannot be separated from the process of moving the body. The touch system *is* the movement system!

Figure 18.1 The touch system is the movement system. Both systems consist of the skin, muscles, and connective tissue of the entire body. Moreover, the process of touching cannot be separated from the process of moving.

One way to deal with the touch system's rebellious nature is to ignore it or downplay its importance. That's what you do with a troublemaker, right? But that may be the wrong move here. It might be better to recognize that the touch system's refusal to play nice with traditional assumptions is at odds with how important it is in both the evolution of species and in daily life.

Evolutionarily, the touch system has been around for hundreds of millions of years—*the touch system is the originator, an innovator, and a trend-setter!* And in daily life, touch provides *nearly continuous support* for performing everyday behaviors such as walking, sitting, standing, reaching, and grasping. It might be that the touch system's tendency to disrupt the status quo is a sign not only that the classic assumptions about how perceiving work are flawed but that the touch system ought to play a larger role in forming a new set of assumptions!

Socratic Question: What makes the touch system "rebellious"? Why might it be the wrong move to ignore or downplay the touch system?

Ecological Haptics

After his dinner party, Fred and Claudia are hanging out and chatting. Keeping eye contact with her, he fumbles in the closet for the broom (to start the process of cleaning up). It's usually hung on the door, so he's able to grasp it without looking except . . . as soon as he grabs what he thought was the broom and starts to move it around, he knows immediately—even without seeing it—that it is not a broom. It has a *short cylindrical handle* that he is holding at the very end, and it seems to have a *narrow rectangular block* on one end. It is *relatively light*, but it feels like he *could use it to pound another object*—it's his long-lost kitchen mallet! What's *that* doing in there?! And hung on the door, no less? Weird.

So, Fred keeps feeling around. He doesn't want to look away from Claudia (she's telling him a really funny story), so he keeps rummaging without looking. He grasps something else, and as soon as he moves it around, he knows immediately that he's found the broom. It has a *long cylindrical handle* that is pointing *straight up from his hand* that he is holding *closer to than the bottom than to the top* so that *more of the object extends above where he is holding it* than below where he is holding it. And it seems to have a *wide and flat triangular* part at one end. It feels *relatively heavy*, but it doesn't really feel like he could use it to pound another object. Instead, it feels like he could use it to *push or move another object*—it *is* his broom (see Figure 18.2)!

It might seem kind of strange that Fred could know about the entire object, including its various properties and what he could do with it, even though he was only holding a small part of that object—whatever portion of the object that happened to be in his hand. In fact, this might sound like some sort of weird magic trick. But we promise you, it's not. In fact, it's no different than what happens when you *visually perceive* properties of an object and what you could do with it.

When you look at a given object, you can never see the *entire object* all at once. At any given moment, you will only be able to see *part* of the object from your *current point of*

Figure 18.2 When Fred reaches into his kitchen closet and grabs items, he can tell a lot about the object without looking.

observation. Nonetheless, you can perceive many different properties and affordances of that object. You can't see the underside of a chair, for example, but you still know you can sit on it. Why? Because from a given point of observation, you are encountering a pattern of structured light in the optic array that is informative about that object and your relationship to it (see Chapters 15 and 16). The same thing happens when you hold an object. Remember—the medium is not the message. You can perceive many different properties and affordances of that object because at that grasp position, you encounter a pattern of structured forces in the haptic array that is informative about that object and your relationship to it.

As we mentioned earlier, animals are not only immersed in an ocean of light and an ocean of sound. They are also immersed in an *ocean of forces.* And like the other oceans of energy surrounding an animal, the ocean of forces is *not uniform.* On the contrary, these forces form an *array.* They differ at different *locations* on the body and in different *directions* at a given location on the body. This is the case both when someone is manipulating an object and when they are not.

Gravity is the primary physical force acting on animals. At a minimum, moving the body, a limb, or an object requires overcoming—and often cooperating with—gravity. This requires generating different forces at different bodily locations in different directions. This is the key to ecological haptics (Carello & Turvey, 2017).

Let's use Fred's broom as an example. His broom weighs about 1kg (a little over 2 pounds). But what does this *mean*, exactly? This means that if he were to put it on a scale, the scale would read 1kg. And if he were to put it on one tray of an old-fashioned balance scale, and he were to put some other thing that weighed 1kg on the other tray (say, a liter of water, a 10-week-old kitten, or a bag of Topsy's peanuts), the two trays would line up exactly.

The mass of an object indicates how much force is required to overcome the pull of gravity to support the object. And if Fred were to grasp the broom at the end and hold it so that it is completely still and pointing straight up (i.e., vertically, see Figure 18.3, left), he would need to apply muscular force that is proportional to the broom's *mass.* This will keep it from falling straight down to the ground.

But if Fred were to hold the broom so that it is completely still and pointing straight out (i.e., horizontally, see Figure 18.3, *right*), he would have to apply muscular force that does more than just prevent the broom from falling straight down. He would also need to

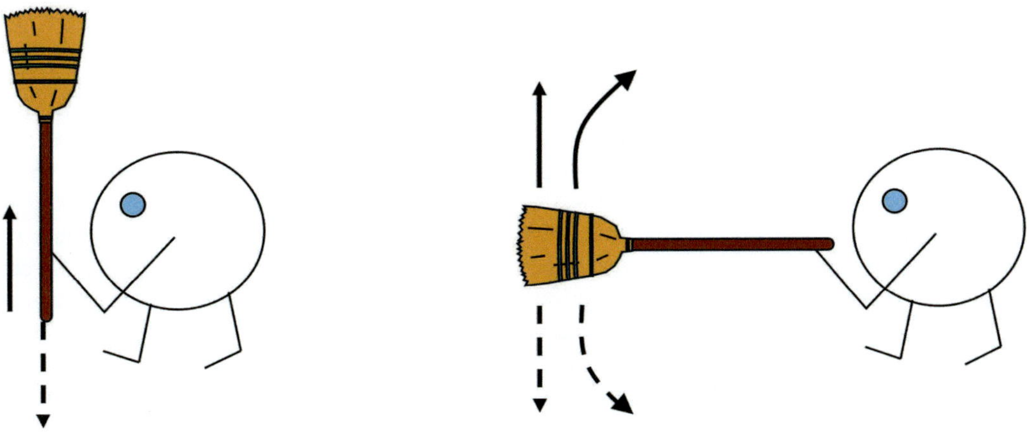

Figure 18.3 When Fred holds the broom still and vertically (left), he only has to apply force (solid lines) to keep it from falling straight down. When he holds the broom still and horizontally (right), he has to apply additional force to keep it from rotating toward the ground.

keep the other end from *rotating toward* the ground. To do this, he would need to apply *rotational force (also known as torque)*. Now, it's not just the *mass* of the broom that determines the forces that he needs to apply. It's also how that mass is *distributed*. Of particular importance is how far the **center of mass**—the point about which the mass of the broom is distributed evenly—is from his hand. In the case of a simple elongated object (like a meter stick), the center of mass is located midway between the two ends of the objects. For a more complex elongated object (like a broom), it will be located a little closer to the end with more mass (in this case, the end with the bristles). So, holding the broom completely still and completely horizontally requires producing a force that is proportional to a *combination* of mass and the distance between the center of mass and his hand—specifically mass × distance to the center of mass.

Center of mass the location at which the distribution of an object's mass is balanced; the average position of the distribution of mass.

But what if Fred wanted to grasp the broom at one end and move it around—like a tennis racket or a sword—*en garde*! Now he would need to do even more work—or at least he would need to *change* how much he is working more often—than when he held it still either vertically or horizontally. Why? When Fred holds the broom completely still—horizontally or vertically—the amount of force he has to apply never changes. It is *static*. However, when he moves it around, the forces that he has to apply are *constantly changing*—this is the "dynamic" in *dynamic touch!* To move the broom, Fred can't just apply muscular forces that *support* the racket and *keep it from rotating*. He has to *make it* rotate. This requires applying muscular forces to increase its velocity from 0 to some other value. He has to *accelerate* it! In doing so, he has to overcome its inertia—its resistance to being moved. Specifically, he has to overcome its ***rotational inertia***—its resistance to being rotated about an axis.

Rotational inertia the resistance of an object to rotation about an axis.

Imagine that Fred moves the broom back and forth across his body—say, from his right to his left and back again like he is swinging a tennis racket. To move it like this, he would need to produce a rotational force in a particular direction about a particular axis—in this case, the axis running vertically through his wrist and perpendicular to the handle of the broom. This required force is still proportional to a combination of mass and the distance between the center of mass and his hand, but now this distance plays an even more important role—mass × (distance to center of mass *squared*).

At some point as the broom makes its way across his body, Fred would need to start to *decelerate the broom* so that it stops moving to the left and *then* apply the muscular forces required to *accelerate* it in the *other* direction.[3] So, he needs to work *harder* when he moves an object around than when he merely holds it still because he has to *continually change* how much force he is applying and in what directions.

But we're still not quite where we need to be yet. Recall that both the optic and acoustic arrays consist of differences in different directions at a particular point of observation. We need to describe the stimulation pattern for perceiving by effortful or dynamic touch in the same way. When you hold an object, you can move it in *lots* of different ways. You could move it up and down—like you would move a hammer—back and forth—like you would move a tennis racket—or twist it—like you would turn a doorknob.

Each of these movements requires applying a *different rotational force* about a *different axis* running through the wrist. So, the "differences in different directions" refer to differences in *resistances to rotations* in different directions. And the "point of observation" refers to the *grasp position* on the object. Where an object is grasped doesn't affect the mass of that object, but it *does* affect the distance between the center of mass and the rotation point. And this will affect the rotational forces required to move that object in different directions—we'll come back to this later. If you've ever wondered why an object like hammer feels so much heavier when held by the handle than when held by the head, that's why!

Box 18.2 A Not-So-Standard Architecture for the Not-So-Standard Touch System

As we described in Box 18.1, unlike the other perceptual modalities, there is no specific organ for touch comparable to the eye, the ear, the nose, or the mouth. The touch system includes the *entire body*—the skin, muscles, tendons, ligaments, and other connective tissue. And all of these bodily tissues are all connected—the touch system is *a continuous system*. How might all of these components be organized in a way that allows them to work together in touching and moving?

Recently, researchers have proposed that the musculoskeletal system is organized as a *biotensegrity system* (de Solórzano, 2020; Turvey & Fonseca, 2014). In a **tensegrity structure**, individual inflexible components are flexibly held together by elastic tension (see Figure 18.4). Considered this way, the bones are analogous to the inflexible components and the muscles and other connective tissue hold them together

Tensegrity structure a self-supporting physical structure in which individual, inflexible components are held in place by a network of continuous tension.

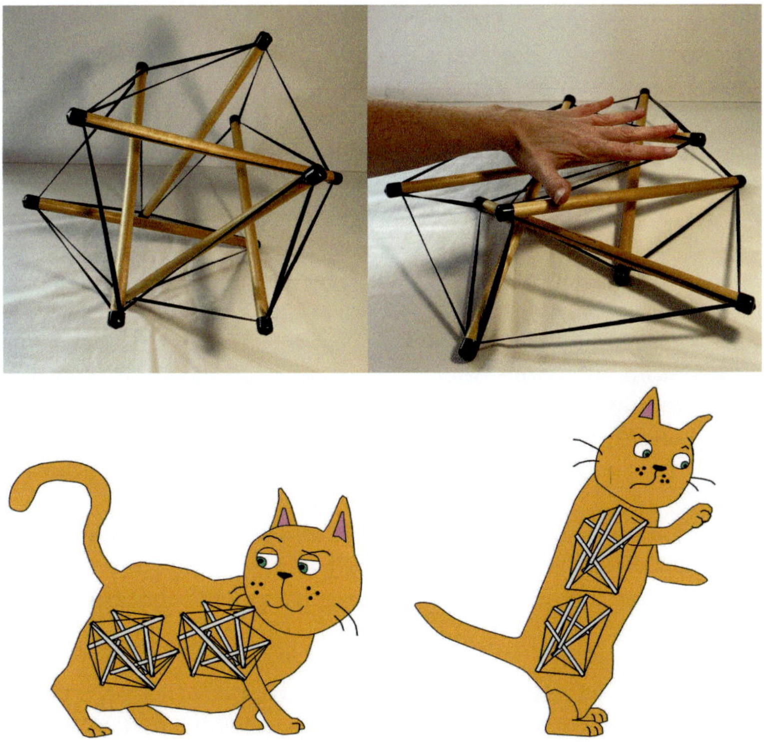

Figure 18.4 A tensegrity structure consists of hard and inflexible components supported by soft and flexible components. It changes shape when compressed but does not collapse. Recently, researchers have suggested that the musculoskeletal system can be understood as a biotensegrity structure.

with elastic tension. Tensegrity systems are strong, stable, resilient, and flexible. This is because, when force is applied to any part of such a system, the entire system reorganizes by changing shape to redistribute those forces across the entire system.

If the musculoskeletal system is organized this way, it would mean that when Fred moves a particular part of his body or manipulates an object, *his entire body* is involved (at least to some degree). It would also mean that the particular body part that he is moving or using to manipulate an object is less important than the overall patterning of forces that occurs when he does so. In other words, it would be consistent with the ecological proposal that the stimulation of relevance to perception by touch is the pattern of *physical forces* on the bodily tissue and not the activity of receptor cells (Wagman et al., 2023).

The Ambient Haptic (Inertial) Array

At every possible grasp location on an object, a person encounters a unique set of resistances to rotations in different directions. The set of resistances to rotations in different directions at a given grasp location is an inertial array. These differences in resistance rotations in different directions can be quantified by something called an *inertia tensor (I)* (see Figure 18.5).

Tensor a quantity that simultaneously varies in magnitude in multiple directions.

Scalar a quantity that varies only in magnitude.

Vector a quantity that simultaneously varies in both magnitude and direction.

Admittedly, a **tensor** is a somewhat complex mathematical concept. Simply put, though, a tensor is a way to describe a quantity that varies along multiple dimensions simultaneously. If a quantity can only vary along one dimension—for example, if it varies only in magnitude—then you only need one value to describe it—called a **scalar**. Values such as temperature, mass, distance, and speed are all scalar quantities. If a quantity simultaneously varies along two dimensions—for example, if it varies in both magnitude *and* direction—then you need to describe how the two scalar values relate to one another. For this, you need a **vector**. The best-known vector quantity is velocity because it describes speed in a given direction.

If a quantity simultaneously varies in multiple directions—for example, if it varies in magnitude in different directions—then you need to describe how the vectors relate to one another. For this you need a tensor. When you stretch an elastic sheet in different directions at the same time, for example, forces of different magnitudes are being applied in different directions[4] (see Figure 18.5).

The last time that Fred went grocery shopping, he happened to get a cart with one bad wheel—annoying, right? When he pushed the cart forward with a particular amount of force, it wobbled off in a different direction—at an angle!—with a different amount of force—slower! A tensor describes how this occurs. It describes how one vector—a given force in

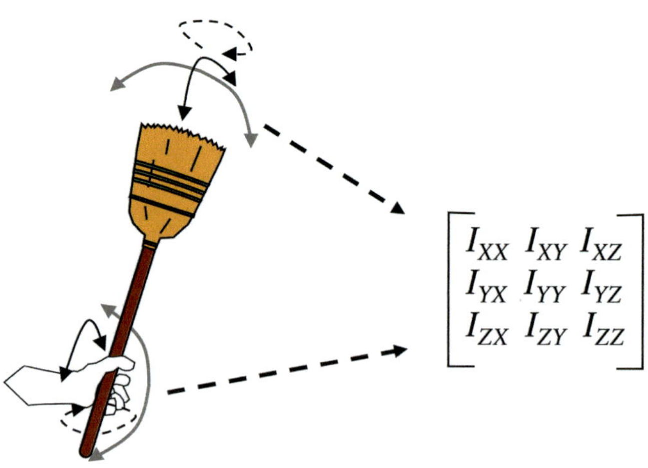

Figure 18.5 The inertia tensor is a 3 x 3 matrix that describes the inertial array—differences in resistance to rotation in different directions at a given grasp position on an object. Note that the matrix is symmetric about the diagonal. The values along the diagonal (I_{XX}, I_{YY}, and I_{ZZ}) are moments of inertia. The values off of the diagonal (I_{XY}, I_{XZ}, and I_{YZ}) are the products of inertia.

a given direction—becomes another vector—a *different force* in a *different direction*. Now imagine that Fred is manipulating a handheld object—maybe a baguette that he is buying at the bakery counter. When he moves the object with a particular amount of force in a particular direction, it will move with a different amount of force in a different direction, depending on its mass distribution. The inertia tensor describes how this occurs!

We can depict the inertia tensor as a 3 x 3 matrix of values (see Figure 18.5). Keep in mind that the matrix is symmetric along the diagonal going from the top left to the bottom right—I_{xy}, I_{yz}, and I_{xz} are redundant with I_{zx}, I_{zy}, and I_{zx}—so it is not quite as complex as it seems.

Socratic Question: What is an inertia tensor? How does it describe an "inertial array"?

Principal moments of inertia values that quantify resistance to rotational acceleration of an object about its main axes.

Each of the values along the diagonal that runs from the top left to the bottom right (I_{xx}, I_{yy}, and I_{zz}) (more or less) describe the resistances to rotational acceleration about the three major axes of the object. I_{xx}—**the major principal moment of inertia**—describes the resistance to rotating an object up and down (toward and away from the ground). I_{yy} describes the resistance to rotating it back and forth. I_{zz}—*the minor principal moment of inertia*—describes the resistance to twisting it (see Figure 18.5).

Ellipsoid of inertia a geometrical representation of the inertia tensor as a three-dimensional ellipse.

These values can be thought of as forming the axes of an "**ellipsoid of inertia**" (an ellipsoid is a three-dimensional ellipse; see Figure 18.6). The height of the ellipsoid depends on the value of I_{xx}, and the width of the ellipsoid depends on the value of I_{zz}. The ellipsoid is what the object "looks like" to the haptic system. The *size* of the

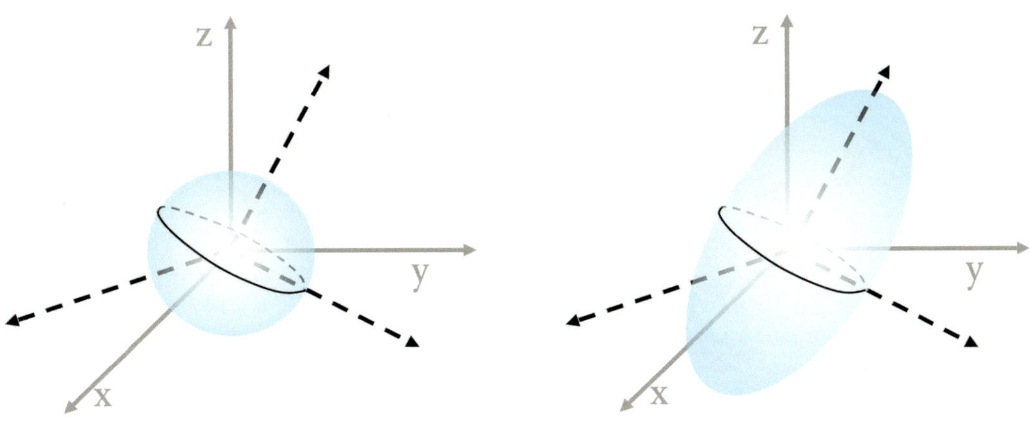

Figure 18.6 An object's resistance to rotation in different directions can be depicted as an ellipsoid of inertia. The ellipsoid is what the object "looks like" to the haptic system.

ellipsoid indicates the overall amount of force that is required to move the object. The *shape* of the ellipsoid indicates the relative amount of force required to move the object in different directions. Specifically, the height of the ellipsoid indicates how hard or easy it is to rotate the end of the object toward and away from the ground, and the width of the ellipsoid indicates how hard or easy it is to twist it like a doorknob.

These "off-diagonal" terms—in the upper right and lower left corners of the matrix (I_{xy}, I_{xz}, and I_{yz})—are the **products of inertia**. These terms each quantify *asymmetries* in the mass distribution. These quantities describe how much the mass distribution of the object "tilts" away from the three main axes of the object. In other words, they describe how the *mass* of the object is distributed relative to the *geometry* of the object.

Products of inertia values that quantify the imbalance or asymmetries in the mass distribution of an object from its main axes.

Collectively, the products of inertia describe the *orientation of the mass distribution*—the orientation of the inertial ellipsoid—in particular how much it is tilted off of the main axes, and in what direction(s) it is tilted (see Figure 18.6). The *orientation* of the ellipsoid of inertia reflects this tilt (see Figure 18.6). Objects in Fred's closet that are bent or tilted relative to the hand—like his hockey stick or his friend Mike's boomerang—will exhibit a more tilted mass distribution than objects that are not—like his broom or his kitchen mallet. Consequently, the products of inertia, in particular *the orientation of the mass distribution*, ought to provide information about how such objects are oriented with respect to the hand.

Socratic Question: What determines the size and shape of the inertial ellipsoid for a given object? How is it that the ellipsoid is what the object "looks like" to the haptic system?

Perceiving Geometric and Functional Properties

Feeling Length

Recall that one of the things that Fred knew about the unseen broom is that it had long handle. One of the first studies conducted on effortful or dynamic touch investigated how

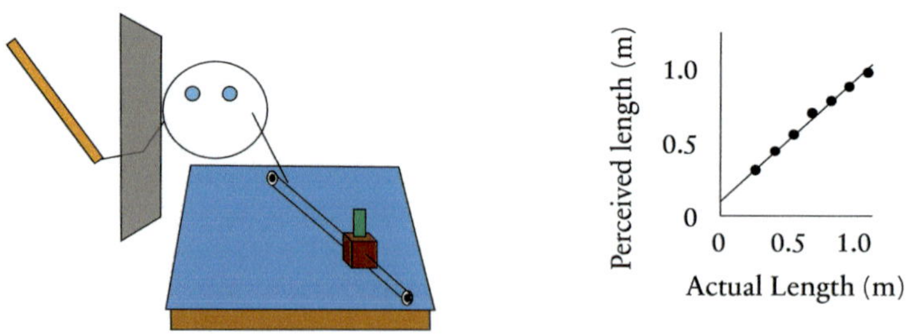

Figure 18.7 Left, in a typical experiment on perception length by effortful touch, a person wields a rod with one hand out of sight and adjusts the distance of a marker with the other hand, so that the marker would be just reachable with the tip of the rod. Right, perceived length isn't perfect, but it very closely tracks actual length.

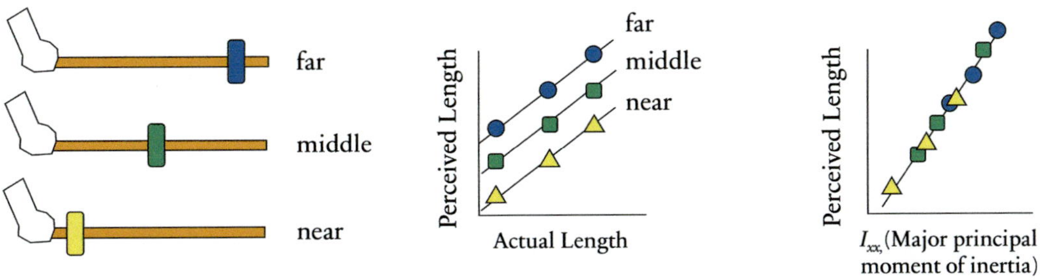

Figure 18.8 Left, experimental conditions. The length of the rod is the same, but the position of the weight is either far from the hand, in the middle, or close to the hand. Middle, perceived length when graphed by actual length and weight placement. Right, perceived length when graphed by moment of inertia (an organism-relevant variable).

this was possible (Solomon & Turvey, 1988). In one experiment, participants sat at a student desk, put their right hand through a curtain, and rested their forearm on the surface of the desk so that their wrist was just over the edge of the desk. An experimenter placed a rod into their hand so that they held it firmly at the very bottom (see Figure 18.7, *left*). The participant's job was to wield the rod with movements of their wrist and adjust the distance of a visible moveable marker with their left hand so that the distance between them and the marker was the same as the length of the rod, so that the marker would be *just reachable* with the other end of the rod. Participants were able to do this task quite well. Perceived rod length closely tracked actual rod length but was slightly underestimated, especially for longer rods (see Figure 18.7, *right*).

The next few experiments showed that perceived length remained constant despite changes in how the rod was wielded—fast or slow, for example. These results suggested that perceiving length depends on a variable that *also* remains constant despite these changes. The researchers proposed that this variable was a particular component of *I*. Specifically, they hypothesized that perceived length would depend on the major principal moment of inertia (*Ixx*, the "height" of the inertial ellipsoid, in Figure 18.6) and not necessarily on the actual length of the object. After all, the touch system works with *forces*, not geometric properties (see Box 18.2).

The researchers ran additional experiments to investigate this hypothesis. In one of these, they used objects consisting of an aluminum rod with a weight attached at a particular location along the length of the rod. Rods were one of three different lengths, and weights were placed at one of three different locations along the length of the rod (see Figure 18.8, *left*). By adding weights to the rods, the researchers were able to create sets of objects that had the *same* length and the *same* mass but *different values* of I_{xx}. So, if perceived length depended on I_{xx} (and not actual length), then rods would feel longer as the weight was moved farther along the length of the rod—even for objects that were the same length! And this is exactly what they found (see Figure 18.8, *middle*). And as they expected, perceived length increased as I_{xx} increased (see Figure 18.8, *right*).

Socratic Question: Why does a rod with a weight placed at the far end feel longer than a rod with a weight placed at the near end (even when those rods are the same length)?

Feeling Shape

Something else that Fred knew about the broom is that it had a wide and flat triangular end. If *I* really *is* the appropriate description of forces on bodily tissues for the touch system, then perceiving shape of a wielded object ought to depend on components of *I* as well. And if perceived object length (or height) depends on I_{xx}—and not necessarily actual object length (or height), then perceived object width should depend on I_{zz}—and not necessarily actual object width. Several experiments have shown that this is the case.

In one experiment, participants wielded three-dimensional rectangular wooden blocks (i.e., shapes known as "parallelepipeds") mounted on handles (Turvey et al., 1998). When the blocks were tall and thin, they were perceived to be tall and thin, and when they were short and wide, they were perceived to be short and wide. In other words, perceived height increased with height (and I_{xx}) and perceived width increased with width (and I_{zz}).

In another experiment, participants wielded strange-looking branched objects called **tensor objects**. These objects consisted of aluminum rods that were fitted together using a moveable joint to create a stem and several branches (see Figure 18.9). What is so useful about such

Tensor objects experimental objects consisting of a stem or handle, a moveable joint, attached branches, and masses.

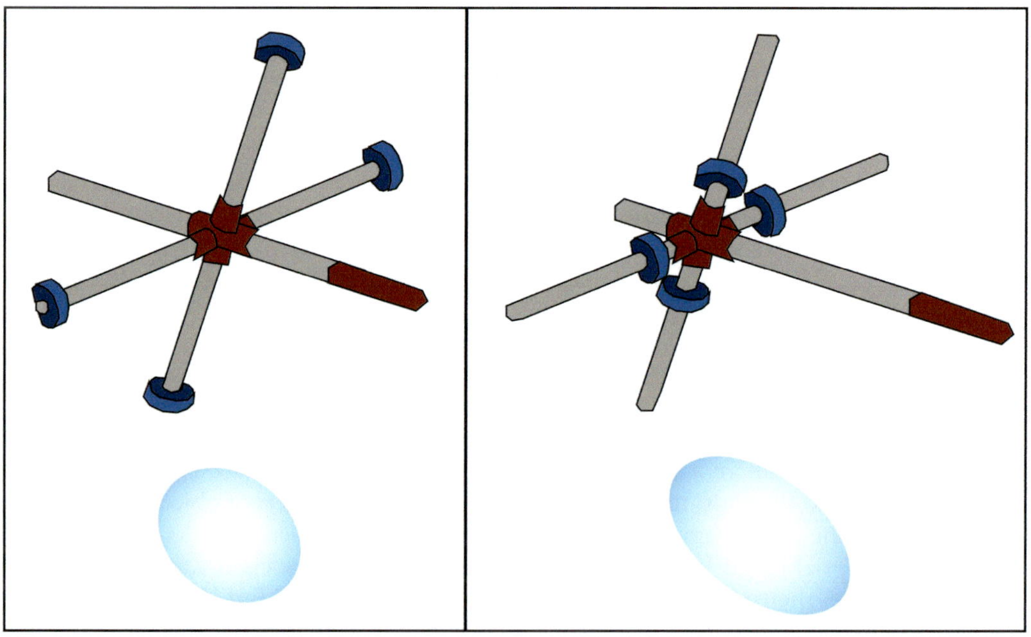

Figure 18.9 "Tensor objects" developed by Amazeen and Turvey (1996) allow researchers to systematically vary the mass distribution of an object—and hence, the inertial ellipsoid of that object. The two objects depicted here (top) have different inertial ellipsoids (bottom), even though the objects themselves are the same length, width, and mass. Given the differences in inertial ellipsoids, the object on the left will feel shorter and wider than the object on the right.

objects is that by carefully positioning the branches along the stem and by carefully positioning weights on those branches, the researchers could create objects that were the same length, width, and mass but that had different values of I_{xx} and I_{zz} (different inertial ellipsoid sizes and shapes). The results showed that people perceived objects to be taller as I_{xx} increased and wider as I_{zz} increased—even though the actual heights, widths, and masses of the objects remained unchanged.

Feeling the Orientation of Objects

One of the other things that Fred knew about the broom was that it was pointing straight up from his hand. Given that the products of inertia (I_{xy}, I_{xz}, and I_{yz}) describe the orientation of the mass distribution, they ought to provide information about object orientation.

In experiments investigating this hypothesis, participants wielded L-shaped objects—consisting of a long stem and a single branch at a 90° angle from the stem (see Figure 18.10, *left*). The researchers handed the object to the participant so that they were holding it with the branch pointing at one of eight different angles—0° to 315° in 45° increments, where 0° was straight up. The participant's job was to report the orientation (the pointing direction) of the branch by rotating a visible pointer with their left hand. Perceived orientation matched object orientation very closely (Turvey et al., 1992).

To conclusively demonstrate that perceived orientation depended on the orientation of the mass distribution (and not necessarily the orientation of the object), researchers conducted a follow-up study in which participants wielded objects with two branches—forming a V—with a small weight placed on one of the two branches (see Figure 18.10, *right*). The results showed that perceived orientation (the pointing direction) of the V was shifted in the direction of the branch with the added weight, even though actual object orientation remained unchanged (Pagano & Turvey, 1992).

Feeling Orientation of the Body

So, the orientation of the mass distribution provides information about the orientation of handheld objects. Does it also provide information about the orientation of parts of the

Figure 18.10 In experiments on perception of orientation of a wielded objects, the participant turns one or more dials to indicate the perceived orientation of the branches of a wielded object.

body? Knowing where your body parts are is an ability known as "proprioception", and at first glance, it seems like a job for the central executive. After all, the central executive ought to know, among other things, the size, shape, and orientation of the body parts.

Body schema a mental representation of the position, size, and shape of the various body parts.

Along these lines, some traditional explanations of proprioception rely on an internal representation of the body called a **body schema**. In many of these types of explanations, the body schema is a brain-based mapping or model of the body's spatial properties that is referenced when performing everyday behaviors and updated when there are changes in the body shape or size, like when wearing a heavy backpack —or a suit of armor (see Figure 14.13).

From the ecological approach, however, perceiving properties of handheld objects and of the body itself ought to occur by the same (lawful) processes. Consequently, *I*—and in particular the orientation of the mass distribution of the limbs—ought to provide information about the orientation of the limbs, not the body schema.

In a study investigating this hypothesis, participants held a cross-shaped object so that the two branches extended horizontally from each side of their fist (see Figure 18.11, *left*). In some cases, weights were attached to one or both branches. What makes this useful is that weighting the branches asymmetrically (right branch or left branch, but not both) changes the orientation of the mass distribution of the arm-plus-object without changing its actual orientation.

Participants held the object under a screen and were asked to point to one of three visible targets (see Figure 18.11, *right*). The results showed that when the weights were placed *asymmetrically*—either on the right or the left branch—participants tended to point slightly off target in the direction of the weight. When the object was weighted on the right branch, participants tended to point slightly to the left of each target and vice versa (see Figure 18.11, *right*). When it was weighted on both sides equally, participants pointed accurately. This pattern showed that participants were pointing with the mass distribution of the arm-plus-object rather than with the arm itself (see van de Langenberg et al., 2007; Pagano & Turvey, 1998).

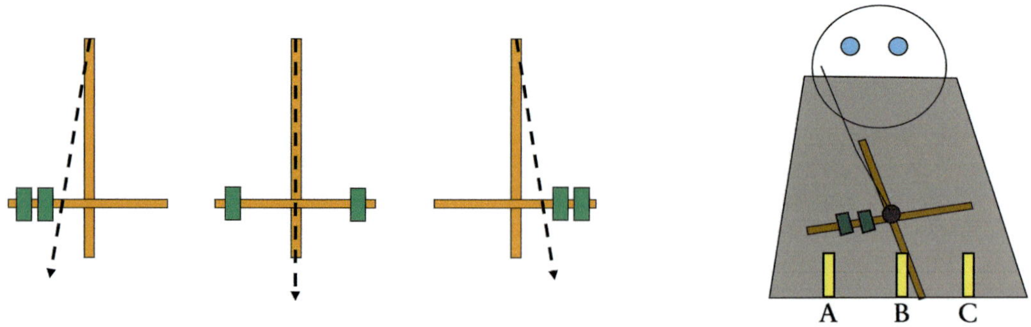

Figure 18.11 Left, the cross-shaped objects used by Pagano and Turvey (1995) to investigate perception of limb orientation. The participant grasps the object where the branches intersect. Right, the participant then points to a target with the unseen tool. Participants tended to point with the mass distribution of the tool+arm and not their anatomical arm.

Socratic Question: What have experiments on effortful touch suggested about the existence of a "body schema" (defined as brain-based mapping or model of the body's spatial properties)?

Feeling Grasp Position and Partial Length

Two other things that Fred knew about the broom were (1) that he was holding it closer to the bottom than to the top and (2) that more of the object extended above his hand than below his hand. In other words, Fred was able to perceive his grasp position on that object and the partial length of the object—the length of the object that extended to one side of that grasp position. Let's take these one at a time.

If you are holding an object in a particular location—like when Fred was holding the broom closer to one end than the other—then it is oriented in a particular way in your hand. In Fred's case, the broom is more *up* than it is *down*, for example. Grasp position affects the orientation of the mass distribution of the object with respect to your hand. Given that the products of inertia (I_{xy}, I_{xz}, and I_{yz}) describe the orientation of the mass distribution, they ought to provide information about grasp position on an object. And they do.

In one study investigating this, participants used their right hand to vertically wield wooden rods of different lengths at different grasp locations along the lengths of those rods (25%, 50%, 75%, or 95% along the length of the rod, Pagano et al., 1994). The participant's job was to wield the rod with movements of their wrist only and then position their left hand on a visible report rod so that the location of their hand along its length corresponded to the felt position of their right hand on the wielded rod (see Figure 18.11). In other words, if they felt that they were grasping the wielded rod exactly in the middle (50% along its length), they were to position their left hand exactly in the middle of the report rod (50% along its length). Not surprisingly, participants were really good at this task. Perceived grasp location very closely matched actual grasp location.

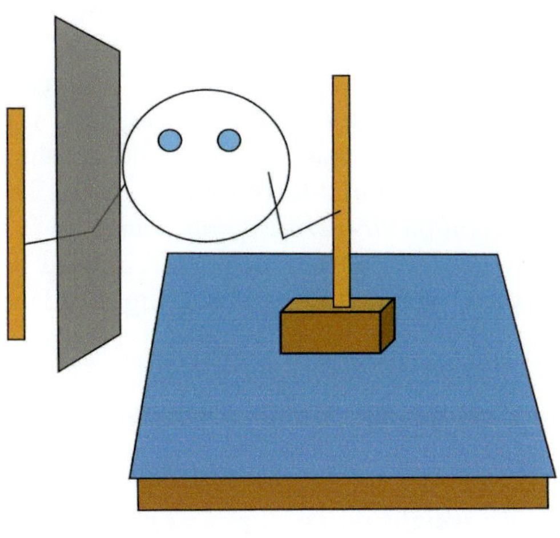

Figure 18.12 When asked to report grip location on an unseen rod, perceived grasp location very closely matched actual grasp location.

To conclusively demonstrate that perceived grasp position depended on the orientation of the mass distribution, researchers conducted a follow-up study in which participants performed more or less the same task except that small weights were placed on the wielded rod—either above or below the grasp position on that rod. The results showed that both the amount and location of added weight mattered—that is, perceived grasp position was influenced by the orientation of the mass distribution.

At first glance, perceiving grasp position on an object and perceiving the partial length of the object that extends to one side of the grasp position might not seem to be different tasks. But they are, for one important reason. Your grasp position on an object is independent of object length. The partial length of the object extending to one side of your grasp position is not. If you are holding a 100cm rod exactly in the middle, your grasp position is 50% of its length and the partial length extending above your hand is 50cm. If you are holding a 200cm rod exactly in the middle, your grasp position is still the same—50% of its length—but the partial length extending above your hand is larger—100cm! So, while perceiving grasp position requires perceiving orientation (or direction), perceiving partial length requires perceiving *a length in a direction*. This means that perceiving partial length ought to depend on both a magnitude and a product of inertia. And it does (Carello et al., 1996).

Feeling Heaviness

Something else that Fred knew about the broom was that it was relatively heavy. For centuries, researchers have known that the mass of the object plays at least some role in how heavy it feels (see Just Noticeable Differences in Chapter 1). For example, his broom (which weighs 1kg) will feel heavier than his kitchen mallet (which weighs 0.3kg). But it also is the case that under the right circumstances two objects of the *same mass*—say, his broom and a bag of Topsy's peanuts—can feel *differently* heavy. And two objects of *different masses*—say, his broom and a full-grown cat—can feel *equally heavy*. Something else must be going on here. In traditional explanations, this something else is representation and computation.[5] In ecological explanations, this something else is *I*.

Recall that *I* describes the forces required to move an object in different directions. Ecological psychologists hypothesized that it is these forces—which depend partly, but not completely, on mass—that determine how heavy an object feels. Researchers investigated this hypothesis using the tensor objects that we described earlier (see Figure 18.9). Remember that by carefully positioning the branches and weights, researchers can create objects that differ in *I*—or specific components of *I*—but that do not differ in other properties, such as mass or size.

They found that objects felt heavier as mass increased and as values of *I* changed, such that larger and more diverse forces were required to move that object. In other words, objects felt heavy to the degree that they were *difficult or challenging to move*. In fact, research has shown that when people report how heavy an object is, they are really reporting how *moveable* that object is (Shockley et al., 2004). Or in other words, they are perceiving affordances for moving the object!

Box 18.3 Which *Feels Heavier*—A Pound of Lead or a Pound of Feathers?

A classic riddle asks, "Which weighs more—a pound of lead or a pound of feathers?"[6] People who are "fooled" by the riddle say that the pound of lead weighs more when, of course, they weigh the same amount. But why might someone be fooled by this riddle?

One possibility is that they just didn't think the question through all that carefully. In other words, they simply "made a mistake" or an "error". But there might be another—perhaps more interesting—reason. As we discussed, psychologists have long known that two objects of the same mass can feel unequally heavy depending on the mass distribution of those objects. And in these cases, the object with the more compact—or asymmetric—mass distribution typically feels heavier. This is because more diverse forces are required to control an object with an asymmetric mass distribution than one with a symmetric mass distribution.

Researchers were curious whether—rather than being a "mistake" or an "error"—being fooled by the riddle might instead have something to do with how the two objects would feel if they were actually held in the hands. So, they did an experiment. They put one pound (about 450g) of lead shot in a plastic bag and taped it on the bottom of small cardboard box, and they put one pound of feathers in plastic bag and put inside an identical cardboard box. Blindfolded participants held each box one at a time in the palm of their hand and reported which box felt heavier. And then they repeated this task 20 times.

Overall, participants said the box containing lead felt heavier on 56% of the trials, which is just a little bit higher than the 50% that would have been expected if they were just guessing. On top of that, over the course of the 20 trials of the experiment, nearly 75% of participants said that the box containing lead felt heavier more often than they said that the box containing feathers felt heavier (Wagman et al., 2007).

So, these results show that a pound of lead feels heavier than a pound of feathers. Most likely, this was because the box containing the lead had a more asymmetric mass distribution than the box containing feathers. That is, whereas the box containing lead was "bottom heavy", the box containing feathers was not. This raises the possibility that being "fooled" by the riddle—"Which weighs more—a pound of lead or a pound of feathers?"—is not about making a mistake or an error but rather about showing sensitivity to how heavy the objects would feel if held in the hands.

Socratic Question: How do experiments show the perception of heaviness is better described as perception of moveableness?

Feeling Affordances for Tool Use

Another thing that Fred knew about the broom was that he could use it to push or move another object. That is, he was able to perceive the *affordances* of the broom just by grasping a small part of it, lifting it, and moving it around a bit. *I* provides information about how an object can be moved in different directions. But using an object as a tool requires moving it *in a particular way*. The powerful pounding movements made with a kitchen mallet—forceful, up and down—are entirely different than the precise pushing or sweeping movements made with a broom—controlled, back and forth—for example. Does *I* provide information about the affordances of a handheld object for use in a specific task?

This hypothesis was investigated by Wagman and Carello (2001). In these experiments, participants wielded unseen objects of different lengths with weights attached at various locations along those lengths. But this time, the participants rated how well they would be able to use each object for a hammering task or a poking task, on a scale of 1 to 7.

Objects were rated as better *hammers* as the values of *I* changed such that larger forces were required to move the object, meaning that more force could be delivered with the object. Objects were rated as better *pokers* as the values of *I* changed such that smaller forces were required to move the object and as the mass distribution of the object oriented more horizontally, meaning that the object tip could be more easily controlled.

More recent studies have shown that *I* not only provides information about *whether* an object can be used to perform a given tool use task; it also provides information about how to grasp or modify a given tool so that it is more appropriate for performing that task. And *I* also provides information about how to use that object to perform that tool use task. *I* even provides information for how to build or assemble an entirely new tool that would be appropriate for performing that task (see Wagman et al., 2023).

The Development of Perceiving by Effortful Touch

The ability to perceive properties of surfaces and objects by touch develops quite early. Infants and toddlers touch all kinds of things—much to Fred's dismay when he is looking after his baby niece Eleanor! When they become mobile, babies probe, poke, and press surfaces—like a visual cliff or a slope or a waterbed—to determine whether that surface will support their weight. And when their hands are free, they heft and wield objects. That is, they can manipulate objects by effortful or dynamic touch.

One study investigated the ability of pre-school-aged children (3 to 5 years old) to perceive the length of wielded objects across several tasks (Fitzpatrick & Flynn, 2010). In one task, children wielded pairs of rods that differed in length and reported which rod in each pair felt longer. Overall, they chose the longer rod more than 80% of the time, and older children were no better at the task than younger children.

In another task, children wielded pairs of rods that were the same length but with weights attached at different locations, creating different values of *Ixx*. Overall, children chose the rod with the larger value of *Ixx* almost 70% of the time, and this time, older children were more likely to do so than younger children. In a third task, children wielded rods that differed in both length and *Ixx* and reported how long each rod felt by positioning a visible marker along a "growth chart". Overall, perceived length increased with *Ixx*, and older children were more sensitive to changes in *Ixx* than younger children.

A related study investigated how pre-school-aged children used a handheld object as a reaching tool (Bongers et al., 2003). In this study, children were asked to hold a rod pointing straight up while walking toward a toy duck on a table (see Figure 18.13). Their task was to come to a complete stop at some point before they got to the table, lower the rod, and then use the rod to slide the duck off the table and into a container of water. The researchers were interested in, among other things, where each child chose to stop walking before performing the task.

In the first experiment, the researchers varied both the length and mass of the rods, and in the second experiment, the researchers varied length, mass, and *Ixx*. Overall, the results of both experiments showed that children chose a stopping distance based on length but not on mass or *Ixx*. In addition, children leaned forward more and extended their arm more when

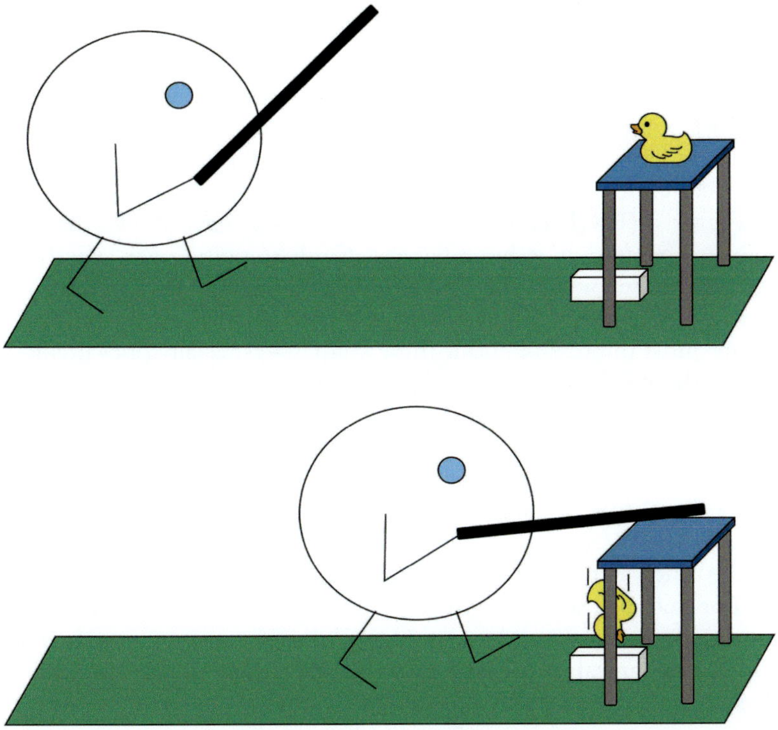

Figure 18.13 When children used a handheld object to displace a toy from a table with a rod, they chose a stopping distance and arm posture based on the length of the rod.

completing the task with shorter rods than with longer rods. And older children chose to stop farther from the table and were generally more successful in performing the task than younger children.

Finally, in a study investigating how children perceive heaviness, pre-school-aged children wielded unseen objects that differed in both size and mass. Researchers (Kloos & Amazeen, 2002) asked them to imagine that the objects they were wielding were pieces of cheese that a mouse would need to carry up a hill to its house. Their job was to instruct the experimenter to mark how far up a hill—depicted on a computer screen—a mouse could walk while carrying the cheese before needing to rest. They used this distance as a measure of perceived heaviness. Clever, huh? Just like adults, children reported that objects felt heavier as mass increased and as values of *I* changed such that larger and more diverse forces were required to move that object—as that object became more difficult or more challenging to move.

Together, these results show that the ability to perceive by effortful touch develops—just like the ability to perceive by vision or hearing. Children can perceive the length, heaviness, and affordances of a wielded object. And, in many of these tasks, they are sensitive to *I*. However, the results also suggest that, like sensitivity to other informative stimulation variables—like optic flow patterns—sensitivity to *I* is not a given. Rather, it *develops*. In this case, children seem to become increasingly sensitive to the relationship between *I* and the various affordances of a given object throughout early childhood and into early adulthood.

Perceiving by Means of an Object Attached to the Body

In Chapter 14, we briefly discussed studies in which blindfolded participants were able to perceive whether a gap affords passing through when exploring the surfaces that form that gap with a handheld object. In fact, they were able to perform this task both when they explored the opening with a wooden rod and when they did so with an "enactive torch"—a handheld device that emits infrared light and converts distance information into vibrations that are felt on the wrist (Favela et al., 2018). Other studies have shown that people can use a handheld object to perceive whether a barrier affords stepping over, whether a gap in the support surface affords stepping across and whether an inclined surface affords standing on (see Wagman et al., 2023).

What is perhaps most impressive about these studies—especially ones involving the enactive torch—is that the participants were blindfolded people who had no experience whatsoever performing such tasks. From the ecological perspective, participants were able to perform such tasks despite this lack of experience because the structure that is informative about a given affordance is analogous across energy forms (e.g., light and the mechanical forces acting on bodily tissues) regardless of the micro-scale differences between those energy forms (see Chapters 14–17).

Even within the touch system itself, though, there are micro-scale differences across different body parts. For example, some body parts are more powerful (e.g., legs), more sensitive (e.g., feet), or more dexterous (e.g., hands) than others. However, given the lawful structuring of the ocean of mechanical forces acting on the body, these micro-scale differences ought not to matter in perception of a given affordance.

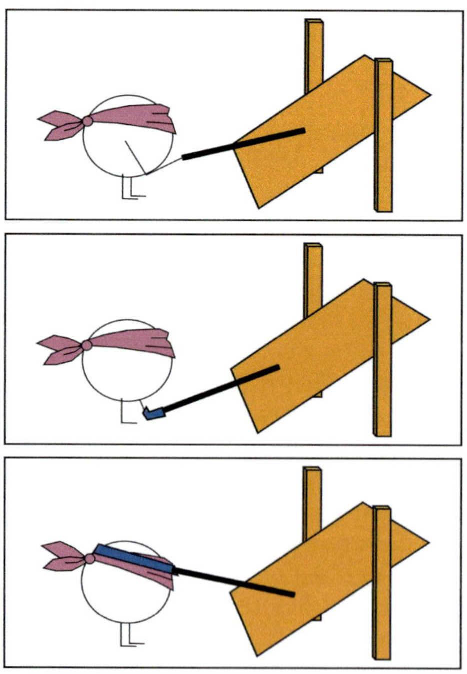

Figure 18.14 Participants can perceive whether a surface affords standing on by probing that surface with an object like a pole. That is true whether the object is held in the hand (top), attached to the foot (middle), or attached to the head (bottom).

In fact, studies have shown that blindfolded participants can perceive whether an inclined surface affords standing on when they explore that surface with an object held in their preferred hand, their non-preferred hand, or both hands (see Figure 18.14). They can even do so when they explore that surface with an object attached to their preferred foot or non-preferred foot and even with an object attached to their head (see Figure 18.14; Wagman & Hajnal, 2014, 2016)! These abilities are comparable to the abilities of other animal species to perceive affordances by means of body parts that are not directly connected to the nervous system like claws, whiskers, antenna, horns, and quills.

So, people can use handheld objects to perceive affordances. But can they also use handheld objects to find their way to different places? Yes, yes, they can. In one experiment that investigated this, blindfolded participants used a handheld soft-tipped long cane to walk back and forth down a narrow pathway between two 30m (100-foot) sections of PVC pipe (Harrison & Turvey, 2010). There was a landmark—a small wooden step—at one end of the path (see Figure 18.15).

Each participant started at a particular unmarked location along the path called "home". They practiced walking in a given direction at a given pace, stopping at a given location, and then turning around and returning to the home location. Then the experimenter led them along another path back to the home position.

After repeating this task a few dozen times, the experimenter told them that certain "repairs" needed to be made to the path before they could complete the next part. For some of the participants, these "repairs" involved shifting the location of the landmark 3m toward the direction of home. For the others, the landmark remained in its original location. Sneaky! Then, the experimenter led the participant along a particular route back and forth along the

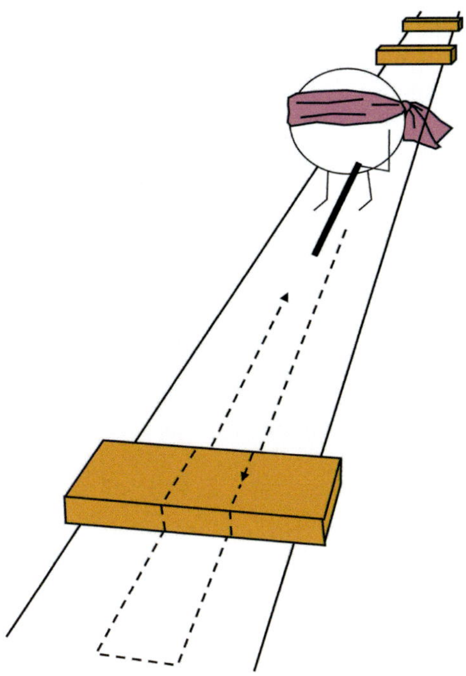

Figure 18.15 Setup of a wayfinding experiment. Blindfolded participants used the handheld cane to find their way back and forth between landmarks.

path, stopped them at a random location, and asked them to find their way back to "home" (i.e., turn in the direction of home, walk to that location, and stop). This task was repeated a few different times, using different routes and different random locations.

So, what happened? Impressively, when the landmark remained in its original location, participants were pretty successful in finding their way back home. On average, participants tended to locate home only about 2m farther away from the landmark than it actually was. This is fairly impressive given that the entire path was 30m long (about the length of a large blue whale!). What is even more impressive, though, is that when the landmark was moved 3m closer to home, participants tended to locate home about 5m farther away from the landmark than it actually was. In other words, changing the location of the landmark by 3m resulted in a corresponding shift in perceived location of home. And this occurred despite the different distances, routes, and locations before the participant was asked to find home. These abilities are comparable to the abilities of other animal species—including fish, insects, and spiders—to learn the locations of places by feeling their way to and from those locations by mechanical contact.

Socratic Question: In Chapter 15 (Box 15.2), we made the argument that the components of your visual system can change depending on what you are doing. Is this also true for the components of your touch system?

Summary

In the ecological approach to perceiving by touch, researchers investigate the mechanical forces acting on bodily tissue at the scale of the relationship between animals and their environments. When people wield or manipulate objects, the forces acting on the body are lawfully structured by the ways in which those objects can be moved. Detecting these forces is how we perceive affordances of and with such objects.

Notes

1 The word "haptic" comes from the Greek word *haptikos*, which means "able to touch or grasp".
2 The skin alone is the largest organ in the body (see Chapter 6).
3 This is along the same lines as putting a car in drive, stepping on the accelerator, stepping on the brake, putting the car in reverse, and stepping on the accelerator again.
4 In fact, the word "tensor" comes from the Latin word *tender* (which means "to stretch").
5 Perceived heaviness is sometimes proposed to be a combination of independent sensations of properties such as mass, size, and density, or a comparison of the expected to actual muscle activity required to lift the object (see Buckingham, 2014).
6 Or its metric equivalent, "Which weighs more—a kilogram of lead or a kilogram of feathers?"

19 But What About . . .?

In this chapter, we discuss several topics that people like to bring up when raising concerns about or objecting to the ecological approach. We hear these concerns often and they usually take the form of questions that start, "But what about . . ." Like . . . but what about illusions? What about improvements in perceiving? What about bottom-up or top-down influences on perception? What about the brain? What about the chemical senses? People ask these questions because they are often convinced that the ecological approach either does not or cannot answer them. In this chapter, we do our best to address these concerns by either answering these questions or showing how they might be answered.

But What About . . . Illusions?

As we have seen in Chapter 9 and elsewhere, illusions have an important place in traditional approaches to perceiving (see Shapiro & Todorović, 2017). And every now and then, a clever illusion takes the internet by storm—remember "the dress" (see Chapter 4)? It is no surprise that illusions get a lot of attention from perceptual scientists and the general public alike. They are fascinating . . . and fun! (see Figure 19.1)[1]

But hang on a minute . . . isn't the fact that we (sometimes) experience illusions a problem for the ecological approach? If perceiving is a process of detecting lawfully structured stimulation, why would we experience illusions *at all*? Shouldn't we experience the world *exactly as it is*? Shouldn't our perceptual experience be *100% accurate* all the time?

Figure 19.1 Left, in the "Café Wall Illusion", the horizontal lines are parallel but they don't look that way. Right, in the Ebbinghaus illusion, the blue inner circle and the red inner circle are exactly the same size, but they don't look that way.

DOI: 10.4324/9781032690964-22

Before we get to those questions, let's back up a bit and review exactly what it means to experience an illusion from more traditional approaches and, consequently, why illusions might be useful in these approaches. From most traditional approaches, perceiving is a process of (unconsciously) interpreting or processing copies to produce mental representations.[2] This process is necessary because, in these approaches, the stimulation reaching the sense organs is ambiguous. Thankfully, the copies—like the pattern of light on the retina—contain *cues* that can inform this process. In these approaches, the *outcome, output, or result* of this processing and interpretation is the basis of our subjective perceptual experience. And, almost all the time, the resulting subjective perceptual experience—more or less[3]—matches objective reality.

How do we know this? Because we can compare our subjective perceptual experience of a given property to a measurement of that same property made by an artificial measuring device that was specifically designed to measure that property. For example, we can compare our subjective visual experience of properties such as length, angle, brightness, or color to measurements made by artificial measuring devices such as a meter stick, a protractor, or a (spectro)photometer. And when we do this, we find out that our experience of these properties—more or less—matches the output of these devices. A short, horizontal, dark line is almost always perceived as a short, horizontal, dark line. And two *identical* short, horizontal, dark lines are almost always perceived as identical. Likewise, two shapes that are the same color are almost always perceived as the same color, and two shapes that are different colors are almost always perceived as different colors (see Figure 19.2).

Likewise, we can also compare our subjective *felt* experience of properties such as temperature, mass, or force to measurements made by different artificial measuring devices such as a thermometer, scale, or a dynamometer. And when we do this, we find that our experience of these properties—again, more or less—matches the output of these devices as well. Two objects that are equal in mass (say, Fred's broom and a bag of Topsy's peanuts) are almost always perceived as equally heavy, and two objects that are unequal in mass (say, Fred's kitchen mallet and an adult cat) are almost always perceived as differently heavy (see Chapter 18).

However, once in a while—under just the right circumstances—the processing or interpreting of copies seems to go awry. In these cases, our subjective perceptual experience of a particular geometric or physical property *does not* match objective reality as measured by an artificial measuring device. For example, under just the right circumstances, two identical short horizontal lines *won't* look identical (see Figure 19.3, *left*). In the figure on the left—called the "Ponzo illusion"—the top horizontal line looks longer than the bottom horizonal line even though they are exactly the same length (as measured by a meter stick). Similarly,

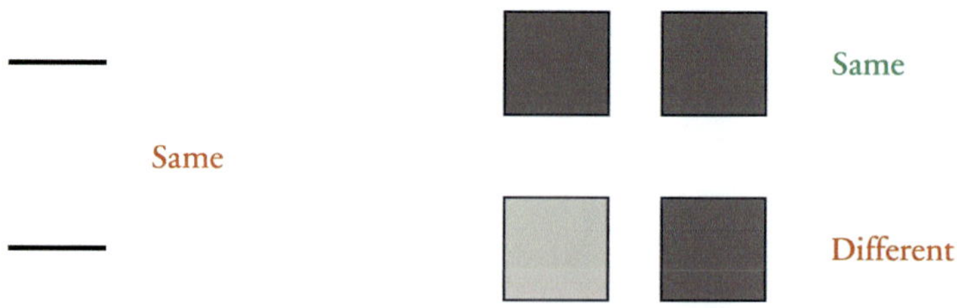

Figure 19.2 Left, two identical short, horizontal, dark lines are almost always perceived as identical. Right, two shapes that are the same color are almost always perceived as the same color, and two shapes that are different levels of brightness are almost always perceived as different levels of brightness.

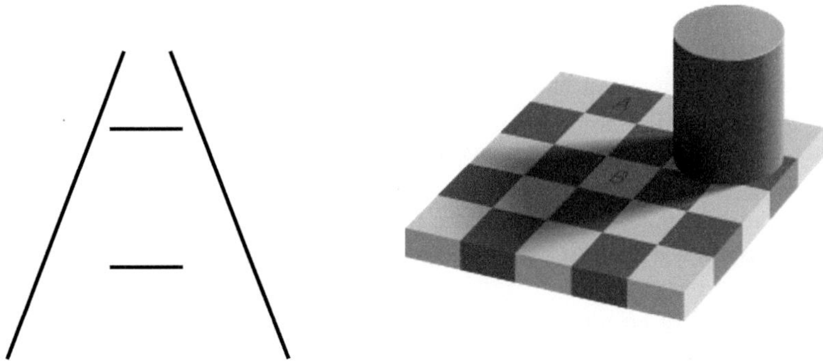

Figure 19.3 Left, in the context of the Ponzo illusion, two identical short, horizontal, dark lines are not perceived to be identical. Right, in the context of the checker shadow illusion, two shapes that are the same color are not perceived to be the same level of brightness.

under just the right circumstances, two shapes that are the same color won't look like the same color. In Figure 19.3 (*right*), the square labeled A looks darker than the square labeled B even though they are exactly the same color (as measured by a spectrophotometer). Weird, right?

And as we have seen in Chapter 18, under just the right circumstances—two objects that are the same mass won't feel equally heavy and two objects that are different masses won't feel differently heavy. From the traditional approach, these are all examples of perceptual illusions—mismatches between subjective perceptual experience and objectively measured reality (Gregory, 2009).

You can understand why perceptual illusions are interesting (and useful!) from the traditional approach. They are rare instances of mistakes or errors in the processing or interpretation of (the cues in) copies. Brain hiccups! So, from the traditional approach, they provide hints about how the processing or interpretations of copies is *supposed to work* under normal circumstances—like how a toilet handle that needs to be jiggled after every flush might give insight about how a properly functioning toilet is supposed to work.

In particular, from the traditional approach, illusions provide hints about the cues available in the copies and what the relevant rules are for interpreting those cues are. At the end of the day, though, occasional mistakes in interpreting or processing the copies are understandable, right? After all, these copies need to be interpreted continuously and immediately, and the stimulation is *always* ambiguous. Bad input is bound to yield bad output at least once in a while, right? The central executive is doing the best it can with the information it has!

From the ecological approach, however, illusions are not what they seem to be. In other words, illusions *themselves* are illusory. There are multiple reasons for this. For one thing, from the ecological approach, perceiving is a *continuously ongoing process or activity*. Specifically, it is a continuous process of detecting, not a momentary act of computing. And so, if it is a continuously ongoing process, then it doesn't ever produce an outcome or output. If there is not an outcome or output, then there is never anything to compare to the output of any kind of artificial measuring device. And if there can be no comparison, there can be no mismatch. And if there can be no mismatch, there can be no illusions.

Second, perceiving is not just any kind of process or activity—it is a lawful one. In particular, it is the process or activity of detecting lawfully structured stimulation patterns. And these lawfully structured stimulation patterns are informative about events and affordances—*not physical or geometric properties* (see Chapter 14). Geometric properties exist, of course, but they don't (necessarily) lawfully structure stimulation patterns. And so, perceptual systems are very much *unlike* artificial measuring devices (see Chapters 15–18). They don't measure the same things, and they don't work in the same way.

Think about it—why would the visual system have evolved to measure geometric properties such as the lengths of lines or the diameters of circles and do so in arbitrary units such as centimeters? It wouldn't have. Why would the touch system have evolved to measure physical properties such as mass (or weight) and do so in arbitrary units such as grams? It wouldn't have. Animals (evolved to) perceive and act on events and affordances, not geometric or physical properties. Asking an animal (even a human animal) to tell you about geometric or physical properties using arbitrary units is a big ask. In fact, it is remarkable how well people (and other animals) can perform such tasks!

Third, perceiving is not just a lawful process, it is an *active process*. Perceiving is an activity. It involves looking, listening, feeling, tasting, smelling. Above all, it involves moving and exploring lawfully structured stimulation patterns. It should be no surprise then that most illusions only work when the perceiver either cannot actively explore at all or cannot actively explore in ways that reveal such structure. For example, when Fred views an illusion on a screen or on a page—say the infamous dress—changing his point of observation in the optic array—leaning to the left or the right, for example—doesn't give him any new information about what is depicted in the image.[4] The illusion only works because he is forced to view it from a very particular point of observation with very limited (or no) context. The same thing is true, of course, about many other illusions such as the Ames room (see Chapter 9) or some kinds of street art (see Figure 19.4).

And so, illusions just don't have the same value in the ecological approach as they do in the traditional approaches. Don't get us wrong. They are still interesting and fun. And they do have *some value* in the ecological approach. It's just that they don't really reveal much about how perceiving works. And they're certainly not mistakes or errors in the perceptual process. *They can't be.* We have already mentioned the reason(s) why. But this is such an important point with such far-reaching implications that we are bringing it back. Ready?

Here it is: In the ecological approach, perceiving is a lawful process or activity that does not produce an outcome. This means that *the accuracy of perceiving can never be evaluated.* Just like any other lawful (and natural) process, perceiving is neither correct nor incorrect.

Figure 19.4 Left, when viewed from one particular angle, the crosswalk appears to "float". Right, viewed from another angle, the arrangement of surfaces is clear and the crosswalk no longer appears to float.

The process is what it is. Full stop. And this is the case in the overwhelming majority of cases in which that process enables us to successfully perform everyday behaviors. But it is *also* the case when that process is unhelpful or—once in a while—even harmful.

Consider baby Eleanor, who refuses to crawl on the (perfectly safe) deep side of the visual cliff—*nope!* (see Chapter 15)—or Fred when he inadvertently walks into a (perfectly solid) glass door—*ouch!* In the first case, the process is somewhat unhelpful—Eleanor *could* crawl on the surface but doesn't. In the second case, it is somewhat harmful—Fred could bump his head and does. However, in neither case is the process of perceiving illusory. In both cases, affordances were perceived (or were not perceived), but only because the information about those affordances was undetected (or was not detectable at all). This doesn't necessarily mean that Eleanor won't eventually learn that that Plexiglas table actually does afford crawling on or that Fred won't eventually learn that the glass door actually does not afford walking through (see *But What About . . . Improvements in Perception?*). What it does mean is that surfaces that do not structure reflected light *will always be invisible* to perceivers who are sensitive to structured reflected light, because the information about the presence of that surface is just not detectable. If not seeing the surface is an illusion, then under these circumstances, the illusion will always occur. Every. Single. Time.

If perceiving is a process or activity of detecting lawfully structured information about events and affordances, then the information detected will determine what events and affordances are perceived (even if those events and affordances do not really exist!). When Fred lost his balance in the moving room (see Chapter 16), is he experiencing an illusion? Or is he merely perceiving (and acting on) affordances by detecting lawfully structured patterns in ambient energy arrays? And if illusions really are errors or mistakes, wouldn't it be a *bigger error or mistake* to be *completely insensitive* to such patterns?

And now you know why any notions of perceiving the world "exactly as it is" or being "100% accurate" don't really make sense in the ecological approach. Perceiving is a process or activity of detecting lawfully structured information about events and affordances. The lawful structuring of stimulation occurs at the level of the animal-environment system. This level includes events and affordances but not abstract geometric or physical properties like color, mass, and distance. Again, such properties exist but they don't (necessarily) lawfully structure stimulation patterns.

Consequently, the ecological approach argues that a theory of perceiving should be developed from the countless everyday successes of perceiving and acting rather than the rare (and often artificial) so-called failures of perceiving. From the ecological approach, illusions are valuable not because they fool perceivers but because they challenge researchers to better understand the lawful process of detecting information about affordances!

> Socratic Question: From the ecological approach, why isn't it (necessarily) an illusion if a person falls over in a moving room or walks into a sliding glass door? And why are illusions themselves illusory?

But What About . . . Improvements in Perception?

Some people are really good at perceiving particular kinds of things. After all, if Fred wanted to have his treasured antique cuckoo clock or an autographed version of this textbook[5] appraised, he wouldn't take it to just anyone. He would take it to his friend Alen, who is an expert appraiser. Given his extensive experience appraising all sorts of items, Alen can tell just by looking at, touching, listening to, and (sometimes) smelling or tasting something what its value is. In other words, Alen is an expert perceiver.

But hang on a minute . . . how could Alen have *become* an expert perceiver? If perception is merely the detection of lawfully structured stimulation, then how does a person get any better at it? After all, if perceiving is a lawful process or activity, then the process is what it is. Full stop. Right? How can there be improvements (or any changes at all) in a lawful process?

Before we get to those questions, let's back up a bit a discuss how learning might occur in perceiving—called "perceptual learning"—from a more traditional approach. If perceiving is a process of (unconsciously) interpreting or processing copies to produce mental representations, then learning likely involves the *modification or enrichment* of such representations or *refinements* in the ability to use such representations. And such learning would result in subjective experience that more closely matches objectively reality. And we'd know this by comparing subjective perceptual experience of a given property to a measurement of that same property made by an artificial measuring device at different points in time (see *What About . . . Illusions?*). If there is less difference over time between the subjective experience and the objective measurement, then learning has occurred. *Voilà*!

Given the objections of the ecological approach to a traditional account of illusions that we just outlined, you can probably guess what some ecological objections to a traditional account of perceptual learning would be. And you'd probably be right. For example, if perceiving doesn't require processing copies into representations, then learning can't be the modification or enrichment of such representations. And so on and so forth. Blah. Blah. Blah. That's all well and good, but then how does the ecological approach explain improvements in perceiving if not for representations? How can improvements (or any changes at all) occur in a lawful process or activity?

The short answer is that while the lawful relationships between stimulation patterns and affordance *do not* (and cannot) change, the ability to detect and use those relationships can change (and *does*). In other words, learning to become a better perceiver is more like learning to use a (special kind of) measuring instrument—like learning to use a telescope to see a distant star—than it is like learning to make better guesses based on bad data. So, a person becomes a better perceiver by learning to detect and use informative stimulation patterns, not by learning how to make meaningless stimulation patterns meaningful (see Figure 19.5).

One of the ways in which the ability to detect and use these stimulation patterns changes is in the selection of which (events and) affordance(s) to perceive in a particular circumstance.

Figure 19.5 In the ecological approach, learning to become a better perceiver is like learning to use a special kind of measuring instrument—like a telescope, a metal detector, or a polar planimeter (see Chapter 13).

Figure 19.6 No, really. How would you suggest that this person does this? This pen is not going to get itself.

Remember, at any given moment, lots of events are occurring, and lots of behaviors are possible. Which events are the right ones to pay attention to right now? And what behaviors are the right ones to perform right now? And *how* should those behaviors be performed? When the pen on Fred's desk fell on the floor in Chapter 14 (see Figure 19.6), one of the things that he could do was pick it up. But how? By reaching with his arm and hand? By crouching *and then* reaching with his arm and hand? By some other means? And, once Fred makes each of these choices, he must then *actively explore* the available energy arrays in a way that reveals the stimulation pattern that might provide information about that affordance. This last point is critical because it means that *learning how to perceive goes hand in hand with learning how to move*. Perceiving is an activity, after all.

So, learning to perceive something very particular—even something as particular as the value of an antique cuckoo clock or an autographed textbook—means learning how to move in a very particular way. For example, people who practice perceiving properties of wielded objects learn to move those objects in particular ways to perceive particular properties of those objects. They tend to rotate it toward and away from the ground—like shaking someone's hand—when attempting to perceive length and tend to twist it—like turning a doorknob—when attempting to perceive width[6] (Arzamarski et al., 2010; see Chapter 18). In general, learning what behaviors to perform, what affordances to perceive, and how to explore to uncover possible information about those affordances is called the **education of intention** (Jacobs & Michaels, 2007).

Education of intention learning what behaviors to perform, what affordances to perceive, and how to explore to uncover information about those affordances.

Another way that this ability changes is through subtle shifts in *what specific aspect* of a given lawfully structured stimulation pattern is detected when intending to perceive a given event or affordance. Ideally, over the course of learning, the person will progress *toward* detecting aspects of stimulation patterns that provide more useful information about the intended event or affordance and *away* from aspects of detecting patterns that provide less useful information about that event or affordance. People who practice perceiving the width of a wielded object shift toward detecting the minimum principal moment of inertia (I_{zz}) and away from detecting other components of I (Arzamarski et al., 2010; see Chapter 18). In general, learning which aspects of a lawfully structured stimulation pattern provide information about a given affordance has been called the **education of attention** (Gibson, 1966).

Education of attention learning which aspects of a lawfully structured stimulation pattern provide information about a given affordance.

The education of intention and education of attention often—but not always—result in changes in *how an animal uses* a given stimulation pattern to perceive a given affordance. But detecting the *appropriate stimulation pattern*—and specifically the appropriate *aspect* of that stimulation pattern—is one thing. Using it properly is another. In other words, finding the useful stimulation pattern is different than knowing how to use that stimulation pattern. People who practice (and get feedback on) perceiving the width of a wielded object will learn to use the minimum principal moment of inertia (*Izz*) to perceive the width of the object based on the specific feedback they receive. Learning *how to use* the information about a given affordance to appropriately perceive a given property or perform a given behavior is called **calibration** (see Jacobs & Michaels, 2007). In other words, calibration is about learning the scaling relationship that exists between the information about a given affordance and perceiving and acting on that affordance.

Calibration learning how to use the information about a given affordance to appropriately perceive a given property or perform a given behavior.

Note that none of these processes—the education of intention, the education of attention, or calibration—affect the status of perceiving as a process or activity of detecting lawfully structured stimulation patterns. Instead, they affect *how* those patterns are uncovered and discovered, *what aspects* of those patterns are detected, and *how* those patterns are used. Nothing about representations at all. In other words, in the ecological approach, expert perceivers are better *detectors*, but not better *detectives*!

Socratic Question: From the ecological approach, perceiving is an ongoing process or activity rather than an outcome or an output. How is this reflected in the ecological explanation of improvements in perception? What does it mean that in the ecological approach "expert perceivers are better *detectors*, but not better *detectives*"?

But What About . . . Bottom-Up and Top-Down Influences on Perception?

Many (if not most) traditional approaches to perceiving can be described in terms of how much they rely on two different kinds of influences on perceptual experience. In so-called bottom-up processing, a perceptual experience is built (more or less exclusively) from "incoming sense data"—especially data relevant to geometric and physical properties.[7] In so-called top-down processing, existing knowledge, hypotheses, or expectations are used to interpret the incoming sense data (see Chapter 10 for examples of bottom-up and top-down approaches to recognizing objects and Part I for discussion of ascending and descending pathways in the sensory systems and brain).

Clearly, it's possible—maybe even *necessary*—for both kinds of processing to influence perceiving, right? So, how much does the ecological approach rely on each one? If the ecological approach explicitly denies that representations and interpretations play any role whatsoever in perceiving, then *surely* it is a completely bottom-up approach, right? And if

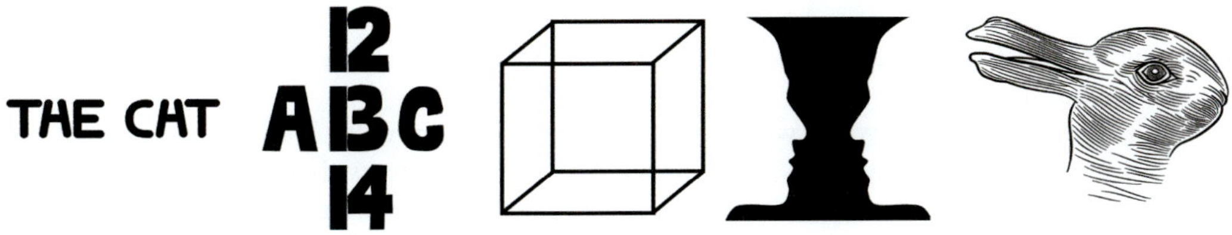

Figure 19.7 Examples of so-called top-down processing in perceiving.

so, then what about seemingly obvious examples in which context and constraints influence perception (see Figure 19.7 and Box 19.1)? Surely, those are examples of top-down processing, right? . . . *right*?

Box 19.1 Practicing Safe Text

One example of context affecting a perceptual task is when a person attempts to perform a cognitive task (like talking or texting on a cell phone) and a perceptual task (like reacting to stimuli while driving) at the same time. In fact, decades of research have conclusively shown that in these situations, performing a cognitive task almost always negatively impacts performance in a perceptual task (see Chabris & Simon, 2011). Does performing a cognitive task also negatively impact performance when perceiving affordances? Yes, but maybe not how you might think and maybe not for the reasons that you might think.

Researchers (Lopresti-Goodman et al., 2012) asked two groups of participants to walk through doorways of different widths—one group did so while actively texting and the other group did so while merely holding their phone. The researchers compared the critical π values (the doorway width at which the participant switched from walking without turning their shoulders to walking while turning their shoulders) for each group. They found that the critical π value was *larger* for the texters than for the non-texters (see Figure 19.8). That is, the texters were being *more cautious* in passing

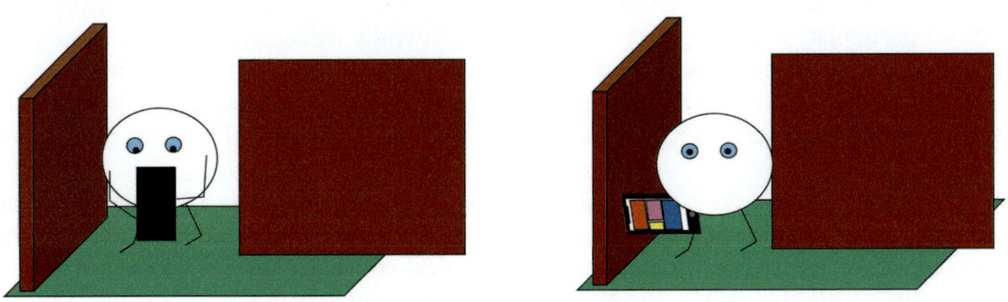

Figure 19.8 Participants who were texting (left) walked slower and were more cautious about the size of the "pass-through-able" gap than participants who merely carried their phones (right).

through the doorway than the non-texters. And the texters walked *more slowly* than the non-texters.

In other words, the texters were distracted, and they knew it. And the fact that the critical π values for both groups were highly consistent suggests that the cognitive task didn't seem to affect their ability to *perceive* affordances for passing through the door so much as it did their ability to *act on* these affordances.

Before we get to those questions, let's back up a bit and discuss why one (or both) kinds of processing are necessary in more traditional approaches. In these approaches, the environment is best described in terms of properties borrowed from Newtonian physics and Euclidean geometry (see Chapters 1, 8, 13, and 14). These properties (e.g., color, mass, and distance) are completely objective and independent of any perceiver. That is, they are context-free and meaningless.

These properties are (ambiguously) copied or represented in the stimulation reaching the sense organs. This is the "sense data" that is eventually used to "build" the perceptual experience (bottom-up processing). But the process of "building" perceptual experience is not merely a process of combining or adding up the sense data. It *can't be* because the stimulation is bad and the representations are ambiguous! Instead, it is a process of making (unconscious) inferences about those representations. And these inferences are interpretations based on existing knowledge, hypotheses, or expectations (i.e., top-down processing). Moreover, once these inferences are made, the resulting subjective perceptual experience can then be used in more "upstream" processes, including moving the body and thinking.

It is true that the ecological approach is a completely non-representational approach to perceiving (see Blau & Wagman, 2022; Turvey, 2019). In fact, this is the *defining feature* of the ecological approach (see Chapters 13 and 14). And it is also true that this would seem to rule out top-down processing. And it does. So then, if top-down processing is ruled out, then only one possibility remains, right? This means that in the ecological approach, perceiving *must* rely exclusively on bottom-up processing. *Bam! End of story.* Except that it doesn't. And it's not. *Wait . . . what?* Let us explain.

Given the objections of the ecological approach to traditional accounts of illusions and perceptual learning, you might be able to guess what the objections would be to top-down processing. As we've discussed, in the ecological approach, perceiving is a lawful process or activity. In particular, it is the process of detecting lawfully structured stimulation patterns. And in the same way that lawful (and natural) processes are neither correct nor incorrect, they are neither top-down nor bottom-up. The processes are what they are. Full stop. And as we've said earlier in this chapter, the same is true about the process of perceiving. It is what it is. Full stop.

In bottom-up processing, a perceptual experience is built from meaningless component pieces—abstract geometric or physical properties such as color, mass, and distance. But there are no meaningless component pieces in the ecological approach. In fact, there are no component pieces *at all.* There are just events and affordances (see Chapter 13 and 14). And events and affordances lawfully structure stimulation patterns. So, we perceive events and affordances by detecting this structure, not by combining component pieces. In the ecological approach, information is not data!

As we pointed out in Chapter 14, events and affordances are nested within one another over different scales. But no matter the scale, events and affordances lawfully structure stimulation patterns. And so, perceiving events and affordances at larger scales is *still* a matter of detecting such lawfully structured stimulation patterns, not a matter of perceiving events and affordances at smaller scales and then combining those component events and affordances (Thomas et al., 2017).

Hopefully, this makes clear why the ecological approach does not rely on either top-down processing (because there are no representations or inferences) or bottom-up processing (because there are no component pieces to combine). Perceiving is neither a matter of building nor interpreting. Instead, it is a matter of detecting. But . . . and this is a *BIG* but . . . this does not mean that the context in which perceiving occurs or the constraints under which perceiving occurs don't matter. It's just that, in the ecological approach, the context and constraints are *baked into the process from the very beginning* so that they do not need to be added in later on (Stoffregen & Wagman, 2024).

In traditional approaches, the context is intentionally stripped away, starting with how the properties of the world are described (see Chapter 8). By definition, the properties of Newtonian physics and Euclidean geometry are context-free—*they exist completely independently of the perceiver*. And the mental representations that form the basis of subjective experience *also* are context-free—but in the complete opposite way—*they exist completely independently of the properties of the world*. In other words, the process of perceiving is completely ungrounded—disconnected from both the perceiver and the world! Connecting the resulting mental representations back up with the perceiver and the world requires adding the context back—in the form of top-down processing. As a reminder, this is known as the *grounding problem* (see Chapter 8).

In the ecological approach, however, the world is described in terms of relationships between animal and environments (i.e., in terms of events and affordances). Animals detect patterns in structured energy that are lawfully related to these relationships. And here is the kicker—*those relationships already include context*! Perceiving is an activity performed by a particular perceiver (say, Fred) in a particular place (say, at his desk) at a particular time (say, right now). Where the animal is, what the animal is doing, and how it is doing it all play a role in the structure that the animal encounters. Therefore, the process of perceiving is *completely grounded* in lawful relations, and the context is an inherent part of these relations. It is there from the beginning. There is no grounding problem!

But . . . wait! What about goals and intentions? Surely, these are top-down influences on perceiving, right? Yes, goals and intentions influence perceiving in the ecological approach, but not in a top-down processing sort of way. Like context and constraints, goals and intentions are *baked into the process from the very beginning* so that they do not need to be added in later on. Perceiving is an activity performed for a particular purpose. Perceiving is not an activity perceived for its own sake. It is performed for the purpose of performing other activities. When Fred is at his desk working on a book manuscript, he could do many different things. That is, there are many different affordances he could perceive and act on. He could continue working, he could reach for the glass of water, he could swat that annoying fly, among many, many others. Fred's goals and intentions will influence whether, when, and how these many affordances are perceived and acted on (Stoffregen & Wagman, 2024).

But rather than influencing the interpretation of incoming sense data, goals and intentions influence how that person actively explores the structured energy, thereby influencing what patterns they detect and how they use those patterns. Again, perceiving is an activity. Fred will explore the structured energy arrays that surround him differently if he intends to reach for the glass of water than if he intends to continue working. And he will also do so differently if he intends to swat the annoying fly but is attempting to figure out exactly how to do so.

> Socratic Question: How is the ecological approach neither a bottom-up approach nor a top-down approach?

But What About . . . the Brain?

In most (if not all) traditional approaches, perceiving is something that happens in or is accomplished by the brain. The sense organs deliver the sense data to the brain. The brain then either builds perceptual experience from the incoming sense data (bottom up), interprets the incoming sense data based on knowledge, hypotheses, or expectations (top down), or both. Scientists can have disagreements about which one of these kinds of process occurs most often under different circumstances but not about *where* such processes take place, right? . . . *right*?

After all, the brain is the only part of the body smart enough to perform the necessary building and interpreting. That's like the brain's *whole deal*, right? And subjective perceptual experience sure feels like it lives right behind the eyes—exactly where the brain lives! In fact, everything about the traditional approaches to perception screams "BRAIN!" And—as if we needed any more evidence—imaging techniques seem to show that the brain "lights up" in specific places during certain kinds of perceptual tasks, and damage to those areas of the brain seems to cause deficits in those same kinds of perceptual tasks (Milner & Goodale, 2006; Humphreys & Riddoch, 2013; see Figure 19.9). So, *clearly* the brain must be at the very

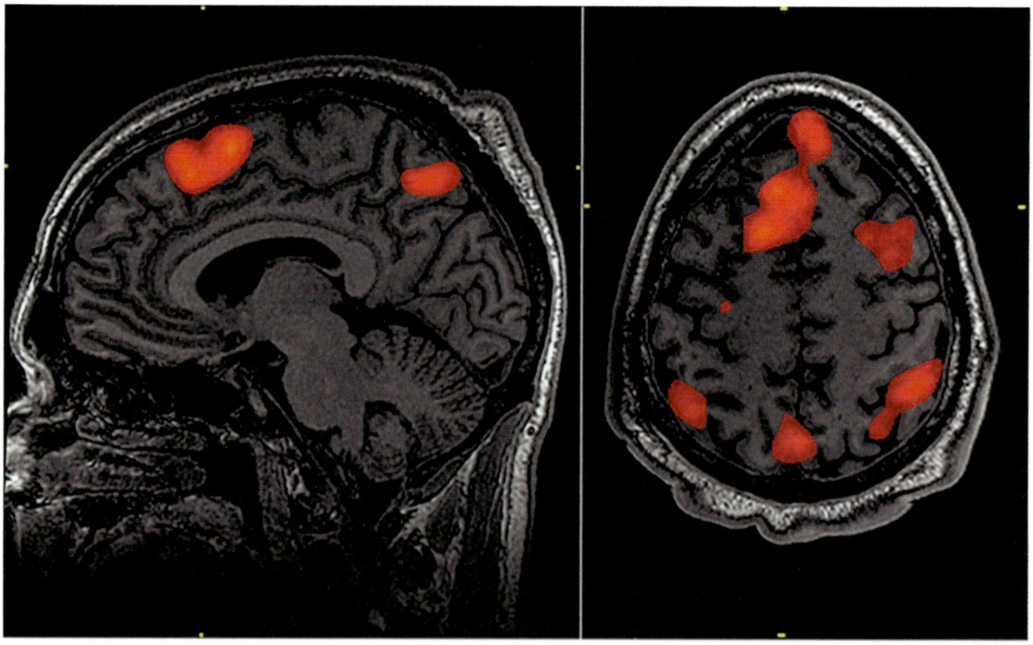

Figure 19.9 Studies have shown that the brain "lights up" in specific places during certain kinds of perceptual or cognitive tasks.

center of *all* approaches to perceiving. But as we have seen, the brain is *not* at the center of the ecological approach to perceiving. In fact, there is very little mention of the brain at all. What in the name of James J. Gibson is going on here?!

Just as we have done for the other "but what about" questions so far, let's back up a bit and discuss why the brain has such an exalted place in traditional approaches to perceiving. To a large extent, this is a necessary and unavoidable consequence of the assumptions of the traditional approach that we outlined *way back* in Chapter 1 (e.g., local causality, simulative assumption, poverty of the stimulus, etc.). Of course, the *primary* consequence of these assumptions is that perceiving *must* be described as a process of (unconsciously) interpreting or processing copies to produce mental representations. But a *secondary* consequence of these assumptions is that the interpreting and processing of copies *must* occur in a particular, identifiable location. Local causality demands that this is so. And the brain, of course, is the most likely candidate for this location. It is the computer that runs the machine!

It is true that the brain is not at the center of the ecological explanations of perceiving. It is also true that, until relatively recently (e.g., Favela, 2024; Raja & Anderson, 2019), ecological explanations of perceiving have not mentioned the brain much at all. But there are good reasons for this. Probably the most important reason is one that we have discussed a few times already. That is, in the ecological approach, perceiving is a lawful process or activity of detecting lawfully structured stimulation patterns that are informative about events and affordances. For one thing, this means that there is just less for the brain to do in the act of perceiving. There are no copies to interpret or process, there are no representations to generate, and there are no inferences to make. In other words, there is very little for the "computer" to compute.

For another thing, the primary value of a lawful process is that it occurs in the same way across circumstances. This means that, in the ecological approach, perceiving works the same way regardless of the anatomical components that are used to detect the structured stimulation patterns that are informative about events and affordances. Fred might be able to perceive the affordances of a surface by probing it with his hand, his foot, or a stick (see Chapter 18). Other animals might be able to perceive the affordances of that same surface by probing it with their tusk, claw, hoof, antler, beak, or antenna (see Figure 19.10). The

Figure 19.10 In the ecological approach, perceiving works the same way regardless of the anatomical components used. A person can perceive affordances for crossing a gap using trekking poles held in their hands (left), and ant can perceive the same affordance using its antenna (right).

anatomy shouldn't matter so long as it enables the animal to detect the structured stimulation patterns that are informative about the affordance. Makes sense, right?

Well, this argument can be applied to the brain as well. *Wait . . . what? Yep.* Let us explain. Fred (whose brain has between 86,000,000 and 100,000,000 neurons; see Chapter 3) might be able to perceive the affordances of a surface by probing it with his hand. An ant (whose *entire nervous system* has just 250,000 neurons) might be able to perceive the affordance of the same surface by probing it with its antenna. As before, the anatomy shouldn't matter so long as it enables the animal to detect the structured stimulation patterns that are informative about the affordance. In both cases, despite their vastly different brains, Fred and the ant perceive affordances by detecting lawfully structured stimulation patterns that are informative about those affordances. So how important can the brain be to the process of perceiving affordances if animals with only 250,000 neurons are doing just fine perceiving affordances? And animals with far fewer neurons do just fine perceiving affordances, too. Earthworms have only 300 or so neurons. And they perceive affordances of leaves for plugging their burrows. They make choices about *which* leaves use, *where* to grasp those leaves, and *how* to drag those leaves into their burrows (see Reed, 1982). And don't get us started on *Difflugia*! As we discussed in Chapter 13, *Difflugia* is a single-celled organism. This means that it has no neurons at all! And yet, it perceives and acts on affordances for selecting and building itself a suit of armor from 200–300 individual silt particles in the ponds where they live. And that's not all! At least one species of *Difflugia* builds teeth-like structures attached to the armor that it uses to catch and eat other single-celled organisms. Amazing!

But there is another important reason why the brain is not at the center of ecological explanations of perceiving. In the ecological approach, the animal itself is not the fundamental unit of analysis—let alone any one of its organs, including its brain. Instead, the *animal-environment system* is the fundamental unit of analysis. This system includes the animal and its brain but also the surrounding surfaces and structured stimulation. This is where the "ecological" in the "ecological approach" comes from, after all (see Chapters 13 and 14). Consequently, understanding the process of perceiving requires staying at this level of analysis. For example, rather than investigating how an animal's brain interprets ambiguous stimulation patterns, it requires investigating how the animal detects the structured stimulation patterns at that animal's point of observation as it moves among surrounding surfaces. Looking for answers inside the animal—or inside the environment, for that matter—won't lead to scientific explanations of perceiving. In fact, doing so will (likely) lead to unsolvable mysteries (see Chapter 13).

Still, this doesn't mean that the brain doesn't play *any role whatsoever* in perceiving and acting on affordances (Fultot et al., 2019). After all, there are good reasons why brains evolved in so many different kinds of animal species.[8] It just means that the brain can't play the lead role in a one-person (er . . . one-organ?) show. Instead, the brain has to play a supporting role in an ensemble cast that includes the animal *and* the environment. But even this supporting role has some limits. It can't be computational or representational, it must respect the animal-environment system as the fundamental unit of analysis, and it must be a role that can be played by less sophisticated brains—like those found in ants.

So, what role *would* the brain play in the ecological approach? Well, one possibility is that rather than generating, modifying, or interpreting ambiguous stimulation patterns, the brain *resonates to* structured stimulation patterns (Raja & Anderson, 2019). Wait. *What?* Let us explain.

The term resonance is typically used in the context of sounds or vibrations—like when one object that is vibrating at a particular frequency (say, a tuning fork) causes a nearby object

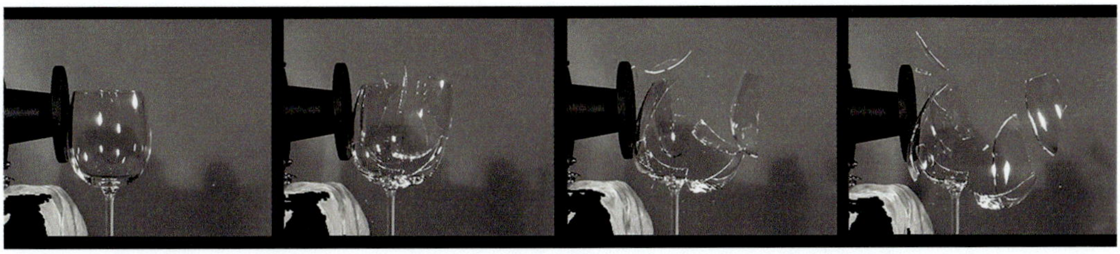

Figure 19.11 Resonance is how a singer (or a machine) can break a wine glass by producing sound waves at just the right amplitude and frequency.

(say, another tuning fork) to vibrate at the same frequency (see Chapter 5).[9] For example, resonance is how a powerful singer—like Fred's favorite rock singer, Dio D. Vicen—can break a wine glass just by singing a loud, sustained note that matches the natural, or resonant, frequency of the glass (see Figure 19.11). In this case, the structured stimulation patterns that are informative about affordances are the notes sung by the singer, and the brain is the wine glass—though hopefully one that doesn't break!

In this way of thinking, the brain is a special kind of antenna that is not only sensitive to structured stimulation patterns that are informative about events and affordances but also reverberates with and amplifies such patterns (Wagman & Thomas, 2026; see Box 10.2). Note that this *reverses* the typical sequence in which activity in the brain and nervous system controls what the animal does. Instead, the activity of the *animal* generates the structured stimulation pattern that controls what the *brain and nervous system* do (Van Orden et al., 2012)! And while it is certainly the case that the brains of people and of ants are very different, the main difference between an animal with a less sophisticated brain (like an ant) and an animal with a more sophisticated brain (like Fred) is not in whether they can perceive events and affordances. They both most certainly can. Instead, the difference is likely in the number of nested levels—the scale or scope—over which they can perceive affordances (see Chapter 14). For example, while an ant might perceive affordances for following a particular kind of trail to the other side of the field, Fred might be able to perceive affordances for following a different kind of trail to the other side of the planet.

Socratic Question: How does an assumption of local causality lead to the brain having a central role in traditional explanations of perceiving? How does an insistence on lawfulness lead to the brain having a peripheral role in explanations of perceiving?

But What About . . . the Chemical Senses?

Most (if not all) children are taught that there are five separate senses—vision, hearing, touch, smell, and taste, each of which is primarily identified with a particular sense organ: the eye, ear, skin, nose, and tongue, respectively. We have already addressed why the notion of separate senses that are each closely identified with anatomical components is likely mistaken (in Chapter 1, no less). But assuming for the moment that there are five separate senses, the ecological approach seems to be able to handle the first three—vision, hearing, and touch—pretty well (see Chapters 15–18). But those are the *easy* ones. But what about *the chemical senses—smell and taste*? What would ecological approach to these senses even look like? And surely, people can't *smell or taste* events and affordances, right? . . . *right?*

Well, an ecological approach to smelling and tasting would be based on the same set of principles as the ecological approach to seeing, hearing, and touching (see Chapters 15–18). One of the consequences of this is that the description "chemical senses" would no longer apply to describe smelling and tasting. Wait, what? That's right—in an ecological approach to smelling and tasting, neither of these descriptors—"chemical" or "sense"—would be appropriate anymore. Let's take these terms one at a time.

First, let's explain why the term "chemical" wouldn't apply. Ecological approaches to seeing, hearing, and feeling required developing an ecological optics, acoustics, and haptics, respectively. Likewise, an ecological approach to smelling and tasting would require developing an **ecological chemistry**—a description of the soluble and volatile substances acting on bodily tissue at the scale of the relationship between animals and their environments (Gibson, 1966).

Ecological chemistry a description of the soluble and volatile substances acting on bodily tissue at the scale of the relationship between animals and their environments.

Some clarification is likely needed here. "Soluble" and "volatile" are not quite everyday words (unless you are an everyday chemist). *Soluble* simply means something that can be dissolved into a liquid. So, sugar is soluble in coffee. And in this context, *volatile* means something that can vaporize into a gas. So, coffee (but especially *steaming hot* coffee) is volatile. Note that in these examples, no mention was made of chemicals. Yes, sugar and coffee (and even the mug the holds the coffee and the air that surrounds the mug) are comprised of chemicals in the same way that *everything* is comprised of chemicals. But the everyday experience of smelling and tasting involves awareness of the soluble and volatile substances *themselves*—sugar and coffee, for example—not the chemicals that comprise those substances (see Chapter 7).

And so, from the ecological approach, investigating how we smell or taste chemicals (e.g., chlorogenic acid lactones)[10] or even how we smell or taste properties like "bitterness" creates unsolvable mysteries in the same way that investigating how we see light at wavelengths of 620–750nm or even how we see "red" creates unsolvable mysteries. We are much better off investigating how we taste a "bitter substance" in the same way we are much better off investigating how we see a "red surface". And take a moment to think about the words you would use to describe what something smells or tastes like. Often, they are words that describe the *substances themselves*—watery, moist, dry, chalky, nutty, fruity, flowery, spicy, earthy, etc.

But really, in an ecological approach to smelling and tasting, we ought to be investigating how we smell and taste events and affordances. At first, you might think that this is just a ridiculous idea. But is it really? Fred can smell whether something affords tasting (or backing away from), and he can taste whether something affords swallowing (or spitting out), right? Might it be possible to smell affordances for behaviors other than those immediately related to eating? Hold that thought for just a few paragraphs.

In the meantime, let's explain why the term "senses" (in "chemical senses") wouldn't apply. The ecological approaches to seeing, hearing, and feeling required describing each of these as activities performed by perceptual systems (see Box 19.1). The same would be true of smelling and tasting. As a reminder, whereas *sense organs* are defined anatomically

Figure 19.12 Blindfolded participants could follow a scent trail much like dogs do.

and passively receive stimulation patterns, *perceptual systems* are defined functionally and actively obtain stimulation patterns. So, smelling and tasting would be defined as activities of perceptual systems that consist of more than just the nose and the tongue, respectively.

So yes—the perceptual system for smelling includes the nose, but also the head, neck, torso, and legs! Imagine what Fred might do if he wanted to locate an alluring aroma source—say, freshly brewed coffee at Richard's house (*yum*)—or maybe an offensive odor—say, the kitty litter box at Pat's house (*ick*). He would sniff, turn his head, sniff again, walk, turn his body, sniff, and so on. And yes—the perceptual system for tasting includes the tongue, but also the lips, teeth, mouth, and jaws. Imagine what Fred would do if he found the freshly brewed coffee at Richard's house (*yum*), poured himself a cup, and wanted to savor it (*mmmm*). He would blow on it (if it was too hot), sip, hold in his mouth, swish it around, hold it again, and swallow. He would do more or less the same thing with solid food, except that he would also chew. Performing these activities changes how food or drink tastes. It's like looking around with your mouth!

And now, we return to the question of whether people can smell affordances. As you surely know, dogs are champion smellers (see Yong, 2022). They can be trained to detect all sorts of things by smelling—explosives, drugs of all kinds, other animals (both living and dead), but also currency, electronics, and perhaps even cancer! And they can follow a scent—especially a scent on the ground, called "scent trail tracking"—to its source over large distances. In other words, they can smell affordances. This smell affords following! And it affords following along *this particular path*! As we have mentioned, it seems pretty clear that people can follow a scent through *the air* to its source (at least to some degree), but they couldn't do this for a scent on the ground, right? . . . *right*?

Dogs seem to have all of the advantages for a task like this—especially in terms of their nose, brain, and nervous system. They have far more olfactory receptors in their nasal cavities than humans (maybe 5 times as many), and the proportion of their brain that "lights up" for smells is much, much larger than in humans—maybe 40 times larger. In addition, their noses are longer and closer to the ground. And, unlike humans, dog noses are shaped in such a way that exhaling actually recirculates inhaled odors back into their nose in a "conveyer belt of smells" rather than just expelling them out of the nose (Yong, 2022; see Chapter 7).

But it turns out that humans can perform a scent trail tracking task pretty well, despite these severe neurological and anatomical disadvantages (Porter et al., 2007; Rosenblum, 2011). Researchers made a 10-meter scent trail in a field using chocolate essential oil (*yum*!). Participants wore an eye mask, earmuffs, knee pads, and work gloves so that they could not see, hear, or feel much of anything. They were brought to a starting position that was 3 meters from the beginning of the scent trail, got down on their hands and knees, put their nose close to the ground, and attempted to *smell* their way to the beginning of the trail and then follow it for the entire 10 meters. Sounds pretty hard, right? It probably was, but nonetheless, two-thirds of the participants (21 of 32 of them) were able to find and follow the scent trail! In other words, these participants were able to smell affordances for following the scent along a particular path!

But that's not all. In a second experiment, four participants practiced this task—without any feedback—three times a day for three days over a two-week period! As you might expect, they got better. They deviated less from the scent trail and increased their tracking speed. And they sniffed more. (See *"But What About . . . Improvements in Perception?"*).

Socratic Question: From the ecological approach, perceiving is an ongoing activity. How does this apply to smelling or tasting?

Summary

There are a number of common concerns about or objections to the ecological approach. We attempted to address the most common examples of these in this chapter. We did so by leaning into the description of perceiving that we developed in Part III of this book. Specifically, from the ecological approach, perceiving is an ongoing and active process of detecting lawfully structured stimulation patterns that are informative about events and affordances. Fully understanding this description—and especially *the implications of* this description—is the best way to address the concerns and objections that we discussed in this chapter, as well as those that we did not.

Notes

1 Check out: https://illusionoftheyear.com.
2 The Gestalt approach is a bit of an exception here. In the Gestalt approach, there is no processing, but there still are representations (see Chapter 9).
3 Remember the lessons of psychophysics!
4 It might, however, might give you new information about the *screen* or the *page* on which the image is displayed!
5 Priceless!
6 Yes, we did just argue that the perceptual systems don't really measure geometric properties. In some cases, though, researchers ask participants to perceive geometric properties when they really want to know about affordances. So, instead of asking someone to report on "how wide would a

space need so that you could fit this object into it?" they just ask the person to report "how wide is this object?"

7 This is the historically popular idea of "Hierarchical Processing" from Chapter 1.

8 And neither of your authors is willing to give up either of their brains any time soon . . . or ever, really.

9 You may have heard someone say, "That really resonates with me" to mean that it really connected with them. This is the same basic idea.

10 These are among the chemicals that can give coffee a bitter taste (Kraehenbuehl et al., 2017).

References

Adolph, K. E. (2019). An ecological approach to learning in (not and) development. *Human Development, 63*, 180–201.

Adolph, K. E., & Hoch, J. E. (2019). Motor development: Embodied, embedded, enculturated, and enabling. *Annual Review of Psychology, 70*, 141–164. https://doi.org/10.1146/annurev-psych-010418-102836

Adolph, K. E., & Kretch, K. S. (2012). Infants on the edge: Beyond the visual cliff. In A. Slater & P. Quinn (Eds.), *Developmental psychology: Revisiting the classic studies* (pp. 36–55). Sage Publications.

Amazeen, E. L., & Turvey, M. T. (1996). Weight perception and the haptic size-weight illusion are functions of the inertia tensor. *Journal of Experimental Psychology: Human Perception and Performance, 22*(1), 213–232. https://doi.org/10.1037/0096-1523.22.1.213

Anderson, M. L. (2014). *After phrenology: Neural reuse and the interactive brain*. MIT Press.

Anstis, S. M. (1997). Experiments on motion aftereffects. In M. Jenkin & L. Harris (Eds.), *Computational and psychophysical mechanisms of visual coding* (pp. 61–74). Cambridge University Press.

Arzamarski, R., Isenhower, R. W., Kay, B. A., Turvey, M. T., & Michaels, C. F. (2010). Effects of intention and learning on attention to information in dynamic touch. *Attention, Perception & Psychophysics, 72*(3), 721–735. https://doi.org/10.3758/APP.72.3.721

Baddeley, A. (1996). Exploring the central executive. *The Quarterly Journal of Experimental Psychology A: Human Experimental Psychology, 49A*(1), 5–28. https://doi.org/10.1080/027249896392784

Bartoshuk, L. M. (1991). Sweetness: History, preference, and genetic variability. *Food Technology, 45*, 108–113.

Barwich, A. S. (2020). *Smellosophy: What the nose tells the mind*. Harvard University Press.

Beidler, L. M., & Smallman, R. L. (1965). Renewal of cells within taste buds. *The Journal of Cell Biology, 27*(2), 263–272.

Berkeley, G. (1709). *An essay towards a new theory of vision*. Aaron Rhames.

Bernstein, L. E., Auer, E. T., Jr., & Takayanagi, S. (2004). Auditory speech detection in noise enhanced by lipreading. *Speech Communication, 44*(1), 5–18. https://doi.org/10.1016/j.specom.2004.10.011

Berwick, R. C., Pietroski, P., Yankama, B., & Chomsky, N. (2011). Poverty of the stimulus revisited. *Cognitive Science, 35*(7), 1207–1242.

Bidet-Ildei, C., Kitromilides, E., Orliaguet, J.-P., Pavlova, M., & Gentaz, E. (2014). Preference for point-light human biological motion in newborns: Contribution of translational displacement. *Developmental Psychology, 50*(1), 113–120. https://doi.org/10.1037/a0032956

Blake, R. (1993). Cats perceive biological motion. *Psychological Science, 4*(1), 54–57. https://doi.org/10.1111/j.1467-9280.1993.tb00557.x

Blakemore, C., & Cooper, G. F. (1970). The development of the brain depends on the visual environment. *Nature, 228*, 477–478. https://doi.org/10.1038/228477a0

Blanchard, J. (1918). The brightness sensibility of the retina. *Physical Review, 11*(2), 81–89. https://doi.org/10.1103/PhysRev.11.81

Blau, J. J. C., & Carello, C. (2020). Perceptual underpinnings for "good" editing: A fractal analysis. *Perception, 49*(3), 281–297. https://doi.org/10.1177/0301006620903166

Blau, J. J. C., Petrusz, S. C., & Carello, C. (2013). Fractal structure of event segmentation: Lessons from reel and real events. *Ecological Psychology, 25*(1), 81–101. https://doi.org/10.1080/10407413.2013.753811

Blau, J. J. C., & Wagman, J. B. (2022). *Introduction to ecological psychology: A lawful approach to perceiving, acting, and cognizing*. Routledge.

Bongers, R. M., Smitsman, A. W., & Michaels, C. F. (2003). Geometrics and dynamics of a rod determine how it is used for reaching. *Journal of Motor Behavior*, *35*(1), 4–22. https://doi.org/10.1080/00222890309602117

Bootsma R. J. (2009). The (current) future is here!. *Perception*, *38*(6), 851–858.

Brainard, D. H., Roorda, A., Yamauchi, Y., Calderone, J. B., Metha, A., Neitz, M., Neitz, J., Williams, D. R., & Jacobs, G. H. (2000). Functional consequences of the relative numbers of L and M cones. *Journal of the Optical Society of America A*, *17*(3), 607–614.

Bregman, A. S. (1990). *Auditory scene analysis: The perceptual organization of sound*. The MIT Press.

Bregman, A. S. (2005). Auditory scene analysis and the role of phenomenology in experimental psychology. *Canadian Psychology / Psychologie canadienne*, *46*(1), 32–40. https://doi.org/10.1037/h0085822

Bridges, J. W. (1912). Doctrine of specific nerve energies. *The Journal of Philosophy, Psychology and Scientific Methods*, *9*(3), 57–65.

Bruce, V., Georgeson, M. A., & Green, P. R. (2014). *Visual perception: Physiology, psychology and ecology*. Psychology Press.

Bruggeman, H., & Warren, W. H. (2010). The direction of walking—but not throwing or kicking—is adapted by optic flow. *Psychological Science*, *21*(7), 1006–1013. https://doi.org/10.1177/0956797610372635

Buckingham, G. (2014). Getting a grip on heaviness perception: A review of weight illusions and their probable causes. *Experimental Brain Research*, *232*(6), 1623–1629. https://doi.org/10.1007/s00221-014-3926-9

Bunge, M. (1979). *Ontology II: A world of systems*. D. Reidel.

Burwick, T. (2014). The binding problem. *Wiley Interdisciplinary Reviews: Cognitive Science*, *5*(3), 305–315. https://doi.org/10.1002/wcs.1282

Cabe, P. A., & Pittenger, J. B. (2000). Human sensitivity to acoustic information from vessel filling. *Journal of Experimental Psychology: Human Perception and Performance*, *26*(1), 313–324. https://doi.org/10.1037/0096-1523.26.1.313

Carello, C., Anderson, K. L., & Kunkler-Peck, A. J. (1998). Perception of object length by sound. *Psychological Science*, *9*(3), 211–214. https://doi.org/10.1111/1467-9280.00040

Carello, C., Santana, M. V., & Burton, G. (1996). Selective perception by dynamic touch. *Perception & Psychophysics*, *58*, 1177–1190.

Carello, C., & Turvey, M. T. (2015). Dynamic (effortful) touch. *Scholarpedia*, *10*(4), 8242.

Carello, C., & Turvey, M. T. (2017). Useful dimensions of haptic perception: 50 years after the senses considered as perceptual systems. *Ecological Psychology*, *29*(2), 95–121. https://doi.org/10.1080/10407413.2017.1297188

Carello, C., & Turvey, M. T. (2020). Challenging the axioms of perception: The retinal image and the visibility of light. In J. B. Wagman & J. J. Blau (Eds.), *Perception as Information detection: Reflections on Gibson's ecological approach to visual perception* (pp. 51–70). Routledge.

Carello, C., Wagman, J. B., & Turvey, M. T. (2005). Acoustic specification of object properties. In J. Anderson & B. Anderson (Eds.), *Moving image theory: Ecological considerations* (pp. 79–104). Southern Illinois Press.

Carroll, S. B. (2005). *Endless forms most beautiful: The new science of evo devo and the making of the animal kingdom*. WW Norton & Company.

Caterina, M. J., Schumacher, M. A., Tominaga, M., Rosen, T. A., Levine, J. D., & Julius, D. (1997). The capsaicin receptor: A heat-activated ion channel in the pain pathway. *Nature*, *389*(6653), 816–824.

Chabris, C., & Simons, D. (2011). *The invisible gorilla: How our intuitions deceive us*. Harmony.

Cheselden, W. (1728). An account of some observations made by a young gentleman, who was born blind, or lost his sight so early, that he had no remembrance of ever having seen, and was couch'd between 13 and 14 years of age. *Philosophical Transactions*, *35*, 447–450.

Cole, J. (1995). *Pride and a daily marathon*. Bradford Books.

Colicchia, G. (2006). Ancient cephalopod scavenges successfully with its pinhole eye. *Physics Education*, *41*(1), 15.

Comalli, D., Franchak, J., Char, A., & Adolph, K. (2013). Ledge and wedge: Younger and older adults' perception of action possibilities. *Experimental Brain Research*, *228*, 183–192. https://doi.org/10.1007/s00221-013-3550-0

Craig, J. C. (1999). Grating orientation as a measure of tactile spatial acuity. *Somatosensory & Motor Research*, *16*(3), 197–206.
Dalton, P. (2002). Odor, irritation and perception of health risk. *International Archives of Occupational and Environmental Health*, *75*(5), 283–290.
Dandan, Y. R. (2025). Ensemble perception in human vision. *Nature Reviews Psychology*, *4*, 310.
Darwin, C. (2004). *The formation of vegetable mould, through the action of worms.* Kessinger Publishing. (Original work published 1881)
Davenport, J. L., & Potter, M. C. (2004). Scene consistency in object and background perception. *Psychological Science*, *15*(8), 559–564.
Davis, T. J., Riley, M. A., Shockley, K., & Cummins-Sebree, S. (2010). Perceiving affordances for joint actions. *Perception*, *39*(12), 1624–1644. https://doi.org/10.1068/p6712
De Agrò, M., Rößler, D. C., Kim, K., & Shamble, P. S. (2021). Perception of biological motion by jumping spiders. *PLoS Biology*, *19*(7), e3001172.
Dennett, D. C. (2010). *Content and consciousness.* Routledge.
Descartes, R. (1993). *Discourse on method and meditations on first philosophy* (D. A. Cress, Trans.). Hackett Publishing Company. (Original work published 1637).
de Solórzano, S. L. (2020). *Everything moves: How biotensegrity informs human movement.* Handspring Publishing.
De Wijk, R. A., & Cain, W. S. (1994). Odor quality: Discrimination versus free and cued identification. *Perception & Psychophysics*, *56*(1), 12–18.
Dicke, M., van Loon, J. J. A., & Soler, R. (2009). Chemical complexity of volatiles from plants induced by multiple attack. *Nature Chemical Biology*, *5*, 317–324.
Djordjevic, J., Lundstrom, J. N., Clément, F., Boyle, J. A., Pouliot, S., & Jones-Gotman, M. (2008). A rose by any other name: Would it smell as sweet?. *Journal of Neurophysiology*, *99*(1), 386–393.
do Couto, C. M., & Carvallo, R. M. M. (2009). The effect external and middle ears have in otoacoustic emissions. *Brazilian Journal of Otorhinolaryngology*, *75*(1), 15–23.
Doron, R., Sterkin, A., Fried, M., Yehezkel, O., Lev, M., Belkin, M., Rosner, M., Solomon, A. S., Mandel, Y., & Polat, U. (2019). Spatial visual function in anomalous trichromats: Is less more? *PLoS One*, *14*(1), e0209662.
Edmonson, A., Iwanaga, J., Olewnik, Ł., Dumont, A. S., & Tubbs, R. S. (2022). The function of the tensor tympani muscle: A comprehensive review of the literature. *Anatomy & Cell Biology*, *55*(2), 113–117.
Eggers, J. (2020). A closer look at the compensating polar planimeter. *The College Mathematics Journal*, *51*(2), 105–116.
Eimas, P. D., & Corbit, J. D. (1973). Selective adaptation of linguistic feature detectors. *Cognitive Psychology*, *4*(1), 99–109. https://doi.org/10.1016/0010-0285(73)90006-6
Einstein, A. (1905). Zur Elektrodynamik bewegter Körper. *Annalen der Physik*, *17*(1), 891–921.
Esch, H. E., Zhang, S., Srinivasan, M. V., & Tautz, J. (2001). Honeybee dances communicate distances measured by optic flow. *Nature*, *411*(6837), 581–583. https://doi.org/10.1038/35079072
Fajen, B. R. (2005). Calibration, information, and control strategies for braking to avoid a collision. *Journal of Experimental Psychology: Human Perception and Performance*, *31*(3), 480–501. https://doi.org/10.1037/0096-1523.31.3.480
Fajen, B. R. (2007). Affordance-based control of visually guided action. *Ecological Psychology*, *19*(4), 383–410. https://doi.org/10.1080/10407410701557877
Favela, L. H. (2024). *The ecological brain: Unifying the sciences of brain, body, and environment.* Routledge.
Favela, L. H., & Chemero, A. (2016). The animal-environment system. In Y. Coello & M. H. Fischer (Eds.), *Foundations of embodied cognition: Perceptual and emotional embodiment* (pp. 59–74). Routledge/Taylor & Francis Group.
Favela, L. H., Riley, M. A., Shockley, K., & Chemero, A. (2018). Perceptually equivalent judgments made visually and via haptic sensory-substitution devices. *Ecological Psychology*, *30*(4), 326–345. https://doi.org/10.1080/10407413.2018.1473712
Finger, T. E., & Kinnamon, S. C. (2011). Taste isn't just for taste buds anymore. *F1000 Biology Reports*, *3*, 20. https://doi.org/10.3410/B3-20
Fink, P. W., Foo, P. S., & Warren, W. H. (2009). Catching fly balls in virtual reality: A critical test of the outfielder problem. *Journal of Vision*, *9*(14), 1–8. https://doi.org/10.1167/9.13.14
Fitzpatrick, P., & Flynn, N. (2010). Dynamic touch perception in preschool children. *Ecological Psychology*, *22*(2), 89–118.

Foster, D. H. (2011). Color constancy. *Vision Research, 51*(7), 674–700.
Fowler, C. A. (2018). Direct perception of speech. In *Oxford research encyclopedia of linguistics.* Oxford University Press. https://doi.org/10.1093/acrefore/9780199384655.013.407
Franchak, J. M., & Adolph, K. E. (2014). Gut estimates: Pregnant women adapt to changing possibilities for squeezing through doorways. *Attention, Perception, & Psychophysics, 76*(2), 460–472. https://doi.org/10.3758/s13414-013-0578-y
Franchak, J. M., Celano, E. C., & Adolph, K. E. (2012). Perception of passage through openings depends on the size of the body in motion. *Experimental Brain Research, 223*, 301–310. https://doi.org/10.1007/s00221-012-3261-y
Franchak, J. M., & Somoano, F. A. (2018). Rate of recalibration to changing affordances for squeezing through doorways reveals the role of feedback. *Experimental Brain Research, 236*, 1699–1711. https://doi.org/10.1007/s00221-018-5252-0
Fultot, M., Adrian Frazier, P., Turvey, M. T., & Carello, C. (2019). What are nervous systems for? *Ecological Psychology, 31*(3), 218–234.
Galantucci, B., Fowler, C. A., & Turvey, M. T. (2006). The motor theory of speech perception reviewed. *Psychonomic Bulletin & Review, 13*(3), 361–377. https://doi.org/10.3758/BF03193857
Gandhi, N. J., & Katnani, H. A. (2011). Motor functions of the superior colliculus. *Annual Review of Neuroscience, 34*(1), 205–231.
Gaver, W. W. (1993). What in the world do we hear? An ecological approach to auditory event perception. *Ecological Psychology, 5*(1), 1–29. https://doi.org/10.1207/s15326969eco0501_1
Genva, M., Kenne Kemene, T., Deleu, M., Lins, L., & Fauconnier, M. L. (2019). Is it possible to predict the odor of a molecule on the basis of its structure? *International Journal of Molecular Sciences, 20*(12), 3018.
Gibson, E. J., & Pick, A. D. (2000). *An ecological approach to perceptual learning and development.* Oxford University Press.
Gibson, E. J., & Walk, R. D. (1960). The "visual cliff". *Scientific American, 202*(4), 64–71. https://doi.org/10.1038/scientificamerican0460-64
Gibson, J. J. (1950). *The perception of the visual world.* Houghton Mifflin.
Gibson, J. J. (1962). Observations on active touch. *Psychological Review, 69*(6), 477–491.
Gibson, J. J. (1966). *The senses considered as perceptual systems.* Houghton Mifflin.
Gibson, J. J. (2015). *The ecological approach to visual perception* (Classic ed.). Psychology Press. (Original work published 1979)
Gilbert, C. D., & Wiesel, T. N. (1990). The influence of contextual stimuli on the orientation selectivity of cells in primary visual cortex of the cat. *Vision Research, 30*(11), 1689–1701.
Gillam, B. (1980). Geometrical illusions. *Scientific American, 242*, 102–111.
Goodale, M. A., & Milner, A. D. (1992). Separate visual pathways for perception and action. *Trends in Neurosciences, 15*(1), 20–25.
Gordon, M. S., & Rosenblum, L. D. (2004). Perception of sound-obstructing surfaces using body-scaled judgments. *Ecological Psychology, 16*(2), 87–113. https://doi.org/10.1207/s15326969eco1602_1
Gottlieb, G. (2000). Environmental and behavioral influences on gene activity. *Current Directions in Psychological Science, 9*(3), 93–97.
Gregory, R. L. (1980). Perceptions as hypotheses. *Philosophical Transactions of the Royal Society B: Biological Sciences, 290*, 181–197.
Gregory, R. L. (2009). *Seeing through illusions.* Oxford University Press.
Gutta, S., & Philomin, V. (2004). *U.S. patent no. 6,812,846.* U.S. Patent and Trademark Office.
Hänig, D. P. (1901). *Zur Psychophysik des Geschmackssinnes.* Engelmann. (As cited in Boring, E. G. (1942). *Sensation and perception in the history of experimental psychology.* Appleton.)
Harrison, S. J., & Turvey, M. T. (2010). Place learning by mechanical contact. *Journal of Experimental Biology, 213*(9), 1436–1442.
Heft, H. (2020). Revisiting "the discovery of the occluding edge and its implications for perception" 40 years on. In J. B. Wagman & J. J. C. Blau (Eds.), *Perception as the detection of information: Reflections on Gibson's ecological approach to visual perception* (pp. 188–204). Routledge.
Heinricher, M. M., Tavares, I., Leith, J. L., & Lumb, B. M. (2009). Descending control of nociception: Specificity, recruitment and plasticity. *Brain Research Reviews, 60*(1), 214–225.
Helmholtz, H. (2000). *Helmholtz's treatise on physiological optics* (Vol. III, J. P. C. Southall, Trans.). Thoemmes. (Original work published 1910)
Heras-Escribano, M. (2019). *The philosophy of affordances.* Palgrave Macmillan.

Hertz, H. (1887, November 10). On electromagnetic effects produced by electrical disturbances in insulators. *Sitzungsberichte der Berliner Akademie der Wissenschaften*.
Hodgkin, A. L., & Huxley, A. F. (1939). Action potentials recorded from inside a nerve fibre. *Nature, 144*(3651), 710–711.
Hofman, P. M., Van Riswick, J. G., & Van Opstal, A. J. (1998). Relearning sound localization with new ears. *Nature Neuroscience, 1*(5), 417–421. https://doi.org/10.1038/1633
Holt, L. L., & Lotto, A. J. (2010). Speech perception as categorization. *Attention, Perception, & Psychophysics, 72*(5), 1218–1227. https://doi.org/10.3758/APP.72.5.1218
Holway, H. A., & Boring, E. G. (1941). Determinants of apparent visual size with distance variant. *American Journal of Psychology, 54*, 21–32.
Horowitz, A., West, E., Ball, M., & Bagwell, B. (2021). Can dogs limbo? Dogs' perception of affordances for negotiating an opening. *Animals, 11*(3), 620. https://doi.org/10.3390/ani11030620
Hubel, D. H. (1982). Evolution of ideas on the primary visual cortex, 1955–1978: A biased historical account. *Bioscience Reports, 2*(6), 435–469.
Humphreys, G. W., & Riddoch, M. J. (2013). *To see but not to see: A case study of visual agnosia*. Psychology Press.
Hurvich, L. M., & Jameson, D. (1957). An opponent-process theory of color vision. *Psychological Review, 64*(6), 384–404.
Ingle, D. (1973). Spontaneous shape discrimination by frogs during unconditioned escape behaviour. *Physiological Psychology, 1*, 71–73. https://doi.org/10.3758/BF03326870
Ingling, C. R., Jr. (1977). The spectral sensitivity of the opponent-color channels. *Vision Research, 17*(9), 1083–1089.
Ishak, S., Assoian, A. B., & Rincon, S. (2019). Experience influences affordance perception for low crawling under barriers with altered body dimensions. *Ecological Psychology, 31*(4), 332–352. https://doi.org/10.1080/10407413.2019.1619456
Jacobs, D. M., & Michaels, C. F. (2007). Direct learning. *Ecological Psychology, 19*, 321–349.
Jansen, A. J., & Fajen, B. R. (2025). Visual control of steering through multiple waypoints. *Scientific Reports, 15*(1), 31261.
Johansson, G. (1973). Visual perception of biological motion and a model for its analysis. *Perception & Psychophysics, 14*, 201–211. https://doi.org/10.3758/BF03212378
Jönsson, E. H., Bendas, J., Weidner, K., Wessberg, J., Olausson, H., Wasling, H. B., & Croy, I. (2017). The relation between human hair follicle density and touch perception. *Scientific Reports, 7*(1), 2499.
Kanizsa, G. (1976). Subjective contours. *Scientific American, 234*(4), 48–53.
Kelso, J. S., & Engstrøm, D. A. (2024). *The squiggle sense: Sixth sense of the complementary nature and the metastable brain~ mind*. Springer Nature.
Kepler, J. (1604). *Ad Vitellionem paralipomena, quibus astronomiae pars optica traditur [Supplements to Witelo, in which the optical part of astronomy is treated]*. Claudium Marnium & Haeredes Ioannis Aubrii.
Kim, S., Carello, C., & Turvey, M. T. (2016). Size and distance are perceived independently in an optical tunnel: Evidence for direct perception. *Vision Research, 125*, 1–11.
Kitaoka, A., & Ashida, H. (2003). Phenomenal characteristics of the peripheral drift illusion. *VISION: The Journal of the Vision Society of Japan*, 261–262. https://doi.org/10.24636/vision.15.4_261
Kloos, H., & Amazeen, E. L. (2002). Perceiving heaviness by dynamic touch: An investigation of the size-weight illusion in preschoolers. *British Journal of Developmental Psychology, 20*(2), 171–183.
Kluender, K. R., Lotto, A. J., & Holt, L. L. (2005). Contributions of nonhuman animal models to understanding human speech perception. In S. Greenberg & W. Ainsworth (Eds.), *Listening to speech: An auditory perspective* (pp. 203–220). Oxford University Press.
Koffka, K. (1935). *Principles of Gestalt psychology*. Harcourt, Brace.
Kraehenbuehl, K., Page-Zoerkler, N., Mauroux, O., Gartenmann, K., Blank, I., & Bel-Rhlid, R. (2017). Selective enzymatic hydrolysis of chlorogenic acid lactones in a model system and in a coffee extract. Application to reduction of coffee bitterness. *Food Chemistry, 218*, 9–14. https://doi.org/10.1016/j.foodchem.2016.09.055
Kuffler, S. W. (1953). Discharge patterns and functional organization of mammalian retina. *Journal of Neurophysiology, 16*(1), 37–68.
Kujawa, S. G., & Liberman, M. C. (2009). Adding insult to injury: Cochlear nerve degeneration after "temporary" noise-induced hearing loss. *Journal of Neuroscience, 29*(45), 14077–14085.
Kunkler-Peck, A., & Turvey, M. T. (2000). Hearing shape. *Journal of Experimental Psychology: Human Perception and Performance, 26*(1), 279–294. https://doi.org/10.1037/0096-1523.26.1.279

Land, E. H. (1977). The retinex theory of color vision. *Scientific American, 237*, 108–128.
Land, M. F. (1999). Motion and vision: Why animals move their eyes. *Journal of Comparative Physiology A, 185*(4), 341–352.
Lederman, S. J., & Klatzky, R. L. (1987). Hand movements: A window into haptic object recognition. *Cognitive Psychology, 19*(3), 342–368.
Lee, D. N., & Aronson, E. (1974). Visual proprioceptive control of standing in human infants. *Perception & Psychophysics, 15*(3), 529–532.
Lee, D. N., Bootsma, R. J., Land, M., Regan, D., & Gray, R. (2009). Lee's 1976 paper. *Perception, 38*(6), 837–858.
Lee, D. N., Davies, M. N., Green, P. R., & Van Der Weel, F. R. (1993). Visual control of velocity of approach by pigeons when landing. *Journal of Experimental Biology, 180*(1), 85–104.
Lee, D. N., & Reddish, P. E. (1981). Plummeting gannets: A paradigm of ecological optics. *Nature, 293*(5830), 293–294. https://doi.org/10.1038/293293a0
Lee, D. N., Reddish, P. E., & Rand, D. T. (1991). Aerial docking by hummingbirds. *Naturwissenschaften, 78*, 526–527.
Lee, D. N., van der Weel, F. R., Hitchcock, T., Matejowsky, E., & Pettigrew, J. D. (1992). Common principle of guidance by echolocation and vision. *Journal of Comparative Physiology A, 171*, 563–571. https://doi.org/10.1007/BF00194105
Lent, R., Azevedo, F. A., Andrade-Moraes, C. H., & Pinto, A. V. (2012). How many neurons do you have? Some dogmas of quantitative neuroscience under revision. *European Journal of Neuroscience, 35*(1), 1–9.
Lewontin, R. C. (2001). *The triple helix: Gene, organism, and environment.* Harvard University Press.
Liberman, A. M. (1996). *Speech: A special code.* The MIT Press.
Liberman, A. M., Harris, K. S., Hoffman, H. S., & Griffith, B. C. (1957). The discrimination of speech sounds within and across phoneme boundaries. *Journal of Experimental Psychology, 54*(5), 358–368. https://doi.org/10.1037/h0044417
Liberman, A. M., & Mattingly, I. G. (1985). The motor theory of speech perception revised. *Cognition, 21*(1), 1–36. https://doi.org/10.1016/0010-0277(85)90021-6
Lishman, J. R., & Lee, D. N. (1973). The autonomy of visual kinaesthesis. *Perception, 2*(3), 287–294.
Locke, J. (1690). *An essay concerning humane understanding* (1st ed., Vol. 1). Thomas Basset.
Lopresti-Goodman, S. M., Rivera, A., & Dressel, C. (2012). Practicing safe text: The impact of texting on walking behavior. *Applied Cognitive Psychology, 26*(4), 644–648.
Loula, F., Prasad, S., Harber, K., & Shiffrar, M. (2005). Recognizing people from their movement. *Journal of Experimental Psychology: Human Perception and Performance, 31*(1), 210–220. https://doi.org/10.1037/0096-1523.31.1.210
Lucaites, K. M., Venkatakrishnan, R., Venkatakrishnan, R., Bhargava, A., & Pagano, C. C. (2020). Predictability and variability of a dynamic environment impact affordance judgments. *Ecological Psychology, 32*(2–3), 95–114. https://doi.org/10.1080/10407413.2020.1741323
Mace, W. M. (2020). Getting into the ambient optic array and what we might get out of it. In J. B. Wagman & J. J. C. Blau (Eds.), *Perception as the detection of information: Reflections on Gibson's ecological approach to visual perception* (pp. 73–89). Routledge.
Macefield, V. G. (2009). Proprioception: Role of joint receptors. In M. D. Binder, N. Hirokawa, & U. Windhorst (Eds.), *Encyclopedia of neuroscience* (pp. 1397–1401). Springer.
Macefield, V. G., & Knellwolf, T. P. (2018). Functional properties of human muscle spindles. *Journal of Neurophysiology, 120*(2), 452–467.
Maloney, L. T., & Wandell, B. A. (1986). Color constancy: A method for recovering surface spectral reflectance. *Journal of the Optical Society of America, A, Optics, Image & Science, 3*(1), 29–33.
Mangalam, M., & Kelty-Stephens, D. (Eds.). (2026). *Beyond computational metaphors of mind and brain.* Cambridge University Press.
Mark, L. S. (1987). Eyeheight-scaled information about affordances: A study of sitting and stair climbing. *Journal of Experimental Psychology: Human Perception and Performance, 13*(3), 361–370. https://doi.org/10.1037//0096-1523.13.3.361
Mather, G., & Harris, J. (1998). Theoretical models of the motion aftereffect. In G. Mather, F. Verstraten, & S. Anstis (Eds.), *The motion after effect: A modern perspective* (pp. 157–185). MIT Press.
Matin, E. (1974). Saccadic suppression: A review and an analysis. *Psychological Bulletin, 81*(12), 899–917.

Matin, L., Picoult, E., Stevens, J. K., Edwards, M. W., Jr., Young, D., & MacArthur, R. (1982). Oculoparalytic illusion: Visual-field dependent spatial mislocalizations by humans partially paralyzed with curare. *Science*, *216*(4542), 198–201.
Mattingly, C. (2011). The machine-body as contested metaphor in clinical care. *Genre: Forms of Discourse and Culture*, *44*(3), 363–380.
McGurk, H., & MacDonald, J. (1976). Hearing lips and seeing voices. *Nature*, *264*(5588), 746–748. https://doi.org/10.1038/264746a0
Metzger, W. (1930). Optische Untersuchungen im Ganzfeld II [Optical investigations in the whole field]. *Psychologizche Forschung*, *13*, 6–29.
Michel, C., Velasco, C., Fraemohs, P., & Spence, C. (2015). Studying the impact of plating on ratings of the food served in a naturalistic dining context. *Appetite*, *90*, 45–50.
Milner, D., & Goodale, M. (1995). *The visual brain in action* (Vol. 27). Oxford University Press.
Milner, D., & Goodale, M. (2006). *The visual brain in action* (2nd ed.). Oxford Psychology Series. Oxford University Press.
Mishkin, M., Ungerleider, L. G., & Macko, K. A. (1983). Object vision and spatial vision: Two cortical pathways. *Trends in Neurosciences*, *6*, 414–417.
Mitchell, M. B., Workman, A. D., Rathi, V. K., & Bhattacharyya, N. (2023). Smell and taste loss associated with COVID-19 infection. *The Laryngoscope*, *133*(9), 2357–2361.
Moayedi, M., & Davis, K. D. (2013). Theories of pain: From specificity to gate control. *Journal of Neurophysiology*, *109*(1), 5–12.
Mock, V. L., Luke, K. L., Hembrook-Short, J. R., & Briggs, F. (2018). Dynamic communication of attention signals between the LGN and V1. *Journal of Neurophysiology*, *120*(4), 1625–1639.
Molyneux, W. (1688). Letter to John Locke.
Morovic, J., Cheung, V., & Morovic, P. (2012, January). Why we don't know how many colors there are. In *Conference on colour in graphics, imaging, and vision* (Vol. 6, pp. 49–53). Society of Imaging Science and Technology.
Nakayasu, T., & Watanabe, E. (2014). Biological motion stimuli are attractive to medaka fish. *Animal Cognition*, *17*, 559–575. https://doi.org/10.1007/s10071-013-0687-y
Newton, I. (1952). *Opticks, or, a treatise of the reflections, refractions, inflections & colours of light*. Courier Corporation. (Original work published 1730)
O'Doherty, J., Kringelbach, M. L., Rolls, E. T., Hornak, J., & Andrews, C. (2001). Abstract reward and punishment representations in the human orbitofrontal cortex. *Nature Neuroscience*, *4*(1), 95–102.
Olivia, A., & Torralba, A. (2007). The role of context in object recognition. *TRENDS in Cognitive Sciences*, *11*(12), 520–527.
O'Neill, S. M., & Russell, M. K. (2017). Impact of postural stability and modality on the perception of passage and surface climbing. *Ecological Psychology*, *29*(1), 54–68. https://doi.org/10.1080/10407413.2017.1270153
Otero-Millan, J., Macknik, S. L., & Martinez-Conde, S. (2012). Microsaccades and blinks trigger illusory rotation in the "rotating snakes" illusion. *Journal of Neuroscience*, *32*(17), 6043–6051.
Pagano, C. C., Kinsella-Shaw, J. M., Cassidy, P. E., & Turvey, M. T. (1994). Role of the inertia tensor in haptically perceiving where an object is grasped. *Journal of Experimental Psychology: Human Perception and Performance*, *20*(2), 276–285. https://doi.org/10.1037//0096-1523.20.2.276
Pagano, C. C., & Turvey, M. T. (1992). Eigenvectors of the inertia tensor and perceiving the orientation of a hand-held object by dynamic touch. *Perception & Psychophysics*, *52*(6), 617–624. https://doi.org/10.3758/bf03211699
Pagano, C. C., & Turvey, M. T. (1995). The inertia tensor as a basis for the perception of limb orientation. *Journal of Experimental Psychology: Human Perception and Performance*, *21*(5), 1070–1087. https://doi.org/10.1037/0096-1523.21.5.1070
Pagano, C. C., & Turvey, M. T. (1998). Eigenvectors of the inertia tensor and perceiving the orientations of limbs and objects. *Journal of Applied Biomechanics*, *14*(4), 331–359.
Parks, R. W., Long, D. L., Levine, D. S., Crockett, D. J., McGeer, E. G., McGeer, P. L., Dalton, I. E., Zec, R. F., Becker, R. E., Coburn, K. L., Siler, G., Nelson, M. E., & Bower, J. M. (1991). Parallel distributed processing and neural networks: Origins, methodology and cognitive functions. *International Journal of Neuroscience*, *60*(3–4), 195–214.
Penfield, W., & Boldrey, E. (1937). Somatic motor and sensory representation in the cerebral cortex of man as studied by electrical stimulation. *Brain: A Journal of Neurology*, *60*(4), 389–443.

Pepping, G. J., & Grealy, M. A. (Eds.). (2007). *Closing the gap: The scientific writings of David N. Lee*. Psychology Press.

Peterson, M. A., & Gibson, B. S. (1993). Shape recognition inputs to figure-ground organization in three-dimensional displays. *Cognitive Psychology*, *25*(3), 383–429.

Peterson, M. A., & Gibson, B. S. (1994). Must figure-ground organization precede object recognition? An assumption in peril. *Psychological Science*, *5*(5), 253–259.

Pickles, J. O. (1992). Tip links and hair cells. *Current Biology*, *2*(1), 48–50.

Pitt, F. H. G. (1944). Monochromatism. *Nature*, *154*(3910), 466–468.

Porter, J., Craven, B., Khan, R. M., Chang, S. J., Kang, I., Judkewitz, B., Volpe, J., Settles, G., & Sobel, N. (2007). Mechanisms of scent-tracking in humans. *Nature Neuroscience*, *10*(1), 27–29. https://doi.org/10.1038/nn1819

Proske, U. (2023). A reassessment of the role of joint receptors in human position sense. *Experimental Brain Research*, *241*(4), 943–949.

Quiroga, R. Q., Reddy, L., Kreiman, G., Koch, C., & Fried, I. (2005). Invariant visual representation by single neurons in the human brain. *Nature*, *435*(7045), 1102–1107.

Raja, V., & Anderson, M. L. (2019). Radical embodied cognitive neuroscience. *Ecological Psychology*, *31*(3), 166–181. https://doi.org/10.1080/10407413.2019.1615213

Ramachandran, V. S., & Anstis, S. M. (1986). The perception of apparent motion. *Scientific American*, *254*(6), 102–109.

Ramón y Cajal, S. (1894). *Die Retina der Wirbelthiere: Untersuchungen mit der Golgi-Cajal'schen Chromsilbermethode und der Ehrlich'schen Methylenblaufärbung*. Bergmann.

Rauschecker, J. P. (2018). Where, when, and how: Are they all sensorimotor? Towards a unified view of the dorsal pathway in vision and audition. *Cortex*, *98*, 262–268.

Reed, C. M., Rabinowitz, W. M., Durlach, N. I., Braida, L. D., Conway-Fithian, S., & Schultz, M. C. (1985). Research on the Tadoma method of speech communication. *The Journal of the Acoustical Society of America*, *77*(1), 247–257. https://doi.org/10.1121/1.392266

Reed, E. S. (1982). Darwin's earthworms: A case study in evolutionary psychology. *Behaviorism*, *10*, 165–185.

Reed, E. S. (1996). *Encountering the world: Toward an ecological psychology*. Oxford University Press.

Reichardt, W. (1961). Autocorrelation, a principle for the evaluation of sensory information by the central nervous system. In W. A. Rosenblith (Ed.), *Sensory communication* (pp. 303–317). MIT Press.

Riehm, C., Chemero, A., Silva, P. L., & Shockley, K. (2019). Virtual auditory aperture passability. *Experimental Brain Research*, *237*, 191–200. https://doi.org/10.1007/s00221-018-5407-z

Robart, R. L., & Rosenblum, L. D. (2009). Are hybrid cars too quiet? *Journal of the Acoustical Society of America*, *125*(4), 2744.

Rodieck, R. W. (2018). *The first steps in seeing*. Sinauer Associates. (Original work published 1998)

Rolls, E. T., & Baylis, L. L. (1994). Gustatory, olfactory, and visual convergence within the primate orbitofrontal cortex. *Journal of Neuroscience*, *14*(9), 5437–5452.

Roper, S. D., & Chaudhari, N. (2017). Taste buds: Cells, signals and synapses. *Nature Reviews Neuroscience*, *18*(8), 485–497.

Rosenblum, L. D. (2005). The primacy of multimodal speech perception. In D. Pisoni & R. Remez (Eds.), *Handbook of speech perception* (pp. 51–78). Blackwell.

Rosenblum, L. D. (2011). *See what I'm saying: The extraordinary power of our five senses*. W. W. Norton.

Rosenblum, L. D., Gordon, M. S., & Jarquin, L. (2010). Echolocating distance by moving and stationary observers. *Ecological Psychology*, *12*(3), 181–206. https://doi.org/10.1207/S15326969ECO1203_1

Rosenblum, L. D., Miller, R. M., & Sanchez, K. (2007). Lipread me now, hear me better later: Cross-modal transfer of talker familiarity effects. *Psychological Science*, *18*, 392–396.

Rosenblum, L. D., & Robart, R. L. (2007). Hearing silent shapes: Identifying the shape of a sound-obstructing surface. *Ecological Psychology*, *19*(4), 351–366. https://doi.org/10.1080/10407410701557844

Rosenblum, L. D., Wuestefeld, A. P., & Anderson, K. L. (1996). Auditory reachability: An affordance approach to the perception of sound source distance. *Ecological Psychology*, *8*(1), 1–24. https://doi.org/10.1207/s15326969eco0801_1

Rosenblum, L. D., Wuestefeld, A., & Saldaña, H. (1993). Auditory looming perception: Influences on anticipator judgments. *Perception*, *22*, 1467–1482.

Rubin, E. (1921). *Visuell wahrgenommene Figuren: Studien in psychologischer Analyse [Visually perceived figures: Studies in psychological analysis]*. Gyldendalske Boghandel.
Runeson, S. (1977). On the possibility of "smart" perceptual mechanisms. *Scandinavian Journal of Psychology*, *18*(1), 172–179.
Runeson, S. (1988). The distorted room illusion, equivalent configurations, and the specificity of static optic arrays. *Journal of Experimental Psychology: Human Perception and Performance*, *14*(2), 295–304.
Russell, M. K., & Brown, S. (2020). Using sound to create and detect occlusion of an unseen sound source. *Auditory Perception & Cognition*, *2*(4), 207–229. https://doi.org/10.1080/25742442.2020.1773731
Russell, M. K. & Turvey, M. T. (1999). Auditory perception of unimpeded passage. *Ecological Psychology*, *11*(2), 175–188. https://doi.org/10.1207/s15326969eco1102_3
Schachar, R. A. (2006). The mechanism of accommodation and presbyopia. *International Ophthalmology Clinics*, *46*, 39–61.
Schoultz, T. W., & Swett, J. E. (1972). The fine structure of the Golgi tendon organ. *Journal of Neurocytology*, *1*(1), 1–25.
Schultze, M. (1866). Zur anatomie und physiologie der retina. *Archiv für mikroskopische Anatomie*, *2*, 175–286.
Scott, T. R., & Plata-Salamán, C. R. (1999). Taste in the monkey cortex. *Physiology & Behavior*, *67*(4), 489–511.
Segundo-Ortin, M., Calvo, P., & Barrett, L. (2026). A world of minds: Ecological psychology as a framework for comparative cognition. In T. Nonaka, V. Romero, M. Segundo-Ortin, & J. B. Wagman (Eds.), *Routledge international handbook of ecological psychology*. Routledge.
Serres, J. R., & Ruffier, F. (2017). Optic flow-based collision-free strategies: From insects to robots. *Arthropod Structure & Development*, *46*(5), 703–717.
Shapiro, A., & Todorović, D. (Eds.). (2017). *The Oxford compendium of visual illusions*. Oxford University Press.
Shapley, R., & Hawken, M. J. (2011). Color in the cortex: Single-and double-opponent cells. *Vision Research*, *51*(7), 701–717.
Shockley, K., Carello, C., & Turvey, M. T. (2004). Metamers in the haptic perception of heaviness and moveableness. *Perception & Psychophysics*, *66*(5), 731–742. https://doi.org/10.3758/bf03194968
Smart, L. J., Jr., Hassebrook, J. A., & Teaford, M. A. (2020). Acting is perceiving: Experiments on perception of motion in the world and movements of the self, an update. In J. B. Wagman & J. J. C. Blau (Eds.), *Perception as information detection: Reflections on Gibson's ecological approach to visual perception* (pp. 174–187). Routledge.
Smart, L. J., Jr., Otten, E. W., Strang, A. J., Littman, E. M., & Cook, H. E. (2014). Influence of complexity and coupling of optic flow on visually induced motion sickness. *Ecological Psychology*, *26*(4), 301–324.
Solomon, H. Y., & Turvey, M. T. (1988). Haptically perceiving the distances reachable with hand-held objects. *Journal of Experimental Psychology: Human Perception and Performance*, *14*(3), 404–427. https://doi.org/10.1037/0096-1523.14.3.404
Sonoda, K., Asakura, A., Minoura, M., Elwood, R. W., & Gunji, Y. P. (2012). Hermit crabs perceive the extent of their virtual bodies. *Biology Letters*, *8*(4), 495–497. https://doi.org/10.1098/rsbl.2012.0085
Spivey, M. (2008). *The continuity of mind*. Oxford University Press.
Srinivasan, M. V., Zhang, S., Altwein, M., & Tautz, J. (2000). Honeybee navigation: Nature and calibration of the "odometer". *Science*, *287*(5454), 851–853. https://doi.org/10.1126/science.287.5454.851
Stanney, K., Lawson, B. D., Rokers, B., Dennison, M., Fidopiastis, C., Stoffregen, T., Weech, S. & Fulvio, J. M. (2020). Identifying causes of and solutions for cybersickness in immersive technology: Reformulation of a research and development agenda. *International Journal of Human-Computer Interaction*, *36*(19), 1783–1803.
Stoffregen, T. A. (2011). Motion sickness considered as a movement disorder. *Science & Motricité*, *74*, 19–30. https://doi.org/10.3917/sm.074.0019
Stoffregen, T. A., Ito, K., Hove, P., Yank, J. R., & Bardy, B. G. (2010). The postural responses of adults who are blind to a moving environment. *Journal of Visual Impairment and Blindness*, *104*, 73–83.
Stoffregen, T. A., Villard, S., Kim, C., Ito, K., & Bardy, B. G. (2009). Coupling of head and body movement with motion of the audible environment. *Journal of Experimental Psychology: Human Perception & Performance*, *35*, 1221–1231.

Stoffregen, T. A., & Wagman, J. B. (2024). Higher order affordances. *Psychonomic Bulletin & Review, 32*, 1–30.
Strijkers, K. (2016). Can hierarchical models display parallel cortical dynamics? A non-hierarchical alternative of brain language theory. *Language, Cognition and Neuroscience, 31*(4), 465–469.
Strogatz, S. (2012). *Sync: The emerging science of spontaneous order*. Penguin.
Swanson, L. W. (2015). *Neuroanatomical Terminology: A lexicon of classical origins and historical foundations*. Oxford University Press.
Taddeo, M., & Floridi, L. (2005). Solving the symbol grounding problem: A critical review of fifteen years of research. *Journal of Experimental & Theoretical Artificial Intelligence, 17*(4), 419–445.
Thaler, L., & Goodale, M. A. (2016). Echolocation in humans: An overview. *WIREs Cognitive Science, 7*(6). https://doi.org/10.1002/wcs.1408
Thomas, B. J., Hawkins, M. M., & Nalepka, P. (2017). Perceiver as polar planimeter: Direct perception of jumping, reaching, and jump-reaching affordances for the self and others. *Psychological Research, 82*, 665–674. https://doi.org/10.1007/s00426-017-0858-6
Tomono, T., Makino, R., Furuyama, N., & Mishima, H. (2019). How does a walker pass between two people standing in different configurations? Influence of personal space on aperture passing methods. *Frontiers in Psychology, 10*, 2651. https://doi.org/10.3389/fpsyg.2019.02651
Treisman, A. (1996). The binding problem. *Current Opinion in Neurobiology, 6*(2), 171–178.
Turvey, M. T. (2019). *Lectures on perception: An ecological perspective*. Routledge.
Turvey, M. T., Burton, G., Amazeen, E. L., Butwill, M., & Carello, C. (1998). Perceiving the width and height of a hand-held object by dynamic touch. *Journal of Experimental Psychology: Human Perception and Performance, 24*(1), 35–48. https://doi.org/10.1037//0096-1523.24.1.35
Turvey, M. T., Burton, G., Pagano, C. C., Solomon, H. Y., & Runeson, S. (1992). Role of the inertia tensor in perceiving object orientation by dynamic touch. *Journal of Experimental Psychology. Human Perception and Performance, 18*(3), 714–727. https://doi.org/10.1037//0096-1523.18.3.714
Turvey, M. T., & Fonseca, S. T. (2014). The medium of haptic perception: A tensegrity hypothesis. *Journal of Motor Behavior, 46*(3), 143–187. https://doi.org/10.1080/00222895.2013.798252
van de Langenberg, R., Kingma, I., & Beek, P. J. (2007). Perception of limb orientation in the vertical plane depends on center of mass rather than inertial eigenvectors. *Experimental Brain Research, 180*(4), 595–607. https://doi.org/10.1007/s00221-007-0891-6
van der Meer, A. L. H., Ramstad, M., & van der Weel, F. R. (2008). Choosing the shortest way to mum: Auditory guided rotation in 6- to 9-month-old infants. *Infant Behavior and Development, 31*, 207–216.
van der Meer, A. L. H., & van der Weel, F. R. (2011). Auditory guided arm and whole body movements in young infants. In P. Strumello (Ed.), *Advances in sound localization* (pp. 297–314). InTech.
van der Meer, A. L. H., & van der Weel, F. R. (2020). The optical information for self-perception in development. In J. B. Wagman & J. J. C. Blau (Eds.), *Perception as information detection: Reflections on Gibson's ecological approach to visual perception* (pp. 110–129). Routledge.
Van Essen, D. C., & Anderson, C. H. (1995). Information processing strategies and pathways in the primate visual system. *An Introduction to Neural and Electronic Networks*, 2, 45–76.
Van Orden, G., Hollis, G., & Wallot, S. (2012). The blue-collar brain. *Frontiers in Physiology, 3*, 207. https://doi.org/10.3389/fphys.2012.00207
Van Valen, L. A. (1973). A new evolutionary law. *Evolutionary Theory, 1*, 1–130.
Vauclin, P., Wheat, J., Wagman, J. B., & Seifert, L. (2023). A systematic review of perception of affordances for the person-plus-object system. *Psychonomic Bulletin & Review, 30*(6), 2011–2029. https://doi.org/10.3758/s13423-023-02319-w
Vilhelmsen, K., Agyei, S. B., van der Weel, F., & van der Meer, A. (2019). A high-density EEG study of differentiation between two speeds and directions of simulated optic flow in adults and infants. *Psychophysiology, 56*(1), e13281. https://doi.org/10.1111/psyp.13281
Vockley, J., & Ensenauer, R. (2006, May). Isovaleric acidemia: New aspects of genetic and phenotypic heterogeneity. In *American journal of medical genetics part C: Seminars in medical genetics* (Vol. 142, No. 2, pp. 95–103). Wiley Subscription Services, Inc., A Wiley Company.
Von Békésy, G. (1960). *Experiments in hearing*. McGraw-Hill.
Wagman, J. B. (2020). A guided tour of Gibson's theory of affordances. In J. B. Wagman & J. J. C. Blau (Eds.), *Perception as the detection of information: Reflections on Gibson's ecological approach to visual perception* (pp. 130–148). Routledge.

Wagman, J. B., Blau, J. J. C., & Duffrin, T. (2023). Perception by effortful touch and a lawful approach to (the evolution of) perceiving and acting. In E. Bruner (Ed.), *Cognitive archaeology, body cognition, and the evolution of visuospatial perception* (pp. 25–51). Elsevier.

Wagman, J. B., & Carello, C. (2001). Affordances and inertial constraints on tool use. *Ecological Psychology, 13*(3), 173–195. https://doi.org/10.1207/S15326969ECO1303_1

Wagman, J. B., & Hajnal, A. (2014). Task specificity and anatomical independence in perception of properties by means of a wielded object. *Journal of Experimental Psychology. Human Perception and Performance, 40*(6), 2372–2391. https://doi.org/10.1037/xhp0000014

Wagman, J. B., & Hajnal, A. (2016). Use your head! Perception of action possibilities by means of an object attached to the head. *Experimental Brain Research, 234*(3), 829–836. https://doi.org/10.1007/s00221-015-4509-0

Wagman, J. B., Zimmerman, C., & Sorric, C. (2007). "Which feels heavier—a pound of lead or a pound of feathers?" A potential perceptual basis of a cognitive riddle. *Perception, 36*(11), 1709–1711.

Warren, W. H., & Verbrugge, R. R. (1984). Auditory perception of breaking and bouncing events: A case study in ecological acoustics. *Journal of Experimental Psychology: Human Perception and Performance, 10*(5), 704–712. https://doi.org/10.1037/0096-1523.10.5.704

Warren, W. H., & Whang, S. (1987). Visual guidance of walking through apertures: Body-scaled information for affordances. *Journal of Experimental Psychology: Human Perception and Performance, 13*(3), 371–383. https://doi.org/10.1037/0096-1523.13.3.371

Weinberg, S. (1983). Why the renormalization group is a good thing. In A. H. Guth, K. Huang, & R. L. Jaffe (Eds.), *Asymptotic realms of physics: Essays in honor of Francis E. Low* (pp. 1–19). MIT Press.

Weiss, T., Soroka, T., Gorodisky, L., Shushan, S., Snitz, K., Weissgross, R., Furman-Haran, E., Dhollander, T. & Sobel, N. (2020). Human olfaction without apparent olfactory bulbs. *Neuron, 105*(1), 35–45.

Weyand, T. G. (2016). The multifunctional lateral geniculate nucleus. *Reviews in the Neurosciences, 27*(2), 135–157.

Whitham, E. M., Fitzgibbon, S. P., Lewis, T. W., Pope, K. J., Delosangeles, D., Clark, C. R., Lillie, P., Hardy, A., Gandevia, S. C., & Willoughby, J. O. (2011). Visual Experiences during Paralysis. *Frontiers in Human Neuroscience, 5*, 160. https://doi.org/10.3389/fnhum.2011.00160

Williford, J. R., & von der Heydt, R. (2013). Border-ownership coding. *Scholarpedia, 8*(10), 30040. https://doi.org/10.4249/scholarpedia.30040

Wundt, W. (1897). *Outlines of psychology* (C. H. Judd, Trans.). Wilhelm Engelmann. (Original work published 1896 as *Grundriss der Psychologie*) (Reprinted 1999, Thoemmes, Bristol)

Yeshurun, Y., & Sobel, N. (2010). An odor is not worth a thousand words: From multidimensional odors to unidimensional odor objects. *Annual Review of Psychology, 61*(1), 219–241.

Yildiz, G. Y., Sperandio, I., Kettle, C., & Chouinard, P. A. (2022). A review on various explanations of Ponzo-like illusions. *Psychonomic Bulletin & Review, 29*, 293–320.

Yilmaz, E. H., & Warren, W. H. (1995). Visual control of braking: A test of the τ hypothesis. *Journal of Experimental Psychology: Human Perception and Performance, 21*(5), 996–1014.

Yokoyama, S., Takenaka, N., Agnew, D. W., & Shoshani, J. (2005). Elephants and human color-blind deuteranopes have identical sets of visual pigments. *Genetics, 170*(1), 335–344.

Yong, E. (2022). *An immense world: How animal senses reveal the hidden realms around us.* Random House.

Yost, W. A., & Killion, M. C. (1997). Hearing thresholds. *Encyclopedia of Acoustics, 3*, 1545–1554.

Young, T. (1832, December). The Bakerian lecture: On the theory of light and colours. In *Abstracts of the papers printed in the philosophical transactions of the royal society of London* (Vol. 1, pp. 63–67). The Royal Society.

Zaal, F. T., & Michaels, C. F. (2003). The information for catching fly balls: Judging and intercepting virtual balls in a CAVE. *Journal of Experimental Psychology: Human Perception and Performance, 29*(3), 537–555.

Zeki, S. (1980). The representation of colours in the cerebral cortex. *Nature, 284*(5755), 412–418.

Zonooz, B., Arani, E., Körding, K. P., Aalbers, P. A. T. R., Celikel, T., & Van Opstal, A. J. (2019). Spectral weighting underlies perceived sound elevation. *Scientific Reports, 9*(1), 1642. https://doi.org/10.1038/s41598-018-37537-z

Index

Note: Page numbers in *italics* indicate figures. Page numbers followed by n indicate notes.

For Product Safety Concerns and Information please contact our
EU representative GPSR@taylorandfrancis.com Taylor & Francis
Verlag GmbH, Kaufingerstraße 24, 80331 München, Germany